The Ethics of Tax Evasion

Robert W. McGee
Editor

The Ethics of Tax Evasion

Perspectives in Theory and Practice

 Springer

Editor
Robert W. McGee
School of Business
Florida International University
3000 NE 151 Street
North Miami, FL 33181, USA
bob414@hotmail.com

ISBN 978-1-4899-8800-3   ISBN 978-1-4614-1287-8 (eBook)
DOI 10.1007/978-1-4614-1287-8
Springer New York Dordrecht Heidelberg London

Printed on acid-free paper

Springer is part of Springer Science+Business Media (www.springer.com)

Contributors

Jaan Alver Institute of Accounting, Tallinn University of Technology, Akadeemia tee 3, Tallinn 12618, Estonia
jaan.alver@ttu.ee

Lehte Alver Institute of Accounting, Tallinn University of Technology, Akadeemia tee 3, Tallinn 12618, Estonia
lehte.alver@ttu.ee

Serkan Benk Zonguldak Karaelmas Universitesi I.I.B.F., Maliye Bolumu, 67100 Zonguldak, Turkey
serkanbenk@hotmail.com

Walter Block Harold E. Wirth Eminent Scholar Endowed Chair and Professor of Economics, Joseph A. Butt, S.J. College of Business, Loyola University New Orleans, 6363 St. Charles Avenue, Box 5, Miller Hall 318, New Orleans, LA 70118, USA
wblock@loyno.edu

Sanjoy Bose Abu Dhabi University, Abu Dhabi, UAE
Sanjoy.Bose@adu.ac.ae

Yiu Yu Butt Hong Kong University, Pokfulam, Hong Kong
yyb@business.hku.hk

Gordon Cohn Touro College, 27-33 West 23rd Street, New York, NY 10010, USA
gordoncohn@juno.com

Marian Eabrasu PhD Department of Economics, Champagne School of Management, 217, Avenue Pierre Brossolette, BP 710, 10002 Troyes Cedex, France
Eabrasu@yahoo.com

Geoff A. Goldman Department of Business Management,
University of Johannesburg, D-Ring 530 (Kingsway Campus), Auckland Park,
PO Box 524, 2006 Johannesburg, Gauteng, South Africa
ggoldman@uj.ac.za

Joseph Horton Department of Economics and Finance, University of Central
Arkansas, Conway, AR 72034-2901, USA
jhorton@uca.edu

Ravi Kumar Jain ICFAI Business School, Hyderabad Campus, IFHE University,
Survey No. 156/157 Dontanpally Village Shankerpally Mandal Ranga Reddy
District – 501 504, Andhra Pradesh, India
rk.bandamutha@gmail.com

Ali Reza Jalili New England College, Division of Management, Henniker,
NH 03242, USA
AJalili@nec.edu

Harun Kılıçaslan Uludağ University, Ivazpasa Mah. Ivazpasa cad. No. 36,
Osmangazi, Bursa, Turkey
harun_iibf@hotmail.com

William Kordsmeier Department of Economics and Finance, University of Central
Arkansas, Conway, AR, USA
billk@mail.uca.edu

Tibor R. Machan Chapman University, PO Box 64, Silverado, CA 92676, USA
tmachan@gmail.com

Tatyana B. Maranjyan Moscow State University of Economics,
Statistics and Informatics, Yerevan Branch, 25 A Nalbandian St., Apt. 29,
Yerevan 0001, Armenia
tmaranjyan@gmail.com

Robert W. McGee School of Business, Florida International University,
3000 NE 151 Street, North Miami, FL 33181, USA
bob414@hotmail.com

Alfonso Morales Associate Professor, Urban and Regional Planning,
University of Wisconsin, 925 Bascom Mall, Old Music Hall 104,
Madison, WI 53706, USA
morales1@wisc.edu

Bouchra M'Zali School of Business, University of Quebec at Montreal,
Montreal, Quebec H2X 3X2 Canada
mbouchraz@yahoo.fr

Yanira Petrides Instituto Tecnológico Autónomo de México, Río Hondo No. 1,
Tizapán San Ángel C.P. 01080, Distrito Federal, Mexico
petrides@itam.mx

Adriana M. Ross School of Accounting, Florida International University,
11200 SW 8th Street, Miami, FL 33199, USA
adrianamross@gmail.com

Georgi Smatrakalev College of Business Administration, Sac,
Florida Atlantic University, 3200 College Avenue 430A, Davie, FL 33314, USA
smatraka@fau.edu

Sheldon R. Smith Accounting Department, Woodbury School of Business,
Utah Valley University, Mail Stop 103, 800 W. University Parkway,
Orem, UT 84058, USA
smithsh@uvu.edu

Benno Torgler School of Economics and Finance, Queensland University
of Technology, GPO Box 2434, Brisbane, QLD 4001, Australia
benno.torgler@qut.edu.au

Part I
Philosophical Foundations

Chapter 1
Four Views on the Ethics of Tax Evasion

Robert W. McGee

Introduction

A few years ago I published an article in the *Journal of Business Ethics* titled Three Views on the Ethics of Tax Evasion (McGee, 2006). Actually, there are four views. The purpose of the present chapter is to update that article and discuss the view that was omitted.

Most articles written on tax evasion are published in tax practitioner journals and take a practitioner or legal perspective. However, some authors have taken a philosophical approach (McGee, 1994a). One of the most comprehensive analyses on tax evasion from a philosophical perspective was a doctoral thesis written by Martin Crowe in 1944. The *Journal of Accounting, Ethics & Public Policy* published a series of articles on tax evasion from various religious, secular, and philosophical perspectives in 1998 and 1999. Most of those articles were also published in an edited book (McGee, 1998a). Since the publication of that book, a few other articles have addressed the issue of tax evasion from an ethical perspective. Those articles are discussed in the next section.

The ethics of tax evasion can be examined from a number of perspectives. Some of these are of a religious nature while others are more secular and philosophical. One approach is to examine the relationship of the individual to the state. Another is the relationship between the individual and the taxpaying community or some subset thereof. A third is the relationship of the individual to God. In other words, if there is a duty to pay taxes, the duty is owed either to God, to the state or to some subgroup of the populations (taxpayers or some other group). Martin Crowe (1944) examined the literature on these approaches, which are the three main approaches that have been taken in the literature over the past five centuries.

R.W. McGee (✉)
School of Business, Florida International University, 3000 NE 151 Street,
North Miami, FL 33181, USA
e-mail: bob414@hotmail.com

R.W. McGee (ed.), *The Ethics of Tax Evasion: Perspectives in Theory and Practice*,
DOI 10.1007/978-1-4614-1287-8_1, © Springer Science+Business Media, LLC 2012

Another possibility is that there is no duty to pay. That possibility has been mentioned in the literature but the treatment has been sparse compared to the various duty arguments. This chapter expands on this "no duty" possibility and explores the various subbranches of this argument.

One empirical study on the ethics of tax evasion was done by Nylén (1998), who did a survey soliciting the views of Swedish chief executive officers (CEOs). McGee (1998e) commented on this study. A study by Reckers, Sanders and Roark (1994) presented participants with a case study and asked them whether they would be willing to evade taxes. Englebrecht et al (1998) did a study involving 199 subjects who replied to 29 ethical orientation questions, some of which had to do with tax evasion. A number of other empirical studies have also been made soliciting the views of various groups on their attitude toward tax evasion. Those studies are discussed in other parts of this book.

Review of the Literature

Although many studies have been done on tax compliance, very few have examined compliance, or rather noncompliance, primarily from the perspective of ethics. Most studies on tax evasion look at the issue from a public finance or economics perspective, although ethical issues may be mentioned briefly, in passing. The most comprehensive twentieth century work on the ethics of tax evasion was a doctoral thesis written by Martin Crowe (1944), titled *The Moral Obligation of Paying Just Taxes*. This thesis reviewed the theological and philosophical debate that had been going on, mostly within the Catholic Church, over the previous 500 years. Some of the debate took place in the Latin language. Crowe introduced this debate to an English language readership. A more recent doctoral dissertation on the topic was written by Torgler (2003), who discussed tax evasion from the perspective of public finance but also touched on some psychological and philosophical aspects of the issue. Alfonso Morales (1998) examined the views of Mexican immigrant street vendors and found that their loyalty to their families exceeded their loyalty to the government.

There have been a few studies that focus on tax evasion in a particular country. Ethics are sometimes discussed but, more often than not, the focus of the discussion is on government corruption and the reasons why the citizenry does not feel any moral duty to pay taxes to such a government. Ballas and Tsoukas (1998) discuss the situation in Greece. Smatrakalev (1998) discusses the Bulgarian case. Vaguine (1998) discusses Russia, as do Preobragenskaya and McGee (2004) to a lesser extent. A study of tax evasion in Armenia (McGee, 1999b) found the two main reasons for evasion to be the lack of a mechanism in place to collect taxes and the widespread opinion that the government does not deserve a portion of a worker's income.

A number of articles have been written from various religious perspectives. Cohn (1998) and Tamari (1998) discuss the Jewish literature on tax evasion and on ethics in general. McGee (1998d, 1999a) comments on these two articles from a secular perspective.

A few articles have been written on the ethics of tax evasion from various Christian viewpoints. Gronbacher (1998) addresses the issue from the perspectives of Catholic social thought and classical liberalism. Schansberg (1998) looks at the Biblical literature for guidance. Pennock (1998) discusses just war theory in connection with the moral obligation to pay just taxes, and not to pay unjust or immoral taxes. Smith and Kimball (1998) provide a Mormon perspective. McGee (1998c, 1999a) comments on the various Christian views from a secular perspective.

The Christian Bible discusses tax evasion and the duty of the citizenry to support the government in several places. Schansberg (1998) and McGee (1994a, 1998a) discuss the biblical literature on this point. When Jesus is asked whether people should pay taxes to Caesar, Jesus replied that we should give to Caesar the things that are Caesar's and give God the things that are God's (Matthew 22:17, 21). But Jesus did not elaborate on the point. He did not say what we are obligated to give government or whether that obligation has limits.

There are passages in the Bible that seemingly take an absolutist position. Romans 13, 1–2 supports the Divine Right of Kings, which basically holds that whoever is in charge of government is there with God's approval and anyone who disputes that fact or who fails to obey is subject to damnation. It is a sin against God to break any law. Thus, according to this viewpoint, Mao, Stalin, and Hitler must all be obeyed, even though they were the three biggest monsters of the twentieth century, because they are there with God's approval. This viewpoint is not widely held in modern liberal societies but it is probably fair to say that some religious fundamentalists still adhere to this view, since it is in the Bible, which they believe to be the literal word of God, a belief that is disputed by McKinsey (1995; 2000), Templeton (1996) and others (Burr, 1987; Lewis, 1926; Barker, 1992).

A few other religious views are also addressed in the literature. Murtuza and Ghazanfar (1998) discuss the ethics of tax evasion from the Muslim perspective. McGee (1998b, 1999a) comments on their article and also discusses the ethics of tax evasion under Islam citing Islamic business ethics literature (McGee, 1997). DeMoville (1998) discusses the Baha'i perspective and cites the relevant literature to buttress his arguments. McGee (1999a) commented on the DeMoville article. McGee (2004) discusses these articles in a book from a philosophical perspective.

Over the centuries, four basic views have emerged on the ethics of tax evasion. One view takes the position that tax evasion is always, or almost always unethical. There are basically three underlying rationales for this belief. One reason is the belief that individuals have a duty to the state to pay whatever taxes the state demands. This view is especially prevalent in democracies, where there is a strong belief that individuals should conform to majority rule.

The second rationale for an ethical duty to pay taxes is because the individual has a duty to other members of the community. This view holds that individuals should not be freeloaders by taking advantage of the services the state provides while not contributing to the payment of those services. A corollary of this belief is the view that if tax dodgers do not pay their fair share, then law-abiding taxpayers must pay more than their fair share.

The third rationale is that we owe a duty to God to pay taxes, or, stated differently, God has commanded us to pay our taxes. This view holds no water among atheists, of course, but the view is strongly held in some religious circles.

View Two might be labeled the anarchist view. This view holds that there is never any duty to pay taxes because the state is illegitimate, a mere thief that has no moral authority to take anything from anyone. The state is no more than a mafia that, under democracy, has its leaders chosen by the people.

The anarchist literature does not address the ethics of tax evasion directly but rather discusses the relationship of the individual to the state. The issue of tax evasion is merely one aspect of that relationship.

There is no such thing as a social contract according to this position. Where there is no explicit agreement to pay taxes there also is no duty. All taxation necessarily involves the taking of property by force or the threat of force, without the owner's permission. Thus, it meets the definition of theft. Stated as an equation, TAXATION = THEFT. A corollary equation is that FAIR SHARE = 0.

View Three holds that tax evasion may be ethical under some circumstances and unethical under other circumstances. This view is the prevalent view, based on the existing literature. The empirical literature on attitudes toward tax evasion, which is discussed later in this book, also finds that the prevailing view among taxpayers is that there is some duty to pay, but the duty is less than absolute.

The fourth view, which was not discussed in any depth in the *Journal of Business Ethics* article (McGee, 2006), is that there can be an affirmative duty not to pay. At least three arguments can be put forth to justify this position – the state is evil or corrupt, and thus is not entitled to receive the fruits of our labor; evading taxes is a positive-sum game, because the private sector is more efficient than the government sector; and tax evasion results in a more just society because there are fewer property rights violations if taxes are evaded.

An Examination of the Four Views

View One: Tax Evasion Is Never Ethical

One strand of this view is that individuals owe a duty to the state to pay whatever taxes the state demands. There is no such thing as taxes that are too high because the people determine the level of taxes. In a democracy, this view is justified under the consent theory. The peoples' representatives are designated to work out the details of democracy because the people are too busy earning a living and dealing with their own problems to actively participate in government. It is an application of the division of labor theory. The legislators, chief government executives, and the government bureaucracy are the specialists. They know best how to run things because they devote their whole working life to the task, and are thus more knowledgeable than the private citizenry can be because private citizens have neither the time nor the inclination to devote to acquiring the expertise and apply their knowledge to the running of government.

There are several criticisms that could be made of this viewpoint. One obvious weakness in this argument is that just because someone lives in a democracy does not mean that the government represents the interests of all the people, or that the government works for the general welfare. Many instances could be cited where the government works for special interests and against the interests of the general public. Trade policy is only one of many examples that may be cited (McGee 1994b, 2003).

The Public Choice School of Economics has examined hundreds of cases where government officials work either for themselves or for some special interest to the detriment of the general public (Tullock 1970, 1983, 1989; Rowley, Tollison & Tullock, 1988; van den Broeck, 1988; Gwartney & Wagner, 1988). All corporate welfare policies fit within this category, as do many other government programs. So it cannot be said categorically that the government represents the will of the people, or even that it usually represents the will of the people. All that can be said is that the government represents the will of some of the people some of the time. Does that justify the moral duty to always pay whatever taxes the government demands?

The argument could be made that, in a democracy, if you don't like the government you have, you have the power to throw out the rascals at the ballot box and replace them with people who better represent your viewpoints and interests. This view is prevalent in democracies, but a close analysis reveals that this possibility is often not realistic. The reason why America has red (Republican) states and blue (Democratic) states is because "the people" cannot agree on the kind of individuals they want running their government. Even in states that usually vote Republican, there is a large minority of democrats who do not agree with the outcome, and vice versa.

One might also point out the rather inconvenient fact that one vote really does not count. The probability that a US Senate or House race will be determined by just one vote is statistically improbable, and even if some member of Congress were to win by a single vote, there really is not much difference between the Democrats and Republicans anymore. It used to be said that, as a general rule, Democrats want to increase federal spending by 8% a year, whereas Republicans want to increase it by a mere 3%, which means there was a 5% difference between the two parties. But even that can no longer be said. President George W. Bush, a supposedly conservative Republican, managed to increase federal spending during his first term more than twice as fast as President Clinton did in his first term. The bottom line is that if you don't like the government you have, you really cannot throw them out and replace them with someone you like better. You are thus left with the option of either putting up with the government you have or move, if you can.

Another argument that has been used to justify the ethical obligation of paying all taxes is what may be called the "vote with your feet" argument. If you don't like the government you live under, move. Go somewhere else. This argument has a certain amount of plausibility. But there are some problems with it. For example, what if you live in a country that does not allow exit? The former Soviet Union is only one of several examples that could be cited. North Korea and Cuba are current examples.

Even if it is theoretically possible to move to another country, it may not be practically possible or feasible. Many people prefer to live close to family and friends, which acts as a barrier to free movement. In some countries it may be difficult to move because other countries don't want to take you or "your kind." If you are young, single, and living in Eastern Europe, the possibility of immigrating to the USA is much lower than if you are Mexican or Canadian and already have 10 or 20 relatives living in the USA. US immigration policy favors some groups over others. So do the immigration policies of many other countries.

If the articles by Cohn (1998) and Tamari (1998) are representative of the Jewish view, one may say that the Jewish view is near absolutist. Since Cohn is an Orthodox rabbi and Tamari is a well-known and highly respected Jewish scholar, one must at least concede that the viewpoints expressed in their articles at least represent some segment of Jewish thought on the issue. Some of the literature Cohn bases his position on goes back 3,300 years. The literature Tamari cites also goes back hundreds of years.

According to Cohn (1998), the Jewish legal perspective on paying taxes has four components:

- There is a duty to follow the country's statutes.
- Laws prohibit lying.
- A Jewish person must not do anything that could discredit the religion.
- Since it is essential for a Jewish person to perform as many commandments and good deeds as possible, it is essential to stay out of jail, since the Jewish religion cannot be practiced properly in prison.

While these reasons for paying taxes may be used as general guidelines, Cohn seems to indicate that they are absolutes or near absolutes according to Jewish law. If they are indeed absolutes, all four rules are subject to criticism. For example, the case can be made that there may not always be a duty to follow all the laws of one's country. Martin Luther King, Gandhi, and numerous other civil rights activists and war protesters would argue that there may at times be a moral obligation to break certain laws if they are evil laws and if the legislature is unlikely to change them any time soon.

One could counter argue that if you don't like the laws of the country where you are living you can move, but, as previously mentioned, that option may not always be attractive, or even possible. Also, what if you are already living in the greatest country on earth? To move to another country would be to move to a place that is not as acceptable as the place you now live.

If one were to play devil's advocate, one might ask whether Jews have an obligation to obey all the laws of the country, and to pay all the taxes they legally owe, if Hitler were the tax collector. I asked Cohn this question via e-mail but he did not reply immediately, perhaps because he felt uncomfortable with the implications of the most logical answer. However, we later coauthored an article that solicited the views of Orthodox Jewish students on tax evasion (McGee & Cohn, 2008).

One of the questions in that survey was whether it would be ethical for a Jew living in Nazi Germany to evade taxes. Of the 18 arguments to justify tax evasion that were included in that survey, the Jews in Nazi Germany argument was the strongest argument to support the view that tax evasion would be ethical in that situation. However, even this situation did not draw absolute support for evasion. Some of the Orthodox Jews who participated in the survey felt that there was some duty to pay taxes even to Hitler, since failure to do so would constitute a breach of the law; a lie; the possibility that other Jews could be viewed in a negative light because if one Jew evades taxes it makes all Jews look bad; and because evasion might lead to jail, which would make it difficult or impossible to do good works (mitzvos).

Thus, while one may state that there is a general obligation to obey the laws of the government of the country where you live, philosophical problems arise when one attempts to make this general guideline an absolute.

The second reason Cohn offers for paying taxes – that laws prohibit lying – may also be an acceptable general rule, subject to exceptions. But there may be situations where lying is the only moral thing to do. For example, what if your neighbor comes running into your house, brandishing a gun or ax, and asks "Where is my wife? I'm going to kill her. Do you know where she is?" If his wife were like the average wife, who is probably less than perfect but probably not bad enough to consider killing, it would be safe to say that you can honestly lie and tell him you do not know where she is, even if you are actually hiding her in the basement… or your bedroom

One might use a similar example to justifiably lie to the government. What if, instead of a husband looking for a wife to kill, it were the Gestapo looking for Jews? Certainly, there would be no moral duty to tell the Gestapo you are hiding a few Jews in your basement, even if lying would tend to tarnish respect for the rule of law.

Cohn's third reason, that one must not do anything that would discredit the religion, may be labeled as self-serving. This argument falls under the category of paying taxes because there is a duty to some segment of the community, the segment in this case being the Jewish community. Also, it is not always clear that the whole religion is seen in a bad light just because one member of the religion engages in activity that is considered dishonest. This argument would be stronger in an Orthodox or Hasidic community than it would be in a Reform Jewish community, where religion plays a lesser role in the life of the average participant.

Cohn's fourth reason, that one should not evade taxes because it would limit the ability to practice one's religion, is basically another way of saying that one must not disobey the laws because you might be punished. As such, it is a strong argument, but one that does not necessarily have anything to do with ethics.

There is another weakness with this argument. The general argument is that if you evade taxes, you might go to jail. There is a duty to perform good works. You will not be able to perform good works if you are in jail. Therefore, you should not evade taxes. The problem with this view is that you might actually be able to perform *more* good works to more deserving individuals if you are *in* jail rather than on the outside. If one were to take this argument to its logical conclusion, and if one believes that the main reason for existence is to perform good works for others, the logical conclusion is that you should evade taxes and also report the evasion to the tax authorities to increase the probability that you will be sent to jail, where you would be able to better fulfill your purpose in life, which is to perform good works.

Tamari (1998) cites some of the same reasons as Cohn for a duty to pay taxes. Tamari points out that the Jewish law states you must follow the laws of the country where you live. But he also points out that the *Mishnah Torah* states that there is no moral obligation to pay taxes where the king usurps power or where the king is arbitrary or capricious or discriminatory or where taxes are confiscatory.

But he also points out that the Jewish literature regards tax evasion as theft. The theft may be from other citizens, who have to pay more taxes if the tax evader pays less. Clark (n.d.), on the contrary, states that the *Mishnah Torah* regards tax evasion as theft from the king. Either way, tax evasion is considered to be theft according to the Jewish literature, at least most of the time.

Christian views are mixed on the issue, although there is a strand within Christianity that is closely akin to the Jewish view. The Mormon view basically agrees with the Jewish view that tax evasion is always unethical, although for different reasons than those advanced by Jewish scholars. In fact, the Mormon view may even be considered more absolutist than the Jewish view because the Mormon view seemingly does not allow for exceptions.

Smith and Kimball (1998) cite several passages from the Mormon literature that support the view that there is a duty to pay taxes. One such argument is that one must obey the laws of whatever government you live under. One passage cited from *The Pearl of Great Price* states that Mormons believe in being subject to kings, presidents, rulers, etc., in obeying, honoring, and sustaining the law. The thirteenth *Article of Faith* states that Mormons believe in being honest which, according to Smith and Kimball, includes honesty in the payment of taxes. The *Encyclopedia of Mormonism* (1992) is also cited as standing for the position that church members are required to obey tax laws. It goes on to say that if a church member disagrees with a particular tax law, he may attempt to change the law or challenge the law in court.

Any member who refuses to file a tax return or to pay whatever income tax is required is in conflict with the teachings of the Church. Smith and Kimball cite secondary Mormon literature that takes the position that tax evasion is a form of theft, although their mention of this position does not state whether it is theft from the government or theft from the taxpaying community. They cite several other sources and conclude that tax evasion is against the teachings of the Church. Nowhere in their article do they mention any exceptions to this rule, leading one to reasonably conclude that there are no exceptions.

One may criticize their absolutist position on several grounds. For example, did the Mormons in nineteenth century New York State have an absolute ethical obligation to pay taxes to the very government that was running them out of the state, sometimes at gunpoint? What about the various governments that prohibit them from practicing their religion? A number of modern governments fall into this category. Ayn Rand might refer to this mentality – the belief that the individual is morally obliged to obey the government even as it is placing its jackboot on your throat – as an example of the "sanction of the victim," which she discusses in several of her works (Rand, 1968; Binswanger, 1986).

DeMoville (1998) presents the Baha'i view on the ethics of tax evasion. Although he mentions the civil disobedience of Henry David Thoreau, Martin Luther King, and Gandhi, their views are not the views of the Baha'i faith. He cites several passages from the Baha'i literature to show that the Baha'i view is absolutist, much like the Mormon view. The reasoning is also similar to that of the Mormons. Individuals must be loyal, faithful, and honest toward the government under which they live.

DeMoville quotes from a letter written by the grandson of the Baha'i faith's founder to the Baha'i community in Germany in 1934, which stated that members are under a sacred obligation to wholeheartedly obey the Nazi regime, at least as long as the regime does not trample on religious freedom. The letter goes on to say that, although individuals should be prepared to sacrifice their own interests to those of the government under which they live, they do not have to endure violations of their religious freedom. But the letter goes on to say that if some government such as that of Germany or Soviet Russia prevents the holding of meetings or the publication of religious literature, Baha'is have a duty to obey. Baha'is are morally obligated to obey their government in all administrative matters. The only time there is no duty to obey is regarding the area of belief. Compromise in this area is not permitted even under threat of death or expulsion.

The Baha'i position may seem abhorrent to liberal democrats in the West, who believe there are limits to what any government may legitimately do. Anyone who believes in freedom of speech, the press and religion certainly would not agree with the Baha'i position. But that does not automatically mean that it is an incorrect position, only that there is room for disagreement. Certainly, no one is forced to be or remain a member of the Baha'i faith, at least not after reaching the age of adulthood, although there may be a lot of peer group pressure not to cast off the religion or even to take a cafeteria approach to the religion's doctrine.

View Two: Tax Evasion Is Always Ethical

The second view, which I label the anarchist view for lack of a better term, begins with the premise that all government is illegitimate. Government is a mere thief, which confiscates assets, percentages of paychecks, etc., without the consent of the owners of the property. The definition of theft is the taking of property without the owner's consent. The fact that it is sometimes some government that does the taking does not alter this basic definition.

The counterargument is that governments that derive their authority from the consent of the governed are legitimate and are thus entitled to some kind of support, although the exact specifics of the amount and type of support may not be easy to agree upon. Some supporters of government would restrict the scope of government to defense functions such as the support of an army, a police force, and some sort of court system. Others would go beyond this night watchman state to include welfare state functions and redistribution of income.

Archists (those who believe in some government legitimacy and are thus not anarchists) often put forth the argument that any kind of workable democracy is legitimate and that individuals who live under the protection of a democratic regime have some duty to obey the laws of the country in which they live. Democracy may not be perfect and may even at times trample on minority rights, but some duty is owed in any event just because some segment of the community supports the regime.

Not all governments are democratically elected, of course, including the government of China, which has the largest population in the world. Thus, not all supporters of government can use the democratic argument. However, even a certain percentage of the Chinese population believes that there is some duty to obey government and its laws. Legitimacy of government is deeply ingrained in Chinese culture. The mere fact that the Chinese government is not a democracy does not alter this pervasive belief.

In the West, the social contract theory is often used to legitimize government. According to this theory, whether it is the version put forth by Locke (1689), Hobbes (1651) or Rousseau (1762; also see Leiker, 1998), some segment of the population, at some point in history decided to give up some portion of their liberty in exchange for government protection. Governments were formed to protect basic rights like the right to life and property. For those who do not believe that such rights exist, there is another argument that governments were formed for protection purposes and that subjects owe some duty to pay for the protection offered by their government.

Anarchists would be quick to dispute this position. They would assert that there never was such a social contract, and even if some group of individuals did, at some point in history, gather around a fire to discuss the formation of government to protect them from external and internal aggression, it does not follow that the current generation is bound by such agreement. It is a well-established principle of law that one person may not be bound by a contractual agreement entered into by another, unless there is some sort of principal agent relationship.

Lysander Spooner (1870), the nineteenth century American lawyer and anarchist, provided one of the best arguments for this position. According to his view, the US Constitution, which was signed by a few people in the last quarter of the eighteenth century, had little legitimacy even on the dates of signing because the individuals who signed it represented only themselves. Even in the cases where the signers were elected by some constituency, they were only elected by some minority of eligible voters. Anyone who did not vote for them cannot be bound by any agreement they enter into. So at most, only a few individuals who were living and who were of the age of majority could be bound by the US Constitution. Anyone not living at the time of the signing certainly cannot be bound. By the time Spooner wrote his pamphlet on this topic (1870), most, if not all of the signers of the US Constitution were dead. Thus, even if one concedes that some laws that are passed by some individuals who represent some part of the eligible electorate are legitimate as of the date of signing, any such laws become null and void at some point, and are not binding on a major part of the populace even while the ink is still wet.

Thomas Jefferson, the third president of the USA and the author of the US Declaration of Independence, was certainly no anarchist. Anarchists do not run for president, as a general rule. However, Jefferson, who died several decades before Spooner's 1870 pamphlet came into existence, agreed with a watered down form of Spooner's argument. In a letter to John Wayles Eppes in 1813, Jefferson states:

> We may consider each generation as a distinct nation, with a right, by the will of its majority, to bind themselves, but none to bind the succeeding generation, more than the inhabitants of another country.

Nearly a quarter of a century earlier (1789), writing to James Madison from Paris, Jefferson said:

> The question Whether one generation of men has a right to bind another, seems never to have been started either on this or our side of the water. Yet it is a question of such consequences as not only to merit decision, but place also, among the fundamental principles of every government … no such obligation can be transmitted … the earth belongs … to the living …

Jefferson believed that laws have a natural expiration date as members of the generation who were of the age of majority when the law was passed start to die. For example, if half of the people who were 21 at the time a particular law was passed are dead 19 years later, the law becomes null and void after 19 years. If half of the adult population dies 22 years after a particular law was passed, then the law dies after 22 years. One generation cannot bind another generation.

The view that one generation cannot bind another was a common view before the American Revolution. English libertarian writers John Trenchard and Thomas Gordon, who were influential in forming intellectual opinion in pre-Revolutionary America, said the following in the early 1720s:

> All men are born free; liberty is a gift which they receive from God himself; nor can they alienate the same by consent, though possibly they may forfeit it by crimes. No man … can … give away the lives and liberties, religion or acquired property of his posterity, who will be born as free as he himself was born, and can never be bound by his wicked and ridiculous bargain (Trenchard & Gordon, 1965).

Archists would be quick to challenge this view of the legitimacy of laws. They would argue that laws, once passed, remain binding on all who live within the jurisdiction for as long as the law exists. Laws disappear only when repealed, unless there is a clause within the law that states that the law is good for only a certain period of time.

Another argument that archists might put forth would be to assert that governments are like corporations. They continue to exist independently of their owners. Just like corporations do not die when a shareholder dies, governments do not go out of existence when a citizen dies.

Governments are not quite like corporations, however. Governments are of necessity a monopoly within any particular jurisdiction. Governments must have a monopoly on force to be effective, or so it has been argued. Corporations, on the contrary, are voluntary associations. One can become a member by buying shares and one can exit by selling the shares. If one wants to cease being part of a particular government, one must move to another jurisdiction where some other government has a monopoly position.

Which argument carries the day? There is a certain amount of disagreement on this point. Although the vast majority of the population subscribes to some form of archism, majorities are not always right. But the interesting point from the perspective of determining when tax evasion is ethical and when it is not is the fact that some people who consider themselves to be archists – believers in the legitimacy of government – sometimes take an anarchist position when it comes to the ethics of tax evasion.

View Three: Tax Evasion Is Sometimes Ethical

View three is the prevalent view, based on the existing literature. This view holds that tax evasion is ethical in some cases and unethical in others. Crowe (1944) spends 177 pages discussing when tax evasion is ethical and when it is not. He summarizes 500 years of theological and philosophical debate on the issue.

Angelus of Clavisio (1494) took the position that there is no ethical obligation to pay taxes if the government does not use the revenues collected to provide for the common good, at least as long as neither lying nor perjury are involved. Berardi (1898) took the position that there is probably no moral duty to pay a tax even if lying or perjury are involved, since the Prince merely dictates what is owed. Taxpayers never enter into a contract with the Prince, and thus are not bound to pay anything.

Genicot (1927) states that partial evasion is justified on the grounds that the government does not have the right to the full amount and that it would be unfair to impose heavier taxes on conscientious men while wicked men usually pay less. Crolly (1877) takes the position that there is no duty to pay taxes unless evasion would result in violence.

Lehmkuhl (1902) takes the position that it is unethical to evade taxes when the result is that nonevaders have to pay more. In other words, there is some moral duty to other taxpayers even if there is no moral duty to the government. But Davis (1938) takes the position that it would be unfair to require honest taxpayers to take up the slack and pay higher taxes to make up for the evasions of others.

The Muslim view toward tax evasion seemingly falls under category three, that evasion is sometimes ethical (McGee, 1997, 1998b, 1999a). Ahmad (1995), citing Yusuf's *Economic Justice in Islam* (1971), lists the following practices that would be considered unethical in an Islamic state:

- It is immoral on the part of the state to use its power and privilege to make monopolistic gains or to tax the common people indirectly for replenishing the exchequer thereby.

- There is no room in Islam for custom barriers, restrictive tariffs, or exchange control. The Islamic state, therefore, must not resort to them.
- It is illegitimate and unlawful for the state to tax directly or indirectly the general body of consumers and to give "protection" to the interests of a class of producers in the name of industrialization.
- Since it is the duty of the state to dispense justice free of charge, therefore, there must not be any court-fees, revenue stamps, or fees of any kind for the transaction of any official business.
- There must not be any "income" tax as such. Besides curbing the initiative it assumes illegitimacy of the income of the rich. The state should levy, if need be, a proportional tax on the pattern of zakat on the accumulated wealth of the capable taxpayers.
- The state should not resort to indirect taxation. If the state has to tax, then it should do so directly so that the taxes represent a conscious contribution of the people to the cause of public interest.
- That there is no justification for imposing death duty. Islamic laws of inheritance take care of the wealth left by the deceased.

If the view of this Islamic scholar (Yusuf, 1971) accurately reflect the Muslim position on the moral obligation to pay taxes, then it would seemingly not be unethical for a Muslim to evade indirect taxes, which include excise taxes, customs duties, and perhaps corporate income taxes. Muslims could also morally avoid paying tariffs and could engage in smuggling, provided the goods being smuggled are not against Islam, such as alcohol or cocaine. Evading income taxes also would not be immoral, although evading a property tax might be. Ahmad (1995) states that there is no moral obligation to pay any tax that has the effect of increasing consumer prices. Sales taxes, excise taxes, and tariffs fall into this category.

Both Yusuf and Ahmad take basically the same position on tax evasion. They believe that evasion is justified in the cases mentioned above. However, not all Muslim scholars agree with their view. Jalili (2012), for example, takes the position that cheating on taxes is absolutely forbidden if the government is a pure Islamic state and follows Sharia Law. The prohibition on any kind of evasion is less than absolute only in cases where the government is not purely Islamic or where it is secular.

An argument can be made that there is nothing unethical about not paying all the taxes that are legally owed if you are a Jew living in Nazi Germany. There is no moral obligation to help pay for the canisters of poison gas that the government plans to use to kill you and your family. Likewise, there is no moral obligation to pay taxes if you are a Mormon living in New York State during the period of the nineteenth century when Mormons were being run out of New York at gunpoint. There is no ethical obligation for a member of the Baha'i faith to pay taxes to the Iranian government when the government is expending funds to kill Baha'is. There is no moral obligation to pay for the rope used in your own lynching or the poison gas or bullets used to kill you, or even for the train ticket to transport you to the gas chambers.

People who agree with any of these above-mentioned positions are not absolutists, since they believe that tax evasion is ethical in some cases. But taking such a position only begins to answer the question. The next question that needs to be answered is, if tax evasion is ethically justified in certain circumstances, what are the limits? At what point does tax evasion become ethically justified? Schansberg (1998) raises this point, as do other scholars (Pennock, 1998; Gronbacher, 1998; McGee, 1994a, 2004).

What if your country is fighting a war that you consider to be unjust? Or what if you are a pacifist and consider all wars to be unjust? Pennock (1998) discusses some of these issues. If 22% of the federal budget is spent on national defense, are you morally justified in evading 22% of the tax you legally owe, or are you ethically justified in evading more than 22%, since all tax collections go into a common pot anyway and whatever taxes you pay might be used to further the war effort?

What if you live under a corrupt government, where a large portion of tax revenue goes to corrupt politicians and their friends and family? Are you any less justified in evading taxes if those corrupt friends and relatives use part of the proceeds to build roads and hospitals than if they send the funds to secret offshore accounts?

What if you are in a high tax bracket and the government takes more than 90% of your marginal income, while taking a much lower percentage from people who have lower incomes? In such cases, you are being treated as a resource, as a means rather than an end, which violates Kantian ethics (1952a, b, c; 1983).

That is not to say that Kant was philosophically opposed to taxes. He was not. He believed that the sovereign has a right to tax and that the people have a duty to pay taxes to support certain government activities. But Kant questioned whether childless people should be forced to pay for the maintenance and support of other people's children and he opposed raising money through lotteries, since he believed that lotteries increased poverty (Kant, 1952d). It is questionable whether Kant would have supported the graduated income tax, since the purpose of this tax is to exploit those who have more. Under this tax regime, people are treated as means rather than ends.

If the government uses the tax system as a means of redistributing income rather than as a means of financing legitimate government functions, are you justified in evading taxes? If not, why not? What if the government's tax system has both the goal of raising revenue for legitimate government functions and also redistribution? Are you justified in evading only the portion that goes for redistribution? What if 80% of your neighbors view redistribution as a legitimate goal of government? Does that change your answer? Even though a strong case has been made that redistribution is inherently unethical (Bastiat, 1968; deJouvenel, 1952), many people, perhaps a clear majority, disagree with this view.

Is there a duty to pay taxes if the government supports the Anglican Church, as is the case in England, if you are a Catholic? Or an atheist? What if the government subsidizes abortions and you think that abortion is murder? What if the government supports affirmation action programs (reverse discrimination programs) and you are a white male?

What if evading a tax actually benefits society? Is there an ethical duty to evade in such a case? If a tax actually does more harm than good, an argument based on utilitarian ethics could be made that evading the tax is a moral obligation since evasion would result in the greatest good for the greatest number. Evading tariffs is one such case where evasion might actually increase societal well-being, since tariffs are negative-sum games. They produce more losers than winners. Evading a tariff would thus prevent a negative-sum game from taking place.

The point is that, once it is conceded that tax evasion is sometimes ethical, there is no clear dividing line that people can agree on regarding when evasion is ethical and when it is not. That does not mean that there is no answer to this question, only that people cannot agree on what the answer is.

View Four: There Is an Affirmative Duty to Evade Taxes

At least three arguments can be put forth to support the view that there is an affirmative duty to evade taxes – the government is evil and funding to evil governments must be cut off to reduce further perpetrations of evil; society benefits by evasion because the result is a positive-sum game; and evading taxes reduces injustice in society because taxes violate property rights and the fewer times property rights are violated, the more justice there is.

The government is evil argument. We have all heard phrases like:

> Silence in the face of evil is itself evil, God will not hold us guiltless. Not to speak is to speak. Not to act is to act (Dietrich Bonhoeffer).
> All that is necessary for evil to triumph is for good men to do nothing (Attributed to Edmund Burke).
> If you're not part of the solution, you're part of the problem (Unknown origin).

The point is that there is an affirmative duty to resist evil. If a government is evil, there is a duty to resist. One form of resistance is tax evasion, which helps to cut off funding to an evil regime. Perhaps fewer people would have been killed in War X if more people would have evaded taxes in Country Y.

Tax resistance has been a part of the strategy of various antiwar groups over the centuries as a means of slamming the brakes on some unjust war. During the Vietnam War, there was a semiorganized effort by a faction of the antiwar movement to evade taxes by claiming a billion dependents on their tax returns. The effort was not very effective. People who took such deductions got audited and had to pay the taxes that were legally owed. They made a statement but their inept attempts at evasion were unsuccessful and they had little or no direct effect on the war effort other than to draw publicity to their antiwar cause.

Eric Metaxas (2010), Bonhoeffer's biographer, paraphrasing Bonhoeffer, states:

> It is sometimes not enough to help those crushed by the evil actions of a state; at some point the church must directly take action against the state to stop it from perpetrating evil.

I don't know if Bonhoeffer evaded taxes as part of his effort to resist Hitler, but I do know that he paid a much higher price than interest and penalties. He was executed in a concentration camp, at Hitler's personal command, for his part in the attempt to assassinate Hitler (Metaxas, 2010). Thus, mere tax evasion might not be enough if one believes there is a moral duty to stop evil. One might be required to do more, on moral grounds.

Those who believe their country is engaged in an unjust war face a moral dilemma if they believe their government also does good things with the tax funds it collects. For example, if 20% of the taxes collected go toward pursuing an unjust war but the other 80% goes toward worthy projects, one must decide how much to evade. Since tax funds go into a common pot, evading a mere 20% of taxes owed will not result in defunding the war effort. In order to accomplish that goal, one must evade 100%.

The same might be said for other cases where the government is evil or is engaging in activities the taxpayer considers immoral. Those who believe that abortion is murder have no moral obligation to fund government-provided abortion facilities. The same could be said for a plethora of other government programs. Forcing fundamentalist Christians to pay for schools that teach evolution is just as abhorrent as forcing atheists to fund schools that teach creationism.

> To compel a man to subsidize with his taxes the propagation of ideas which he disbelieves and abhors is sinful and tyrannical (Thomas Jefferson).

If the activities the government is engaging in are considered to be evil, the argument could be made that there is an affirmative duty to resist. One form of resistance is tax evasion. Whether that resistance should include killing abortion doctors – or killing those who kill abortion doctors - is a question we will leave for another day.

The question of how much one may morally evade defunding an evil government remains unanswered in cases where the government is not totally evil. Anything less than total evasion defeats the purpose, since all tax collections are put into a common fund, but total evasion results in not paying a tax one has a moral duty to pay to support other projects, assuming there is a moral duty to pay something.

The utilitarian ethics argument. I have not seen any arguments to justify tax evasion on the basis of utilitarian ethics. Perhaps others have applied utilitarian ethical principles to the issue of tax evasion, but I have not seen any writings using this approach. I hesitate to say that the approach I am about to take is unique. Nothing is new under the sun, as they say. Someone else has probably made this argument before, and my apologies to whoever has made a utilitarian argument to justify tax evasion, since I am not citing you.

Actually, there are at least two utilitarian-based arguments that could be used to justify tax evasion on ethical grounds.

Argument 1: The first argument goes something like this. The ethical choice is the choice that increases efficiency or societal wealth. The private sector is more efficient than the government sector. Therefore, money should be kept in the private sector rather than transferred to the government sector. Tax evasion is a means of keeping money in the private sector. Therefore, tax evasion is ethical and there is an ethical duty to evade, since failure to evade does not result in maximization of societal wealth.

The efficiency argument has its roots in classical utilitarianism and has thrived in the law and economics literature (Barnes & Stout, 1992; Cooter & Ulen, 1988;

Table 1.1 Comparison of high-cost municipal to low-cost contract refuse collection

Productivity measure	Rochester (municipal)	Utica (contract)
Loads per crew/day	1.75	2.12
Time available for collection (based on 8-h day)	3.04	6.77
Stops per crew/h	93.5	190.8
Stops per crewman/h	23.4	79.5
Average crew size	4	.24
Annual cubic yards per crew	6,898	16,859
Annual tons per crew	1,725	5,619
Annual cubic yards per crewman	1,725	7,024
Annual tons per crewman	431	2,341
Productivity index	1.00	5.43

Source: Stevens (1980: 75)

Goetz, 1984; Harrison, 1995; Katz, 1998; Malloy, 1990; Mercuro & Medema, 1997; Posner, 1983, 1998). The basic utilitarian argument is that an act is ethical if it produces the greatest good for the greatest number (Bentham, 1988; Mill, 1962). Sidgwick, in his *The Methods of Ethics*, expands on that view by taking the position that an action is justified only if it results in at least as much net happiness as any other action the individual could have taken. Otherwise, it is wrong. Thus, merely increasing overall happiness is not sufficient to make an act ethical. One must maximize net happiness. If two acts can increase happiness and a decision is made to perform the act that produces less happiness than the other alternative, one is acting unethically according to Sidgwick.

It should come as no surprise that the private sector is more efficient than the government sector. The private sector can do just about anything more efficiently, cheaper and better than government. There should be no need to provide examples, since they are all around us. However, some blind referees in the past have criticized my prior work for merely making such a statement without references or examples to support this position, so I will provide a few examples and references for those who insist on documenting every obvious statement of truth (Donahue, 1991; Finley, 1989; Fitzgerald, 1988; Goodman, 1985; Greene, 2001; Kemp, 2007; Lauder, 1992; Letwin, 1988; Ohashi & Roth, 1980; Pirie, 1988; Pitcher, 2003; Poole, 1980; Savas, 1982, 2005; Veljanovski, 1989; Walker, 1988).

Table 1.1 shows the much greater efficiency of private refuse collection. The productivity index is 5.43. The private sector collectors were much more efficient by any measure.

Here are some additional statistics:

- Refuse collection – Nationwide surveys of the USA, Canada, and Switzerland found that municipal collections are 29–37% more costly than contract collections, if one compares the cost of municipal collection to the price of private collection. If one compares just the relative costs (by adjusting for profits and taxes), the cost of municipal refuse collection would be between 61 and 71% higher than the cost of private collection (Savas, 1982: 93).

- Fire protection – is 89% more costly if done by government (Savas, 1982: 96).
- Airlines – private airlines are 204% more efficient in terms of tons of freight and mail carried per employee, 122% more efficient in terms of passengers carried per employee, and 113% more efficient in terms of revenue earned per employee (Savas, 1982: 97).
- Buses – Government buses in Germany cost 160%/km more to run than do privately owned buses (Savas, 1982: 97).
- Package delivery – UPS delivers packages faster than the US Postal Service and has a damage rate that is one-fifth of the government rate (Savas, 1982: 98).
- Nursing care – A comparative study of nursing homes operated by the Veterans Administration with privately operated nursing homes found that the cost per patient day was 82% higher in the government facilities (Savas, 1982: 99).
- Health insurance administration – It costs 35% more to process health insurance claims when the processing is done by government workers (Savas, 1982: 101).
- Cleaning government offices – In Germany, it costs between 42 and 66% more to clean government offices when the cleaning is done by government workers. The cost of cleaning government offices in Hamburg is 30–80% cheaper when done by private firms (Savas, 1982: 106).
- Tree trimming – Private firms can trim trees for one-third the cost of government employees in Detroit (Savas, 1982: 107).
- Towing cars – A car that is illegally parked in New York City can be towed by a private firm for 46% of what it would cost for government employees to do it (Savas, 1982: 107).

Hundreds of additional examples of government inefficiency could be given, but enough is enough. Much evidence of government inefficiency can be found in any study of privatization. The reason governments all over the world have privatized or are in the process of privatizing various functions is because of the substantial cost savings that result when tasks formerly performed by governments are turned over to the private sector. The http://www.privatization.org website provides numerous studies to document the savings that can be had through privatization.

A government study of waste in the federal government of the USA has documented hundreds of billions of dollars of waste that is difficult or impossible to eliminate because of the way governments are structured (GAO, 2011). Governments are not run on the profit motive. They are run on the principle that if we do not spend all of this year's budget by year-end, next year's budget will be reduced. There is no way to eliminate this mentality by hiring efficiency experts because the incentive system does not change.

Also, government programs that do not work are not eliminated. If some government agency fails to do a good job, it is likely to receive increased funding so that it can do a better job in the future. The public (government) school system is a perfect example. Whenever it is pointed out that American students perform relatively poorly, someone inevitably suggests we need to spend more on education. We spend more on education in the USA, per capita, than any other nation on earth, so money is not the problem.

The problems are monopoly and government control. Parents do not have choices. They must send their children to the school that is closest to their home. As is the case with any monopoly, the cost is higher and the quality is lower than would be the case in a competitive system. It is a structural problem that is caused by the way government is structured and the perverse incentive system that is inherent in government. The solution is not to throw more money into the failed system but to prevent money from being taken out of the more efficient private sector to be thrown into the black hole that is government.

The law and economics literature applies utilitarian ethical principles to arrive at the conclusion that what is efficient is ethical. Stated in Christian terms, it is a sin to waste. Ronald Coase takes the position that policy should focus on maximizing the wealth of society (Coase, 1960:43; 1964: 195; 1988: 28). Richard Posner, one of the founders of the law and economics movement, states that:

> ... the criterion for judging whether acts and institutions are just or good is whether they maximize the wealth of society (Posner, 1983: 115).

In another place he states that morality and efficiency are consistent (Posner, 1998: 284–285).

Since the private sector is much more efficient than the government sector, the moral thing to do would be to prevent as much money as possible from being transferred from the private sector to the government sector. One way to do that is by evading taxes. One cannot maximize societal wealth by transferring assets from the more efficient sector to the less efficient sector.

Argument 2: There is another utilitarian argument to support tax evasion. The underlying premise of utilitarian ethics is that an act is ethical if it increases happiness or decreases pain. People who can keep the fruits of their labor are happier than people who have the fruits of their labor confiscated and they experience less pain than people who have the fruits of their labor confiscated. People who evade taxes are able to keep more of the fruits of their labor. Therefore, tax evasion is ethical and there is a duty to evade taxes because doing so increases total happiness in society.

Of course, this latter argument assumes there is no penalty for evasion. If one has to worry about being penalized for getting caught, that factor must be included in the utilitarian calculus. If the pleasure to be gained by evasion exceeds the pain to be incurred by getting caught and having to pay penalties, evasion is the ethical choice, according to utilitarian ethical theory. One might include probability theory into the equation if one is able to predict the probability of getting caught and the penalties that must be paid upon being caught.

The point may be raised that tax evasion results in both winners and losers and that the above argument is incomplete because it ignores the effects that tax evasion will have on people whose happiness will decrease as a result of the evasion. Let's examine that argument.

First of all, we must determine who all the winners and losers are. The obvious winners are those who get to keep more of the fruits of their labor. The losers are the government employees who will not be paid or the beneficiaries of the government's largesse, which would include welfare cheats, people on Medicaid, Medicare, and Social Security, among others. Wealth is shifted from those who produce it to those who consume it.

If we were to stop the analysis at this point, it would appear that the winners and losers cancel each other out. The money transferred from the private sector to the government sector increases the happiness of those who receive it and decrease the happiness of those who are forced to pay. But that is not the end of the analysis. There are really two losers for every winner.

Frédéric Bastiat (1801–1850) addressed this wealth transfer issue in the 1840s in his classic essay, *What Is Seen and What Is Not Seen* (Bastiat, 1964: 1–50). Bastiat would point out that there are two losers for each winner. Let's say that Peter is taxed and his tax payments are transferred to Paul. Peter is the loser and Paul is the winner. But that is not the end of the story. Sam also loses because Peter would have used those funds to pay for a vacation at Sam's restaurant and motel if he had not had to pay Paul. Thus, there are two losers – Peter and Sam – and only one winner.

Taxing Peter to pay Paul makes one person happier and two people less happy. If Peter evades the tax, two people are happy – Peter and Sam – and only one person is unhappy – Paul. Thus, the utilitarian ethics solution would be to evade taxes.

The rights argument. A just society is a society where injustice is absent (Bastiat, 1968). A society is just if individuals are free to live their lives as they see fit without interference, provided they do not violate the rights of others.

Plunder – the taking of property without the owner's consent – is an injustice. Plunder is of two types – illegal and legal. An example of illegal plunder would be where a thief takes the property of another by force or fraud. Legal plunder occurs when the government does the taking. Bastiat (1968: 21) identifies legal plunder as follows:

> See if the law takes from some persons what belongs to them, and gives it to other persons to whom it does not belong. See if the law benefits one citizen at the expense of another by doing what the citizen himself cannot do without committing a crime.
>
> Then abolish this law without delay, for it is not only an evil itself, but also it is a fertile source for further evils because it invites reprisals. If such a law – which may be an isolated case – is not abolished immediately, it will spread, multiply, and develop into a system.

For Bastiat, tax funds that are used to support government functions that protect the life, liberty and property of all the people are raised legitimately. Tax funds that are taken with the intent of redistribution are examples of plunder and increase the injustice that exists in society.

Taking that argument one step further than Bastiat, a logical extension would be to assert that there is no duty to participate in the act of injustice that results from redistributive taxation, and one is performing a beneficial act to society by resisting this redistributive injustice. Tax evasion in such cases decreases the amount of injustice in society, and thus increases justice. Refusing to have one's property confiscated for redistributive purposes leads to a more just society. One might even go a step further and assert that we all have a duty to eliminate injustice, and that one way to achieve that goal would be to evade redistributive taxes.

Nozick (1974) looks at things somewhat differently. For him, taxation is a form of slavery. Let's say that the government takes 40% of a person's income in taxes.

In substance, that is the same as forcing that person to work for free 2 days a week. That person is a slave to the extent that he is not able to keep the fruits of his labor.

Nozick's view is based on entitlement. The individual who earns the income is more entitled to it than anyone else. If a portion of that income is taken in the form of taxes, it is little more than theft. That person's property rights have been violated.

Societies that have strong property rights regimes tend to be more peaceful, more just, and wealthier than societies that disparage property rights. If one lives in a society where property rights are being disparaged, one can commit a positive act by doing things to reduce the amount of property rights violations that take place. One of those things is to evade taxes. Not only does it benefit the individual who is protecting his own property but it also benefits society because it reduces the amount of property rights violations that take place.

I would like to end this section with a quote from Walter Williams, who does an excellent job of summarizing the entitlement position in a way that can be understood by most readers.

> But you might say, if government didn't do all that it's doing we wouldn't have a *just* society. What's *just* has been debated for centuries but let me offer my definition of social justice: I keep what I earn and you keep what you earn. Do you disagree? Well then tell me how much of what I earn *belongs* to you – and why? (Williams, 1987: 62).

Concluding Comments

The argument that tax evasion is never justified is the weakest of the options. To argue that a taxpayer is never justified in evading a tax, no matter how unfair the tax or corrupt the government, is simply untenable (McGee, 1999a). To hold otherwise would be to assert that Jews have a moral obligation to pay taxes to Hitler so that the Nazi government will be able to afford the poison gas that will be used to exterminate a segment of the population. If this is true, then it could also be argued that Jews have a moral obligation to reimburse the Nazi government for the cost of the train ride to the death camps. The absolutist view is simply untenable.

The other views are not so easy to dismiss. Taxpayers who live under a government that does more *to* them than it does *for* them have a strong moral argument to evade at least a portion of the tax (Crowe, 1944; McGee, 1999a). If one begins with the premise that the government is the servant and the people are the masters, then an argument could be made that there is some obligation to pay at least some taxes to reimburse the government for the services it provides, just as a master is obligated to pay the salary of his servant. But it does not follow that one must pay whatever the government demands, even in a democracy, just like there is no absolute moral duty for a master to pay whatever the servant demands.

Some scholars have asserted that democracy has become the new God (Hoppe 2001). If this is the case, then to criticize democracy is to blaspheme. Any decisions arrived at by the democratic process are necessarily the correct decisions, which must be obeyed no matter what.

Hamilton, Madison, and Jay (1961) and others (Acton, 1985) have warned against the dangers of untrammeled majoritarianism. It could also be pointed out that both Hitler and Mussolini gained power through the democratic process. If two wolves and a sheep voted to determine what to have for lunch, the sheep would not be bound by any adverse decision, even though it was arrived at democratically. Indeed, the sheep would be morally justified in resisting the democratic decision with deadly force. In other words, just because some democratically elected government imposes a tax, it does not automatically follow that there is a duty to pay. Whether there is a duty to pay depends on the facts and circumstances. Or perhaps there is never any duty to pay, if one takes the Spooner (1870) position that all government is illegitimate. If government is really no more than a mafia where the victims get to choose their godfathers and capos, then it seems that there is no ethical duty to pay anything. However, space does not permit a full discussion of the issue of government legitimacy, so we save it for another day.

What if the government provides services that certain taxpayers do not want, need or use? Do they still have an ethical obligation to pay? If so, *why* do they have a duty to pay? If the government is the servant and the people are the masters, it seems like the masters should not have to pay the servants for services they do not want, need, or use.

Do evangelical Christians, Orthodox Jews and Muslims have a moral duty to fund abortion clinics? I think not. Politicians who force these people to fund abortion clinics are acting immorally. If funding for abortion clinics is considered a legitimate function of government, it should be funded on a user fee basis, or by the segment of the taxpaying public that thinks that funding abortion clinics is a legitimate function of government. This way, taxpayers who do not approve of abortion will not be forced to pay for them.

Under present law, it is not possible for taxpayers to pick and choose which functions of government they will support. However, this need not be the case. Podolsky (2002) has suggested that tax forms include a list of government functions and that taxpayers be allowed to check off the functions of government they want their taxes to be spent on. Implementation of this proposal would do much to alleviate the problem of forcing taxpayers to fund activities that they deem abhorrent or unwanted.

The abortion clinic argument is a strong one. But it is not the only example that could be given. Should childless couples be forced to pay for the education of other people's children? Should parents who send their children to private schools be forced to pay for public education? It seems inherently unfair to make some individuals pay for the education of other people's children. Yet it is done on a universal basis. If there is no moral duty to pay, then there is nothing immoral about not paying.

One could argue that since the older generation paid for your education, you have a moral duty to pay for the education of the younger generation. But this argument does not hold up under analysis. For one, it is a non sequitur. One might just as easily say that since your father beat your mother, you have an obligation to beat your wife. If there is a moral obligation to pay for the education of other people's children, some other argument must be found.

The argument has been made that there is some moral obligation to society, and that paying for the education of other people's children is an example of that obligation. However, this argument suffers from several weaknesses. Perhaps the strongest counterargument is that "society" does not exist. *Society* does not eat, sleep, breathe, or flatulate. Only individuals do these things. Society is merely a collective term that is used to describe a group of individuals who live within a certain geographic area and who perhaps share some common values or experiences.

Hayek (1967, 1976) has pointed out this misuse of language in several of his writings (Nishiyama and Leube, 1984). It is a convenient term to use at times but merely using it does not result in bringing society to life. When someone makes the argument that there is a duty to society, what they are really saying is that some individuals have a moral obligation toward other individuals. But it does not follow that this duty is absolute, or even that such a duty exists in certain cases.

There is no moral obligation to force Muslims to pay for the education of Christian or Jewish children who attend religious schools. Indeed, it is immoral to force them to do so. Is it any less immoral to force Shiite Muslims to pay for the education of Sunni Muslim children? Or atheists to pay for the education of theist children? Or childless individuals to pay for the education of anyone's children?

The point is that it cannot be stated categorically that the moral obligation to pay for the education of other people's children is absolute. If such an obligation exists, it is conditional and subject to limitation.

If there is such an obligation, where does it come from? The argument that we owe it to society does not hold up under analysis. So if forcing some people to pay for the education of other people's children is ethical, another justification must be found. The existing literature does not discuss this point much. An obligation is merely assumed to exist. This point needs to be examined in greater depth.

The whole redistribution argument is constructed on a shaky foundation, as Bertrand de Jouvenel pointed out a few generations ago (1952). Taxing some people more than others just because they have more than others fails the Kantian ethics test (Kant 1952a, b, c, 1983). Such individuals are being used as means rather than ends in themselves, which Kant concludes is unethical.

The graduated income tax, which is one example of this approach to taxation, fails the test of utilitarian ethics because the primary and secondary effects of the graduated income tax result in what economists call a negative sum game (Blum and Kalven, 1953; McGee, 2004, pp. 111–119). There are more losers than winners. The small amount that is gained by soaking the rich is more than offset by reduced economic growth rates and inefficient allocation of resources.

The argument that taxpayers in a democracy have consented to be taxed is a weak one. As has been pointed out in the literature, only some people have consented to be taxed. It is difficult to justify the argument that politicians actually represent the best interests of the people who have elected them. Many politicians do not even know what the best interests of their constituents are. If they did, the Democrats and Republicans would never disagree on anything.

Special interest politics is alive and well. Politicians tend to represent special interests rather than the general public, as the Public Choice School of Economics and others have been pointing out for decades (Tullock 1970, 1983, 1989, 2004a, b; Rowley et al., 1988). This phenomenon is not new. America's Founding Fathers were aware of this tendency when they were constructing America's constitution (Hamilton, Madison and Jay, 1961; Peters, 1987).

That being the case, what obligation do taxpayers have to their government? Are they obligated to pay taxes just because they receive something in return? Does it depend on what they receive in return? Is there an ethical obligation to pay taxes if the government takes your car and gives you a bicycle in return? Or two cars? What is the relationship between what you receive from government and what you are obligated to pay? These are all questions that have not been adequately addressed in the literature. More research is needed. Presumably, there should be some relationship between the amount received from government and the amount paid, but the details of this relationship have yet to be worked out in the literature.

Another strand in the existing literature mentions a relationship between taxpayers. One argument that has been made for the ethical duty to pay taxes is that if one person evades paying taxes, other taxpayers must pay more. The evader becomes a free rider, but only in cases where the evader receives benefits from government. One cannot be a free rider if one receives no benefits.

Is there an ethical obligation to others when it comes to paying taxes? Such an obligation has been asserted but not really discussed or analyzed. The argument that an evader owes a duty to taxpayers even in cases where the evader does not receive benefits from government is a weak one. The free rider arguments to justify forced payment cannot be used in such instances. If an obligation exists, some other arguments must be found.

The argument that taxpayers who *do* receive benefits from government have an ethical obligation to other taxpayers is a stronger one. But it does not follow that this obligation is unlimited or absolute.

Many people receive less in benefits than what they have to pay in taxes. Leona Helmsley, who has paid many millions of dollars in taxes over her long life, received free room and board for a few years at government expense (prison) because she paid a few million less than what the government said she owed. H. Ross Perot, who during one of the US presidential campaigns boasted about paying one billion dollars in taxes over the years, undoubtedly received much less than a billion dollars in benefits from the government.

While the argument has been made that people who receive benefits from the government somehow have an ethical duty to pay taxes, the statement has merely been asserted, not sufficiently analyzed. The fact that others might have to pay more if evaders pay nothing is a separate question.

Let's assume for the sake of argument that if some people evade taxes, others will have to shoulder a larger portion of the total tax burden. This assumption may not be accurate, since government may cut back on spending or resort to financing its expenditures if it does not collect enough from taxpayers. But let's assume that if some pay less because of evasion, others will have to pay more. What duty do the evaders owe to the taxpaying community?

In the case of Jews paying taxes to Hitler, it would seem that there is no obligation to other taxpayers. If non-Jews must have their taxes increased to pay for the poison gas, it seems that it is the German government that is treating the taxpayers unfairly, not the Jews. Thus, it cannot be said that evaders always owe a duty to taxpayers. If evaders owe a duty to those who must shoulder the tax burden, it is a duty that exists only under certain conditions. What are those conditions? The literature has been silent on this point. Although a duty has been asserted, it has not been adequately discussed or analyzed in the literature. Thus, there is a need for further research on this point. It is not intellectually adequate to merely assume that such a duty exists. The specifics need to be spelled out.

Let's say that an armed mugger walks into a café and orders the patrons to collectively give him $100. The patrons discuss among themselves how this burden should be allocated and they decide that each patron should pay an equal percentage of the cash that is in their wallets and purses. Does Jack, one of the patrons, have an ethical duty to reveal that he has $20 in his hat? Is he ethically obligated to include this $20 in the calculation? If he does not, his share will be less than would otherwise be the case and the shares of the other patrons would be more. If Jack keeps silent, is he violating an ethical duty to the other patrons? Surely the patrons as a group are being treated unfairly because they are having their property rights violated. But it appears to be the mugger who is treating them unfairly, not Jack. If Jack keeps silent he is merely being treated less unfairly than the other patrons, but it is the mugger who is acting unethically, not Jack.

Let's take another example. Let's say that someone who works in the property tax office of some local community manages to manipulate the agency's software program that computes the amount of tax liability so that the perpetrator owes $1,000 in property tax rather than $10,000. In effect, manipulating the software has resulted in a $9,000 tax evasion. Since the municipality incurs the same exact expenses regardless of whether the software has been manipulated or not, the other taxpayers in the community must have their taxes increased as a result of the software manipulation. What duty does the software manipulator, let's call him Tom, have to the other taxpayers in the community?

Let's say that the budget for this particular community goes mostly to fund elementary and secondary education. Does Tom's duty to the other taxpayers in the community depend on whether he sends his children to the public school? What if Tom sends his children to private schools? Or what if he does not have any children? Is Tom's duty to the other taxpayers in the community dependent on whether he receives benefits from the local government? If not, why not? This point has not been addressed in the literature.

If it can be argued that Tom has a duty to the other taxpayers in the community even if he derives no benefit from the local government, can it also be argued that Jews have an obligation to other German taxpayers even though they receive no benefits from the Nazi government? Merely asserting that Tom has an obligation to other taxpayers is not sufficient. If Tom has a duty to other taxpayers but Jews living in Nazi Germany do not, some justification must be found for treating the two cases differently.

The argument has been made that there is a duty to resist a government that is involved in an unjust war (Pennock 1998; Crowe 1944). One form of resistance is tax evasion. Although breaking laws has a tendency to chip away at respect for the law and for government, sometimes that is a good thing. The mere fact that the governments of Hitler and Mussolini were duly elected does not mean that they are worthy of citizen respect. Tax evasion in such cases might actually be good from the perspective of utilitarian ethics, since reducing respect for an evil government tends to delegitimize it. An argument could be made that there is a duty to evade taxes in a corrupt or oppressive state, at least in cases where potential punishment is remote. There may be a duty even where punishment is swift and guaranteed. The extent of such a duty needs to be explored.

The argument that tax evaders always have a duty to government or to other taxpayers does not hold up under analysis. If such an obligation exists, it is less than absolute. Or perhaps no duty ever exists. Some framework has to be constructed to determine under what conditions an evader has an obligation to others. That framework has not yet been constructed in the literature.

More work needs to be done on the question of when there is an affirmative duty to evade taxes, or when evasion benefits society. If taxation is theft, then reducing the amount of theft in society is a good thing. If evasion results in a positive-sum game, then perhaps we should have more of it.

References

Acton, John Emerich Edward Dalberg. 1985. *Essays in the History of Liberty*, Volume I, J. Rufus Fears, editor. Indianapolis: Liberty Press, pp. 220–221.

Ahmad, Mushtaq. 1995. *Business Ethics in Islam*. Islamabad, Pakistan: The International Institute of Islamic Thought and the International Institute of Islamic Economics.

Angelus of Clavisio. 1494. *Summa Angelica*, as cited in Martin T. Crowe, *The Moral Obligation of Paying Just Taxes*, The Catholic University of America Studies in Sacred Theology No. 84, 1944 at p. 29.

Ballas, Apostolos A. and Haridimos Tsoukas. 1998. "Consequences of Distrust: The Vicious Circle of Tax Evasion in Greece," *Journal of Accounting, Ethics & Public Policy*, 1(4): 572–596, reprinted in Robert W. McGee, editor, *The Ethics of Tax Evasion*. Dumont, NJ: The Dumont Institute for Public Policy Research, 1998, pp. 284–304.

Barker, Dan. 1992. *Losing Faith in Faith*. Madison, WI: Freedom from Religion Foundation.

Barnes, David W. and Lynn A. Stout. 1992. *Cases and Materials on Law and Economics*. St. Paul: West Publishing Co.

Bastiat, Frédéric. 1964. *Selected Essays on Political Economy*. Irvington-on-Hudson, NY: Foundation for Economic Education.

Bastiat, Frédéric. 1968. *The Law*. Irvington-on-Hudson, NY: Foundation for Economic Education.

Bentham, Jeremy. 1988. *The Principles of Morals and Legislation*. Amherst, NY: Prometheus Books.

Berardi, Aemilio. 1898. *Praxis Confessariorum II*, as cited in Martin T. Crowe, *The Moral Obligation of Paying Just Taxes*, The Catholic University of America Studies in Sacred Theology No. 84, 1944 at p. 35.

Binswanger, Harry, editor. 1986. *The Ayn Rand Lexicon: Objectivism from A to Z*. New York: New American Library.

Blum, Walter J. and Harry Kalven, Jr. 1953. *The Uneasy Case for Progressive Taxation*. Chicago: University of Chicago Press.

Burr, William Henry. 1987. *Self-Contradictions in the Bible*. Buffalo: Prometheus Books. Originally published in 1860 in New York by A.J. Davis & Company.

Clark, Eli D. (n.d.) "Paying Taxes: Time to Stop the Evasion," *Business Ethics and Integrity* (Jerusalem) http://www.besr.org/.

Coase, Ronald H. 1960. The Problem of Social Cost. *Journal of Law and Economics*, 3, 1–44.

Coase, Ronald H. 1964. Discussion of "Direct Regulation and Market Performance in the American Economy," by Richard E. Caves, and "The Effectiveness of Economic Regulation: A Legal View," by Roger C. Cramton. *American Economic Review*, 54, 194–197.

Coase, Ronald H. 1988. *The Firm, the Market, and the Law*. Chicago: University of Chicago Press.

Cohn, Gordon. 1998. "The Jewish View on Paying Taxes," *Journal of Accounting, Ethics & Public Policy* 1(2): 109–120, reprinted in Robert W. McGee, editor, *The Ethics of Tax Evasion*. Dumont, NJ: The Dumont Institute for Public Policy Research, 1998, pp. 180–189.

Cooter, Robert and Thomas Ulen. 1988. *Law and Economics*. Glenview, IL and London: Scott, Foresman and Company.

Crolly, George. 1877. *Disputationes Theologicae de Justitia et Jure III* at pp. 1001ff, as cited in Martin T. Crowe, *The Moral Obligation of Paying Just Taxes*, The Catholic University of America Studies in Sacred Theology No. 84, 1944 at p. 38.

Crowe, Martin T. 1944. *The Moral Obligation of Paying Just Taxes*, The Catholic University of America Studies in Sacred Theology No. 84.

Davis, Henry. 1938. *Moral and Pastoral Theology*, p. 339, as cited in Martin T. Crowe, *The Moral Obligation of Paying Just Taxes*, The Catholic University of America Studies in Sacred Theology No. 84, 1944 at p. 40.

deJouvenel, Bertrand. 1952. *The Ethics of Redistribution*. Cambridge: Cambridge University Press. Reprinted by The Liberty Fund, Indianapolis, 1990.

DeMoville, Wig. 1998. "The Ethics of Tax Evasion: A Baha'i Perspective," *Journal of Accounting, Ethics & Public Policy* 1(3): 356–368, reprinted in Robert W. McGee, editor, *The Ethics of Tax Evasion*. Dumont, NJ: The Dumont Institute for Public Policy Research, 1998, pp. 230–240.

Donahue, John D. 1991. *The Privatization Decision: Public Ends, Private Means*. New York: Basic Books.

Encyclopedia of Mormonism. 1992. New York: Macmillan Publishing Company.

Englebrecht, Ted D., Buky Folami, Choongseop Lee and John J. Masselli. 1998. "The Impact on Tax Compliance Behavior: a Multidimensional Analysis," *Journal of Accounting, Ethics & Public Policy* 1(4): 738–768, reprinted in Robert W. McGee, editor, *The Ethics of Tax Evasion*. Dumont, NJ: The Dumont Institute for Public Policy Research, 1998, pp. 372–402.

Finley, Lawrence K. (Ed.) 1989. *Public Sector Privatization: Alternative Approaches to Service Delivery*. New York, Westport & London: Quorum Books.

Fitzgerald, Randall. 1988. *When Government Goes Private: Successful Alternatives to Public Services*. New York: Universe Books.

Genicot, E.-Salsmans. 1927. *Institutiones Theologiae Moralis I*, as cited in Martin T. Crowe, *The Moral Obligation of Paying Just Taxes*, The Catholic University of America Studies in Sacred Theology No. 84, 1944 at p. 37.

Goetz, Charles J. 1984. *Cases and Materials on Law and Economics*. St. Paul: West Publishing Co.

Goodman, John C. (Ed.) 1985. *Privatization*. Dallas: National Center for Policy Analysis.

Government Accountability Office. 2011. Opportunities to Reduce Potential Duplication in Government Programs, Save Tax Dollars, and enhance revenue. United States Government Accountability Office. GAO-11-318SP.

Greene, Jeffrey D. 2001. *Cities and Privatization: Prospects for the New Century*. Upper Saddle River, NJ: Prentice Hall.

Gronbacher, Gregory M.A. 1998. "Taxation: Catholic Social Thought and Classical Liberalism," *Journal of Accounting, Ethics & Public Policy* 1(1): 91–100, reprinted in Robert W. McGee (Ed.), *The Ethics of Tax Evasion* (pp. 158–167). Dumont, NJ: The Dumont Institute for Public Policy Research, 1998.

Gwartney, James D. and Richard E. Wagner, editors. 1988. *Public Choice and Constitutional Economics*. Greenwich, CT and London: JAI Press.

Hamilton, Alexander, James Madison and John Jay. 1961. *The Federalist Papers*. New York: New American Library.

Harrison, Jeffrey L. 1995. *Law and Economics in a Nutshell*. St. Paul: West Publishing Co.

Hayek, F.A. 1967. *Studies in Philosophy, Politics and Economics*. New York: Simon and Schuster.

Hayek, F.A. 1976. *Law, Legislation & Liberty*, Volume 2, *The Mirage of Social Justice*. Chicago: University of Chicago Press.

Hobbes, Thomas. 1651. *Leviathan*.

Hoppe, Hans-Hermann. 2001. *Democracy: The God That Failed: The Economics and Politics of Monarchy, Democracy and Natural Order*. New Brunswick, NJ: Transaction Publishers.

Jalili, Ali Reza. 2012. The Ethics of Tax Evasion: An Islamic Perspective, in Robert W. McGee (Ed.), *The Ethics of Tax Evasion in Theory and Practice*. New York: Springer.

Jefferson, Thomas. 1789. "Letter of Thomas Jefferson to James Madison," Paris, September 6, 1789, reprinted in *Thomas Jefferson: Writings*. New York: The Library of America, 1984, pp. 959–964.

Jefferson, Thomas. 1813. "Letter of Thomas Jefferson to John Wayles Eppes," June 24, 1813, reprinted in *Thomas Jefferson: Writings*. New York: The Library of America, 1984, pp. 1280–1281.

Kant, Immanuel. 1952a. *Fundamental Principles of the Metaphysics of Morals*. Great Books of the Western World, Volume 42, Chicago: Encyclopedia Britannica, pp. 251–287.

Kant, Immanuel. 1952b. *General Introduction to the Metaphysics of Morals*. Great Books of the Western World, Volume 42, Chicago: Encyclopedia Britannica, pp. 381–394.

Kant, Immanuel. 1952c. Preface and Introduction to the *Metaphysical Elements of Ethics*. Great Books of the Western World, Volume 42, Chicago: Encyclopedia Britannica, pp. 363–379.

Kant, Immanuel. (1952d). *Introduction to the Science of Right*. *Great Books of the Western World*, Volume 42, Chicago: Encyclopedia Britannica, pp. 397–458.

Kant, Immanuel. 1983. *Ethical Philosophy*, James W. Ellington, translator. Indianapolis and Cambridge: Hackett Publishing Company.

Katz, Avery Wiener (Ed.) 1998. *Foundations of The Economic Approach to Law*. New York: Foundation Press.

Kemp, Roger L. 2007. *Privatization: The Provision of Public Services by the Private Sector*. Jefferson, NC: McFarland & Co.

Lauder, Ronald S. 1992. Privatization for New York: Competing for the Future. A Report of the New York State Senate Advisory Commission on Privatization. Albany, NY: New York State Senate Advisory Commission on Privatization.

Lehmkuhl, A. 1902. *Theologia Moralis I*, as cited in Martin T. Crowe, *The Moral Obligation of Paying Just Taxes*, The Catholic University of America Studies in Sacred Theology No. 84, 1944 at p. 76.

Leiker, Bret H. 1998. "Rousseau and the Legitimacy of Tax Evasion," *Journal of Accounting, Ethics & Public Policy* 1(1): 45–57, reprinted in Robert W. McGee, editor, *The Ethics of Tax Evasion*. Dumont, NJ: The Dumont Institute for Public Policy Research, 1998, pp. 89–101.

Letwin, Oliver. 1988. *Privatising the World: A Study of International Privatisation in Theory and Practice*. London: Cassell.

Lewis, Joseph. 1926. *The Bible Unmasked*. New York: The Freethought Press Association.

Locke, John. 1689. *Two Treatises on Government*.

Malloy, Robin Paul. 1990. *Law and Economics: A Comparative Approach to Theory and Practice*. St. Paul: West Publishing Co.

McGee, Robert W. 1994a. "Is Tax Evasion Unethical?" *University of Kansas Law Review* 42(2): 411–435. Reprinted at http://ssrn.com/abstract=74420.

McGee, Robert W. 1994b. *A Trade Policy for Free Societies: The Case against Protectionism*. New York and Westport, CT: Quorum Books.

McGee, Robert W. 1997. "The Ethics of Tax Evasion and Trade Protectionism from an Islamic Perspective," *Commentaries on Law & Public Policy* 1: 250–262. Reprinted at http://ssrn.com/abstract=461397.

McGee, Robert W., editor. 1998a. *The Ethics of Tax Evasion.* Dumont, NJ: The Dumont Institute for Public Policy Research.

McGee, Robert W. 1998b. "The Ethics of Tax Evasion in Islam: A Comment," *Journal of Accounting, Ethics & Public Policy* 1(2): 162–168, reprinted in Robert W. McGee, editor, *The Ethics of Tax Evasion.* Dumont, NJ: The Dumont Institute for Public Policy Research, 1998, pp. 214–219.

McGee, Robert W. 1998c. "Christian Views on The Ethics of Tax Evasion," *Journal of Accounting, Ethics & Public Policy* 1(2): 210–225. Reprinted at http://ssrn.com/abstract=461398.

McGee, Robert W. 1998d. "Jewish Views on the Ethics of Tax Evasion," *Journal of Accounting, Ethics & Public Policy* 1(3): 323–336. Reprinted at http://ssrn.com/abstract=461399.

McGee, Robert W. 1998e. "Ethical Views on Tax Evasion among Swedish CEOs: A Comment," *Journal of Accounting, Ethics & Public Policy* 1(3): 460–467. Reprinted at http://ssrn.com/abstract=713903.

McGee, Robert W. 1999a. "Is It Unethical to Evade Taxes in an Evil or Corrupt State? A Look at Jewish, Christian, Muslim, Mormon and Baha'i Perspectives," *Journal of Accounting, Ethics & Public Policy* 2(1): 149–181. Reprinted at http://ssrn.com/abstract=251469.

McGee, Robert W. 1999b. "Why People Evade Taxes in Armenia: A Look at an Ethical Issue Based on a Summary of Interviews," *Journal of Accounting, Ethics & Public Policy* 2(2): 408–416. Reprinted at http://ssrn.com/abstract=242568.

McGee, Robert W. 2003. "Trade Policy as Corporate Welfare: The Case of the U.S. Steel Industry." In Jerry Biberman and Abbass F. Alkhafaji, editors, *Business Research Yearbook: Global Business Perspectives*, Volume X, Saline, MI: McNaughton & Gunn, Inc., 2003, pp. 585–589. A longer version of this manuscript was presented at the Fifteenth Annual Conference of the International Academy of Business Disciplines, Orlando, Florida, April 3–6, 2003. Reprinted at http://ssrn.com/abstract=410817.

McGee, Robert W. 2004. *The Philosophy of Taxation and Public Finance.* Boston, Dordrecht and London: Kluwer Academic Publishers.

McGee, Robert W. 2006. "Three Views on the Ethics of Tax Evasion," *Journal of Business Ethics* 67(1): 15–35.

McGee, Robert W. and Gordon M. Cohn. 2008. Jewish Perspectives on the Ethics of Tax Evasion. *Journal of Legal, Ethical and Regulatory Issues*, 11(2): 1–32.

McKinsey, C. Dennis. 1995. *The Encyclopedia of Biblical Errancy.* Amherst, NY: Prometheus Books.

McKinsey, C. Dennis. 2000. *Biblical Errancy: A Reference Guide.* Amherst, NY: Prometheus Books.

Mercuro, Nicholas and Steven G. Medema. 1997. *Economics and the Law.* Princeton: Princeton University Press.

Metaxas, Eric. 2010. *Bonhoeffer: Pastor, Martyr, Prophet, Spy.* Nashville: Thomas Nelson.

Mill, John Stuart. 1962. *Utilitarianism; On Liberty; Essay on Bentham.* New York: Signet.

Morales, Alfonso 1998. "Income Tax Compliance and Alternative Views of Ethics and Human Nature," *Journal of Accounting, Ethics & Public Policy* 1(3): 380–399, reprinted in Robert W. McGee, editor, *The Ethics of Tax Evasion.* Dumont, NJ: The Dumont Institute for Public Policy Research, 1998, pp. 242–258.

Murtuza, Athar and S.M. Ghazanfar. 1998. "Taxation as a Form of Worship: Exploring the Nature of Zakat," *Journal of Accounting, Ethics & Public Policy* 1(2): 134–161, reprinted in Robert W. McGee, editor, *The Ethics of Tax Evasion.* Dumont, NJ: The Dumont Institute for Public Policy Research, 1998, pp. 190–212.

Nishiyama, Chiaki and Kurt R. Leube, editors. 1984. *The Essence of Hayek.* Stanford, CA: Hoover Institution Press.

Nozick, Robert. 1974. *Anarchy, State & Utopia.* New York: Basic Books.

Nylén, Ulrica. 1998. "Ethical Views on Tax Evasion among Swedish CEOs," *Journal of Accounting, Ethics & Public Policy* 1(3): 435–459, reprinted in Robert W. McGee, editor, *The Ethics of Tax Evasion*. Dumont, NJ: The Dumont Institute for Public Policy Research, 1998, pp. 260–282.

Ohashi, T.M. and T.P. Roth. 1980. *Privatization Theory & Practice: Distributing Shares in Private and Public Enterprises*. Vancouver: The Fraser Institute.

Pennock, Robert T. 1998. "Death and Taxes: On the Justice of Conscientious War Tax Resistance," *Journal of Accounting, Ethics & Public Policy* 1(1): 58–76, reprinted in Robert W. McGee, editor, *The Ethics of Tax Evasion*. Dumont, NJ: The Dumont Institute for Public Policy Research, 1998, pp. 124–142.

Peters, William. 1987. *A More Perfect Union: The Making of the United States Constitution*. New York: Crown Publishers.

Pirie, Madsen. 1988. *Privatization: Theory, Practice and Choice*. Aldershot, UK: Wildwood House.

Pitcher, M. Anne. 2003. *Transforming Mozambique: The Politics of Privatization, 1975–2000*. New York: Cambridge University Press.

Podolsky, Robert E. 2002. *Titania: The Practical Alternative to Government*. Boca Raton, FL: The Titania Group, Inc.

Poole, Robert W., Jr. 1980. *Cutting Back City Hall*. New York: Universe Books.

Posner, Richard A. 1983. *The Economics of Justice*. Cambridge, MA and London: Harvard University Press.

Posner, Richard A. 1998. *Economic Analysis of Law*, 5th edition. New York: Aspen Law & Business.

Preobragenskaya, Galina G. and Robert W. McGee. 2004. "Taxation and Public Finance in a Transition Economy: A Case Study of Russia." In Carolyn Gardner, Jerry Biberman and Abbass Alkhafaji, editors, *Business Research Yearbook*: *Global Business Perspectives* Volume XI, Saline, MI: McNaughton & Gunn, Inc., 2004, pp. 254–258. A longer version, which was presented at the Sixteenth Annual Conference of the International Academy of Business Disciplines in San Antonio, March 25–28, 2004, is available at http://ssrn.com/abstract=480862

Rand, Ayn. 1968. *For the New Intellectual: The Philosophy of Ayn Rand*. New York: New American Library.

Reckers, Philip M.J., Debra L. Sanders and Stephen J. Roark. 1994. "The Influence of Ethical Attitudes on Taxpayer Compliance," *National Tax Journal* 47(4): 825–836.

Rousseau, Jean Jacques. 1762. *The Social Contract*.

Rowley, Charles K., Robert D. Tollison and Gordon Tullock, editors. 1988. *The Political Economy of Rent-Seeking*. Boston, Dordrecht and Lancaster: Kluwer Academic Publishers.

Savas, E.S. 1982. *Privatizing the Public Sector: How to Shrink Government*. Chatham, NJ: Chatham House Publishers.

Savas, E.S. 2005. *Privatization in the City: Successes, Failures, Lessons*. Washington, DC: CQ Press.

Schansberg, D. Eric. 1998. "The Ethics of Tax Evasion Within Biblical Christianity: Are There Limits to 'Rendering Unto Caesar'?" *Journal of Accounting, Ethics & Public Policy* 1(1): 77–90, reprinted in Robert W. McGee, editor, *The Ethics of Tax Evasion*. Dumont, NJ: The Dumont Institute for Public Policy Research, 1998, pp. 144–157.

Smatrakalev, Gueorgui. 1998. "Walking on the Edge: Bulgaria and the Transition to a Market Economy," In Robert W. McGee, editor, *The Ethics of Tax Evasion*. Dumont, NJ: The Dumont Institute for Public Policy Research, 1998, pp. 316–329.

Smith, Sheldon R. and Kevin C. Kimball. 1998. "Tax Evasion and Ethics: A Perspective from Members of The Church of Jesus Christ of Latter-Day Saints," *Journal of Accounting, Ethics & Public Policy* 1(3): 337–348, reprinted in Robert W. McGee, editor, *The Ethics of Tax Evasion*. Dumont, NJ: The Dumont Institute for Public Policy Research, 1998, pp. 220–229.

Spooner, Lysander. 1870. No Treason: The Constitution of No Authority, originally self-published by Spooner in Boston in 1870, reprinted by Rampart College in 1965, 1966 and 1971, and by Ralph Myles Publisher, Inc., Colorado Springs, Colorado in 1973.

Stevens, Barbara J. 1980. *Handbook of Municipal Waste Management Systems: Planning and Practice.* New York: Van Nostrand Reinhold, as cited by Barbara J. Stevens in Ronald S. Lauder (Ed). 1992. Privatization for New York: Competing for a Better Future. Albany, NY: New York State Senate Advisory Commission on Privatization, p. 236.

Tamari, Meir. 1998. "Ethical Issues in Tax Evasion: A Jewish Perspective," *Journal of Accounting, Ethics & Public Policy* 1(2): 121–132, reprinted in Robert W. McGee, editor, *The Ethics of Tax Evasion.* Dumont, NJ: The Dumont Institute for Public Policy Research, 1998, pp. 168–178.

Templeton, Charles. 1996. *Farewell to God.* Toronto: McClelland & Stewart.

Torgler, Benno 2003. *Tax Morale: Theory and Empirical Analysis of Tax Compliance.* Dissertation der Universität Basel zur Erlangung der Würde eines Doktors der Staatswissenschaften.

Trenchard, John and Thomas Gordon. 1965. "Cato's Letters, no. 59," in D.L. Jacobson, editor, *The English Libertarian Heritage.* Indianapolis: Bobbs-Merrill, 1965, p. 108, as cited in Murray N. Rothbard, *The Ethics of Liberty.* New York and London: New York University Press, 1998, p. 147, n. 17.

Tullock, Gordon. 1970. *Private Wants, Public Means: An Economic Analysis of the Desirable Scope of Government.* New York: Basic Books. Reprinted by University Press of America, in 1987.

Tullock, Gordon. 1983. *Welfare for the Well-To-Do.* Dallas: The Fisher Institute.

Tullock, Gordon. 1989. *The Economics of Special Privilege and Rent Seeking.* Boston, Dordrecht and London: Kluwer Academic Publishers.

Tullock, Gordon. 2004a. *Virginia Political Economy. The Selected Works of Gordon Tullock,* Volume 1. Indianapolis: Liberty Fund.

Tullock, Gordon. 2004b. *The Economics of Politics. The Selected Works of Gordon Tullock,* Volume 4. Indianapolis: Liberty Fund.

Vaguine, Vladimir V. 1998. "The 'Shadow Economy' and Tax Evasion in Russia." In Robert W. McGee, editor, *The Ethics of Tax Evasion.* Dumont, NJ: The Dumont Institute for Public Policy Research, 1998, pp. 306–314.

Van den Broeck, Julien, editor. 1988. *Public Choice.* Dordrecht, Boston & London: Kluwer Academic Publishers.

Veljanovski, Cento (Ed.) 1989. *Privatisation & Competition: A Market Prospectus.* London: Institute of Economic Affairs.

Walker, Michael (Ed.) 1988. *Privatization: Tactics and Techniques.* Vancouver: The Fraser Institute.

Williams, Walter. 1987. *All It Takes is Guts: A Minority View.* Washington, DC: Regnery Books.

Yusuf, S.M. 1971. *Economic Justice in Islam.* Lahore: Sh. Muhammad Ashraf.

Chapter 2
Duty to Whom?

Robert W. McGee

There is no moral obligation to pay a homeless person who does an inferior job of washing your windshield without your permission while you are stuck at a stop light. Why should there be a moral obligation to pay government for providing some inferior service that you do not want and did not ask for?

(McGee, 2012).

Introduction

If we have a duty to pay taxes, to whom do we owe a duty? The literature over the last few thousand years has discussed three possibilities – to God, to some segment of the community, or to the state. The next few sections of this chapter review this literature and the various arguments that have been put forth that assert we have a duty to pay taxes.

Duty to God

Some religious literature has stated that we owe a duty to God to pay taxes. Sometimes, the duty is directly to God and sometimes the duty is to the state, but that God will punish us if we do not pay (Jalili, 2012). The argument often takes the form of a command – God commands us to pay taxes. Does he really? Who says so?

There are passages in the Bible that seemingly take an absolutist position. Romans 13, 1–2 supports the Divine Right of Kings, which basically holds that

R.W. McGee (✉)
School of Business, Florida International University, 3000 NE 151 Street,
North Miami, FL 33181, USA
e-mail: bob414@hotmail.com

R.W. McGee (ed.), *The Ethics of Tax Evasion: Perspectives in Theory and Practice*,
DOI 10.1007/978-1-4614-1287-8_2, © Springer Science+Business Media, LLC 2012

whoever is in charge of government is there with God's approval and anyone who disputes that fact or who fails to obey is subject to damnation.

> Let every soul be subject unto the higher powers. For there is no power but of God: the powers that be are ordained of God. Whosoever therefore resisteth the power, resisteth the ordinance of God: and they that resist shall receive to themselves damnation (Romans 13:1–2).

Jalili (2012) interprets the Muslim literature to hold that there is an absolute duty to pay the state whatever it demands, but only in cases where the state is a purely Islamic state, the belief being that in a purely Islamic state, the rulers are God's representatives on earth and are there with God's approval. Such a state currently does not exist, but even if one did exist, it is doubtful that the people in charge of running the state would do it honestly, since humans are imperfect. History has shown time and time again that when individuals are given power, they become corrupt. The trick is to structure governments so that no one individual has too much power. The least corrupt governments tend to be the ones that have checks and balances built into the system.

Almost no one believes this gibberish these days that God commands us to pay whoever is in charge. Governments are corrupt and often evil. To believe such a statement would be to support the regimes of Hitler, Mao, Stalin, Pol Pot, and all the other dictators who have killed millions of people. Such a belief would give credence to the Marxist view that religion is the opiate of the people.

Presumably, some religious fundamentalists still adhere to this view, since it is in the Bible, which they believe to be the literal word of God, a belief that is disputed by McKinsey (1995; 2000), Templeton (1996), and others (Burr, 1987; Lewis, 1926; Barker, 1992).

Since God did not write the Bible, we must discount anything and everything that is in it. We must apply the rules of logic and fairness before we decide whether the Biblical position on any issue is the position we should adopt. Applying those rules, it would be fair to conclude that God did not command us to pay taxes to evil states, since the people who run those evil states are likely to use the funds to do evil things.

Several other passages in the Bible have something to say about taxes. In the New Testament, when Jesus was asked whether it was legal to give tribute to Caesar, he said: "Render therefore unto Caesar the things which are Caesar's; and unto God the things that are God's" (Matthew 22:21). But all this statement really says is that we are supposed to give individuals and institutions (the state) what they are entitled to. It does not address the main issue, which is what the state might be entitled to. One might infer from this passage that Jesus said it is all right to evade the tax if the state is not entitled to the tax. In fact, such would be the logical conclusion to draw from this statement.

St. Paul made a similar statement in Romans 13:7: "Render therefore to all their dues: tribute to whom tribute is due; custom to whom custom; fear to whom fear; honour to whom honour."

Schansberg (1998), a Biblical scholar, interprets the Bible to permit wiggle room, an escape clause when the government is evil or engages in immoral activities, such as subsidizing abortion or engaging in an unjust war, a topic also addressed by Pennock (1998). Thus, even if God does command us to pay taxes, the command is less than absolute.

Duty to Others

Another argument is that we have a duty to others to pay taxes. Others may include the religious community or other taxpayers.

Cohn (1998) states that Jews have a duty to pay taxes in order not to make other Jews look bad, a strain of thought that is contained in the Jewish literature but is also contained in the Muslim literature, applying the same concept to Muslims (Jalili, 2012). The argument goes something like this. Jews may not do anything that disparages other Jews. A Jew who evades taxes makes all other Jews look bad. Therefore, a Jew must not evade taxes.

This argument sounds good on the surface. It is a special application of the broader rule that we should not do anything that harms others. However, a closer analysis reveals weaknesses in the argument. For example, must a Jew pay taxes to Hitler in order not to be called a bad Jew?

This issue was addressed in a survey instrument distributed to a group of Orthodox Jewish students (McGee and Cohn, 2008). The survey instrument consisted of 18 statements. Participants were asked to select a number from 1 to 7 to indicate the extent of their agreement or disagreement with each statement. One of the statements was "Tax evasion would be ethical if I were a Jew living in Nazi Germany." The 18 statements were ranked in terms of strength. Although this statement was the strongest argument to justify tax evasion, its score was 3.12 which, on a scale of 1–7, where 1 represents strong agreement, means that even Orthodox Jews believe there is some duty to pay taxes to Hitler.

This belief seemingly defies rationality. Ayn Rand (1961) would probably assert that it is an example of the sanction of the victim. However, their reason for concluding that Jews have an obligation to pay taxes even to Hitler is based on two strains of thought in the Jewish literature – one must not do anything to disparage another Jew, and the law is the law (Cohn, 1998).

Both of these rationales can be criticized. It seems stupid that Jews should assert they have a duty to help pay for the purchase of the poison gas that is used to kill them in the death camps just so that no one refers to them as bad Jews. A better argument would be that Jews have an obligation to other Jews to evade paying taxes to Hitler so that it would be a bit more difficult for Hitler to kill Jews.

The "law is the law" argument can also be criticized. The basic argument is that all laws must be obeyed. Gandhi, Martin Luther King, and other rebels would disagree, and might even state that there is a moral obligation to break unjust laws. Even the Jewish literature makes a provision for breaking unjust laws.

> Taxes may not be confiscatory nor arbitrary nor discriminatory. Mairmorides for example, rules that a king who usurps power or whose laws are capricious or discriminating may be disobeyed and his laws including tax, disregarded (Tamari, 1998, citing Mishnah Torah Hilkhot Gezeilah Cpat. 5 halakhah 11).[1]

---

[1] Jewish scholars may point out that I have misspelled "Maimonides" and "Mishneh." In my defense, my excuse is that I am merely quoting Tamari, letter for letter. Possibly, the differences arise because of translation. The original version of the Mishneh Torah was in Hebrew. In some versions of Hebrew, they leave out the vowels, leaving the reader to guess which vowel best fits.

Another reason given in the Jewish literature for not evading taxes is because tax evasion might result in jail, which makes it difficult or impossible to perform good works (mitzvos). That argument goes something like this. Jews have a duty to perform good works (mitzvos). Jews who evade taxes might go to jail. If they go to jail, it would be difficult or impossible to perform good works. Therefore, Jews must not evade taxes.

This view may be criticized on several grounds. Going to prison might actually avail one or more opportunities to do good deeds than staying on the outside. Also, evading taxes might be considered doing a good deed, especially if Hitler is the tax collector. Evading the payment of taxes to an evil regime might result in the perpetration of less evil.

Another variation of the argument that there is a duty to others is the belief that we owe a duty to other taxpayers to pay our fair share. If we pay less than our fair share, others must pay more than their fair share.

This argument also sounds good on the surface. However, analyzing the argument uncovers flaws. For example, how does one determine fair share? What if everyone is paying more than their fair share because tax rates are too high or because government is doing a lot of things it should not be doing? Failure to pay all that the government demands in such cases does not automatically mean that other taxpayers are being unfairly harmed by the evader. If those taxpayers are being harmed, it is by the government that is overcharging them for the services it provides.

If "taxation of earnings from labor is on a par with forced labor" (Nozick, 1974: 169), then evading this forced labor is perfectly ethical. If the government has to force others to perform more labor because evaders have escaped it, then it is the government that is perpetrating the injustice, not those who have found a way to reduce the amount of forced labor the government extracts from them.

One might also point out that it is not necessarily true that if an evader pays less, others will be forced to pay more. If I pay less than is legally due, it has no effect on my neighbor down the hall or on anyone else in the building. If the government runs on a balanced budget (a rarity these days), then if I pay less, government will have less money to waste and squander, which is a benefit to a society that values efficiency. That is also true if the government runs a deficit. The less money it has to spend, the less it can waste and squander.

Duty to the State

Numerous scholars over the years have asserted that there is a duty to pay taxes to the state.

> The state has to be maintained for the common good, peace and security, and therefore it is part of legal justice that the citizens should contribute their just share when it is claimed (Davis, 1938: 339).
>
> A tax is not due as a penalty but since the magistrates and princes serve the Republic they have a *strict right* to demand those things which are necessary. Therefore those who defraud this right commit an injustice (La Croix, 1739: III, pars II).

> By the very fact that the people have transferred the authority and administration of the republic to the prince, they tacitly promise to give him a just stipend and whatever is necessary for carrying on the business of the state (Billuart, 1874: 215).

> … just as the king is bound to work for the good of the people by administering justice and performing other duties, so on the other hand are the people bound from justice and natural law to pay taxes for the maintenance of the prince (Liguori, 1907).

Concina (1774) compares the state to a servant. "Therefore the stipend, just as a servant's wage, is due in strict justice." Patuzzi (1770) compares the relationship of the state and the individual to that of an employee and employer.

> According to Patuzzi, the relations between the citizen and the state are comparable to the relations between employer and employee. The state, i.e., the government, is hired by the citizens. It has certain obligations which require the expenditure not only of time but also of money. In return the state has a strict right to compensation from the employer, i.e., from the citizens (Crowe, 1944: 57, summarizing the views of Patuzzi).

However, even if we concede that there is some moral obligation to pay something for the services the state renders to the citizenry, it does not follow that we must pay whatever the state demands. What if the state is evil, corrupt, or inefficient? What if it spends on things we abhor? Should pro-life people be forced to pay for abortions? Should agnostics or atheists be forced to subsidize religion? Should Catholics be forced to support the Church of England if they happen to live in the UK? Should childless people be forced to pay for the education of other people's children? Or for their health care? Or for the pensions of their parents or grandparents?

Is tax evasion ethical if a large portion of the funds collected wind up in the pockets of corrupt politicians or their families and friends? What if tax rates are too high and we cannot afford to pay? What if the tax system is unfair? Is there a duty to pay if the government does not provide me with any services? Is it ethical to evade some portion of the tax if the government does more *to* me than it does *for* me? What if the government discriminates against people on the basis of race, religion, or ethnicity, or if it imprisons and/or tortures people for their political beliefs? Is it ethical for a Jew living in Nazi Germany to evade taxes?

These are all questions that need to be answered or at least addressed. Part of the answer lies in whether the state is a just state.

The Just State

When trying to determine whether, or under what circumstances, one has a duty to pay taxes to the state, one approach to determine the answer is to ask whether the state is a *just* state. If the answer is *yes*, then there is a duty to pay; if the answer is *no*, there is less than an absolute duty to pay, although there might be some duty to pay even if the state is not purely just, or so the argument goes. Perhaps, the duty to pay might be viewed as on a sliding scale, where the duty to pay drops as the extent of injustice increases. One might illustrate this relationship by the following linear continuum:

Unjust State	Just State
No Duty to Pay	Absolute Duty to Pay

If we accept this rule of thumb, the next step is to determine what makes a state just and what makes it unjust. The concept of justice has been discussed for thousands of years, going back to Plato (The Republic; The Laws, among other places) and Aristotle (The Politics; Nicomachean Ethics) in ancient Greece.

One might also refer to social contract theory, which includes the presumption that where the state performs the functions it has been hired to perform, there is a duty to contribute to the support of the state. Numerous writers over the centuries have discussed various versions of the social contract theory, including Hobbes (1651), Locke (1689), and Rousseau (1762).

We can discuss social contract theory another time. At this time, all that is necessary to point out is that there are major problems with the social contract theory, not least of which is the fact that no group of humans ever got together and entered into such a contract, and even if they did, their contract is not binding on anyone who did not sign. It is a well-established principle of law that no one can bind anyone else to a contract against his will. Thus, any contract we did not sign is not binding on us (Spooner, 1870).

Another concept that might be mentioned at this juncture is the Biblical command that we should pay those who deserve to be paid.

> Render therefore unto Caesar the things that are Caesar's; and unto God the things that are God's (Matthew 22:21).
> Render therefore to all their dues: tribute to whom tribute is due; custom to whom custom; fear to whom fear; honor to whom honor (Romans 13:7).

Both of these Biblical quotes beg the question because they do not provide clear guidance regarding when there is a duty to pay. All we can gather from these commands is that we should do what is the fair thing to do.

Doing what is fair reminds me of a conversation I had over lunch while visiting the Foundation for Economic Education (FEE) in Irvington-on-Hudson, New York, during the 1980s. FEE is located on an expensive piece of real estate in Westchester County, just north of New York City. Because it is a nonprofit organization, it is exempt from property taxes. Were it not a nonprofit, it would be forced to pay an exorbitant amount of taxes to support a wide range of government services it does not use, including the local school system.

The people I was dining with, a rabid group of libertarians, told me that FEE voluntarily sends a check to the local government every year to pay for the water, fire, and police services it uses. They determine what they consider to be a fair price and they send the check. It seems like this approach is fair and honorable. They are not free riding, but they also are not being exploited by a state that would otherwise force them to pay for services they do not use and do not value.

Getting back to the issue of justice, Frédéric Bastiat's view might be adopted as a means of guiding us to the solution. For Bastiat (1801–1850), the only legitimate functions of government are the protection of life, liberty, and property. All other actions are illegitimate because they redistribute wealth by taking from some and giving to others. He might be labeled an advocate of the night watchman state.

He was a negative rights theorist. To paraphrase Bastiat, "My right to life, liberty and property do not conflict with your right to life, liberty or property." In other words, my liberty to throw out my fist stops where your nose begins.

> … this negative concept of law is so true that the statement, *the purpose of the law is to cause justice to reign*, is not a rigorously accurate statement. It ought to be stated that *the purpose of the law is to prevent injustice from reigning*. In fact, it is *injustice*, instead of justice, that has an existence of its own. Justice is achieved only when injustice is absent (Bastiat, 1968: 29).

A state is acting illegitimately when it enforces positive rights (rights created by government), since such rights necessarily come at someone else's expense. For example, the right to free health care comes at the expense of those who are forced to pay. The right of a retired worker to social security comes at the expense of others who are still working. The right to a free education comes at the expense of those who do not have children or have children who attend private schools.

The right of the landlord to charge $1,500 per month rent on a property he owns is violated if some government has a rent control law restricting the rent to $500. In such a case, the landlord is being forced to subsidize the rent of his tenant to the tune of $1,000 per month. In substance, the law is taxing the landlord $1,000 and transferring that amount to the tenant, to whom the government has granted the right to subsidized rent. One person's right is gained only at the expense of another person's right.

Such laws are inherently unjust for Bastiat. He calls such laws legal plunder.

> But how is this legal plunder to be identified? Quite simply. See if the law takes from some persons what belongs to them, and gives it to other persons to whom it does not belong. See if the law benefits one citizen at the expense of another by doing what the citizen himself cannot do without committing a crime.
> Then abolish this law without delay, for it is not only an evil itself, but also it is a fertile source for further evils because it invites reprisals. If such a law – which may be an isolated case – is not abolished immediately, it will spread, multiply, and develop into a system (Bastiat, 1968: 21).

Walter Williams has the following to say on the subject:

> But you might say, if government didn't do all that it's doing we wouldn't have a *just* society. What's *just* has been debated for centuries but let me offer my definition of social justice: I keep what I earn and you keep what you earn. Do you disagree? Well then tell me how much of what I earn *belongs* to you – and why? (Williams, 1987: 62).

In other words, to the extent that a state engages in redistribution it is unjust. Unjust states need not be obeyed. Indeed, the dictates of unjust states should be resisted. Thus, one may say, at a minimum, that there is no moral duty to pay taxes to a state to the extent that the tax funds paid are used for redistribution rather than to pay for essential government services that protect the lives, liberty, and property of the vast majority.

Can we take this argument a step further? Can one make an argument that the duty to pay is less than absolute even if the state confines its functions to the protection of life, liberty, and property? For example, what if one chooses not to use the services the state provides? Is there still a duty to pay? If so, why is there a duty to pay and where does this duty come from? It seems like it would be an uphill battle to try to argue that there is a duty to pay in cases where the taxpayer does not benefit.

Robert Nozick (1974), the eminent Harvard philosopher, raises this point, indirectly, at least. Both Nozick and Bastiat (1968) assert that the state cannot legitimately do anything that individuals cannot do. The reason states came into existence is to more efficiently protect the lives, liberty, and property of their constituents. Individuals have the right to protect their lives, liberty, and property. They merely delegated these inherent rights to some government. It is a principal–agent relationship, where the state is the agent of the citizenry.

If some individuals choose not to avail themselves of the services the state provides, it seems inherently unfair that they should be forced to pay for services they do not want. Even though the state may be the dominant provider of security, it may not be the only provider of security. Private security agencies also provide security for a fee, and individuals who prefer to hire one of these private security agencies should be able to do so without also being forced to pay for state security, which they do not use.

The same could be said for pensions, education, or any other service the state provides. People should not be forced to pay for social security if they are willing to forego receiving social security benefits. People who do not have children or who send their children to a private school should not be forced to pay for the education of other people's children. Such forced payments are inherently unfair. Evasion of payments for such services would seem justified.

One might think that we have solved the problem at this point, but there is another issue to discuss. What if the government provides services that you use? Is there a moral obligation to pay for them? We all benefit from the government's provision of police and fire protection. We all use government roads. Is there a moral obligation to pay for them?

Nozick (1974: 265) asks the question – Would you pay for the service if the compulsion were removed? If the answer is *yes*, then an argument could be made that there is a moral duty to pay. The example of the FEE sending a check to the local government is an example of how to do the right thing in the absence of compulsion.

But that is not the end of the analysis. What if the government provides a service you use but does so inefficiently? It is a valid statement that government is less efficient than the private sector. Hundreds of studies over the years have documented the fact that the private sector can do just about anything more efficiently than government (Fitzgerald, 1988; Greene, 2001; Kemp, 2007; Poole, 1980; Savas, 1982, 2005). Is there a moral obligation to reimburse the government for its costs if its monopoly price is higher than what would exist in a free market, where government did not prevent private providers from offering the same or better service?

Government is a monopolist in the areas where it operates. Since the government uses force to prevent private individuals and firms from entering the market, it would seem unfair to force people to pay the monopoly price the government charges to reimburse it for its inefficiently provided services. If one would voluntarily pay for the service the government provides, it seems fair that the correct price to pay would be the price that would exist if the government did not abuse its power by preventing private firms from entering the market.

The post office could be used as an example. The federal government of the USA has a monopoly on the delivery of first-class mail. The absence of competition allows it to charge above-market prices and provide below-market levels of service. Wherever the private sector has been allowed to compete, such as in the delivery of packages, it has been able to do the job cheaper and better than the government alternative. Where individuals would be willing to pay for a service currently provided by government, it seems that the fair price would be the price they would pay in the absence of monopoly. To insist on a higher price would be to force people to pay a price that would result in the unjust enrichment of government, since it has done nothing to earn an above-market price.

Concluding Comments

As was mentioned previously, there may be a duty not to pay in some cases. Where the state is evil and would use the funds to finance its evil projects, there is a duty not to pay. The same could be said where the state is engaging in an unjust war.

One might also apply utilitarian ethics to conclude that there is a duty not to pay. The argument goes something like this. The state is not as efficient as the private sector. We have a duty not to waste resources. We can minimize or reduce waste (increase efficiency) by not transferring resources to the less-efficient government sector. Therefore, we have a duty to evade taxes because the result will be a more efficient, and therefore more prosperous society. The result will be a positive-sum game because there will be more winners than losers. To my knowledge, no one has applied utilitarian ethics to the issue of tax evasion in quite this way. Perhaps, mention of it here will start a dialog among ethicists and policy makers.

Evasion of taxes also strengthens property rights, since taxation violates property rights. A just society is a society, where property rights are not violated. The more tax evasion we have, the fewer property rights are violated. If "taxation of earnings from labor is on a par with forced labor," as Nozick asserts (Nozick, 1974: 169), then evasion would also reduce the amount of forced labor we must endure. Tax evasion may be seen as a form of self-defense, where the state is little more than a robber.

The strongest case to support the position that there is a moral duty to pay taxes is the case where the state limits its activities to the defense of life, liberty, and property. This is the reason why governments were formed, according to Bastiat (1968) and a host of other political theorists. When governments go beyond these basic functions, they venture into the realm of redistribution and confiscate the property of some to dole out to others, which is always unethical and never justifiable. In such cases, the government need not be obeyed.

However, even in cases where the state limits its activities to the defense of life, liberty, and property, it is difficult to justify on ethical grounds the confiscation of property to pay for these functions if the person whose property is confiscated does not want to utilize the government services. Individuals who are willing to forego access to the services the state provides should not be forced to pay for those services. People who prefer not to use government services to protect their life, liberty, and property should not be forced to pay. People who want to opt out of social security or Medicare or Medicaid should be able to do so. People who do not have children enrolled in government schools should not be forced to pay for the (inferior) education of the children who attend those schools. People who abhor abortion should not be forced to pay to support clinics that supply abortion services. There is nothing unethical about refusing to pay for services you do not want.

References

Aristotle. *Nicomachean Ethics.*

Aristotle. *The Politics.*

Barker, Dan. (1992). *Losing Faith in Faith.* Madison, WI: Freedom from Religion Foundation.

Bastiat, Frédéric. (1968). *The Law.* Irvington-on-Hudson, NY: Foundation for Economic Education. Originally published in 1850 as a pamphlet, *La Loi,* reprinted in *Sophismes Économiques,* Vol. I. *Oeuvres Complètes de Frédéric Bastiat,* 4th edition, Paris: Guillaumin et Cie, 1878, pp. 343–394.

Bulluart, F.C.R. (1874). *Summa Sancti Thomae hodiernis academiarum moribus accommodate,* VI, dissert. IX, art. VII, para. II (Lyons), VI, as cited in Martin T. Crowe, *The Moral Obligation of Paying Just Taxes.* The Catholic University of America Studies in Sacred Theology No. 84, p. 56.

Burr, William Henry. (1987). *Self-Contradictions in the Bible.* Buffalo: Prometheus Books. Originally published in 1860 in New York by A.J. Davis & Company.

Cohn, Gordon. (1998). The Jewish View on Paying Taxes. *Journal of Accounting, Ethics & Public Policy,* 1(2), 109–120, reprinted in Robert W. McGee (Ed.), *The Ethics of Tax Evasion* (pp. 180–189). Dumont, NJ: The Dumont Institute for Public Policy Research, 1998, pp. 180–189.

Concina, Daniel F. (1774). *Theologia Christiana Dogmatico-Moralis* (Naples), as cited in Martin T. Crowe, *The Moral Obligation of Paying Just Taxes.* The Catholic University of America Studies in Sacred Theology No. 84, p. 55.

Crowe, Martin T. (1944). *The Moral Obligation of Paying Just Taxes.* The Catholic University of America Studies in Sacred Theology No. 84.

Davis, Henry (1938). Moral and Pastoral Theology, 3rd ed. New York: Sheed and Ward, as cited in Martin T. Crowe, *The Moral Obligation of Paying Just Taxes.* The Catholic University of America Studies in Sacred Theology No. 84, p. 40.

Fitzgerald, Randall (1988). *When Government Goes Private: Successful Alternatives to Public Services.* New York: Universe Books.

Greene, Jeffrey D. (2001). *Cities and Privatization: Prospects for the New Century.* Upper Saddle River, NJ: Prentice Hall.

Hobbes, Thomas. (1651). *Leviathan.*

Jalili, Ali Reza (2012). The Ethics of Tax Evasion: An Islamic Perspective. In Robert W. McGee (Ed.), *The Ethics of Tax Evasion in Theory and Practice* (forthcoming). New York: Springer.

Kemp, Roger L. (2007). *Privatization: The Provision of Public Services by the Private Sector.* Jefferson, NC: McFarland & Co.

La Croix, C. (1739). *Theologia Moralis*, III, pars. II (Coloniae), as cited in Martin T. Crowe, *The Moral Obligation of Paying Just Taxes.* The Catholic University of America Studies in Sacred Theology No. 84, p. 55.

Lewis, Joseph. (1926). *The Bible Unmasked.* New York: The Freethought Press Association.

Liguori, St. Alphonsus (1907). *Theologia Moralis* (ed. Gaudé, Rome), III, as cited in Martin T. Crowe, *The Moral Obligation of Paying Just Taxes.* The Catholic University of America Studies in Sacred Theology No. 84, p. 58. Crowe does not cite the exact page number.

Locke, John. (1689). *Two Treatises on Government.*

McGee, Robert W. and Gordon M. Cohn. (2008). Jewish Perspectives on the Ethics of Tax Evasion. *Journal of Legal, Ethical and Regulatory Issues*, 11(2), 1–32.

McGee, Robert W. (Ed.) (2012). *The Ethics of Tax Evasion: Perspectives in Theory and Practice.* New York: Springer.

McKinsey, Dennis C. (1995). *The Encyclopedia of Biblical Errancy.* Amherst, NY: Prometheus Books.

McKinsey, Dennis C. (2000). *Biblical Errancy: A Reference Guide.* Amherst, NY: Prometheus Books.

Nozick, Robert (1974). *Anarchy, State & Utopia.* New York: Basic Books.

Patuzzi, J. (1770). Ethica Christiana sive Theologia Moralis (Venice), I, as cited in Martin T. Crowe, *The Moral Obligation of Paying Just Taxes.* The Catholic University of America Studies in Sacred Theology No. 84, p. 57.

Pennock, Robert T. (1998). Death and Taxes: On the Justice of Conscientious War Tax Resistance. *Journal of Accounting, Ethics & Public Policy*, 1(1), 58–76, reprinted in Robert W. McGee (Ed.), *The Ethics of Tax Evasion* (pp. 124–142). Dumont, NJ: The Dumont Institute for Public Policy Research, 1998.

Plato. *The Laws.*

Plato. *The Republic.*

Poole, Robert W. (1980). *Cutting Back City Hall.* New York: Universe Books.

Rand, Ayn (1961). *For the New Intellectual.* New York: Penguin.

Rousseau, Jean Jacques. (1762). *The Social Contract.*

Savas, E.S. (1982). *Privatizing the Public Sector: How To Shrink Government.* Chatham, NJ: Chatham House Publishers.

Savas, E.S. (2005). *Privatization in the City: Successes, Failures, Lessons.* Washington, DC: CQ Press.

Schansberg, Eric D. (1998). The Ethics of Tax Evasion within Biblical Christianity: Are There Limits to "Rendering Unto Caesar"? *Journal of Accounting, Ethics & Public Policy*, 1(1), 77–90, reprinted in Robert W. McGee (ed.), The Ethics of Tax Evasion (pp. 144–157). The Dumont Institute for Public Policy Research, Dumont, NJ, 1998.

Spooner, Lysander. (1870). *No Treason: The Constitution of No Authority*, originally self-published by Spooner in Boston in 1870, reprinted by Rampart College in 1965, 1966 and 1971, and by Ralph Myles Publisher, Inc., Colorado Springs, Colorado in 1973.

Tamari, Meir. (1998). Ethical Issues in Tax Evasion: A Jewish Perspective. *Journal of Accounting, Ethics & Public Policy*, 1(2), 121–132, reprinted in Robert W. McGee (Ed.), *The Ethics of Tax Evasion* (pp. 168–178). Dumont, NJ: The Dumont Institute for Public Policy Research, 1998.

Templeton, Charles. (1996). *Farewell to God.* Toronto: McClelland & Stewart.

Williams, Walter (1987). *All It Takes Is Guts: A Minority View.* Washington, DC: Regnery Books.

Chapter 3
An Analysis of Some Arguments

Robert W. McGee

Introduction

Morality can exist only when there is choice. Stated alternatively, where there is no choice there is no morality. If a commanding officer orders a soldier to either kill someone or be killed for disobeying an order, the soldier is not morally responsible for executing the person who has been chosen for execution because he has no choice.

From that basic premise, one may also state that paying taxes does not raise any moral issues because one does not have a choice. Paying taxes is neither moral nor immoral. It is merely something one is forced to do. Paying taxes to an evil or corrupt government is not immoral because we have no choice. Paying taxes to the Nazi war machine does not constitute an unethical act because we have no choice.[1]

But that is not quite correct because it is possible to refuse to pay (evade) taxes that are legally owed if one is willing to suffer the penalty. Some theologians have argued that it is not immoral to evade taxes if one is willing to pay the penalty for nonpayment (Angelus of Clavisio 1494; Crolly 1877; Merkelbach 1938: 287; Navarrus 1618). Other theologians have disagreed with this position (Antoninus 1571).

There have been instances historically where individuals have refused to pay taxes for one reason or another. One moral reason that has been given for refusing to pay taxes is when the taxpayer is confronted with the option of paying taxes to support an unjust war or being punished for failure to pay. Some Vietnam War protesters refused to pay taxes for this reason. This reasoning goes back hundreds of years in the philosophical and theological literature (Pennock and Robert 1998).

---

[1] This latter position has been disputed and we will discuss it below.

R.W. McGee (✉)
School of Business, Florida International University, 3000 NE 151 Street,
North Miami, FL 33181, USA
e-mail: bob414@hotmail.com

R.W. McGee (ed.), *The Ethics of Tax Evasion: Perspectives in Theory and Practice*,
DOI 10.1007/978-1-4614-1287-8_3, © Springer Science+Business Media, LLC 2012

But what if someone refuses to pay taxes just because they do not want to pay and what if they have an opportunity to evade and perhaps not get caught? This possibility raises a different set of issues because they do have a choice. Where there is choice, there is an opportunity to act morally or immorally. The remainder of this paper examines the main arguments that have been put forth to claim that tax evasion is either ethical or unethical.

Duty to Whom?

The literature discusses duty to three possible entities – God, the state, and other individuals. To these three duties mentioned above, one might add a fourth category – duty to clients. Tax practitioners have a fiduciary duty to do what is in the best interest of their clients. If the cost of evading taxes exceeds the benefits to be gained by evading, then practitioners have a fiduciary duty to their clients not to help them evade taxes, even if evading the tax itself does not constitute an unethical act.

Another point about tax evasion by practitioners is worth mentioning. Local bar associations, state boards of accountancy, and associations of certified public accountants have rules that sanction their members for aiding and abetting tax evasion. In cases where tax evasion does not constitute an unethical act, it seems inherently unfair that practitioners should be subject to sanctions, loss of their license, and so forth, on ethical grounds because they have not done anything unethical (McGee 1998).

The Relationship of the Individual to the State

The relationship of the individual to the state is one of the main determining factors of what the duty is to pay taxes. Stated differently, the duty to pay taxes is determined by the relationship of the individual to the state. The two polar extremes are that the individual is the master and the state is the servant, or the state is the master and the individuals are the servants. Either the state exists for the benefit of individuals or individuals exist for the benefit of the state. These two polar positions can be represented by the following continuum.

State is Master	Individuals are Masters
Individuals are Servants	State is Servant

At the extreme left side of the spectrum is the view that the state is the master and the people are the servants, who exist for the benefit of the state. Various totalitarian regimes over the centuries have been at or near this end of the spectrum. The underlying philosophy of those who support this view of the state might be stated thus: "Ask not what your country can do for you – ask what you can do for your country." (Kennedy 1961).

At the other extreme is the view that the state exists only to provide services for the citizenry. Most liberal democracies hold this view to some extent.

It is probably fair to say that historically very few states have been at either extreme. Most states are between these two extremes and have elements of both polar positions.

Ancient Greece and ancient Rome had slaves, and so did many more modern societies, including the United States prior to the Civil War of 1861–1865 (or War of Northern Aggression, depending on one's perspective). However, these societies also had citizens who were not slaves.

The Soviet Union did not have slaves, per se, although its citizens were not free to choose their occupation, their place of residence, their political beliefs or their religion, and they were not free to leave the country. One could say the same of ancient Egypt. The Nazi regime in Germany generally allowed its citizens to choose their occupations, their place of residence and their religion but not their political beliefs. Those who disobeyed the state or who even said anything negative about the state were subject to severe punishment under both the Nazi and Soviet regimes.

At the other end of the spectrum is the view that the state is the servant of the people. The question then becomes, "What services should the state provide to its citizens?" Those who believe in minimal government believe that the functions of the state should be limited to the protection of life, liberty, and property and that all other functions of the state are illegitimate. Others believe that the legitimate functions of the state go beyond these basic protections and into the realm of social welfare. However, once one goes beyond the basic functions of protecting life, liberty, and property, some individuals are forced to contribute to the welfare of other individuals, which some political philosophers would say is an illegitimate use of state power (Nozick 1974).

The duty to pay taxes is not absolute, partly because the duty to the state is not absolute. The duty to pay may be viewed on a continuum as well.

No duty to pay _____ Absolute duty to pay

As a general rule, one might assert that there is no duty to pay where taxpayers are treated like slaves of the state, and that there is an absolute duty to pay where the state is a true servant of the people, when services are limited to the protection of life, liberty, and property. As one approaches the left side of the spectrum, the duty to pay declines, and as one approaches the right side of the spectrum, the duty to pay increases.

However, there are problems at the right side of this spectrum. For example, what if some citizens would rather provide for their own protection? Do they still have a duty to pay taxes to support protections that they do not want? If so, where does this duty come from? How can one say that the state is justified in extracting taxes from those people when they would agree not to burden the state by using the services that the state provides? It seems like an unfair trade, since the parties at one end of the bargain do not want the services the state provides. Rather than being a voluntary exchange, it is a forced exchange.

There is also the problem of a democracy that devolves into untrammeled majoritarianism, as James Madison and some of America's other Founding Fathers feared. If some majority comes to power through the electoral process and uses its power to exploit some minority (usually rich people), do those who are exploited still have a duty to pay whatever taxes the democratically elected government demands? If two wolves and one sheep vote on what's for dinner, not only does the sheep not have to obey the majority but also has an absolute right to use deadly force to prevent the will of the majority from being implemented. Could one say the same of some other minority that is exploited by the majority?

How much force is justified in defending one's life, liberty, or property is a basic question of political philosophy. When one's life is being threatened unfairly, it seems reasonable that the individual being attacked can use deadly force to prevent being killed, but what if it is mere property that is threatened with confiscation? May one still use deadly force to prevent the confiscation?

It seems reasonable that one may use the same amount of force to defend property as the other side uses to attempt to confiscate the property. If the state uses deadly force to unjustly confiscate property, one might reasonably argue that the individual whose property stands to be confiscated is justified in using equal force to prevent the unjust confiscation. Arguing that the individual whose property is at risk is not justified in using equal force to that used by the aggressor is an untenable position.

Arguments Pro and Con

A number of arguments have been used over the centuries to justify both major positions – that there is a duty to pay taxes or that there is no duty to pay taxes. We will now examine those arguments.

Taxes Are the Price We Pay for Civilization

Oliver Wendell Holmes, Jr. (1841–1935), an eminent American jurist, has been quoted as saying that "Taxes are the price we pay for civilization." It is carved on the façade of the Internal Revenue Service building in Washington, DC (Block 1997). Actually, the quote has been attributed to him with several variations. In Felix Frankfurter's biography of Holmes he quotes Holmes as saying "I like paying taxes. With them I buy civilization." (Frankfurter 1961: 71).

The Holmes quote has permeated the accounting, tax, legal, economics, public finance, and popular literature and is perhaps the most frequently quoted utterance about taxes. When Franco Modigliani, the Nobel Prize winning economist heard it, his response was "That is a very non-Italian attitude." (Samuelson 1999: 354).

Elaborate upon the meaning of the quote in a *Chicago Tribune* newspaper article published the day before the April 15 tax filing deadline in the United States (Holmes and Sunstein 1999b). They responded to taxpayer arguments that "It's our money and we want to keep it" and "Why should the IRS take our money, when the government wastes it and we want to spend it on ourselves?" with some counterarguments. They ask whether the money in our pockets and bank accounts is fully ours. They ask whether we could have inherited it without the assistance of a probate court or whether we could have saved it without bank regulators. They argue that without taxes there would be no property and we would have no assets worth defending. Homeowners depend of fire and police protection as well as registry titles and deeds, all services provided by government. Taxes pay for armies to protect us from external aggression. They conclude that there is no liberty without dependency on government to protect our rights.

They raise some good points and they should not be faulted for not offering counterarguments to the many criticisms that could be made of the tax system. After all, there is limited space in newspaper article and it is not possible to fully analyze all the issues and respond to opponents, although they did elaborate on some of these points in a book on the same topic (Holmes and Sunstein 1999b).

However, their argument is incomplete on several counts, as is the Holmes position in general. While a case can be made for using force to collect revenue that is used to protect the rights to life, liberty, and property, the argument for using force to support other government functions is more difficult to justify. Government functions that redistribute wealth from those who have earned it to those who have not are difficult to justify. Whole books have been written that analyze this question (de Jouvenel 1952). Frederic Bastiat (1801–1850), a French political economist, has the following view on this abuse of government power, which he refers to as legal plunder:

> But how is this legal plunder to be identified? Quite simply. See if the law takes from some persons what belongs to them, and gives it to other persons to whom it does not belong. See if the law benefits one citizen at the expense of another by doing what the citizen himself cannot do without committing a crime.
>
> Then abolish this law without delay, for it is not only an evil itself, but also it is a fertile source for further evils because it invites reprisals. If such a law – which may be an isolated case – is not abolished immediately, it will spread, multiply, and develop into a system (Bastiat 1968: 21).

Then there is the question of how much civilization do we want to pay for. There is a difference between government and society. Society can exist without government but government cannot exist without society. Even in places that do not have a fully functioning government, like Somalia, Afghanistan, and post-earthquake Haiti, there is society and a civilization. There is no doubt that more protection of life, liberty, and property would be a good thing in these places. However, having more government and more taxes is only one of several possible solutions. In some cases society itself is oppressive and violates basic rights like the right of free speech and press and the right to property. There are certain factions in Afghanistan that think women should not go to school or receive medical care from male doctors. But since women are not permitted to go to school, there are no female doctors. In such cases it is not lack of government that is the problem but rather society.

The "Government Couldn't Exist Without Taxes" Argument

The underlying assumption to the "Government couldn't exist without taxes argument" is that it is desirable that government exist. A variation of that argument is that functions that are now provided by government could no longer be provided by government without taxes. But that does not mean that some or all of the functions now provided by government would no longer be provided. The market would provide the services that are demanded by consumers and the nonprofit sector would provide the most important charitable functions. Functions that government should not provide would no longer be provided by government if it could no longer generate the tax funds to pay for those functions. If governments did not have the funds required to invade or bomb other countries they would be far less likely to invade or bomb other countries, which is generally a good thing. If government could not raise the funds to engage in wasteful spending projects like building bridges to nowhere,[2] it would no longer build bridges to nowhere.

An underlying premise of the argument that government could not exist without taxes is that all government funds come from taxes, which is blatantly not true. Governments can also raise funds by user fees, lotteries and voluntary contributions. Thus, it cannot be said that government cannot exist without taxes because it can. What would be more accurate to say is that government cannot exist at the present level without taxes. The scope of government would have to be cut back if its only sources of funding were user fees, lotteries, and voluntary contributions, and that might be a good thing.

The voluntary contribution option might seem ridiculous. One might validly ask who in their right mind would voluntarily send a check to the government when government already takes perhaps 20–40% of a person's income and squanders a good deal of what it collects? That is a valid point. However, if government were to drastically shrink in size because it could no longer extract taxes from the populace, it would have to shed its wasteful spending habits and people would be less inclined

---

[2] I am referring to the scandal surrounding Congressional approval to spend hundreds of millions of dollars to build a bridge from mainland Alaska to Gravina Island, an island that was nearly uninhabited and which already had a ferry service connecting it to the mainland. The main issue was whether taxpayers from Florida, Kansas, and other states should be forced to pay for a bridge in Alaska that was not needed and was pushed by a member of the Alaska Congressional delegation mostly as a means of creating jobs (and obtaining Alaskan votes at the expense of the taxpayers of the other 49 states).

to view government as a wasteful and corrupt behemoth. Some people may even view government as worthy of receiving contributions if those contributions were to be spent on worthy projects, such as relief to Haitian or other disaster victims (although making a donation to the Red Cross would probably be a more rational option). After natural disasters like the earthquake in Haiti and Hurricane Katrina numerous individuals donated millions of dollars to help in the relief effort. Various Hollywood celebrities and others have donated to such causes on numerous occasions. Ted Turner made news by donating $1 billion to the United Nations (United Nations 2006). In such cases, government would compete with private charities such as the Red Cross.

There is a body of literature that shows how government services can be provided privately. Space does not permit a full discussion and analysis of this literature. However, there are many cases where the market or the nonprofit sector have been able to provide services that had previously been provided by government, usually at lower cost and higher quality (Donahue 1991; Fitzgerald 1988; Greene 2001; Kemp and Roger 2007; Letwin 1988; Pitcher 2003; Poole and Robert 1980; Savas 2005).[3]

The "What If Everybody Did It" Argument

The "What if everybody did it" argument, known in philosophical circles as the Kantian Categorical Imperative (Kant 1997, 1998, 2001), is an argument that has been used in the philosophical literature to determine whether an act can be justified on ethical grounds. It has become a form of ethical reasoning (Baron et al. 1997).

When applied to the issue of the morality of tax evasion, the conclusions are interesting. Of course, if everyone refused to pay all taxes, government would not be able to garner any revenue to perform its functions, unless it resorted to the printing press to print money, user fees, lotteries, or voluntary contributions. But what if everyone merely refused to pay unjust taxes? The obvious answer is that soon there would be fewer unjust taxes and more justice. What if everyone refused to pay taxes to an oppressive or corrupt government? Soon there would be fewer oppressive and corrupt governments. What if everybody refused to pay for wasteful spending? Soon there would be less wasteful spending.

Étienne de la Boétie (1530–1563) asked a similar question a few centuries ago. His basic question was why do people support the governments that oppress them? His conclusion is that our slavery is voluntary (Boétie 1577; de la Boétie 1974, 1975; Keohane 1977; Walter 1966).

---

[3] www.privatization.org provides a wealth of information, including a database, of numerous cases where functions once performed by government have been successfully transferred to the private or nonprofit sector.

The Taxation Is Theft/Slavery Argument

This argument basically states that taxation is theft because it constitutes the taking of property without the owner's consent. When a thief takes property without the owner's consent it is called theft but when the government does it, it is called taxation. The only difference between the two is who does the taking.

A corollary of this position is that taxation is slavery. Nozick (1974) makes this argument in *Anarchy, State and Utopia*. The argument derives from the body as property doctrine. Individuals own their bodies. They use their bodies to produce income. This income is the fruits of their labor. They are entitled to the fruits of their labor. Their entitlement is superior to that of all others. Anyone who takes these fruits without the owner's consent does so without moral justification. If some government takes 40% of the fruits of one's labor, it is the substantial equivalent of enslaving that person for 2 days a week, given a 5-day workweek. "Taxation of earnings from labor is on a par with forced labor." (Nozick 1974: 169).

Those who object to this line of reasoning might argue that taxation is not really theft because we consent to it. But that is not always the case, as is discussed elsewhere in this paper. It might also be pointed out that coercion would not be needed if there were consent, and since coercion is required, we may reasonably conclude that consent is not present.

Tamari (1998) turns the "taxation is theft" argument on its head by stating that tax evasion is theft. Of course that implies that the funds that would be taken in taxes really belong to the government, even though the income has been earned by the citizenry. Nozick's entitlement theory would challenge that assertion.

The Law Is the Law

Another argument against the moral case for tax evasion is that "The law is the law" (Cohn 1998). In other words, one may never disobey a law. One may further argue that if you don't like the law you can change it, which may or may not be true, even in a democracy.

One criticism of this view is that it does not take unjust laws into account. There is a strain of thought within the philosophical and political science literature that unjust laws need not be obeyed. In some cases one might even assert that there is a moral duty to disobey unjust laws. Protesters who practice civil disobedience would agree with this position. Thus, a better position might be that there is a moral duty to obey just laws but not unjust laws.

The "We Have a Duty to Pay Taxes" Argument

The "We have a duty to pay taxes" argument can be subdivided into at least three subparts. According to the literature, this duty can be to God, to the government or to some portion of the population. The duty to God argument and the duty to the government argument are discussed elsewhere in this paper, so let's focus on the third case, the duty to some group.

The group can include other taxpayers. If I pay less, others must pay more is one argument that has been used historically. This argument is discussed in another part of the present paper, so let's move on to a related argument. There is a strain of thought within the Jewish literature (Cohn 1998) that holds that one Jew must never do anything to disparage another Jew. In other words, if one Jew does something bad it makes all other Jews look bad. That being the case, no Jew should ever evade taxes because doing so would make all other Jews look bad.

This view may be criticized on the grounds of a lack of duty. The argument can be made that one individual may have a duty to another individual but not to a group, unless there is a duty to each member of the group. But more importantly, if the tax itself is unjust or if the proceeds from the tax are used for evil purposes, there may be a positive duty to evade the tax so that evil enterprises cannot be funded.

The Ability to Pay Argument

The ability to pay argument is based on a non sequitur: You have more, therefore you must pay more. That is not the case when you go to the supermarket. Why should it be the case when you are called upon to pay for government services?

The ability to pay argument has a long if undistinguished history in the literature. Discussions of the concept appear in the Catholic theological literature going back hundreds of years (Crowe 1944). Karl Marx advocated it in his *Critique of the Gotha Program* (1875).

The underlying assumption of the ability to pay argument is that some people have a moral right to live at the expense of others or that some individuals can be used as resources for other individuals rather than as ends in themselves. There are basically just two positions on the relationship of the individual to the state. One view holds that the people are the masters and the state is the servant. The other view holds that the state is the master and the people are the servants, who may be considered resources to be used for whatever purpose the state sees fit. The ability to pay concept (I cannot call it a principle because it is the absence of principle) is a corollary of this second view because it treats individuals as resources, to be milked as needed.

The "It's OK If Everyone Is Doing It" Argument

This argument might seem outrageous on its face, but Catholic theologians have defended this view on the basis of fairness. Martin Crowe (1944: 37), discussing the view of Genicot E.-Salsmans (1927), states that "…it would be unjust to burden conscientious men with heavier taxes while wicked men usually pay less."

Crowe (1944: 40), quoting Henry Davis (1938: 339), states:

> It appears unreasonable to expect good citizens, who certainly are in the minority, to be obliged in conscience to pay taxes, whereas so many others openly repudiate the moral obligation, if there is one. It seems unjust that good people should feel an obligation to be mulcted and to pay readily, in order to balance the evasions of so many.

Thus, it appears a case can be made on the basis of fairness for evading taxes if everyone else is doing it.

The Majority Rule Argument

In a democracy, the majority rules. In cases where there is not unanimity, which is in nearly all cases, that means that the minority must be content to take their lumps. The argument is sometimes made that if they don't like it they should leave, an argument that is discussed elsewhere in this paper.

One of the differences between a democracy and a republic is that the majority rules in a democracy whereas in a republic the minority has rights. For example, in a democracy, if two wolves and one sheep vote on what to have for lunch, the sheep must comply with the majority vote of the wolves, whereas in a republic the sheep has rights that are superior to any majority and would have a right to resist with whatever force is needed.

The point is that one may not assert that there is always a moral duty to pay any tax that some majority has voted to enact. More is needed. If taxes are imposed in order to suppress some segment of the population, or perhaps all segments of the population, one must look for some moral justification. One may not merely assume that the tax is always morally justified.

A related argument is that we have elected representatives to do our bidding. It is a more efficient system of government than having debates and town hall meetings every day. Most people are too busy working and living their lives to study the issues and arrive at conclusions regarding a wide range of policy issues, so they delegate that task to their elected representatives, who are supposed to become specialists who work only in the best interests of their constituents. No one actually believes that, and the literature of the Public Choice School of Economics has documented numerous cases where public officials use their offices to work for their own interests rather than those of their constituents (Tullock 1970, 1989, 1993).

The Representative Government Argument

The representative government argument is a variation of the contract theory or "we consent to be taxed" argument, which is discussed below. This argument basically states that we consent to be taxed because we elect representatives who do our bidding. It is an application of the principal–agent theory. The taxpayers (voters) are the principals. The elected representatives are the agents. They do what we tell them to do and we delegate authority, since we are too busy leading our lives to become enmeshed in the details of government. If they vote to tax us, it is OK because we elected them to represent us. Thus, we agreed to be taxed and we should have no complaints. If we no longer want them to represent us, we can throw them out in the next election and choose a different set of representatives.

There are several weaknesses with this argument. While it is true that we elect our representatives, it does not necessarily follow that they do our bidding. More often than not they do the bidding of some special interest group, or they do their own bidding, working on their own behalf instead of the behalf of the people who elected them. The Public Choice School of Economics has been documenting this phenomenon since the 1970s or so. It is also obvious whenever we read the newspaper (or the Internet) or watch television. Very few people believe that Congress or the various state legislatures represent them or their views.

Even if we are able to elect a representative who does represent our views, it is likely that the individual elected will only agree with us on 60 or 70% of the issues, and that representative is one of many. If I live in Florida, the representatives from California (on the left coast) and New York and other liberal states will override any votes that are cast by my representative (who, as of this writing, does not represent my views anyway). Thus, it cannot be said with a straight face that our representatives actually do our bidding and that we therefore have no room to complain.

The Contract Theory Argument (We Consent to Be Taxed)

The Contract Theory argument and the consent argument are not quite the same but they will be lumped together here for the sake of efficiency. The underlying premise of the Contract Theory is that some group of individuals got together at some time in the past and agreed to form a government to protect life, liberty, and property. No documentation can be found of such a meeting, of course, but from a philosophical perspective no documentation is needed in order to discuss the issue.

Various forms of the Contract Theory have emerged over the centuries. According to some versions of the theory, individuals give up their rights in exchange for government protection whereas in other versions individuals retain their rights and merely delegate their rights to government because of efficiency. Three versions of the theory that have stood the test of time in the philosophical literature are those of Hobbes (1651), Locke (1689) and Rousseau (1762). We will not debate the differences and nuances of their three versions in this paper but will discuss some criticisms that have been made of all contract theories.

Lysander Spooner (1870) raises some strong legal objections to all contract theories. He pointed out that it is a long and well-established principle of common law that no one may be bound by a contract without his consent. He analyzed the United States Constitution as an example. His argument was that the U.S. Constitution was signed by a small group of individuals who represented no one but themselves and that those individuals are all now dead. If they bound anyone it was only themselves. No one else was bound and certainly future generations were not bound by any agreement they entered into. Any contract they had died with them. They did not obligate their children or anyone else's children to abide by the Constitution they signed.

Since taxation is compulsory upon all, voters and nonvoters alike, it cannot be said that those who vote thereby consent to be taxed (Spooner 1870, p. 14). Many people who vote do so to protect their property. A modern version of this argument would be that we do not vote *for* certain candidates, we vote *against* them by voting for their opponent, whom we consider to be the lesser evil. Merely voting for the lesser evil is not the same as consenting to be taxed by the winner of the election. Voting is seen as a means of protecting property against those who would confiscate it without consent of the owner. Voting for individuals who promise to confiscate less than their opponents cannot be confused with consenting to the future confiscations.

Spooner points out that the main difference between government tax officials and a highwayman is that the highwayman will just rob you once and let you go. He will not rob you repeatedly and give you moral lectures about why he is taking your property without your consent for your own good and that you are morally obligated to pay (Spooner 1870, p. 17).

In another place, Spooner states:

> ... no man can be taxed without his personal consent ... Taxation without consent is as plainly robbery, when enforced against one man, as when enforced against millions ... If the government can take a man's money without his consent, there is no limit to the additional tyranny it may practise upon him (Spooner 1852, p. 222).

He goes on to state that all legitimate government is no more than a mutual insurance company where individuals consent to pay some agreed upon fee in exchange for the services that insurance companies provide. Those who agree receive protection and those who decide not to pay are not entitled to protection.

One may point out that this approach would result in free rider problems, since some people would be afforded protection without paying. It is a valid point. If a policeman sees someone being assaulted he probably will not ask the victim whether his insurance payments are up to date before coming to his aid. In cases where a nonparticipant receives police or fire protection, some kind of premium billing arrangement might be used whereby nonsubscribers are charged a premium for using police or fire services. Such an arrangement would be fair to subscribers, since it is the subscribers who are paying to support the service.

The "If You Don't Like It, Leave" Argument

We have all heard the "If you don't like it, leave" argument. It is often heard whenever someone is complaining about the government, the society, or a job. The underlying premise of such arguments is that if you decide to stay you consent to whatever rules are established by the people in charge.

Several criticisms may be made of this argument. Perhaps the main criticism is that wherever you go you are faced with another imperfect political jurisdiction. Merely deciding to stay where you are does not mean that you consent to all of the rules. It merely implies that you have decided that your current residence is the least unacceptable choice, all things considered.

There also may be economic reasons for not leaving, such as the inability to find suitable employment or the inability to buy a plane or train or bus ticket. The point is that consent to submit to the rules of the political jurisdiction may not be inferred merely because the individual in question has not voted with his feet to leave.

Another problem with this argument is that not everyone is free to leave. The vast majority of those who lived in the former Soviet Union were not free to leave the country without government permission, and permission was usually not granted. In many cases, individuals who asked for permission were punished for merely asking. Communist Cuba and North Korea may be cited as other examples where individuals are not free to leave as of this writing.

Recent legislation enacted in the United States imposes an exit tax on certain individuals if they decide to leave permanently (Arsenault 2009), which has been referred to as America's Berlin Wall (Anonymous 2008). However, whereas people who left Berlin during the communist era had to do so without government permission and had to pay a 100% tax, in the sense that they had to leave all their assets behind, the U.S. tax is somewhat less than 100%, although the principle is the same.

It seems inherently unfair to tax individuals who decide to leave a political jurisdiction. If they are willing to forego the benefits that the government provides, they should not be forced to pay, since they have given up the right to receive future benefits by leaving. If there is any moral duty to pay taxes, such a duty exists only in cases where the government provides services to the taxpayer. Since the government will not provide future services to people who leave the country permanently, it seems that there would be nothing unethical about evading such exit taxes.

The "We Must Pay Our Fair Share" Argument

The fair share argument is prevalent in the literature. It is a moral argument, since not paying one's fair share means that someone else must pay for your benefits. One who does not pay one's fair share is a free rider, a leech on the body politic.

The problem with the fair share argument is that no one can agree on what one's fair share is. If it means that individuals should pay for the value of the government services they receive, then most people are paying more than their fair share, since they receive less in government benefits than what they pay. That is certainly true in the case of federal taxes in the United States. It is often difficult to see what benefits one receives from the federal government, but it is easy to see the costs, or at least some of them, especially on pay day when a percentage of wages earned are withheld from paychecks.

If that is the case, then could it be said that those who pay more than their fair share have a moral justification to evade at least a portion of their taxes? It would seem so, since it would be difficult to justify being forced to pay *more* than one's fair share on moral grounds.

Internal Revenue Service data for the United States reveals that the top 1% of U.S. taxpayers pay more than 40% of all federal income taxes and that the top 5% pay nearly 61% of total taxes, which means that the bottom 95% pay 39% (Tax Foundation 2009). In other words, the top 1% of income earners pay more than the bottom 95% of income earners (Prante and Robyn 2010). Given those statistics it would be difficult to justify the argument that the top 1 or 5% of income earners are not paying their fair share. A more realistic argument would be that they are paying far more than their fair share, that they are actually being exploited.

The problem with the fair share argument is that "fair share" is never defined. If one begins with the premise that there is a moral obligation to pay one's fair share, one might also reasonably assert that there is no duty to pay more than one's fair share. Since the top 1 and 5% of income earners are obviously paying more than their fair share, one may reasonably conclude that those income groups may morally evade at least some of the taxes that are legally owed.

The "Tax Evasion Is a Sin" Argument

Some theologians believe that tax evasion is a sin. The Christian Bible seems to indicate that there is a duty to support the government, whether it be a king or Caesar (Matthew 22: 17–21). There is a long line of debate on the specific nature of the sin in the Catholic literature. Some theologians have said that it is a mortal sin to evade taxes (Saint Antoninus 1571), meaning that the offender is destined to go to hell for eternity. Other theologians believe tax evasion is a mortal sin if the amount is "sufficient for a mortal sin of theft." (Molina 1611). At least one theologian believed it is not a mortal sin to secretly transport grain and other merchandise from the city without paying a tax on it, provided he does not resist the tax collectors with violence and force of arms (Beia 1591). Bonacina states: "Those who defraud taxes imposed on the necessities of life (pro usualibus) probably can be excused from mortal sin and from the obligation of making restitution." (Bonacina 1687: 449).

The current edition of the Baltimore Catechism states that tax evasion is a sin but does not get more specific than that. Some Catholic theologians have held that tax evasion is not a sin at all, provided that the government is corrupt or provided the evader is willing to pay the price if caught (Crowe 1944).

Some theologians have held that tax evasion is not a sin at all, at least in some cases.

> But I say that when those who impose these taxes do not provide for the common good, for example, in caring for roads, bridges, the safety of people and other things, according to their ability as they are bound to do, the subjects do not sin if they evade the tax without

lying and perjury, nor are they bound to restitution … Nor do I believe that those sin who defraud taxes, even when the aforesaid (i.e., those who impose the taxes) do provide for the common good." (Angelus Carletus de Clavisio 1494).

Since theologians cannot agree on the nature of tax evasion, it is difficult to arrive at any clear-cut answer to the question on theological grounds. That, coupled with the fact that there are many atheists and agnostics, and that many believers do not necessarily value the opinions of their clergy, makes it impossible to reach a consensus on theological grounds.

Finding a view one feels comfortable with is probably religion specific. For example, the Mormon literature states that tax evasion is always unethical (Smith and Kimball 1998), and it is reasonable to expect that Mormons do not place much value on the opinions of Catholic theologians. The Baha'i literature states that tax evasion is always unethical except in cases where members of the Baha'i faith are oppressed by the government in question (DeMoville 1998). Speaking from a Jewish perspective, Tamari (1998) states that tax evasion is theft, which is a sin, although he does make exceptions in cases where the government is corrupt. Another Jewish scholar (Cohn 1998) takes the position that tax evasion goes against Jewish teachings, at least most of the time.

The "If I Pay Less, Others Must Pay More" Argument

The "If I pay less, others must pay more" argument is a variation of the fair share argument but it is not quite identical. It also involves some assumptions that may not be accurate. Since governments often resort to deficit financing to fill the gap between tax expenditures and tax receipts, the fact that one taxpayer pays less does not necessarily mean that others must pay more, at least not directly. It merely means that the deficit increases.

But there is more to it than that. If one looks at the taxing and spending pattern in the United States for the last few decades, one sees that merely raising more in tax collections does not result in reducing the deficit. In fact, for every dollar collected in new taxes, federal government spending has increased by more than one dollar. That being the case, it is difficult to state that evading $20 in taxes means that other taxpayers have to pay that $20 because the amount of funds spent is not that closely related to the amount of taxes collected. If you pay $20 less than you should, it does not mean that someone else must pay $20 more.

In the rare event that a government has a balanced budget, paying less than your fair share means that the government has less money to operate with, but that is not necessarily a bad thing. If the government wastes and squanders money, then paying less means there will be less waste and squandering. If the government engages in evil activities, failure to pay your fair share means the government will not be able to engage in as many evil activities.

Also, in the case of those who are already paying more than their fair share, it would be illogical to assert that they must continue to do so lest others be forced to pick up their slack. If the taxpayer's moral obligation to pay taxes has already been met by paying the fair share amount, it cannot be said that failure to pay beyond that amount constitutes an unethical act because other taxpayers must pay the extra amount. If there is any moral question, it involves that tax collector who insists that you must continue to pay more than your fair share.

If an armed robber bursts into a restaurant and demands that the patrons give him 50% of what is in their wallets and purses, is it unethical not to tell the robber you have $50 in your shoe? What if the robber instead demands that the people in the room give him $1,000 so that he can pay his medical bills or buy an airplane ticket to visit his girlfriend, and that the amount to be collected from each patron will be based on the ratio of what is in their purses and wallets? Is it unethical not to tell the person in charge of the collection that you have $50 in your shoe? If it is not unethical to hide money from the thief, why is it unethical to hide money from the government if the government is little more than a thief? Does it make any difference that your failure to disclose the $50 will mean that others will have to pay more? It is the thief who is acting unethically, not you.

The Redistribution/False Philanthropy Argument

The redistribution/false philanthropy argument consists of several branches. One view is that the tax system should be used not only to raise the revenue needed for government to function but also to redistribute income from the rich to the poor. This view is a close cousin to the ability to pay argument. It is based on a non sequitur – You have more, therefore you should pay more. The public finance literature justifies redistribution on marginal utility grounds (Musgrave 1959; Musgrave and Musgrave 1976; Pantaleoni 1883), in spite of the fact that it is impossible to compare interpersonal marginal utilities (Kaldor 1939; Rothbard 1970, 1997).

Some advocates of this view even go so far as to say that the rich have a moral obligation to give to the poor. This view is expressed in the literature of several religions.

Perhaps there is an obligation to give to those who are less fortunate and perhaps there is not. Whether such an obligation exists is beside the point and merely distracts us from the main issue, which is whether the use of the tax code to redistribute income is fair, or whether it is a just use of the government's use of force. Bertrand de Jouvenel (1952) wrote an entire book addressing this question.

The fact that force or the threat of force is used to collect taxes erases the possibility of acting morally, since all morality involves choice. Since people are forced to pay, it cannot be said that they are acting morally. People cannot be forced to act morally. It is an example of false philanthropy. Those who advocate the use of the tax system to take money from those who have earned it and give it to those who have not earned it are not acting out of compassion or love for humankind. They could do that only if they used their own funds. Encouraging the use of government force to pay for one's favored pet projects or to further one's personal agenda cannot be said to be a moral act. One may actually categorize it as immoral.

Walter Williams, talking about justice, sums up the counterargument to the redistributionists as follows:

> But you might say, if government didn't do all that it's doing we wouldn't have a *just* society. What's *just* has been debated for centuries but let me offer my definition of social justice: I keep what I earn and you keep what you earn. Do you disagree? Well then tell me how much of what I earn *belongs* to you – and why? (Williams 1987, p. 62)

The other branch of the redistribution argument goes in exactly the opposite direction. This view argues that, while there may or may not be a moral obligation to pay taxes to a government whose functions are limited to the protection of life, liberty, and property, there is no moral obligation to pay for functions that go beyond those basic functions. Once the tax law is used to redistribute income rather than raise funds for necessary government functions, the moral obligation to pay ceases.

The "I Receive Benefits, Therefore I Must Pay" Argument

> There is no more justification for using the state apparatus to compel some citizens to pay for unwanted benefits that others desire than there is to force them to reimburse others for their private expenses (Rawls 1971, p. 283).

Another argument that there is a moral duty to pay taxes is that one should pay if one receives benefits – I receive benefits from government; therefore I have a duty to pay. The underlying premise of the argument is that there is a moral duty not to be a free rider. If one receives benefits but does not pay, then someone else must pay for your benefits. Such people are leeches on the body politic.

That very well may be true in some cases but that is not the end of the story. Just because one receives benefits does not mean that there is an automatic duty to pay all that is demanded. What if what you receive from the government is the equivalent of a bicycle but they want you to pay the equivalent of a car?[4] Or what if you give the government the equivalent of a bicycle in taxes but the government gives you the equivalent of a car in benefits? Is there less of an obligation to pay in the first case than in the second case? What if you did not want the car but they gave it to you anyway? What if you tell them you do not want the bicycle or car that they offer to give you in exchange for your tax payments? Do you have an obligation to pay anyway?

Let's take a concrete example. Social Security[5] is a bad investment. A private pension plan would yield a much higher return and the nest egg that builds up could be passed on to beneficiaries of one's choice. It has been called a government Ponzi

---

[4] I do not know the origin of this example. Marshall Fritz used it in a speech I heard in the 1980s but it did not originate with him.

[5] For more on these and other points, see www.socialsecurity.org.

scheme, since one group pays into it and another group takes the funds out of the system. There is no real trust fund in the finance sense of that term. One advantage of a private sector Ponzi scheme is that contributions are voluntary. In a government Ponzi scheme the payments are forced and taxpayers may be lectured on why they have a moral obligation to pay.

Medicare is also a bad investment compared to the market alternative if one takes the total costs into account. Everyone who earns a salary must pay into the system but only a relatively few people qualify for benefits. At least with a private plan everyone who pays is entitled to benefits. Is there a duty to pay for such programs when there either are no benefits or when benefits are forced down your throat? If so, where does this duty come from? Neither the public finance literature nor the ethical literature addresses this point, perhaps because there is no duty in these situations.

That does not mean that there is never a duty to pay if benefits are received from some governmental entity. The author knows of a nonprofit entity in Westchester County, New York, just north of New York City that makes an annual voluntary contribution to the local government. There is no legal duty to pay because non-profit entities are tax exempt, but their board felt they had a moral duty to pay their fair share for the police and fire protection, water and sewage services they received from the local government. Thus, there might be a duty to pay taxes in some cases where benefits are received but it cannot be said categorically that there is always a duty to pay just because benefits are received. The duty argument is especially weak in cases where the benefits are unwanted or where the benefits received cost sub-stantially more than the market alternative.

The "I Do Not Receive Benefits, Therefore I Do Not Have to Pay" Argument

The benefit theory in its extreme form developed during the eighteenth century as a protest against the unjust tax systems of France and other countries. According to this theory, a person should pay taxes in direct proportion to the benefits he receives from the state. If an individual could prove that the state conferred no benefits upon him, he could not be held to pay anything. According to this basis a poor man should be taxed more than a rich man because the state does more in the matter of support and protection for the poor than for the rich. (Crowe 1944: 24–25, citing Seligman 1931: 73).

There are a number of cases where the individuals who are taxed do not qualify for the benefits. Social Security and Medicare were mentioned above but they are not the only examples that could be given. If the benefits are "separable," a case can be made that those who do not use the service should not be forced to pay. For example, if some individuals do not use a public park, a moral case could be made that they should not have to pay to maintain the park. In reality it would be an uphill battle to construct a plausible argument that there is a moral obligation to pay for the use of a park one does not use. A fair solution would be to charge user fees so that only those who benefit from the service would be paying for it.

The way the current federal tax system is structured, people who live in Florida and Maine are forced to subsidize the construction of bridges in Alaska and roads in California, even though there is only a very remote chance that they will use them. If there is a duty to pay for such bridges and roads, it is difficult to see where such a duty comes from. Where there is no duty to pay, evasion is ethically justifiable.

In some communities there is a free bus service that is available only for senior citizens, yet all taxpayers are forced to pay for it. Likewise, local governments sometimes offer entertainment events that only a small fraction of the local population ever takes advantage of. In some Florida communities, some of those who take advantage of these free services are retired multimillionaires. These free services are paid for by the lower and middle income classes. If there were a way for nonusers to evade the taxes used to support these activities it seems like they would be morally justified in doing so, since they receive no benefit from them and are forced to pay for benefits that are enjoyed by individuals who have more assets and income than they have. It is a kind of reverse redistribution, since the group being subsidized is generally in better financial condition than the group that pays.

Being forced to educate other people's children is one of the more expensive examples of a separable cost that is unfairly assessed. Most education in the United States and many other countries is free, in the sense that the parents of the children who attend government schools do not have to write a check to the owner of the school. It is inherently unfair to the parents of children who attend private schools to be forced to pay to educate other people's children as well as their own children. And how can an argument be made that childless individuals have a moral duty to pay for the education of other people's children? If there were some way to evade payment of these taxes it seems like the evaders would be morally justified in doing so.

The usual argument that is made to counter this charge is that the prior generation paid to educate you; therefore, you have a moral duty to educate the next generation. There are several problems with this line of reasoning. For one, it is a non sequitur – Peter paid to educate Paul; therefore Paul has a moral duty to educate Jane. The argument is not logical.

But that is not the only weakness in the argument. Not all people had their education paid by taxpayers. Those who went to private schools had their educations paid for by parents or grandparents or through scholarship funds that were given up voluntarily by the donors. It seems inherently unfair to force these people to pay for the education of others, since they have not received any benefits from the government system. It is also inherently unfair to force childless people to pay to educate other people's children. It is difficult to see how a moral argument can be constructed that would give them this obligation.

A fair solution would be to have a user fee approach. Those who benefit pay and those who do not benefit do not pay. Those who cannot afford to educate their children should seriously consider not having children, since they would be placing a burden on everyone else. Alternatively, private charities and nonprofit organizations could be used to educate the children of the poor. Such a system has worked in the past. There is no reason to believe it would not work in the future (Blumenfeld 1985; Burleigh 1973; West 1970).

The "We Owe It to the Future/Past Generation" Argument

This argument is similar to the previous argument but it is not identical. It takes several forms. The common element is that the present generation somehow owes a moral duty either to the future generation or the past generation to pay taxes. One form of this argument involves the supposed duty to pay Social Security taxes. It goes something like this. The older generation has paid Social Security taxes so that their parents could receive Social Security benefits; therefore our generation has to pay Social Security taxes to support our parents' generation.

The argument involves a non sequitur, of course. But there are other problems with it as well, not the least of which is that Social Security is a poor investment, as was mentioned above. Should orphans be relieved of paying Social Security taxes, since they did not have parents? Should the current generation be relieved of paying Social Security taxes when their parents die? Should those who do not want to pay be relieved of payment obligations if they agree not to take benefits when they would otherwise be eligible to do so? If not, why not? What moral argument could be constructed to justify making them pay when they agree not to take the benefits at the end of the pipeline?

Social Security is another example of a separable payment situation. In a just society, individuals should be able to choose whether they want to participate in the government system. If they choose not to participate they should not be forced to pay. It is difficult to construct a moral case that argues they should be forced to pay for something they do not want. That, coupled with the fact that Social Security is a bad investment, makes it appear that evading the Social Security tax might be justifiable on ethical grounds.

The "Government Is Evil/Corrupt/Oppressive" Argument

All governments are less than perfect. Some are downright evil. Is there a moral obligation to pay taxes to such governments anyway? Is it unethical for Jews living in Nazi Germany to evade taxes where Hitler is the tax collector? This question was actually asked in a number of surveys distributed to various groups in the United States and elsewhere (Some of these surveys are discussed elsewhere in this book). Those surveys consisted of a series of 18 statements that began with the phrase: "Tax evasion is ethical if …" Respondents were asked to select a number from 1 to 7 to indicate the extent of their agreement or disagreement with each statement. The Jews in Nazi Germany statement often received the most support. Other strong arguments for justifying tax evasion were in cases where the government wastes money or is corrupt or engages in human rights abuses. There is also some support for tax evasion in the philosophical and theological literature in cases where the government is corrupt or oppressive or where there is inability to pay (discussed elsewhere in this book).

The "We Have a Duty to Evade Taxes" Argument

The argument has been made that there may be a moral duty to evade taxes, at least in some cases. The theological literature states that there is a duty to evade immoral taxes, such as in cases where the funds are used to pursue an unjust war. War protesters during the Vietnam War asserted this reason, as have others in different wars (Pennock 1998).

This argument may be expanded to include other issues. For example, a strong case can be made that it would not be unethical to evade taxes if you lived in Nazi Germany, regardless of your religion, since the Hitler war machine was evil. There may even be a duty to evade taxes to defund such an evil regime to the extent possible.

It seems abhorrent to force Orthodox Jews, Muslims, and some Christians to pay taxes to fund abortion, since these groups believe that abortion is murder. It is reasonable to expect that some members of these groups believe that tax evasion might be not only justified but required to prevent their funds from being used for such purposes.

But a solution is not that simple. For example, if only one-tenth of 1% of their taxes is used to fund abortions, would they be justified in evading only one-tenth of 1% of their taxes? Doing so would not prevent the remaining 99.9% of their tax payments from being used to fund abortions, since the funds are poured into a common fund to pay for a wide range of government services, including abortions. The only way to be sure that their taxes will not be used to fund abortions would be to evade *all* taxes. If this line of moral reasoning were expanded to include other abhorrent government expenditures, then any taxpayer who disapproved of just one-tenth of 1% of government expenditures on moral grounds would be justified in evading 100% of taxes, since any lesser percentage would not prevent their tax funds from being used to pay for the abhorrent activity. One way to prevent this kind of thing from happening would be for governments to refrain from spending on abhorrent activities and confine their expenditures to the protection of life, liberty, and property.

Let's look at another argument that espouses a duty to evade taxes on moral grounds. There is a strain of thought within utilitarian ethics that holds actions that increase efficiency to be moral (Posner 1979, 1983, 1998). Some utilitarians hold the view that one is not acting ethically unless one chooses the most efficient option available (Shaw 1999).

If we begin with that premise and take into account the fact that the private sector can provide just about anything more efficiently than government, we are led to the conclusion that we have a moral duty to evade taxes so that our funds are not transferred out of the more-efficient private sector and into the less-efficient government sector. It is a point that is seldom discussed in the literature.

Some scholars, including eminent Harvard philosopher Robert Nozick (1974), have called taxation theft and the income tax a form of involuntary servitude, since it confiscates the fruits of people's labor. If one wants to reduce the extent of theft and involuntary servitude in a society, one way to do that would be to engage in tax evasion. Doing so prevents theft and slavery.

There is a strain of thought within the political science, philosophy, and religious literature that we have an affirmative duty to resist evil. Dietrich Bonhoeffer, a German theologian, was executed on direct orders from Hitler for his participation in a plot to assassinate him.

> Silence in the face of evil is itself evil. God will not hold us guiltless. Not to speak is to speak. Not to act is to act (Dietrich Bonhoeffer).
> All that is necessary for evil to triumph is for good men to do nothing (Attributed to Edmund Burke).

As this page is being written, federal agents of the United States government are groping the sex organs of men and women at airports throughout America as a condition of allowing them to board airplanes. In some cases they are conducting body cavity searches. Has the time come to resist? If not, what else would they need to do to the citizenry before resistance is called for?

References

Angelus Carletus de Clavisio. 1494. *Summa Angelica*. Lyons, as cited by Martin T. Crowe, The Moral Obligation of Paying Just Taxes, The Catholic University of America Studies in Sacred Theology No. 84, 1944, p. 28–29.

Anonymous, 2008: 'America's Berlin Wall', *The Economist*, June 14, p. 39.

Antoninus, Saint. 1571. *Summa Sacrae Theologiae, Iuris Pontificii, et Caesarei*, II, p. 63 ff, Venice, as cited by Martin T. Crowe (1944). The Moral Obligation of Paying Just Taxes, The Catholic University of America Studies in Sacred Theology No. 84, 1944, p. 42.

Arsenault, Steven J.: 2009, 'Surviving a Heart Attack: Expatriation and the Tax Policy Implications of the New Exit Tax', *Akron Tax Journal* **24**, 37–67.

Baron, Marcia W., Philip Pettit & Michael Slote: 1997, *Three Methods of Ethics* (Blackwell, Oxford).

Bastiat, F.: 1968, *The Law* (Foundation for Economic Education, Irvington-on-Hudson, NY). Originally published in 1850 as a pamphlet, *La Loi*. Reprinted in *Sophismes Économiques, Ouevres Complètes de Frédéric Bastiat*, Vol. I, 4th edition. Paris: Guillaumin et Cie, 1878: 343–394.

Beia, F. Lodovicus de. 1591. *Responsiones Casuum Conscientiae*. Venice, at cas. 13, p. 53 ff., as cited by Martin T. Crowe, The Moral Obligation of Paying Just Taxes, The Catholic University of America Studies in Sacred Theology No. 84, 1944, p. 32.

Block, Julian: 1997, 'Tax Report: The Judicial View of Taxes', *The Network Journal* **5**(3), 20.

Blumenfeld, Samuel L.: 1985, *Is Public Education Necessary?* (The Paradigm Company, Boise, Idaho).

Boétie, Étienne de la. 1577. *Discours de la Servitude Volontaire*.

Boétie, Étienne de la. 1974. *The Will to Bondage*. Colorado Springs: Ralph Myles Publisher.

Boétie, Étienne de la. 1975. *The Politics of Obedience: The Discourse of Voluntary Servitude*. New York: Free Life Editions.

Bonacina, Martinus. 1687. *Operum de Morali Theologia*, "Tractatus de Restitutione," disp. II, q. IX, n. 5 (Venice), II, p. 449, as cited by Martin T. Crowe, The Moral Obligation of Paying Just Taxes, The Catholic University of America Studies in Sacred Theology No. 84, 1944, p. 46.

Burleigh, Anne Husted: 1973, *Education in a Free Society* (Liberty Fund, Indianapolis).

Cohn, Gordon: 1998, 'The Jewish View on Paying Taxes', *Journal of Accounting, Ethics & Public Policy* **1**(2), 109–120.

Crolly, George: 1877, *Disputationes Theologicae de Justitia et Jure* (Gill and Son, Dublin), cited in Martin T. Crowe: 1944, *The Moral Obligation of Paying Just Taxes*. Catholic University of America Studies in Sacred Theology No. 84, p. 38.

Crowe, Martin T.: 1944, *The Moral Obligation of Paying Just Taxes*. Catholic University of America Studies in Sacred Theology No. 84.

Davis, Henry. 1938. Moral and Pastoral Theology, 3rd ed. New York: Sheed and Ward, as cited in Martin T. Crowe, *The Moral Obligation of Paying Just Taxes*. The Catholic University of America Studies in Sacred Theology No. 84, p. 40.

DeMoville, Wig. 1998. The Ethics of Tax Evasion: A Baha'i Perspective. *Journal of Accounting, Ethics & Public Policy*, 1(3), 356–368, reprinted in Robert W. McGee (Ed.), *The Ethics of Tax Evasion* (pp. 230–240). Dumont, NJ: The Dumont Institute for Public Policy Research, 1998.

Donahue, John D.: 1991, *The Privatization Decision: Public Ends, Private Means* (Basic Books, New York).

Fitzgerald, Randall: 1988, *When Government Goes Private: Successful Alternatives to Public Services* (Universe Books, New York).

Frankfurter, Felix: 1961, *Mr. Justice Holmes and the Supreme Court* (Harvard University Press, Cambridge, MA).

Genicot, E.-Salsmans: 1927, *Institutiones Theologiae Moralis I*, as cited in Martin T. Crowe, *The Moral Obligation of Paying Just Taxes*, The Catholic University of America Studies in Sacred Theology No. 84, 1944, p. 37.

Greene, Jeffrey D.: 2001, *Cities and Privatization: Prospects for the New Century* (Prentice Hall, Upper Saddle River, NJ).

Hobbes, Thomas: 1651, *Leviathan*.

Holmes, Stephan & Cass B. Sunstein: 1999a, 'Why We Should Celebrate Paying Taxes', *The Chicago Tribune*, April 14: 19. http://home.uchicago.edu/~csunstei/celebrate.doc. Accessed February 2, 2010.

Holmes, Stephan & Cass B. Sunstein: 1999b, *The Cost of Rights: Why Liberty Depends on Taxes* (W.W. Norton, New York & London).

Jouvenel, Bertrand de: 1952, *The Ethics of Redistribution* (Cambridge University Press, Cambridge).

Kaldor, Nicholas: 1939, 'Welfare Propositions in Economics and Interpersonal Comparisons of Utility', *The Economic Journal* **49**, 549–552.

Kant, Immanuel: 1997, *Critique of Practical Reason* (Cambridge University Press, New York).

Kant, Immanuel: 1998, *Groundwork for the Metaphysics of Morals* (Cambridge University Press, New York).

Kant, Immanuel: 2001, *Lectures on Ethics* (Cambridge University Press, New York).

Kemp, Roger L.: 2007, *Privatization: The Provision of Public Services by the Private Sector* (Jefferson, NC, McFarland & Co.).

Kennedy, 1961. Presidential Inaugural Address.

Keohane, Nannerl O. 1977. The Radical Humanism of Étienne de la Boétie. *Journal of the History of Ideas* **38**(1): 119–130.

Letwin, Oliver: 1988, *Privatising the World: A Study of International Privatisation in Theory and Practice* (Cassell, London).

Locke, John: 1689, *Two Treatises on Government*.

Marx, Karl: 1875, *Critique of the Gotha Program*.

McGee, Robert W. 1998. Should Accountants be Punished for Aiding and Abetting Tax Evasion? *Journal of Accounting, Ethics & Public Policy*, **1**(1), 16–44.

Merkelbach, H.B. 1938. *Theologiae Moralis*, 3rd ed., I. Paris: Dersclee De Brouwer & Soc., as cited by Martin T. Crowe, The Moral Obligation of Paying Just Taxes, The Catholic University of America Studies in Sacred Theology No. 84, 1944, p. 28.

Molina, Louis. 1611. *De Justitia et Jure*, tr. II., Disp. 674, n.3, III, col. 555 ff., Venice, as cited by Martin T. Crowe, The Moral Obligation of Paying Just Taxes, The Catholic University of America Studies in Sacred Theology No. 84, 1944, p. 43.

Musgrave, Richard A.: 1959, *The Theory of Public Finance* (McGraw-Hill, New York).

Musgrave, Richard A. and Peggy B. Musgrave: 1976, *Public Finance in Theory and Practice*, 2nd ed. (McGraw-Hill New York).

Navarrus, Martinus (1618). *Opera Omnia*. Venice, as cited by Martin T. Crowe, The Moral Obligation of Paying Just Taxes, The Catholic University of America Studies in Sacred Theology No. 84, 1944, p. 31.

Nozick, Robert: 1974, *Anarchy, State and Utopia* (Basic Books, New York).

Pantaleoni, Maffeo: 1883, 'Contributo alla teoria del riparto delle spese pubbliche', *Rassegna Italiana*, October 15; reprinted in Maffeo Pantaleoni: 1904, *Scritti varii di Economia*, Vol. 1 (Rome), pp. 49–110; Translated from Italian by D. Bevan and reprinted under the title 'Contribution to the Theory of the Distribution of Public Expenditure' and reprinted in Richard A. Musgrave and Alan T. Peacock (eds.): 1958, *Classics in the Theory of Public Finance* (Macmillan, London & New York), pp. 16–27.

Pennock, Robert T. 1998. Death and Taxes: On the Justice of Conscientious War Tax Resistance. *Journal of Accounting, Ethics & Public Policy*, 1(1), 58–76, reprinted in Robert W. McGee (Ed.), *The Ethics of Tax Evasion* (pp. 124–142). Dumont, NJ: The Dumont Institute for Public Policy Research, 1998.

Pitcher, M. Anne: 2003, *Transforming Mozambique: The Politics of Privatization, 1975–2000* (Cambridge, Cambridge University Press).

Poole, Robert W., Jr.: 1980, *Cutting Back City Hall* (Universe Books, New York).

Posner, R. A.: 1979, 'Utilitarianism, Economics, and Legal Theory', *The Journal of Legal Studies* 8(1), 103–140.

Posner, R. A.: 1983, *The Economics of Justice* (Harvard University Press, Cambridge, MA)

Posner, R. A.: 1998, *Economic Analysis of Law*, 5th edition (Aspen Law & Business, New York).

Prante, Gerald and Mark Robyn: 2010. Summary of Latest Federal Individual Income Tax Data. Fiscal Fact No. 249 (October 6). Washington, DC: Tax Foundation.

Rawls, John: 1971, *A Theory of Justice* (Harvard University Press, Cambridge, MA).

Rothbard, Murray N.: 1970, *Man, Economy and State* (Nash Publishing, Los Angeles).

Rothbard, Murray A.: 1997, *The Logic of Action One: Method, Money, and the Austrian School* (Edward Elgar, Cheltenham, UK).

Rousseau, Jean Jacques: 1762, *The Social Contract*.

Samuelson, Paul A.: 1999, 'Samuelson's Economics at Fifty: Remarks on the Anniversary of Publication', *Journal of Economic Education* 30(4), 352–363.

Savas, E.S.: 2005, *Privatization in the City: Successes, Failures, Lessons* (CQ Press, Washington, DC).

Seligman, E.R. 1931. *Essays in Taxation*. New York: Macmillan.

Shaw, W.H.: 1999, *Contemporary Ethics: Taking Account of Utilitarianism* (Blackwell Publishers, Oxford).

Smith, Sheldon R. and Kevin C. Kimball. 1998. Tax Evasion and Ethics: A Perspective from Members of The Church of Jesus Christ of Latter-Day Saints. *Journal of Accounting, Ethics & Public Policy*, 1(3), 337–348, reprinted in Robert W. McGee (Ed.), *The Ethics of Tax Evasion* (pp. 220–229). Dumont, NJ: The Dumont Institute for Public Policy Research, 1998.

Spooner, Lysander: 1852, *An Essay on the Trial by Jury* (John P. Jewitt and Company, Boston), reprinted in Lysander Spooner: 2008, *Let's Abolish Government* (The Ludwig von Mises Institute, Auburn, AL).

Spooner, Lysander: 1870, *No Treason: The Constitution of No Authority* (Self-Published, Boston), reprinted in Lysander Spooner: 2008, *Let's Abolish Government* (The Ludwig von Mises Institute, Auburn, AL).

Tamari, Meir: 1998, 'Ethical Issues in Tax Evasion: A Jewish Perspective', *Journal of Accounting, Ethics & Public Policy* 1(2), 121–132.

Tax Foundation: 2009, Summary of the Latest Federal Income Tax Data, 1980–2007. www.taxfoundation.org/taxdata/show/23408.html.%20Accessed%20February%2026 Accessed February 26, 2010.

Tullock, Gordon. 1970. *Private Wants, Public Means: An Economic Analysis of the Desirable Scope of Government*. New York: Basic Books.

Tullock, Gordon. 1989. *The Economics of Special Privilege and Rent Seeking*. Boston, Dordrecht & London: Kluwer Academic Publishers.

Tullock, Gordon. 1993. *Rent Seeking*. Hants, UK & Brookfield, VT: Edward Elgar Publishing.

United Nations: 2006, 'Ted Turner's United Nations Foundation Delivers $1 Billion to UN Causes', Press Release DEV/2594, Department of Public Information, News and Media Division, United Nations, New York, 11 October. Posted at www.un.org/partnerships/Docs/PR_TED_TURNERFOUNDATION1BILLION.pdf

Walter, Nicolas. 1966. Etienne de la Boetie's Discourse of Voluntary Servitude: Introduction. *Anarchy* **6**(5): 129–152.

West, E.G.: 1970, *Education and the State* (Institute of Economic Affairs, London).

Williams, Walter: 1987, *All It Takes Is Guts: A Minority View* (Regnery Books, Washington, DC).

Chapter 4
Taxation: The Ethics of Its Avoidance or Dodging

Tibor R. Machan[*]

Introduction

What I aim to do here is to offer a case, albeit a necessarily brief one, in support of tax dodging or avoidance. I do not plan to survey all the arguments for and against the institution of taxation but take up the position of the defense, as it were, in light of the widespread and rarely disputed condemnation that has been aired about tax-avoidance/dodging/evasion.

It is going to be an uphill effort, given how widely it is believed, especially among academicians who, probably not entirely incidentally, earn their living in state and thus tax supported institutions, that Justice Oliver Wendell Holmes, Jr. was right when he said, reportedly, that taxation is the price we pay for civilization. (See footnote 10, below.) I base this case on the idea that each of us has an unalienable right to his or her life, liberty, and property and taking it without one's permission is morally and should be legally wrong. And those rights are, in turn, derived from an understanding of human beings as moral agents who require a sphere of sovereignty, personal authority to carry on as such. I begin the chapter with some background on why taxation is inconsistent with the American political tradition, despite its having been endorsed, in very limited form, in the US constitution. I then defend the morality of dodging taxes. I also address some skepticism about the position I defend.

Essays like this one cannot possibly do full justice to all aspects of the issue being considered. This short treatment and defense of tax resistance, by the way of dodging or avoiding or escaping it, should serve as a clear hint about how at least some moral and political theorists would show that it is morally acceptable, maybe

[*]Reprinted from *Contemporary Readings in Law and Social Justice* 2(2): 80–91 (2010). Copyright © 2010 Tibor R. Machan.

T.R. Machan (✉)
Chapman University, PO Box 64, Silverado, CA 92676, USA
e-mail: tmachan@gmail.com

R.W. McGee (ed.), *The Ethics of Tax Evasion: Perspectives in Theory and Practice*,
DOI 10.1007/978-1-4614-1287-8_4, © Springer Science+Business Media, LLC 2012

even required, for citizens to reject this institution, to deny its moral and political validity. But the full case in support of my position is likely to take a lot more than can be produced here.

Neglecting Basics

Instead of all acrimony among candidates running for high or low public office, it would be refreshing to have candidates engage in serious and in depth political and public policy discussions. For example, judging by the frequency of tax protests and tax resistance during recent times (e.g., by means of organizations such as the Tea Party Express) and over the decades, quite possibly many American voters would appreciate the close examination of the nature of taxation given that the federal income tax, in particular, appears on its face to conflict with the Fifth Amendment's "takings clause" in the US Constitution and with the strong tradition of the language of the right to private property in the country's history. Moreover, problems with taxation – levied without proper representation – had a powerful role in precipitating the American Revolution and, furthermore, taxation is very much wedded to monarchical type governments one of which, at least, that revolution helped overthrew.

In the USA – a supposedly free country – the issue of how a robust system of confiscatory taxation can be reconciled with the basic principles of the country sketched in the Declaration of Independence (principles that were learned from John Locke and which are supposedly based on human nature and thus universal so far as human community life is concerned) could use intense public discussion. In this revolutionary statement of a radical political philosophy – wherein we learn that human beings are equal in having unalienable rights to, among other things, their lives, liberty, and pursuit of happiness – it seems quite arguable that a government's confiscation of a citizen's resources would amount to morally wrongful conduct and policy.

But why bother about such a quintessentially American document as the Declaration of Independence, especially in light of the pervasive doctrine of multiculturalism that does not recognize universal principles of community organization? Because its principles were proposed as universal and because, since they were recorded, those principles have had enormous influence in global political discussions. (All the human rights watch organizations, such as Amnesty International, owe a good deal to them, to start with.) What is the theory underlying the document?

It is John Locke's doctrine of natural rights, whereby, in virtue of one's being a human being, certain principles of human community life need to be respected and implemented. This is a normative stance based on the fact that human beings are best off when they flourish in their lives. And this is supposed to be an objective fact about the values of community life and not a mere opinion or bias, within the arguably sound framework of natural law and rights theory. (Dominant contemporary thinking on the matter is quite different but not for that correct – see footnote 4 below).

Let us briefly consider the alleged right to life everyone possesses, a right that in the Lockean tradition is basic – "the right to one's person and estate." To understand this, it is necessary to consider what, most generally, life consists of. Without endeavoring to write a treatise on the topic, it is arguable that much of a human being's life consists of actions, including conduct that aims to earn one the resources to support one's various needs and wants, including the housing, feeding, clothing, and education of one's family. Having an unalienable right to one's life means, in turn, that one may not lose one's life and its fruits to other people unless one freely gives them away.

To proceed with the argument, it needs to be noted that confiscatory taxation is not a case of having one's resources contributed freely or lost by means of misfortune, not even by the most postmodern interpretation of the words being used here. What, in turn, is it to have an unalienable right to one's liberty? It pertains to one's not having anyone else, including government, dictate to one what one will do, how one will act, what course of conduct one will undertake. No one is authorized to be in control of one since the right to liberty, too, is unalienable – that is to say incapable of being lost unless one's humanity has vanished somehow. The notion that one might implicitly consent to having a significant portion of one's labor and its results confiscated via taxation is sophistry – one cannot consent, either explicitly or implicitly, to confiscating other people's resources, nor having one's basic rights violated (that is what "unalienable" means).

Once again, taxation is inconsistent with the principle that one has this unalienable right to one's liberty for such taxation coerces one to hand over a goodly part of one's earnings to people one has not freely chosen to receive them. (And the claim that taxation is ultimately voluntary or that majority vote may void one's unalienable rights is indefensible and gains its plausibility from a way of speaking that involves assertions about how "we" gave permission, which ignores that some of us did not! It is, in any case, untrue that what no individual is morally justified in doing to another, a large group, the majority, is. Also, it is important to remember that enforcing tax laws involves coercing the citizenry to perform many time-consuming and costly chores – i.e., what the late Robert Nozick so aptly dubbed something "on par with forced labor."[1])

As to the pursuit of happiness, that too is supposed to be one's unalienable right, yet when some get the legal power to force one to devote resources to goals one has

---

[1] Robert Nozick, *Anarchy, State, and Utopia* (New York: Basic Books, 1974), 169. A worthwhile scholarly exploration of how Nozick's arguments have been dealt with by defenders of taxation may be found in Edward Faser, "Taxation, Forced Labor, and Theft," *The Independent Review* 4(2): 218–235. I should note that my position on taxation is not that it is theft but that it is extortion. It involves stating to citizens, "You must hand over a portion of your resources or you will be prosecuted and when convicted you will go to jail and if you resist you will be forcibly recaptured and might be killed in the process, all according to law."

not chosen to pursue, that right is also quite arguably violated.[2] None of the rights listed in the Declaration is optional and all, if valid, place severe restrictions on what other people may do to one (which may be understood to be the source of due process considerations in the law). Indeed, this is just what rendered the American rejection of British rule not merely some internal dispute but a bona fide revolution, removing sovereignty from the crown or government and resting it with individuals. The fact that contrary ideas and ideals are also very much part of the American system need not count against those ideas. After all, the American political tradition introduced quite novel notions into the world community which had, until then, been mostly under the influence of one or another form of statism – regimes ruled from the top down by pharaohs, kings, emperors, Caesars, tribal chiefs, etc. – and hardly influenced by a Lockean type individualism that, once fully developed, regards everyone a sovereign person.

Negative Rights Only

The rights referred to in the Declaration are just a few among the "certain unalienable" ones. Indeed, by the Lockean doctrine (or theory), human beings have unalienable rights to do anything that's peaceful, anything that does not violate someone else's rights. This is because they are understood to be moral agents who must choose to act and without "borders" around them afforded by their rights this choosing would be impossible.

Even the Bill of Rights gives support to this idea in its inclusion of the Ninth Amendment among the constitutional principles it lists that restrict the powers of governments. It clearly refers to prelegal (not legally granted) rights we all have that are not enumerated in or by the Constitution. So, to use some simple examples, we all have the right to laugh, sing, and hold parties in our back yards, and so forth, even though these rights are not listed. They would take volumes to list in the Constitution.

It is true enough that reference is made in the Constitution to taxation but that is, arguably and I do so argue, an unfortunate mistake that's itself worthy of discussion since it is, in fact, an inconsistency given that taxation cannot be part of a bona fide free country – with everyone having the basic right to private property – properly understood, any more than could be serfdom or involuntary servitude. Maybe the pressure to fund a free government and the lack of a tradition wherein such funding is possible without taxation explain this. But in any case, it is irrelevant; after all, slavery, too, was tolerated in the US Constitution despite how inconsistent it was

---

[2] Some have misunderstood this right to amount to one that legally guarantees one's happiness but in fact it amounts to requiring respect for one's right to the freedom to pursue happiness, including by means of establishing a legal order that will secure one's rights.

with the philosophy of the Declaration. Furthermore, since possession of the right to private property amounts to one's right to freedom to engage in obtaining, producing, and holding valued items, this right is implicit in the unalienable right to human liberty, to do what one chooses to do provided others' rights are not violated in the process.

One might however wonder then, how are the proper functions of government to be funded without taxes? How, if not by means of what by any reasonable account would have to be seen as an extortionist scheme? Despite rarely being considered, there are valid alternatives to taxation, ones not involving elements of coercion, confiscation, and extortion (all parts of the tax system when one admits that individuals have unalienable rights to their lives, liberty, and property). These are not studied because so many people accept that taxation is legitimate and, also, because opposition to taxation can, if well grounded, amount to threats to many officials' favored position in a society. Such could be said about slavery, too – for centuries – alternatives to which were not studied because influential people complacently accepted the practice, as they now accept taxation. But that does not make either practice justified!

As a very brief hint suggested by me elsewhere, the legal services governments provide can be funded by a contract fee – anyone who enters into a contract would need to pay a fee so it would gain legal backing. Given the enormous popularity of freely entered into contracts, and given that one need not make use of them if one can get by "with a handshake," the method would provide ample resources to fund government's proper functions.[3] In any case, if what taxes fund could not be funded without it, this still does not justify the institution. The answer may have to be, as libertarian anarchists argue, that government is inherently immoral and unacceptable.

Most public policy and public finance scholars tend now to regard the wealth of the population as public wealth, not consisting of (taken) private property. How to get publicly – i.e., taxpayer – funded health insurance and care is as basic a question in this area as it gets these days.[4] In the current political climate, with most academicians virtually completely on board about the kind of society that America needs – consider the recent essay by the late Tony Judt showing that apart from ordinary Americans, the educated classes are mostly democratic socialists[5] – explorations of alternatives to the welfare state are meager at best.

---

[3] For a discussion of this idea, see Tibor R. Machan, "Dissolving the Problem of Public Goods: Financing Government without Coercive Measures," in T. R. Machan (ed.), *The Libertarian Reader* (Totowa, NJ: Rowman and Littlefield, 1982), 201–208. For another similar position, see Ayn Rand's "Government Financing in a Free Society," *The Virtue of Selfishness* (New York: Signet Books, 1964), 135–140.

[4] For more on this, see Tibor R. Machan (2006), "Rights, Values, Regulation and Health Care," *Journal of Value Inquiry* 40(2–3): 385–391.

[5] Tony Judt (2009), "What's Living and What's Dead in Social Democracy," *The New York Review of Books* 56 (December 17).

In light of the above, it can be appreciated why some thoughtful, prudent Americans, as well as others simply aiming to gain some economic advantage, resort to some type of tax avoidance, tax evasion, and tax dodging – I do not distinguish between these when they rely on the conviction that taxation is wrong – not unlike those Americans who recognized the inconsistency of conscription or military draft in the past and have resorted to draft avoidance, draft evasion, and even draft-dodging. What kind of case could be made for such actions? Why could such conduct amount to something morally justified?

Now in light of what I have said so far, it seems quite reasonable to expect that taxation will be resisted – including avoided and dodged – by many citizens who take to heart the very possibly universal political principles of the Declaration of Independence, ones reflecting the ideals of classical liberalism and libertarianism. But perhaps those principles are bogus? That is what such scholars as Stephen Holmes and Cass R. Sunstein, among others[6], argue. What arguments may be advanced in support of such resistance?

Ethics and Tax Resistance

Essentially tax resistance may be defended on grounds nearly identical to those associated with defending resistance to aggression against oneself – one's life, liberty, etc. If one is accosted on some city street and threatened with bodily harm, let alone murder, one has the right to defend oneself against the attacker. (One must take care, however, not to involve others other than accidentally – for example, if they were to become obstacles to one's self-defense.) This right of self-defense is derivable from the basic right one has to one's life, one that rests on one's nature as a human being, on one's moral agency. If one carries on in one's life peacefully and is nonetheless attacked, one is justified – has the right to – resist this. This is also the case if the attack is aimed at confiscating one's resources, including one's labor,

---

[6] Stephen Holmes and Cass Sunstein, *The Cost of Rights: Why Liberty Depends on Taxes* (W. W. Norton & Co., 1999). See, also, Cass R. Sunstein, *The Second Bill of Rights: FDR's Unfinished Revolution and Why We Need It More than Ever* (New York: Basic Books, 2004), which defends what are usually referred to as positive or welfare rights which impose involuntary obligations – servitude? – on all who are able to fulfill them. There are other approaches than Sunstein's to defending such "rights". See, in particular, James Sterba, *How to Make People Just: a Practical Reconciliation of Alternative Conceptions of Justice* (Lanham, MD: Rowman and Littlefield, 1988), who argues the enigmatic view that negative rights imply positive ones because in some (in my view exceptionally rare) cases not being coerced isn't sufficient for people to take the actions required for their survival and flourishing in life. Cf., Tibor R. Machan (1976), "Prima Facie v. Natural (Human) Rights," *Journal of Value Inquiry* 10(1): 119–131, which argues, among other points, that the existence of such extraordinary cases is no reason for fashioning a legal system by what they seem to imply. As the saying goes, "hard cases make bad law".

property, and whatever one has a right to keep and hold for one's own use and, yes, misuse (wastefulness may not be criminalized in a free society unless it involves dumping, imposing it on others, as in pollution). Although some distinguish between aggression upon a person versus upon a person's property, in Locke and as I, too, understand and have argued the point in numerous publications "person and estate" are property and so the aggression is nearly equivalent.

A more systematic approach to self-defense, taken against governments that are operating under a legal system that sanctions slave labor or conscription – the draft – can involve more complicated forms of resistance. For example, arguably the military draft may be dodged by leaving the realm wherein it is imposed or by taking measures that make the draft inapplicable to oneself (such as pursuing graduate studies in fields that the government has selected as legally justifying noncompliance with it). More Draconian cases could be cited here, such as slaves or concentration camp victims taking measures to escape their conditions that are imposed on them by governments in line with the "laws" that they enforce.[7] Given the widely understood wrongness of such institutions, there is little doubt about whether resisting being subjected to them is ethically justified (although in nearly all such cases the perpetrators tend to defend themselves by reference to the above mentioned doctrine of implied collective consent or some kind of greater good)!

The case I am outlining here is one that is akin not so much to resisting slavery or internment but to serf rebellions. Serfdom was integral to certain political systems, such as types of feudalism, and so was taxation. Both institutions rested, ultimately, on the view that, essentially (and put simply) the monarch or ruler owns the realm – the country – and is owed service or payment from those who live and work there. This system gained its justification, for what it was worth, by the way of various narratives, some of them involving the divine rights of monarchs, some hypothetical social contracts. These may be deemed to be precisely the sort of systems that came under serious scrutiny and opposition from classical liberal and democratic political theorists. The gist of the criticism of such systems can be seen in the Declaration of Independence wherein instead of governments having sovereignty, it is individuals who do. Or, in other words, instead of divine rights for monarchs and such, it is individual human beings who have basic, unalienable rights, including to their lives, liberty, and property (the term Thomas Jefferson used in an early draft based on the Virginia Declaration of Rights, which referred to "property and pursuing happiness"[8]).

---

[7] Whether orders that governments issue in societies that fail to meet the proper criteria of legitimacy should still be dubbed "laws" is a widely debated matter among those concerned with the foundations of legal systems, including, especially, natural law theorists. Perhaps it would be clearer to label those edicts "rules," and the "governments" involved as "rulers," as in "the ruler or rulers of Dubai".

[8] http://www.lonang.com/curriculum/2/s21b.htm and Jean M. Yarbrough, "Jefferson and Property Rights," in Ellen Frankel Paul and Howard Dickman (eds.), *Liberty, Property, and the Foundations of the American Constitution* (Albany, NY: State University of New York Press, 1989).

Rational, Ethical Tax Resistance

At any rate, once it is clear that taxation is extortion and has no place, any more than serfdom, in a just legal order, the issue of whether it is ethically justified to dodge or avoid it should not pose an insurmountably difficult problem. There are, of course, considerations as to the proper means by which tax laws, as others that are unjust within a substantially just system of laws, would need to be resisted. Are dodging and avoiding them among these? Might it not be more ethical to work for the abolition of taxation, instead?

Here, I believe one faces the kind of issues that had confronted abolitionists in the era of chattel slavery who were often urged to refrain from using radical means by which to resist the institution. Yet that is not the central topic here. Arguably, one size does not fit all in how oppression of any kind ought to be resisted, opposed, combated, and so forth. Different victims could be justified in taking very different steps to counter the oppression involved, including taxation. For some it would be most appropriate to make use of the available political processes, for some other means could be best. And it is also possible that for some citizens, with more important tasks facing them, resisting taxation could be an inapplicable goal. Taxation could, for some, be a minor although impermissible imposition, especially if they are wealthy enough so it makes little difference to the way they choose to live their lives. The context of the situation is relevant to how one is justified in addressing oppressive measures just as this is so with how one ought to respond to aggressive actions from others in one's personal and social circumstances. (For a simple example, if one is a large, powerful individual then having someone else assault one could be nearly inconsequential and not worth spending the time and resources to resist it. Both are normative matters but one of politics while the other of ethics.[9])

Suffice it to conclude here that although there could be variations in how one ought to resist (dodge, avoid, legally contest, etc.) taxation, the basic question of whether those subject to the institutions are ethically justified in making the effort to resist it can be answered in the affirmative. Yet, as with all matters of conduct involving other people, a sort of moral due process is required. One may not resist a trespasser by killing him and that kind of consideration would apply in how one goes about resisting an evil such as taxation. In any case, the often-voiced objections to tax dodging and tax avoidance are without merit.

---

[9] For a discussion of the general principles of revolutionary action, see Tibor R. Machan, "Human Rights, Political Change and Feudalism," in A. Rosenbaum, (ed.), *Philosophies of Human Rights* (Greenwich, CT: Greenwood Press, 1981).

Last Considerations

A few points remain, however, to be addressed. First, might it not be at least quite unfair to successfully dodge or avoid taxation while millions of others keep being subject to it and, indeed, comply with the law that mandates that they pay taxes? And what of the famous quip from Justice Oliver Wendell Holmes, Jr. that "I like paying taxes. With them I buy civilization."[10]?

As to the former matter, unfairness could not be decisive. It would then be impermissible for men and women in a free or nearly free society to enjoy their favorable legal status while millions across the world are in bondage. It would have been impermissible for draft age young people during the Vietnam War to escape being conscripted while many thousands of others were successfully drafted. All those who escaped slavery, serfdom, internment, and so forth could be condemned since it was and in many cases still is unfair that others haven't fared well in their own efforts to be free. And to insist that everyone be subjected to oppression instead of only those who are not successful in resisting it in the name of fairness is morally perverse. It is akin to insisting that all the healthy people become ill because some are.

As to the quip from Justice Holmes, well it is entirely gratuitous or, at best, misguided. Turning to the latter possibility, what Holmes might have been after is the point that submitting to laws is the price we pay for civilization but whether those laws need to include taxation per se is open for debate. What if there are other ways to secure the resources required to support a just legal system, one not involving coercive measures? Would it then still be taxation itself that is required for civilization? No. It would be the legal system, leaving the question of how it is to be funded separate. And then the famous Holmes quip could well turn out to have been gratuitous because it is, well, merely a dismissive quip instead of a seriously defended proposition.

Finally, there is the prominent political economic argument for taxation or the confiscation of private property based on the view that the problem of public goods or free riders demands it. But this is ethically toothless. If one produces something for people who cannot be charged for it since they cannot be kept from making use of it, that is just how it is. Millions of people benefit others by various means, even by simply being attractive or inventive, while they cannot be charged for this since it is not possible to isolate the ones who benefit from those who do not. This simply is no excuse for imposing burdens on them all. The so-called public good being produced, such as a radio broadcast many can enjoy without paying for, is (a) not really public at all – meaning needed to sustain a just legal order for all – and (b) not something

---

[10] Quoted in Felix Frankfurter, *Mr. Justice Holmes and the Supreme Court*, (New York, NY: Atheneum, Originally Published by Harvard University Press, 1965), 71.

the beneficiaries have chosen to obtain on mutually agreeable terms. If I produce something my neighbors benefit from but have not paid for, I am not authorized to confiscate "payment" from them without their consent.

Conclusion

Are tax dodgers and avoiders acting unethically? Not as a general rule. Indeed, as such they are doing what is fully justified, given that taxation is itself an oppressive, tyrannical institution comparable to serfdom. There can be valid inquiries as to the precise form that tax dodging and avoidance ought to take for a citizen – one size does not fit all. But there is no reasonable doubt for many that making the effort to escape taxation is morally unobjectionable and, indeed, justified by the virtue of prudence, just as is self-defense of any sort that stays within the limits of what is necessary instead of over-stepping them by becoming reckless.[11]

---

[11] It is worth mentioning in this connection that a strong clue to the truth of this conclusion comes from discussions in families, usually around April 15th, as to the variety of ways that earnings by family members ought to be protected, including by means of competent tax advisors who may well indicate what might by champions of taxation be construed as dubious – illegal (?) – forms of tax dodging and avoidance. But see, for an enthusiastic, dogmatic call for merciless action against all tax evasion and dodging – that is, against all those who would escape the extortion that is taxation – Raymond Baker and Eva Joly (2009), "Illicit Money: Can it Be Stopped?" *The New York Review of Books*, December 3: 61–64. (The authors try to lump together escaping taxation with all sorts of looting by various criminal agents but their sophistry is blatant.)

Chapter 5
Understanding and Interpreting Tax Compliance Strategies Among Street Vendors

Alfonso Morales

> *Judgments about values are judgments about conditions and the results of experienced objects; judgments about that which should regulate the formation of our desires, affections and enjoyments.*
>
> (John Dewey, *The Construction of the Good*)

Introduction

For centuries street markets have been vibrant multiuse spaces providing economic opportunities for immigrants and native populations alike. Only over the last 70–80 years have a number of laws – food safety, tax, and others – been adopted that criminalize street markets and vendors. Over the last 30 years we have witnessed some loosening of legal regimes to accommodate a number of public policy goals (such as access to healthy food) but tax law and policy have not kept pace with the emergent purposes associated with street markets and merchants. Thus, we need to know more about tax-related values and practices of vendors, the deeper aspirations and contextual sources of those values and practices, and how law and policy might be revised to enhance individual welfare and realize public goals.

One government goal is to maximize citizen compliance with tax law. Besides providing resources to the state, tax compliance serves as a route for state–society relations. The Boston Tea Party, India's Salt Sathyagraha, and Thoreau's civil disobedience demonstrate the mixed motives for tax deviance. As these examples suggest, tax compliance (as well as noncompliance) illuminates complex amalgamations of ideas and behavior in practice. These examples also suggest that these behaviors

A. Morales (✉)
Urban and Regional Planning, University of Wisconsin, 925 Bascom Mall,
Old Music Hall 104, Madison, WI 53706, USA
e-mail: morales1@wisc.edu

R.W. McGee (ed.), *The Ethics of Tax Evasion: Perspectives in Theory and Practice*,
DOI 10.1007/978-1-4614-1287-8_5, © Springer Science+Business Media, LLC 2012

overlap, inform, and are informed by other conflicting or congruent ones. Besides such rather esoteric institutional concerns, government must understand and address causes of noncompliance. Connecting the institutional and the individual is a question: how might state policy be modified to increase compliance and still allow markets to accomplish other laudable public goals?

In order to answer this question we need contextually rich knowledge of vendors' behavior, the sort of knowledge that will help revise the behavioral assumptions associated with tax policy and suggest promising avenues for policy experimentation. When considering the street merchant our proximate problem is locating merchants in socioeconomic context, with respect to their expectations about the state, the organization of their income-earning and household practices, and the changing content of their household aspirations. In doing so, we understand how they deliberate and make choices – choices that produce conflicts with the state and law, but choices that under a different policy regime could fulfill the goals of both household and state. Such an understanding synthesizes the mutual interaction that determines the economic values held by different parties; how such values are working hypotheses that can become law or convention; and how people's practices and state laws are revised in light of experience, conditions, and goals. Accepting the social construction of values invites us to examine Dewey's two sources of value judgments: proximate experiences and the question of what should form our desires. Doing so moves us toward new policy possibilities and new research questions.

This interaction of household and state values and practices is examined and reinterpreted in this chapter through the study of "rationalizations" for tax evasion. By discovering household-level tax "policies" including different degrees of compliance, we discover how household-level decisions are amenable and even adaptable to revised public policies aimed at community economic development. We can further analogize such policies as household-level versions of local, state, and national level concerns with community economic development. This chapter shows empirically how street vendors relate their experience and behavior to their context and desires. Income earned from vending replaces inadequate services from local and state government and substitutes for inadequate workplace wages. It pays for hobbies and private school tuition for children, makes home and car repairs possible, and, in short, becomes capital for both consumption and investment. This chapter uses examples such as these to argue for reconstructed policies that enhance vending as a tool for community economic development.

We begin by reviewing tax compliance literature and locating vending in historical context. A discussion of research methods indicates how policy prescriptions flow from the findings. The data shows the tax beliefs and practices merchants developed, why those change, and how those are reflective of their perceptions of society as well as the relationship between their personal circumstances and the rather complex integument of their economic and familial goals. The policy section suggests that improvements to the tax system, which incorporate and accommodate these motivations may encourage compliance, and, more importantly, foster economic activity, mobility, and citizenship.

Research on Tax Compliance and Evasion

Historical Changes in Taxation

Taxation changes with changing economic conditions, particularly as income-earning activities, are deemed (il)legitimate. Therefore, we should expect that historical changes in tax policy would reflect the changing relationship between state and society. Consider two facts: In 1913, the USA initiated its first "modern" income tax, aimed at the wealthy, and so the vast majority of wage earners were exempted. In Chicago in 1912 and elsewhere, over previous decades (Tangires 2003), cities were encouraging street vending and public markets to employ new immigrants, socialize the foreign-born, and help provide food and consumer goods to isolated parts of rapidly growing cities (Morales 2000). Taxing the wealthy and commissioning street vendors were both deemed legitimate contributions to the common good.

Over the subsequent 50 years, a wage and salaried labor force concentrated in large organizations offered the opportunity to tax the working class in a new and highly cost-effective way. Compliance rates are highest with third-party reporting or withholding, so the system originally intended to tax the wealthy was harnessed to tax this "captured" population (Browlee 2000).[1] At the same time, the changing structures of retail trade marginalized street vendors. For instance, the increasing emphasis on new technology, the advent of national and global supply chains and ever increasing political clout (Mayo 1993), city governments (and social scientists) expected street vendors to disappear (Bromley 2000). Though new retail activities and regulations slowly delegitimized vending and vendors, their inheritors, new immigrants and members of aspiring populations seeking economic mobility, constantly renewed many marketplaces around the country.

Such small-scale activity may have remained mostly ignored but for the 1960s, farmers' markets led renaissance in marketplaces around the country. The growth of farmers' markets was motivated initially by the middle-class interest in organic food (Friedlander 1976). However, cities around the country reconstructed their perceptions of such markets, reconceiving them as amenities attractive to the "creative" class. Thus, academics and policy makers have recently recuperated their historic interest in marketplaces and street vendors as tools of community economic development (Morales 2009). Likewise, urban planners and policy makers are seeking the tools and rationale for incorporating street-level commerce into development plans of various kinds (Morales and Kettles 2009a, b). Thus, markets and merchants have come full circle, slowly returning to legitimacy, but in a coarse tax policy regime unable to incorporate merchants and markets into the public goals associated

---

[1] The wealthy move their money to places where they can avoid third-party reporting and withholding taxes.

with the revenue system.[2] Worse, existing tax systems are incapable of integrating vendors into other public policies to achieve other public goals. However, over the previous decade, a stream of innovative compliance research has emerged providing new policy opportunities.

Recent Research on Compliance

A typical account of research on merchants assumes they are self-interested economic players rationally responding to maximize profits in largely unregulated economic environments. In this view vendors who do thwart the tax system simply *want* to cheat, and therefore they produce various rationalizations for their behavior (Morales 1998). This approach is superficially powerful in that it simplifies human nature, behavior, and cognition to a collection of parallel, but disconnected, decision-making processes and focuses – for instance, on how people rationalize noncompliance and evasion. These approaches enjoy significant traction from analytical and enforcement perspectives as their assumptions simplify research and policy. Because researchers need only focus on one element of social life, economic decision making, they can use concepts accepted among researchers (and recognizable to the researched), which easily capture the fact of noncompliance – even if doing so oversimplifies the empirical reality. Likewise, under these assumptions policy is streamlined and reducible to enforcement or education that "sharpens" how people identify and act on the relationship between law and behavior. In short, adopting "undersocialized" or "unembedded" views of behavior (Wrong 1961; Granovetter 1985) simplifies our research, but in such simplification they also rob us of greater understanding and moreover, responsive and constructive policy choices.

We can contrast this approach with recent research using ethnographic and mixed methods approaches that capture the diverse motives and complex organization of tax-related behavior, from off-shore sheltering processes to street vendors (Rossotti 2002; Morales 1998; Braithwaite 2003). These researchers transform oversimplified assumptions about behavior into research questions that contextualize behavior and locate it in social processes. Once we disprove the idea that people simply *want*

---

[2] Unpaid income tax makes up about half of the tax gap (Internal Revenue Service, 2005a). Of this, the largest component (80%) involves the underreporting of income, mostly from business activities (Internal Revenue Service, 2005b). The tax gap for the tax year 2001 in the USA is estimated at $312 billion to $353 billion (Internal Revenue Service 2005a, b). The tax gap does not include taxes that could have been paid on income earned in legal activity for which the earner did not acquire appropriate permits, for instance, street vending in many jurisdictions. The tax gap does not cover taxes owed on income from illegal activities like drug trafficking and smuggling (Internal Revenue Service, 2005a), but presumably also excludes activities that may be legitimate, like street vending, in jurisdictions that bar vending or when such activities are undertaken without obligatory permits or licenses. Furthermore, untaxed cash income is often earned legitimately. The cash economy varies in size between countries and the estimation methods produce different guesses, for the USA range from 6 to 14% of GNP (Morales 2009).

to cheat on their taxes, we can then analyze the source of their rationalizations as nuanced and interpenetrating streams of thought and action. Doing so helps us understand the larger state-person derived value judgments people make about their noncompliance. We come to see how evasion varies by aspirations, circumstances, and perspectives. In this way research answers the "why" of evasive behavior as well as the "how" – and in so doing indicates how policy might be amended to understand such behavior, legitimize it, and harness it to public purposes (according to circumstances.)

Findings are the foundation of our contemporary belief, as Braithwaite states, "perceptually, people are capable of linking different forms of taxation to each other and to the quality of governance" (2009: 4). The implications for research and policy are significant, as ethnographic methods uncover various streams of experience and variation in how the ideas and behaviors of those streams influence each other. In terms of policy, we come to see the utility of contingency. The most comprehensive policy begins by incrementally and contingently fulfilling the goals of both state and citizen by legitimizing natural economic activities. Then, moreover, it indicates to citizens other conventional means the state makes available to them to more fully realize their aspirations. In doing so the government can work within existing functional infrastructure and most efficiently promote its own interests by working in concert with, instead of against, the people it serves.

Braithwaite (2009: 15) articulates this approach arguing that individual deliberation and choice about taxation is an important element of the tax system. For her, these deliberative choices produce three "opportunities for conflict with the tax authority… (1) benefits accrued from contributions; (2) obligation or coercion to make contributions; and (3) justice in collecting contributions" (2009: 15). All three have to do with the perceived qualities of local governance, and furthermore tie individually held aspirations, behaviors, and values to the supply of services in an area. An important element of governance is the reciprocal relationship between state and society that characterizes taxpaying in most stable democracies (Frey and Feld, 2001; Feld and Frey, 2007; Rawlings, 2003; Scholz and Lubell, 1998a, b). Reciprocity is subjective, and rarely perfect. People recognize that "you get what you pay for," but the idea is made much more complicated when evaluating the quality of goods and services "paid" for through income taxes. Still, research can reveal how governance can be revised to enhance reciprocity and so both achieve state goals and enhance the prospects of these small business people.

The absence of felt reciprocity helped produce Moran's (2003: 378) definition of taxation: "a tax occurs when a government requires contributions for its operations from individuals, firms, or groups within its jurisdiction without returning a clear quid pro quo." Certainly such a definition works to understand why some people evade taxes. However, by reducing reciprocity to bilateral relationships between the state and elements of society, the definition oversimplifies complex social situations and processes. Clearly the context for a street vendor or any other actor involves a variety of factors, including changing notions of how to participate in society and the dynamic role of the state as the actor's interests and aspirations fluctuate. So, we should expect the emergence, persistence, and erosion of felt reciprocity to vary by organizational context, and not simply with respect to services rendered. We argue here to amplify the type of "psychological contract" between the taxpayer and the state argued by Frey and Feld (2001; 2007), by understanding taxpayers' constellations of attitudes and practices (and how they change over time) with respect to similar diverse collections of ideas from other socio-organizational contexts.

Methods

The analyses reported here specify how street vendors adjust their compliance with respect to their expectations about the state, their income-earning and household practices, and in light of their household aspirations. Such adjustments are not automatic, but neither are they random. Often the lag between information and change is due to double-checking and considering the impact on the business. Ethnographic methods are suited to exploring these dynamics, and we are particularly interested in the composition of ideas and behaviors, how they mediate between forms of tax and governance or other social contexts, how they structure decision making, and how such structures change over time.

I collected these ethnographic data between 1989 and 1992 when I became a participant observer and ethnographer of Chicago's Maxwell Street Market. I met and learned about street vending from the Market's dominant ethnic groups, African-Americans, Whites, and Mexican-Americans, inclusive of both genders. I conducted hundreds of formal and informal interviews about various aspects of the vending process, including business start-up, merchandise acquisition, business practices, and, for our purposes, accounting and tax compliance. I sampled to include variation in merchandise sold, vendor ethnicity, gender, age, and household composition. In sum I interviewed members of 56 households, split between Spanish-speaking (mostly immigrant Mexican), Black, and White families. Interview questions were open ended, but directed from an interview guide. For Spanish speakers, questions were translated to Spanish and back-translated to English to ensure reliable translations. The same process was used to ensure reliable translations of responses from Spanish to English. The data reported below are representative of the ideas and behaviors of these households.

In addition, I was a vendor at Maxwell Street Market for almost 2 years. I became a vendor to adopt the mindset of a participant by practicing their lifestyle. This practice legitimized my presence in both vendors' and consumers' eyes, and gave me insight into the vendors' lifestyle and day-to-day circumstances. I sold used items for 8 months and new bathroom accessories the remaining 12 months. When I conducted this research, the Market was open every Sunday.[3] There were two kinds of vendors, the regular and the irregular. The vast majority of vendors were

---

[3] In 1994 the City of Chicago closed the Market and moved it to a new location, changing it completely (Martel 1996; Walker 2000). Readers interested in the Market's history can also see Morales (1993; 2000).

regular. They had vended for many years and expected to continue to do so. A small number of vendors conducted "garage sales" at the market, vending only a few Sundays, usually on the periphery of the market. This chapter reports data gathered from regular vendors. There were 846 licensed vendors, but the Market actually employed between 700 and 2,600 people per Sunday. Seasonal variation is the source of this range (Morales et al. 1995). Typical vendors had at least one partner, who was either a co-owner or employee. In many cases these employees were family members.

This report will discuss tax compliance related to vending income. For some merchants vending and nonvending income streams were inseparable. For others, different sources of income remain strictly divided. For most vendors, vending in the market represented one component of their household income. This means that most vendors had at least one other job that occupied some part of the rest of a typical week. I have data on this variation but a complete analysis cannot be forthcoming here (see Morales, 1997 for a partial account). My sample of vendors indicates significant variation in length of residence in Chicago. Ethnic White residents were often fourth generation Chicagoans. African-American vendors were often second, or sometimes third generation Chicagoans, but occasionally were also migrants to Chicago from elsewhere as adults. Mexican vendors were almost exclusively migrants, with a few being born in the City, but most having children born in Chicago. Most merchants became vendors after falling on hard times, or they took up vending to augment household income, the latter being the predominant reason for African-American or Mexican vendors (see Morales 2009a, b).

Our methods must elicit answers to our research questions to help us structure our theories, or test them, as the case may be. Ethnographic methods are well-suited to understanding complex social situations. The approach assumes that street vendors, like anyone else, live in the milieu of social, moral, and governmental regulation of ideas and behavior. Like the rest of us, merchants engage these combinations of contexts as compelled and as they see fit. Oftentimes this is to serve their own purposes, as in when disparate factors clash in reconciling the demands of employment with those of a needy child. Demands may be made on the child, or perhaps demands are made on another family member or friend to fill the caretaker role. In practice, the particular elements of these influences on behavior may be supportive and reinforcing, or they can be in conflict with each other. Understanding this enables us to predict people's behavior in complex situations, but such predictions of course cannot be guaranteed since people's choices are influenced by new inspirations and information. Indeed, it is when accounting for change in such choice circumstances that our social theories begin to fulfill their role informing policy practice.

Ethnographic methods provide the data that pragmatist theory uses to bridge social–psychological and social–organizational aspects of situations. Pragmatism examines the flow of interaction, interruptions in that flow, and how such are resolved and interactions resumed. The larger pragmatist literature is rich with concepts for describing, predicting, and understanding social behavior, but most accounts begin with understanding people in "problem" situations and how they assess their interests and the immediate constellation of related ideas and behaviors (Mead 1934; Tamanaha 1997; Morales 2009b). Locating interruptions to the flow in the larger social context clarifies the conflicting interests or information that structure a particular disruption. Resolutions and the return to "typical" interaction develop through negotiations with the self and others. Such "self-making" and relational processes involve adopting the roles others are playing, varying one's attitudes, interests, and behaviors with respect to others; even adapting concepts from one behavior with ideas from another.

Merchant Tax Behavior [4]

From the merchant's perspective, tax compliance practices can invoke three systems of ideas/behaviors. The first is economic, meaning the activities of business including profit, loss, and risk, merchandise acquisition, and other management activities. The second is the household or kinship ideas and behaviors that include the roles household members play, as well as their aspirations. Finally, political ideas relating to the market, its condition, and the roles government plays at the market bring into play concepts of public service and governance. What we look for are problems and opportunities, the resulting thoughts and behaviors, and how those thoughts and behaviors are rooted in experience and motivated by aspirations. All these elements are autocatalytically related, but similarly result in resolutions that return to habitual behavior. Such findings provide the reasoning underlying policy change. In the following we begin with how vendors harness political ideas of reciprocity to understand a problem situation – nascent conflict between merchants and the state.

Governance and Reciprocity

The initial core complaint all merchants have deals with the notion of reciprocity, in both specific and generalized forms. Merchants have specific complaints that the license fees or taxes paid to government are not returned in the form of services or improvements to the market, as well as generalized complaints that their payments to the state are not returned as improvements to neighborhoods or schools. These complaints represent the absence of benefits from the contributions merchants make – this is in keeping with Braithwaite's first conflict opportunity. Notice how one African-American merchant, Virgilee, articulated this generally perceived lack of reciprocity with questions, asking:

> The money they collect, the taxes that people pay, where does that money go? I mean does it go back into that area or does it go into the general city fund or something like that? I think that the neglect of the market has caused the destruction of the market itself. Not just

---

[4] Readers interested in a detailed example of how pragmatist theory, especially a Meadian theory of interaction, applies in interpreting behavior can see Matsueda (2006) for criminological thought and Morales (2010) who uses Matsueda's insights for understanding self-governance among street vendors.

the neglect of the market, but the city not putting things into the market. I know that over the years, you know, millions of dollars have been paid to the city from people who have been down there (at the market) but none of it is ever put back.

These "millions" of dollars were partly comprised of license fees for vendors, but also of money extorted from vendors by corrupt regulators (Morales 1993). Virgilee asks if reciprocity is specific, with reference to "that area" or generalized with respect to the "general city fund." Either way, this constellation of ideas includes "neglect" and the absence of investment, "not putting things into the market."

Merchants of both genders and all ethnicities consistently level the reciprocity critique. Such consistency is hardly surprising. This concern with reciprocity is central to anyone affected by city services and it surfaces in many ways, regarding poor schools (Morales 1998, where merchants use income to send children to private school), potholed streets, inadequate garbage removal, and even a general malaise or distrust of the city. A more extensive example echoes Virgilee, but extends the general critique to particular ideas and organizational practices that show how these Mexican immigrant merchants develop household level "policy" in response to the situation. Cecilia and her husband Felix both vend and both feel that the state fails to provide adequate schools in their neighborhood. Felix is well aware of what the tax money should help subsidize:

I know that the [tax] money is for the good of the neighborhood, but what happens to it? Where are the workers? Only the politician's friends get help. I understand that there are neighborhoods with good schools, good streets, and less crime, but these are also more expensive homes. I work hard at the factory and still can only make enough money for the home we have here. I want to live in a better neighborhood but this is what we can afford and so we vend and we put up with canyons in the streets and sidewalks.

The "canyons" or potholes that Felix refers to are indicative of the poorly maintained public infrastructure people observe and often complain about. Felix and Cecilia assess their compliance choices in light of the level and quality of services available in their neighborhood. Cecilia's perspective and expectations for the services focuses on education:

Our neighborhood schools only teach the children to join gangs. Oh, some [children] do well, but I pay for my children's parochial education and I know it is a better education. But every year it gets higher and higher. It started out at five hundred dollars every month (for four children) and most of the time all the money I make vending goes for tuition.

Cecilia rarely pays taxes on her vending income, instead she pays for her children's education. Her choice is to decrease the chances her children will become a burden on society and instead increase the chances for achievement and economic integration into the mainstream. In the choice between the state and her family, the family won. She makes the choice between tax and tuition pointed:

I know taxes should be paid, my husband started paying some taxes from his vending income. But my situation is different, he thinks of all of us, but I think first, always first, about my children. I know that education is important and they need it, so I try to help them get it.

Thus, we see how their desires are formed by distinct impressions of what they value. Cecilia is clear about her wish to support her children's education and many families with children echo her sentiments (in my sample mostly Black and Mexican families, since the White vendors were mostly older with grown children who benefitted from income at the Market, or else younger and childless). Felix admits to paying some income taxes, mostly to help establish credit worthiness in hopes of eventually moving to a nicer neighborhood. He was clear that part of income he earned occasionally subsidized tuition and other expenses, but it was mostly devoted to broader household concerns. This experience illustrates the clashing demands of kin, economic, and political constellations of ideas.

Within the household, wishes can be oriented to distinct purposes, may be rooted in gendered roles, and in practice can modify vendors' organization and outcomes (see also Morales 2009b). Immigrant vendors are not the only vendors who withhold income tax for these "supply of service" reasons (Morales 1998), but among the most recent immigrants, this logic was pervasive. Among the older migrants and among vendors of many years of experience, desirable neighborhoods and schools were less important because, as implied by Felix, those vendors had already purchased homes in neighborhoods they liked better.

Context counts, and context provides ideas and examples of how they are used. People take and modify those ideas and use them in divining responses to their circumstances. Felix and Cecilia exemplify those who struggle to make relatively one stable wage income job stretch as far as possible. In that effort they have developed general (and, in this case, gender-based) heuristics for how to organize and deploy their vending income. These practices evince an overall interest in stability in the household's routines, but can be rooted in gendered understandings of the household in context. Thus they exemplify the multilateral relationship between state and society. Merchants' choices compensate for inadequate services, or, put more positively, they choose to invest in their families and homes, using less-stable income that they have more control over.

In short, the reciprocal obligations street vendors have with respect to the state go mostly unfulfilled by either party. The Market provided no services or support in lieu of the city or state. Neighborhood infrastructure was in disarray, and schools approached 40% drop out rates. Merchants actually subsidized the state by self-organizing participation and Market organization and helped achieve broad public and private goals by paying private school tuition for their children (Morales 2009, 2010). Vendors' appreciation of and response to reciprocity illustrates Braithwaite's first opportunity for conflict with the tax authority. Vendors' beliefs about what the governmental authority should provide are violated, with tax evasion as a behavioral outcome of that violation.

Dimensions of Obligation

Braithwaite's second conflict opportunity is associated with obligation. This is illuminated by cases of unpaid taxes where vendors are either naïve about required tax-related licenses or regulations, or else avoid understanding them entirely. This means vendors are noncompliant with tax law because they are not complying with business law. Not only does this underestimate business activity, it also reminds us that there are a number of steps in creating a business, steps that are recognized by the state and by financial organizations, and steps that can release financial resources from both to emerging businesspeople. However, vendors might react in different ways to the same regulatory stimulus, contingent on who they are, their aspirations, and social–organizational context. In the following example we see how the race of vendor influences whether or not the vendor acquires and maintains a vending license. In this way we learn how changing aspirations motivate merchants to change their "policy" via licensing – that is, acquiring a license and therefore beginning to pay taxes.

Local Licenses

Street vendors or other businesspeople escape taxation by failing to fully investigate and subscribe to the legal requirements of their commercial endeavors.[5] Merchants who sell for a few weeks at a time, or those with little business experience or from other countries, may make sales periodically for months or even years at a time and not discover the need for a license. When they finally understand that a permit or license is required, they may continue to forego such in favor of their habitual practices.

Street vending is an activity that is nominally counted by the State of Illinois. Vendors are expected to have a license. To obtain a license, a vendor must have a State of Illinois sales tax number. Thus, licensing is the precursor to taxation. Licenses expire every March 31, cost \$25 per year (all dollar figures cited here are 1990 dollars, multiply by 1.5 for approximate 2010 value) and were purchased through the City of Chicago Department of Revenue. Vendors who did not report income or pay taxes could be denied a license. Many vendors avoided paying sales taxes and dodged income taxes by circumventing the licensing process. Police rarely patrolled the market, but when they did they exercised much discretion in checking licenses, usually ignoring White merchants, and typically checking merchants of color. White merchants recognized their privilege, Bert noted:

> Yeah, look at this, (referring to his license, which he wears backward, when he wears it) ain't changed it in nine years, hell, who needs to when the blueboys know you?

Vendors of color recognized this inequality and its consequences. Pedro commented:

> The biggest danger at the market is the police. Even if you have a license they often just tell you to pack up and go. Representatives of the law abuse it more than the rest; people they know don't have licenses and are never questioned.

---

[5] The role enforcement agents play in compliance is the complex study of "street-level" bureaucrats, e.g. Schorr (1997).

What is perceived as real is also real in consequence with the result that vendors of color found that whether they acquired a license or not, they might be ejected from the market. Still, vendors sought stable relationships with the police, because these relationships might substitute for a license. They developed those relationships even while performing rudimentary cost/benefit calculations about whether or not to get a license. Many Black and Mexican vendors got to know the beat patrolmen, and like me, those relationships often developed into substitutes for obtaining a license.

At face value, it seems that vendors have a simple choice: get a license or not. However, this choice is made more complex by ethnicity and by experience at the market. Thus, many (mostly Mexican) vendors, relatively new to vending and with a lower competency in English, noticed the uneven enforcement of license regulations and struggled to learn (the relatively simple) process for purchasing a license by their experiences at the market alone. Many tried substituting relationships with neighbors for the legitimacy of a license. Neighbors vouch for each other as "legitimate" vendors, in terms of acquiring space at the market (Morales 1993). On many occasions I witnessed or was part of these "self-legitimizing" exchanges with police. The form of the interaction was simple. A patrolman was seen down the street, a new vendor would ask what the officer might demand. The experienced vendor would reply, "a license" and follow that by saying, "don't worry, I'll tell him you're with me," or "don't worry, if he asks you for a license just say you forgot it at home, or that you're only here this week replacing a regular." In brief, what seems a fairly simple set of alternatives to the license dilemma can be, contingent on the merchant, a much more complex set of choices, a set of choices that will change with vendor experience.

Other Obligations: International Tariffs

Many vendors are foreign-born and cater to the tastes of their fellow expatriates. Often this means importing items required to reproduce the culture left behind. Music and clothing are two items that are in demand and imported by enterprising vendors. There are two kinds of examples I will discuss, both involve the opportunity to avoid taxation.

Mario and Guillermo's parents emigrated from Mexico, but they were born in the USA. They make regular trips to Mexico to visit family; on those trips they make purchases for resale at the Market. They avoid the USA–Mexico border tariff by under-invoicing merchandise they purchase, and they count the value of taxes and one airline ticket against the sales:

> Then from the $1,400 (that week's profits) we take out for airfare, and we send somebody to Mexico to get the stuff and they bring it back on the plane. We pay 30% taxes on things you bring back. So you figure, you invest $600 in merchandise, and tell them you paid $300, so you pay $90, (in taxes at the border). We say we spent $300 and the [Customs agents] ask

"yeah, well what do you have?" we say "Ah, baby clothes that we bought for my daughters," (Guillermo has twin girls) so they don't know it's for business.

The $600 dollar purchase when sold grosses about $3,600 in sales. The same merchandise in the USA would have cost them about $2,000, and grossed the same $3,600. The difference is striking. Besides the larger profit, there are two further benefits, first, visiting relatives, and second, is that no paper trail remains to trace the transactions.

Julle, a Korean merchant, runs an import business and a retail outlet. He describes how he employs under-invoicing for avoiding import tariffs:

> A shipment will arrive in San Francisco, there, taxes are paid,...but no, not fully, less is paid than declared,...no, we select different items to declare less, each shipment will be different.

Here, Julle engages a similar process. Even though a paper trail exists, he avoids patterns in his declarations and thus reduces the chances the transactions will be detected.

Accounting practices and paper trails are key in avoiding tariffs. The next topic, avoiding income tax, encompasses the previous two, and afterwards I will return to the role of accountants and accounting practices for avoiding taxation.

Income Tax Evasion

Vendors at Maxwell Street could make a lot of money, grossing as much as $2,000 in one 10–12 hour Sunday. The vast majority of this income goes undeclared. A Black merchant, Ace, discusses the fairness of taxing all components of multiple-income earning household:

> Well really man, you're working on a job and you figure, man, at the end of a workday, you got to share your earnings with somebody, that burns you up. You're up there sweating and you're working hard and you have your partner [the government] that's not even there. That's the way I look at it, [the government is a] stick up man without a gun, and then he try to make you feel kinda good, givin' you a little of your money back.

On another occasion he provided this analogy:

> If you have a job, the government knows what you make. But I feel like this, when I get up on Sunday morning I'm doing something that's what I want to do, not because I have to, but because I want to. I feel like the government is not supposed to interfere with what I do on those Sunday mornings. I really strongly believe, "Hey I do this on Sunday, I prefer laying in bed until 12 or 1 o'clock but hey I wouldn't have nothing." I got kids to bring up, I could be out there selling drugs, but I prefer getting up and doing it the old fashioned way.

The ideas Ace suggests are clear: in wage labor jobs, government, the invisible partner, shares earnings, but returns little in either goods or services. The wage laborer, in order to get ahead in society, plays the wage game, but could engage in other games, selling drugs, or "doing it the old fashioned way." Ace shows us how he plays the games he wants to, without much remorse and in fact in a positive fashion, with particular goals in mind and often choosing the least of several perceivable evils.[6] Ace rationalizes breaking the law, but policy makers should take advantage of vendors' desire to "do it the old fashioned way" and in doing so, contribute positively to community and society. A distinct, but complimentary position sees such rationalization as analogous to an executive's reasoning when fighting labor directly or co-opting labor or political leaders.

The obvious problem with income tax compliance enforcement is that the income is not recorded and cash transactions predominate. The replacement value of this activity is quite high. Ace commented:

> You'd have to give me an extra 50 or 60 thousand a year (1990 dollars) for me to forget about my Sundays. You really would, like I just explained to you. The money you make down there is tax-free money. I don't have to report nothing I make down there. Everything I make at [a meat processing plant] is recordable. If I want to buy something that cost $500 for my kids I can go buy it. If I buy it with my checks it might take two checks, but I can do it in one day, before noon, at the market.

It is clear that this "tax-free money" is income unrecorded by the state. Furthermore, it became clear, when Ace showed me his check and W-2 form, that he is frustrated by the small amount of money he makes in the formal labor market ($27,000/year, 1990 dollars), and that his own business sense is what has afforded him the chance to acquire things and pay for household needs. Vending then is at least an opportunity to exercise control over income, and/or express a business sense otherwise stifled. Still, what might convince a vendor to change their mind about complying with the law? Felix's interest in establishing credit gave one indication and the following elaborates these notions.

Changes in the Vendor's Behavioral Orientation

Over the years many vendors remain content with the income they earned at the Market. But other vendors sought to establish businesses outside the market, and over the years many did so with great success (Eastwood 2002; Eshel and Schatz 2004; Morales 2006). Ace, for instance, owned 27 apartment buildings with units rented to some 60–70 families. Ace, Felix, and other vendors learned that establishing storefront businesses required they work with banks and other financial organizations – and banks will not provide financial support without demonstrable cash flow. Accordingly, merchants sought licenses and permits and began to declare income (often even more income than they were strictly liable for). Purchasing

---

[6] Willis (1977) is among the authors who describe how particular opportunities became linked with particular segments of society.

homes and securing business or investment properties required vendors to interface with a more complex organizational environment. One merchant, Louis, exemplifies how changing desires led to changing experiences and compelled him to learn and engage a more complex constellation of economic ideas and organizations,

> Credit man, humph, money makes money, you see I didn't know that. When I was a young man I just liked getting paid. I had my car, my cash in pocket; I did what I wanted and when I wanted to. I got older, got into trouble, got out, and got back in the market. I had to think, "I got a wife, I got a son, I got some business ideas, what am I gonna do?" So, I went legit, it took me some time to convince myself. I got a license, then after a while I learned about contracting and did some of that, then I got a contractor's license. Then I worked with my brother and set up a business and started doing some taxes, then I was able to get some credit, I got a house, started getting more equipment and more contracts and the busier I got, the easier it was to let the pros handle things and hand me back my money.

The "pros" never handled *all* the cash Louis earned at the market or in contracting, but without demonstrable cash flow he may have never achieved the high level of income and business success he enjoyed. We can see how Louis's life was modified and made more complex by the "trouble" he was in, but it was also made more complex and more rich by adopting the ideas of family life. The consequences of his experience and intersecting economic and kin-related ideas and behaviors induced him to pursue private business. This was done initially at the market, where even without a license his earned income covered his household expenses and provided the resources and relationships to expand into contracting. However, he knew that he needed a license and other businesses licenses to become "legit," and such legitimacy served him as his activities grew and changed to meet his aspirations.

Martin also characterizes the process of legitimization in terms of investment. His comments help us understand how merchants come to see the advantages of becoming legitimate:

> If I file low taxes year after year [then that means] my business isn't doing much in terms of sales. So when I go to sell my company or if I go to the bank and want to borrow money, they want your income taxes. So you understand that it's to your benefit to pay your taxes. I'm going to sell my business when I don't want it anymore and so because my time and effort is worth a lot of money and [I have] my clients and my repeat customers, you know, my records and documents, *that's* what selling a business is about. I can show records of how much my business has been making over the years and so other vendors won't be able to do that.

Of course, other vendors cannot demonstrate those sales since they do not keep the records. In short, many merchants choose not to "go legit" simply because they do not share the same aspirations. Eventually, every household chooses how to resolve said conflicts in favor of compliance or not. Framing this choice is not only experience and reciprocity but also aspirations and goals.

The larger point I am making here is twofold. First, with respect to Braithwaite, the coercion or obligation to pay taxes creates a conflict, but such conflicts are resolved by merchants and need not only be resolved by the state's enforcement agents. Indeed, the state can restructure law to extract rents from those not seeking storefront growth, and simultaneously incentivize and support vendors who do.

These matters are a matter of perspective, and recognizing the relativity of perspective is important in designing flexible policy responses. The second part of this larger point is theoretical. Our accounts of vendors' behavior should acknowledge that they adjust their practices incrementally as they understand the fit between their circumstances and different pieces of the regulatory puzzle. Vendors, especially those who seek storefront businesses, will come to understand how subscribing to state policies can enhance their business prospects.

As an example, Martin was trained in leather craft in his native Mexico and he made and sold custom leather goods, as well as mass-produced leather goods at the Market. His hope was to expand his business to a storefront and his behavior is supportive of this aspiration:

> I report taxes quarterly, not on every dollar I make, but pretty close. I understand that bankers pretty much predict how much business you're doing based on your taxes and if I file year after year of very low taxes my business isn't doing much in terms of sales and so when I go to the bank and want to borrow money they want your income taxes and so they won't give me much... For a lot of people who aren't looking to get bank loans or selling their business well, that's one thing. But if I'm going to get a loan, and I'm sure I will, or if I'm going to sell my business when I don't want it anymore, well, my time and effort and my clients and my repeat customers, they are all worth a lot of money...then I can show the bank, in records, how much my business has been making over the years. Others won't be able to do that if they don't pay their taxes... So, I pay some [taxes] since it is to my benefit.

Martin may have only an elementary understanding about how financing works, but he demonstrates a growing knowledge, and a knowledge oriented to developing equity, which is useful for business growth or deployable to other purposes. Such knowledge is not uncommon, and the attitude and practices is found and communicated among many merchants. Martin is similar to many vendors in planning for a future in business or for a home in a more expensive neighborhood. But he is cognizant that his choice is with respect to his circumstances and goals, he recognizes others operating in the same conceptual context might make other choices:

> Look, I don't pay all my taxes; I have other things I want to buy. My wife takes care of our children and life is expensive. I know, look around you (referring down the street to fellow vendors Cecilia and Felix), many people have children and they want their kids in the best schools they can. Myself, I want the best neighborhood I can, it's like the old saying, "*cada chango su columpio*," [every monkey has his swing].

People operate with similar conceptual and behavioral choices, but these are nuanced according to experience, aspiration, relationships and immediate circumstances. Becoming "legit" is a process involving acquiring a language, professional relationships, new attitudes and the like. The concepts merchants have in common, as well as those they learn, make communication between them and others possible. Furthermore, the same concepts make our understanding of their behavior possible. Finally, and perhaps most importantly, they help us to understand how relatively similarly-placed people can make very distinct choices based on their differences in aspirations, relationships, and experience.

The point is simple. Vendors realize that there are multiple and occasionally competing principles on which to act, and they act considering the situation as they perceive it and the worth of each choice in that context. Furthermore, as contexts change, so do the choices. Vendors deploy components of these behaviors and concepts as they are catalyzed through experience, relationships, and aspirations. Cecilia and Felix and Martin exemplify learning processes. They know that vending may mean economic mobility, but they also recognize that such mobility comes in different forms. Inherent in this is different requirements for how they organize themselves and their income, and different concepts to learn and practice with. For instance, vendors must choose how much income earning from vending to declare. We can see that this is rarely a linear or simple choice, but is instead influenced by the intersection of many behaviors and ideas, as well as organizational complexities, to which we now turn.

Complexities in Constellations of Behavior in Tax Compliance

We have learned three things from the foregoing discussion: first, that we can identify salient constellations of ideas and behavior; second, that we can understand how choices are organized by these constellations; and third, that we see how behavioral contexts change with respect to new goals or sources of information. We see that Braithwaite correctly summarizes opportunities for conflict with taxing authority, especially in the bilateral relationship between vendor and the state. We have also learned how pressing and influential competing ideas and practices can be on vendors as they justify noncompliance according to personal circumstances or service inequalities. These are relatively straightforward rationalizations, implied in bilateral situations where aspirations dominate or injustices are perceived. However, the complexities of the tax code and information asymmetries are also implicated in noncompliance. Are these opportunities for conflict in Braithwaite's sense? Yes – if we adopt a multilateral analysis of "taxp(l)aying"[7] to include institutionally-validated organizations that influence street vendors' compliance behavior. Here I am referring to tax professionals who populate the immigrant neighborhood and whose advice and services complicate the conceptualization of compliance that vendors may use.

Tax professionals are an additional layer of experience and source of judgment about compliance. Here, my emphasis will be on tax professionals as either a wholly-negative problem or a necessary evil for merchants. Tax professionals provide a useful service, saving vendors time and money. They can be a vehicle for unwittingly sheltering income, but can also be a problem when behaving contrary to professional norms. About half the vendors I interviewed had help with their taxes.

---

[7]Term coined by the author for the 1991 U.S. Internal Revenue Service Annual Research Conference, the IRS provided transcript of the lecture available from the author.

Some developed that support by educating children or recruiting family members, some went to friends for help, some hired help. A Puerto Rican merchant, Bori, trusts a friend for help with the taxes:

> I have to pay taxes for what I earn; I got a number for that, (referring to his tax or "whole-sale" number received with his license). See the government asks for my taxes, and the company where I buy stuff is gonna say, "he showed me a tax number," or whatever, so then they (the government) gonna ask me why I haven't paid the taxes, on the merchandise I buy from the guy, I think that's how it works. But I don't do the tax paper, another guy does the paper, every three months, he charges me about 50 or 75 dollars, like this time of the year it's slow, a lot of people don't pay nothing, so I don't pay much.

Like other merchants Bori under-invoices his purchases and declares less than he sells. Furthermore, caught up with the business of business as well as being a husband and father, Bori reveals how vendors put their trust in friends or professionals to make sure their taxes are done.

Not all these friends or professionals are trustworthy – is this a question of honor between thieves? Don Pedro does a brisk business and he maintains various assets (including rental buildings and a storefront business). The simplest way to maximize his income is to avoid income taxes, and the easiest way to do that is to do all business deals in cash. But nonetheless, his personal ambitions and lifestyle often require the services of accountants, bankers, or lawyers. The following example demonstrates the difficulties faced by business owners without reliable information about local professionals:

> Alfonso: Does this person have their own business or are they a friend?
> Don Pedro: No, they have their own business, with computers and everything and they don't charge me much, very low prices. The first one I had was a Mexican and he stole money from me. The one I have now is White. She charges me $50 a month. The Mexican charged me $100 a month and did a terrible job. He got me into problems with the State and the City and she had to get me out. She had to fix everything up. When you start a business you don't know anything, then it seems that I got this guy by bad luck. I had been in business for a week when he came by and I hired him. He made a mess and after about six months I figured it out. I asked him for records, I thought I was about $1,400 short, and he said, "I can't give you copies of the records," he said that he needed to keep them, but he also said for me to make my own copies. Well… No… then I found this woman accountant, found her in the papers. I called her, and told her that I had an accountant but it seemed like it was not going well. That's what I said. She said she would take my accounts. Then I had to buy my records from that shameless guy. He said, "You want your papers, you give me $100 for them or you won't get your papers." I wanted to jump on him. I gave him the money but told him to take the papers to the address of my new accountant. This woman put a scare into him saying, "How could you be so irresponsible? What are you doing? Your work is hardly worth the trash can!"

Fraud, exploitation, unprofessional conduct, racketeering, and professional inter-accountability are all present in this example. One consequence of such behavior is how such stories spread and influence other vendors. Besides deterring the use of tax professionals, this story might encourage unethical behavior by modeling it. The second part of the example is Don Pedro's problem finding a suitable accountant. Coethnics discovered through personal networks proved unreliable, and therefore many merchants supplied their own expertise as children or relatives demonstrated suitable talent and acquired the skills. Don Pedro turned to the newspapers to hire help, although initially language proved a barrier to their relationship. These problems demonstrate how difficult it can be to secure a suitable accountant. But even after the process of finding the accountant is through, a vendor must choose the information to submit to the accountant. As indicated above, there are circumstances where merchants willingly report income, but not always. Don Pedro's response about how he minimized his tax liability is typical:

> Well, she does her work, the papers you give her are what she works with. Like for example the business I have, the things I buy, usually I don't have a receipt. Why report to her those things? Sure, when you get a receipt or give one out, well, that is different. But all the things that you get on the side. Those are the things you make money on, because you don't worry about taxes. How will they know that you bought or sold? No one can know that you bought or sold or what you bought or sold. You bought ten refrigerators. Will you ask for a receipt? Why would you want to report? Are you going to say, - "Oh look I am a very honorable man and I bought ten refrigerators here, for $500 I sold them for $1,500, I made $1,000, charge me (enormous laughter). I owe you this much, I am very honorable..." No, no, there are no people like that in the world, no such innocents. If there is a person of such honor they will die of starvation.

Don Pedro purposely leaves his accountant ignorant of many of his transactions. Clearly this is not her fault, but to any outside observer the records she prepares look like complete and accurate business records. The example demonstrates how it is possible to shelter income in the absence of a paper trail, particularly for households that mix different sources of income. Again, the general point made here is that a comprehensive analysis of compliance behavior is multilateral and inclusive of tax professionals as well as perhaps other parties.

Policy Implications: Substituting Self-Service Provision for Taxation

Tax laws help define the state (Stiglitz, 2002: 177). Roughly speaking, adding the "what and how" of public services to the "what and how" of taxation equals governance. In this chapter we have learned that the citizen's perception of governance is with respect to various compositions of ideas and behavior, within which perceptions of governance and of the state structure the vendor's compliance strategy. This focus on the vendor and their understanding of the common good in addition to how they reconcile that understanding with their household needs and aspirations may humanize them for us. However, it should also point to policy implications that expand economic opportunity, and perhaps more important, it should help us consider how governance processes might be modified to create stronger citizens *and* a more effective state.

From the collective interest, asking people to relate to the state and thereby to each other is important to our collective well-being. The evidence presented here indicates that we need a paradigm shift in terms of policy prescriptions, especially with regards to certain marginalized populations like street vendors. We need to supplement, and even replace, policy focused on enforcement with policy that incorporates the interconnectivity of vendor aspirations, practices, and their relationship to the state. Law itself may be too difficult to write in such a manner, but licenses can be crafted, issued, and audited to ensure that the income is used for the purposes intended. I contend we should be much more flexible in our treatment of merchants, and that the same resources deployed to enforcement could and should be used to identify and support vendors who wish to expand business and occupy storefronts. I would suggest policy experiments that permit vendors to spend the income they earn on increased or improved human or physical capital and investments in themselves and their families, thus decentralizing the provisional role of the government where it has proved insufficient, and allowing for a more individualized approach to providing needed services.[8]

In the absence of adequate services to neighborhoods and Market Street, vendors invest taxable income in children and homes. In effect, they tax themselves. Yet, merchants willingly establish a tax trail to support business aspirations. These are not contradictory behaviors, nor do they rest on impulsive decision making. Instead, many vendors consider the competing logic of state and family and make choices cognizant of both, but are especially mindful of the long-term implications associated with diverting taxable income to education or other household needs.

Thus, enhancing vendors' economic prospects means recovering legitimate practices and adopting various economic, educational, and other social policies that enable the transition to more conventional economic activities. To enhance policy flexibility we need to resolve the contradiction in the state that fails to adequately support the range of economic activity, inclusive of the smallest entrepreneurs among us. We need to erase artificial "formal" and "informal" divisions in economic activity and be aware of the effects of criminalizing activities in each realm. Street vending historically has been not just legitimate, but has been counted as an occupation by the US Census (until 1940 "peddler" was an occupation category). In terms of the latter, the concern with justice in tax collections should compel governments to reduce the public perception that free-riding individuals and corporations fail to pay their fair share of taxes. These perceptions not only mock the hardworking entrepreneur and spawn defiant attitudes in the public (Mason and Calvin, 1984; Braithwaite et al. 2003), but they erode the resources required to integrate the public more fully into the economy and society more generally.

Before offering brief recommendations, let us recognize that the malfunction of government is twofold. First, there are the problems associated with addressing the failures of service provision; second, and more importantly, government measures favor the large over the small, thus ignoring the *community development potential*

---

[8] Obviously this makes for interesting research questions including an assessment that discovers if the costs associated with enforcement weigh less than the benefits accruing to vendors and society from spending that income.

of the street merchant. We should also recognize the problem of "institutional incompleteness" (Breton 1964), meaning that around the state and the taxp(l)ayer are found other organizations, persons, and professionals not all of whom willingly support compliance. In sum, an appreciation of the organizational and professional environment amplifies Braitwaite's paradigms for understanding compliance behavior. It is important to consider elements of this environment that might be supportive of compliance – for instance, legitimate financial institutions – but we should not assume a uniformly supportive organizational or professional environment.

In short, we should understand that the pursuit of private purposes is not incompatible with the pursuit of public purposes, and, especially in business, the two actually owe much to each other. Seeking policies that explicitly incorporate emergent purposes that vendors or others have or develop will change their relationship to the tax system, not only by increasing compliance, but also by implying or creating explicit opportunities to realize larger purposes. The approach taken here was to unpack the rationalizations associated with noncompliance. We discovered that it is not simply that people want to cheat (the economic assumption) and they come up with an excuse to justify their self-interest (the policy implications of which would be enforcement/cognitive sharpening). Rather, the rationalizations are emergent from a complex and dynamic social context. Since this is the case, the description of vendors I provided also suggests that evasion by wealthy is not a haphazard or rationalizing excuse for self-interest, but also emerges from effects of their social context. In saying this, we clearly need more research focused on many socioeconomic groups and classes about the context and practices and the view of the common good that their taxes help supply. This specific focus of research reconstructs our current emphases on the *decision* to evade taxes alone (which appears to be a local decision reflecting attitudes about taxes) into a complimentary and more comprehensive approach that focuses research and policy on state–individual relations in a more general sense.

Conclusion

This chapter has characterized the tax deviance and motives observed among street merchants in Chicago. The research reported here extends policy-practical knowledge by showing how people adopt and *adjust* their tax compliance ideas and practices and by showing how people relate those ideas to important and changing conditions of ideas and behaviors. Whether it is through avoiding tariffs or skirting income taxes, tax deviance was clearly pervasive throughout the merchant community. Instead of curbing vending because of tax noncompliance, government agencies should support this industry. Furthermore, they should seek simple ways for merchants to participate in the economy to promote a sense of cooperation and agency, whether they wish to grow beyond their business at the market or not. Designing policies that privilege the norms of the state or big business will impact individuals in unpredictable and undesirable ways. Policy makers cannot control how individuals interpret and share their experience with others. However, as Braithwaite (2009: 397–98) concludes:

> …they can experiment with policies that assume non or partly compliant taxpayers share basically the same goals and aspirations as their compliant neighbors in other parts of the jurisdiction. The connection between quality services and realizing those aspirations can inform policy about the interdependent nature of taxpaying, the promise of the state for its citizens, and the promise of the citizens to each other and those coming in the future. This research shows how taxpayers orchestrate income-earning activities into a mix of defiant and obedient practices as they contemplate their relationships, to the state, to each other, and to their hopes and dreams. Tax authorities can no longer afford to design their systems as they please and ignore public perceptions. Nor is the answer one of bringing the community on board through "spin," which is a short-term approach to a serious problem. Tax authorities need to engage in a reflective process with the community about tax design, tax administration, tax benefits, moral obligation, coercion, justice and alternative tax authorities. This discussion needs to be augmented by evidence acquired through field experiments and rigorous data analysis. Only then will tax authorities have the knowledge and moral authority required to manage the difficult problems of evasion and avoidance currently besetting tax systems. (tax handbook).

In this way we can work together to advance the common good.

Acknowledgment I would like to thank Valerie Braithwaite for encouraging this project and for her many helpful revisions to the chapter. I am also indebted to Robert McGee and Robert Rosen for their constructive comments. Finally, thanks to Austin Outhavang and especially Jessi Moths for research and editorial assistance.

References

Braithwaite, V., Schneider, F., Reinhart, M. & Murphy, K. 2003. Charting the shoals of the cash economy. In Valerie Braithwaite (ed.), *Taxing Democracy: Understanding Tax Avoidance and Evasion*. Aldershot: Ashgate.

Braithwaite, Valerie 2009. Tax Evasion. In M. Tonry (Ed.), *Handbook on Crime and Public Policy (pp. 381–405)*. Oxford: Oxford University Press.

Breton, Raymond. 1964. Institutional Completeness of Ethnic Communities and the Personal Relations of Immigrants. *American Journal of Sociology* 70 (2):193–205.

Bromley, Ray. 2000. Street vending and public policy: A global review. *International Journal of Sociology and Social Policy* 20 (1/2):1–28.

Browlee, W. E. 2000. Historical perspective on U.S. tax policy toward the rich. In J. Slemrod (Ed.), *Does Atlas Shrug? The Economic Consequences of Taxing the Rich* (pp. 29–73). New York: Russell Sage Foundation.

Eastwood, Carolyn. 2002. *Near West Side Stories: Struggles for Community in Chicago's Maxwell Street Neighborhood*. 1st ed. Chicago: Lake Claremont Press.

Eshel, Shuli, and Roger Schatz. 2004. *Jewish Maxwell Street Stories*. Charleston, SC: Arcadia.

Friedlander, Harriet. 1976. If You Want to Be a Customer at a Farmers' Market-Start One. *Organic Gardening and Farming*, 108–109.

Feld, Lars and Bruno Frey. 2007. Tax compliance as a result of a psychological tax contract: The role of incentives and responsive regulation *Law and Policy* 29 (1).

Frey, Bruno S. and Lars P. Feld. 2001. The Tax Authority and the Taxpayer: An Exploratory Analysis. Paper presented at the Second International Conference on Taxation, Centre for Tax System Integrity, Australian National University, Canberra 10–11 December.

Granovetter, Mark. 1985. Economic Action and Social Structure: The Problem of Embeddedness. *American Journal of Sociology* 91 (13, November):481–510.

Internal Revenue Service. 2005a. Understanding the Tax Gap FS-2005-14. http://www.irs.gov/newsroom/article/0,,id=137246,00.html.

Internal Revenue Service. 2005b. New IRS Study Provides Preliminary Tax Gap Estimate IR-2005-38. http://www.irs.gov/newsroom/article/0,,id=137247,00.html.

Martel, Elise. 1996. From market to market: The reinstitutionalization and legitimation of Chicago's Maxwell Street Market. Master's thesis, University of Illinois, Chicago.

Mason, Robert and Lyle D. Calvin. 1984. Public confidence and admitted tax evasion. *National Tax Journal* 37, 489–496.

Matsueda, Ross L. 2006. Criminological Implications of the Thought of George Herbert Mead. In *Sociological theory and criminological research: Views from Europe and the United States*, (pp. 77–108). Oxford, UK: Elsevier Science.

Mayo, James M. 1993. *The American Grocery Store: The Business Evolution of an Architectural Space*. Westport, CT: Greenwood Press.

Mead, George Herbert, and Charles W. Morris. 1934. *Mind, self & society from the standpoint of a social behaviorist*. Chicago, Ill.: University of Chicago Press.

Morales, Alfonso. 1993. Making money at the market: The social and economic logic of informal markets, Department of Sociology, Northwestern University, Evanston, IL.

Morales, Alfonso. 1997. How Street Vendors Organize Risk. *The International Journal of Sociology and Social Policy*.

Morales, Alfonso. 1998. Income Tax Compliance and Alternative Views of Ethics and Human Nature. *Journal of Accounting, Ethics and Public Policy* 1 (3):380–400.

Morales, Alfonso. 2000. Peddling Policy: Street vending in historical and contemporary context. *International Journal of Sociology and Social Policy* 20 (3):14.

Morales, Alfonso, Steve Balkin, and Joe Persky. 1995. "The Value of Benefits of a Public Street Market: The Case of Maxwell Street.". *Economic Development Quarterly* (9):17.

Morales, Alfonso. 2006. *New Maxwell Street Market: It's Present and Future*. Maxwell Street Foundation.

Morales, Alfonso. 2009. Public Markets as Community Development Tools. *Journal of Planning Education and Research* 28(4):426–440.

Morales, Alfonso. 2010. Planning and the Self-Organization of Marketplaces. *Journal of Planning Education and Research*. 30(2):182–197.

Morales, Alfonso, and Gregg Kettles. 2009. Healthy Food Outside: Farmers' Markets, Taco Trucks, and Sidewalk Fruit Vendors. *The Journal of Contemporary Health Law and Policy* 26 (20):20–48.

Morales, Alfonso, and Gregg Kettles. 2009. Zoning for Markets and Street Merchants. *Zoning Practice* 25 (1).

Moran, B. I. 2003. Taxation. In P. Cane & M. Tushnet (Eds.), *The Oxford Handbook of Legal Studies* (pp. 183–201): Oxford University Press.

Rawlings, G. 2003. Cultural narratives of taxation and citizenship: Fairness, groups and globalisation. *Australian Journal of Social Issues, 38*(3), 269–306.

Rossotti, C. O. 2002. *Report to the IRS Oversight Board: Assessment of the IRS and the Tax System*. Washington D.C., September.

Scholz, John T. and Mark Lubell. 1998a. Adaptive political attitudes: Duty, trust and fear as monitors of tax policy *American Journal of Political Science* 42, 903–920.

Scholz, John T. and Mark Lubell. 1998b. Trust and taxpaying: Testing the heuristic approach to collective action *American Journal of Political Science* 42, 398–417.

Schorr, Lisbeth, B. 1997. Common Purpose: Strengthening Families and Neighborhoods to Rebuild America. New York, NY: Doubleday.

Stiglitz, Joseph. 2002. *Globalization and its Discontents* New York: W. W. Norton.

Tamanaha, Brian Z. 1997. *Realistic socio-legal theory: pragmatism and a social theory of law, Oxford socio-legal studies*. Oxford: Clarendon Press.

Tangires, Helen. 2003. Public Markets and Civic Culture in Nineteenth-Century America. Baltimore, MD: Johns Hopkins University Press.

Walker, Janelle L. 2000. Saving Maxwell Street: People, power, and the politics of urban aesthetics in Chicago. Dissertation, Indiana University, Bloomington.

Willis, P. 1977. *Learning to Labor: How Working Class Kids Get Working Class Jobs*. New York: Columbia University Press.

Wrong, Dennis H. 1961. The Oversocialized Conception of Man in Modern Sociology. *American Sociological Review* 26:11.

Chapter 6
Towards a Convergence of the Ethics of Tax Evasion and Secession

Marian Eabrasu

Introduction

Tax evasion and secession usually receive different treatments. Secession is perceived as a distinguished argument in ethics. It is at stake in numerous philosophical debates and very often embedded within the mainstream democratic theory for defending minority rights. On the contrary, if we consider the number of occurrences in philosophical debates, tax evasion appears to be a far less significant argument. With the exception of a minority of libertarian scholars (who in every way perceive the State as immoral), mainstream philosophers discard tax evasion as unethical. In any event, it is important to note that most scholars who seem disposed to grant secession rights to minorities disagree on the morality of tax evasion. Why do these theories of secession and tax evasion remain separated? Is there a logical obstacle to their association? These are precisely the questions that this chapter aims at addressing.

The pertinence of this study lies in the fact that our very simple intuitions suggest important similarities between secession and tax evasion. All secessionists are tax evaders at least in respect to the State from which they are seceding, and all tax evaders are secessionist in the sense that they are at odds with the institutional framework of the State where they were making profits. Insofar as secession is not a constitutional provision, both tax evaders and secessionists are illegal. Nevertheless their illegality, secession and tax evasion might altogether be morally acceptable if they are carried out against illegitimate governments. At any rate, if the act of seceding is morally acceptable, then ipso facto tax evasion is also morally acceptable and vice versa.

This chapter precisely plans to demonstrate the theoretical validity of these intuitions. It does not simply aim at assessing the morality of tax evasion but rather

M. Eabrasu (✉)
Department of Economics, Champagne School of Management,
217, Avenue Pierre Brossolette, BP 710, 10002 Troyes Cedex, France
e-mail: Eabrasu@yahoo.com

R.W. McGee (ed.), *The Ethics of Tax Evasion: Perspectives in Theory and Practice*,
DOI 10.1007/978-1-4614-1287-8_6, © Springer Science+Business Media, LLC 2012

at arguing that whenever secession is considered moral, so should tax evasion. The current argumentation will be displayed through a systematic and step-by-step inquiry into the alleged differences between these theories. We will begin with the core of the secessionist argument (the territorial claim) in order to show that it is shared by both secession and tax evasion theories. Second, we discuss the commonly assumed opposition between secession (lying on a collective territorial claim) and tax evasion (lying on an individual territorial claim) in order to show that there are more connections than differences between these two theories. Third, we will argue that both theories have a common normative structure. Therefore, the justification of secession must imply *ceteris paribus*, a justification of tax evasion.

Territorial Claim

Secession is built upon a strong claim, which we may call the *territorial claim* following Brilmayer's seminal study on this topic. "When individuals seek to secede, they are making a claim to territory. They wish a piece of land for their future, a piece of land on which they will be able to make their own claims of integrity of territorial borders. Their claim is typically centred on a piece of land that they possessed in the past, and upon which they claim territorial integrity" (Brilmayer 1991: 201). The territorial claim underlines the fact that some scarce resources such as land have particular characteristics in the sense that they cannot be transported. It is precisely in this sense that the right to secession is designed to complement the right to emigration. When a person takes advantage of the right to emigrate, there remain some resources in her property, such as land and real estate, which cannot be transported. Hence, the territorial claim upgrades the right to the free movement of persons and property by taking into account the claims on immutable goods (Brilmayer 1991: 187).

However, the territorial claim is not only at the core of the theory of secession but also central to the theory of tax evasion. Just like secessionists, tax evaders want to keep control of their movable and unmovable property instead of emigrating (which implies leaving or selling their land and real estate). Tax evaders and secessionists assume their property rights on land and thus feel legitimate to continue to live on the respective territory. Furthermore, by evading taxes, a person demonstrates her aversion for the public budget. Hence, not only the action of seceding but also the action of evading taxes is directed against the State. While the former consists in rejecting the whole institutional framework of the State, the latter is set up to keep one's revenues away from the State. Consequently, both the secessionist and the tax evader formulate altogether an implicit claim for redistributing the taxes according to their own preferences: either by creating a different political entity (as secessionists do) or by simply separating private and public budgets (as tax evaders do). Even thought their aims might differ – political for secessionists and personal for tax evaders – both kinds of territorial claims contest the authority of a given coercive political arrangement over the respective territory in raising taxes. In a nutshell, in spite of their different forms of action, a secessionist and a tax evader altogether formulate a territorial claim.

Since the territorial claim is at the core of both theories, it becomes important to grasp its justifications. Who is entitled to formulate a territorial claim? When does a territorial claim become morally acceptable? While the answer to the former question will be discussed in the next section, let us now focus on the latter one. In a nutshell, we have to understand how to discern a legitimate territorial claim from an illegitimate moral claim. Two arguments converge in justifying secession: the *preexistence* of an ethnically homogenous group of individuals on a given territory and the *permanent occupation* of the respective territory by the respective group. These justifications are discussed one after another, and we demonstrate their convergence with the arguments in favor of tax evasion.

The former argument "is based on a claim to indigenousness. Many groups in all parts of the world claim to be indigenous" (Moore 2001: 184). According to this line of argumentation, the territorial claim is justified when secessionists can attest the anteriority of their presence on the respective territory with regard to other groups of individuals or to the State from which they intend to secede. "The claim to territory which flows from indigenousness is primarily a claim to prior, rightful ownership, based on first occupancy. Since the indigenous people are rightful owners of the land, the later arrivals were engaged in 'theft'. This is the suggestion behind the title of a recent book on American history, *Stolen Continents: The 'New World' Through Indian Eyes* and it has intuitive plausibility in so far as everyone can understand the idea that I have a right to evict unwelcomed guests from my home, or to set the terms under which guests can stay" (Moore 2001: 184).

This justification of the territorial claim consists in formulating property rights on land on the model of the Lockean homesteading principle. "Whatsoever, then, he removes out of the state that Nature hath provided and left it in, he hath mixed his labour with it, and joined to it something that is his own, and thereby makes it his property" (Locke 1980: 111–12). The homesteading principle maintains that a person is the rightful owner of a resource if she was the first one to occupy it. If two persons contend the same piece of land, the earliest one arrived on that land is morally entitled to own it. This type of justification is mainly brought into play when an indigenous secessionist demand is at stake but also when the current State has obviously been more recently created than the secessionist part. For instance, it may uphold the Basque call for secession in Spain.

From this point of view, the structure of the justification in favor of secession bears a salient resemblance to the argument in favor of tax evasion. Inasmuch as we refer to freely produced and/or acquired resources, tax evasion (just like secession) is morally acceptable from the point of view of the Lockean homesteading theory. Tax evaders and secessionists assume their property rights on land and feel legitimate to continue to live on the respective territory. In spite of their different forms of action, a secessionist and a tax evader ground their territorial claim on the fact that they are legitimate successors (i.e., they legitimately inherited from their ancestors the respective piece of land).

Yet, the interpretation of land inheritance provided by most of the scholars defending secession remains superficial. Following this rationale, the Basques would have the right to secede from Spain because their ethnic group was there before the Castilians. This type of moral argument would grant ownership right only to the most ancient civilizations, cultures, ethnical groups, etc. The preexistence argument does not take into account the possibility that the *most ancient* ethnic group we know today might not be the *first come* ethnic group and that it might have wrongfully occupied the respective territory. From this point of view, one can neither sell nor rent a piece of land, nor can she associate with other groups. These are important insufficiencies of this interpretation of inheritance and they can be found at the origin of important territorial disputes. Indeed, there are secessionist conflicts, such as ex-Yugoslavia, where both sides justify their territorial claim by their earlier presence (Transchel 2006). Moreover, there are territorial claims where the preexistence on the respective territory may be questionable as it is in the case of Padania (Agnew 2002: 178).

However, these limits of the interpretation of inheritance within the mainstream theory of secession can be overcome if we add to the Lockean homesteading a provision regarding the morality of property title transfer. From this point of view, the ethics of tax evasion may shed a new light on this issue. While indigenes refer to ethnical, cultural, or linguistic footprints, tax evaders refer to a variant of the natural law which anchors ownership rights on voluntary transaction. It is precisely in the merit of this difference that we can better explain why it is more difficult for secessionists than it is for tax evaders to prove their preexistence. For determining who came first, it is far easier to investigate the voluntary character of each past transaction on land than it is to identify the origins of a homogenous culture, language, or ethnic group. Undoubtedly, the voluntary character of a transaction might also be questionable and/or difficult to determine. However, comparatively, it must be easier to assess if the land was acquired through a voluntary transaction than it is to say if the land was first occupied by a given ethnic group.

As to the second justification of the territorial claim, secessionists are entitled to secede provided that they were permanently occupying the respective territory. "The people who inhabit a certain territory form a political community. Though custom and practice as well as by explicit political decision they create laws, establish individual or collective property rights, engage in public works, shape the physical appearance of the territory. Over time this takes on symbolic significance as they bury their dead in certain places, establish shrines or secular monuments and so forth. All these activities give them an attachment to the land that cannot be matched by any rival claimants. This in turn justifies their claim to exercise continuing political authority over that territory. It trumps the purely historical claim of a rival group who argue that their ancestors once ruled the land in question" (Miller 1998: 68).

Contrary to the previous type of justification referring to the preexistence of the secessionist group, this justification grounded on the continuous presence of the respective secessionist group is more comprehensive. It suits not only the Basques in Spain but also the political communities derived from compact immigration such as the Quebecois in Canada. In this case, it should be far easier to attest the presence of secessionists than to prove their preexistence. It is maybe for this reason that most separatist demands are justified on the grounds of a permanent continuity on the respective territory. However, this type of justification often engenders incompatible secessionist demands. The territorial claims formulated by Quebecois in Canada concur with the territorial claims formulated by the English-speaking community. It goes the same for most of the secessionist demands. Based on their continuous presence, why should the Catalans or the Flemish be more entitled to formulate their territorial claims than the Spaniards or the Belgians? In all these cases, additional justification is required to discern which territorial claim is moral.

The continuous presence of an ethnic cultural or linguistic group remains a highly unsatisfactory criterion for discerning the moral acceptability of a territorial claim. The *de facto* presence of a given group cannot say much about who ought to occupy the respective territory. The fact that a person has been sitting on a chair for several hours does not inform the observer regarding the identity of the owner of the chair. Deleting the distinction between effective control and legitimate ownership would create even greater confusion regarding the morality of territorial claims. Therefore, at least for the sake of clarity, the scholars who justify the secession right should consider improving the argument of continuous presence with a more consistent moral argument. The ideas of homesteading and voluntary exchange usually used for legitimizing tax evasion would perfectly suit this purpose. It would be far more unambiguous to settle territorial disputes by assigning moral rights on a given piece of land to specific persons, instead of letting different groups of persons formulate incompatible territorial claims on the same piece of land.

Up to now, we showed that beyond their different justifications, secession and tax evasion formulate altogether the same territorial claim. This is to say that, whatever the reason – preexistence or continuous presence – if the territorial claim is morally acceptable it works for secession but also for tax evasion. As to the justification's rationale, we added that the moral argument usually engaged in support of tax evasion is suitable to augment the mainstream secessionist arguments. Notwithstanding this demonstration, most scholars who uphold secession are still reluctant when it comes to defending tax evasion. They usually distinguish collective and individual rights on land and in the meantime dismiss individual territorial claims as immoral. Since the territorial claim that a tax evader formulates is more akin to individual property rights, there must be no logical obligation to derive the morality of tax evasion from the morality of secession. Let us now take a step further and address this issue in the next section.

Individual Versus Collective Territorial Claim

Our most basic intuitions lead us to think that it is morally permissible for a slave to evade or for a citizen to emigrate. Most scholars sharing the same intuitions consider that these rights, derived from the right to self-ownership, must be assigned individually to each person *qua* person. However, when it comes to secession, the same right to self-ownership – accounting for the morality of slave resistance and emigration – is renamed as a right to self-determination and is assigned collectively to some groups of people, based on the fact that these people speak the same language, have the same ethnic background or a common culture. Indeed, the mainstream defense of secession insists on its collective character and contrasts it with individual rights such as the right to free-speech and to emigration. From this point of view, the secessionists' collective territorial claim appears to be at the opposite of individual territorial claims formulated by tax evaders. This section plans to explain why this opposition is superficial.

At the outset, it is important to note that the collective territorial claim formulated by secessionists differs from Locke's homesteading principle (Locke 1980: 111–12) and is more akin to the Hobbesian right to "live in." Hobbes lists the "live in" right among the rights that individuals retain while they are supposed to adhere to the social contract. "As it was necessary that a man should not retain his right to every thing, so also was it that he should retain his right to some things: to his own body (for example) the right of defending, whereof he could not transfer to the use of fire, water, free air, and place to live in, and to all things necessary for life" (Hobbes 2004: 61). This Hobbesian right has two essential features: it *can be assigned collectively* and it *is enforceable against the State*. "[The Hobbes's right to 'live in'] is not, indeed, to a particular place, but it is enforceable against the State, which exists to protect it; the State's claim to territorial jurisdiction derives ultimately from this individual right to place. Hence the right has a collective as well an individual form, and these two come into conflict" (Walzer 1983: 43). The conflict mentioned by Walzer is actually a conflict between the two types of territorial claims which can be both enforceable against the State: an individual one (grounded on the Lockean principle of "homesteading") and a collective one (grounded on the Hobbesian right to "live in").

Yet, none of these features (the collective assignment and enforceability against the State) suffices to distinguish secession from tax evasion. On the contrary, they denote a significant convergence between these theories. Just like a secessionist, a tax evader believes that her rights are enforceable against the State and that she may associate with others in order to claim her rights collectively. This is the case because the territorial claim formulated by secessionists and tax evaders is grounded on *moral rights* and not on the *legal rights* established by the State itself. Indeed, it would be absurd to justify a separation from the State on the ground of the legal rights assigned by the State.

Although, it is not entirely inconceivable to make the moral right to secede a legal right by inserting it explicitly in a constitution (McGee 1992), it is much more difficult to imagine a constitution explicitly granting the right to tax evasion. If secession and tax evasion are morally acceptable, it is precisely because their territorial claims have a moral foundation which is independent from the State's institution of private property. "If every person has a right to defend – even by force – his person, his liberty, and his property, then it follows that a group of men have the right to organize and support a common force to protect these rights constantly. The law is the organization of the natural right of lawful defense. It is the substitution of a common force for individual forces. And this common force is to do only what the individual forces have a natural and lawful right to do: to protect persons, liberties, and properties; to maintain the right of each, and to cause *justice* to reign over us all" (Bastiat 1950: 6–7). Tax evaders share with secessionists the aim to "break the compulsory ties with a government which they no longer accept" (Hülsmann 2003: 410).

However, beyond the agreement on the fact that the territorial claim must be morally enforceable against the State, most scholars defending secession insist on the fact that secession is essentially a collective claim. "Group rights are ascribed to collections of individuals and can only be exercised collectively or at least on behalf of the collective, usually through some mechanism of political representation. The right to secede, as we have been understanding it, is a group right" (Buchanan 1991: 74–75). Whatever a collective right may be, its main characteristic is that it is assigned collectively to a group of individuals *qua* group by virtue of their group identity.

Unlike an individual right, which considers the single individual as the basic moral unit, a collective right takes a specific group of individuals – apparently homogenous from one or more points of view (religion, language, ethnicity, etc.) – to be the basic moral unit. Yet, there should be no disagreement between scholars maintaining the morality of tax evasion and secession based on the fact that the territorial claim may be formulated collectively. There is no logical obstacle to conceive tax evaders formulating a collective territorial claim. Also, the collective territorial claim formulated by secessionists includes a collection of independent individual claims or shares of individual territorial claims. "There is no theoretical reason why the size of the seceding group cannot be as small as a single individual, although there may be some technical difficulties involved when the entity seceding is this small" (McGee 2004: 137).

In order to better assess the pertinence of this idea of a collective territorial claim, let us turn back to the question that was left aside in the previous section: Who is entitled to formulate a territorial claim? Supposing that the territorial claim is justified (either by the preexistence or by continuous presence), we still need to formulate a criterion for identifying those who may legitimately formulate territorial claims. In case we admit that only groups *qua* groups are eligible to secede, we still have to specify who these groups are. Is any group of people entitled to secede provided that their ancestors were preexistent or that they have ancestors who marked their continuous presence on the respective territory? Which are the pertinent criteria for assigning collective territorial claims?

At the outset, it is important to note that for identifying groups *qua* groups, we must select highly homogenous groups. Yet the very idea of a homogenous ethnic group is notoriously fuzzy (O'Reilly 2001). There is no general agreement on the essential properties that might define it (Brubaker 1998: 238). The idea of homogenous ethnicity must be confronted with increasing mixed marriages and multilingualism (Brubaker 1998: 256). Immigration, exchanges, and mass tourism are also important challenges for the durability of a compact ethnic group. Inasmuch as the justification of secession depends upon the particular definition of ethnicity, nation, and culture, a disagreement with one of these conceptions would suffice for refuting the right to secede to a particular group of persons. For example, it would suffice to assert that the fact of speaking the same language does not account for a strong ethnic tie in order to deny the right to secession of the Quebecois. Most of the scholars agree that it is "hopelessly unrealistic to assume that the only means of political organisation available is one in which territorially sovereign bounded states must mirror the location of cultural and national groups as they themselves adapt and change" (Bishai 1998: 104).

Furthermore, even if we might identify a homogenous ethnic group, it should be very difficult to consider it to be a genuine ethnic group especially if we take into account the multiplicity of allegiances (Balibar and Wallerstein 1991). For instance, within an ethnic group, there may be individuals having original religious beliefs or cultural practices. The difficulty of identifying a genuine homogenous group (i.e., preexistent or independent of the State's action) becomes even more patent, especially if we agree with Kymlicka that "the idea of State's ethnocultural neutrality is simply a myth" (Kymlicka 2002: 19). Indeed, one can simply argue that what we might consider today as a homogenous ethnic group is actually the implicit result of a previous State's policies of assimilation or segregation (Cook 2003). On top of these difficulties in identifying a homogenous ethnic group, we must add that it is practically impossible to separate ethnic territorial claims from their economic motivations (Wallerstein 1961: 88).

A group of persons planning to separate from a larger political arrangement might call the attention on the fact that they have similar economic interests. "These triggering mechanisms have existed throughout history. One example is from the beginning of recorded history: the secession of the ten northern tribes of Israel was economic in nature: it was triggered by the coming to power of Rehoboam, son of Solomon (in 930 BC), who increased taxes upon taking power. The population, dissatisfied with the high rates of taxation that they were forced to pay, declared their secession" (Bookman 1993: 170). In order to better grasp this argument, it is important to note that any secessionist group is obviously composed of definite individuals. It is not the group as such who is economically disadvantaged but the concrete particular persons. Individuals might be disadvantaged in virtue of their belonging to an ethnic group or a social class but there is no such thing as an abstract collective territorial claim (Burg 2004). For all these reasons, it must be difficult to circumscribe a group *qua* group on an ethnic criterion in order to grant it a moral right to secede.

At any rate, there are obvious technical obstacles for circumscribing territories that are exclusively inhabited by homogenous ethnic groups. Actually, all territorial claims formulated by secessionists also concern people from different ethnic groups. Why should the territorial claim of some ethnic group prevail over another? Even if we admit that the Basques are eligible for secession as a homogenous ethnic group, it must be difficult to identify pieces of land inhabited only by Basques. The map of a hypothetical Basque country would surely have a lot of holes. However, the actual map claimed by Basque secessionists does not overlap the portions exclusively inhabited by Basques but all the parts of a declared historic Basque country. With different words, the collective territorial claim formulated by secessionists does not simply overlap with the sum of individual property rights formulated by secessionists.

> We might think initially that what is at stake here is an aggregate of property rights: I own this plot, you own that, and so all of us together own the territory that we call Britain. If that were the right way to think about the problem, then a secessionist group occupying a compact area would simply have to assert their joint property rights to establish a conclusive claim to the land they want to take with them. But as Buchanan has argued, the relationship between a people and their territory cannot properly be understood in these terms. When we say that Iceland belongs to Icelanders (to take a simple case), we do not mean that they own it as property; we mean that they have a legitimate claim to exercise authority over Iceland, to determine what happens in that island, including what individual property rights there are going to be. This authority is exercised in practice by the state on the people's behalf, but the Icelanders' claim to authority is not reducible to the authority of the Icelandic state, as we can see if (per impossible) we were to imagine a revolutionary upheaval in that country which established an entirely new set of political institutions. The Icelanders' claim to control Iceland would survive such political cataclysm (Miller 1998: 68).

We emphasized this long quotation because it perfectly illustrates the key feature of the alleged specificity of secession with respect to tax evasion: the *political* territorial claim, i.e., a territorial claim that can only be exercised collectively and that can only be used for exercising the authority on the respective land. However, we first have to assess the pertinence of this political territorial claim before using it to distinguish secession from tax evasion.

In line with most scholars defending secession, Miller argues that the secessionist territorial claim does not simply overlap the sum of individual property rights. Yet, why could an ethnic group (whatever its definition might be) be entitled to formulate a territorial claim without *effectively* owning the respective territory? To be sure, the effective ownership must refer to moral property rights and not to the legal property rights defined by the current State. In this case, it would be difficult to see why the political territorial claim formulated by the Flemish over Brabant would be more legitimate than the property rights acquired by Walloons in the region of Brussels. Asserting that past people spoke roughly the same language or had the same customs as the people who assert today their Flemish origins remains highly unconvincing insofar as the Walloons may refer to their Roman ancestors. Secession and tax evasion are properly understood as moral claims as opposed to legal claims.

In a nutshell, the territorial claim formulated by the Basques (or any other secessionist group) must be grounded on *moral* (not legal) and *concrete* property rights. Otherwise, the respective claims would remain just claims and, in addition, various and incompatible territorial claims might be formulated over the same piece of land. If secessionists aim to show that their claimed territory is not randomly chosen, they need to justify within a moral framework that they concretely *own* the land which is claimed. Secessionists may refer for instance to the homesteading principle in order to prove that, individually or collectively, they voluntary received the land (as present or inheritance) or bought it. Inasmuch as reference is made to moral rights and not to legal rights, these transactions are independent from the State's institutions.

From this point of view, there is no difference between secession and tax evasion. Both actions must refer to *concrete moral rights* over the respective territory. Just like secessionists, tax evaders must effectively own the resources on which they do not pay taxes. Such ownership must necessarily be grounded on *moral* property rights. This is to say that each tax evader must have voluntarily acquired the resources on which she does not pay taxes. By all moral standards, a person cannot claim moral property rights on a stolen commodity. Hence, tax evasion cannot be defended on moral grounds in a case where the goods were stolen. Indeed, the scholars who defend tax evasion associate taxes with theft, so they can justify tax evasion as self-defence against a coercive (and therefore immoral) form of payment. This argument leads us to discuss the core of the convergence between secession and tax evasion: the normative claim.

Normative Claim

When the secessionists formulate a territorial claim, they challenge the ongoing political order and by the same token they plan to substitute it (Brilmayer 1991: 186). Besides various justifications of the territorial claim discussed in the previous sections, it is important to note that secession is unanimously justified when it is directed against a totalitarian regime. Hence, the *normative claim*: secession is legitimate every time it opposes an illegitimate government. This *normative claim* is *a fortiori* applicable to taxation: tax evasion is legitimate every time it opposes an illegitimate government. Taxation is morally unacceptable not only for libertarians who dismiss as immoral any form of nonprovoked violence – and the State in particular – but also for those who dismiss as illegitimate a particular political arrangement (Bagus et al. 2011). Such a fine-tuning should contribute to unveil a neglected line of defence for tax evasion and eventually to fill to gap between the ethics of secession and tax evasion.

To begin with, we can first note that the justification of secession or tax evasion is very often derived from the justification of revolution. In other words, the occasions in which secession or tax evasion appear to be legitimate are roughly the same as the cases where revolution would be legitimate. Insofar as secession is perceived as a form of self-defence and self-resistance, its justification roughly follows the same pattern of argumentation as the justification of the revolution. As John Locke puts it, "whosoever uses force without right, as every one does in society, who does it without law, puts himself into a state of war with those against whom he so uses it; and in that state all former ties are cancelled, all other rights cease, and every one has a right to defend himself, and to resist the aggressor" (Locke 1980: 202). Just like a revolutionary movement, the acts of seceding or evading taxes appear to be adequate and suitable replies to an illegitimate political arrangement.

However, the drives for opposing an illegitimate political arrangement may be very different. A revolutionary wants to dissolve the political order, while a secessionist wants to reorganize the territory. "He that will with any clearness speak of the dissolution of government, ought in the first place to distinguish between the dissolution of the society and the dissolution of the government" (Locke 1980: 193). From this point of view, tax evasion is much more akin to secession than it is to revolution. "The object of the exercise of the right to secede is not to overthrow the government, but only to sever the government's control over that portion of the territory" (Brubaker 1998: 231). *Ceteris paribus*, tax evasion does not depose the government but restricts its control. Given the difficulties of the Italian government in collecting taxes in Sicily (Gambetta 1996: 163), we can observe that tax evasion does not cause the downfall of the Italian government but restrains its control on this specific area.

The normative claim we previously outlined maintains that secession (or tax evasion) is legitimate when these actions oppose an illegitimate government. It is commonly stated that a government loses its legitimacy "when the people suffer prolonged and serious injustices" (Brubaker 1998: 231). At the outset, it is important to see that this expression still does not help us very much in circumscribing illegitimate government and, hence, legitimate secession (tax evasion). Nevertheless, we need to spell out what prolonged and serious injustice exactly means. Still, "what is needed is a coherent set of principles to distinguish legitimate from illegitimate secession" (Buchanan 1997: 303). In order to determine such a theoretical framework, we necessarily need to refer to current theories of justice. Different standards of justice may account for different strategies of legitimating secession (or tax evasion). "So, depending upon which type of theory of justice, libertarian or welfarist, we espouse, the question of whether the secessionists are the better off may make a crucial difference as to whether we judge secession to be justified" (Buchanan 1991: 17). To put it differently, secession might be morally acceptable within a definite normative framework and at the same time morally unacceptable within another normative framework.

The broadest normative view maintains that secession is "one solution to the problem of tyranny" (Freeman 1998: 12). This idea rests on a common presupposition describing tyranny as a political arrangement which violates some basic individual rights such as the right to emigration (Beran 1977: 268). Therefore, according to most authors, secession is legitimate insofar as it is directed against a government denying the right to free movement of persons. Clearly, if secession is legitimate in this situation so should tax evasion be. However, secession can be justified beyond a totalitarian regime. "Even though they live in prosperous liberal states, with firm guarantees of their civil and political rights, the Flemish and Québécois may be moving down to the road to independence. The threat to secession has arisen in both capitalist and communist countries, in both democracies and military dictatorships, in both prosperous and impoverished countries"(Kymlicka 1998: 110). There are territorial claims even in democratic states granting most individuals rights to free-speech and free movement (Höffe 2007 278–81). It is possible to justify secession within a democratic framework precisely because, as we emphasized since the beginning of this chapter, the territorial claim is logically independent from the right to emigrate, although both of them rest on the rhetoric of consent.

However, "the rhetoric of consent obscures the importance of territorial claims. Consent theory seems to suggest that the only important factor is whether an individual chooses to be part of the existing state. The rhetoric does not distinguish, however, between those who may avoid state authority only by leaving and those who may avoid state authority while remaining where they are" (Brilmayer 1991: 189). Although the right to emigrate might be granted, it still does not suffice to ensure the absence of coercion. The citizens of the former state of RDA did not cease to be free only when the Berlin wall was erected. More generally, this assimilation would conceal the very nature of theft and aggression. An aggression is not less an aggression because the aggressor releases her victim. It is precisely the dehomogenization of consent and emigration that makes possible the secessionist's claim in a democratic state. Although they are free to quit Spain, the inhabitants of the Basque Country still feel coerced by the Spanish democratic political arrangement. The normative claim is a natural complement of the territorial claim.

In the light shed by this idea, the convergence between tax evasion and secession appears more clearly. Tax evasion can thus be justified even in respect to a democratic State granting all basic liberties. The justification of tax evasion in a democracy follows roughly the same pattern as the justification of secession, previously emphasized. The point we want to stress here is that whatever the justification of secession might be, tax evasion can be defended on the same grounds. Therefore, if secession is defended within a democratic framework, so should tax evasion. Furthermore, in light of this idea, we can now see that there should be more than one line of defence for tax evasion. In addition to the classical libertarian justification (Bagus et al. 2011), the case for tax evasion is implicitly defended also by a variety of arguments usually formulated in favor of secession: communitarian, (Gilbert 1998: 220), democratic (Beran 1998: 41), etc.

All these normative frameworks share the presupposition that secession rights ought to be assigned as a solution to a discriminating redistribution of resources between different regions often between a state and its colonies. "But if discriminatory redistribution can justify secession from an imperial state that happens to lie across the sea (as in the case of Belgium or France and their African colonies or, for that matter, as in the case of the thirteen American colonies and Britain), why does it not justify secession from an empire (such as the Soviet Union) whose subject peoples happen to occupy the same landmass as their exploiters" (Buchanan 1997: 312). The discrimination of a specific group of citizens (such as an ethnic or religious minority group) in respect to other groups belonging to the same State legitimizes the secessionist movement of the respective discriminated group. Indeed, "to ignore discriminatory redistribution is to neglect what is probably the most common grievance secessionists raise. Discriminatory redistribution was universally, if not implicitly, recognised as *a* major justification, if not *the* major justification for the legitimacy of that wave of secessionist movements that has received the widest and firmest support from international legal doctrine and institutional practice so far: cases in which peoples severed colonial territory from colonial empires, cast the yoke of colonialism, and established their own independent states" (Buchanan 1997: 312). This is the case, precisely because "a State which encouraged or even merely turned a blind eye to hostility directed at minority identities would risk undermining its own legitimacy" (Preece 2005: 161).

Yet, wouldn't it be arbitrary to restrict the right to secede only to given ethnic groups? We saw in the previous section the difficulties in pertinently circumscribing genuine and homogenous groups. Since the definition of such groups depends on contingent parameters, the right to secession would be arbitrarily assigned if it were restricted to ethnic communities (Höffe 2007: 278–81). Let aside the rare discriminatory policies such as the special rights constitutionally granted to Muslims under Shariah Law or to Malaysia's Malay majority (Jomo 2004), it should be difficult to justify most of the secessionist claims (Basques, Quebecois, Flemish, etc.). Given the manifest difficulties in distinguishing homogenous groups of net tax payers and net tax receivers, we may reasonably limit to identifying individual net tax payers and grant them the right to secede.

Eventually, inasmuch as it is effectively feasible, they may associate with each other and formulate a collective territorial claim. "A number of government actions could thus be seen as illegitimate: taxing people who work and giving the proceeds to people who do not work; taxing all the people to pay for the construction of a bridge in one state (a number of pork-barrel projects fall under this genre); taxing all the people and using the proceeds to fund scholarships for persons of a certain race; preventing landlords from charging the market rate for their apartments (rent control laws); and so on. The list can go on and on, especially in welfare states, which hold redistribution of wealth to be one of the highest goals" (McGee 1994: 19). In light of this argumentation, secession and tax evasion converge whatever their ethical grounds.

Furthermore, if we agree on the injustice of the discriminatory policy, wouldn't it be discriminatory to reserve the right to secession only to genuinely homogenous ethnic groups? By all moral standards, restricting the access to fundamental rights (such as the right to emigration or free-speech) only to persons belonging to a genuine homogenous group would be inacceptable. Why, then, should we proceed differently when it comes to secession (which for most scholars is also a fundamental right)? If we set aside any personal prejudice against secession and we refer exclusively to the argument's coherence, we must admit that territorial claim should receive the same treatment as the claims to free movement and to free-speech. Either we admit that discriminatory policies are acceptable (and in this case there is scarcely any reason to grant secession rights to any particular group of persons) or we consider that the discriminatory policies are unacceptable (but in this case we can no longer maintain that individual discrimination is acceptable). To put it differently, there is no logical reason to consider collective discrimination unacceptable and at the same time to maintain that individual discrimination is acceptable. By all logical standards, discriminatory policies are not directed against *qua* groups but are targeting individuals as such or as members of a definite ethnic, religious, linguistic, or cultural group.

In line with this argument, if the right to secede is to be assigned on an individualistic basis (i.e., to individuals as such or as member of one or more groups), then there is a perfect convergence with the ethics of tax evasion. "Individuals who were despised as a result of their race, ethnicity, religion or language for example, would have serious grievances against the state which allowed such (mis)treatment. Why should they pay taxes or serve in the armed forces or in other ways be responsible citizens if that were the case?" (Preece 2005: 161). The State's quintessence is the redistribution of resources among its citizens and, consequently, the unremitting discrimination. By appealing to tax evasion, a citizen demonstrates that she is considering herself to be discriminated against with respect to the other citizens and aims at protecting her revenues while formulating a territorial claim. Although most scholars focus on ethnic, religious, and linguistic groups, it is important to keep in mind that only individuals are the ultimate victims of discriminatory policies. Tax evasion and secession denote complementary territorial claims with a similar normative scaffold.

To sum all up, if an individual (or a group of individuals) is entitled to secede, then – for coherence reasons – the same individual (or group of individuals) has a moral right to evade taxes.

Conclusion

This chapter revealed important paths of convergence between the theories of secession and tax evasion. The attentive study of the main arguments in favor of secession showed that there are no important differences with the arguments in favor of tax evasion. Moreover, not only the justifications for secession can also be used for defending tax evasion, but their accuracy may even be improved when they are applied to tax evasion. Based on the previous argumentation, we conclude that secession and tax evasion bear a salient resemblance both from a descriptive and normative perspective. As a final point, we will recapitulate the main points of this convergence and suggest a few directions for future research opened in the merit of this convergence.

Certainly, tax evasion is illegal with regard to the State, but so is secession. Save constitutional specifications (McGee 1992), the seceding region is seen as illegal from the point of view of its former State. Besides their position with respect to the law, secession and tax evasion also have other formal similar characteristics. A State that ceases to collect taxes ceases to be a State. When a State ceases to enforce taxation in a given region, the respective region becomes ipso facto a different entity. An accurate illustration of this idea can be found in all political entities with limited international recognition such as the secessionist parts of the former Soviet Union (Transnistria, Nagorno-Karabakh, Abkhazia, South-Ossetia) (Bremmer 1991: 41). From a formal political point of view, these territories are a part of the former States to which they used to belong. The members of these political entities remain citizens of the former State and they even retain their passports. Yet, de facto the former States ceased to collect taxes in the secessionist regions. This is to say that the former States do not have any effective influence in the respective region and they have only a declarative claim on the respective territory. In descriptive terms, there is no difference between tax evasion and secession.

As we showed in this chapter, this is so because the theories of tax evasion and secession have a common theoretical structure. Tax evasion and secession denote territorial claims which distinguish them from emigration. Even when they are collective, the territorial claims are grounded on concrete individual property rights. There are important obstacles in conceiving a collective territorial claim due to the difficulty of identifying the groups eligible to formulate such a claim. Given the absence of a commonly accepted definition of ethnicity and the difficulties in conceiving an ethnically homogenous group, it must be complicated to justify an indivisible territorial claim. On the contrary, there is no logical obstacle in reducing collective territorial claims to individual property rights or shares of property rights. In a nutshell, when an individual (or group of individuals) concretely secede or evade taxes she aims at separating from a coercive order while remaining on the territory on which she claims moral property rights.

In addition, this chapter demonstrated that these theories are alike even from a normative point of view. Since both claims (secession and tax evasion) are directed against the State, they cannot lay on the legal rights defined by the State's institution of property rights but only on the moral rights defined according to a specific normative background. Why should the territorial claim formulated by Basques prevail over the territorial claim formulated by Castilians? There would be no reason in the absence of a normative background. Although most scholars discussing the issue of secession share the idea that not all forms of secession are legitimate, they are in profound disagreement as to which criterion should be used for distinguishing just and unjust secession (Buchanan 1997: 319). However, whatever the normative background, if some individuals are entitled to secede, they are also entitled to evade taxes.

This is so because of the common argumentative structure of tax evasion and secession. Both theories rest on effective territorial claims, i.e., on territorial claims formulated by concrete individual property rights. These property rights are assigned on the moral basis of voluntary transactions (exchange, endowment, inheritance) and they do not necessarily overlap legal property rights. However, this idea does not say that tax evasion or secession is intrinsically ethical. It is precisely the voluntary chain of past transactions that may help us to categorize them as such. This chapter only argued that the moral acceptability of tax evasion and secession are intrinsically bound.

This argumentation designed to fill the gap between secession and tax evasion should open new research perspectives regarding the strategies of separation. At the outset, this convergence between tax evaders and secessionists should lead to a reconsideration of the moral status of tax evaders and persuade against numerous prejudices regarding this practice. Tax evaders are not merely free-riders externalizing the costs and internalizing the benefits; they are also secessionists. Further research may inquire as to the social role of tax evaders as pacifist and discrete secessionists. From this point of view, tax evasion appears to be a particular type of action situated somewhere between *exit* and *voice* options (Hirschman 1970).

Tax evaders exit the State and, at the same time remain on the relevant territory. Yet, this particular tie that tax evaders have with their land makes them probably the most important whistleblowers regarding discriminatory policies in the respective state. Just like the "parents who home-school their children, or send them to private schools, have seceded from the government school system. People who charter their businesses in foreign countries are seceding from the American bureaucratic regulatory agencies, and firms that locate plants in Kansas or other right-to-work states do so to avoid politically imposed requirements to allow unionization. Cash markets and barter trade are common ways to secede from state monitoring of retail markets in order to collect taxes. Increasing numbers of Canadian citizens travel to the U.S. for rapid delivery of complex medical treatment, seceding from the Canadian system of socialized medicine" (Benson 1998: 243).

References

Agnew, J. A. 2002. *Place and Politics in Modern Italy.* Chicago: Chicago University Press.

Bagus, Ph, Block, W., Eabrasu, M., Howden, D. & Rostan, J. 2011. 'The Ethics of Tax Evasion.' *Business and Society Review*, 116:3, 375–401.

Balibar, E. & Wallerstein, I. 1991. *Race, Nation, Class. Ambiguous Identities.* London: Verso.

Bastiat, F. 1950. *The Law.* Irvington-on-Hudson, N.Y.: Foundation for Economic Education.

Benson, B. L. 1998. 'How to Secede in Business Without Really Leaving: Evidence of the Substitution of Arbitration for Litigation.' In D. Gordon (Ed.) *Secession, State & Liberty:* 243–87. New Brunswick: Transaction Publishers.

Beran, H. 1977. 'In defence of the consent theory of political obligation and authority.' *Ethics,* 87:3, 260–71.

Beran, H. 1998. 'Democratic Theory of Political Self-Determination.' In P. B. Lehning (Ed.) *Theories of secession:* 32–59. London: Routledge.

Bishai, L. 1998. 'Secession and the Problems of Liberal Theory.' In P. B. Lehning (Ed.) *Theories of secession:* 92–110. London: Routledge.

Bookman, M. Z. 1993. *The Economics of Secession.* Palgrave Macmillan.

Bremmer, I. 1991. 'Fraternal Illusions; Nations and Politics in the USSR.' *American Association for the Advancement of Slavic Studies.* Miami.

Brilmayer, L. 1991. 'Secession and self-determination. A territorial interpretation.' *Yale Journal of International Law,* 16, 177–202.

Brubaker, R. 1998. 'Myths and misconceptions in the study of nationalism.' In M. Moore (Ed.) *National self-determination and secession.* Oxford: Oxford University Press.

Buchanan, A. 1991. Secession. The morality of political divorce from Fort Sumter to Lithuania and Quebec. San Francisco: Westview.

Buchanan, A. 1997. 'Self-determination, secession and the rule of law.' In R. M. a. J. McMahan (Ed.) *The morality of nationalism.* Oxford: Oxford University Press.

Burg, D. F. 2004. A World History of Tax Rebellions. An Encyclopedia of Tax Rebels, Revolts, and Riots from Antiquity to the Present. New York: Routledge.

Cook, T. E. 2003. Separation, Assimilation, Accomodation. Contrasting Ethnic Minory Policies. London: Greenwood Publishing Group.

Freeman, M. 1998. 'The priority of function to structure. A new approach to secession.' In P. B. Lehning (Ed.) *Theories of secession.* Londres: Routledge.

Gambetta, D. 1996. The Sicilian Mafia. The Business of Private Protection. Harvard: Harvard University Press.

Gilbert, P. 1998. 'Good and bad causes for national secession.' In P. B. Lehning (Ed.) *Theories of secession.* London: Routledge.

Hirschman, O. A. 1970. *Exit, Voice and Loyality.* Cambirdge, Mass: Harvard Univesity Press.

Hobbes, T. 2004. The Elements of Law Natural and Politic. Kessinger Publishing.

Höffe, O. 2007. Democracy in an Age of Globalisation. Springer.

Hülsmann, G. 2003. 'Secession and the Production of Defense.' In H.-H. Hoppe (Ed.) *The Myth of National Defense*. Hans-Hermann Hoppe: Ludwig von Mises Institute.

Jomo, K. S. 2004. 'The New Economic Policy and Interethnic Relations in Malaysia.' New York: United Nations Research Institute for Social Development.

Kymlicka, W. 1998. 'Is Federalism a Viable Alternative to Secession ?' In P. B. Lehning (Ed.) *Theories of Secession:* 111–50. London: Routledge

Kymlicka, W. 2002. 'Western Political Theory and Ethnic Relations in Eastern Europe.' In K. W. a. O. M. (Ed.) *Managing Diversity in Plural Societies: Minorities, Migration and Nation-Building in Post-Communist Europe*: 13–105. Ottawa: Forum Eastern Europe

Locke, J. 1980. *Second Treatise of Government*. Hackett Publishing.

McGee, R. 1992. 'A Third Liberal Theory of secession.' *The Liverpool Law Review*, 14:1, 45–66.

McGee, R. 1994. 'Secession Reconsidered.' *Journal of Libertarian Studies*, 11:1, 11–33.

McGee, R. 2004. The philosophy of taxation and public finance. Dordrecht: Springer.

Miller, D. 1998. 'Secession and the principle of nationality.' In M. Moore (Ed.) *National self-determination and secession*. Oxford: Oxford University Press.

Moore, M. 2001. *The ethics of nationalism*. Oxford: Oxford University Press.

O'Reilly, C. 2001. 'Introduction.' Minority Languages, Ethnicity and the State in the European Union: 1–20. Palgrave Macmillan.

Preece, J. J. 2005. Minority Rights: Between Diversity And Community. Cambridge: Polity.

Transchel, K. 2006. *The Break Up of Yugoslavia (Arbitrary Borders)*. London: Chelsea House Publications.

Wallerstein, I. 1961. *Africa: The Politics of Independence*. New York: Vintage.

Walzer, M. 1983. Spheres of Justice. A Defense of Pluralism and Equality. Basic Books.

Chapter 7
Attitudes on the Ethics of Tax Evasion: A Survey of Philosophy Professors

Robert W. McGee

Methodology

An 18-statement survey was constructed and distributed via the Internet to the members of the Association for Practical and Professional Ethics, the American Association of Philosophy Teachers, Philosophy in Europe, and PHILOSOP. A total of 39 responses were received.

This study could be criticized on several counts. The sample size could have been larger. However, a sample size of 39 is sufficiently large to reach tentative conclusions. Another criticism might be the method used to select the sample. Participants were self-selecting rather than random, leaving open the possibility that the sample was not representative of the general philosophy professor population.

Only nine individuals identified themselves as female, which makes the female statistics highly tentative. However, the responses for the females in this survey were consistent with other surveys (Gupta and McGee 2010; McGee, Alver and Alver 2008; McGee and Andres 2009; McGee and Bose 2009; McGee and Cohn 2008; McGee and Guo 2007; McGee and Lingle 2008; McGee and López 2007, 2008), which also reported that the female scores were higher than the male scores.

Tables 7.1–7.3 show the demographic data. The sample was mostly male, mostly Caucasian, with a smattering of different religious beliefs, with Christian having the largest plurality.

Table 7.4 shows the 18 statements and the mean scores for each statement. The overall mean score was 5.36, indicating a fair degree of aversion to tax evasion.

R.W. McGee (✉)
School of Business, Florida International University, 3000 NE 151 Street,
North Miami, FL 33181, USA
e-mail: bob414@hotmail.com

R.W. McGee (ed.), *The Ethics of Tax Evasion: Perspectives in Theory and Practice,*   125
DOI 10.1007/978-1-4614-1287-8_7, © Springer Science+Business Media, LLC 2012

Table 7.1 Responses by gender

Male	28
Female	9
Unspecified	2
Total	39

Table 7.2 Responses by ethnicity

Caucasian	26
African-American	1
Other	1
Unspecified	11
Total	39

Table 7.3 Responses by religious affiliation

Christian	16
Atheist	6
Universalist	2
Other	5
Unspecified	10
Total	39

Table 7.5 ranks the arguments based on mean score from strongest to weakest. The range of scores is 3.82–6.46, which indicates a wide range of attitudes, depending on which statement is being considered.

Table 7.6 splits the responses into three categories, based on mean score:

1–2 Slight opposition to tax evasion
3–5 Moderate opposition to tax evasion
6–7 Strong opposition to tax evasion

The category having the highest percentage was the strong opposition (6–7) category for 15 of the 18 statements. The slight opposition (1–2) category had the highest percentage for the Jews in Nazi Germany statement. The moderate opposition group (3–5) had the highest percentage for the other two human rights statements.

Table 7.7 compares the mean scores for each statement by gender.

The female mean scores were higher for all 18 cases and the total mean scores were more than a full point apart (5.07 for men vs. 6.21 for women), which leads

Table 7.4 Summary of responses (1 = strongly agree; 7 = strongly disagree)

Statement number	Statement	Mean
1	Tax evasion is ethical if tax rates are too high	5.18
2	Tax evasion is ethical even if tax rates are not too high because the government is not entitled to take as much as it is taking from me	6.10
3	Tax evasion is ethical if the tax system is unfair	4.59
4	Tax evasion is ethical if a large portion of the money collected is wasted	5.37
5	Tax evasion is ethical even if most of the money collected is spent wisely	6.23
6	Tax evasion is ethical if a large portion of the money collected is spent on projects that I morally disapprove of	5.15
7	Tax evasion is ethical even if a large portion of the money collected is spent on worthy projects	6.16
8	Tax evasion is ethical if a large portion of the money collected is spent on projects that do not benefit me	6.19
9	Tax evasion is ethical even if a large portion of the money collected is spent on projects that do benefit me	6.22
10	Tax evasion is ethical if everyone is doing it	5.72
11	Tax evasion is ethical if a significant portion of the money collected winds up in the pockets of corrupt politicians or their families and friends	4.53
12	Tax evasion is ethical if the probability of getting caught is low	6.46
13	Tax evasion is ethical if some of the proceeds go to support a war that I consider to be unjust	5.04
14	Tax evasion is ethical if I cannot afford to pay	5.06
15	Tax evasion is ethical even if it means that if I pay less, others will have to pay more	6.37
16	Tax evasion would be ethical if I were a Jew living in Nazi Germany in 1940	3.82
17	Tax evasion is ethical if the government discriminates against me because of my religion, race, or ethnic background	4.06
18	Tax evasion is ethical if the government imprisons people for their political opinions	4.14
Average score		5.36

one to fairly conclude that female philosophy professors are significantly more averse to tax evasion than are male philosophy professors. However, for those nit-pickers who insist on statistical testing even in cases where the a priori conclusion is obvious, Table 7.8 provides the relevant data.

The p-value is 0.00034, which indicates that female philosophy professors are significantly more averse to tax evasion than are male philosophy professors.

Table 7.5 Ranking (1 = strongly agree; 7 = strongly disagree)

Rank	Statement	Mean
1	Tax evasion would be ethical if I were a Jew living in Nazi Germany in 1940	3.82
2	Tax evasion is ethical if the government discriminates against me because of my religion, race, or ethnic background	4.06
3	Tax evasion is ethical if the government imprisons people for their political opinions	4.14
4	Tax evasion is ethical if a significant portion of the money collected winds up in the pockets of corrupt politicians or their families and friends	4.53
5	Tax evasion is ethical if the tax system is unfair	4.59
6	Tax evasion is ethical if some of the proceeds go to support a war that I consider to be unjust	5.04
7	Tax evasion is ethical if I cannot afford to pay	5.06
8	Tax evasion is ethical if a large portion of the money collected is spent on projects that I morally disapprove of	5.15
9	Tax evasion is ethical if tax rates are too high	5.18
10	Tax evasion is ethical if a large portion of the money collected is wasted	5.37
11	Tax evasion is ethical if everyone is doing it	5.72
12	Tax evasion is ethical even if tax rates are not too high because the government is not entitled to take as much as it is taking from me	6.10
13	Tax evasion is ethical even if a large portion of the money collected is spent on worthy projects	6.16
14	Tax evasion is ethical if a large portion of the money collected is spent on projects that do not benefit me	6.19
15	Tax evasion is ethical even if a large portion of the money collected is spent on projects that do benefit me	6.22
16	Tax evasion is ethical even if most of the money collected is spent wisely	6.23
17	Tax evasion is ethical even if it means that if I pay less, others will have to pay more	6.37
18	Tax evasion is ethical if the probability of getting caught is low	6.46

Concluding Comments

Although the sample size was small, some useful information was gained. The survey discovered which arguments to justify tax evasion were the strongest and which were the weakest in the eyes of philosophy professors. It also found that female philosophy professors were significantly more opposed to tax evasion than were male philosophy professors. It is hoped that this study will pique interest in the views of philosophy professors on this topic and perhaps lead to other, more comprehensive studies.

Table 7.6 Range of scores (1 = strongly agree; 7 = strongly disagree)

Statement number	Statement	Score	Range of scores (%)		
			1–2	3–5	6–7
1	Tax evasion is ethical if tax rates are too high	5.18	11	22	67
2	Tax evasion is ethical even if tax rates are not too high because the government is not entitled to take as much as it is taking from me	6.10	10	3	87
3	Tax evasion is ethical if the tax system is unfair	4.59	16	37	47
4	Tax evasion is ethical if a large portion of the money collected is wasted	5.37	11	34	55
5	Tax evasion is ethical even if most of the money collected is spent wisely	6.23	8	3	89
6	Tax evasion is ethical if a large portion of the money collected is spent on projects that I morally disapprove of	5.15	16	24	60
7	Tax evasion is ethical even if a large portion of the money collected is spent on worthy projects	6.16	8	5	87
8	Tax evasion is ethical if a large portion of the money collected is spent on projects that do not benefit me	6.19	8	5	87
9	Tax evasion is ethical even if a large portion of the money collected is spent on projects that do benefit me	6.22	8	5	87
10	Tax evasion is ethical if everyone is doing it	5.72	8	0	92
11	Tax evasion is ethical if a significant portion of the money collected winds up in the pockets of corrupt politicians or their families and friends	4.53	22	31	47
12	Tax evasion is ethical if the probability of getting caught is low	6.46	5	3	92
13	Tax evasion is ethical if some of the proceeds go to support a war that I consider to be unjust	5.04	14	29	57
14	Tax evasion is ethical if I cannot afford to pay	5.06	16	30	54
15	Tax evasion is ethical even if it means that if I pay less, others will have to pay more	6.37	6	11	83
16	Tax evasion would be ethical if I were a Jew living in Nazi Germany in 1940	3.82	45	33	22
17	Tax evasion is ethical if the government discriminates against me because of my religion, race, or ethnic background	4.06	29	43	29
18	Tax evasion is ethical if the government imprisons people for their political opinions	4.14	26	38	35

Table 7.7 Comparison of male and female scores (1 = strongly agree; 7 = strongly disagree)

Statement number	Statement	Overall	Score Male	Female	Score larger by Male	Female
1	Tax evasion is ethical if tax rates are too high	5.18	4.88	5.89		1.01
2	Tax evasion is ethical even if tax rates are not too high because the government is not entitled to take as much as it is taking from me	6.10	5.83	6.94		1.11
3	Tax evasion is ethical if the tax system is unfair	4.59	4.30	5.28		0.98
4	Tax evasion is ethical if a large portion of the money collected is wasted	5.37	5.07	6.39		1.32
5	Tax evasion is ethical even if most of the money collected is spent wisely	6.23	5.99	6.94		0.95
6	Tax evasion is ethical if a large portion of the money collected is spent on projects that I morally disapprove of	5.15	4.70	6.61		1.91
7	Tax evasion is ethical even if a large portion of the money collected is spent on worthy projects	6.16	5.95	6.83		0.88
8	Tax evasion is ethical if a large portion of the money collected is spent on projects that do not benefit me	6.19	5.99	6.78		0.79
9	Tax evasion is ethical even if a large portion of the money collected is spent on projects that do benefit me	6.22	5.98	6.89		0.91
10	Tax evasion is ethical if everyone is doing it	5.72	5.57	6.67		1.10
11	Tax evasion is ethical if a significant portion of the money collected winds up in the pockets of corrupt politicians or their families and friends	4.53	4.07	5.78		1.71
12	Tax evasion is ethical if the probability of getting caught is low	6.46	6.30	6.94		0.64

(continued)

Table 7.7 (continued)

Statement number	Statement	Overall	Score		Score larger by	
			Male	Female	Male	Female
13	Tax evasion is ethical if some of the proceeds go to support a war that I consider to be unjust	5.04	4.87	5.63		0.76
14	Tax evasion is ethical if I cannot afford to pay	5.06	4.93	5.10		0.17
15	Tax evasion is ethical even if it means that if I pay less, others will have to pay more	6.37	6.23	6.80		0.57
16	Tax evasion would be ethical if I was a Jew living in Nazi Germany in 1940	3.82	3.21	5.90		2.69
17	Tax evasion is ethical if the government discriminates against me because of my religion, race, or ethnic background	4.06	3.65	5.17		1.52
18	Tax evasion is ethical if the government imprisons people for their political opinions	4.14	3.74	5.20		1.46
Average mean scores		5.36	5.07	6.21		

Table 7.8 Statistical comparison of male and female mean data

	Mean	SD	SE
Male	5.07	0.97171	0.22903
Female	6.20778	0.70464	0.16609
$p = 0.00034$			

References

Gupta, Ranjana and Robert W. McGee. (2010). A Comparative Study of New Zealanders' Opinion on the Ethics of Tax Evasion: Students v. Accountants. *New Zealand Journal of Taxation Law and Policy*, 16(1), 47–84.

McGee, Robert W. and Zhiwen Guo. (2007). A Survey of Law, Business and Philosophy Students in China on the Ethics of Tax Evasion. *Society and Business Review*, 2(3), 299–315.

McGee, Robert W. and Silvia López Paláu. (2007). The Ethics of Tax Evasion: Two Empirical Studies of Puerto Rican Opinion. *Journal of Applied Business and Economics*, 7(3), 27–47 (2007). Reprinted in Robert W. McGee (editor), *Readings in Accounting Ethics* (pp. 314–342). Hyderabad, India: ICFAI University Press, 2009.

McGee, Robert W., Jaan Alver and Lehte Alver. (2008). The Ethics of Tax Evasion: A Survey of Estonian Opinion, in Robert W. McGee, editor, *Taxation and Public Finance in Transition and Developing Economies* (pp. 461–480). New York: Springer.

McGee, Robert W. and Gordon M. Cohn. (2008). Jewish Perspectives on the Ethics of Tax Evasion. *Journal of Legal, Ethical and Regulatory Issues*, 11(2), 1–32.

McGee, Robert W. and Christopher Lingle. (2008). The Ethics of Tax Evasion: A Survey of Guatemalan Opinion, in Robert W. McGee, editor, *Taxation and Public Finance in Transition and Developing Economies* (pp. 481–495). New York: Springer.

McGee, Robert W. and Silvia López Paláu. (2008). Tax Evasion and Ethics: A Comparative Study of the USA and Four Latin American Countries, in Robert W. McGee, editor, *Taxation and Public Finance in Transition and Developing Economies* (pp. 185–224). New York: Springer.

McGee, Robert W. and Susana N. Vittadini Andres. (2009). The Ethics of Tax Evasion: Case Studies of Taiwan, in Robert W. McGee, *Readings in Business Ethics* (pp. 200–228). Hyderabad, India: ICFAI University Press. An abbreviated version was published in Marjorie G. Adams and Abbass Alkhafaji, editors, *Business Research Yearbook: Global Business Perspectives*, Volume XIV, No. 1 (pp. 34–39). Beltsville, MD: International Graphics: Beltsville, MD, 2007.

McGee, Robert W. and Sanjoy Bose. (2009). The Ethics of Tax Evasion: A Survey of Australian Opinion, in Robert W. McGee, *Readings in Business Ethics* (pp. 143–166). Hyderabad, India: ICFAI University Press.

Part II
Religious Views

Chapter 8
Hindu Ethical Considerations in Relation to Tax Evasion

Sanjoy Bose

Introduction

The subject of Hindu ethics, and literature pertaining to it, stretches through 3,000 years of history and represents a vast array of research and analysis by both Indian and Western scholars. Yet, discerning a clear set of ethical principles based on definitional and methodological clarity remains elusive. This is not surprising because the study of ethics, related closely to Hindu philosophy, traces its origins back to the Vedic age, which over the centuries has spawned a plethora of scholars to offer views in their own understanding of Hindu ethics. Ancient literature on religion, philosophy, and ethics are numerous: Vedic ethics appears to be the original source; followed by the ethics of the Upanishads; then the Bhagavad Gita; the Dharma Shastras; the six orthodox systems of Indian philosophy, followed by the ethics of Jainism and Buddhism. In recent times philosophers such as Radhakrishnan, Mahatma Gandhi, Pandit Nehru, and Sri Aurobindo have all contributed to the vast body of knowledge on Hindu ethics.

It is, at times, difficult to distinguish the lines separating philosophy, ethics, and religion. Yet reference to the Rig Veda, one of the earliest sources of literature, shows the view that man's faith could not have been what it was, had it not been for the particular form of the cumulative tradition to that point. Yet it was not simply the product of that previous tradition; if this poet had perchance died of disease as a child, probably few would wish to argue that hymn in just that form would have been written anyway. Therefore, the subsequent form of the Hindu cumulative tradition, including this hymn, is not simply the continuation or extrapolation of its earlier history. Rather, its later history is the prolongation and enrichment of its earlier existence "as modified" by the intervention of the faith and activity of this man.

S. Bose (✉)
Professor of Finance and Assistant Dean, College of Business Administration,
Abu Dhabi University, Abu Dhabi, UAE
e-mail: Sanjoy.Bose@adu.ac.ae

R.W. McGee (ed.), *The Ethics of Tax Evasion: Perspectives in Theory and Practice*,
DOI 10.1007/978-1-4614-1287-8_8, © Springer Science+Business Media, LLC 2012

Smith (1964) continues by stating if one multiplies this kind of incident a thousand million times, he is then able to envisage the development of the Hindu religious tradition. It is a part of this world; it reflects the product of human activity; it is diverse, it is fluid; it grows, its changes, it accumulates.

Smith's words are relevant to the study of ethics, as ethical studies of necessity involve the interaction of persons, which is fundamental to most definitions of ethics or of morality. However, specific references to commercial ethics is not evident, and, thus, the interpretation of ethical standards relating to finance, accounting, and taxes must be constructed from the large amounts of literature and anecdotal evidence that is available to scholars on the subject. Many philosophers have observed that throughout the ages Hindu tradition has been renewed and revitalized in times of crisis by men like Sankara, Ramanuja, Madhva, and Caitanya – men who have had the creative genius to create a synthesis of the old and the new. He states that the dynamic, sacred centre of Hinduism is, in fact, the enlightened guru, whose charismatic leadership creates the institution for philosophical, religious, and social change.

While the study of Hindu religion and philosophy is copious and substantial, the actual scientific study of ethics is much less so. Much of Hindu ethics is therefore interpretative, a logical extension of established, but dynamic principles, possessing enough characteristics of a flexibility to adapt to the change of age. There are, thus, plenty of discussions in Hindu in literature about proper conduct, of moral standards, and the application of such standards and norms of behaviour in many situations of life. The nuclei of ethics – standards of morality, good versus bad, virtue versus vice – found in most modern literature on ethics, had already been evident in the Srutis or Vedas.

Maitra (1925) states that the morality of the performance of one's duties is the groundwork of Hindu ethics. As constituting their concrete moral life, it furnishes the positive basis of Hindu ethical concerts and norms. It is also preparatory to the higher morality of self-purification, which necessarily presupposes the mediation of an objective code of right and wrong actions. While Maitra does not provide elaborations on what constitutes ethics and ethical considerations, his list in the *Sadharanadharmas* may be logically extended to what constitutes ethical actions in commerce and finance and tax.

The Taxation System in India and Ethical Considerations

Taxation is a prime source of revenue earned by the government of India from the populace, with an objective to redistribute the wealth and thereby to maintain growth and stability in the country. Therefore, payment of tax is regarded as a civic duty.[1]

---

[1] Kiabel, B.D., and N. G. Nwokah, 2009 "Curbing Tax Evasion and Avoidance in Personal Income Tax Administration: A Study of the South-South States of Nigeria." *European Journal of Economics, Finance and Administrative Sciences.*

However, one of the prolonged issues facing in the Indian tax collection system is the problem of tax evasion. In fact, tax evasion has assumed an important subject of inquiry in India over a long period of time. Though many structural deficiencies can be identified in the prevailing Indian taxation procedures that led to tax evasions, the ethical considerations enjoyed by Hindus in tax exemptions are often criticized as a notable anomaly in the Indian taxation procedures.

As tax evasion is described as intentional illegal behaviour, or as behaviour involving a direct violation of tax law to escape the payment of tax,[2] the deliberate under-reporting of income and over claiming of tax deductions are common tax-avoiding practices in India. Apparently, in societies where one or few religions are dominant, the overarching core values of these religions are likely to be considered as non-codified social norms,[3] which perhaps regulate everyday activity and lead them to enjoy ethical considerations. Consequently, these types of ethical consideration for Hindus regarding tax payments were initially introduced in the Indian Taxation Law after the amendment of the Hindu Succession Act in 1937. This move was initiated by the British who later came to be blamed for their alleged aim to pamper the Hindu feudal families to earn their loyalty by creating an ameliorated place for them in the society.[4]

Not much literature exists on the view that tax evasion is ethical, and early literature indicates that whatever justifications were provided were inadequate for some reason.[5] However, some part of a body of literature that examines tax evasion from an ethical perspective concludes that tax evasion may be justified in certain situations, although the reasons differ.[6] The same philosophy is followed in Hinduism to justify their ethical considerations for tax evasions.

Hinduism is considered to be an ancient religion. It is followed as a way of life with certain customs, traditions, and rituals that are centuries old. Hinduism holds

---

[2] Olayinka Marte Uadiale, Temitope Olamide Fagbemi, and Jumoke Omowumi Ogunleye (2010), An Empirical Study of the Relationship between Culture and Personal Income Tax Evasion in Nigeria. European Journal of Economics, Finance and Administrative Sciences, ISSN 1450-2887 Issue 20 (2010).

[3] K. Praveen Parboteeah, Martin Hoegl, John B. Cullen (2008), Ethics and Religion: An Empirical Test of a Multidimensional Model, Journal of Business Ethics, Springer, DOI 10.1007/s10551-007-9439-8.

[4] Anurag Sanyal (1995), The Hindu Undivided Family; Effects on the Indian Tax System, The Park Place Economist, Vol. 3 (1), Article 17, p. 73.

[5] (a) Block, W. (1989). The Justification of Taxation in the Public Finance Literature: A Critique. *Journal of Public Finance*; (b) Cohn, G. (1998). The Jewish View on Paying Taxes. *Journal of Accounting, Ethics & Public Policy*, 1(2), 109–120, reprinted in R. W. McGee (Ed.), *The Ethics of Tax Evasion* (pp. 180–189). Dumont, NJ: The Dumont Institute for Public Policy Research, 1998.

[6] (a) Crowe, M. T. (1944). *The Moral Obligation of Paying Just Taxes*. The Catholic University of America Studies in Sacred Theology No. 84. (b) Schansberg, D. E. (1998). The Ethics of Tax Evasion within Biblical Christianity: Are There Limits to "Rendering Unto Caesar"? *Journal of Accounting, Ethics & Public Policy*, 1(1), 77–90, reprinted in R. W. McGee (Ed.), *The Ethics of Tax Evasion* (pp. 144–157). Dumont, NJ: The Dumont Institute for Public Policy Research, 1998.

certain divine concepts and ethics that form the foundation for spiritual life. The Hindu ethics were drawn from the spiritual texts such as the Upanishads,[7] Bhagavad-Gita, and Brahma Sutra that guide the Hindus through their daily life. Hindu ethics differ from modern scientific ethics in discharge of life's duties. While the scientific ethics aim to secure the maximum utility for a society by eliminating friction and guaranteeing harmonious existence for its members, the Dharmashastra of Manu Smrithi and Arthashastra of Chanakya discipline the Hindus for a practical life with spiritual sense that are to be observed consciously or unconsciously as long as they are alive.

Ancient literature speaks much about taxation in India. The earliest evidences of taxation are depicted in ancient Aryan writings – the Rig Veda, which state that the Rig Vedic people had developed some sort of political organization under the rule of the king.[8] Vedic literatures reveal that for the maintenance of royalty, i.e., in return for the services in war and peace, people's obedience and their contribution to the royal exchequer were natural corollaries as well as necessities.[9] Hence, the state derived its revenue from people's contribution, which was technically named as "Bali."[10] Perhaps the use of the term Bali was not restricted exclusively to collection of revenue but also to "offerings to a god" and to tributes paid by hostile tribes to the king.

The Atharvaveda also refers to the existence of taxation, which was considered as almost a regular and compulsory system. For instance, the hymns of Atharvaveda mention the regular share of king in the agricultural produce and cattle of his subjects. However, there is no clarity as to the share the king was entitled to in agricultural produce and in the wealth of his subjects. There is no doubt about the fact that as a system of taxation, the subjects were to regularly part with certain portion of their produce/wealth or income for the royal exchequer.[11]

According to Hindu notions taxes are considered as king's wages for the services of protection. Further, the king is entitled to his share of treasure and minerals because he is the lord of all.[12] However, in Hindu ethics there was no room for arbitrary collection of tax by the king.[13]

[7] Upanishad:http://sanatan.intnet.mu/upanishads/pdf/upanishads_nikhilananda.pdf.

[8] Rig Veda, Book – 1, HYMNN XX, Rbhus 7 & 8: http://keithbriggs.info/documents/rv.pdf.

[9] Spengler, Joseph J (1971) Indian Economic Thoughts, Durham, NC: Duke University Press

[10] Kunwar Deo Prasad (1987),Taxation in Ancient India: From the Earliest Times to up to Guptas, New Delhi, Mithil Publications, P.34.

[11] Atharvaveda XI. 4.19; X. I. 20; VI. 117.1. www.vedah.com/org/literature/PDFs/Atharva Veda. PDF.

[12] Mahabaratha Book 11 Volume 7 cited in James L. Fitzgerald (2003), The Mahabaratha, Volume 7, Book No 11, Chicago, University Press.

[13] Kunwar Deo Prasad (1987),Taxation in Ancient India: From the Earliest Times to up to Guptas, New Delhi, Mithil Publications, p. 76.

Interestingly, review of several past literatures such as Kathak Samhita, Taittiriya Upanishad, and Aitareya Brahmana[14] reveal the gradual transformation of Bali from a voluntary contribution to an established regular payment to the exchequer.

In the early period of Hinduism, several ethical considerations were offered to the public in relation to tax evasions based on their *Varna* (caste). For instance, the Brahmanas, the first *Varna*, were totally exempt from taxation with a belief that the king could censure all except Brahmanas. However, the third *Varna*, Vaishyas were depicted as the sole payers of taxes, since they were the only *Varna*, engaged in trade and economic activities.[15] It is not clear whether the other *Varnas* were also compelled to contribute towards state exchequer. But, in case other Varnas were spared from paying taxes in reality, it may be safely assumed that the Vedic texts failed to extend any justification excepting an excuse based on religion.[16]

Literatures reveal that in the initial stages Bali was levied occasionally and voluntarily, but when it commenced being applied in regular form it might have met with subjects' displeasure and resentment. The use of the metaphor, "balihrit" (devourer of subjects) for the king in the literature of this period was nothing but a show of people's anger and annoyance.

In this context, it is significant to analyse Chanakya's ethics on taxation. According to him taxation should not be a painful process for the people. There should be leniency and caution while deciding the tax structure. Ideally, governments should collect taxes like a honeybee, which sucks just the right amount of honey from the flower so that both can survive. Taxes should be collected in small and not in large proportions."[17] However, Hindu Vedic texts do not deal much with taxation policies of governments but are applicable only in the work of collection of taxes.

Taxation in India

Among the major taxation powers vested by the Indian constitution to both the Union and the States, the personal income tax is one of the most important sources of revenue. According to the Indian Income Tax Act 1956[18] personal income tax is levied on the total income of all individuals, Hindu Undivided Families (HUF), unregistered firms, and other "associations of persons." The process of tax collection done through one or more of four different processes: first, deductions or

---

[14] Kathak Samhita. Chapter XXIX.7.9, and Taittiriya Upanishad. Chapter I. 5.3.

[15] Aitareya Brahmana, Chapter VII. 29 & VII. 34. cited in Keith. A.B. (1998), Aithra Brahmana, Rig Veda Brahamanas (English translation); Banaras, India. Motilal Publishers.

[16] Prasad. B, Systems of Taxation During the Vedic Age.

[17] Chanakya, Arthashastra, cited in Shamasastry, R. (1956) Kautilya's Arthashastra, 8th ed., Mysore India: Mysore Printing and Publishing House.

[18] Indian Income Tax Act, 1956.

withholding at source at the time of payment of income; second, advance payment of tax by the tax payer himself; third, provisional assessment and demand by the income tax officer; and fourth, regular assessment and final demand by the Income Tax officer.[19] However, the prevailing considerations in respect of HUF in tax payment are identified as the primary complication in the calculation and collection of income tax in India.[20]

Hindus and Ethical Considerations for Tax Evasions

Hindus constitute a majority of the Indian population. Hindus include all the persons who are Hindus by religion. According to Section 2 of the Hindu Succession Act, 1956, Hinduism elaborately declares that it applies to any person, who is a Hindu by religion in any of its forms or developments, including a Virashaiva, a Lingayat, or a follower of Brahmo, Prathana, or Arya Samaj, a Buddhist, Jain, or Sikh.[21]

Generally, Hindu ethics believes in the concept of joint family system in community living. Under this system all the members of a family, including married brothers, their children, and grandchildren live together under a common roof. This fundamental principle of *Spindaship* or family relationship [22] promises better living to Hindu families offering certain values and principles through sharing their common house, properties, business, income, wealth, and food. Moreover, in India, this joint Hindu family system enjoys a separate legal entity status called "Hindu Undivided Family" (HUF) that is shared and enjoyed by all the members of the family who follows this system. Such joint families are included in the group or communities who gain "ethical considerations in tax evasions."

Vedic-period literatures insist on certain element of certainty in Hindu tax – system. According to Hindu ethics, taxes had to be certain and made known to the tax payers – the amount of tax, articles to be taxed and the time frame for payment – otherwise the tax collectors could realize more than what is prescribed and appropriate a part of the collection for their own benefit.[23] This maxim of certainty in the Hindu fiscal thoughts appears to be close to the second principle of Adam Smith's

---

[19] Cutt. J. (1969), Taxation and Economic Development in India. New York:Frederick Praeger, Inc. p.87

[20] Anurag Sanyal (1995), The Hindu Undivided Family: Effects on the Indian Tax System, The Park Place Economist, Vol. 3 (1), Article 17, p. 74.

[21] In CWT. Smt. Champa Kumari Singh (1972) 83 ITR 720, the Supreme Court held that the HUF includes Jain Undivided Family.

[22] Chawla, O.P (1972) Personal Taxation in India. 1947–1970. Bombay: Somaiya Publications. P.103.

[23] Chanakya, Arthashastra, Shamasastry, R. (1956) Kautilya's Arthashastra, 8th ed., Mysore India: Mysore Printing and Publishing House

philosophy, i.e., "the tax which each individual is bound to pay ought to be certain and not arbitrary. The time of payment, the manner of payment, the quality to be paid, all ought to be clear and plain to the contributor and to every other person."[24]

Later in history, two ancient schools of thoughts led by Dayabhagh and Mitakshara, emerged on Hindu law to define special ethical considerations to the members of a Hindu joint family in acquiring property or wealth. While the Dayabhagh system is specifically followed by the Hindus in West Bengal and Assam, Hindus in the rest of the country followed the ethics of Mitakshara School in exercising their rights on ownership, devolution, and taxation of properties.[25]

A Mitakshara joint family consisted of father and son.[26] On death of a son, the father and the widow of the son constitute the HUF. According to this school, till the Hindu family remains joined, no member of the HUF can have a specific share in the HUF property. However, on partition of HUF, the share of a member is decided, but then the member receiving the property will be said to hold it as HUF and not as his individual property, subject to the condition that there is more than one member in the family. Moreover, if any addition is made to a partitioned HUF property, then the addition also would also receive the status of HUF property. In this context, it should be noted that the property received by inheritance under the Hindu Succession Act is, in truth, only the individual property of the person inheriting it and does not have the HUF status property. Moreover, it also explains that if some loans are taken by that HUF and an immovable property or a movable property is purchased by the HUF, the property so purchased will be known as HUF property.

Exploiting this privilege in respect of numerous financial transactions, people buying or selling immovable property or any movable property, it has become a common practice to declare their status as that of HUF. However, according to Indian Law, a mere declaration by a Hindu buyer or seller of real estate, or any other asset, that his status is that of an HUF cannot be accepted; however, there are certain legal requirements to be furnished to proof his or her valid HUF status.

Under the Income-Tax Act, 1961 ("the Act") and Wealth Tax Act, 1957, an "HUF" is treated as a separate entity for the purpose of assessment. Whatever the procedures, the concept of HUF is an excellent tax saving device for the Hindus. For instance, the members of HUF enjoy specific considerations such as they can file two income tax returns, one in their personal individual capacity and the other in the name of HUF.

Perhaps, the *Distinct and Separate Legal Entity Status* granted to HUF under Indian Tax Law would often lay down some forms of ethical consideration for Hindus in relation to tax evasions. A Hindu can divide his or her taxable income between two entities and also double deductions and expenses in both capacities. This brings down his or her total taxable income and tax liability substantially.

---

[24] Adam Smith (1776), An Inquiry into the Nature and Causes of the Wealth of Nations, London, W.Strahan & T Cadell.

[25] Goyal, P.C, (1956), Effect of Hindu succession act, 1956, on direct taxation of Mitakshara Hindus, 2d ed, Allahabad, Central Law Agency.

[26] Cited in the case file of A.G. v. A.R. Arunachalam Chettiar, 34 ITR 421 (PC).

Expressing an HUF status to evade taxation is a common practice prevailing among the Hindu families in India. There is no formal procedure to form an HUF as this is deemed to be automatically created in law. As the name suggests, HUF means a family of Hindus. However, under the Indian tax law,[27] to form an HUF, the family must have at least two members, of which at least one is male. An HUF can also consist of female members, being the wives and unmarried daughters of the male members.

An HUF is formed in two ways. If any of the members of an HUF receives ancestral property from a relative three generations preceding him, then that property will automatically be regarded as his HUF's property. Or if a member receives an asset or property by way of gift from a lineal "ascendant" (meaning from a relative of a generation earlier) with a specific instruction by the donor that the same is being gifted to the HUF, the HUF would be automatically formed. However, generally, an HUF always exists in a Hindu family, from a tax point of view the common HUF property are evaded from taxation and only when any additional assets or property comes to the family or they engage in any new commercial activities, the assets are considered for taxation.

Thus, a Hindu as an individual enjoys a general exemption[28] on his or her taxable wealth as well as the HUF's property he or she is eligible to a further general exemption. Hence, persons having immovable property and jewellery and motorcars under HUF status stand to gain from the extra exemption under Wealth Tax Act as well.[29]

Similar to HUF, the Hindu Coparcenary also enjoys tax benefits and considerations. A Hindu coparcenary is a smaller body than the HUF as it can only consist of male members of the family who are entitled to or acquire a right to, by birth, an interest in the joint or coparcenary property. The most senior member is called the Karta (Manager), who generally manages the joint or coparcenary property, belonging to all coparceners. An HUF must consist of at least two male members but, in the event of a partition of the HUF, the smaller family can form an HUF even with a single male member if it receives a part of the property.

So, in brief, under the Hindu law, a Hindu enjoys tax exemptions or is ethically considered for tax evasions on their property if he or she has property owing to him or her, his or her spouse, sons and unmarried daughter, including sons wives and children or otherwise even if the grandsons also have wives and children.[30]

In order to evade tax a Hindu at any time may devolve his self-acquired property into the common stock of an HUF and, thereby, he or she could create a new HUF, which was hitherto non-existent. Obviously, this enables the individual to transfer part of his property to his wife and children and consequently circumvent the Income Tax Act (section 64).[31] Income Tax Act, 1961 has provisions for Hindus to repeat the above act any number of times.

---

[27] Indian Income Tax Act – 1961 Section 171.

[28] Indian Income Tax Act, 1961 Section 2(31).

[29] Indian Wealth Tax Act, 1957.

[30] CIT v. M.M.Khanna 49 ITR 232 (Bombay) cited in http://www.indiankanoon.org/doc/1147903.

[31] Indian Income Tax Act, 1961.

However, though the principles of *Spindaship* are not followed in general, on paper, to gain tax exemptions the Hindu families could stand to be HUFs. Perhaps, the prime reason for this system could be that the beneficiaries can then save a greater proportion of their income by protecting it under the cover of high exemptions and transfer facilities available to an original HUF. These benefits get multiplied even more because of the small size of these families.[32]

Listed below are some other tax exemptions enjoyed by HUF.

1. To enjoy the benefits of tax exemption, bank accounts of HUF should be opened in the name of either the HUF or in the name of the *Karta* by specifically declaring that the account is that of the HUF only. However, only the funds belonging to the HUF should be deposited in such an account that could be eligible for tax exemptions. The aforementioned "ethical considerations" for the Hindus provide them with a good deal of income tax and wealth tax saving.[33]

2. Though the law specifically insists that only the *Karta* of the HUF is entitled to sign the bank transactions, however, in practice he could also permit the other adult members of the family to sign on behalf of the HUF.

3. If a Hindu family member wants to evade tax on his or her property on ethical consideration he or she could show that the property is transferred to his or her son by Will or as gift. Moreover, this would result into a good deal of income tax and wealth tax saving for the persons inheriting such property by will as mentioned above.

4. Even after the death of the sole male member or *Karta* so long as the original property of the Joint Family remains in the hands of the widows of the members of the family and the same is not divided amongst them; the Joint Hindu Family continues to exist and the properties are ethically considered for tax evasion.

5. It is frequently argued that the existence of nucleus or joint family property is necessary to recognize the claim of HUF status in respect of any property or income of an HUF. It has been established now that since the HUF is a creation of Hindu Law, it can exist even without any nucleus or ancestral joint family property and can still be considered for tax exemptions.

6. In the case of certain joint HUFs property, if the tax liability on the property occurs above the permitted level, it may be reduced by partitioning the property. This can be easily achieved in a case where the partition results in separate independent taxable units but comes below the permitted slab. Such a partition of HUF will reduce the tax liability considerably. (Partial partition of HUF is also a very effective device for reducing its tax liability. Partial partition is recognized under the Hindu Law. However partial partition of an HUF has now been prohibited by the provisions of section 171(9) of the Income Tax

---

[32] Gulati, L S., and Gulati, K. S. The undivided Hindu Family: A Study of Its Tax Privileges. Bombay: Asia Publishing House, 1962.

[33] Lakhotia. R.N. *51 Tips for Saving Income Tax,* New Delhi, Vision Books.

Act, 1961, according to which any partial partition affected after 31.12.78, will not be recognized).

7. It is also noticeable that on partition between father and sons, the shares that sons obtain on partition of the HUF with their father is the ancestral property. Therefore, one of the sons who is not married at the time of partition will receive the property as his HUF property, and he enjoys an ethical consideration for tax evasion on the property till the date of his marriage.

8. It is also important to mention that the motive for partition in a Hindu family cannot be questioned by the tax authorities.

9. Notwithstanding the provisions of section 171(9) partial partition, can still be used as a device for tax planning in certain cases. An HUF not hitherto assessed as undivided family can still be subjected to partial partition because it is recognized under the Hindu Law and such partial partition does not require recognition under Section 171 of the Income Tax Act of 1961. Thus a bigger HUF already assessed as such, can be partitioned into smaller HUFs and such smaller HUFs may further be partitioned partially before being assessed as HUFs. Besides any HUF not yet assessed for tax can be partitioned partially and thereafter enjoy tax concessions. However, the distribution of the assets of an HUF in the course of partition would not attract any capital gains tax liability as it does not involve a transfer.

10. Family settlements or arrangements are also effective devices for the distribution of ancestral property. The object of the family settlement should be to settle existing or future disputes regarding property, amongst the members of the family. For instance, suppose a family consists of Karta, his wife, two sons, and their wives and children and its income is assumed to be Rs. 600,000. According to 2007–08 financial years the tax burden on the family will be quite heavy. If by family arrangement, income the yielding property is settled on the Karta, his wife, his two sons, and two daughters-in-law, then the income of each one of them would be Rs. 100,000, which would attract no tax since the tax liability would be reduced from Rs. 100,000 to nil for the financial year.

11. The other important method to enjoy ethical consideration under Hinduism for the evasion of tax is to pay remuneration to the Karta and/or other members of the HUF for services rendered by them to the family business. The remuneration so paid would be allowed as a deduction from the income of the HUF and thereby tax liability of the HUF would be reduced, provided the remuneration is reasonable and its payment is bonafide. The payment must be for service to the family for commercial or business expediency.

12. In recent times, some states like Maharashtra and Tamil Nadu have amended the Indian Succession Act to provide that all daughters who were unmarried as on the date of the amendment would be regarded as coparceners in much the same manner as the sons in the family. Subsequently, in these states, unmarried daughters as well as daughters married after the date of the amendment (in the case of Maharashtra, it was June 22, 1994) were regarded as coparceners. They are, therefore, eligible to demand partition of an HUF, and receive a share (equal to that of male coparceners) of the HUF property.

13. *The Hindu Succession (Amendment) Act, 2005 (39 of 2005)* comes into force
    from 9th September, 2005 with an objective to remove gender discriminatory
    provisions laid down in the Hindu Succession Act, 1956 and gives the follow-
    ing rights to daughters under Section 6:

    (a) The daughter of a coparcener cell by birth become a coparcener in her own
        right in the same manner as the son;
    (b) The daughter has the same rights in the coparcenary property as she would
        have had if she had been a son;
    (c) The daughter shall be subject to the same liability in the said coparcenary
        property as that of a son; and any reference to a Hindu Mitakshara coparce-
        ners shall be deemed to include a reference to a daughter of a coparcener;
    (d) The daughter is allotted the same share as is allotted to a son;
    (e) The share of the pre-deceased son or a pre-deceased daughter shall be allot-
        ted to the surviving child of such pre-deceased son or of such pre-deceased
        daughter;

As mentioned earlier, the ethical consideration for tax evasions for Hindus can
cause immense losses to the exchequer. Past research on these aspects identifies that
the maximum tax avoidance available to an HUF, through varied combinations of
complete partition, partial partition, and transfers by gifts shows that by dexterous
employment of avoidance techniques an HUF can earn up to eight times the actual
exemption limit without incurring any income tax liability.

In India, which is described a Sovereign, Socialist, Secular, Democratic, Republic,
defining Hindus under a separate entity and treating HUF with special consideration
are challenged as a threat to the basic essence of secularism by the think tanks of the
country.

However, examining the aforementioned arguments, it is not entirely justified to
comment that the problems of avoidance and evasion – the major issues of the
Indian personal income tax – are solely due to the existence of the HUF. In fact, it
is true that leakage in revenue may occur either through evasion or avoidance, but
evasion is a more serious issue and found to be more controversial since it has the
colour of legality in India.

Conclusion

The subject of Hindu ethical considerations in respect of tax evasion is complicated,
inter alia, by its long history and the intertwining with traditions sourced in ancient
literature and modern economic considerations. Aspects of colonial rule by Muslim
invaders and latterly by the British over a thousand years until independence in 1947
have complicated the attitudes, beliefs, and traditions in respect of the ethics of tax
evasion. Given its long history, it is hard to imagine that a concrete and clear set of
principles regarding the ethics, or otherwise, of tax evasion have not evolved. What
creates even more difficulty in gauging ethical considerations is the composition of

the nation comprising all the world's major religious groups, each paying taxes under different norms. However, Hindus enjoy special considerations in tax law, which arguably may be interpreted as legalized tax evasion. The government is, nevertheless, moving to a standardized tax system for all religious groups, which will be capable of discerning ethical versus unethical attitudes to tax evasion.

References

Kiabel, B.D., and N. G. Nwokah, 2009 "Curbing Tax Evasion and Avoidance in Personal Income Tax Administration: A Study of the South-South States of Nigeria". *European Journal of Economics, Finance and Administrative Sciences*.

Praveen P., Martin H., Cullen, J.B., (2008), Ethics and Religion: An Empirical Test of a Multidimensional Model, Journal of Business Ethics, Springer, DOI 10.1007/s10551-007-9439-8

Sanyal, A., (1995), The Hindu Undivided Family; Effects on the Indian Tax System, The Park Place Economist, Vol. 3(1) 17, p. 73

Block, W. (1989). The Justification of Taxation in the Public Finance Literature: A Critique. *Journal of Public Finance*.

Cohn, G. (1998). The Jewish View on Paying Taxes. *Journal of Accounting, Ethics & Public Policy*, 1(2), 109–120, reprinted in R. W. McGee (Ed.), *The Ethics of Tax Evasion* (pp. 180–189). Dumont, NJ: The Dumont Institute for Public Policy Research.

Crowe, M. T. (1944). *The Moral Obligation of Paying Just Taxes*. The Catholic University of America Studies in Sacred Theology No. 84.

Schansberg, D. E. (1998). The Ethics of Tax Evasion within Biblical Christianity: Are There Limits to "Rendering Unto Caesar"? *Journal of Accounting, Ethics & Public Policy*, 1(1), 77-90, reprinted in R. W. McGee (Ed.), *The Ethics of Tax Evasion* (pp. 144-157). Dumont, NJ: The Dumont Institute for Public Policy Research

Maitra, S. K. (1932), Public Policy in Ancient India: An Interpretation of the Upashinads, Calcutta University Press.

Maitra, S. K. (1932), Rig Veda: An Interpretation of Religion and Morality, Calcutta University Press

Spengler, Joseph J (1971) Indian Economic Thoughts, Durham, NC: Duke University Press.

Kunwar, D. P. (1987), Taxation in Ancient India: From the Earliest Times to up to Guptas, New Delhi, Mithil Publications, P. 34

Maitra, S. K. (1934), Atharvaveda: An Investigation into the Practices of Taxation in Ancient India, Calcutta University Press

Fitzgerald, J. L. (2003), Mahabaratha, Book 11 Volume 7, Chicago, University Press

Kunwar, D. P (1987),Taxation in Ancient India: From the Earliest Times to up to Guptas, New Delhi, Mithil Publications, p. 76

Kathak S., (1989) Taittiriya Upanishad, Ramkrishna Press.

Keith. A. B. (1998), Aitareya Brahmana, cited in Aithra Brahmana, Rig Veda Brahamanas (English translation); Banaras, India. Motilal Publishers.

Kunwar, D. P (1987),Systems of Taxation During the Vedic Age.

Shamasastry, R. (1956) Chanakya, Arthashastra, cited in Kautilya's Arthashastra, 8th ed., Mysore India: Mysore Printing and Publishing House.

Seth, R. J. (1971) A Guide to The Indian Income Tax Act, 1956

Cutt. J. (1969), Taxation and Economic Development in India. New York: Frederick Praeger, Inc. Publishers

Chawla, O.P (1972) Personal Taxation in India. 1947-1970. Bombay: Somaiya Publications Pvt. Ltd., 1972

Smith, A., (1776) Wealth of Nations: An Enquiry into Nature and Cause, Strahan and Cadell, London.

Goyal, P.C, (1956), Effect of Hindu succession act, 1956, on direct taxation of Mitakshara Hindus, 2d ed, Al, Central Law Agency Central Law Agency, Allahabad.

Goyal, P.C, (1961), An Interpretation of the Indian Income Tax Act - 1961 Section 171, Central Law Agency, Allahabad.

Goyal, P.C, (1961), An Interpretation of the Indian Income Tax Act, 1961 Sec. 2(31), Central Law Agency, Allahabad.

Goyal, P.C, (1957), An Interpretation of the Indian Wealth Tax Act, 1957, Central Law Agency, Allahabad.

Lakhotia. R.N. (1982) *51 Tips for Saving Income Tax*, New Delhi, Vision Books

Gulati, L S., & Gulati, K. S. (1962) The Undivided Hindu Family: A Study of Its Tax Privileges. Bombay: Asia Publishing House.

Cutt, James (1969), Taxation and Economic Development in India. New York: Frederick Praeger, Inc. Publishers, p.89

Maitra, S.K., (1925), The Ethics of the Hindus, Calcutta: The University of Calcutta Press, India.

Smith, W. C., (1964), The Meaning and End of Religion, Mentor Books, New York.

Chapter 9
The Traditional Jewish View of Paying Taxes

Gordon Cohn

Introduction

This paper presents the Orthodox Jewish view regarding the obligation to pay taxes. This paper is meant to provide a philosophical approach to the obligations to pay taxes, not a practical guide as to under what conditions one is required to pay. Due to the complexity of the subject, it is impossible to include all relevant information in this article. If after reading this document the reader has questions whether he is obligated to pay taxes, he is advised to consult a knowledgeable Rabbi who can ascertain his obligation.

The opinions which are presented herein are based on the Orthodox Jewish approach. This approach defines the obligation of Jewish persons according to the oral tradition. The oral tradition consists of Rabbinic teachings from when the Torah was given (around 3,300 years ago) until today.

The main source of the oral tradition is the Talmud. The Talmud is the compilation of Jewish oral law. It explains the meanings behind the Torah's verses. According to the Jewish tradition, the Torah cannot be properly understood without examining Talmudic interpretations.

The Talmud consists of the Mishna and Gemara. The Mishna was compiled and edited approximately 1,800 years ago. The Gemara was written a few hundred years later. It focuses on presenting commentaries on the Mishna. Since the compilation of the Talmud, Rabbis have used it to develop a system of laws which are compatible with the complexities of modern times. Two of the most important post-Talmudic Rabbinical works are those by Maimonides (Egypt, 1135–1204) and the *Shulchan Aruch* [Joseph Caro (Safed, 1488–1575)].

G. Cohn (✉)
Touro College, 27-33 West 23rd Street, New York, NY 10010, USA
e-mail: gordoncohn@juno.com

R.W. McGee (ed.), *The Ethics of Tax Evasion: Perspectives in Theory and Practice*,
DOI 10.1007/978-1-4614-1287-8_9, © Springer Science+Business Media, LLC 2012

The volumes by these authors are important. They codify and simplify the more complex Talmud. *The Shulchan Aruch* is considered a fundamental text and is referred to as *The Code of Jewish laws*. An important commentary that appears with the *Shulchan Aruch* is by the *Rama* [Rabbi Moshe Isserles (1530–1572)]. According to Jewish tradition, people whose ancestry is from the Northern European countries follow the opinion of the *Rama*. Alternatively, those who lived in Mediterranean countries went after the view of the *Shulchan Aruch*. Unless noted otherwise, for simplification, whenever this paper refers to a Jewish person, it means one who follows Orthodox tradition.

The Jewish Philosophy Behind Paying Taxes

An Orthodox Jewish person is preoccupied with obeying laws. From the beginning to the end of his day, his every move is regimented. The Rabbis prescribe which shoe should be put on first, what side to sleep on in the bed, the proper posture when walking in the street, etc. These laws of everyday conduct are in addition to a multitude focusing on frequently performed religious rituals. Thus, obeying laws regarding payment of taxes is merely one of the many laws which a Jewish person accustoms himself to follow.

Adherence to tax laws has a different flavor for the Jewish person than for the general population. First, as is discussed in the next section, Jewish law requires an individual to listen to the government and to pay taxes. Thus, when a Jewish person pays taxes, he is not only discharging his secular responsibility, but also fulfilling a religious obligation. Second, the Mishna in *Ethics of our Fathers*[1] (4:21) (the classic collection of Jewish ethical statements) says that this world is similar to a corridor before the next world. The same Mishna also advises that one should fix himself up in this world in order that he should be ready for the next world. In other words, the Mishna advises that a Jewish person is not supposed to consider this world as his "true" home; rather, it is only a place of preparation for one's future dwelling.

Therefore, based on the above, a Jewish person's principal reason for keeping the tax laws is not only because he is afraid of punitive action. Rather, an effort to diligently follow the tax laws gives him a larger share in the next world. Paying taxes helps one gain more eternity in the same way as keeping laws of Kashrus or praying the required three times a day.

When a person adopts the aforementioned attitude toward paying taxes, he is no longer a citizen who the government must scrutinize in order to insure tax law compliance. Rather, he independently wants to make sure that he pays what is required. A story regarding Rabbi Yaakov Kamenetsky captures the spirit which the Jewish person is supposed to have regarding paying taxes.

---

[1] The work appears in most standard prayer books.

Rabbi Kamenetsky was one of the most prominent Rabbis in America until his passing away in 1985. Once, an appreciative congregant gave Rabbi Kamenetsky a silver kiddish cup for a present. Subsequently, it was discovered that Rabbi Kamenetsky took this cup to a silversmith for appraisal. It seemed unusual that such a distinguished person receives a gift and was preoccupied with determining its value. However, later was discovered Rabbi Kamenetsky's true intention in seeking the appraisal.

The cup was received for performing Rabbinical services; therefore, Rabbi Kamenetsky decided that its value was taxable income. Rabbi Kamenetsky's diligence must be attributed to his giving intrinsic value to paying taxes. Fear of Internal Revenue Service citations could not motivate such extraordinary dedication.

Rabbi Kamenetsky's behavior is called lefnim mashorus hadin [Tractate *Baba Mitziah*. (24b)]. This term refers to righteous people being so careful not to violate any prohibition that they go out of their way to insure that their behavior is consistent with even an extreme interpretation of a law. It is unlikely that the IRS expects a clergyman to report small gifts from congregants. However, the spirit of the law looks at certain gifts as income. Rabbi Kamenetsky felt compelled to comply with the spirit. Since Torah law requires paying income taxes, the Rabbi wanted to be sure that he was fulfilling his responsibility according to all interpretations.

People like Rabbi Kamenetsky consider that there is a large reward for fulfilling the Torah properly and a significant loss for transgressions. They exceed normal efforts to insure that all their behaviors are proper.

Finally, two Talmudic statements explain why a Jewish person would want to give a high priority to fulfilling his tax obligation despite its steep cost. A principal reason for a person not paying taxes is that he wants to amass as much money as possible. He sees happiness as a function of having more wealth. However, in *Ethics of our Fathers* (4:1), it is explained that a rich person is not someone who has accumulated large amounts of wealth; rather, it is someone who is happy with what he has.

An individual who contemplates this Mishna is less likely to shrug his civic obligation in order to acquire more wealth. He realizes that allowing himself to remain with the personal quality of greed, a common motivation for tax evasion, can be more detrimental to his well-being than forfeiting the money necessary to fulfill his tax obligation.

Furthermore, in Tractate *Shabbos* (31a), the questions which are asked on the day of judgement are discussed. The first inquiry is, was one ethical in his business dealings? This question precedes inquiries regarding performing good deeds and ritually based commandments. A person who uses unscrupulous tactics to avoid paying taxes, in the final calculations, is immediately held responsible for not giving the government the portion which it is entitled to from his business dealings. The passage informs one that even if he has not been called for a review by the IRS, in the end he will still to have his records examined. A person who studies the aforementioned Talmudic passage before filling out his/her income tax form reconsiders making illegal deductions and not reporting income.

Halachik Perspective on Paying Taxes

The *Halachik* (Jewish legal) perspective on paying taxes has four components. First, there are laws related to a citizen's duty to follow his/her country's statutes. This is called *dina damalchusa dina*. Second, laws discuss the prohibition of lying. Third, it is forbidden for a Jewish person to do anything that could discredit the religion. This is known as *chillul Hashem*. Fourth, a Jew is required to have integrity.

Dina Damalchusa Dina

Dina damalchusa dina literally means that one is required to keep the laws which the king has established. This principle provides the basis for a Jew's *Halachik* requirement to follow the country's laws. It appears in several places in the Talmud [Tractates *Baba Kamma* (113a), *Nadorim* (28a), *Gittin* (10b) and *Baba Basra* (25a)] and also in the *Choshen Mishpat* section of the *Code of Jewish Laws*, Chap. 369.

As with many *Halachos*, there are disagreements among Rabbis when *dina damalchusa dina* applies. However, generally speaking, the *Shulchan Aruch* and the *Rama* are relied upon to resolve the disputes and present the final opinion which one must follow. This section discusses the disagreement in opinions regarding *dina damalchusa dina* and presents the final conclusion. Through examining a variety of opinions, readers gain greater insight into issues related to the requirement to follow their country's tax laws. Unless otherwise noted, all opinions appear in either the *Shulchan Aruch* or the *Rama* in the *Choshen Mishpat* section of the *Code of Jewish Laws*, Chap. 369.

There are three principal reasons for *dina damalchusa dina*. First, it can be claimed that the king owns the country and therefore everyone is required to give him a portion of their income. The payment is a type of rent. Second, a country can be considered as a type of partnership or corporation. The king or president is the organizational leader. Third, according to the Torah, the sons of Noah were assigned seven laws to follow. One of these laws is that each nation should establish a government which provides for the welfare of its citizens.

The first reason is that the king is considered the owner of the entire country. Thus, he is entitled to receive rent from all inhabitants. According to this reason, there is a question whether *dina damalchusa dina* applies only to laws related to land. Since all the land belongs to the king, he is entitled to rent for their use.

However, according to this view, the king owns the land and nothing else. Therefore, he has no right to income which is not dependent on land. On the other hand, some opinions hold that not only does the land belong to the king, but the people are also considered his property. Therefore, the people must also give the king a portion of their labor. The fact that a ruler has a right to force people to work or draft them into the army is an indication that their labor is owned by the king.

The Rama concludes that *dina damalchusa dina* applies even to laws which are not related to land.

Alternatively, if a king forces himself onto the people and the people do not accept him, there is no law of *dina damalchusa dina*. Rather, *dina damalchusa dina* applies only when there is a legitimate monarch or leader. Thus, for example, in Cuba or Eastern European countries which were invaded by Russia, the governments were kept in power by brute force and there would not be a rule of *dina damalchusa dina*. Thus, in these cases where the king or leader is not legitimate, *dina damalchusa dina* is not a reason to forbid tax evasion.

The reason for *dina damalchusa dina* which was described above applies only to a monarch. However, the next two reasons for *dina damalchusa dina* are also relevant to democracies. Maimonides in the Laws of Stealing (5:8) describes the quality one must have to be considered a legitimate ruler and for *dina damalchusa dina* to be applicable.

He says that people should agree that a person is their ruler and they see themselves as servants to him. From Maimonides and similar writings, commentaries claim that whenever a populace elects a government and they agree to its laws dina damalchusa dina applies. Thus, in a country such as the USA, there should be a rule of *dina damalchusa dina*. This is due to the apparent agreement among the populace that they will follow the decisions of their elected officials.

According to this last reason, *dina damalchusa dina* can be thought of as similar to rules which are enforced by a partnership. When people join a partnership, they implicitly agree to go along with all rules which are made by the ruling body. If someone feels that he cannot abide by the partnership's rulings, he is expected to withdraw.

Similarly, everyone in a democracy implicitly agrees to abide by the government's decisions. One who is not satisfied with the tax system, for example, is expected to concede and pay his/her obligation or move to a different country. Continuing to live in a country indicates an implicit agreement to abide by its rules. If one does not pay, he has violated this implicit agreement.

The third and final legitimacy of *dina damalchusa dina* to be discussed here is based on the laws which were given to Noah. These laws are discussed in Tractate *Sanhedrin* (56b). According to the Jewish tradition, these laws provide the guiding moral principles which non-Jews are expected to follow. One of the laws is the requirement for each state to convey statutes which provide for the welfare of its people. Included in this category of laws are those which are related to taxes. Thus, since the Torah requires the nations of the world to set up a tax system, Jewish people are also expected to obey these laws.

The reason for *dina damalchusa dina* which is based on the monarch owning all land has stronger implications than the other two reasons. Maimonides [Laws of Stealing (5:11)] says that one who does not pay taxes violates the Biblical prohibition of stealing [Leviticus (19:11)]. Thus, when tax evasion transgresses this important prohibition, it becomes a more serious offense. The commentaries explain that Maimonides' conclusion is only consistent when the king owning all the land is the reason for *dina damalchusa dina*.

According to this rationale, if a person does not give the king a portion of the crop, he is not paying the rent which is rightfully the king's. Thus, he is stealing from the king. He is holding onto the king's rent money. However, if *dina damalchusa dina* is due only to there being a law that one must pay taxes, but the country has no intrinsic ownership of its citizens' income, if one does not pay taxes, he/she has violated a law, but has not transgressed the stealing prohibition.

Besides the reason of an illegitimate ruler which was discussed earlier, the *Shulchan Aruch* addresses another justification for not having to follow the government's tax statutes. It says that taxes have to be paid only if there is a fair tax system. For example, there is a set scale regarding how much people have to pay. Alternatively, deciding each individual's tax burden separately is not within the rights of a government. Under this circumstance, the *dina damalchusa dina* rule does not require paying taxes.

Finally, the *Rama* discusses another government practice for which there are mixed opinions whether it is considered legitimate. Suppose the government decides to give a special excise tax to one group of people or to one particular profession, for example, if all Jews, all Italians, or all people living in Alabama have to pay more federal income tax.

The *Rama* says that according to one opinion such a tax system is considered unfair and *dina damalchusa dina* does not apply. However, he concludes that since the discrimination is against a whole group of people rather than particular individuals, the government is permitted to do it and *dina damalchusa dina* does apply.

Prohibitions Regarding Lying

The Torah gives a stronger warning about lying than other sins. It says "keep a distance from speaking false" [Exodus (23:7)]. The Torah not only prohibits lying, but it warns that a person should not say anything that would be close to lying. Stay away from it. Maimonides [laws of the *Sanhedrin* (21:10)] gives an example of what is meant by keeping away from lying. He says that a judge must be careful to not even smile at one of the litigants.

Such behavior can cause the second litigant to conclude that the judge looks more favorably to the first litigant. As a result, the second litigant makes less effort to fully present his position. Consequently, a false din could result. Thus, although the judge smiling at one litigant in itself is not a falsehood, it is still forbidden. The verse warns that one must keep away from anything that could come to a falsehood. Smiling at one litigant is considered in this category.

Even though the verse from Exodus which was mentioned above refers to speaking, there are several places in the Talmud which indicate that writing a falsehood is also a violation of the Biblical warning [*Baba Basra* (172a), *Gittin* (26b), and

Sanhedrin (30a)]. Based on these sources, one who evades taxes by signing a falsified tax form has violated the stay-away-from-falsehood warning.

Furthermore, there is disagreement among Rabbinical sources if *dina damalchusa dina* is a law which derives from the Torah or is only a decree made by Rabbis of later generations. If it is only a decree, then it is a less serious offense. However, since submitting a falsified tax statement involves lying, this form of tax evasion is definitely violating a Biblical prohibition and is automatically considered a more serious offense.

Not only is lying considered a sin, but even saying something that could look like a lie is to be avoided. Tractate *Baba Basra* (82a) discusses the mitzvah of bringing the first fruits. When these fruits are brought, verses are read which thank *Hashem* for providing the owner of the fruit land to grow it.

The Tractate discusses that even though there is a mitzvah to read these verses, if there is any question regarding if the land actually belongs to the bearer of the fruits, the verses are omitted. One could justify the reading as just reciting a verse from the Torah and it does not matter who owns the land. But instead, the fulfillment of the mitzvah is relinquished in order that the reading should not look like a lie. It should not appear that the fruit bearer claims to own land that in actuality does not belong to him.

However, it should be noted that according to Jewish Law if, for example, a merchant tells a customer that he does not have to pay sales tax if he pays in cash, the purchaser is committing a less serious offense than by not paying his full share of income taxes. As we just mentioned, when one does not pay income taxes, he/she is over at least one and possibly two Biblical prohibitions. However, when one does not pay sales tax, he/she has perhaps violated no Biblical transgression. This is because lying is not necessary in order to avoid paying sales tax.

Finally, the reader should realize that Jewish law considers the prohibition of lying as only a relative iniquity. This means that under certain conditions one is allowed to lie in order to prevent a larger injustice from being perpetrated. For example, in regards to taxes, a person is allowed to lie regarding his/her income to an illegal government. Under this circumstance, he/she is not considered to have violated the Biblical prohibition of keeping away from falsehoods.

Evidence that lying is permitted under this circumstance is found in Tractate Nadorim (62b). It is described how a Rabbi allows a congregant to say that he was a servant of a priest in order to avoid paying a tax which the government did not have a right to collect.

However, even though lying is sometimes permitted in order to circumvent an injustice, one is never allowed to swear falsely or give false testimony in court [*Shavous* (31a)]. Furthermore, since it can be difficult to differentiate when lying is permitted and when it is forbidden, some Rabbis suggest that only someone who is very learned in Jewish law should be permitted to lie. They say that if less-learned individuals are allowed to lie, they might wrongly infer that lying is permitted in other situations, where it is actually forbidden.

Chillul Hashem

In Tractate *Yuma* (86a), it is discussed how *chillul Hashem* is considered from the most reprehensible of all transgressions. *Chillul Hashem* has two meanings. First, it refers to any action which makes people look down at the Jewish religion. For example, if someone who is a Torah scholar and keeps all rituals is convicted of stealing money, this is a *chillul Hashem*. It makes people think that following the Torah does not lead one to become a more ethical person.

Second, *chillul Hashem* is when people see a distinguished person doing a transgression causes them to be willing to perform similar transgressions. For example, if a distinguished Rabbi is seen eating in a McDonalds restaurant, other Jewish people might infer that they do not have to be careful about Kashrus.

The Talmud discusses that a person can violate *chillul Hashem* even by doing something that is permissible. For example, it says that a *chillul Hashem* is a distinguished Torah scholar buying on credit and people becoming suspicious if he actually paid his bill.

Causing people to talk about a Torah scholar is called a *chillul Hashem* even if the bill was actually paid immediately and the gossip had no substance. Similarly, if the Rabbi mentioned above only eats a coke and apple at McDonalds, items which are allowed, his action may still not look proper.

Onlookers may not realize what he is eating or they may think if the Rabbi had a coke they can have a non-kosher hamburger. For this Rabbi to eat at McDonalds is called a *chillul Hashem* even though he violated no specific transgression. Furthermore, as people assume more respected positions, they must be more careful regarding their actions. When someone is more distinguished, the public is more likely to observe, talk about, and learn from their actions.

This section presented another transgression that can be violated by a person who evades paying taxes. As mentioned, the Talmud considers *chillul Hashem* to be one of the most serious violations. Even if there is a type of tax evasion which did not require lying and did not violate *dina damalchusa dina*, if it could come to *chillul Hashem*, it would not be allowed. Alternatively, it a tax evasion is a violation of din damalchusa dina and necessitates lying and can also come to *chillul Hashem* if it is revealed, it is considered an extremely serious offense.

While *chillul Hashem* has its basis in the Talmud and technically applies only to the Jewish religion, it is a general concept which can have ramifications for many types of people. Elected officials, for example, should be overly careful that all of their actions appear ethical. The discovery that public officials are involved in scandals or have not practiced exemplary behavior can cause citizens to lose respect for them. As a result, it is more difficult for them to govern.

Furthermore, if the public sees that elected officials appear to not pay proper respect for the laws, they are more likely to become lax. If, for example, it is discovered that an elected official paid no taxes for 1 year, citizens could be more willing to not report all their income or do other illegal manipulations to avoid paying taxes. This could be the case even if the elected official publicly justifies his not paying taxes.

Integrity

Over and above not telling a lie, a Jewish person is expected to have integrity. Not only must he not be bad and tell a lie, but he must be good and honest. There are many discussions how one cannot give up his principles for money and is expected to stay by his word. Paying taxes requires the same amount of integrity as any other part of one's life.

The most striking example of the importance of integrity regarding making money appears in the Rashbam commentary in *Baba Basra* (68a). There, he describes how Rav Safra made up his mind on a price to sell merchandise, let us say $50, did not tell anyone his decision, and then went to pray. While Rav Safra was praying, the customer came over to him and said he would offer him $50. Rav Safra could not answer since he was praying.

The customer assumed that Rav Safra did not respond because he was dissatisfied with the price. By the time Rav Safra finished his prayers, the customer was bidding $100. After he finished praying, Rav Safra responded that he would only charge the original price he had decided on of $50. To take advantage of the customer's misinterpretation of his silence would be dishonest. One would expect that Rav Safra who was ultracareful regarding money matters would behave similarly regarding paying taxes. He would not want to do any action that even looks like tax evasion.

The verse in the Prophet *Tsafonya* (3:13) illustrates the integrity required by the Torah. It says that Jewish people cannot do a sin and are not allowed to speak like liars. The Talmud uses the verse in several places in order to make an assumption that a religious person always keeps his word and means what he/she says. In Tractate *Kiddoshun* (46a), a husband agrees to his wife's insistence that their daughter marries her relatives rather than his. In the case of the Talmud, the daughter can only get married with the father's consent.

Subsequently, his relative comes and performs a marriage ceremony with the daughter. However, the wedding is declared null and void. The father had previously promised the girl to the wife's family. Therefore, based on the verse, it is assumed he could not have consented to his relative marrying her.

Similarly, Tractate *Pasuchim* (91a) says that if a prisoner is in a jail run by a religious warden who promises to release him, you can order for him his own paschal sacrifice and not worry about his not showing up. On the other hand, if the warden is not religious, you cannot depend upon a promise that the prisoner will be freed. The Gemorah also uses the verse in *Tsafonya* as a proof for this injunction.

When a religious person promises something, he keeps his word. Not keeping one's word is lying, which is not permissible. Once the warden says he will let the prisoner go, one does not have to worry that he will change his mind. Analogously, regarding the responsibility to pay taxes, the verse in *Tsafonya* teaches us that a person must give the IRS a straightforward account regarding his/her income. No form of lying can be condoned.

Conclusion

This chapter has shown that there are several reasons based on Jewish law why a Jewish person should not be a tax evader. The reasons include *dina damalchusa dina*, prohibitions regarding lying, *chillul Hashem*, and the importance of maintaining integrity. Probably, several other reasons could also be found.

In Leviticus (19:2), the Jewish people are commanded to be a holy nation. Furthermore, in verse 22:32, there is a commandment for the Jewish people to sanctify *Hashem's* name. These mitzvos are the opposite of *chillul Hashem*. The Torah teaches that the Jewish people have a special mission of bringing morality into the world.

Through a Jewish person attempting to strictly follow his/her nation's laws, staying away from falsehoods, and making sure that all his/her actions are a credit for the Jewish people, he/she fulfills the mitzvah of making *Hashem's* name great. People then see that being an Orthodox Jew is more than just practicing many ritualistic mitzvos.

Tax evasion is frequently performed only because a person wants to hold on to his/her wealth. When a Jewish person is convicted of this transgression, it causes the populace to lose respect for Judaism. Even if ethical or technical leniencies can be found which would make tax evasion permissible, the damage to the image of Judaism which can result if one's actions become public requires every Jewish person to make substantive efforts to refrain from controversial activities.

Chapter 10
The Ethics of Tax Evasion in Islam: A Comment

Robert W. McGee

A Note to Readers

I first started writing about the ethics of tax evasion in 1994 (McGee, 1994). As I became increasingly interested in the topic, I searched the literature in an attempt to find various religious perspectives on the issue. I could find only two discussions on the ethics of tax evasion from an Islamic perspective (Ahmad, 1995; Yusuf, 1971) and I wrote an article (McGee, 1997) that discussed the views of the two Islamic scholars I found.

I was not completely satisfied with the coverage of the topic in the literature, so I solicited the views of scholars from a variety of religious perspectives, inviting them to write an article from their religious perspective for publication in the journal I edit, with the possibility of reprinting their article in a book I planned to edit (McGee, 1998b). Several scholars accepted my invitation and wrote articles from the Jewish (Cohn, 1998; Tamari, 1998), Christian (Gronbacher, 1998; Pennock, 1998; Schansberg, 1998; Smith & Kimball, 1998), Muslim (Murtuza & Ghazanfar, 1998), and Baha'i (DeMoville, 1998) perspectives. The Murtuza and Ghazanfar article discussed zakat but did not address some of the issues regarding tax evasion that I wanted to have them address, so I wrote another article (McGee, 1998a) to address the issues that they left out of their article. Again, my main sources of information on the Islamic view were the only two sources I could find from my prior search (Ahmad, 1995; Yusuf, 1971).

Some of the other work I did on tax evasion from a religious perspective included a discussion of the Islamic view (McGee, 1999, 2004, 2006), again incorporating the views of Ahmad and Yusuf, since those were the only two sources I was aware of, other than the Murtuza and Ghazanfar (1998) article. Somewhere along the line,

R.W. McGee (✉)
School of Business, Florida International University, 3000 NE 151 Street,
North Miami, FL 33181, USA
e-mail: bob414@hotmail.com

R.W. McGee (ed.), *The Ethics of Tax Evasion: Perspectives in Theory and Practice*,
DOI 10.1007/978-1-4614-1287-8_10, © Springer Science+Business Media, LLC 2012

Ali Reza Jalili read some of these works and contacted me, pointing out that the Islamic view I presented was incorrect. As a result of our correspondence, I invited him to submit a chapter presenting his views for the present book, which he accepted (Jalili, 2012). Actually, his chapter does not present *his* views, but rather his interpretation of the Islamic view on tax evasion.

Needless to say, his view differs from the views of Ahmad (1995) and Yusuf (1971), and also from the views I expressed in my various articles and books. In my opinion, the Jalili chapter presents the most comprehensive treatment of the Islamic view on the ethics of tax evasion ever written, although I may be wrong on this point. I have searched the English language literature and have not found anything nearly as comprehensive (or as well written) as the Jalili chapter included in this book. However, I have not searched the literature in other languages, since my language skills are more or less limited to some of the Indo-European languages. Thus, there may be a more extensive treatment in existence in some other language, but if there is, I am unaware of it.

The discussion below is a slightly edited version of the article I wrote in 1998. It is presented so that the reader will become acquainted with the views of Ahmad and Yusuf, which were the only views widely available as of 1995, and even their views were not that widely available, since their views were published in books originating from the Middle East. I had to use the interlibrary loan services of the university where I was then teaching to get my hands on them.

Introduction

My distinguished colleagues have done a superb job of outlining the Islamic tax system in the previous article (Murtuza and Ghazanfar), so I will not rehash what they have already said. According to Islam, Muslims have a moral obligation to pay zakat for the support of the poor and for the legitimate functions of government. Thus, evading one's duty to pay zakat is classified as an immoral act. The Islamic system of taxation is a voluntary one, at least partially, although Islamic literature makes it clear that a government is justified in forcing people to pay taxes if the amount raised by zakat is insufficient to cover all the legitimate costs of government. However, "This right of interference with the individual's personal property will be limited to the extent required by the general welfare of the society ..." (Ahmad, 1995: 134).

Also, it does not follow that Muslims have a moral obligation to pay whatever taxes the government demands (Yusuf, 1971: 96), and it does not follow that any and all forms of taxation are legitimate. Thus, a case can be made that some forms of tax evasion, under certain conditions, may not be immoral. For example, if the government engages in activities that are beyond its legitimate functions, it might not be immoral to withhold taxes.[1] It might also not be immoral to evade certain kinds of taxes.

---

[1] For more on the legitimate role of the government under Islam, see Siddiqi 1996.

Ahmad (1995: 135–136) cites Yusuf's *Economic Justice in Islam*, which provides a list of practices that would be immoral for an Islamic state to engage in:

(a) It is immoral on the part of the state to use its power and privilege to make monopolistic gains or to tax the common people indirectly for replenishing the exchequer thereby (Yusuf, 1971: 96).

(b) There is no room in Islam for custom barriers, restrictive tariffs, or exchange control. The Islamic state, therefore, must not resort to them (Yusuf, 1971: 68, 101).

(c) It is illegitimate and unlawful for the state to tax directly or indirectly the general body of consumers and to give "protection" to the interests of a class of producers in the name of industrialization (Yusuf, 1971: 9–10).

(d) Since it is the duty of the state to dispense justice free of charge, therefore, there must not be any court-fees, revenue stamps, or fees of any kind for the transaction of any official business (Yusuf, 1971: 67).

(e) There must not be any "income" tax as such. Besides curbing the initiative, it assumes illegitimacy of the income of the rich. The state should levy, if need be, a proportional tax on the pattern of zakat on the accumulated wealth of the capable tax payers (Yusuf, 1971: 67).[2]

(f) The state should not resort to indirect taxation. If the state has to tax, then, it should do so directly so that the taxes represent a conscious contribution of the people to the cause of public interest (Yusuf, 1971: 67).

(g) That there is no justification for imposing death duty. Islamic laws of inheritance take care of the wealth left by the deceased (Yusuf, 1971: 67).

If these are the parameters, then it would seemingly not be immoral for a Muslim not to pay indirect taxes, which include excise taxes, customs duties, and perhaps corporate income taxes.[3] Muslims could also morally evade paying tariffs and could engage in smuggling, as long as the good smuggled is not against Islam, such as alcohol or cocaine. Evading income taxes would also not be immoral although evading a property tax might be. The evasion of inheritance, estate, and gift taxes would not be immoral.

---

[2] Since there must not be any income tax, there definitely must not be any graduated income tax, which necessarily treats the rich less favorably than the poor. According to Yusuf (p. 67): "There is no tax on income, which curbs initiative and enterprise. The progressive taxation assumes illegitimacy of the income of the rich. The rising slabs represent taxation with vendetta. Only a proportional tax at a fixed rate (on the pattern of Zakat) is to be levied on the accumulated wealth of the capable taxpayers without any distinction."

[3] A simplified definition of a direct tax is a tax that individuals or corporations pay directly (Stiglitz, 1988: 387). Indirect taxes are taxes on commodities. However, the burden of a corporate income tax is ultimately borne by individuals, either shareholders, consumers, or the corporation's employees. So a case can be made that a corporate income tax is actually an indirect tax. For more on the distinction between direct and indirect taxes, as well as the ethics of tax evasion in general, see McGee (1994).

Ahmad elaborates on some of the points made by Yusuf. Protectionism is condemned because it amounts to a direct or indirect tax placed upon consumers by the state. The general public must pay higher prices because the favored few (domestic producers) are being enriched. Traders and consumers are not morally bound to pay the increased price, whether the price increase is the result of protectionism or price fixing (Ahmad, 1995: 122).

According to Ahmad, "the adoption of any methods that create an artificial rise in the prices is strictly forbidden."(Ahmad, 1995: 123). Price fixing and protectionism are only two actions that cause prices to artificially rise. Other causes mentioned by Ahmad include the sales tax and excise taxes.

> The term *maks* is used for sales-tax. The Prophet (peace be on him) had reportedly said: 'He who levies *maks* shall not enter Paradise'. Since the imposition of sales-tax (or, for that matter, of octroi and excise duties) results in raising the prices unjustly, therefore, Islam does not approve of it. The Caliph 'Umar ibn 'Abd al-'Aziz had abolished *maks*, interpreting it as *bakhs* (diminution in what is due to others) which is expressly prohibited by the Qur'an. (Ahmad, 1995: 123)

This prohibition on sales taxes places Muslims in a bit of a quandary, since nearly every state in the USA levies a sales tax. Many European and other countries levy value-added taxes, which are basically the same thing as a sales tax. While it might be expedient for a Muslim consumer to pay a sales tax, and for a Muslim merchant to charge a sales tax, because they are required to do so by law, there is apparently nothing immoral about not collecting or paying them according to Islam.

Excise taxes are more difficult to avoid paying, since they are incorporated into the price of certain products. Of course, the excise tax on alcohol is easy to avoid. Just refrain from purchasing alcoholic beverages. But the excise tax on gasoline is more difficult (but not impossible) to avoid. In fact, the only way I can think of offhand to avoid paying the excise tax on gasoline is to buy gas from certain gas stations on Long Island, where the local mafia has made the evasion of the excise tax on gasoline into a profitable business. However, doing business with the mafia might run afoul of other Islamic tenets.

Another, less obvious form of tax evasion that is not immoral is the evasion of compliance with certain government regulations. A number of studies have pointed out that regulations can be equivalent to a tax,[4] and many examples can be given. One of the more obvious examples is rent control. If a landlord who owns a rent controlled building is prohibited from charging more than $500 a month for an apartment that would fetch $1,500 in a free market, he is, in effect, being forced to subsidize his tenant to the tune of $1,000 a month. The effect of this regulation is exactly the same as if the landlord were allowed to charge the $1,500 market rate, then pay a tax of 66 2/3 percent. Rent control laws force the transfer of wealth from property owners to a favored group (tenants), which is immoral according to the tenets of Islam.

---

[4] For examples, see Utt 1991; Payne 1992; Weidenbaum and DeFina 1978; MacDonnell 1989; U.S. General Accounting Office 1993; Gray 1987; Hopkins 1991; Yandle 1994; Adler 1996.

The strongest argument for complying with government regulations is when the regulation benefits the general public. However, many regulations are not of this genre. At least two other categories of regulations exist, those that benefit some special interest at the expense of the general public and those that are actually harmful to the general public. A number of trade regulations fall into one or both of these categories. The US Trade Representative publishes a book each year that summarizes some of these protectionist regulations.[5]

Numerous studies in recent years have attempted to measure the cost of various regulations. Some of these studies have concluded that certain regulations cost more than they are worth, or actually do more damage than good.[6]

Since there is no moral obligation for a Muslim to comply with a law that causes prices to rise unnecessarily or that enhances the wealth of some protected group at the expense of the general public – such as price fixing and protectionist trade legislation – and since some regulations cause prices to rise unnecessarily or protect some favored group at the expense of the general public, it is logical to conclude that Muslims have no moral duty to comply with regulations that either cause prices to rise unnecessarily or that protect some special interest at the expense of the general public. It would also be logical to conclude that there is no moral duty for a Muslim (or anyone, for that matter) to comply with a regulation that is actually harmful to the general public.

Whether, and under what circumstances, a Muslim has a duty to evade certain taxes or regulations is a question we will leave for another day.

References

Adler, Jonathan H. 1996. Property Rights, Regulatory Takings, and Environmental Protection. Washington, DC: Competitive Enterprise Institute.

Ahmad, Mushtaq. 1995. *Business Ethics in Islam*. Islamabad, Pakistan: The International Institute of Islamic Thought and the International Institute of Islamic Economics.

Cohn, Gordon. (1998). The Jewish View on Paying Taxes. *Journal of Accounting, Ethics & Public Policy*, 1(2), 109–120, reprinted in Robert W. McGee (Ed.), *The Ethics of Tax Evasion* (pp. 180–189). Dumont, NJ: The Dumont Institute for Public Policy Research, 1998, pp. 180–189.

DeMoville, Wig. 1998. The Ethics of Tax Evasion: A Baha'i Perspective. *Journal of Accounting, Ethics & Public Policy*, 1(3), 356–368, reprinted in Robert W. McGee (Ed.), *The Ethics of Tax Evasion* (pp. 230–240). Dumont, NJ: The Dumont Institute for Public Policy Research, 1998.

Gray, Wayne B. 1987. The Cost of Regulation: OSHA, EPA and the Productivity Slowdown. *American Economic Review* 77: 998–1006.

---

[5] For example, see US Trade Representative, 1997 National Trade Estimate Report on FOREIGN TRADE BARRIERS (Washington, DC: Superintendent of Documents).

[6] For a study that discusses some regulations that actually make things worse rather than better, see Stroup and Goodman (1989).

Gronbacher, Gregory M.A. 1998. Taxation: Catholic Social Thought and Classical Liberalism. *Journal of Accounting, Ethics & Public Policy*, 1(1), 91–100, reprinted in Robert W. McGee (ed.), *The Ethics of Tax Evasion* (pp. 158–167). Dumont, NJ: The Dumont Institute for Public Policy Research, Dumont, NJ, 1998.

Hopkins, Thomas D. 1991. Cost of Regulation. An RIT Public Policy Working Paper, Rochester Institute of Technology.

Jalili, Ali Reza. 2012. The Ethics of Tax Evasion: An Islamic Perspective, in Robert W. McGee (Ed.), *The Ethics of Tax Evasion in Theory and Practice*. New York: Springer.

MacDonnell, Lawrence J. 1989. Government Mandated Costs: The regulatory burden of environmental, health and safety standards. *Resources Policy* 15(1): 75–100. March 1.

McGee, Robert W. 1994. Is Tax Evasion Unethical? *The University of Kansas Law Review* 42:2 (Winter): 411–435.

McGee, Robert W. 1997. The Ethics of Tax Evasion and Trade Protectionism from an Islamic Perspective, *Commentaries on Law & Public Policy*, 1, 250–262.

McGee, Robert W. 1998a. The Ethics of Tax Evasion in Islam: A Comment. *Journal of Accounting, Ethics & Public Policy,* 1(2), 162–168, reprinted in Robert W. McGee, editor, The Ethics of Tax Evasion (pp. 214–219). Dumont, NJ: The Dumont Institute for Public Policy Research, 1998.

McGee, Robert W. (Ed.). 1998b. *The Ethics of Tax Evasion*. Dumont, NJ: The Dumont Institute for Public Policy Research.

McGee, Robert W. 1999. Is It Unethical to Evade Taxes in an Evil or Corrupt State? A Look at Jewish, Christian, Muslim, Mormon and Baha'i Perspectives. *Journal of Accounting, Ethics & Public Policy*, 2(1), 149–181. Reprinted at http://ssrn.com/abstract=251469.

McGee, Robert W. 2004. *The Philosophy of Taxation and Public Finance*. Norwell, MA and Dordrecht: Kluwer Academic Publishers.

McGee, Robert W. 2006. Three Views on the Ethics of Tax Evasion. *Journal of Business Ethics*, 67(1), 15–35.

Murtuza, Athar and S.M. Ghazanfar. 1998. Tax as a Form of Worship: Exploring the Nature of Zakat. *Journal of Accounting, Ethics & Public Policy* 1(2): 134–161, reprinted in Robert W. McGee (ed.), *The Ethics of Tax Evasion* (pp. 190–212). The Dumont Institute for Public Policy Research: Dumont, NJ, 1998.

Payne, James L. 1992. Unhappy Returns: The $600-Billion Tax Ripoff. *Policy Review* (Winter): 18–24.

Pennock, Robert T. 1998. Death and Taxes: On the Justice of Conscientious War Tax Resistance. *Journal of Accounting, Ethics & Public Policy*, 1(1), 58–76, reprinted in Robert W. McGee (Ed.), *The Ethics of Tax Evasion* (pp. 124–142). Dumont, NJ: The Dumont Institute for Public Policy Research, 1998.

Schansberg, D. Eric. 1998. The Ethics of Tax Evasion within Biblical Christianity: Are There Limits to "Rendering Unto Caesar"? *Journal of Accounting, Ethics & Public Policy*, 1(1), 77–90, reprinted in Robert W. McGee (ed.), The Ethics of Tax Evasion (pp. 144–157). The Dumont Institute for Public Policy Research, Dumont, NJ, 1998.

Siddiqi, M. Nejatullah. 1996. *Role of the State in the Economy: An Islamic Perspective*. Leicester, UK: The Islamic Foundation.

Smith, Sheldon R. and Kevin C. Kimball. 1998. Tax Evasion and Ethics: A Perspective from Members of The Church of Jesus Christ of Latter-Day Saints. *Journal of Accounting, Ethics & Public Policy*, 1(3), 337–348, reprinted in Robert W. McGee (Ed.), *The Ethics of Tax Evasion* (pp. 220–229). Dumont, NJ: The Dumont Institute for Public Policy Research, 1998.

Stiglitz, Joseph E. 1988. *Economics of the Public Sector*, second edition. New York: W.W. Norton & Company.

Stroup, Richard L. and John C. Goodman. 1989. Making the World Less Safe: The Unhealthy Trend in Health, Safety, and Environmental Regulation. NCPA Policy Report #137, Dallas: National Center for Policy Analysis.

Tamari, Meir. 1998. Ethical Issues in Tax Evasion: A Jewish Perspective. *Journal of Accounting, Ethics & Public Policy*, 1(2), 121–132, reprinted in Robert W. McGee (Ed.), *The Ethics of Tax Evasion* (pp. 168–178). Dumont, NJ: The Dumont Institute for Public Policy Research, 1998.

U.S. General Accounting Office. 1993. Regulatory Burden: Recent Studies, Industry Issues, and Agency Initiatives. GAO/GGD-94-28. December.

Utt, Ronald. 1991. The Growing Regulatory Burden: At What Cost To America? IPI Policy Report No. 114, Lewisville, TX: Institute for Policy Innovation. November.

Weidenbaum, Murray L. and Robert DeFina. 1978. The Cost of Federal Regulation of Economic Activity. Washington, DC: American Enterprise Institute. May.

Yandle, Bruce. 1994. Regulatory Takings, Farmers, Ranchers and the Fifth Amendment. Center for Policy Studies, Clemson University.

Yusuf, S.M. 1971. *Economic Justice in Islam*. Lahore: Sh. Muhammad Ashraf.

Chapter 11
The Ethics of Tax Evasion: An Islamic Perspective

Ali Reza Jalili

Introduction

Tax structures, tax systems, and tax policies are among the most important factors affecting economic and social affairs of any society. At the same time, the public's reaction to them, specifically the public attitudes regarding tax evasion and tax avoidance, can substantially influence these systems and policies to the point of either facilitating and promoting or undermining and defeating their original purposes and intentions. In all societies, while tax avoidance is permitted, evasion of taxes is illegal. Tax evasion, however, is probably a practice as old as taxation itself (Adams, 1993). The relevant point, nonetheless, is when if ever, different people evade taxation and view their behavior to be ethically justified. A correlated question is determination of the degree that culture or ideology influences attitudes toward tax evasion.

Review of the Literature

The modern economics, accounting, and law literatures have investigated the issue of tax evasion from efficiency, public finance, technical, and legal points of view. The coverage of morality or ethical aspects of tax evasion, however, have been primarily overlooked until fairly recently. One of the modern attempts to study tax evasion from ethical, mainly Catholic, perspective is the work by Crowe (1944) that covers 500 years of philosophical and theological debate on the subject. A number of more recent articles have studied the tax evasion issue from a variety of perspectives. Many of these studies have appeared in pages of *The Journal of Accounting,*

A.R. Jalili (✉)
New England College, Division of Management, Henniker, NH 03242, USA
e-mail: AJalili@nec.edu

R.W. McGee (ed.), *The Ethics of Tax Evasion: Perspectives in Theory and Practice,*
DOI 10.1007/978-1-4614-1287-8_11, © Springer Science+Business Media, LLC 2012

Ethics & Public Policy. A collection of articles on the subject has also appeared in an edited book (McGee, 1998g).

Cohn (1998), Tamari (1998), McGee (1998e), and McGee and Cohn (2008) have examined the issue of tax evasion from a Jewish perspective. Schansberg (1998) and McGee (1994) explore Biblical views on tax evasion while Gronbacher (1998) presents a Catholic and classical liberal views. A Mormon point of view is discussed by Smith and Kimball (1998) and McGee and Smith (2006). An Islamic view on the ethics of tax evasion is provided by Murtuza and Ghazanfar (1998) as well as McGee (1997, 1998h), and a Baha'i interpretation on the subject is given by DeMoville (1998). Other researches covering various Christian as well as secular views on ethics and morality of tax evasion include McGee (1998b, 1998g, 1999a). Moral and philosophical discussions of the issue and justifiability of taxation and tax evasion are, *inter alia*, presented in Block (1993), Leiker (1998), McGee (1994, 1998a, 1998f, 1999a, 2004, 2006a), Pennock (1998), Torgler (2003), and Nickerson, et al. (2008).

A monumental survey of 200,000 individuals in 81 countries has been conducted by Inglehart et al. (2004), covering a host of issues including tax evasion. Utilizing this data, as well as additional surveys, numerous empirical studies have been carried out by scholars in the field among various ideologies, cultures, communities, and groups.

The list includes Argentina (McGee and Rossi 2006), Armenia (McGee 1999b, McGee and Maranjyan 2006b), Bosnia and Herzegovina (McGee, Basic, and Tyler 2006), Bulgaria (Smatrakalev 1998), China (McGee and An 2006; McGee and Guo 2006), Germany (McGee, Nickerson, and Fees 2005), Greece (Ballas and Tsoukas 1998), Guatemala (McGee and Lingle 2005), Hong Kong (McGee & Butt, 2006; McGee and Ho 2006), Iran (McGee and Nazemi 2009), Macau (McGee, Noronha, and Tyler 2006), Poland (McGee and Bernal 2006), Romania (McGee 2006b), Russia (Vaguine 1998; Preobragenskaya and McGee 2004), Slovakia (McGee and Tusan 2006), Thailand (McGee 2006c), Ukraine (Nasadyuk and McGee 2006), the UK (McGee and Sevic 2008), and Vietnam (McGee 2006e).

Comparative studies of attitudes toward tax evasion encompass studies of Egypt, Iran, and Jordan (McGee and Bose 2008), Asian countries (McGee 2007), Australia, New Zealand, the USA (McGee and Bose 2007), Southern China and Macau (McGee and Noronha 2007), the USA with six Latin American countries (McGee and Gelman 2009), the USA and Hong Kong (McGee, Ho, and Li, 2006), a comparative demographic study of 33 countries (McGee and Tyler 2007), ten transitional countries (McGee 2008), and the states of Utah and New Jersey (McGee and Smith 2006).

Studies concentrating on specific groups include philosophy teachers (McGee 2006d), accounting and tax practitioners (Armstrong and Robinson 1998; Oliva 1998, McGee and Maranjyan 2006a), Mexican immigrants (Morales 1998), Swedish CEO's (McGee 1998c; Nylén, 1998), international business academics (McGee 2005), and participants in hypothetical case studies and questioners (Reckers, Sanders and Roark, 1994; Englebrecht, Folami, Lee, and Masselli 1998).

Most of the aforementioned studies indicate that, under certain circumstances, tax evasion is considered as an ethical behavior at both philosophical and practical levels by a majority of people covered by the surveys. Several arguments have also been provided to discuss the results and present justifications for those positions on tax evasion from different perspectives.

McGee (2006a), following the classification and criterion proposed by Crowe (1944), divided these arguments into three categories.

Accordingly, he states that examination of the work of scholars throughout the centuries reveals that views on tax evasion may be classified into three groups. Those who consider tax evasion never to be ethical; those who believe tax evasion could be ethical under certain circumstance; and those who view tax evasion as always ethical. McGee refers to these three groups as "Absolutists," "Rationalists," and "Anarchists," respectively.

The "Absolutist" view asserts that tax evasion is always, or nearly always unethical. The underlying rationale for this belief is a three-prong duty, duty to State, duty to fellow members of the society, and duty to God. The "Rationalist," "Social Contract Theorist," or "Relativist" view holds that, depending on the circumstances, tax evasion may be sometimes ethical and other times unethical. "Anarchists," on the other hand, reject the existence of any "Social Contract" and hold that citizens never have any duty to pay taxes to the state since there is no explicit agreement between the citizens and the states to do so.

They view states as thieves and illegitimate entities that have no moral authority to take anything from anyone. Each group, obviously, discusses the issue in detail and provides logic, reasoning, and theoretical justification for its position. Particulars of the philosophical propositions, issues surrounding the question, and arguments, along with results of specific studies, may be found, among other places, in the previously cited works of Cohn, Crowe, Ballas and Tsoukas, Block, De Moville, Gronbacher, Leiker, McGee, Smatrakalev, Smith and Kimball, Tamari, and Vaguine.

According to these discussions and experiments, the rationalist view appears to be the most widely held position among people studied. The basic conclusion of most experimental works and surveys may be stated in one sentence: "Most people find tax evasion to be ethical in some situations, although some arguments to justify tax evasion are stronger than others." (McGee, Basic and Tyler, 2007). It also appears that in each society or culture, several factors shape the public opinion on taxation. Whether these factors are real or perceived is irrelevant, and their heavy influence on people's attitude toward tax evasion is rather clear.

Among the identified factors, perceived fairness of the prevailing tax system, legitimacy of the government collecting taxes, availability and quality of public goods provided to the society, and level of governmental corruption appear to exert the most influence on people's attitude regarding tax evasion.

Methodology

The current study is an attempt to present and explain an Islamic view on tax evasion and address some of the ethical questions surrounding this issue from that perspective. Prior to examination of ethical considerations of tax evasion and as a point of entry, one might pose and probe some questions. For instance, are taxes in general ethical? Is there any moral obligation to pay any kind of taxes? Is there any kind of tax that might be morally justified? Is there a time and situation in which tax evasion may be ethical or justified? If yes, are there boundaries to this behavior? If tax payments somehow depend on legitimacy of the government in question or fairness of the tax system or the government's level of corruption, then how might one define, determine, and measure the legitimacy, corruption, and fairness?

What makes a government legitimate or illegitimate? What makes a system fair or unfair? How are these attributes measured? What should a citizen expect in return for tax payments? How may the adequacy of return on taxes be defined and evaluated? These and numerous similar questions should be addressed before one could carry out an adequate and meaningful discussion of the issues surrounding tax evasion. Since the present work is informative rather than evaluative in nature, and since these concerns are sufficiently addressed in the previously noted literature, particularly the numerous works of Robert McGee and the citations contained therein, and in consideration of time and space, the aforesaid questions are minimally addressed here and the full arguments are avoided.

Discussion and evaluation of any emotionally charged issue, such as religion or belief system is always a delicate and sensitive balancing act. This is true even when the issue under question is only a peripheral one in relation to the totality of the ideology. Islam is no exception to this rule. Islam as a doctrine has developed over the years and has been interpreted in a variety of ways. As such, it inevitably contains ambiguity and contradictions.

Through time, several Islamic Schools of Thoughts have emerged. The two basic branches are Sunnis and Shiites. The Sunnis are divided into four major Schools, namely Maleki, Shafei, Hanafi, and Hanbali. Shiites contain two major groups, Jaafari and Ismaeili. The evolution of Islamic Thoughts over the years along with inherent vagueness and flexibility of some Islamic principles, have produced a vast body of literature on a variety of issues that embodies many contradictions and varied interpretations.

Assorted Muslim writers and jurists with diverse ideological tendencies and in consideration of their specific time, place, and circumstances, have taken different positions, offered distinct explanations, or put forth various arguments. Each author or jurist draws on a portion of available sources to support his position. These writings are often influenced by biases and sectarianism and frequently contain unsubstantiated assertions and conclusions.

The claims and explanations reflect a given author's response to a specific time and place and often contain views or wishes of the writers rather than being rooted in the original Islamic Law. Therefore, while it is necessary to be aware of what Muslim writers have to offer on any given issue, one should not be oblivious to their inherent shortcomings. Exclusive reliance on these sources most likely will lead inquirers to a conclusion that is the intension of the source-authors and may have little or nothing to do with the letter or the spirit of Islamic Thought itself.

Shariah or Islamic Law is what theoretically governs all Muslim societies. There are two main sources for this Law, the Muslim holy book (Qur'an) and reported traditions and actual practices of Muhammad (Sunnah). Although there is a high degree of consensus among Muslim jurists on basic Principles and Fundamentals of Shariah, there are several differences in details and on secondary issues. This stems from the fact that sometimes the Qur'anic verses are interpreted differently and that at times the details and validity of Muhammad's reported behavior are disputed.

Moreover, there are issues facing contemporary Muslims that were not applicable in the early years of Islam and therefore do not have any direct references in the original sources. Consequently, in settling some issues, various jurists, depending on their particular bent, have arrived at different conclusions and established different rules. The current study, deliberately avoids extensive utilization of interpretations and secondary sources. It also refrains from engaging in a deep probe of each point based on all existing viewpoints. This is done since detailed comparative discussion is neither fruitful here nor within the scope of this study.

To be mindful of potential traps, to consider different sensitivities, and to evade unnecessary trajectories, the main reliance is on facts and sources that are uncontroversial and universally accepted by Muslims. All assertions and inferences are based on the explicit letter of the Law as stated in the Qur'an and undisputed reported actions and traditions of Muhammad. Interpretations or conjectures by the author are completely avoided and whenever any kind of interpretation is adopted, it is by a third party and only from reliable and unanimously accepted sources and interpretations.

Other secondary sources are occasionally and marginally used and only as a point of reference. All references to the Qur'an are cited by chapter and verse and adopted through a comparison of four different English translations matched against the Arabic text. Whenever more than one verse in the Qur'an addresses a given point, except in some instances, only a few such verses are presented to support an assertion. The final product, nonetheless, should provide all readers with a substantial comprehension of the Islamic view on tax evasion.

The Framework

Studying any aspect of Islam is not fruitful unless the subject is approached within a proper holistic framework. The topic should be evaluated based on its place within the Islamic doctrine as a whole and its connection to other facets of Islamic Thought. The discussion of tax evasion in Islam will not be complete and proper comprehension will not be attained without reasonable knowledge of several categories within the Islamic Doctrine.

The most fundamental and pertinent of these concepts are an understanding of the Hereafter, the purpose of life, Justice, the role of the individual in Muslim society, ownership and property rights, consumption patterns, the concentration of wealth, the role of the state, and the function of taxes. The essence of an Islamic position on these categories is presented below. More details on the Islamic perspective on these categories may be found, among other sources, in Abdul Rauf (1979), Abdel Rahman (1977), Ahmad, K. (1980), Ahmad, M. (1995), Ahmad, Z. (1991),

Al Hassani and Mirakhor (1989), Azhar (2009), Chapra (1992, 1996), Choudhury (1980, 2010), de Zayas (1960), El Ashker and Wilson (2006), Harrigan and El-Said (2009), Haq (1995), Iqbal and Lewis (2009), Izadi (1974), Khaf (1978), Khan (1983), Khan, M.F. (2009), Kuran (1983 and 2010), Mannan (1989 and 2008), Niazi (1977), Nomani and Rahnema (1994), Qardawi (1997), Rahman (1986, 1990, and 1995), Shaik (1980), Singer (2008), Yusuf (1996), and Zaman (1981).

God and the Law

Based on Islamic beliefs, the Qur'an and Sunnah make up the Islamic Law (Shariah), which governs the public and private lives of Muslims everywhere and at all times. Shariah is Commands of the All Knowing God and encompasses all that is good and needed for a faithful to be blessed and delivered, both in this world and in the Hereafter.

The Qur'an itself states that "And with Him are the keys of the unseen. None but Him knows them. And He knows whatever is in the land and the sea. Not a leaf falls but He knows, not a grain amid the darkness of the earth, nor anything wet or dry but it is recorded in the clear Book." (6:59) or "Do you not know that Allah knows whatever is there in the heavens and earth. Indeed that is in a Record. Indeed, that is easy for Allah." (22:70).

Muslims must uphold that the Qur'an is the direct word of God as revealed to Muhammad and accept it in its totality and follow it in its entirety. "And if you are in doubt about that which we sent down (Qur'an) to our slave (Muhammad), then produce a chapter like that." (2:23) or "O you who believe, believe in Allah and His messenger and the Book which He has sent down to His messenger and the Scripture which He sent down before. And whoever disbelieves in Allah, and His angels, and His Scriptures, and His messengers, and the Last Day, then indeed he has strayed far away." (4:136), or "And thus We have sent it (the Qur'an) down to be a judgment of authority." (13:37).

In all their deeds, Muslims must constantly be conscious of the Omnipresent All Knowing All Powerful God who sees and hears everything and keeps track of all deeds of all people for use in the Day of Reckoning.

"When the heaven is cleft asunder. And when the stars have fallen and scattered. And when the seas are burst forth. And when graves are overturned." A person shall know what he has sent forward and what he has left behind. "O man what has made you careless regarding your Lord, the most generous? Who created you, fashioned you perfectly, and gave you due proportion. In whatever form He willed, He put you together. Nay, but you deny the Judgment. And indeed there are above you guardians. Honorable recorders. Who know all you do." (82:1–12)" or "Do they not think that they will be resurrected? On a Great Day. The Day when mankind shall stand before the Lord of the worlds. Nay, indeed, the record of the wicked is in sijjeen. And what do you know what sijjeen is. A written record."

(83:4–9) and "Nay, indeed, the record of righteous is in illiyun. And what do you know what illiyun is? A written record to which bear witness those nearest to Allah." (83:18–21). The same concepts have been enumerated and stressed many more times in the Qur'an, which indicates its vital role and crucial importance in a proper understanding of the Islamic perspective.

A sample includes "Do you not know that Allah has power over all things." (2:106), or "Indeed Allah is all Seer of all you do." (2:110) or "And He is Allah in the heavens and in the earth. He knows your secrets and what you reveal." (6:3), as well as "And Allah encompasses all that they do" (8:47). Also "And he is the all hearer, the all knower." (2:137), and "And to Allah belongs the east and the west. So wherever you turn there is Allah's face. Indeed Allah is all encompassing all knowing." (2:115), or "Indeed Allah knows the unseen of heavens and earth. And Allah is the all seer of all you do." (49:18). Additionally, "Indeed Allah is all powerful, all mighty." (58:21), and "And indeed, We have given you from Us a reminder. Whoever turns away from it, he verily will bear a burden in the Day of Resurrection." (20:99–100), or "Then do you believe in part of the Scripture and disbelieve in other parts? Then what is the recompense of those who do so among you, except disgrace in the worldly lives and severest punishment in the Day of Resurrection. And Allah is not unaware of what you do." (2:85).

Hereafter

According to Islam, all people resurrect to stand before God and answer for their deeds in this world. All that emphasis on the fact that God knows and keeps track of everything is to remind everyone of the Day of Judgment and its consequences. One cannot doubt or deny this and be a Muslim or expect salvation. "Woe to deniers on that Day. Those who deny the Day of Judgment. And no one denies it except every sinful transgressor. When our verses are recited to him, he says tales of ancient people. Nay, but that which they have earned is rust upon their hearts. Nay, surely on that day, they will be debarred from mercy of their Lord. Then, surely they shall burn in Hellfire. Then, it will be said this is what you used to deny. (83:10–17)." The Hereafter is eternal while this world is a transitory stage in the life of an individual. People pass through this world to reach the eternal salvation.

Accordingly, Muslims must dedicate their lives to this task. To accomplish that, however, they must follow the rules and codes of conduct as prescribed by God in the Qur'an and Sunnah. People must live well in this world and seek material well-being. They, however, must also take advantage of the opportunity on earth to prepare for Hereafter. "And seek to attain by means of what God has given you the abode of the Hereafter, but neglect not your share in this world, and do good to others as God has done good to you, and seek not corruption on earth. Surely God loves not the corruptors." (28:77).

Justice and Equality

Muslim jurists almost unanimously believe that seeking social and economic justice and establishment of a Just and Righteous Society on earth is the main goal of Islam. The Qur'an declares, "We verily sent Our messengers with clear signs, and sent with them the Scripture and the Balance so that mankind may stand by justice." (57:25). Being just, based on the Qur'an, is one of the fundamental attributes of an individual Muslim as well as an Islamic society. Therefore, Islam orders the believers to always be just and follow the path of justice in all they do.

That includes dealing in the affairs of daily lives and activities as well as establishing social norms and standards that should prevail in an Islamic society. "O you who believe, be steadfast witnesses for Allah in justice, and let not hatred of some people make you not to deal justly. Be just: that is nearer to piety. And fear Allah. Verily, Allah is informed of what you do." (5:8) or "Give full measure and full weight, in justice. We burden not any soul beyond its capacity. And when you speak, do justice, even if it be against a kinsman." (6:152). Similarly, "Woe to the defrauders. Those who, when they have to receive from people by measure, demand full measure. And when they have to give to others by measure, give less than due." (83:1–3) or "Verily Allah commands you to justice and kindness." (16:90).

All human beings are created from the same origin and thus are equal before God and the Law. The Qur'an asserts that Muslims are "brothers-in-faith" (9:11) and declares "Verily, the most honored of you before God is the most righteous of you." (49:13). This equality before the God and the Law, however, does not imply social or economic equality as well. Islam acknowledges that some people are above others in income, wealth, and position. "And it is He who made you His vice-regents of the earth, and raised some of you above others in ranks, that He may try you in what He had given you." (6:165) or "Truly your Lord enlarges the provision for whom He wills and strains (it for whom He wills). Verily, He is ever knower, all seer of His slaves." (17:30). However, the principles of justice and unity dictates that Muslims to be mindful of each other and provide for their brothers in need. In fact, the Qur'an states that the poor have a right and a share in the wealth of more affluent Muslims.

Concentration of Wealth

Under Islam, when all individuals receive what is due them, economic justice is achieved. Under a Just system, there is no guarantee of equity or equality of the outcome. Concentration of wealth in few hands and hoarding of idle wealth, however, is not viewed favorably by Islam. God dislikes concentration of wealth and any wealth amassed through illegal or immoral activities. The Qur'an states "Those who hoard up gold and silver and do not spend it in the way of Allah, unto them give tidings of a painful punishment. On the day when it will be heated in the fire of Hell, and their foreheads and their flanks and their backs will be branded with it. Here is what you hoarded for yourselves, now taste of what you used to hoard." (9:34–35). Or "Woe to every slanderer, defamer, who amasses wealth and counts; thinking that his wealth would make him last forever. Nay, he will surely be thrown into the crushing place." (104:1–4).

Given the Islamic position on concentration of wealth and its subscription to social and economic justice, it is not surprising that Islam prescribes mechanisms that mandates transfer of wealth from upper income to lower income Muslims in the community.

Property Rights and Ownership

Unquestionably, Islamic property rights are not absolute. Ownership of everything belongs to God and he is the ultimate owner of all there is. Allah is the only real, actual, and final owner of everything in the universe. The Qur'an declares, "Whatever is in the heavens and the earth belongs to Allah." (2:284), or "to Him alone belongs everything in the heaven and the earth and everything in between. To Him alone belongs whatever is below the soil." (20:6). God, however, provides the resources as gifts for use by human beings "He is who created for you all that is on earth." (2:29) and "Allah has subjected to you, as from Him, all that is in heavens and on earth." (14:13). Also, "And to Allah belongs whatever is in the heavens and whatever is on earth. And indeed We instructed you and those who were given the Book before you to fear Allah." (4:131).

The Qur'an commands believers to "bestow upon them, of the wealth of Allah which he has bestowed upon you." (24:33). Humans are selected and appointed by God as trustee over His gifts. "Believe in Allah and His Messenger, and spend of that whereof He has made you trustees." (57:7). The Qur'an leaves no doubt that people are merely entrusted with wealth for their livelihood in this world. They are allowed to hold property and enjoy the benefits so long as they understand that they are holding the property in trust and follow God's Rules. "It is We who placed you with authority on earth, and provided you therein with means for your life." (7:10). "It is Allah who has subjected the sea to you, that ships may sail through it by His command, that you may seek of His bounty, and that you may be grateful." (14:12). It follows, then, that the distribution of wealth and the outcome of economic activities and policies, including taxes, must be "Just" and in accordance with the will of the "Ultimate Owner." God's Will is manifested in the principles laid down by Him in the Qur'an. Thus, following the Qur'an is the only way to satisfy Him and achieve eternal salvation.

Consumption Pattern

Muslims' consumption pattern, except for some specific items, is not limited or constrained. "Eat and drink of that which God has provided and act not corruptly, making mischief in the world." (2:60). Or "Say: who has forbidden the gifts of Allah which He has provided for His servants, and the good things of His providing?" (7:32). Also, "O you believers, eat of the good things that We have provided for you, and be grateful to Allah if it is Him you worship." (2:172). Despite this freedom, however, "moderate" and "lawful" consumption and spending as well as avoiding extravagance are repeatedly recommended by Islam.

The Qur'an says, "O mankind, eat of what is lawful and good on earth and follow not the footsteps of the devil." (2:168). Or "O you who believe, forbid not the good things which Allah has made lawful for you and do not transgress. For Allah does not love transgressors. And eat of the lawful and good things that Allah has given you. And fear Allah in whom you believe." (5:87–88). In general, Islam prohibits "extravagance" (Israf) and spending ones money on impermissible items (Tabzir). According to the Qur'an, "Squanderers are indeed brothers of the devil." (17:27), and "Allah does not love people who waste what they have." (6:141).

The prohibition of "extravagance" and "wasting of one's wealth" is repeated at least in 13 Qur'anic verses while moderation has always been prescribed. "Don't make your hand shackled to your neck, nor stretch it forth to the utmost of its stretching for you will be sitting rebuked, destitute." (17:29). Many other places in the Qur'an, including 6:142, 7:31, 7:160, 16:114, 20:81, 23:51, 34:15, and 67:15 repeat the same theme. Accordingly, Muslim writers, almost invariably, assert that Islam advocates a modest life and an average standard of living.

Individual and Society

Muslim society as well as individual Muslims should have some attributes, characteristics, and behavioral code of conduct. The Islamic code of conduct is elaborated in some detail in the Qur'an and Sunnah and all Muslims unanimously agree upon it. Muslims must subscribe to this code of conduct and follow it to create a virtuous society and lead a righteous life. This is the path of Islam in this world and the only way to achieve eternal salvation in the Hereafter.

In general, Muslims must be honest and upright and Muslim communities must be free from fraud, deception, greed, lying, cheating, and all other activities considered by Islam to be unjust or immoral. Muslims, naturally, must strive to cleanse themselves from undesirable characteristics and be as close to the ideal model as possible. To facilitate this journey, two Islamic principles of Promotion of Good Deeds and Prevention of Bad Deeds are prescribed. It is incumbent upon each and every Muslim to promote good behavior and prevent the bad ones. Each Muslim has a duty to himself/herself and his/her fellow Muslims to behave in an ethical and exemplary manner and vigilantly safeguard the society against any violation of good behavior.

Muslims are ordered to be charitable and spend part of their wealth to help their fellow Muslims in need. Three charitable categories mentioned in the Qur'an are "Sadaghaat," "Ihsaan," and "Infaagh." These acts amount to helping the needy, the impoverished, and the destitute. Performing them pleases Allah and is rewarded by Him. The emphasis on these acts is so strong that they resemble an obligatory duty of Muslims and constitute a right for the receivers. Qur'an declares "And in their wealth the beggar and the outcast had due share." (5:19) or "And in whose wealth there is a right acknowledged for the beggar and the destitute." (70:24–25) and "By no means shall you attain to righteousness until you spend in the way of Allah out of that which you cherish most and whatsoever you spend, Allah is aware of it." (3:92).

Many more verses in the Qur'an encourage Muslims to perform these charitable acts. A partial list includes 2:3–5, 2:195, 2:177, 2:245,, 2:254, 2:261, 2:265, 2:271–272, 2:274, 3:133–134, 4:36, 8:60, 9:111, 9:120, 11:3, 11:52, 16:90, 16:97, 17:23–6, 28:77, 30:38–39, 35:29, 57:7, 57:18, 63:10, 64:17, 76:8–11, and 92:5. Therefore, unquestionably these charitable acts constitute as part of a Muslim's duty to society and are intended to alleviate poverty and promote justice and harmony.

The State and the Ruler(s)

According to Islamic doctrine, the primary objective and task of an Islamic state is to implement and strictly follow the Shariah. For it is strict following of this Law and the Islamic code of conduct that provides and maintains an environment that enables flourishing of virtuous attributes, honorable, and prosperous lives during the transitory life on earth and guarantees eternal salvation in the Hereafter. This is the only true path of salvation in both words. Therefore, the role and function of an Islamic state is nothing but strict following of this course.

All programs and policies of a true Islamic state must be rooted in and be in accordance with the Shariah Laws. Qur'an states that "Say: Obey Allah and obey the messenger, but if you turn away he is only responsible for the duty placed on him and you for that which is placed on you. And if you obey him you will be rightly guided." (24:54). Also, "And fear the fire which is prepared for the disbelievers. And obey Allah and the messenger that you may obtain mercy." (3:131–132).

This command has been repeated so frequently that it leaves no doubt that teachings of the Qur'an and Muhammad must be continuously and unconditionally obeyed by all Muslims. The state ruled by Muhammad's successors, then, must follow the same path to be a worthy Islamic state. If it does, it will be a state that is ruled by "Those who, if We give them authority in the land, establish prayer and pay Zakaat and enjoin what is right and forbid what is wrong. And with Allah rests the outcome of all matters." (22:41).

The Qur'an refers to such a legitimate government or ruler as Ulul-Amr. Following the Ulul-Amr is mandatory and constitutes as a part of a Muslim's duty. "O you who believe, obey Allah, and obey the messenger and Ulul-Amr (those who are vested with authority), and if you have a dispute amongst yourselves concerning any matter, refer it to Allah and the messenger if you truly believe in Allah and the Last Day. That is better and more suitable in the end." (4:59).

Also, "And when there comes to them some matter or news concerning safety or fear, they spread it. And only if they had referred it to the messenger and to the Ulul-Amr, the competent investigators would have understood it directly from them. If it had not been for the grace of Allah upon you and His mercy all of you but a few would have followed Satan (4:83)". Thus, it follows that such a righteous Islamic state must be continuously and unconditionally supported and obeyed by all Muslims since it is representative of Allah on earth and successor to Muhammad.

This obedience, just like the one to Muhammad, must be unremitting, unmitigated, and unconditional. That is, Muslim's are obligated to heed the rules and mandates of their legitimate rulers or governments. Naturally, the necessary and sufficient condition is that the state must be a legitimate Islamic state. A state can have this legitimacy if and only if it follows the Shariah Laws. When this legitimacy is established, any violation of the rules is forbidden and illegal and therefore punishable in this world as well as the Hereafter.

Islamic Taxes

It is extremely difficult to present a concise, coherent, and uniform understanding of the Islamic tax system. In addition to many conceptual vaguenesses and generalities in Islamic economic doctrine, several other factors contribute to this phenomenon. The list of these factors include subjective interpretations by different authors, the writers' ideological tendencies, large and frequently conflicting accounts of events, and outright mistakes in translation of sources. The outline, intent, and spirit of the original Islamic tax laws, nonetheless, are rather clear.

The Islamic tax system contains both "general" and "selective" or "classified" taxes, and it considers both the nature of the property and the owner's conditions in the calculations. Different categories of wealth and real properties are treated and taxed differently. In some cases, even items within the same class of property are treated dissimilarly, e.g., treatment and taxation of real properties and personal properties, tangible and intangible assets, farm and residential lands.

Despite all these, a generally accepted mechanics and intent of Islamic taxes may be stated as idle or uncirculated, accumulated, and hoarded wealth plus certain categories of annual income are subject to taxation. The taxes are levied against the taxable base after deduction of an exemption level (Nisaab), as well as an allowance equal to a "reasonable amount for one's annual expenditure that is commensurate with the taxpayer's status in life." In addition to the financing the regular functions of the Islamic state, the main objectives of Islamic tax system are alleviation of poverty, improving income distribution, and creation and maintenance of a just society.

Islamic jurisprudence recognizes individuals as the taxpaying units. As such, households, corporations, and other entities are not taxed. They are merely conduits that all income and taxable items pass through them to individual owners and are taxed at that level. The first Islamic tax was Khums, which was imposed after the

Battle of Badr in the second year of Hijra (Muhammad's migration from Mecca to Medina on 622 AD). Zakaat-ul-Fitr was also made mandatory in the same year. Kharaaj was imposed on the 7th year, Zakaat, which was voluntary at first, was declared mandatory on the 8th year and Jizya was established in 7th or 8th year after Hijra (Sadr 1989, p. 123 and 143, Ijtihadi 1985, p. 187, Zaman 1981, p. 44).

The Islamic taxes are mainly levied against and calculated based on actual taxable items. That is, these taxes are in-kind taxes. The payment, however, may be either in-kind or in equivalent value. Some of the taxable items are specified in the Qur'an or by Muhammad himself, while others have been added in later years by analogy and extension. In all cases, taxes are collected by the state and are kept in the Public Treasury (Bayt-ul-Maal). The money, then, is spent on certain categories specified in Shariah. The manner of disbursing some of the collected taxes is specific and on pre-prescribed items while spending of other parts is more flexible with less restriction.

Most of the Islamic taxes mentioned in the Qur'an come under the category of Zakaat. The term refers to a generic compulsory tax and literally means to cleanse, to purify or to grow. Zakaat is one of the pillars of the Islamic faith and an extremely important aspect of Islamic Code of Conduct. It is called a duty from God (Farizatan min Allah) and a form of worship that cleanses and purifies the soul and heart and the wealth of the Zakaat payer.

Zakaat has been mentioned in the Qur'an 60 times. Twenty-seven of those are right after Salaat or daily prayer, which itself is referred to as "the Pillar of the Religion." It is among the duties of the righteous Muslims and is a necessary condition of being a Muslim. "Establish regular prayer and pay Zakaat." (2:110), or "Indeed, those who believe and do the righteous deed, and establish regular prayer and pay Zakaat, their reward is with their Lord and there shall be no fear upon them, nor shall they grieve." (2:277), and "He it is Who produces gardens trellised and untrellised, and the date palms, and crops of divers flavor, and the olive and the pomegranate, like and unlike. Eat of their fruits when they bear fruits, and pay its due on the day of its harvest and waste not by excess. Indeed, He does not love those who are extravagant." (6:141).

Or "So establish worship, pay Zakaat, and hold fast to Allah." (22:78) and "And they were not commanded except to worship Allah, being sincere and true to Him in faith, and to establish prayer and to pay Zakaat, and that is the true religion." (98:5). The same command may be found in numerous other verses such as: 2:43, 2:83, 2:177, 4:30, 4:58, 4:77, 4:162, 5:12, 5:13, 5:58, 7:156, 9:5, 9:11, 9:18, 9:71, 9:103, 19:31, 19:55, 21:73, 23:4, 24:37, 24:56, 30:39, 31:4, 33:33, 41:7, 58:13, 73:20. The emphasis leaves no doubt about the importance of Zakaat in a Muslim society and Muslim's lives. The Qur'an, it should be noted, sometimes uses the term "Sadaqah" (alms), in place of Zakaat. The consensus among Muslim jurists, though, is that whenever the payment is compulsory, it is Zakaat while Sadaqah refers to voluntary payments or charity.

Zakaat is payable by all free Muslims who are in possession of the taxable items and have the ability to utilize and make decisions about the properties (de Zayas 2003, Khoie 1982, Khomeini 1980, Montazeri 1986; Rahman, 1986). For payment of Zakaat to be valid, the Zakaat payer must have the intention of paying Zakaat, pay it for prescribed categories, and unconditionally transfer the ownership to the recipient.

While the majority of jurists believe that the Zakaat payer must not receive any direct benefit from the payment, some argue that even an indirect benefit from Zakaat is not permitted (Zaman 1981). A general categorization along with a brief description of Islamic taxes is presented below. A more detailed description of Islamic taxes may be found in several places, including Abu Yusuf al Qadi (1979), Abu Zahra (1965), Awan (1980), Chapra (1992), de Zayas (1969, 2003), Ijtihadi (1985), Jalili (2006), Mannan (2008), Qardawi (1969), Rahman, F. (1986), Rahman, M. (2003), Sadr (1989), Shaik (1980), and Zaman (1981).

1. Zakaat of land or Ushr, which is a flat percentage tax on some agricultural products. Views vary on the taxability of various crops, but most agree that crops, such as wheat, barley, rice, and most fruits, are taxable. The rates for Ushr are specified in Sunnah as 5% of the agricultural produce on artificially irrigated lands and 10% on produce of the lands benefiting from rain or natural spring only (Khomeini 1980; Rahman 1986; Shad 1986).

2. Zakaat on livestock, which applies to cattle, camels, and sheep older than 1 year. By analogy, this tax is extended to animals, such as goats, water buffaloes, and alike. Horses and riding animals, holdings of fish, poultry, and wild games are exempt from taxation unless they constitute the owners' trade or when they are sold. In general, animals kept for personal consumption are not subject to taxes unless they are sold. Some believe in taxability of animals kept for any business purpose while others do not. Each category of animal has a certain threshold amount called "Nisaab" that is exempt from taxation. Zakaat is applicable based on the number of holdings beyond Nisaab in each category. The rate structure is expressed in quantity and type of animals. Taxes are calculated and are due in kind, but they may also be paid in equivalent monetary value.

3. In addition to items taxed under Zakaat of livestock and Zakaat of land, three other categories are taxed under what may be referred to as general Zakaat. Although opinions vary on specifics, generally jurists agree that gold, silver, and "other assets" above prescribed thresholds (Nisaabs) are subject to Zakaat at the rate of 2.5%. Zakaat is due whenever the taxable item remains in the taxpayer's possession for 1 year. The gold and silver categories are straightforward. There is no unanimous agreement, however, on what constitutes the appropriate tax base for "other assets." Although many candidates, such as "wealth," "income," "idle wealth," "hoarded wealth," "merchandise," "articles of trade," "all types of wealth," "capital of various types," etc., have been proposed, a well-defined and universally acceptable tax base and list of taxable items is still elusive.

Debates on the taxable items and treatment of other concepts, such as valuation of Nisaab, amount of Nisaab, Zakaat on capital and inventory, effects of inflation, handling of depreciation, etc., continues without a generally acceptable resolution in sight. A partial list of topics and authors engaged in the debate may be found in Siddiqi (1981).

4. Khums, literally meaning one-fifth, in its original form was applied at the rate of 20% to spoils of war. The origin of this tax is a verse in the Qur'an stating "And know that whatever you take as spoils of war, verily one fifth of it is for Allah, and for the messenger, and for close kinsman, and orphans, and the needy, and the wayfarer. If you believe in Allah and that what We sent down to our slave." (8:41). Later, the tradition extended this tax to treasure-troves, mines, and all materials extracted from sea or earth. Currently, the Sunni jurisprudence maintains that Khums is only applicable to the excavated articles from land, sea, mines, buried treasures, and spoils of war at the rate of 20% (Abu Ubayd 1968; Ahmad, M 1995; Qardawi 1997; Shaik 1980). In this sense, Khums is partly a "windfall tax" and partly a tax on selected natural resources.

   The Shiite school of thought, while agreeing with this assessment, extends Khums to larger categories of income and hoarded wealth. Formally, based on Shiite interpretation, Khums is applicable to seven items, including business profits and proceed of mines at the rate of 20%. It is an in-kind tax but may be paid either in kind or equivalent value. The equivalent value must be the fair market value of the taxable item. Unlike Zakaat, which is applicable until the holding falls below the appropriate Nisaab, Khums is a one-time tax. Thus, when Khums on an item is paid, that item will be forever exempt from Khums (Khoie 1982; Khomeini 1980; Montazeri 1986; Rizvi 1992; Sadr, 1989).

5. Zakaat-ul-Fitr, or "Sadaghat-ul-Fitr," or "Soul Zakaat" is a poll tax due once a year at the end of fasting month of Ramadan. All sane and free adult Muslims, who are not poor by Islamic standards, must pay this tax. Additionally, each person must pay this tax on behalf of those dependents that are not qualified to pay the tax themselves. Even if the dependents do not live with the taxpayer or they are not Muslim, this tax must still be paid by the person on whom they depend (Khoie 1982; Khomeini 1980; Montazeri 1986; Sadr 1989).

   The amount of this tax is either in kind, about 3 kg (6.6 lb) of the main local staple, such as wheat, rice, barley, etc., or its equivalent monetary value. There is no specific mention of this tax in Qur'an, but it has been expressly prescribed by Muhammad. The Qur'anic reference is said to be "And render to the kinsman his due as to the needy and wayfarer. If you believe in Allah and that what We sent down to Our slave." (17:26).

6. Kharaaj is another form of land tax applicable to lands conquered by Muslims or entered into treaty with Muslims without war. The tax has some precedent, albeit not clearly defined and established, from Muhammad's time. The term itself originates from the Persian word "Kharaag." The structure and operation of this tax is essentially patterned after the Persian land tax. Formalization and extension of Kharaaj and some other taxes along with appropriate structural changes came during the reign of Umar, the second Caliph. The coverage, amount, or rate for Kharaaj is not uniform or pre-prescribed and varies from land to land and place to place based on several criteria. Kharaaj has been collected sometimes as a fixed amount and sometimes as a percentage of the harvest. It has also been collected based on factors, such as acreage, the crop or type of agricultural produce, fertility of land, methods of irrigation, the location and proximity of the

land to the market and roads, "tax-bearing ability" of the land, and several other factors. Some authors assert that the maximum rate has been set at 50% (Mannan 2008). Others claim that in practice Kharaaj has been set at a level that makes the tax equal to the rent on that land (Ijtihadi 1985; Sadr 1989). No Nisaab is mentioned and no deduction of expenses is allowed for Kharaaj purposes.

7. Jizya or "Poll Tax" is a tax levied on non-Muslims living under Islamic jurisdiction. The reference to this tax in the Qur'an is said to be: "Fight those who do not believe in Allah and the Last Day, and do not forbid what God and His messenger have forbidden, and those, being among the people who were given the Scripture but do not acknowledge the religion of truth, until they pay tribute (Jizya) with submission and utterly subdued." (9:29).

    Women, children not yet at puberty, slaves, poor, unemployed, blind, sick, insane, beggars, priests, and the monks of monasteries are exempt from Jizya (Abu Ubayd 1968; Dennett, 1975; Qardawi 1997; Zaman 1981). Non-Muslims living in "Treaty Towns" are also free from Jizya payments and instead pay taxes as assessed by their own officials. Rates or amounts of Jizya are not mentioned in Qur'an or specified by Muhammad. Traditionally, different amounts have been suggested and used.

8. Kaffaraat, or expiation money, are not technically taxes. They are fines and penalties for some of the wrongdoings and transgressions committed by Muslims. They, however, constitute part of any Islamic state's revenue and as such are stated here. Examples of finable offenses include breaking one's fast without a proper cause, breaking one's oath, transgressions during the month of Haj, etc. The Qur'an states: "Allah will not punish you for that which is unintentional in your oaths, but He will take you to task for the oaths which you have sworn in earnest. So its expiation is the feeding of ten needy individuals with the average of that which you feed your own folks or clothing of them, or freeing of a slave." (5:89). The amount of these fines vary in each case and depends on the particulars of each situation. These penalties may be paid in cash or in-kind.

9. Other taxes may also be levied by an Islamic government on a need basis. All variants of Islamic jurisprudence allow levying of additional taxation by an Islamic government (Chapra 1992). In fact, throughout Islamic history, additional taxes with no reference in Shariah have been imposed on Muslims by their governments. Taxes, such as "transaction taxes," "sales taxes," and several other taxes along with fees like "Minters' Charge," "the Book Charge," "the Army Charge," "Tariffs," and "Custom Duties," have been reported in several Islamic regions and territories (Zaman 1981).

Uses and Purposes of Tax Revenue

For some of the taxes, the Islamic Shariah clearly mandates the categories on which the tax revenues must be spent. In other cases, there are no specifications. Expenditure of Ushr, Zakaat of animals, and general Zakaat are specifically devoted by the

Qur'an to be on eight items. "Zakaat expenditures are only for poor, and the needy, and those who collect them, and those whose hearts are to be reconciled, and to free the slaves, and the debtors, and for the cause of Allah, and for the wayfarers, a duty imposed by Allah. And Allah is All Knower, All Wise." (9:60). The relative share of each category and the percentage devoted to each group is not indicated in the Qur'an. Neither are the exact definitions of some of these categories and what may be covered by these funds.

Of the spending categories mentioned in the Qur'an, one category is devoted to the payment of slaves' ransom to buy their freedom. Another category is earmarked for the administrative cost of collection and distribution of Zakaat. Two categories are rather ambiguous "cause of Allah" and "those whose hearts to be reconciled." The ambiguity, however, allows some flexibility on spending these amounts.

Generally, they have been interpreted as spending on activities that in some form and manner benefit Islam and Muslims. Four other categories, notwithstanding the details of the debates surrounding them and based on the spirit of the Qur'anic verses along with the consensus of Muslim jurists, are aimed at alleviation of poverty and need. These are the poor, the needy, the wayfarer, and the debtor.

The need and poverty may be temporary as in the case of a wayfarer in need, or an unemployed person, or a debtor, or it may be permanent as in the case of a disabled individual, or someone who is unable to work. Details and procedures, however, are not provided in the Qur'an and the issues are resolved by Sunnah or through consensus of the jurists. In general, however, the general agreement is that the raison d'être for Zakaat is to alleviate poverty and move the Islamic community toward achieving the Just Islamic society. Therefore, the collected funds must be spent in such a way to accomplish these goals.

These expenditures could be on anything that a worthy Muslim state or ruler sees fit, including spending to reduce the income and wealth gap among members of the society, welfare projects, ensuring minimum standard of living, healthcare, education, scientific and cultural matters, maintenance of religious institutions and missionaries, public goods, war and defense efforts, propaganda, social projects, security, support of the warriors in the cause of Allah, and other similar activities. Distribution and utilization of Khums, based on Sunni Muslims, is identical to those of Zakaat. According to the Shiites, however, the treatment is different.

For Shiites, Khums should be divided into two parts. One half is earmarked for the direct descendants of Muhammad and must be disbursed to them. The other half must be surrendered to the religious leaders or the Islamic state for proper disposal. The usage of this portion appears to be similar to those of Zakaat. Under certain circumstances, the taxpayer may directly spend a portion of Khums on allowable uses (Khoei, 1982; Khomeini, 1980; Montazeri, 1986; Rizvi, 1992).

The origin of this distribution comes from the allocation of booty, which was the first item subject to Khums. According to the original verse, one fifth of the booty belonged to Muhammad, his family, orphans, needy, and wayfarers. The remaining four-fifth went to the conquering army. In another verse, however, the Qur'an indicates that: "They ask you about the spoils of war. Say: all spoils of war belong to Allah and the Messenger. So, fear Allah and set things right between you, and obey

Allah and His Messenger, if you are believers." (8:1). This verse, then, could be interpreted as that the spoils of war belong to the Islamic state. Since mines and natural resources are also subject to Khums, then permissibility of taxing these items by the Islamic state may be inferred.

Recipients of Khums or Zakaat must be Muslim (except those categories that are specifically permitted), poor, do not openly commit sins, and do not spend the funds on sinful activities. The receipts should not be more than the recipient's annual expenditure. The recipients may not be a dependent of the taxpayer and should not themselves be subject to payments of Zakaat or Khums unless they are eligible to receive from these funds under different categories, such as Zakaat collectors or wayfarers. Zakaat-ul-Fitr is spent on the same items as Zakaat and the conditions of the recipients are also the same (Khoei, 1982; Khomeini, 1980; Montazeri, 1986; Rahman, 1986; Rizvi, 1992). The uses of Jizya, Kharaaj, Kaffaraat, and other taxes, for the most part, are not specified. Thus, they may go to the general fund and along with other revenues be utilized at the discretion of the Islamic state. The uses, however, must not contradict or violate Islamic Principles, Codes, and Laws.

Hence, it is clear that Islamic taxes are designed to support the functioning of an Islamic state, which must establish Shariah Law and function within its framework. This Islamic state, accordingly, is required to strive to establish justice and create a just society. Among the major steps to accomplish these tasks are alleviation of poverty, promotion of the welfare of Muslim community, prevention of bad behavior, promoting good deeds, and eliminating extreme concentration of wealth in a few hands. Thus, collection of taxes and spending the funds to accomplish its goals constitute a primary function of an Islamic state and it is incumbent upon all Muslims to contribute to this process and assist the state in this path.

Ethics of Tax Evasion

The first step in addressing the ethics of tax evasion is to answer a fundamental question. Is taxation, in general, legitimate? If the answer is negative, then taxation amounts to theft. In that case, tax evasion is simply an act of defending one's property against theft, and defending one's property against thieves not only does not constitute an unethical act but it may even be considered a duty. In this situation, the discussion boils down to discuss the proper role of the state and means and methods of its financing. If, on the other hand, the answer is affirmative and the legitimacy of taxation in general is acknowledged, then the discussion may proceed to explore and specify the limitations, conditions, and parameters of taxation.

Following the "Social Contract" tradition of Hobbes, Locke, and Rousseau, most social philosophers assert that as the general rule some form of taxation is necessary for proper functioning of the state and the society. The assertion stems from the idea that when a person lives in a community, he/she enters into some sort of a Social Contract with other members of that society and thus must share the burden of running that community. One major way of assuming this responsibility is the payment of taxation.

This position, however, needs to resolve several other issues. For instance, is the responsibility to pay taxes absolute? Are there cases under which tax evasion becomes ethical? Should taxes be paid to corrupt or evil states? What determines the level of corruption or evil? How corrupt or evil should a state be for tax evasion to become ethical? What determines the legitimacy of a state? Who and what determines that legitimacy? Are there limits to the taxes or tax rates? What is a fair tax system? What determines the fairness of taxes? How should each taxpayer's fair share of taxation be determined? Is tax evasion ethical when tax rates are too high? What determines that the tax rate is high? Is tax evasion ethical if one disagrees with the government policies? Is evading discriminatory redistributive or capricious taxes ethical?

Do factors such as Human Rights abuse, nepotism, lack of political or economic freedom, level and quality of public goods, inadequate income distribution, etc., change one's position on the ethics of tax evasion? What is the appropriate threshold before tax evasion becomes ethical? The answers to these and numerous similar questions, while an integral part of a proper discussion on the ethics of tax evasion, are deeply rooted in ideology and accordingly are subject to intense ongoing debates. A sample of these discussions may be found in Gronbacher (1998), Pennock (1998), Schansberg (1998), and many works of McGee (e.g., 2004, 1999a, 1998a, 1998d, 1998f, 1998g, and 1994) and thus will not be reproduced here since they fall outside of the scope of this work.

The tax evasion issue, from an Islamic perspective, may be considered under two different scenarios. First, the state is a pure Islamic state and its ruler(s) can be considered as Ulul-Amr. Second, when the state is either not a pure Islamic state (Mixed) or it is Secular or non-Islamic. These two possibilities are examined in the remaining pages.

The Case of a Purely Islamic State

As noted previously, Islam teaches: That Allah is an Omnipresent All-Seer, All-Hearer, and All-Knower of all things. He keeps a record of everything that people do and will Judge and hold them accountable in the Day of Reckoning. That God is the owner of all things in heaven and earth and people are mere trustees of whatever material things is in their possession. That humans are placed temporarily on this earth and will live in eternity in the Hereafter. That Islam strives for justice in this world and does not approve of concentration of wealth and conspicuous consumption. That the Qur'an is infallible since it is the direct words of the all Powerful and all Wise Allah. That the Qur'an and the traditions of Muhammad and his righteous successors must be obeyed by Muslims totally and unquestionably. That Muslims and the Islamic state must seek to establish Justice by following the Shariah. That Muslims and the Islamic state must be in a relentless struggle against evil by promoting good behavior and prevent bad deeds. And that Muslims are duty bound to look after, support, and take care of each other.

Given all abovementioned undisputable basics and the general Islamic frame of mind, then, if a government qualifies as a true Islamic state, its ruler or rulers must be considered as the Ulul-Amr or representative of Allah on earth. Accordingly, unconditional allegiance to this state and total obedience of its demands becomes mandatory for all Muslims. Consequently, it is amply clear that tax evasion in such a state is not only immoral and unethical, but a great sin. The Qur'an repeatedly orders Muslims to pay Zakaat, and reminds them that the wealth does not belong to the Zakaat payers and is really the recipients' Rights as ordained by Allah. Muslims are frequently warned not to abandon this duty or expect the most severe punishments in this world as well as the Hereafter.

Evading Zakaat, or any other tax levied by a true Islamic state, is blatant disobedience of Allah's Command, an act that puts the tax evaders in the direct path of war against Allah and His messenger. The Islamic taxes prescribed by the Qur'an or an Islamic state are compulsory and not voluntary. All Islamic taxes must be paid without any hesitation, reservation, or question. The necessary and sufficient condition, categorically, is that the state must be an Islamic one as determined by that state's subscription and adherence to the Shariah Law.

The authorities of such a state, if needed, may collect any and all taxes by force and punish the tax evader. For any form of evading any kind of taxes in an Islamic state undermines the functioning of the state and the Islamic society. It retards the Islamic state's drive to develop the society into a just, compassionate, and harmonious society. It constitutes stealing from the community of Muslims and amounts to failure to fulfill one's duties to Allah, the Muslim society, and fellow Muslims. It is committing injustice against the society and depriving others from their rightful shares. These are some of the reasons why paying Islamic taxes is one of the pillars of Islam and a precondition for being a true Muslim. It should also be noted that evaders of Islamic taxes have no possibility of escaping punishment since this transgression cannot be concealed from God and tax evaders will be taken into task and punished by God.

Some writers and researchers assert that under some circumstances or regarding certain type of taxes, tax evasion by Muslims may not be unethical. Among categories mentioned are indirect taxes, income tax, gift tax, property tax, sales tax, excise tax, value added tax, tariffs, custom duties, taxes, and policies that raise prices unjustly or artificially, taxes and policies that redistribute wealth, preferential taxes and policies, targeted taxes and policies, and progressive taxes (e.g., Ahmad, M. 1995; McGee, 1997 and 1998h; Murtuza and Ghazanfar 1998; and Yusuf 1996).

Although a critical analysis of these writings is beyond the scope of the present work, a brief exploration of these assertions may be useful to shed light on the issue itself and as such worthy to carry out. To start, one has to decide which of the two aforementioned cases are meant by these authors, the case of a true Islamic state or the case of a non-Muslim state or not-purely Islamic state? The latter scenario is discussed later in these pages. The propositions under the former case, however, are explored and examined first.

Under Islam, there is no specific prohibition of amount or form of taxes over and above the taxes mentioned in Qur'an. Taxes may be direct or indirect and on income or wealth. They may be excise, sales, property, value added, gift, or any other tax. Ushr, Khums, and Zakaat on "proceeds of business activities," for instance, are essentially taxes on income. The taxpayer must pay taxes on these proceeds and gains after subtraction of a prescribed amount (Nisaab) and deduction of "reasonable business and individual expenses." The system of taxation can also be progressive, proportional, or regressive. Moreover, avoiding taxes on the grounds, such as objecting to the state's policies, redistributive effect of taxes and policies, spending the funds on expenditures that are beyond limits, spending tax revenues on categories that are not for the public's general welfare, the wastefulness of government expenditures, does not provide adequate defense basis.

This is so because one has to ask, who determines what is "beyond the legitimate function of the state?" Who defines "general welfare of society?" Who decides the "sufficiency of government expenditure?" Human beings or God? Muslims have no choice but to attest that it is God and His Commands as revealed to Muhammad and reflected in the Qur'an and Muhammad's tradition (Sunnah) that answers these questions. A true Islamic state, by definition, follows the Shariah Law. Therefore, provided that the state adheres to Shariah Law, Muslim cannot consider it to be engaged in any wasteful or unnecessary policy. None of the activities, laws, programs, and regulations of a true Islamic state contradicts Shariah. They are either directly commanded by it or are in accordance with it and are aimed to establish and promote God's Commands. As such, all these activities must be considered as necessary, legitimate, unobjectionable, desirable, and for the general welfare of the society.

From an Islamic perspective, transfers of wealth among different groups, as well as targeted and discriminatory policies are not forbidden and may not be used as a basis to justify tax evasion. One should remember that Islamic taxes, including Zakaat, are not applicable to all income and wealth. Some categories of wealth and some individuals are exempt from some taxes. Further, the applicable rates, minimum thresholds, and allowable deductions are not uniform. Moreover, in addition to heavy emphasis on paying the "poor due" and calling it the "right of the poor" in the possessions of wealthy members of the society, the Qur'an specifically devotes few categories of Zakaat funds to be used on poor, needy, destitute, and orphans.

Buying back the slaves' freedom, supporting wayfarers in need, paying-off the debtors' debts, and financing the administrators of Zakaat funds are other expenditures permitted by Shariah. These payments are clearly redistributive in nature and are aimed at reducing poverty, eliminating needs, and helping the impoverished. Specific percentages of distributing the inheritance among the heirs mentioned in the Qur'an is another example of discriminatory and redistributive policy regarding wealth in an Islamic community. The declaration that discriminatory, targeted taxes and redistributive policies might cause animosity among people ignores the fact that the Qur'an asserts that these Commands are God's Will. He is the One who orders dispensing of the wealth, which is His in the first place, according to what He sees fit.

The claim that all fluctuations in prices are the work of Allah and thus any governmental policy or law that raise prices "unjustifiably," "unnecessarily," or "artificially" is opposed by Islam and illegitimate, has no validity in Islamic Doctrine.

Firstly, it is not clear what is meant by "unnecessary" or "unjustified" rise in prices. This assertion can only make some sense if the doctrine of "Just Prices" is explicitly accepted. Furthermore, there is no directive in the original Islamic sources that substantiate this assertion.

The statement that Muslims do not have the moral obligation to comply with "harmful" policies is not acceptable either. Included in these policies, presumably, are tariffs, quotas, and other protectionist policies, as well as targeted taxes, distribution policies, work-safety and environmental regulations, as well as similar legislation and regulations. The problem, again, is who is going to determine what is harmful and what is beneficial to the society? What constitutes a necessary and just price? What is real and what is artificial? Once more, if a true Islamic state enacts these policies, they become legally and morally binding for all Muslims.

Accordingly, one might reiterate, that Islamic taxes, those that are specified by Shariah as well as those imposed by a true Islamic state are not voluntary, but mandatory under the Islamic state. Regardless of the reason, logic, or motive, evading Islamic taxes is illegal and never ethical or moral. This assertion stems from the fact that Islamic taxes and policies are ordained and ordered by Allah and is the manifestation of His Will. God knows everything and knows what is best for all. The pivotal condition, of course, is that the state must be a legitimate and true Islamic state and nothing else. The legitimacy, obviously, is solely derived from the state's strict adherence to the letter and spirit of Shariah Law without any violation of or contradiction to it.

Under these conditions, and only these conditions, all taxes imposed and policies enacted by the state, regardless of their shape, form, amount, procedure, purpose, etc., are considered legitimate and beneficial. Therefore, paying these taxes or adhering to these policies is obligatory for all Muslims. Evading or circumventing them is immoral, unethical, and illegal which makes it an offense punishable by God and the state in this world and on Judgment Day.

The Case of Secular Non-Islamic and Mixed States

The question of the ethics of tax evasion for Muslims becomes more problematic when a state is either secular or non-Islamic or mixed (i.e., an Islamic state that does not strictly follow Shariah Law). In these cases, the aforementioned arguments for Muslims' unconditional allegiance and obedience to the state will no longer apply. Consequently, all debates and arguments regarding various aspects of taxes and tax evasion advanced by numerous philosophers and social thinkers throughout the ages are invigorated and pertinent. The piercing questions must still be answered and the burning issues must be addressed.

Before proceeding with the discussion, however, one point should be cleared and underlined. That is, irrespective of where and under what circumstances a Muslim lives, all Islamic taxes specifically mentioned by the Qur'an must still be paid. The mixed, non-Islamic, or secular characters, or even corrupt or outright evil nature, of the state in this case is irrelevant since the Islamic taxes are not collected by any state other than the purely Islamic state. Under these circumstances, the Islamic taxes must either be surrendered to the appropriate religious authorities, who are separate and independent from the governing authorities, or may be dispensed by the taxpayer himself/herself in a specific manner and on specified categories sanctioned by Shariah Law. No evasion of these taxes is permitted under any circumstances and for any reason. Tax evaders in these cases are dealt with for their transgression by Allah and in accordance with His Will and Judgment. Therefore, the following discussion refer to taxes not specifically ordered by Shariah and are levied by a state other that a true Islamic one.

To be a Muslim, an individual must follow a certain Code of Conduct regardless of the place of domicile and the kind of government running the society. Conceptually, in their dealings with the society, Muslims should not lie, must behave ethically, must not be deceitful, must honor their contracts, must fulfill their promises, and must be exemplary in all they do. In short, Muslims should lead an honorable and commendable life and should not engage in activities that may disgrace themselves or Islam. Muhammad is reported to have said "the hypocrite has three characteristics: he tells lies, breaks his promise and breaches the trust." (Reported by Al-Bukhari and Muslim).

Also, "the one who cheats is not of us" (Muslim, Tirmidhi, and Abu Dawud) and "the one who does not fulfill trusts has no faith, and the one who does not fulfill commitments has no religion." (Reported in Ahmad, M. 1995). Hence, one might argue that, based on Islam, lying, cheating, and deceiving to evade paying taxes is an unethical act in itself, as is the act of evading taxes.

Furthermore, tax revenues may finance activities that are beneficial and vital for the proper functioning of the society. In that case, evading taxes may amount to free riding and could qualify as stealing from the public. Consequently, the obligation and necessity of paying some taxes may be asserted. Additionally, an argument may be advanced that individuals, including Muslims, by virtue of living in a society, enter into a contract with that society and as such must honor that contract and observe the social norms and social codes of conduct. This notion, in abstraction, will render tax evasion as an immoral and unethical act under all circumstance and independent of time and place.

The problem, nevertheless, is that concepts such as social contract, stealing from the public, obligation to the society, legitimacy of taxation, validity of different types of taxes and systems of taxation, and universal unacceptability of lying or deceit may be challenged from a variety of perspectives. Moreover, many questions and concerns, such as those stated at the beginning of the segment on the ethics of tax evasion, further complicate the mix and the debate.

Questions like how to deal with corrupt or evil states, what determines and measures the level of corruption or evilness of a state, the policies financed by taxes, fairness of taxes, and so on. As noted above, full discussion and evaluation of all arguments and questions surrounding the ethics of taxes and tax evasion is well outside of the scope of this work and accordingly will not be pursued. Details of these issues and debates may be found in the works already cited, specially the many works of Robert McGee on the subject. Considering the spirit as well as some letter of the Islamic Law, however, one can deduce an Islamic position on the ethics of tax evasion under non-Islamic or mixed Islamic states.

Islam orders Muslims to always promote good deeds and prevent bad deeds. Some of the good and bad deeds are specified, e.g., murder, stealing, and cheating as bad and feeding the hungry, honoring one's contracts, and defending communities as good. By analogy and deduction, other unspecified acts may also be categorized as good or bad deeds. Generally, one might infer that an act is deemed as a good deed and should be promoted if it is not in flagrant contradiction to Shariah, does not contradict any of the established Islamic codes and concepts, and is beneficial to humanity and communities. On the other hand, if an action is harmful to others or contradicts the Islamic Laws, it is considered as a bad deed and must be prevented.

Conceptually, for individual Muslims or the community of Muslim jurists, the distinction between good and bad in accordance with Shariah is not an insurmountable act. Then, it follows that, if a state is engaged in good deeds, it may be regarded as a state that must be supported, and therefore a social contract between that state and Muslims living in that society is in effect. In such cases, one can argue that, payment of taxes to the state, regardless of the type and method of taxation, is really promotion of good deeds and evading them constitutes an unethical act. If, on the other hand, the state is committing bad deeds, Muslims have a duty to oppose and disobey the laws governing those bad deeds by all means available to them.

Tax evasion is one such method and, under these circumstances, not only is ethical but rather a moral obligation for all Muslims. Financing a bad deed is not acceptable and, to the extent possible, payment of taxes in any form, shape, or amount, should be avoided. Tax evasion in these cases amounts to prevention of bad deeds and obligatory for all Muslims. Thus, depending on the circumstances, and interpretation of Muslim jurists, tax evasion may at times be ethical while at other times unethical.

Concretely, however, classifying acts into good or bad is complex and ambiguous. Things are not always straightforward and definite. To begin with, "good" and "bad" are subjective and largely function of one's background and ideological persuasion. Moreover, these concepts themselves are not universal and rigid. An act that is viewed as noble under one set of conditions may be assessed as appalling under a different scenario. Even the Shariah Law permits temporary suspension of good acts as well as engaging in acts that are normally banned by Islam. For instance, lying or deceit to save a life is allowed. So is stealing or eating forbidden foods if one is hungry and truly does not have another alternative.

The daily prayer, fasting, or other religious duties may be suspended or altered under dire circumstances or threats to health and life. Falsification of information and concealment of one's true feelings are tolerated under extraordinary situations and whenever a threat to health and lives of people exist. Revolting against an evil or oppressive regime is not only acceptable but in some cases is mandatory.

A revolution, naturally, may entail death and destruction. Nevertheless, for practical purposes, the classifications must be made. The categorization of an act as good or bad or modification of behavior or suspension of the Islamic rules, however, must not be arbitrary and resulting solely from one's interpretation and short-term narrowly defined self-interest. Rather, it must be based on the broad societal long-term interests and considerations. When a bad act is committed or a good act is suspended, the actions must be truly necessary and unavoidable. Therefore, to arrive at a decision in these instances, a Muslim's decision and evaluation of various acts must be informed by and be based on permission granted or precedent established by trusted religious leaders and credible jurists. Once more, then, it is apparent that tax evasion, depending on circumstances, could be ethical or unethical.

The assertion, however, begs the question. Theoretically, Muslims' duties regarding tax payments and tax evasion under non-Islamic or mixed states are clear. The vicious circular argument is present nonetheless. Except for a few instances, classifying states into corrupt or evil is not an easy task. Neither is categorizing deeds into good and bad. Currently, there is no state, and probably there has never been, a state that meets the criteria of a truly Islamic state.

All contemporary states are either secular, non-Islamic, or mixed states. This fact suggests that at best all states in all societies are engaged in a mixture of activities that entail good and bad. Some of these activities might contradict Shariah and are thus objectionable to Muslims while other activities may be good deeds. Since tax revenues are mixed and expenses are disbursed from the general funds, Muslims, as well as all others who might find those acts objectionable, face a challenging situation. That is, how can a Muslim promote the state's good deeds while preventing its bad ones?

If there are practical ways to object to bad deeds and withhold taxes proportionate to the extent that they finance bad deeds, the solution is rather clear. This option, however, is not available in the existing world. Thus, the circle is completed and one is faced again with the same set of questions on ethics of tax evasion as one started with. It becomes incumbent on each person to resolve his or her dilemma. Legal and moral precedents, as well as one's conscience and principles along with trusted opinions may serve as guideposts.

Concluding Remarks

With a perfect unanimity, Muslim jurists and theologians believe that the only purpose of Islam is to guide humanity and reveal the path of virtuous and righteous living. Following this path, in turn, will establish justice on earth and prepare humans for eternal salvation in the Hereafter. It follows that Muslims should believe that the functions and intentions of all Islamic Laws, including Islamic taxes, are to enable the societies to accomplish those goals. An Islamic state collects and disburses taxes to finance its functions and to facilitate the establishment of a blissful Islamic society. Since such a state follows Shariah Law, it must enjoy the full and unconditional support and allegiance of all Muslims at all times. Disobeying any of its laws, including tax evasion, is disobeying Allah and His representative, the Ulul-Amar.

This act undermines the Islamic state and obstructs accomplishing the Islamic ideals. Therefore, it is an act of war against Allah, His messenger, and His representative. Consequently, tax evasion for Muslims in this case, not only is illegal, immoral, and unethical, but also constitutes a mortal sin, an offense worthy of the most severe punishments. Ordinarily, one might argue that people, whenever they can, may disobey the mandates of evil or corrupt states and try to undermine it.

Faced with an undesirable state, people may change their situations by revolting against the government, voting the officials out of office, or leaving the country. This situation, however, is not applicable to an Islamic state and these options are not available to Muslims. This is so because a true Islamic state follows Shariah Law and, from a Muslim perspective, cannot be evil or corrupt. For Muslims living in non-Islamic, secular, or mixed societies, it may be asserted that they have some obligations to pay taxes when the government's actions and policies are viewed as virtuous and noble as measured by the Islamic standards, and are not in direct opposition or violation of Shariah. If, however, the state does not measure up against these standards or it is an evil or corrupt state, Muslims may resort to acts of disobedience and undermining of the government.

One such act would be to refuse financing the functioning of that state or bad deeds through tax evasion. In this case, tax evasion will be moral and ethical, and may even be a duty and an obligation incumbent upon all Muslims. That is, to the extent that it is practically feasible, Muslims should evade taxes and refuse to finance immoral acts. The benchmark for this assessment, obviously, must be the Islamic Laws as specified in the Qur'an and Sunnah. The decision must not be rooted in narrow self-indulgence at the expense of the community's long-term interests. A Muslim's decision should be made based on legal and religious precedent established by trustworthy religious leaders and reliable jurists.

References

Abdel Rahman, Moussa Ibrahim, 1977. "Zakaat, Social justice and Social Security," in *Outlines of Islamic Economics*, Proceedings of the first Symposium on the Economics of Islam in North America, Association of Muslim Social Scientists, Indianapolis, Indiana, USA.

Abdul Rauf, Muhammad, 1979. *The Islamic Doctrine of Economics and Contemporary Economic Thought*, American Enterprise Institute for Public Research, Washington, DC.

Abu Ubayd, Qasim bin Sallam, 1968. *Kitabul Amwal* (Book of Possessions), Edited by Muhammad Khalil Harras, Cairo, Al-Azhar University.

Abu Yusuf al Qadi, Yaqub bin Ibrahim, 1979. Kitab-al-Kharaaj (Book of Tributes), Dar-al- Marifa, Beirut, Lebonan.

Abu-Zahra, Mohammad, 1965. The Zakaat, in *Proceedings of the Second Conference*, Al Azhar, the Academy of Islamic Research, Cairo.

Adams, C. 1993. *For Good or Evil: The Impact of Taxes on the Course of Civilization*. New York: Madison Books.

Ahmad, Khurshid, Ed. 1980. *Studies in Islamic Economics*, London, Redwood Burn, Ltd.

Ahmad, Mahmud Shaikh. 1995. *Economics of Islam: A Comparative Study*, Shah Muhammad Ashraf Publishers, Lahore, Pakistan.

Ahmad, Mushtaq. 1995. *Business Ethics in Islam*. Islamabad, Pakistan: The International Institute of Islamic Thought and the International Institute of Islamic Economics.

Ahmad, Ziauddin. 1991. Islam, Poverty and Income Distribution. The Islamic Foundation, UK.

Al Hassani, Baqir and Abbas Mirakhor (Eds.). 1989. Essays in Iqtisad: The Islamic Approach to Economic Problems. Nur Corp., USA.

Armstrong, Mary Beth and Jack Robison. 1998. "Ethics in Taxation," *Journal of Accounting, Ethics & Public Policy*, 1(4): 535–557. Reprinted in Robert W. McGee (Ed.), *The Ethics of Tax Evasion*. Dumont, NJ: The Dumont Institute for Public Policy Research, 330–348.

Awan, Muhammad Mahmood. 1980. "Economic Policy for Development- A Treatise on Zakah," in M. Raquibuz Zaman, (Ed.) *Some Aspects of the Economics of Zakah*, Association of Muslim Social Scientists, Plainfield, Indiana: 184–208.

Azhar, Rauf A. 2009. *Economics of an Islamic Economy*. Themes in Islamic Studies, Brill.

Ballas, A. A. & H. Tsoukas. 1998. "Consequences of Distrust: The Vicious Circle of Tax Evasion in Greece," *Journal of Accounting, Ethics & Public Policy*, 1(4), 572–596, reprinted in Robert W. McGee (Ed.), *The Ethics of Tax Evasion,* 284–304. Dumont, NJ: The Dumont Institute for Public Policy Research.

Block, Walter. 1993. "Public Finance Texts Cannot Justify Government Taxation: A Critique," Canadian Public Administration, (36): 225–62. Reprinted in Robert W. McGee (Ed.), *The Ethics of Tax Evasion,* as "The Justification for Taxation in the Economics Literature," *36*–88, Dumont, NJ: The Dumont Institute for Public Policy Research.

Chapra, M. Umer. 1992. *Islam and Economic Challenge*, The Islamic Foundation, UK.

Chapra, M. Umer. 1996. *Objectives of the Islamic Economic Order*, the Islamic Foundation, UK.

Choudhury, Massudul Alam, 1980. "The Role of Az-Zakah in resource Allocation," in M. Raquibuz Zaman, (Ed.), *Some Aspects of the Economics of Zakah*, Association of Muslim Social Scientists, Plainfield, Indiana: 159–169.

Choudhury, Massudul Alam, 2010. *Comparative Economic Theory: Occidental and Islamic Perspectives*. Springer Publishers.

Cohn, Gordon. 1998. "The Jewish View on Paying Taxes," *Journal of Accounting, Ethics & Public Policy* 1(2): 109–120, reprinted in Robert W. McGee, (Ed.), *The Ethics of Tax Evasion*. Dumont, NJ: The Dumont Institute for Public Policy Research, 180–189.

Crowe, Martin. T. 1944. *The Moral Obligation of Paying Just Taxes*. Doctoral dissertation, the Catholic University of America Studies in Sacred Theology No. 84.

DeMoville, Wig. 1998. "The Ethics of Tax Evasion: A Baha'i Perspective," *Journal of Accounting, Ethics & Public Policy* 1(3): 356–368, reprinted in Robert W. McGee (Ed.), *The Ethics of Tax Evasion*. Dumont, NJ: The Dumont Institute for Public Policy Research, 230–240.

Dennett, Daniel. 1975. *Convention and Poll Tax In Early Islam*. Translated into Persian by Muhammad Ali Movahed, 2nd Edition, Kharazmi Publication, Tehran, Iran

de Zayas, Farishta. 1960. *The Law and Philosophy of Zakaat*, Al-Jadidah Press, Damascus, Syria. Reprinted, as *The Law and Institution of Zakat*, 2003, The Other Press, Malaysia.

deZayas, Farishta. 1969. "The Functional Role of Zakaat in the Islamic Social Economy," *Islamic Literature*, March, 5–10, Lahore, Pakistan.

de Zayas, Farishta G. 2003. The Law and Institution of Zakat. The Other Press, Malaysia.

El Ashker, Ahmed and Rodney Wilson. 2006. *Islamic Economics: A Short History*. Themes in Islamic Studies, Brill

Englebrecht, Ted D., Buky Folami, Choongseop Lee and John J. Masselli. 1998. "The Impact on Tax Compliance Behavior: a Multidimensional Analysis," *Journal of Accounting, Ethics & Public Policy* 1(4): 738–768, reprinted in Robert W. McGee, (Ed.), *The Ethics of Tax Evasion*. Dumont, NJ: The Dumont Institute for Public Policy Research, 372–402.

Gronbacher, Gregory M.A. 1998. "Taxation: Catholic Social Thought and Classical Liberalism." *Journal of Accounting, Ethics & Public Policy*, 1(1): 91–100, reprinted in Robert W. McGee (Ed.), *The Ethics of Tax Evasion*, 158–167. Dumont, NJ: The Dumont Institute for Public Policy Research.

Harrigan, Jane R. and Hamid El-Said. 2009. *Economic Liberalization, Social Capital and Islamic Welfare Provision*. Palgrave Macmillan Publisher.

Haq, Irfan Ul, 1995, *Economic Doctrines of Islam*, The International Inst. Islamic Thought, USA.

Ijtihadi, Abolqasim. 1985. *The Fiscal and Tax Situation of the Muslims*, Sorush Publication, Tehran, Iran.

Inglehart, R., M. Basanez, J. Diez-Medrano, L. Halman & R. Luijkx (Eds.), 2004. *"Human Beliefs and Values: a crosscultural sourcebook based on the 1999–2002 values surveys."* Siglo XXI: Mexico. An expanded dataset of this study is available at http://www.worldvaluessurvey.org.

Iqbal, Zafar and Mervyn K. Lewis. 2009. *An Islamic Perspective on Governance.* Published by Edward Elger Publishing, Inc. Northampton, USA.

Izadi, Ali M. 1974. "The Role of az-Zakaat in the Islamic System of Economics in Curing the Poverty Dilemma," in *Proceedings of the Third National Seminar* of the Association of Muslim Social Scientists, Gary, Indiana, May, 9–18.

Jalili, Ali Reza. 2006. "A Descriptive Overview of Islamic Taxation." *The Journal of American Academy of Business,* Cambridge. March, 8(2):16–28.

Khaf, Monzer. 1978. *The Islamic Economy*, Plainfield, Indiana, Muslim Association of the U.S. and Canada. Reprinted in 1993 by the American trust Publications.

Khan, Akram Muhammad (1983). Islamic Economics, Annotated Sources in English and Urdu, The Islamic Foundation, Leicester.

Khan, M. Fahim. 2009. Essays in Islamic Economics. Islamic Foundation, 2009.

Khoie, Aboulquasem. 1982. *Resaleh Towzih-ul-massael*, Elmiyeh Publisher, Qum, Iran.

Khomeini, Rouhollah. 1980. *Resaleh Towzih-ul-massael*, Rooh Publisher, Qum, Iran. Available at http://al-shia.com/html/far/books/fegh/resaleh.

Kuran, Timur. 1983. "Behavioral Norms in the Islamic Doctrine of Economics," *Journal of Economics Behavioral Organization*, 4, December: 353–379.

Kuran, Timur. 2010. *The Long Divergence: How Islamic Law Held Back the Middle East.* Princeton University Press, 2010.

Leiker, B. H. 1998. "Rousseau and the Legitimacy of Tax Evasion," *Journal of Accounting, Ethics & Public Policy*, 1(1): 45–57, reprinted in Robert W. McGee (Ed.), *The Ethics of Tax Evasion*, 89–101. Dumont, NJ: The Dumont Institute for Public Policy Research.

Mannan, M. A. 1989. *Economics Development and Social Peace in Islam.* Ta-Ha Publishers, Ltd. Publishers, London, UK.

Mannan, M. A. 2008. *Islamic Economics: Theory and Practice*, Shah Muhammad Ashraf Publishers, Lahore, Pakistan.

McGee, Robert W. 1994. "Is Tax Evasion Unethical?" *University of Kansas Law Review* 42(2): 411–435. Available at http://ssrn.com/abstract=74420.

McGee, Robert W. 1997. "The Ethics of Tax Evasion and Trade Protectionism from an Islamic Perspective," *Commentaries on Law & Public Policy* 1: 250–262. Available at http://ssrn.com/abstract=461397.

McGee, Robert W. 1998a. "Are Discriminatory Tax Rates Ethically Justifiable?" *Journal of Accounting, Ethics & Public Policy,* 1(4), 527–534.

McGee, Robert W. 1998b. "Christian Views on the Ethics of Tax Evasion," *Journal of Accounting, Ethics & Public Policy* 1(2): 210–225. Available at: http://ssrn.com/abstract=461398.

McGee, Robert W. 1998c. "Ethical Views on Tax Evasion among Swedish CEOs: A Comment," *Journal of Accounting, Ethics & Public Policy* 1(3): 460–467. Available at: http://ssrn.com/abstract=713903.

McGee, Robert W. 1998d. "Is the Ability to Pay Principle Ethically Bankrupt?" *Journal of Accounting*, Ethics & Public Policy, 1 (3): 503–511.

McGee, Robert W. 1998e. "Jewish Views on the Ethics of Tax Evasion," *Journal of Accounting, Ethics & Public Policy* 1(3):323–336. Available at http://ssrn.com/abstract=461399.

McGee, Robert W. 1998f. "The Case for a Maximum Tax: A Look at Some Legal, Economic and Ethical Issues," *Journal of Accounting, Ethics & Policy*, 1 (2): 294–299.

McGee, Robert W. (Ed.). 1998g. *The Ethics of Tax Evasion.* Dumont, NJ: The Dumont Institute for Public Policy Research.

McGee, Robert W. 1998h. "The Ethics of Tax Evasion in Islam: A Comment," *Journal of Accounting, Ethics & Public Policy* 1(2): 162–168, reprinted in Robert W. McGee, (Ed.), *The*

Ethics of Tax Evasion. Dumont, NJ: The Dumont Institute for Public Policy Research, 214–219.

McGee, Robert W. 1999a. "Is It Unethical to Evade Taxes in an Evil or Corrupt State? A Look at Jewish, Christian, Muslim, Mormon and Baha'i Perspectives," *Journal of Accounting, Ethics & Public Policy* 2(1): 149–181. Available at http://ssrn.com/abstract=251469.

McGee, Robert W. 1999b. "Why People Evade Taxes in Armenia: A Look at an Ethical Issue Based on a Summary of Interviews." *Journal of Accounting, Ethics & Public Policy,* 2(2), 408–416. Available at http://ssrn.com/abstract=242568.

McGee, Robert W. 2004. *The Philosophy of Taxation and Public Finance.* Boston, Dordrecht and London: Kluwer Academic Publishers.

McGee, Robert W. 2005. *"The Ethics of Tax Evasion: A Survey of International Business Academics,"* Presented at the 60th International Atlantic Economic Conference, New York, October 6–9. Available at http://www.ssrn.com. Published in the *Journal of Accounting, Ethics & Public Policy,* 6(3), 301–352 (2006).

McGee, Robert W. 2006a. "Three Views on the Ethics of Tax Evasion," *Journal of Business Ethics,* 67(1), 15–35. Available at http://www.ssrn.com.

McGee, Robert W. 2006b. "The Ethics of Tax Evasion: A Survey of Romanian Business Students and Faculty," in Robert W. McGee and Galina G. Preobragenskaya, *Accounting and Financial System Reform in Eastern Europe and Asia.* Springer: New York, 299–334. Available at: http://ssrn.com/abstract=813345.

McGee, Robert W. 2006c. *"The Ethics of Tax Evasion: A Case Study of Opinion in Thailand."* Andreas School of Business, Working Paper Series, Barry University. Available at: http://ssrn.com/abstract=934645. Reprinted in Robert W. McGee, editor, *Taxation and Public Finance in Transition and Developing Economies* (pp. 609–620). New York: Springer, 2008.

McGee, Robert W. 2006d. *"The Ethics of Tax Evasion: A Survey of Philosophy Teachers."* Andreas School of Business Working Paper Series, Barry University. Cited in McGee and Gelman (2009).

McGee, Robert W. 2006e. *"The Ethics of Tax Evasion: A Survey of Vietnamese Opinion."* Academy of International Business Southeast Asia Regional Conference, Bangkok, December 7–9. Available at http://www.ssrn.com. Reprinted in Robert W. McGee, editor, *Taxation and Public Finance in Transition and Developing Economies* (pp. 663–674). New York: Springer, 2008.

McGee, Robert W. 2007. "Ethics and Tax Evasion in Asia," *ICFAI Journal of Public Finance,* 5(2), 21–33 (May). Reprinted in Business Ethics: A 360 Degree Appraisal, ICFAI University Press. Hyderabad, India. Available at: http://papers.ssrn.com/sol3/papers.cfm?abstract_id=934644.

McGee, Robert W. (2008). Changing Attitudes toward the Ethics of Tax Evasion: An Empirical Study of 10 Transition Economies. *Accounting and Finance in Transition,* 5, 145–154. Also Fifth International Conference on Accounting and Finance in Transition. London, July 12–14, 2007. Reprinted in Robert W. McGee (Ed.), *Taxation and Public Finance in Transition and Developing Economies* (pp. 119–136). New York: Springer, 2008, under the title Trends in the Ethics of Tax Evasion: An Empirical Study of Ten Transition Economies.

McGee, Robert, W. and Yuhua An. 2006. "The Ethics of Tax Evasion: A Survey of Chinese Business and Economics Students." Published in the *Proceedings of the International Academy of Business and Public Administration Disciplines* (IABPAD), Orlando, Florida. January 3–6. Available at: http://ssrn.com/abstract=869280. Reprinted in Robert W. McGee, editor, *Taxation and Public Finance in Transition and Developing Economies* (pp. 409–421). New York: Springer.

McGee, Robert W. and Arkadiusz Bernal. 2006. *"The Ethics of Tax Evasion: A Survey of Business Students in Poland."* Sixth Annual International Business Research Conference, co-sponsored by the Coggin College of Business, University of North Florida and the School of Management, Warsaw University, February 10–11, Jacksonville, Florida. Available at: http://ssrn.com/abstract=875434. Published in *Global Economy -- How It Works* (Mina Baliamoune-Lutz, Alojzy Z. Nowak & Jeff Steagall, eds.) (pp. 155–174). Warsaw: University of Warsaw & Jacksonville: University of North Florida. Reprinted at http://ssrn.com/abstract=875434.

McGee, Robert W. and Sanjoy Bose. 2007. "The Ethics of Tax Evasion: A Comparative Study of Australian, New Zealand and USA Opinion." International Academy of Business and Public Administration Disciplines (IABPAD) May 3–6, Dallas. Published in The IABPAD *Conference Proceedings,* 951–964. Available at: http://ssrn.com/abstract=979408. Published in Robert W. McGee, *Readings in Business Ethics* (pp. 125–142). Hyderabad, India: ICFAI University Press.

McGee, Robert and Sanjoy Bose. 2008. *"Attitude toward Tax Evasion in the Middle East: A Comparative Study of Egypt, Iran and Jordan,"* Working Papers, November. Available at: http://ssrn.com/abstract=1310454. Published in Accounting and Finance in Transition 3: 23–34 (2006).

McGee, Robert W. and Y.Y. Butt. 2006. *"The Ethics of Tax Evasion: A Survey of Hong Kong Opinion."* Cited in McGee 2009. Published as An Empirical Study of Tax Evasion Ethics in Hong Kong. Proceedings of the International Academy of Business and Public Administration Disciplines (IABPAD), Dallas, April 24–27: 72–83 (2008).

McGee, Robert W. & Gordon M. Cohn, 2008. "Jewish Perspectives on the Ethics of Tax Evasion." *Journal of Legal, Ethical, and Regulatory Issues,* 11(2): 1–32. Available at: http://papers.ssrn.com/sol3/papers.cfm?abstract_id=929027.

McGee, Robert W. and Wendy Gelman, 2009. "Opinions on the Ethics of Tax Evasion: A Comparative Study of the USA and Six Latin American Countries." *Akron Tax Journal* 24(69):69–91. Available at: http://uakron.edu/law/lawreview/taxjournal/atj24/docs/McGee.pdf.

McGee, Robert W. and Zhiwen Guo. 2006. "The Ethics of Tax Evasion: A Survey of Law, Business and Philosophy Students in China." Published in *the Proceedings of the International Academy of Business and Public Administration Disciplines* (IABPAD), Orlando, Florida, January 3–6. Available at http://ssrn.com/abstract=869304. Published as A Survey of Law, Business and Philosophy Students in China on the Ethics of Tax Evasion. *Society and Business Review,* 2(3), 299–315 (2007).

McGee, Robert W. and Simon S.M. Ho. 2006. "The Ethics of Tax Evasion: A Survey ofAccounting, Business and Economics Students in Hong Kong." Published in the *Proceedings of the International Academy of Business and Public Administration Disciplines* (IABPAD), Orlando, Florida. Available at: http://ssrn.com/abstract=869306. Reprinted as A Comparative Study on Perceived Ethics of Tax Evasion: Hong Kong vs. the United States. *Journal of Business Ethics,* 77(2), 147–158 (2008).

McGee, Robert W. and Christopher Lingle. 2005. *"The Ethics of Tax Evasion: A Survey of Guatemalan Opinion."* Presented at the 60th International Atlantic Economic Conference, New York, October 6–9. Available at: http://ssrn.com/abstract=813288. Reprinted as The Ethics of Tax Evasion: A Survey of Guatemalan Opinion, in Robert W. McGee, editor, *Taxation and Public Finance in Transition and Developing Economies* (pp. 481–495). New York: Springer, 2008.

McGee, Robert W. and Tatyana B. Maranjyan, 2006a. *"The Ethics of Tax Evasion: A Survey of Accounting Practitioners,"* Andreas School of Business Working Paper Barry University. Cited in McGee and Bose, 2008. Reprinted as Opinions on Tax Evasion in Armenia, in Robert W. McGee, editor, *Taxation and Public Finance in Transition and Developing Economies* (pp. 277–307). New York: Springer, 2008.

McGee, Robert W. and Tatyana B. Maranjyan. 2006b. *"Tax Evasion in Armenia: An Empirical Study."* Presented at the Fourth Annual Armenian International Policy Research Group Conference, Washington, DC, 1/ 14–15. Available at: http://ssrn.com/abstract=869309.

McGee Robert W. and Mahdi, Nazemi Ardakani .2009. *"The Ethics of Tax Evasion: A Case Study of Opinion in Iran,"* Florida International University Working Paper, January. Available at: http://ssrn.com/abstract=1323059.

McGee, Robert W. and Carlos Noronha. 2007. *"The Ethics of Tax Evasion: A Comparative Study of Guangzhou and Macau Opinion."* Andreas School of Business Working Paper Series, Barry University. Available at: http://papers.ssrn.com/sol3/papers.cfm?abstract_id1015882. Reprinted as The Ethics of Tax Evasion: A Comparative Study of Guangzhou (Southern China) and Macau Opinions. *Euro Asia Journal of Management,* 18(2), 133–152, 2008.

McGee, Robert W. and M. J. Rossi. 2006. *"The Ethics of Tax Evasion: A Survey of Law and Business Students in Argentina,"* 6th Annual International Business Research Conference, co-sponsored by U. of North Florida and the School of Management, Warsaw University, February 10–11, Jacksonville, Florida. Available at: http://ssrn.com/abstract=875892. Reprinted as A Survey of Argentina on the Ethics of Tax Evasion, in Robert W. McGee, editor, *Taxation and Public Finance in Transition and Developing Economies* (pp. 239–261). New York: Springer, 2008.

McGee, Robert W. & Z. Sevic. 2008. *"The Ethics of Tax Evasion: A Survey of UK Opinion,"* Cited in Nickerson, Pleshko, and McGee, 2008.

McGee. Robert W. and Sheldon R. Smith. 2006. *"Ethics, Tax Evasion, Gender and Age: An Empirical Study of Utah Opinion."* Andreas School of Business Working Paper, Barry University, January. Available at: http://www.ssrn.com/abstract=934649.

McGee, Robert W. and Michael Tyler. 2007. Tax Evasion and Ethics: A Comparative Study of 33 Countries. *Proceedings of the International Academy of Business and Public Administration Disciplines* 4 (1), 709–729. A different version is available at: http://ssrn.com/abstract=940505. Reprinted as Tax Evasion and Ethics: A Demographic Study of Thirty-three Countries. *International Journal of Business, Accounting, and Finance*, 1(1), 95–114, 2007.

McGee, Robert W. and Radoslav Tusan. 2006. *"The Ethics of Tax Evasion: A Survey of Slovak Opinion."* Andreas School of Business Working Paper Series, Barry University, available at http:// ssrn.com/abstract=932990. Reprinted as The Ethics of Tax Evasion: A Survey of Slovak Opinion, in Robert W. McGee, editor, *Taxation and Public Finance in Transition and Developing Economies* (pp. 575–601). New York: Springer, 2008.

McGee, Robert W., Meliha Basic, and Michael Tyler. 2006. The Ethics of Tax Evasion: A Survey of Bosnian Opinion, available at http://papers.ssrn.com/sol3/papers.cfm?abstract_id=899609. Reprinted as The Ethics of Tax Evasion: A Survey of Bosnian Opinion, *Journal of Balkan and Near Eastern Studies*, 11(2), 197–207, 2009.

McGee, Robert W., Simon S.M. Ho, and Annie Y.S. Li. 2006. *"A Comparative Study on Perceived Ethics of Tax Evasion: Hong Kong vs. the United States,"* September. Available at: http://ssrn. com/abstract=930533.

McGee, Robert W., Inge Nickerson, and Werner Fees. 2005. "When Is Tax Evasion Ethically Justifiable? A Survey of German Opinion." *Proceedings of the Academy of Legal, Ethical and Regulatory Issues*, 9 (2): 35–38, Las Vegas, October 12–15. Available at: http://www.allieda-cademies.org/pdf/vegas05/paleri-9-2.pdf. Reprinted in Robert W. McGee, editor, *Readings in Accounting Ethics* (pp. 365–389). Hyderabad, India: ICFAI University Press, 2009.

McGee, Robert W., Carlos Noronha, and Michael Tyler. 2006. *"The Ethics of Tax Evasion: A Survey of Macao Opinion."* Presented at the Fifteenth Annual World Business Congress of the International Management Development Association (IMDA), Sarajevo, Bosnia, June 18–21. Reprinted as The Ethics of Tax Evasion: a Survey of Macau Opinion. *Euro Asia Journal of Management*, 17(2), 123–150 (2007). Reprinted in Robert W. McGee (editor), *Readings in Accounting Ethics* (pp. 283–313), Hyderabad, India: ICFAI University Press, 2009.

Montazeri, Housain Ali. 1986. *Resaleh Towzih-ul-massael*, Qum, Iran. Available at: http://www. montazeri.com/html/books/resaleh.

Morales, A. 1998. "Income Tax Compliance and Alternative Views of Ethics and Human Nature." *Journal of Accounting, Ethics & Public Policy*, 1(3): 380–399, reprinted in Robert W. McGee (Ed.), *The Ethics of Tax Evasion*. Dumont, NJ: The Dumont Institute for Public Policy Research, 242–258.

Murtuza, Athar and S.M. Ghazanfar. 1998. "Taxation as a Form of Worship: Exploring the Nature of Zakat," *Journal of Accounting, Ethics & Public Policy* 1(2): 134–161, reprinted in Robert W. McGee, (Ed.), *The Ethics of Tax Evasion*. Dumont, NJ: The Dumont Institute for Public Policy Research, 190–212.

Nasadyuk Irina and Robert W. McGee. 2006. *"Lessons for Emerging Tax Regimes: The Ethics of Tax Evasion in the Ukraine,"* Open Society Institute, Higher Education Support Program, Regional Seminar for Excellence in Teaching, Odessa, July 23-August 4, published in the *Proceedings*: 47–66.

Niazi, Kausar. 1977. *Economic Concepts in Islam*, Shah Muhammad Ashraf Publishers, Lahore, Pakistan.

Nickerson, Inge, Larry Pleshko, and Robert W. McGee, 2008. "Presenting the Dimensionality of an Ethics Scale Pertaining to Tax Evasion," *Journal of Legal, Ethical and Regulatory Issues*, May, available at: http://papers.ssrn.com/sol3/papers.cfm?abstract_id=113133.

Nylén, Ulrica. 1998. "Ethical Views on Tax Evasion among Swedish CEOs," *Journal of Accounting, Ethics & Public Policy* 1(3): 435–459, reprinted in Robert W. McGee, (Ed.), *The Ethics of Tax Evasion*. Dumont, NJ: The Dumont Institute for Public Policy Research, 260–282.

Nomani, Farhad and Ali Rahnema. 1994. Islamic Economic Systems, Zed Books, London, UK.

Oliva, R. R. 1998. "The Schism between Tax Practitioners' Ethical and Legal Obligations: Recommendations for the Fusion of Law and Ethics," *Journal of Accounting, Ethics & Public Policy*, 1(4): 603–628, reprinted in R. W. McGee (Ed.), *The Ethics of Tax Evasion*, Dumont, NJ: The Dumont Institute for Public Policy Research: Dumont, NJ, 350–371.

Pennock, Robert T. 1998. "Death and Taxes: On the Justice of Conscientious War Tax Resistance," *Journal of Accounting, Ethics & Public Policy* 1(1): 58–76, reprinted in Robert W. McGee (Ed.), *The Ethics of Tax Evasion*. Dumont, NJ. Inst. for Pub. Pol. Res.

Preobragenskaya, Galina G. and Robert W. McGee. 2004. "Taxation and Public Finance in a Transition Economy: A Case Study of Russia." In Carolyn Gardner, Jerry Biberman and Abbass Alkhafaji, (Eds.), *Business Research Yearbook: Global Business Perspectives*, Volume XI, Saline, MI: McNaughton & Gunn, Inc., 2004, 254–258.

Qardawi, Yusuf Al, 1969. *Figh-al-Zakaat*, (Jurisprudence of Zakaat), Beirut, Dar al-Irshad Publishing.

Qardawi, Yusuf Al. 1997. *Economic Security in Islam*, translated by Muhammad Iqbal Siddiqi, Islamic Book Services, New Delhi, India.

Rahman, Fazlur. 1995, 1990, 1986. *Economic Doctrines of Islam*, Four Volumes published at different dates, Islamic Publication Ltd. Lahore, Pakistan.

Rahman, Mushfiqur. 2003. *Zakat Calculation*, the Islamic Foundation, London, UK.

Reckers, Philip M.J., Debra L. Sanders and Stephen J. Roark. 1994. "The Influence of Ethical Attitudes on Taxpayer Compliance," *National Tax Journal* 47(4): 825–836.

Rizvi, S. M. 1992. *An Introduction to the Islamic Economic System*, 3rd edition, published by S. M. Rizvi, Ontario, Canada.

Sadr, Kazim. 1989. Fiscal Policies in Early Islam, in Al-Hasani, Baqir, and Mirakhor, Abbas, Editors, *Essays on Iqtisad: The Islamic Approach to Economic Problems*, 115–167, Nur Corporation, Silver Spring, MD, USA.

Schansberg, D. Eric. 1998. "The Ethics of Tax Evasion Within Biblical Christianity: Are There Limits to 'Rendering Unto Caesar'?" *Journal of Accounting, Ethics & Public Policy* 1(1): 77–90, reprinted in Robert W. McGee, (Ed.), *The Ethics of Tax Evasion*. Dumont, NJ: The Dumont Institute for Public Policy Research, 144–157.

Shad, Abdur Rahman. 1986. *Zakaat and Ushr*, Kazi Publications, Lahore, Pakistan.

Shaik, Abdul Aziz. 1980. Concepts of Zakah: "A Survey of Qur'anic Texts and Their Explanations in Shariah and Contemporary Economics," in M. Raquibuz Zaman, (Ed.), *Some Aspects of the Economics of Zakaat*, Association of Muslim Social Scientists, Plainfield, Indiana, 3–68.

Siddiqi, Muhammad Nejatullah. 1981. *Muslim Economic Thinking: A survey of contemporary literature,* The Islamic Foundation, London, United Kingdom.

Singer, Amy. 2008. *Charity in Islamic Societies*. Cambridge University Press.

Smatrakalev, G. 1998. "Walking on the Edge: Bulgaria and the Transition to a Market Economy," in Robert W. McGee (Ed.), *The Ethics of Tax Evasion*, 316–329. Dumont, NJ: The Dumont Institute for Public Policy Research.

Smith, Sheldon R. and Kevin C. Kimball. 1998. "Tax Evasion and Ethics: A Perspective from Members of The Church of Jesus Christ of Latter-Day Saints," *Journal of Accounting, Ethics & Public Policy* 1(3): 337–348, reprinted in Robert W. McGee, (Ed.), *The Ethics of Tax Evasion*. Dumont, NJ: The Dumont Institute for Public Policy Research, 220–229.

Tamari, Meir. 1998. "Ethical Issues in Tax Evasion: A Jewish Perspective," *Journal of Accounting, Ethics & Public Policy* 1(2): 121–132, reprinted in Robert W. McGee, (Ed.), *The Ethics of Tax Evasion*. Dumont, NJ: The Dumont Institute for Public Policy Research, 1998, 168–178.

Torgler, Benno. 2003. *Tax Morale: Theory and Empirical Analysis of Tax Compliance.* Dissertation der Universität Basel zur Erlangung der Würde eines Doktors der Staatswissenschaften. Cited in McGee and Gelman (2009).

Vaguine, V. V. 1998. "The Shadow Economy" and Tax Evasion in Russia," in Robert W. McGee (Ed.), *The Ethics of Tax Evasion*: 306–314. Dumont, NJ: The Dumont Institute for Public Policy Research.

Yusuf, S. M. 1996. *Economic Justice in Islam*, Shah Muhammad Ashraf Publishers, Lahore, Pakistan.

Zaman, S. M. hasan-Uz, 1981. *The Economic Functions of the Early Islamic State*, International Islamic Publishers, Karachi, Pakistan.

Chapter 12
Christian Views on the Ethics of Tax Evasion

Robert W. McGee

Introduction

One hesitates to make general statements about "Christian" views on anything, given the fact that Christians of various sects have persecuted and even killed each other (not to mention Jews and Muslims) over the centuries because of doctrinal disputes.[1] Nevertheless, I will attempt to make some general statements regarding Christian doctrine on the ethics of tax evasion. The literature on this topic is scant, or at least was scant until recently (McGee 1998). Therefore, I will necessarily be limited in my discussion to some Biblical passages, a few recent articles (Pennock; Schansberg; Gronbacher; Smith and Kimball; McGee 1994a), the views of some Popes, and a doctoral dissertation that was written in the 1940s (Crowe).

The Popes' Views

Pope John Paul II's view, as expressed in the most recent edition of the Baltimore Catechism, is that tax evasion is a sin (Newsweek; Economist). Unfortunately, it does not go into any detail, nor does it explain how that conclusion was arrived at. One wonders whether the view, as expressed in the most recent edition – the first since 1566 – would consider tax evasion to be a sin if Hitler were the tax collector, or if the tax were so high as to deprive a poor family of basic needs. I think not, based on my understanding of Catholic doctrine. In fact, Christian scholars have

---

[1] As someone who has gone through the Catholic school system to grade 16 (university) I even hesitate to claim to know what Roman Catholic doctrine is, since I learned several, contradictory versions of it during the course of my studies.

R.W. McGee (✉)
School of Business, Florida International University, 3000 NE 151 Street,
North Miami, FL 33181, USA
e-mail: bob414@hotmail.com

R.W. McGee (ed.), *The Ethics of Tax Evasion: Perspectives in Theory and Practice*,
DOI 10.1007/978-1-4614-1287-8_12, © Springer Science+Business Media, LLC 2012

taken the position that it is probably not a sin to evade a tax that is imposed on the necessities of life or to evade a tax if the burden is too large (Bonacina).

Thus, even though a publication approved by the Pope states that tax evasion is a sin, serious Catholic scholars cannot take seriously the possibility that tax evasion is always a sin. Furthermore, the Pope is not speaking *ex cathedra*, meaning that his statement cannot be taken as the word of God,[2] but is merely his opinion, at best. I say at best because the Pope did not write the new edition of the Baltimore Catechism but only approved it after numerous scholars spent many years revising it.

Other Popes have addressed taxation from time to time. Leo XIII recognized the right to property and thought that the advantages of private property could be attained only if private wealth was not drained away by crushing tax burdens. He also rejected the concept of egalitarian and redistributive taxation. An American Bishop's letter issued in 1933 agreed with this position (Gronbacher: 163–164).

Another interesting point, which was not mentioned either in the Baltimore Catechism or by any Popes (to my knowledge) in any of their statements, is how tax evasion can be an offense against God, which is necessary in order for something to be a sin. If tax evasion is an offense at all, it is an offense against the state.[3] If one stretches a bit, one might argue that evading a tax makes it necessary for others to pay more, since the tax evader is paying less. But that argument leaves a lot to be desired, especially if the tax is an unfair one, or one where the proceeds are used to do evil things. Thus, the recent Roman Catholic Church view, as expressed in the Baltimore Catechism, must be deeply discounted, since it leaves out so much detail.

Other Christian Views

If one wants more detail than is provided by the Baltimore Catechism – which represents only one branch of Christianity in any event – it is possible to find some detail in the ethical and religious literature. Perhaps the most comprehensive treatise on the ethics of tax evasion from a Christian – mostly Catholic[4] – perspective was that done by Martin Crowe in 1944. Crowe's review of the Christian literature quickly reveals that tax evasion is not always unethical. Christian scholars over the centuries have often conceded that, at times at least, tax evasion is not unethical. However, they do not always agree on the fine points.

---

[2] Roman Catholic doctrine has considered the Pope to be infallible, meaning incapable of stating error on Catholic doctrine or morals, only since 1870, when the doctrine was approved by majority vote of some council. Even then, infallibility applies only to certain statements.

[3] Crimes such as murder are considered crimes against the state for some reason. In fact, they are crimes against some individual. Yet the state is the one that prosecutes and punishes rather than the individual, or more accurately the surviving family of the murdered individual. Whether, and under what circumstances, something can be a crime against the state is an interesting question that is, unfortunately beyond the scope of the present paper.

[4] I say mostly Catholic because some of Crowe's references were to Christian scholars who wrote before the Reformation. Prior to the Reformation, there was no distinction between Christian and Catholic.

If one were to summarize Crowe's thesis in a single sentence, it would be that there is a moral obligation to pay just taxes, but there is no moral obligation to pay unjust taxes. That conclusion begs the question, of course, since one must first determine what is a just tax and what is not. But before we examine that question, let's try to define exactly what a tax is. Crowe's definition of a tax is as follows:

> A tax is a compulsory contribution to the government, imposed in the common interest of all, for the purpose of defraying the expenses incurred in carrying out the public functions, or imposed for the purpose of regulation, without reference to the special benefits conferred on the one making the payment (Crowe: 14–15).

This definition seems fairly comprehensive on its face. However, it leaves out a number of things that could be considered taxes. For example, any so-called tax that benefits some private interest at the expense of the general public would seemingly not fit this definition. Exactions by government that do not fit this definition could therefore logically be considered to be exactions that could ethically be evaded. What are some of these so-called taxes that benefit special interests at the expense of the general public? Tariffs, for one, because, in most modern societies at least, tariffs are less a means of raising revenue than a means of reducing foreign competition (McGee 1990; 1994b). Tariffs raise the prices of products that the general public buys while special interests benefit due to the decreased competition.

Another, perhaps less obvious special interest exaction is Social Security. The only people who benefit from Social Security taxes are people who receive benefits, which is a distinct minority. Those who must pay the tax, on the other hand, constitute the majority. Thus, Social Security taxes benefit special interests (those who receive benefits) at the expense of the general public. One might push the point farther by pointing out that Social Security is a bad investment, since a much higher rate of return – and pool of cash at the time of retirement – could be had by investing in the average mutual fund. Forcing people to make a bad investment cannot be deemed in the public interest even if they get some or all of their money back eventually.

Another special interest tax is the property tax, to the extent that it is used to finance public schools. Anyone who owns a house has to pay property taxes. Tenants also pay indirectly, since landlords try to pass along the tax as part of the rent. Yet many people do not have children, and many people who do have children do not send them to public schools. Thus, the portion of the property tax that goes to finance public education constitutes special interest subsidization at the expense of the general taxpaying public. Thus, according to Crowe's definition, it appears that there is no ethical duty to pay these taxes, since they benefit special interests rather than the general public. A letter issued by the American Bishops in 1933 seems to justify this position.

> ...state taxation could never be justified for special interests. The placing of the interest of one group of people over another, in terms of taxation, was unjust. The state should not be permitted to tax particular groups within society to benefit other specific groups. Thus, taxation should serve the citizenry in common and not a particular group as the redistributive tax system of socialism is constructed to do. (Gronbacher: 165)

For Crowe (22–26), a tax is just only if it meets three criteria. It must (1) be imposed by legitimate legislative authority, (2) for a just cause, and (3) where there is just distribution of the tax burden. Presumably, there is no ethical duty to pay any tax that meets less than all three of these criteria. Thus, failing to pay taxes to Hitler would not be unethical because the taxes were not used for a just cause, although it could not be said that his authority was illegitimate because he, as well as the Nazi legislature, was elected. This conclusion lends evidence to the argument that tax evasion is not always a sin, even though the revised Baltimore Catechism states that tax evasion is a sin.

While Crowe's doctoral thesis provides an excellent review of the Christian literature on the topic of tax evasion, his logic and line of reasoning sometimes leave a lot to be desired. For example, he states that "moralists are unanimous in their teaching that the ultimate basis of apportioning a tax is the ability of the citizen to pay." (Crowe: 24).[5] There are several problems with this statement. For one, moralists are not unanimous in this view. Secondly, even if they were unanimous, it does not follow that a tax should be based on ability to pay. Morality and ethics are not majoritarian. If the world consisted of 100 moralists and they all agreed that the world is flat, it would not mean that the world is flat, but only that the moralists are unanimously wrong in their opinion.

The most important flaw in Crowe's reasoning is his premise: that some individuals should be exploited for the sake of others. There are basically only two kinds of taxes, those based on the premise that individuals are the masters and the state is the servant, and those based on the premise that the state is the master and the people are the servants. The ability to pay viewpoint is based on the premise that the state is the master and the people are the servants. Karl Marx said it best when he stated: "From each according to his ability, to each according to his needs." (Marx 1875) The Marxian view treats people as ends rather than means. It exploits the most productive citizens by forcing them to pay for benefits that others receive just because they have the funds to do so. It begins with the premise that individuals exist to serve the state rather than the other way around. The ability to pay principle is parasitical because it forces the producers in society to transfer wealth to wealth consumers, those who consume government benefits.

Modern democracies are based on the premise that the only reason for the state to exist is to benefit the people, to perform functions that benefit the vast majority, such as providing police protection from internal thugs and military protection from external threats.[6] The Marxian premise, on the other hand, is that the people exist to serve the state. How else could Marx have made such an utterance? Thus, Crowe's

---

[5] He cites several Christian scholars to buttress his position. For example, "There is an obligation in justice for all the subjects to contribute to the expenses of the state according to the ability and means of each." (LeCard 504).

[6] Even these functions are not necessarily monopolies that only the state can provide. The majority of police protection in the United States, for example, is provided by private security guards, who are retained by shopping malls, warehouses, and businesses to protect their customers and property. There are thousands of private roads, private schools, private parks, etc. as well. Many of these things are provided by the private sector better and cheaper than by the state, which leads one to wonder what we need a state for anyway.

view, that taxes should be based on the ability to pay, is morally bankrupt, even if a majority of "moralists" agree with him.

The other view of taxation, that the state provides services for the people, is more tied in to the cost–benefit principle. The cost of government services should be borne by those who benefit. The purest form of "tax" in this regard is actually a user fee. An example would be a gasoline tax, since the only people who pay gasoline taxes are those who use the roads. If the gasoline tax is used solely to build and maintain roads, then those who pay gasoline taxes are not being exploited to pay for services that others use. Another example of a user fee would be charging admission to a public park or a museum. The only people who have to pay for such things are the people who use the facility. This is the fairest kind of tax, since it does not require one group of people to pay for the benefits that other people receive.

In the strictest sense, however, such user fee taxes are not really taxes at all, since they do not involve the force of government. A real tax involves coercion. People must be forced to pay because they will not pay voluntarily. A user fee is different because no one is forced to pay park admission fees. If they don't want to pay, they don't have to pay. But if they don't pay, they are not entitled to the service. That seems fair. No one is forced to pay anything and no one is being used to pay for someone else's benefit. Neither Crowe nor most of the moralists he refers to, however, mention this point. The Christian literature neglects this very important distinction between coercion and volunteerism.

Some Christian scholars take the position that one is morally bound to pay direct taxes but not indirect taxes. Other Christian scholars have held that whether a tax is direct or indirect has nothing to do with the morality of paying or not paying (Crowe: 17 and elsewhere). The matter is further complicated by the fact that people (and governments) cannot agree on what is a direct tax and what is an indirect tax. For example, in the United States, income taxes are considered to be direct taxes but in France they are classified as indirect taxes (Crowe 139), which put one in the curious position of committing a sin if one evades the U.S. income tax but not if one evades the French income tax. I wonder what God would have to say about this?

Some Christian scholars have taken the position that it is a sin to break any law. This position was common during the period when it was thought that the King derived his power from God. This view is supported in the Bible. In Romans 13, 1–2, for example, it states:

> Let every soul be subject unto the higher powers. For there is no power but of God: the powers that be are ordained of God. Whosoever therefore resisteth the power, resisteth the ordinance of God: and they that resist shall receive to themselves damnation.

Almost no one believes this gibberish these days. To believe such a statement would be to support the regimes of Hitler, Mao, Stalin, Pol Pot, and all the other dictators who have killed millions of people. Such a belief would give credence to the Marxist view that religion is the opiate of the people.

Several other passages in the Bible have something to say about taxes. In the Old Testament, it says that the King taxed people according to their ability to pay (2 Kings 23:35) but it does not say whether such a practice is moral. In the New Testament, when Jesus was asked whether it was legal to give tribute to Caesar, he said: "Render therefore unto Caesar the things which are Caesar's; and unto God the things that are God's." (Matthew 22:21). But all this statement really says is that we are supposed to give individuals and institutions (the state) what they are entitled to. It does not address the main issue, which is what the state might be entitled to. One might infer from this passage that Jesus said it is all right to evade the tax if the state is not entitled to the tax. In fact, such would be the logical conclusion to draw from this statement.

St. Paul made a similar statement in Romans 13:7: "Render therefore to all their dues: tribute to whom tribute is due; custom to whom custom; fear to whom fear; honour to whom honour."

The "paying one's fair share" argument also leaves a lot to be desired. Must one pay one's fair share of whatever taxes the state sees fit to impose, or only the fair share of the taxes that are not squandered or given to special interests? This is a very real question at present, since every western democracy squanders large sums of taxes and spends vast quantities of taxpayer dollars (or Euros, Pesos, Yen, or Kroner) on questionable projects. Does it make sense for one person to pay more so that others will be exploited by the state less?

What about the "everybody does it" argument, which states that it is all right to evade taxes since everybody does it? One Christian scholar makes the following point:

> It appears unreasonable to expect good citizens, who certainly are in the minority, to be obliged in conscience to pay taxes, whereas so many others openly repudiate the moral obligation, if there is one. It seems unjust that good people should feel an obligation to be mulcted and to pay readily, in order to balance the evasions of many. (Davis 339)

While a case might be made that there is no moral duty to pay a tax where no benefits are received – such as a tariff where the benefits go to some special interest like the textile industry, or Social Security payments, which are transferred directly to people who do not work – what about the case where some benefits are received? Does it depend on how much benefit is received compared to the amount of tax paid, or are taxes morally due in cases where any benefit whatsoever is received?

Most of the time, individuals receive less in benefits from government than they pay in taxes. There are several reasons for this. For one, there is an administrative fee associated with the collection of taxes. Taxpayers in Oregon who send their money to Washington, for example, do not necessarily get it all back. The bureaucracy eats up a substantial portion of their tax payments. If their Senator or Congressman is more skilled than his colleagues, he might be able to push through legislation that results in a higher than average return of tax dollars to Oregon. But half the members of Congress are less skilled than average at this sort of thing. For some federal programs, only about 10% of their budget goes to the people intended to be helped. The other 90% goes for administration costs.

Another problem with the view that individuals owe some duty to pay taxes if they receive benefits is that the benefits they receive are often benefits they would not pay for if they had to get them from the market rather than the government.

Also, the benefits the government bestows on the populace might be of inferior quality compared to what the market would provide, or more costly than what could be had if the market were permitted to provide the same or a similar service. What then? Is one morally obligated to pay the full cost, including the waste that is inherent in the government provision of services? Or is one only obligated to pay the price that would exist if the market provided the service instead of the government?

What about barter? We all engage in it at some point, even if it is only to take turns carpooling our children to school – You do it today and I will do it tomorrow. Barter transactions are taxable (but probably not the present example). If I pay someone to take my child to school, the person who receives the money is subject to the income tax, or at least that is the case in some countries. What if, instead of paying someone, we agree to take turns instead? Isn't it basically the same as if I got paid for my services and the other person got paid for hers? Is it ethically any different whether we decided to barter to evade the tax rather than because barter would be more convenient? As Schansberg points out (151), I Corinthians 4:5 states that God will judge men by their motives. So if tax evasion is a sin (a big IF), and if I barter to evade taxes, then I will be guilty of a sin. Of course, I could always estimate the value of the service I receive and declare that on my tax return.

The pacifist wing of Christianity, represented by Quakers among others, does not place much emphasis on whether a tax is just. Their emphasis is on what the tax is used for. If it is used to finance war, the moral thing to do is resist and evade (Pennock). Some pacifists refuse to pay only that portion of the tax that represents military expenditure. For example, if military expenditures represent 40% of the budget, some objectors will refuse to pay 40% of their income taxes.

Resisters generally respect and obey the law, but recognize that there is a higher law that must be obeyed. The moral law is higher than the law of the state, so when the two conflict, the state loses. They take the position that it is not only not immoral to break an immoral law but also that one has a moral duty to break it.

The pacifist argument against paying taxes leaves something to be desired. It begins with the premise that some taxes are legitimate; it is merely the use to which some taxes are put that makes them immoral. Consistent pacifists would resist paying taxes to repel an invading army. Many pacifists think that taxes should be used on social programs like Social Security or welfare, which are merely transfer payments. Many pacifists also think that there is nothing morally wrong with the graduated income tax or other taxes that are based on the ability to pay. They often see nothing wrong with using the force of government to pay for their social agenda. They only see the force of government as evil when it involves killing people. They see nothing wrong with a government that fleeces its people or threatens to imprison them if they resist the fleecing.

Some pacifists are selective in their resistance to war taxes. They would resist payments of taxes to support some wars but not others. They are not consistent in their pacifism. Perhaps they should not be called pacifists in such cases, since war tax resister seems more descriptive.

> If much of what government does is sinful or promotes sin, a case could be made for a
> subsequent level of tax evasion … If taxation is so stringent that it prevents a believer from
> giving to God, tax evasion would be a conceivable alternative. (Schansberg: 155)

Thus, if government supports sinful activity, there may not be any ethical duty to pay to support such activities. There may even be an ethical duty not to pay, as in cases where the government supports or subsidizes abortion, systematically disparages property rights, etc. Likewise, if the tax burden makes it difficult or impossible to give to the church, tax evasion might not be considered unethical. Schansberg sums up his view on tax evasion as follows:

> …the Bible does not endorse tax evasion except in cases where obedience to God supersedes obedience to the state. Moreover, a spirit of the law interpretation recognizes that tax
> evasion of some sorts is a necessary aspect of life. The bottom line from the perspective of
> a Biblical Christian ethic is to "render unto Caesar" – most of the time. (Schansberg: 157)

Some Catholic scholars point out that the Catholic view is not completely internally consistent. For example, traditional Catholic sources like Encyclicals and bishops' letters take a more or less classical liberal view of taxation, whereas the recent views of American bishops are more statist and collectivist (Gronbacher: 159).

Another interesting view is that presented by the Church of Jesus Christ of Latter-day Saints, also known as the Mormons. While the authors of the only article I could find on this viewpoint (Smith and Kimball) are quick to point out that the views in their article are their own and do not represent the views of their church, they also state that they "derived their conclusions from a historical background unique to the Church." (220). Their conclusion is basically that tax evasion is both legally and ethically wrong. Section 134, Verse 5 of the Mormon Doctrine and Covenants states that individuals should support their governments (221).

> We believe that all men are bound to sustain and uphold the respective governments in
> which they reside, while protected in their inherent and inalienable rights by the laws of
> such governments; and that sedition and rebellion are unbecoming every citizen thus protected, and should be punished accordingly; and that all governments have a right to enact
> such laws as in their own judgments are best calculated to secure the public interest; at the
> same time, however, holding sacred the freedom of conscience. (222)

This view that governments should be supported is also contained in the Articles of Faith, *The Pearl of Great Price*: "We believe in being subject to kings, presidents, rulers, and magistrates, in obeying, honoring, and sustaining the law." (222). To further bolster their position, Smith and Kimball (224) also quote the *General Handbook of Instructions* of the Church of Jesus Christ of Latter-day Saints, which is reprinted in the *Encyclopedia of Mormonism*, Volume 3:

> Church members in any nation are to obey applicable tax laws. If a member disapproves of
> tax laws, he may attempt to have them changed by legislation or constitutional amendment,
> or, if he has a well-founded legal objection, he may attempt to challenge them in the courts.
> A member who refuses to file a tax return, or to pay required income taxes, or to comply
> with a final judgment in a tax case is in direct conflict with the law and with the teachings
> of the Church.

Based on this quote, it seems that there is little room for disputing the Mormon position that tax evasion is considered unethical. One of the Mormon twelve apostles, who later became the president of the Mormon Church, likened tax evasion to theft (224). He likened tax evaders to meter robbers and purse snatchers (225).

One might ask whether the Mormon doctrine would view tax evasion as unethical even if the tax collector were Hitler (one of my rules of thumb for judging the absolutism of someone's position on tax evasion). But in the Mormon case, the Mormon Church was persecuted and some church members were killed, not by Hitler but by fellow nineteenth century Christians who were equally tolerant of different lifestyles as was Hitler. So it could reasonably be concluded that the Mormon doctrine would support the payment of taxes to the Hitlers of the world. According to the Mormon authors of this article (Smith and Kimball), "tax evasion is not consistent with gospel principles." (228)

Conclusion

What conclusions can be drawn from this review of Christian literature? The main conclusion is that Christian writers cannot agree on whether, and under what circumstances, tax evasion might be unethical. Some Christians believe that tax evasion is always unethical. Others believe that it is not unethical at least sometimes. Jesus's oft-quoted view that we should render unto Caesar what is Caesar's is also subject to differing interpretations.

The Catholic Popes apparently do not agree on whether tax evasion is unethical. Neither do the American Catholic Bishops. Christian scholars cannot even agree on whether the ability to pay principle is morally bankrupt or the ethical way to tax. Some scholars believe that there is nothing ethically wrong with evading indirect taxes and others think that it is ethically improper to evade any tax, even if the state does evil things with the proceeds. In short, the only thing that can be said about the Christian position on tax evasion is that there is no coherent, unified, noncontradictory position.

References

Bonacina. 1687. *De Morali Theologia, Tractatus de Restitutione*, disp. II, q. IX, n. 5 (1687), II, p. 449, as quoted in Crowe at 48.

Crowe, Martin T. 1944. *The Moral Obligation of Paying Just Taxes.* Catholic University of America Studies in Sacred Theology No. 84. Doctoral Dissertation.

Davis, H. 1938. *Moral and Pastoral Theology*, as quoted in Crowe at 40.

Gronbacher, Gregory M.A. 1998. Taxation: Catholic Social Thought and Classical Liberalism. 1 *Journal of Accounting, Ethics & Public Policy* (Winter), 91–100, reprinted in Robert W. McGee, editor, *The Ethics of Tax Evasion*. South Orange, NJ: The Dumont Institute for Public Policy Research, 1998: 158–167.

LeCard, S.E. 1869. *Gousset, Theologie Morale I*, as quoted in Crowe at 59.

Marx, Karl. 1875. *Critique of the Gotha Program.*

McGee, Robert W., editor. 1998. *The Ethics of Tax Evasion*. Dumont, NJ: The Dumont Institute for Public Policy Research.

McGee, Robert W. 1994a. Is Tax Evasion Unethical? 42 *University of Kansas Law Review* 411–435 (Winter).

McGee, Robert W. 1994b. *A Trade Policy for Free Societies: The Case Against Protectionism*. Westport, CT: Quorum Books.

McGee, Robert W. 1990. The Trade Policy of a Free Society. 19 *Capital University Law Review* 301–341.

New Rules for an Old Faith. 1992. *Newsweek*, November 30, p. 71.

Pennock, Robert T. 1998. Death and Taxes: On the Justice of Conscientious War Tax Resistance. 1 *Journal of Accounting, Ethics & Public Policy* (Winter), 58–76, reprinted in Robert W. McGee, editor, *The Ethics of Tax Evasion*. South Orange, NJ: The Dumont Institute for Public Policy Research, 1998: 124–142.

Schansberg, D. Eric. 1998. The Ethics of Tax Evasion Within Biblical Christianity: Are There Limits to "Rendering Unto Caesar"? 1 *Journal of Accounting, Ethics & Public Policy* (Winter), 77–90, reprinted in Robert W. McGee, editor, *The Ethics of Tax Evasion*. South Orange, NJ: The Dumont Institute for Public Policy Research, 1998: 144–157.

Sins, Ancient and Modern. 1992. *The Economist*, November 21, p. 50.

Smith, Sheldon R. and Kevin C. Kimball. 1998. Tax Evasion and Ethics: A Perspective from Members of The Church of Jesus Christ of Latter-day Saints. 1 *Journal of Accounting, Ethics & Public Policy* (Summer), forthcoming, reprinted in Robert W. McGee, editor, *The Ethics of Tax Evasion*. South Orange, NJ: The Dumont Institute for Public Policy Research, 1998: 220–229.

Chapter 13
Ethics, Tax Evasion, and Religion: A Survey of Opinion of Members of the Church of Jesus Christ of Latter-Day Saints

Robert W. McGee and Sheldon R. Smith

Introduction

Most studies that have been done on tax evasion take a public finance perspective. Very few studies look at tax evasion from the perspective of ethics, philosophy, or religion. However, there are some exceptions. A study by McGee (1994) took a philosophical approach. One of the most comprehensive analyses of tax evasion from an ethical and religious perspective was a doctoral thesis written by Martin Crowe in 1944. The *Journal of Accounting, Ethics & Public Policy* published a series of articles on tax evasion from various religious, secular, and philosophical perspectives in 1998 and 1999. Most of those articles were also published in an edited book (McGee 1998a). Since the publication of that book, a few other articles have addressed the issue of tax evasion from an ethical perspective.

The ethics of tax evasion can be examined from a number of perspectives. Some of these are of a religious nature while others are more secular and philosophical. One approach is to examine the relationship of the individual to the state. Another is the relationship between the individual and the taxpaying community or some subset thereof. A third is the relationship of the individual to God. Martin Crowe (1944) examined the literature on these approaches, which are the three main approaches that have been taken in the literature over the past five centuries.

A review of the literature reveals that three basic viewpoints on the ethics of tax evasion have emerged over the centuries. Some scholars have taken the position that tax evasion is always unethical (Cohn 1998; DeMoville 1998; Smith & Kimball 1998;

R.W. McGee (✉)
School of Business, Florida International University, 3000 NE 151 Street,
North Miami, FL 33181, USA
e-mail: bob414@hotmail.com

S.R. Smith
Accounting Department, Woodbury School of Business, Utah Valley University,
Mail Stop 103, 800 W. University Parkway, Orem, UT 84058, USA

R.W. McGee (ed.), *The Ethics of Tax Evasion: Perspectives in Theory and Practice*,
DOI 10.1007/978-1-4614-1287-8_13, © Springer Science+Business Media, LLC 2012

Tamari 1998). Others believe that tax evasion is always ethical because there is absolutely no duty to the State (Spooner 1870). A third group believes that tax evasion can be ethical under certain circumstances (Crowe 1944; Gronbacher 1998; Pennock 1998; Schansberg 1998).

One empirical study on the ethics of tax evasion was done by Nylén (1998), who did a survey soliciting the views of Swedish chief executive officers (CEOs). McGee (1998e) commented on this study. A study by Reckers, Sanders and Roark (1994) presented participants with a case study and asked them whether they would be willing to evade taxes. Englebrecht et al. (1998) did a study involving 199 subjects who replied to 29 ethical orientation questions, some of which had to do with tax evasion. Inglehart et al. (2004) conducted a large survey of more than 200,000 people in more than 80 countries that asked more than 100 questions, 1 of which was about tax evasion. McGee and Cohn (2006) surveyed the views of Orthodox Jews on the ethics of tax evasion. Not many empirical studies have been done on the ethics of tax evasion from an ethical or religious perspective. The present study is aimed at partially filling this gap in the literature.

Review of the Literature

Although many studies have been done on tax compliance, very few have examined compliance, or rather noncompliance, primarily from the perspective of ethics. Even fewer studies have looked at tax evasion from a religious perspective. Most studies on tax evasion look at the issue from a public finance or economics perspective, although ethical issues may be mentioned briefly, in passing. The most comprehensive twentieth century work on the ethics of tax evasion was a doctoral thesis written by Martin Crowe (1944), titled *The Moral Obligation of Paying Just Taxes*. This thesis reviewed the theological and philosophical debate that had been going on, mostly within the Catholic Church, over the previous 500 years. Some of the debate took place in the Latin language. Crowe introduced this debate to an English language readership. A more recent doctoral dissertation on the topic was written by Torgler (2003), who discussed tax evasion from the perspective of public finance but also touched on some psychological and philosophical aspects of the issue. Alfonso Morales (1998) examined the views of Mexican immigrant street vendors and found that their loyalty to their families exceeded their loyalty to the government.

There have been a few studies that focus on tax evasion in a particular country. Ethics are sometimes discussed but, more often than not, the focus of the discussion is on government corruption and the reasons why the citizenry does not feel any moral duty to pay taxes to such a government. Ballas and Tsoukas (1998) discuss the situation in Greece. Smatrakalev (1998) discusses the Bulgarian case. Vaguine (1998) discusses Russia, as do Preobragenskaya and McGee (2004) to a lesser extent. A study of tax evasion in Armenia (McGee, 1999b) found the two main reasons for evasion to be the lack of a mechanism in place to collect taxes and the widespread opinion that the government does not deserve a portion of a worker's income.

A number of articles have been written from various religious perspectives. Cohn (1998) and Tamari (1998) discuss the Jewish literature on tax evasion and on ethics in general. Much of this literature is in Hebrew or a language other than English. McGee (1998d, 1999a) commented on these two articles from a secular perspective. Another study, which used the same methodology as the present study, solicited the views of Orthodox Jews (McGee & Cohn 2006). That study found that Orthodox Jews were generally opposed to tax evasion, but some arguments were more persuasive than others.

A few articles have been written on the ethics of tax evasion from various Christian viewpoints. Gronbacher (1998) addresses the issue from the perspectives of Catholic social thought and classical liberalism. Schansberg (1998) looks at the Biblical literature for guidance. Pennock (1998) discusses just war theory in connection with the moral obligation to pay just taxes, and not to pay unjust or immoral taxes. Smith and Kimball (1998) provide a Mormon perspective. McGee (1998c, 1999a) commented on the various Christian views from a secular perspective.

The Christian Bible discusses tax evasion and the duty of the citizenry to support the government in several places. Schansberg (1998) and McGee (1994, 1998a) discuss the biblical literature on this point. When Jesus is asked whether people should pay taxes to Caesar, Jesus replied that we should give to Caesar the things that are Caesar's and give God the things that are God's (Matthew 22:17, 21). But Jesus did not elaborate on the point. He did not say what we are obligated to give to the government or whether that obligation has limits.

There are passages in the Bible that may be interpreted to take an absolutist position. For example, Romans 13, 1–2 is read by some to support the Divine Right of Kings, which basically holds that whoever is in charge of government is there with God's approval and anyone who disputes that fact or who fails to obey is subject to damnation. It is a sin against God to break any law. Thus, according to this viewpoint, Mao, Stalin, and Hitler must all be obeyed, even though they were the three biggest monsters of the twentieth century, because they are there with God's approval.

A few other religious views are also addressed in the literature. Murtuza and Ghazanfar (1998) discuss the ethics of tax evasion from the Muslim perspective. McGee (1998b, 1999a) comments on their article and also discusses the ethics of tax evasion under Islam citing Islamic business ethics literature (McGee, 1997). DeMoville (1998) discusses the Baha'i perspective and cites the relevant literature to buttress his arguments. McGee (1999a) commented on the DeMoville article. McGee (2004) discusses these articles in a book from a philosophical perspective.

If one were to summarize the views of the various religious groups in a few words, one could say that Jews, Mormons, and Baha'is are strongly opposed to tax evasion, whereas other Christians, including Catholics, and also Muslims take a more flexible approach. Jews, Muslims, and Baha'is all take the position that one must obey the laws in the country in which one lives. The Jewish literature also says that one must never do anything to place another Jew in a bad light. If a Jew were found guilty of tax evasion, it would place shame on the entire Jewish community. Thus, Jews should not engage in tax evasion.

The Christian literature (Crowe 1944; Gronbacher 1998; McGee 1998c, 1999a; Pennock 1998; Schansberg 1998) would consider tax evasion to be ethical where the tax system is perceived as unfair, where the government is corrupt or where the tax collector is engaged in an unjust war. According to the Muslim business ethics literature, Muslims believe that there is no duty to pay any tax that results in prices being raised, such as sales taxes, value added taxes, or tariffs. This literature also indicates that there is no duty to pay a tax that is based on income (Ahmad, 1995; McGee 1997, 1998b, 1999a; Yusuf 1971). However, a conversation one of the present authors had with a Muslim scholar found that not all Muslims take this position. That scholar said that the literature cited in those Islamic business ethics books is a complete misreading of the Quran and that God commands Muslims to pay taxes. Thus, there is apparently room for discussion on the Muslim view.

The Church of Jesus Christ of Latter-day Saints (LDS) looks to several literary sources for spiritual guidance. Church members use the Christian Bible, of course, but they also have some religion-specific literature. *The Doctrine and Covenants* is a collection of divine and inspired revelations. *The Pearl of Great Price* touches on many significant aspects of the LDS religion and doctrine. Both of these religious books take the position that LDS members have a moral duty to support government.

One of the basic statements on the relationship of the individual to the State is as follows:

> We believe that all men are bound to sustain and uphold the respective governments in which they reside, while protected in their inherent and inalienable rights by the laws of such governments; and that sedition and rebellion are unbecoming every citizen thus protected, and should be punished accordingly; and that all governments have a right to enact such laws as in their own judgments are best calculated to secure the public interest; at the same time, however, holding sacred the freedom of conscience. (The Doctrine and Covenants, Sec. 134, Verse 5).

This view was reiterated in a letter from Joseph Smith to the editor of the *Chicago Democrat*: "We believe in being subject to kings, presidents, rulers, and magistrates, in obeying, honoring, and sustaining the law." (*The Articles of Faith*, in The Pearl of Great Price) Another Church document refers more specifically to obedience to tax laws:

> Church members in any nation are to obey applicable tax laws. "If a member disapproves of tax laws, he may attempt to have them changed by legislation or constitutional amendment, or, if he has a well-founded legal objection, he may attempt to challenge them in the courts. A member who refuses to file a tax return, to pay required income taxes, or to comply with a final judgment in a tax case is in direct conflict with the law and with the teachings of the Church." (General Handbook of Instructions, as quoted in Encyclopedia of Mormonism, vol. 3, p. 1097)

Smith and Kimball (1998) cite a number of other Church documents and statements by Church leaders, all of which say basically the same thing – tax evasion is not in keeping with Church law. Church doctrine views tax evasion as a form of dishonesty, even fraud. None of the documents Smith and Kimball cite make exceptions for unfair tax laws, tax rates that are deemed to be too high, or taxes that are paid to an evil or corrupt State.

The Church of Jesus Christ of LDS has addressed the issue of tax evasion on more occasions than most other churches. The views of the Church are also consistent. Tax evasion is wrong.

Several criticisms have been made of the absolutist positions espoused by some religions (McGee 1999a). For one, religious doctrine would apparently require individuals to comply with even the worst laws of an extremely corrupt or evil State, which does not make sense to those political philosophers who believe there are limits to what the State may demand or extract from the population. Political theory for the last few hundred years recognizes cases where obedience to the State is not absolute. These political thinkers (including Gandhi, Martin Luther King, and others) begin with the basic premise that the State exists to serve the individual and that evil laws may (or must) be disregarded, a possibility the absolutists do not consider.

Any issue relating to tax fairness could also be raised to criticize the absolutist position (Crowe 1944; McGee 2004, 1999a). Assuming there is such a thing as paying one's "fair share," (McGee 1999c) it might be argued that if one is forced to pay well beyond one's fair share, there is no longer any moral duty to pay. Excessive redistribution and taxes that aim at social engineering rather than raising revenue for legitimate governmental purposes might also be cited as legitimate reasons for evasion. Using tax proceeds to kill Jews, Palestinians, Christians, Muslims, or Baha'is might also be used to justify evasion according to some scholars. The absolutist views do not take any of these cases into consideration. However, the purpose of the present study is not to criticize any absolutist view, but merely to present the results of a study aimed at discovering the state of present thinking by members of The Church of Jesus Christ of LDS.

The Present Study

Methodology

A survey instrument was constructed that included all three views on the ethics of tax evasion that Crowe (1944) identified in his thesis. Eighteen statements covering the 15 arguments that Crowe identified plus three more recent arguments were included. The survey was distributed to 638 students at a large college in the western USA, 562 of which belonged to The Church of Jesus Christ of LDS. The statements generally began with the phrase "Tax evasion is ethical if ..." Participants were asked to select a number from 1 to 7 to reflect the extent of their agreement or disagreement with each statement. Results were tabulated and the arguments favoring tax evasion were ranked from strongest to weakest. Male and female scores were also compared, as well the scores by major area of study.

Table 13.1 shows the number of male and female responses. Table 13.2 shows the number of responses by major.

Table 13.1 Responses by gender

Male	456
Female	180
Total	636

Two of the responses had missing data for gender

Table 13.2 Responses by major

Major	
Accounting	202
Business and economics	300
Legal studies	35
Technology (IS, IT, etc.)	34
Unspecified or other	67
Total	638

Survey Findings

Table 13.3 shows the scores for each of the 18 statements. Respondents were asked to select a number from 1 to 7 to indicate the extent of their agreement or disagreement with each statement, where 1 indicated strong agreement and 7 indicated strong disagreement. Non-LDS members were excluded, since the purpose of this study is to learn the views of LDS members.

One of the main goals of the present study was to determine which of the arguments favoring tax evasion over the past few centuries were strongest and which were weakest. Table 13.4 shows how the arguments were ranked.

The strongest argument favoring tax evasion is in a case where the taxpayer is a Jew and the government is Nazi Germany. This argument was not discussed by Crowe but was added to test the limits. Surely if tax evasion is ever ethical it would be ethical in this case, since it is reasonable to expect that some of the proceeds collected would be used to exterminate Jews. Or at least that was the intent of including this argument in the present survey, to test the limits.

Although it was not surprising that this argument was the strongest of the 18, what was surprising was the lack of support for it. On a scale of 1 to 7, where 1 represents strong agreement, it received a score of 5.144, which means respondents thought that even Jews in Nazi Germany have an ethical duty to pay taxes to Hitler.

One explanation for such a high score might be because the respondents were members of the Church of Jesus Christ of LDS. The literature of this religion (Smith & Kimball 1998) strongly indicates that tax evasion is never justified. Another recent study (McGee & Cohn 2006) found that even Orthodox Jews strongly believe that Jews had an obligation to pay taxes to Hitler. The score for this statement in the Orthodox Jewish survey also ranked as the strongest argument to support tax

Table 13.3 Scores for LDS members (562)

Statement number	Statement	Mean scores
1	Tax evasion is ethical if tax rates are too high	6.34
2	Tax evasion is ethical even if tax rates are not too high	6.415
3	Tax evasion is ethical if the tax system is unfair	5.973
4	Tax evasion is ethical if a large portion of the money collected is wasted	6.044
5	Tax evasion is ethical even if most of the money collected is spent wisely	6.507
6	Tax evasion is ethical if a large portion of the money collected is spent on projects that I morally disapprove of	6.18
7	Tax evasion is ethical even if a large portion of the money collected is spent on worthy projects	6.449
8	Tax evasion is ethical if a large portion of the money collected is spent on projects that do not benefit me	6.468
9	Tax evasion is ethical even if a large portion of the money collected is spent on projects that do benefit me	6.48
10	Tax evasion is ethical if everyone is doing it	6.523
11	Tax evasion is ethical if a significant portion of the money collected winds up in the pockets of corrupt politicians or their families and friends	5.815
12	Tax evasion is ethical if the probability of getting caught is low	6.553
13	Tax evasion is ethical if some of the proceeds go to support a war that I consider to be unjust	6.457
14	Tax evasion is ethical if I cannot afford to pay	6.142
15	Tax evasion is ethical even if it means that if I pay less, others will have to pay more	6.566
16	Tax evasion would be ethical if I were a Jew living in Nazi Germany in 1940	5.144
17	Tax evasion is ethical if the government discriminates against me because of my religion, race, or ethnic background	5.742
18	Tax evasion is ethical if the government imprisons people for their political opinions	5.641
	Average score	6.191

1 = strongly agree; 7 = strongly disagree

evasion, with a score of 3.12 using a similar survey instrument. Perhaps the reason why even Orthodox Jews believe there is an obligation to pay taxes to Hitler is because the Jewish literature takes the view that tax evasion is always, or almost always, unethical (Cohn 1998; Tamari 1998).

Three of the 18 statements in the survey (S16, 17 and 18) might be labeled as "human rights" arguments to justify tax evasion. These were the three arguments that Crowe (1944) did not identify in his research. These were also the three arguments that scored highest in the present survey, meaning that they were the three strongest arguments justifying tax evasion. But even these arguments were not regarded as strong by the participants, since their scores were 5.144, 5.742, and 5.641, respectively.

Table 13.4 Ranking of arguments – LDS members. Ranked from strongest to weakest. Arguments supporting tax evasion

Rank	Statement	Scores
1	Tax evasion would be ethical if I were a Jew living in Nazi Germany in 1940 (S16)	5.144
2	Tax evasion is ethical if the government imprisons people for their political opinions (S18)	5.641
3	Tax evasion is ethical if the government discriminates against me because of my religion, race or ethnic background (S17)	5.742
4	Tax evasion is ethical if a significant portion of the money collected winds up in the pockets of corrupt politicians or their families and friends (S11)	5.815
5	Tax evasion is ethical if the tax system is unfair (S3)	5.973
6	Tax evasion is ethical if a large portion of the money collected is wasted (S4)	6.044
7	Tax evasion is ethical if I can't afford to pay (S14)	6.142
8	Tax evasion is ethical if a large portion of the money collected is spent on projects that I morally disapprove of (S6)	6.18
9	Tax evasion is ethical if tax rates are too high (S1)	6.34
10	Tax evasion is ethical even if tax rates are not too high (S2)	6.415
11	Tax evasion is ethical even if a large portion of the money collected is spent on worthy projects (S7)	6.449
12	Tax evasion is ethical if some of the proceeds go to support a war that I consider to be unjust (S13)	6.457
13	Tax evasion is ethical if a large portion of the money collected is spent on projects that do not benefit me (S8)	6.468
14	Tax evasion is ethical even if a large portion of the money collected is spent on projects that do benefit me (S9)	6.48
15	Tax evasion is ethical even if most of the money collected is spent wisely (S5)	6.507
16	Tax evasion is ethical if everyone is doing it (S10)	6.523
17	Tax evasion is ethical if the probability of getting caught is low (S12)	6.553
18	Tax evasion is ethical even if it means that if I pay less, others will have to pay more (S15)	6.566

(1 = strongly agree; 7 = strongly disagree)

It was found that the arguments to justify tax evasion were stronger in cases where the government was corrupt or inefficient or where the system was perceived as being unfair. Inability to pay also ranked high, which lends support to the arguments put forth by a scholar who discussed tax evasion in the Mexican culture (Morales 1998). Inability to pay was also identified as one of the most popular arguments favoring evasion in the Catholic religious literature (Crowe 1944).

The weakest arguments were found to be the arguments that might be labeled as selfish reasons. Chart 13.1 shows the range of responses to the 18 statements, with the statements ordered as they were in Table 13.4. As can be seen, some arguments had less disagreement than others, but none of the arguments received much support.

Table 13.5 compares male and female scores for each statement. Some studies in gender ethics have found that women are more ethical than men (Akaah & Riordan 1989; Baird 1980; Brown & Choong 2005; Sims, Cheng & Teegen 1996), while other studies found that there is no statistical difference between men and women

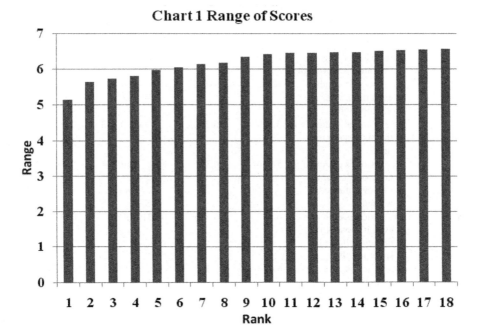

Chart 13.1 Range of scores

when it comes to ethics (Roxas & Stoneback 2004; Sikula & Costa 1994; Swaidan, Vitell, Rose & Gilbert 2006). A few studies have found that men are more ethical than women (Barnett & Karson 1987; Weeks, Moore, McKinney & Longenecker 1999). It was thought that comparing the male and female scores would be interesting, although the comparison could not lead to any conclusion regarding the relative ethics of men and women, since, to arrive at that conclusion, one must begin with the premise that tax evasion is unethical, which may not always be the case. All that one may conclude from the present study is that Mormon women are more strongly opposed to tax evasion than are Mormon men.

Table 13.5 shows that the female scores were higher than the male scores in 16 of 18 cases. But applying Wilcoxon tests to the data found that female scores were significantly higher than male scores in only five cases. However, these findings do not allow us to conclude that women are more ethical than men. In order to arrive at that conclusion we must begin with the premise that tax evasion is unethical, which may or may not be the case. At least one author of the present study believes that tax evasion is not unethical for Jews living in Nazi Germany. Thus, all we can conclude is that Mormon women are sometimes more opposed to tax evasion than are Mormon men.

Table 13.5 Comparison of LDS male and female scores

Statement number	Statement	Male score	Female score	Score larger by Male	Score larger by Female	p-Value
1	Tax evasion is ethical if tax rates are too high	6.276	6.503		0.227	0.1389
2	Tax evasion is ethical even if tax rates are not too high	6.382	6.476		0.094	0.3649
3	Tax evasion is ethical if the tax system is unfair	5.859	6.252		0.393	0.09375***
4	Tax evasion is ethical if a large portion of the money collected is wasted	5.936	6.35		0.414	0.02174**
5	Tax evasion is ethical even if most of the money collected is spent wisely	6.537	6.406	0.131		0.4925
6	Tax evasion is ethical if a large portion of the money collected is spent on projects that I morally disapprove of	6.113	6.343		0.23	0.1671
7	Tax evasion is ethical even if a large portion of the money collected is spent on worthy projects.	6.472	6.378	0.094		0.8913
8	Tax evasion is ethical if a large portion of the money collected is spent on projects that do not benefit me	6.451	6.49		0.039	0.8765
9	Tax evasion is ethical even if a large portion of the money collected is spent on projects that do benefit me	6.458	6.537		0.079	0.5853
10	Tax evasion is ethical if everyone is doing it	6.5	6.566		0.066	0.758
11	Tax evasion is ethical if a significant portion of the money collected winds up in the pockets of corrupt politicians or their families and friends	5.711	6.056		0.345	0.2036

(continued)

Table 13.5 (continued)

Statement number	Statement	Male score	Female score	Score larger by Male	Score larger by Female	p-Value
12	Tax evasion is ethical if the probability of getting caught is low	6.527	6.608		0.081	0.8426
13	Tax evasion is ethical if some of the proceeds go to support a war that I consider to be unjust	6.426	6.51		0.084	0.727
14	Tax evasion is ethical if I cannot afford to pay	6.044	6.385		0.341	0.03**
15	Tax evasion is ethical even if it means that if I pay less, others will have to pay more	6.556	6.573		0.017	0.8717
16	Tax evasion would be ethical if I were a Jew living in Nazi Germany in 1940	4.843	5.892		1.049	6.348E-05*
17	Tax evasion is ethical if the government discriminates against me because of my religion, race, or ethnic background	5.602	6.085		0.483	0.02986**
18	Tax evasion is ethical if the government imprisons people for their political opinions	5.53	5.896		0.366	0.1013
	Average score	6.123	6.349		0.226	

*Significant at the 1% level
**Significant at the 5% level
***Significant at the 10% level

How does the Mormon view differ from the view held by non-Mormons? We answer that question in Table 13.6 by comparing the LDS and non-LDS responses. The sample consisted of 562 LDS and 59 non-LDS participants. The LDS scores were higher than the non-LDS scores in all 18 cases. The difference was significant at the 1% level in all 18 cases as well, leading to the strong conclusion that LDS members are significantly more opposed to tax evasion than are non-LDS members, regardless of the issue.

Table 13.6 Comparison of LDS and non-LDS scores

Statement number	Statement	LDS score	Non-LDS score	Score larger by LDS	Score larger by Non-LDS	p-Value
1	Tax evasion is ethical if tax rates are too high	6.34	5.263	1.077		1.003E−08*
2	Tax evasion is ethical even if tax rates are not too high	6.415	5.737	0.678		7.973E−06*
3	Tax evasion is ethical if the tax system is unfair	5.973	4.491	1.482		7.234E−10*
4	Tax evasion is ethical if a large portion of the money collected is wasted	6.044	4.877	1.167		3.94E−08*
5	Tax evasion is ethical even if most of the money collected is spent wisely	6.507	6.14	0.367		0.0004795*
6	Tax evasion is ethical if a large portion of the money collected is spent on projects that I morally disapprove of	6.18	5.158	1.022		9.119E−07*
7	Tax evasion is ethical even if a large portion of the money collected is spent on worthy projects	6.449	6.175	0.274		0.007003*
8	Tax evasion is ethical if a large portion of the money collected is spent on projects that do not benefit me	6.468	5.786	0.682		1.054E−06*
9	Tax evasion is ethical even if a large portion of the money collected is spent on projects that do benefit me	6.48	5.86	0.62		7.216E−05*
10	Tax evasion is ethical if everyone is doing it	6.523	6.097	0.426		0.0006032*
11	Tax evasion is ethical if a significant portion of the money collected winds up in the pockets of corrupt politicians or their families and friends	5.815	4.509	1.306		2.351E−06*

(continued)

Table 13.6 (continued)

Statement number	Statement	LDS score	Non-LDS score	Score larger by		p-Value
				LDS	Non-LDS	
12	Tax evasion is ethical if the probability of getting caught is low	6.553	5.677	0.876		4.235E–07*
13	Tax evasion is ethical if some of the proceeds go to support a war that I consider to be unjust	6.457	5.129	1.328		1.603E–07*
14	Tax evasion is ethical if I cannot afford to pay	6.142	4.581	1.561		1.367E–09*
15	Tax evasion is ethical even if it means that if I pay less, others will have to pay more	6.566	5.968	0.598		3.89E–05*
16	Tax evasion would be ethical if I were a Jew living in Nazi Germany in 1940	5.144	4.323	0.821		0.001178*
17	Tax evasion is ethical if the government discriminates against me because of my religion, race, or ethnic background	5.742	4.839	0.903		0.0007172*
18	Tax evasion is ethical if the government imprisons people for their political opinions	5.641	4.419	1.222		1.104E–05*
	Average score	6.191	5.279	0.912		

*Significant at the 1% level

Concluding Comments

The goal of the present study was achieved. The major arguments that have been put forward to justify tax evasion in recent centuries have been ranked. As expected, some arguments proved to be stronger than others. None of the arguments proved to be very strong, however, as indicated by the high scores received for even the strongest arguments.

The results show that Mormon men are more tolerant of tax evasion than are Mormon women where the system is seen as unfair, if a large portion of tax revenues are wasted, where the taxpayer does not have the ability to pay, if the taxpayer is a Jew living in Nazi Germany, or if the government discriminates against the taxpayer on the basis of religion, race, or ethnic background. The study also found that Mormons are significantly more opposed to tax evasion than are non-Mormons, regardless of the issue.

References

Ahmad, Mushtaq (1995). Business Ethics in Islam. Islamabad, Pakistan: The International Institute of Islamic Thought and the International Institute of Islamic Economics.

Akaah, Ishmael P. and Edward A. Riordan. (1989). Judgments of Marketing Professionals about Ethical Issues in Marketing Research: A Replication and Extension. *Journal of Marketing Research* 26(1): 112–120.

Baird, J.S. (1980). Current Trends in College Cheating. *Psychology in the Schools* 17(4): 515–522, as cited in Brown & Choong (2005).

Ballas, Apostolos A. and Haridimos Tsoukas. 1998. "Consequences of Distrust: The Vicious Circle of Tax Evasion in Greece," *Journal of Accounting, Ethics & Public Policy*, 1(4): 572–596, reprinted in Robert W. McGee, editor, *The Ethics of Tax Evasion*. Dumont, NJ: The Dumont Institute for Public Policy Research, 1998, pp. 284–304.

Barnett, John H. and Marvin J. Karson. (1987). Personal Values and Business Decisions: An Exploratory Investigation. *Journal of Business Ethics* 6(5): 371–382.

Brown, Bob S. and Peggy Choong. (2005). An Investigation of Academic Dishonesty among Business Students at Public and Private United States Universities. *International Journal of Management* 22(2): 201–214.

Cohn, Gordon. 1998. "The Jewish View on Paying Taxes," *Journal of Accounting, Ethics & Public Policy* 1(2): 109–120, reprinted in Robert W. McGee, editor, *The Ethics of Tax Evasion*. Dumont, NJ: The Dumont Institute for Public Policy Research, 1998, pp. 180–189.

Crowe, Martin T. 1944. *The Moral Obligation of Paying Just Taxes*, The Catholic University of America Studies in Sacred Theology No. 84.

The Doctrine and Covenants. 1989. The Church of Jesus Christ of Latter-day Saints.

DeMoville, Wig. 1998. "The Ethics of Tax Evasion: A Baha'i Perspective," *Journal of Accounting, Ethics & Public Policy* 1(3): 356–368, reprinted in Robert W. McGee, editor, *The Ethics of Tax Evasion*. Dumont, NJ: The Dumont Institute for Public Policy Research, 1998, pp. 230–240.

Encyclopedia of Mormonism. 1992. New York: Macmillan Publishing Company.

Englebrecht, Ted D., Buky Folami, Choongseop Lee and John J. Masselli. 1998. "The Impact on Tax Compliance Behavior: a Multidimensional Analysis," *Journal of Accounting, Ethics & Public Policy* 1(4): 738–768, reprinted in Robert W. McGee, editor, *The Ethics of Tax Evasion*. Dumont, NJ: The Dumont Institute for Public Policy Research, 1998, pp. 372–402.

General Handbook of Instructions (1989). The Church of Jesus Christ of Latter-day Saints.

Gronbacher, Gregory M.A. 1998. "Taxation: Catholic Social Thought and Classical Liberalism," *Journal of Accounting, Ethics & Public Policy* 1(1): 91–100, reprinted in Robert W. McGee (Ed.), *The Ethics of Tax Evasion* (pp. 158–167). Dumont, NJ: The Dumont Institute for Public Policy Research, 1998.

Inglehart, Ronald, Miguel Basanez, Jaime Diez-Medrano, Loek Halman and Ruud Luijkx, editors. 2004. Human Beliefs and Values: a cross-cultural sourcebook based on the 1999–2002 values surveys. Mexico: Siglo XXI Editores.

McGee, Robert W. 1994. "Is Tax Evasion Unethical?" *University of Kansas Law Review* 42(2): 411–435. Reprinted at http://ssrn.com/abstract=74420.

McGee, Robert W. 1997. "The Ethics of Tax Evasion and Trade Protectionism from an Islamic Perspective," *Commentaries on Law & Public Policy* 1: 250–262. Reprinted at http://ssrn.com/abstract=461397.

McGee, Robert W., editor. 1998a. *The Ethics of Tax Evasion*. Dumont, NJ: The Dumont Institute for Public Policy Research.

McGee, Robert W. 1998b. "The Ethics of Tax Evasion in Islam: A Comment," *Journal of Accounting, Ethics & Public Policy* 1(2): 162–168, reprinted in Robert W. McGee, editor, *The Ethics of Tax Evasion*. Dumont, NJ: The Dumont Institute for Public Policy Research, 1998, pp. 214–219.

McGee, Robert W. 1998c. "Christian Views on The Ethics of Tax Evasion," *Journal of Accounting, Ethics & Public Policy* 1(2): 210–225. Reprinted at http://ssrn.com/abstract=461398.

McGee, Robert W. 1998d. "Jewish Views on the Ethics of Tax Evasion," *Journal of Accounting, Ethics & Public Policy* 1(3): 323–336. Reprinted at http://ssrn.com/abstract=461399.

McGee, Robert W. 1998e. "Ethical Views on Tax Evasion among Swedish CEOs: A Comment," *Journal of Accounting, Ethics & Public Policy* 1(3): 460–467. Reprinted at http://ssrn.com/abstract=713903.

McGee, Robert W. 1999a. "Is It Unethical to Evade Taxes in an Evil or Corrupt State? A Look at Jewish, Christian, Muslim, Mormon and Baha'i Perspectives," *Journal of Accounting, Ethics & Public Policy* 2(1): 149–181. Reprinted at http://ssrn.com/abstract=251469.

McGee, Robert W. 1999b. "Why People Evade Taxes in Armenia: A Look at an Ethical Issue Based on a Summary of Interviews," *Journal of Accounting, Ethics & Public Policy* 2(2): 408–416. Reprinted at http://ssrn.com/abstract=242568.

McGee, Robert W. 1999c. An Ethical Look at Paying Your 'Fair Share' of Taxes. Journal of Accounting, Ethics & Public Policy 2(2): 318–328, reprinted at http://ssrn.com/abstract= 242549.

McGee, Robert W. 2004. *The Philosophy of Taxation and Public Finance*. Boston, Dordrecht and London: Kluwer Academic Publishers.

McGee, Robert W. and Gordon Cohn. 2006. Jewish Perspectives on the Ethics of Tax Evasion. Andreas School of Business Working Paper Series, September.

Morales, Alfonso 1998. "Income Tax Compliance and Alternative Views of Ethics and Human Nature," *Journal of Accounting, Ethics & Public Policy* 1(3): 380–399, reprinted in Robert W. McGee, editor, *The Ethics of Tax Evasion*. Dumont, NJ: The Dumont Institute for Public Policy Research, 1998, pp. 242–258.

Murtuza, Athar and S.M. Ghazanfar. 1998. "Taxation as a Form of Worship: Exploring the Nature of Zakat," *Journal of Accounting, Ethics & Public Policy* 1(2): 134–161, reprinted in Robert W. McGee, editor, *The Ethics of Tax Evasion*. Dumont, NJ: The Dumont Institute for Public Policy Research, 1998, pp. 190–212.

Nylén, Ulrica. 1998. "Ethical Views on Tax Evasion among Swedish CEOs," *Journal of Accounting, Ethics & Public Policy* 1(3): 435–459, reprinted in Robert W. McGee, editor, *The Ethics of Tax Evasion*. Dumont, NJ: The Dumont Institute for Public Policy Research, 1998, pp. 260–282.

The Pearl of Great Price. 1989. The Church of Jesus Christ of Latter-day Saints.

Pennock, Robert T. 1998. "Death and Taxes: On the Justice of Conscientious War Tax Resistance," *Journal of Accounting, Ethics & Public Policy* 1(1): 58–76, reprinted in Robert W. McGee, editor, *The Ethics of Tax Evasion*. Dumont, NJ: The Dumont Institute for Public Policy Research, 1998, pp. 124–142.

Preobragenskaya, Galina G. and Robert W. McGee. 2004. "Taxation and Public Finance in a Transition Economy: A Case Study of Russia." In Carolyn Gardner, Jerry Biberman and Abbass Alkhafaji, editors, *Business Research Yearbook*: *Global Business Perspectives* Volume XI, Saline, MI: McNaughton & Gunn, Inc., 2004, pp. 254–258. A longer version, which was presented at the Sixteenth Annual Conference of the International Academy of Business Disciplines in San Antonio, March 25–28, 2004, is available at http://ssrn.com/abstract=480862

Reckers, Philip M.J., Debra L. Sanders and Stephen J. Roark. 1994. "The Influence of Ethical Attitudes on Taxpayer Compliance," *National Tax Journal* 47(4): 825–836.

Roxas, Maria L. & Jane Y. Stoneback. (2004). The Importance of Gender Across Cultures in Ethical Decision-Making. *Journal of Business Ethics* 50:149–165.

Schansberg, D. Eric. 1998. "The Ethics of Tax Evasion Within Biblical Christianity: Are There Limits to 'Rendering Unto Caesar'?" *Journal of Accounting, Ethics & Public Policy* 1(1): 77–90, reprinted in Robert W. McGee, editor, *The Ethics of Tax Evasion*. Dumont, NJ: The Dumont Institute for Public Policy Research, 1998, pp. 144–157.

Sikula, Andrew, Sr. and Adelmiro D. Costa. (1994). Are Women More Ethical than Men? *Journal of Business Ethics* 13(11): 859–871.

Sims, Ronald R., Hsing K. Cheng & Hildy Teegen. (1996). Toward a Profile of Student Software Piraters. *Journal of Business Ethics* 15(8): 839–849.

Smatrakalev, Gueorgui. 1998. "Walking on the Edge: Bulgaria and the Transition to a Market Economy," In Robert W. McGee, editor, *The Ethics of Tax Evasion*. Dumont, NJ: The Dumont Institute for Public Policy Research, 1998, pp. 316–329.

Smith, Sheldon R. and Kevin C. Kimball. 1998. "Tax Evasion and Ethics: A Perspective from Members of The Church of Jesus Christ of Latter-Day Saints," *Journal of Accounting, Ethics & Public Policy* 1(3): 337–348, reprinted in Robert W. McGee, editor, *The Ethics of Tax Evasion.* Dumont, NJ: The Dumont Institute for Public Policy Research, 1998, pp. 220–229.

Spooner, Lysander. 1870. No Treason, the Constitution of No Authority, originally self-published by Spooner in Boston in1870, reprinted by Rampart College in 1965, 1966 and 1971 and by Ralph Myles Publisher, Inc., in Colorado Springs in 1973.

Swaidan, Ziad, Scott J. Vitell, Gregory M. Rose and Faye W. Gilbert. (2006). Consumer Ethics: The Role of Acculturation in U.S. Immigrant Populations. *Journal of Business Ethics* 64(1): 1–16.

Tamari, Meir. 1998. "Ethical Issues in Tax Evasion: A Jewish Perspective," *Journal of Accounting, Ethics & Public Policy* 1(2): 121–132, reprinted in Robert W. McGee, editor, *The Ethics of Tax Evasion.* Dumont, NJ: The Dumont Institute for Public Policy Research, 1998, pp. 168–178.

Torgler, Benno 2003. *Tax Morale: Theory and Empirical Analysis of Tax Compliance.* Dissertation der Universität Basel zur Erlangung der Würde eines Doktors der Staatswissenschaften.

Vaguine, Vladimir V. 1998. "The 'Shadow Economy' and Tax Evasion in Russia." In Robert W. McGee, editor, *The Ethics of Tax Evasion.* Dumont, NJ: The Dumont Institute for Public Policy Research, 1998, pp. 306–314.

Weeks, William A., Carlos W. Moore, Joseph A. McKinney & Justin G. Longenecker. (1999). The Effects of Gender and Career Stage on Ethical Judgment. *Journal of Business Ethics* 20(4): 301–313.

Yusuf, S.M. (1971). Economic Justice in Islam. Lahore: Sh. Muhammad Ashraf.

Part III
Public Finance and Economic Aspects
of Tax Evasion

Chapter 14
The Failure of Public Finance

Walter Block, William Kordsmeier, and Joseph Horton

Introduction

A number of explanations are commonly given as reasons why government intervention in the economy will improve performance. This chapter questions the validity of each of them. They are presented in popular public finance textbooks.[1] If, as we believe, these arguments have not been demonstrated to be correct, much of public finance as presented in typical textbooks is not positive economics but rather relies on rather dubious normative judgments.

The arguments given are merit goods, equity considerations, growth and development, and stabilization. Each of these will be considered in turn. An earlier paper (Block, Kordsmeier, and Horton) considered the arguments of divergence from perfect competition and the supposed problem of externalities.

---

[1] A.B. Atkinson and J.E. Stiglitz, LECTURES ON PUBLIC ECONOMICS, New York, McGraw- Hill, 1980; A. L. Auld and F.C. Miller, PRINCIPLES OF PUBLIC FINANCE: A CANADIAN TEXT (Toronto: Methuen, 1982); J.F. Due, GOVERNMENT FINANCE: AN ECONOMIC ANALYSIS, Homewood (Illinois), Irwin, 1963, third edition: Richard A. Musgrave, Peggy B. Musgrave, and Richard M. BIRD, PUBLIC FINANCE IN THEORY AND PRACTICE, first Canadian edition (Toronto: McGraw-Hill Ryerson, 1987); Douglas J. McCready, THE CANADIAN PUBLIC SECTOR (Toronto: Butterworths, 1985); C. S. Shoup, PUBLIC FINANCE, Chicago, Aldine, 1969; Charles Wolf, Jr., MARKETS OR GOVERNMENTS: CHOOSING BETWEEN IMPERFECT ALTERNATIVES (Cambridge, MA: MIT Press, 1988).

W. Block (✉)
Loyola University, 6363 St. Charles Avenue, Box 5, Miller Hall 318,
New Orleans, LA 70118, USA
e-mail: wblock@loyno.edu

W. Kordsmeier • J. Horton
Department of Economics and Finance, University of Central Arkansas, Conway, AR, USA
e-mail: billk@mail.uca.edu

R.W. McGee (ed.), *The Ethics of Tax Evasion: Perspectives in Theory and Practice*,
DOI 10.1007/978-1-4614-1287-8_14, © Springer Science+Business Media, LLC 2012

Merit Goods

In the case of merit goods, the public finance writers, instead of arguing that the
market is deficient because it misallocates resources, maintain that although the free
enterprise system does not misallocate resources from the vantage point of consumer sovereignty, government should still be brought in precisely because the market does allocate goods in accord with the wishes of individual consumers!

> What are merit wants? According to Shoup (p. 43), Certain private-sector outlays are
> deemed so laden with a public purpose that they are stimulated by tax laws or subsidies;
> philanthropic and religious outlays are examples.
>
> Musgrave (p. 13) holds that merit wants are considered so meritorious that their satis-
> faction is provided for through the public budget, over and above what is provided for
> through the market and paid for by private buyers…. Public services aimed at the satisfaction
> of merit wants include such items as publicly furnished school luncheons, subsidized
> low-cost housing, and free educations. Alternatively, certain wants may be stamped as
> undesirable, and their satisfaction may be discouraged through penalty taxation, as in the
> case of liquor…. *The satisfaction of merit wants, by its very nature, involves interference
> with consumer preferences,* In view of this, does the satisfaction of merit wants have a place in
> a normative theory of public economy, based upon the premise of individual preference in a
> democratic society? A position of extreme individualism could demand that all merit wants
> be disallowed, but this is not a sensible view.
>
> Atkison and Stiglitz (p. 8) describe merit wants as, a category of goods where the state
> makes a judgement that certain goods are "good" or "bad," and attempts to encourage
> the former (e.g., education) and discourage the latter (e.g., alcohol). *This is different from
> the arguments concerning externalities and public goods in that with merit wants, the
> "public" judgement differs from the private evaluation, rejecting a purely individualistic
> view of society.* (emphasis added)

But these arguments will not do at all. The public finance economists cannot
have it both ways. If it was so important not to misallocate resources from the perspective of consumer sovereignty before (e.g., as argued in their analysis of the role
of the state, perfect competition and externalities), how can the very opposite now
be required, namely, a setting aside of the sovereign consumer's desire for alcohol
and a wish to neglect education? Alternatively, if resource allocation in service of
the sovereign consumer is so unimportant that it can be set aside in favor of these
paternalistic merit wants, why should anyone pay attention to arguments purporting
to show that the market misallocates resources by being imperfectly competitive
and subject to externalities? The public finance writers cannot both have their cake
and eat it. Their merit want concept makes a mockery of their allocational concerns.
The two are contradictory. At least one set of arguments must go by the board.

If nothing else, the concept of "merit goods" is a public relations success of vast
proportions.[2] Our authors could have characterized those items for which they
wanted to promote subsidies or special protections as "our favorite goods." Had

---

[2] For a group of people who purport to dislike advertising, the public finance economists do very
well in this regard.

they done so, no one would have paid them much mind, dismissing the idea as that of yet another special interest group – not a financially motivated one, but rather one that acts out of ideological purposes.[3] Instead, they hit upon a brilliant ploy: they called their pet projects and favorite commodities "merit goods," thus effusing them with a spurious objectivity. At least in the upper reaches of the halls of academia, this justification for government intervention is actually seriously deliberated upon by otherwise thoughtful scholars.

How does the doctrine of merit wants relate to the issue of democracy? At first glance, there would appear to be a downright contradiction between the two. If people are smart enough to pick their leaders, how can they not be able to spend their families' budgets without "help" from their political masters? MM&B (p. 71) give some evidence of concern:

> The concept of communal needs (which underlies the doctrine of merit goods)...carries the frightening implications of dictatorial abuse. But this does not go far enough. It is not just dictators we need to worry about. There is also the totalitarianism of the majority, dictating minute choices over our everyday lives.

In any case, Musgrave (1959, p. 14) was far less worried about this problem:

> While consumer sovereignty is the general rule, situations might arise, within the context of a democratic community, where an informed group is justified in imposing its decisions upon others.

In conclusion, it is difficult to see how any economist who sees value freedom as an important part of the methodology of the profession can embrace the concept of merit goods.

Equity

The public finance writers often argue for government intervention to redistribute income to enhance equity. A&M state (p. 3):

> Without government intervention, the distribution of income would depend upon who owns the various factors of production and the price they command in the market. There is nothing to say that this distribution, even if determined by perfect competition in product and factor markets, is the most socially desirable distribution. Governments must attempt to determine the consensus of the population as to whether there should be more assistance to the lower-income groups, and if so, who should bear the burden of higher taxation to provide this assistance in a situation where there is an unequal pattern of income distribution.

A&M's argument is fraught with difficulties. First we are given no independent measure of "socially desirable distribution." Yet, without it, there would appear to be no way to unambiguously determine whether the income distribution that arises

---

[3] The near universal inclusion of education among merit goods by college professors might, however, give one pause about possible financial interest.

from market activity is "desirable" or not. The government is to determine a consensus of the population. How this is to be done is not specified. However, Arrow's impossibility theorem tells us that there is no way of aggregating individual preferences to provide decisions that are consistent and rational as we would expect them to be for individuals (Arrow, 1963). Second, even if we were given this independent measure, it would appear difficult to reconcile this with positive economics. How does one deduce what should be from what is? Third, why resort to a "consensus of the population"? Even the public finance writers admit that democratically derived consensuses fail to be efficient due to problems inherent in majority rule such as logrolling, etc. Fourth, there is the conflation of equity and equality by these authors. According to A&M:

> Governments must attempt to determine the consensus of the population as to whether there should be more assistance to the lower-income groups.

Contrary to A&M's implicit presumption that such assistance enhances equity, it is not clear that more equal incomes are indeed more equitable. The implicit premise in A&M is that the two concepts are indistinguishable.

McCready (p. 5) also addresses the issue of equity:

> …there are always some persons unable to exist in the market structure, either through disabilities of one sort or another, or because they lack advantages in education, upbringing, and the like. In earlier times, the accepted method of dealing with these persons was by way of religious and charitable organizations of one sort or another. It is now generally accepted that government must play some role in distributing income and wealth to coincide with the humanitarian values of our society.

There are grave difficulties with McCready's argument as well. Charity, whatever its drawbacks, and none are mentioned here, is part and parcel of the system of laissez faire capitalism (Hughes, 1992). It is a commercial interaction, after all, between consenting adults. These "earlier times" have certainly given way to modern times. Nowadays, our welfare system creates dependency, promotes crime, fosters illegitimacy, and family breakup (Murray, 1984, 1988). Wolf (p. 41) scathingly points to the

> …failure to realize that expanded welfare programs, such as Aid for Families with Dependent Children, although intended to provide help for poor families, might have the subsequent effect of seriously weakening the structure of the family.

Why is the substitution of public for private charity an improvement, given that family breakup leads to crime, poverty, and other indices of social disarray? Indeed in 1997, the US government, explicitly recognizing the problems inherent in the AFDC program, abandoned it. Unfortunately, AFDC was replaced by a new federal program, Temporary Assistance for Needy Families (TANF). While the new stopgap welfare program may be less offensive than its predecessor, it still perpetuates public charity as a substitute for the voluntary exchanges that characterize private charity.

McCready continues (pp. 7–8):

Initially, the state of distribution depends on the distribution of factor endowments. Factors are priced in the marketplace depending on competitive circumstances and the value of the marginal products. This determines the distribution of income. Hence an individual's income depends on factor supplies and factor demands, plus in some cases inherited wealth.

The resulting distribution may or may not be in line with society's desires. Influenced by social philosophers and value judgments, society must somehow determine the "just" state of distribution…

Economists include distribution as an important aspect of public policy. Adequacy of income at the lower end of the income scale appears to have become a widespread concern, which is in contrast with earlier concern about relative income positions or about excessive incomes at the top of the scale. Current discussion rather involves trying to determine a tolerable minimum level of income.

McCready is clearly unhappy with the state of distribution in Canadian and other modern societies. He correctly acknowledges, however, that it "depends" upon factor endowments. This leads to an interesting speculation. Suppose that we did not have it within our power to change the distribution of wealth, but only to alter the pattern of initial endowments. That is, while we could not redistribute purchasing power, we could do so for IQ, beauty, endurance, persistence, charm, musical, and athletic talent, and all of the other human attributes that together determine the variance of income. Would we do so? The result would be a situation that would make the one depicted in BRAVE NEW WORLD look like a Libertarian Nirvana, but based on McCready's comments, he would appear to be logically committed to welcoming such a spectre. The public education system in the USA is a program that seeks to equalize intelligence, learning, and skills among our youth. Instead of nurturing exceptionally good students, it generally pulls all students down to the lowest common denominator. It is just such a spectre that frightens market devotees.

How, then, does McCready's argument represent an improvement over that of A&M? In two regards. First, McCready clearly concedes that "value judgments" play a critical part in the determination of equity. Unfortunately, he does not conclude from this that the economist, qua economist, has absolutely *no* role to play in this determination. Second, McCready's discussion of income distribution has the virtue of depicting it accurately along the lines of concern over style changes in hemline lengths: initially, focus on the adequacy of income at the lower end of the income scale; then, on relative income positions; after that, on excessive incomes at the top of the scale; finally, try to determine a tolerable minimum level of income, but do not take it as a serious scientific endeavor.

And what has Wolf to add to our deliberations? There is one aspect of his analysis that is vastly preferable to that of A&M and McCready: his willingness to consider the merits and demerits of imperfect markets and imperfect governmental institutions vis-a-vis one another. This is a distinct advantage over the other commentators, who all too often compare perfectly functioning benevolent state organizations with what they are pleased to see as highly imperfect markets.

Wolf's contribution to the discussion of equity focuses, reasonably enough, on the role of private charity.[4] Unfortunately, he categorizes such efforts under the rubric of nonmarket activity, alongside those of government (p. 6):

> Although government is the largest member of the nonmarket sector, the others (foundations, universities, and nonproprietary hospitals) are numerous, vast, and growing. The behavior and deficiencies of those other nonmarket organizations should be included in a comprehensive theory of nonmarket failure that can highlight similarities and differences among them, as well as permit suitable comparisons to be made between the market sector and the nonmarket sector.[5]

There is a certain amount of truth to the Wolf position. After all, neither governmental nor private charitable activities are market driven. Neither relies upon prices, profits, buying, and selling. However, in lumping them together, Wolf makes it awkward to evaluate the benefits of the laissez faire capitalist system, which very much includes philanthropy, but not the state. Charity, it must be repeated, is part and parcel of the complex of voluntary interactions; governments, and taxes and regulations, hardly qualify.

Notwithstanding the above, when it comes time for Wolf to criticize the institution of private charity, he does so from a perspective that sees this as market, not nonmarket, failure (pp. 28, 29):

> … it is theoretically correct to consider distributional *in*equity as an example of market failure. From this perspective, income distribution is a particular type of public good. An "equitable" redistribution does not result from freely functioning markets because philanthropy and charity yield benefits that are external to, and not appropriable by, the donors, but are instead realized by society as a whole. Left to its own devices, the market will

---

[4] It is marred, however, by the simplistic identification of equity with equality: "Even when the central importance of distributional equity is acknowledged, the question remains, What standard should be used to evaluate it? The answer will be very different, and often ambiguous, depending on whether equity is interpreted in the sense of equality of outcome or equality of opportunity (p. 19). That's it? That is how far equity can stretch? Between one or another type of *equality*? Nonsense. Equity means justice, or fairness, and need have nothing whatever to do with equality. An equitable division of the points between two football teams is whatever points they have *earned*, not a tie score; an equitable division of the haul in a fishing expedition is whatever had been agreed upon beforehand, not necessarily equal shares.

[5] Later on in his analysis, Wolf sees this relationship as "complex. . .difficult and ambiguous" (pp. 87–91).

therefore produce less redistribution than is "efficient" (that is, socially desirable), because of the usual "free rider" problem associated with externalities, public goods, and incomplete markets.[6]

But this externalities defense of the welfare state is open to several telling criticisms.

Let us grant this unproven and logically unprovable contention in any case, just for the sake of discussion. Why does the argument lead to the conclusion that poverty must be alleviated? If it is a negative externality, perhaps it should instead be *prohibited*. Instead of seeing *helping* the poor as an external economy to be encouraged, we could with equal logical rigor interpret *being* poor as an external diseconomy to be *punished* (this, after all, is the message of Coase, 1960). There is ample historical precedent for such a policy, including laws against vagrancy. Frederick William I, father of Frederick the Great, instituted the first War on Poverty. He drove around Prussia in his carriage, and every time he spotted a beggar he would leap out of the carriage and beat the tar out of him with his cane. This did wonders to diminish the number of beggars in Prussia. It is not clear if it actually reduced poverty, but no doubt it reduced the supposed negative visual externality of poverty.

But there are still other difficulties with this argument. One man's meat is another man's poison, as we have seen. Some people may be distressed by the sight of poverty, but others might relish this state of affairs, perhaps as a means of lording it over others. Giving welfare to the poor, then, might promote the welfare of the men of good will, but it will reduce that of the misanthropes among us. Since there is not and cannot be any scientific method of making interpersonal utility comparisons, we cannot rigorously conclude that welfare programs unequivocally improve the well being of society as a whole.

Then, too, with this perspective, there is a great difficulty of accounting for the generous amount of charity that does indeed take place, given governmental efforts in this regard. For, according to the theory, we are all going to refuse to help the poor unless everyone does so. Why, then, in a society where government gives a historically unprecedented amount of money to the poor, are people still making charitable contributions? There should be little or none according to the externalities argument, but on the contrary there is much private giving.

---

[6] Wolf continues: "Another perspective for viewing distributional equity is quite unrelated to market failure in the strict sense. From this perspective, the equilibrium redistribution previously referred to may be quite inequitable in terms of one or another ethical norm. Even if the market could surmount the narrow type of 'finance' discussed above, its distributional outcome might still be socially and ethically unacceptable from the standpoint of one or more such norms. On these groups, the distributional outcomes of even perfectly functioning markets can be justifiably criticized." Much as it pains the present authors to appear to defend "perfectly functioning markets" (We maintain there is no such thing, and that the perfectly competitive model is a vast red herring), this last statement of Wolf's does not logically follow the foregoing. The distribution arising from market interaction can only be justifiably criticized if the ethical norms to which Wolf refers are themselves valid. But no such proof has been even considered, much less offered. In any case, to do so would be to take us very far afield indeed from the realm of (positive) economics.

Indeed, one of the problems with this argument is that government action or even the argument itself may reduce voluntary charitable giving. News reports in 1997 told that Vice President Al Gore contributed only $353 to charity. This may well indicate the amount to be expected from a person who genuinely cares for others but who believes that it is the responsibility of government, rather than voluntary giving, to aid them. The externality argument, to be extent that it is widely believed, may have the effect not only of encouraging acceptance of government programs that trap the poor but of lessening support for voluntary programs, thus diminishing freedom as well.

Then there is also the difficulty of explaining the level of private charitable contributions made before government began its activity in this field. According to Wolf's theory, donations should have then been virtually nonexistent, as we each all wanted to contribute, but were waiting for someone else to do it so that we could free ride on their efforts, or would only do so if given an assurance that everyone else would do so, too. The point is, we have overwhelming evidence suggesting that people do not wait for the assurances that others will give before doing so themselves. On the contrary, they give in any case, and they give generously, even when they know that others will *not* give as generously, or indeed, give at all.

One way to comprehend this state of affairs is to realize that externalities, should they exist,[7] can be internalized through the operation of a free society. This is done in many different ways. People are given buttons to denote their contributions. Those without them are looked down upon. High society patrons hold charity balls. It is of great importance, in some circles, to be invited. But guest lists are highly correlated with charitable giving. Making a contribution, especially a highly public one, is good advertising for businessmen. This must be a large part of the explanation of the endeavors, not to say the very existence of, groups such as the Rotary, the Elks, the Moose, and similar institutions. People of a religious persuasion are convinced that helping the poor in this vale of tears can help square their accounts in the world to come. These motivations are hardly compatible with the Wolfian account we are contemplating.

Even if all of these objections were somehow countered, the argument does not suffice to establish anything like the welfare state now in existence. It is vulnerable to all sorts of reductio ad absurdum. For example, this argument applies as much to foreigners as to domestic citizens. Are we more distressed by the abject poverty of Americans than we are by that of Ethiopians or Bangladeshians? In some sense, there really *are* no poor people in America, at least not as this phrase is used in the latter two countries. So if our distress is correlated with the degree of immiseration, virtually all of our tax money devoted to fighting poverty will be used up for foreigners; none will be left over for our fellow countrymen. And yet our welfare system most certainly does not include the poorest people in the world. On the contrary, it focuses almost entirely on the relatively well off "poor" people in the USA. This can hardly be explained on the grounds that we are distressed by poverty.

---

[7] Until they are one day proven to exist, we can now only accept them on the basis of faith.

Another reductio ad absurdum concerns the level of welfare payments. Some people, perhaps not Wolf, are distressed not merely by the sight of poverty, but by the sight of inequality of income or wealth. In their view, anything less than absolute egalitarianism is "distressful." If these arguments justify coercive taxation in order to "help" the poor, then they also justify anything that anyone else finds distressful, such as the absence of egalitarianism. But why stop here? Why just equality of money income or physical wealth? Why not equality of some rather more important things, such as intelligence, beauty, musical talent, etc., on the assumption, of course, that it were physically possible to redistribute such things. There is simply no stopping point to the argument of redressing the absence of absolute equality of some characteristic about which someone, somewhere, is distressed. So much for Wolf.

What can MM&B[8] contribute to the equity argument? Starting out on a high note, they concede that Pareto optimality can play no role (p. 10):

> This criterion... cannot be applied to a redistributional measure which by definition improves A's position at the expense of B's and C's" (p. 10). As well, they admit that "the answer to the question of fair distribution involves considerations of social philosophy and value judgement".

Most important, MM&B recognize that interpersonal utility comparisons are fraught with logical dangers (p. 11):

> ...it is ... impossible to compare the levels of utility which various individuals derive from their income.

With a base as sound as this, it is hard to believe that their argument would come to grief. Nevertheless, this is precisely what occurs. For in almost their next mention of the topic they are busily drawing two-person utility frontiers and social indifference curves (p. 53). So quickly did the "impossibility of comparing the levels of utility which various individuals derive from their income" vanish from memory.

Their other contribution to the equity argument consists of a defense of the principles of benefits received and ability to pay, for determining "equitable" taxation.[9] A moment's reflection will convince us that both are iniquitous and do not promote equity at all. This can be shown by applying the two precepts to any other area of life besides the relationship between the citizen and the state.

First, let us ponder about the benefits received principle (p. 209):

> ... each taxpayer contributes in line with the benefits which he or she receives from public services.

But according to the theory adumbrated by MM&B, there is no way to be sure that taxpayers – any one of them, let alone all of them – actually benefit from so-called public services at all.

---

[8] These authors, unfortunately, ascribe fully to the version of the externalities theory we have been attributing to Wolf. (See p. 91).

[9] The ability to pay principle is deeply flawed. For discussions of this point, see McGee (1998a, b, c).

In their view (p. 6):

> But where the benefits are available to all, consumers will not voluntarily offer payments to the suppliers of social goods. I will benefit as much from the consumption of others as from my own, and with thousands or millions of other consumers present, my payment is only an insignificant part of the total. Hence, no voluntary payment is made....

And again (pp. 48, 49):

> ... the crucial fact (is) that social goods are provided without exclusion. Because of this, consumer preferences for such goods (the value which they assign to successive marginal units of consumption) will not be revealed voluntarily.

MM&B simply *assume,* without any proof whatsoever, that consumers gain from social goods. But what kind of grounding for the economic science of public finance is that? An unsupported assumption, hanging in the air, with no foundation. As we have seen, there is reason to believe that at least some members of the public (pacifists) might well *be hurt* by some "public" goods (defense). MM&B concede that there is no way, as in the private sector, for consumers to reveal, or demonstrate, their positive preferences for these so-called "public goods." In the absence of any evidence, the only rational conclusion is a healthy skepticism.

But doesn't the government provide services? Even though people will not reveal their preferences for these goods, don't we know "in our hearts" that they do indeed provide benefits? The obvious objection to this scenario is that it is not enough to give out "benefits," even if we stipulate that everyone recognizes them as "good." It is also necessary that people value the item they are given more highly than the money they give up in order to get it. People must agree to the transaction, else how on earth can we ever tell that they valued the item more than the money taken from them? Thus, the MM&B theory cannot be maintained. What is missing is the *acquiescence* on the part of the victim/taxpayer.[10]

Now, let us appraise the ability to pay principle (p. 210):

> ... each taxpayer is asked to contribute in line with his or her ability to pay.

How would this principle work in the area of consumer purchases? Currently, when Rockefeller and a poor man buy a loaf of bread, they pay the identical price.[11] In a fiscal context, this would appear as a very severe regressive "tax." In contrast, on the assumption that Rockefeller is one million times richer than the poor man, if the latter paid $1 for the loaf, Rockefeller would pay $1 million under the ability to pay assumption. The problem with this scenario, at the very least, is that if it were carried out consistently over all people and all goods and services in the economy, our economy would have been reduced to one of absolute income equality.

---

[10] Those who maintain that paying taxes, or voting, or living in the country, or swearing allegiance, or singing the national anthem, or maintaining citizenship is sufficient to establish willingness to pay taxes are invited to peruse Spooner (1870) 1966.

[11] We abstract from such irrelevancies as quality, associated services (e.g., delivery), location of the vendor, etc.

Rockefeller's budget would enable him to buy no more cars, bicycles, fishes, or loaves of bread than would that of the poor man. All people would have identical standards of living. Apart from the pragmatic difficulty (what would be the point of trying to become rich?), this result would only be satisfactory to those whose concept of equity meant strict equality.

Take another example. Suppose a thief (Robin Hood) robs from people in proportion to their wealth; he takes much from the rich, and little from the poor. Or, to make him even more palatable, he steals only from the rich, in proportion to their wealth. Say what you will about such a robber, but it is difficult to see why his actions could best be characterized as "equitable." This is theft, pure, and simple. The only reason Robin Hood can be successfully depicted as being on the side of the angels is *not* because he plunders the rich, but because he does so to people who were thieves themselves. If a modern day Robin Hood burglarized Jane Fonda, Bjorn Borg, Madonna, Magic Johnson, Mike Tyson, Steven Spielberg, Woody Allen, and Arsenio Hall – all exceedingly rich people – he would not be seen in a positive light at all.

Growth and Development

The market is also said to misallocate resources between present and future consumption, i.e., it is charged that the rate of growth is not optimal under free enterprise, and that this, too, is a justification for government taxation and expenditure policy. In the view of Musgrave (p. 7):

> Other discrepancies may arise from differences between public and private…time preferences.

Shoup maintains (pp. 38, 39) that:

> …the rate at which income per head will grow under full employment can be increased by public finance measures that restrain certain types of consumption, thus freeing resources for investment in the broadest sense, including education, medical care, and improvements in the pattern and level of nutrition for children and working age adults that increase their productive capacity, present or future, by more than the cost of these improvements (all discounted to a given date). Some of those whose consumption is restricted for this purpose will object, not agreeing that the present sacrifice is worth the gain, present and future, even if that gain materializes in time to be enjoyed by them rather than only by a future generation.

According to McCready (p. 5):

> There is an argument that government should be involved in the economy because public valuations of future (relative to present) consumption will differ from private values. Typically, the time horizon perceived by an individual is extremely short, with the resultant rate of discount being relatively high. A reasonable case can be made for government valuing the future at a higher rate than individuals would, and therefore, the discount rate used in valuing consumption of goods and services would have to be lessened (p. 5).

MM&B agree with these assessments (p. 169):

> Individuals are said to suffer from "myopia," so that, in arranging their private affairs, they underestimate the importance of saving and overestimate that of present consumption. Hence, the consumers' time discount is too high and government should correct this error by applying a lower rate.

Unfortunately, there is much about which one can object within these short statements. Note, first, that none of the authors come right out and claims that private time preference rates *are* too high. Each maintains this position in the passive voice: "There is an argument that..." "Individuals are said to suffer from 'myopia'..." Perhaps this is because a more forthright statement of the view would open them up to questions of proof or evidence. In plain point of fact, there are no criteria put forth to determine the truth of these assertions. The rate of time preference, the choice between saving and investment, is subjective. None of the veneer of objectivity mentioned by these public finance writers is able to undermine this cold hard fact. Further, even if it can somehow be shown that the market's desire for present consumption is intemperate, it by no means follows, as we have seen, that government can or "should correct this error."

If anything, public finance theorists have got things exactly backwards; if there is any difference between government and the market system with regard to the rate of time preference, it is not that the latter is too present oriented. It is the very opposite: the time horizon of the politician rarely stretches past the next election, in a few years time. When the bill comes in for capital improvements, he will likely be retired, or in jail, or in higher office; so, why worry about these things now? In contrast to the politician, the manager of the modern corporation may have a very long-term view. The typical financial management text presents the role of the manager as maximizing stockholder wealth (Block and Hirt, pp. 11, 12). The value of stock depends upon the earnings of the firm out to infinity. There is no cut-off point such as the next election. Thus, the value of investments to people yet unborn is, at least in principle, considered in corporate decisions. There is no similar assurance of considerations of future generations, even in principle, in decisions made by politicians.

Let us follow up in some detail on MM&B, since they are the most thorough in their analysis of social discount rates (p. 169):

> Next come several arguments related to the welfare of future generations. One argument is that people are too greedy and do not care sufficiently about the welfare of those who follow them. If they did, they would save more so as to leave future generations with a larger capital stock and hence higher level of income. The government, as guardian of future generations, can offset this by using a lower rate of discount and investing more. Saving is viewed as a merit good. This may be a decision faced by the planning board of a developing country, which must choose between more rapid development and an early increase in the level of consumption.

Again, no objective criterion is proffered to determine the "proper" level of greed[12]; nor is it possible to do so. What is the evidence for the declaration "government (I)s the guardian of future generations"? No one in any future generation ever elected any member of any present parliament. If the government represents anyone[13] it is surely the *present* generation, the one that elected it. We have already seen the fallacy of "merit goods," but "the planning board of a developing country," is a contradiction in terms. To the extent that a nation really is developing economically (Hong Kong, Singapore, South Korea) this is precisely the extent to which it has eschewed "planning boards." And to the extent that a nation really has a planning board – for example, many of the nations of Africa and South America, The "People's" Republic of China, North Korea, Vietnam, Cuba, the former USSR. and Eastern Europe until a few years ago, this is precisely the extent to which it is *not* developing economically. This is the extent to which, and precisely why, it is on the way to becoming an economic basket case. It is perhaps easy to see this now, from the vantage point of late 1998, from which we have seen the move of socialism toward the dustbin of history.

Stabilization

A recurring claim all throughout the public finance literature is that the unencumbered market is subject to sudden bouts of depression and that government intervention is thus needed to keep the economy on an even keel. Musgrave's statement (p. 22) is symptomatic of the genre:

> A free economy, if uncontrolled, tends towards more or less drastic fluctuations in prices and employment; and apart from relatively short-term swings, maladjustments of a secular sort may arise towards unemployment or inflation. Public policy must assume a stabilizing function in order to hold within tolerable limits departures from high employment and price stability.

This view amounts to the reiteration of the old familiar standby, "market failure." But here, as in all other cases where this charge is made, it is "government failure" that is really responsible for the flaw mistakenly ascribed to the market.

---

[12] To be fair to MM&B, they do note that "with technical progress raising future productivity, the capital stock needed to sustain the consumption standard may fall, calling for a higher discount rate" (p. 169). But this admission is marred in two ways. First, they base their conclusion on the discredited notion of (intergenerational) equity. Second, they still call for government intervention into the economy. This is problematic because they do so if the present generation is "too greedy," and they *also* do so if the present generation is not greedy enough (due to the fact that future generations will be richer than they because of improved technology). In other words, the verdict is in: market failure, the need for government intervention; the only open question is whether there is too much or too little greed. Talk about angels dancing on the tip of a pin.

[13] There are serious arguments to the effect that it does not. See Rothbard (1970, 1973, 1982), Friedman (1989), Spooner (1870) 1966.

Unemployment, for example, is not intrinsic to the capitalist order. On the contrary, it is brought about through all sorts of unwise and mischievous government interventions: minimum wage legislation; legal support for unions to raise wage rates above productivity levels; the Davis-Bacon Act; occupational licensure; and excessive taxation.

Similarly, Musgrave to the contrary notwithstanding, inflation is always a strictly governmental phenomenon (Rothbard, 1983; Mises, 1971; Friedman and Schwartz, 1963). Price inflation depends crucially upon excessive monetary creation, and in the modern era of central banking, this is solely a prerogative of the state. It can only be alleged that the market is responsible for inflation from a perspective that is innocent of basic economics.

The 1929 depression is commonly thought to be a product of the unhampered market place. This is perhaps "exhibit A" of the public finance point of view on this matter. But even here, despite widely accepted man-in-the-street opinion, there is strong evidence to indicate that far from being a result of the working of the free economy, the great depression, too, came about because of unwise government policies: the collapse of the money supply (Friedman and Schwartz, 1963), the Smoot–Hawley tariff, wage-price controls that kept them inflexible in a downward direction; and the previous bout of inflation during the 1920s, which artificially encouraged and overstimulated basic industries and round about methods of production (see Rothbard, 1975; 1933).

Conclusion

We have considered the common normative justifications for government action given in popular public finance texts. We have found each of them to be wanting, often demonstrating nothing more than a desire to use government force to impose personal preferences on others. The most obvious case is merit goods, which are merely the favorite goods of those who advocate them. Equity is taken to mean equality in income or at least more equality, again with no positive justification for imposing this preference on unwilling people. Voluntary charitable actions tend to be ignored or belittled. The call for the government to find a consensus ignores the Arrow impossibility theorem. The demand that government act to increase economic growth relies upon the undemonstrated positive conclusion that it is capable of doing so as well as the value judgment that it should. In fact, there is reason to believe that corporate managers seeking to maximize the wealth of stockholders will be more concerned about the more distant future than will politicians concerned about the next election. Likewise, the claim that government should act to stabilize the economy depends upon the positive conclusion that the government is capable of making the economy more, rather than less, stable. Yet the evidence is that both unemployment and inflation are government caused phenomena. Given this evidence, the normative claims that greater stability than free markets provide is desirable and should be imposed by government does not even require consideration.

Thus, we find that the common normative justifications for government interference with free markets lack a basis in positive economics or consist merely of the preferences of those writing on public finance. Public finance would be strengthened as an intellectual endeavor if it gave up these supposed reasons supporting government as a means of correcting defects in the market.

References

Kenneth Arrow, SOCIAL CHOICE AND INDIVIDUAL VALUES, 2nd ed., New York: Wiley, 1963.

Rothbard M.N, The Mystery of Banking, New York, Richardson and Snyder, 1983.

Murray N. Rothbard, America's Great Depression, Princeton, NJ, D. Van Nostrand Co., [1963] 1975. Also published by Nash Publishing Co., Los Angeles, 1972 with an introduction to the 2nd edition. Revised edition, New York University Press, 1975.

Ronald Coase, *The Problem of Social Cost,* JOURNAL OF LAW AND ECONOMICS, October 1960.

David Friedman, The Machinery of Freedom: Guide to a Radical Capitalism, 2nd ed., La Salle, IL: Open Court, 1989.

Milton Friedman, and Anna J. Schwartz, A MONETARY HISTORY OF THE UNITED STATES, 1867–1960, New York: National Bureau of Economic Research, 1963.

F. A. Hayek, ed., COLLECTIVIST ECONOMIC PLANNING, Clifton, N. J.: Kelley, 1975 (1933).

Mark Hughes, THE TIES THAT BIND, Vancouver: The Fraser Institute, 1992.

Douglass J. McCready, THE CANADIAN PUBLIC SECTOR, Toronto, Butterworths, 1984.

Robert W. McGee, *Is the Ability to Pay Principle Ethically Bankrupt?* 1 Journal of Accounting, Ethics & Public Policy (Summer 1998a).

Robert W. McGee, *Are Discriminatory Tax Rates Ethically Justifiable?* 1 JOURNAL OF ACCOUNTING, ETHICS & PUBLIC POLICY (Fall 1998b).

Robert W. McGee, *Should Rich People Pay More than Poor People? An Ethical Look at the Graduated Income Tax,* COMMENTARIES ON THE LAW OF ACCOUNTING & FINANCE (1998c).

Ludwig von Mises, The Theory of Money and Credit, Irvington-on-Hudson, NY, Foundation for Economic Education, [1912] 1971.

Richard A. Musgrave, THE THEORY OF PUBLIC FINANCE, New York: McGraw-Hill, 1959.

Charles Murray, LOSING GROUND: AMERICAN SOCIAL POLICY FROM 1950 TO 1980, New York: Basic Books, 1984.

Charles Murray, IN PURSUIT: OF HAPPINESS AND GOOD GOVERNMENT, New York, Simon & Schuster, 1988.

Murray N. Rothbard, POWER AND MARKET: GOVERNMENT AND THE ECONOMY, Menlo Park Cal.: Institute for Humane Studies, 1970.

Murray N. Rothbard, FOR A NEW LIBERTY, Macmillan, New York, 1973.

Murray N. Rothbard, THE ETHICS OF LIBERTY, Humanities Press, Atlantic Highlands, N.J., 1982.

Murray N. Rothbard, MAN, ECONOMY AND STATE, Los Angeles, Nash, 1970.

Lysander Spooner, NO TREASON, Larkspur, Colorado, (1870) 1966.

Part IV
Practitioner Perspectives

Chapter 15
Attitudes Toward Tax Evasion: An Empirical Study of Florida Accounting Practitioners

Robert W. McGee and Tatyana B. Maranjyan

Introduction

People have been evading taxes ever since the first ruler attempted to tax his subjects (Adams, 1982, 1993; Webber & Wildavsky, 1986). There have been tax revolts (Baldwin, 1967; Beito, 1989) and talk of tax revolts (Laffer & Seymour, 1979; Larson, 1973; Rabushka & Ryan, 1982). There have been discussions of tax fairness (Boortz & Linder, 2005; Graetz & Shapiro, 2005; McCaffery, 2002) and reform (Champagne, 1994; DioGuardi, 1992; Grace, 1984; Payne, 1993; Schlaes, 1999; Shughart, 1997) and criticisms of the graduated income tax (Blum & Kalven, 1953) and of government abuses (Burnham, 1989; Frankel & Fink, 1985; Gross, 1995; Hansen, 1984). Some scholars have called for the abolition of the income tax (Champagne, 1994; Chodorov, 1954; Curry, 1982; Sabrin, 1995). Others have complained about the leakage that occurs as a result of cheating on taxes and call for a crackdown, reform, or increasing taxes on the rich (Cowell, 1990; Johnston, 2003, 2007; Lewis & Allison, 2002). Some authors defend the present system (Greenwood, 2007) while others question the legitimacy of the state (Martinez, 1994).

A number of books have been written from the perspective of public finance, some taking a taxpayer or public choice perspective (Buchanan, 1967; Buchanan & Flowers, 1975; Cullis & Jones, 1998) and others taking a more statist perspective (Musgrave, 1959, 1986; Musgrave & Musgrave, 1976; Musgrave & Peacock, 1958). Buchanan and Musgrave debated the relative merits of both approaches (Buchanan & Musgrave, 2001).

R.W. McGee (✉)
School of Business, Florida International University, 3000 NE 151 Street,
North Miami, FL 33181, USA
e-mail: bob414@hotmail.com

T.B. Maranjyan
Moscow State University of Economics, Statistics and Informatics,
Yerevan Branch, 25 A Nalbandian St., Apt. 29, Yerevan 0001, Armenia

R.W. McGee (ed.), *The Ethics of Tax Evasion: Perspectives in Theory and Practice*,   247
DOI 10.1007/978-1-4614-1287-8_15, © Springer Science+Business Media, LLC 2012

A few articles (Martinez, 1994; McGee, 1994, 2006a) and books (Crowe, 1944; McGee, 1998a, 2004) have taken a philosophical approach to the ethics of tax evasion. Some studies have been done from a religious perspective. Cohn (1998), Tamari (1998), and McGee (1998e) discuss the issue from the Jewish perspective. Crowe (1944) reviewed 500 years of Catholic literature on the subject. More recent Catholic- or Christian-oriented studies have been done by Gronbacher (1998), McGee (1998b), Pennock (1998), and Schansberg (1998). DeMoville (1998) discussed the Baha'i perspective. Smith and Kimball (1998) discussed the Mormon literature on the topic. Murtuza and Ghazanfar (1998) provide a perspective on the Muslim practice of zakat. McGee (1997, 1998c, 1998d) discussed the Muslim view of tax evasion as put forth by two Muslim scholars (Ahmad, 1995; Yusuf, 1971). Jalili (2012) presents a much different view from the Muslim perspective. McGee (1999) critiques some of the religious literature on the subject.

In recent years, several studies have been done that examine opinions on tax evasion. However, most of those studies involve student surveys (Brown & Choong 2005). Very few have solicited the opinions of accounting practitioners. The purpose of the present study is to partially fill that gap in the literature.

The authors developed a survey instrument that included 18 statements incorporating the three major views on the ethics of tax evasion that have emerged in the literature over the last 500 years. The survey was distributed to the Atlantic, Broward, East Coast, Jacksonville, and South Miami-Dade chapters of the Florida Institute of Certified Public Accountants (FICPA) and the Tampa Bay chapter of the Association of Latino Professionals in Finance and Accounting (ALPFA). This chapter reports on the results of that survey.

Methodology

After reviewing the literature that exists on the ethics of tax evasion, a survey was constructed and distributed to a group of accounting practitioners in South Florida in order to learn their views on the ethics of tax evasion. The survey consisted of 18 statements. Using a seven-point Likert scale, respondents were asked to place the appropriate number in the space provided to indicate the extent of their agreement or disagreement with each statement. The statements in the survey reflected the three main viewpoints on the ethics of tax evasion that have emerged over the centuries. A total of 171 usable responses were received.

Survey Findings

The next few sections report on the study's findings.

Table 15.1 Demographics

	Sample	%
Ethnicity		
Non-Hispanic white	114	66.7
Hispanic	35	20.5
Asian	4	2.3
African-American	1	0.6
Other	7	4.1
Not specified	10	5.8
	171	100.0
Gender		
Male	101	59.1
Female	60	35.1
Not specified	10	5.8
	171	100.0

Demographics

Table 15.1 shows the demographics. The sample consisted mostly of non-Hispanic whites, although over 20% of the sample was Hispanic. More than 59% was male.

Table 15.2 shows the mean scores for each of the 18 statements. The average mean score was 6.45, indicating strong opposition to tax evasion.

Table 15.3 ranks the argument for justifying tax evasion, from strongest to weakest. The three strongest arguments were the three human rights arguments. The strongest reason to justify tax evasion was the case of Jews living in Nazi Germany. In second place was the case, where the government discriminates against the taxpayer on the basis of religion, race, or ethnicity. The third strongest reason was in cases, where the government imprisons people for their political beliefs. All three of these rationales had mean scores of less than 6.0, although they were all more than 5.3, indicating a strong resistance to tax evasion even in cases of human rights abuses.

The other 15 arguments all had means scores above 6.0. Corruption, unfairness, and waste ranked relatively high in terms of justification for tax evasion, although, with mean scores above 6.0 on a scale of 1–7, the arguments were not strongly supported by the practitioners. Inability to pay was another reason to justify tax evasion, as was the case where the government spends money on projects that the taxpayer morally disapproves of. Among the weakest rationales for justifying tax evasion were cases where the government spends the money wisely or on worthy projects or where the taxpayer benefits by the expenditures.

Gender Differences

A number of studies have examined the relationship between gender and ethical values. Some studies have concluded that women are more ethical than men (Tang & Zuo, 1997; Singhapakdi, Vitell, & Franke, 1999; Beu, Buckley, & Harvey, 2003).

Table 15.2 Mean scores

S#		
1	Tax evasion is ethical if tax rates are too high (S1)	6.65
2	Tax evasion is ethical even if tax rates are not too high because the government is not entitled to take as much as it is taking from me (S2)	6.71
3	Tax evasion is ethical if the tax system is unfair (S3)	6.34
4	Tax evasion is ethical if a large portion of the money collected is wasted (S4)	6.37
5	Tax evasion is ethical even if most of the money collected is spent wisely (S5)	6.81
6	Tax evasion is ethical if a large portion of the money collected is spent on projects that I morally disapprove of (S6)	6.55
7	Tax evasion is ethical even if a large portion of the money collected is spent on worthy projects (S7)	6.80
8	Tax evasion is ethical if a large portion of the money collected is spent on projects that do not benefit me (S8)	6.71
9	Tax evasion is ethical even if a large portion of the money collected is spent on projects that do benefit me (S9)	6.76
10	Tax evasion is ethical if everyone is doing it (S10)	6.59
11	Tax evasion is ethical if a significant portion of the money collected winds up in the pockets of corrupt politicians or their families and friends (S11)	6.06
12	Tax evasion is ethical if the probability of getting caught is low (S12)	6.68
13	Tax evasion is ethical if some of the proceeds go to support a war that I consider to be unjust (S13)	6.61
14	Tax evasion is ethical if I cannot afford to pay (S14)	6.53
15	Tax evasion is ethical if I cannot afford to pay (S15)	6.65
16	Tax evasion would be ethical if I were a Jew living in Nazi Germany in 1940 (S16)	5.37
17	Tax evasion is ethical if the government discriminates against me because of my religion, race, or ethnic background (S17)	5.93
18	Tax evasion is ethical if the government imprisons people for their political opinions (S18)	5.98
	Average score	6.45

1 = strong agreement; 7 = strong disagreement

Other studies have concluded that there is no statistical difference between men and women in terms of ethics (Dubinsky & Levy, 1985; Babakus, Cornwell, Mitchell, & Schlegelmilch, 2004; McCabe, Ingram, & Dato-on, 2006). Barnett & Karson (1987) concluded that men are more ethical than women. Weeks, Moore, McKinney, & Longenecker (1999) concluded that women are more ethical than men on some issues and men are more ethical than women on other issues.

Table 15.4 shows the mean scores by gender. Female scores were higher in 13 of 18 cases, indicating a stronger aversion to tax evasion. The average mean score for females was also higher than for males, 6.55 compared to 6.39.

Table 15.5 summarizes the mean comparisons.

Table 15.3 Ranking of arguments

Rank		Mean
1	Tax evasion would be ethical if I were a Jew living in Nazi Germany in 1940 (S16)	5.37
2	Tax evasion is ethical if the government discriminates against me because of my religion, race, or ethnic background (S17)	5.93
3	Tax evasion is ethical if the government imprisons people for their political opinions (S18)	5.98
4	Tax evasion is ethical if a significant portion of the money collected winds up in the pockets of corrupt politicians or their families and friends (S11)	6.06
5	Tax evasion is ethical if the tax system is unfair (S3)	6.34
6	Tax evasion is ethical if a large portion of the money collected is wasted (S4)	6.37
7	Tax evasion is ethical if I cannot afford to pay (S14)	6.53
8	Tax evasion is ethical if a large portion of the money collected is spent on projects that I morally disapprove of (S6)	6.55
9	Tax evasion is ethical if everyone is doing it (S10)	6.59
10	Tax evasion is ethical if some of the proceeds go to support a war that I consider to be unjust (S13)	6.61
11	Tax evasion is ethical if tax rates are too high (S1)	6.65
11	Tax evasion is ethical if I cannot afford to pay (S15)	6.65
13	Tax evasion is ethical if the probability of getting caught is low (S12)	6.68
14	Tax evasion is ethical even if tax rates are not too high because the government is not entitled to take as much as it is taking from me (S2)	6.71
14	Tax evasion is ethical if a large portion of the money collected is spent on projects that do not benefit me (S8)	6.71
16	Tax evasion is ethical even if a large portion of the money collected is spent on projects that do benefit me (S9)	6.76
17	Tax evasion is ethical even if a large portion of the money collected is spent on worthy projects (S7)	6.80
18	Tax evasion is ethical even if most of the money collected is spent wisely (S5)	6.81

1 = strong agreement; 7 = strong disagreement

Table 15.6 shows the significance of the differences in means. In most cases, the differences are not significant. The exception is Statement 16 (the Jews in Nazi Germany statement). In that case, men were significantly less opposed to tax evasion.

Differences by Ethnicity

Table 15.7 compares the differences in mean scores by ethnicity. The Hispanic and non-Hispanic white samples were sufficiently large to make a comparison. The overall mean score for Hispanics (5.98) was lower than for non-Hispanic whites (6.53), which indicates that Hispanics were less averse to tax evasion.

Table 15.8 shows that the Hispanic mean score was higher in only 1 of the 18 cases, meaning that Hispanics were less opposed to tax evasion in 17 of 18 cases.

Table 15.4 Mean scores by gender

S#		Overall	Female (sample size 60)	Male (sample size 101)	Female	Male
1	Tax evasion is ethical if tax rates are too high	6.65	6.72	6.61	0.11	
2	Tax evasion is ethical even if tax rates are not too high because the government is not entitled to take as much as it is taking from me	6.71	6.72	6.71	0.01	
3	Tax evasion is ethical if the tax system is unfair	6.34	6.53	6.23	0.30	
4	Tax evasion is ethical if a large portion of the money collected is wasted	6.37	6.42	6.34	0.08	
5	Tax evasion is ethical even if most of the money collected is spent wisely	6.81	6.70	6.88		0.18
6	Tax evasion is ethical if a large portion of the money collected is spent on projects that I morally disapprove of	6.55	6.58	6.53	0.05	
7	Tax evasion is ethical even if a large portion of the money collected is spent on worthy projects	6.80	6.77	6.81		0.04
8	Tax evasion is ethical even if a large portion of the money collected is spent on projects that do not benefit me	6.71	6.70	6.71		0.01
9	Tax evasion is ethical even if a large portion of the money collected is spent on projects that do benefit me	6.76	6.63	6.83		0.20

10	Tax evasion is ethical if everyone is doing it	6.59	6.72	6.51	0.21
11	Tax evasion is ethical if a significant portion of the money collected winds up in the pockets of corrupt politicians or their families and friends	6.06	6.08	6.04	0.04	0.11
12	Tax evasion is ethical if the probability of getting caught is low	6.68	6.77	6.62	0.15
13	Tax evasion is ethical if some of the proceeds go to support a war that I consider to be unjust	6.61	6.68	6.56	0.12
14	Tax evasion is ethical if I cannot afford to pay	6.53	6.65	6.46	0.19
15	Tax evasion is ethical if I cannot afford to pay	6.65	6.58	6.69	
16	Tax evasion would be ethical if I were a Jew living in Nazi Germany in 1940	5.37	6.12	4.92	1.20
17	Tax evasion is ethical if the government discriminates against me because of my religion, race, or ethnic background	5.93	6.21	5.77	0.44
18	Tax evasion is ethical if the government imprisons people for their political opinions	5.98	6.28	5.80	0.48
	Average score	6.45	6.55	6.39	

1 = strong agreement; 7 = strong disagreement

Table 15.5 Gender mean summary

	Frequency	%
Female mean higher	13	72.2
Male mean higher	5	27.8
	18	100.0

Table 15.6 Gender statistical data

S#	Female–Male	Probability, assuming null hypothesis	t	SD
1	Tax evasion is ethical if tax rates are too high	0.48	0.708	0.891
2	Tax evasion is ethical even if tax rates are not too high because the government is not entitled to take as much as it is taking from me	0.96	0.471E-01	0.867
3	Tax evasion is ethical if the tax system is unfair	0.16	1.41	1.33
4	Tax evasion is ethical if a large portion of the money collected is wasted	0.71	0.375	1.31
5	Tax evasion is ethical even if most of the money collected is spent wisely	0.10	1.64	0.678
6	Tax evasion is ethical if a large portion of the money collected is spent on projects that I morally disapprove of	0.77	0.293	1.02
7	Tax evasion is ethical even if a large portion of the money collected is spent on worthy projects	0.68	0.418	0.664
8	Tax evasion is ethical if a large portion of the money collected is spent on projects that do not benefit me	0.92	0.961E-01	0.821
9	Tax evasion is ethical even if a large portion of the money collected is spent on projects that do benefit me	0.13	1.53	0.793
10	Tax evasion is ethical if everyone is doing it	0.29	1.06	1.06
11	Tax evasion is ethical if a significant portion of the money collected winds up in the pockets of corrupt politicians or their families and friends	0.87	0.161	1.65
12	Tax evasion is ethical if the probability of getting caught is low	0.37	0.907	0.966
13	Tax evasion is ethical if some of the proceeds go to support a war that I consider to be unjust	0.45	0.757	0.964
14	Tax evasion is ethical if I cannot afford to pay	0.28	1.09	1.07
15	Tax evasion is ethical if I cannot afford to pay	0.47	0.728	0.925

(continued)

Table 15.6 (continued)

S#	Female–Male	Probability, assuming null hypothesis	t	SD
16	Tax evasion would be ethical if I were a Jew living in Nazi Germany in 1940	0.0019	3.16	2.30
17	Tax evasion is ethical if the government discriminates against me because of my religion, race, or ethnic background	0.15	1.43	1.86
18	Tax evasion is ethical if the government imprisons people for their political opinions	0.12	1.56	1.82

Table 15.7 Scores by ethnicity

S#		Hispanic (sample size 35)	Non-Hispanic white (sample size 114)	Hispanic	Non-Hispanic white
1	Tax evasion is ethical if tax rates are too high	6.31	6.75		0.44
2	Tax evasion is ethical even if tax rates are not too high because the government is not entitled to take as much as it is taking from me	6.40	6.85		0.45
3	Tax evasion is ethical if the tax system is unfair	5.60	6.41		0.81
4	Tax evasion is ethical if a large portion of the money collected is wasted	5.26	6.52		1.26
5	Tax evasion is ethical even if most of the money collected is spent wisely	6.46	6.90		0.44
6	Tax evasion is ethical if a large portion of the money collected is spent on projects that I morally disapprove of	5.77	6.69		0.92
7	Tax evasion is ethical even if a large portion of the money collected is spent on worthy projects	6.23	6.90		0.67
8	Tax evasion is ethical if a large portion of the money collected is spent on projects that do not benefit me	6.14	6.81		0.67

(continued)

Table 15.7 (continued)

S#		Hispanic (sample size 35)	Non-Hispanic white (sample size 114)	Hispanic	Non-Hispanic white
9	Tax evasion is ethical even if a large portion of the money collected is spent on projects that do benefit me	6.40	6.86		0.46
10	Tax evasion is ethical if everyone is doing it	5.94	6.70		0.76
11	Tax evasion is ethical if a significant portion of the money collected winds up in the pockets of corrupt politicians or their families and friends	5.74	6.10		0.36
12	Tax evasion is ethical if the probability of getting caught is low	6.20	6.75		0.55
13	Tax evasion is ethical if some of the proceeds go to support a war that I consider to be unjust	6.06	6.69		0.63
14	Tax evasion is ethical if I cannot afford to pay	5.85	6.58		0.73
15	Tax evasion is ethical if I cannot afford to pay	6.31	6.75		0.44
16	Tax evasion would be ethical if I were a Jew living in Nazi Germany in 1940	5.38	5.32	0.06	
17	Tax evasion is ethical if the government discriminates against me because of my religion, race, or ethnic background	5.76	6.02		0.26
18	Tax evasion is ethical if the government imprisons people for their political opinions	5.84	5.89		0.05
	Average score	5.98	6.53		

1 = strong agreement; 7 = strong disagreement

Table 15.8 Ethnicity score summary

	Frequency	%
Hispanic score higher	1	5.6
Non-Hispanic white score higher	17	94.4
	18	100.0

Table 15.9 shows the significance of the differences in mean score on the basis of ethnicity. In many cases, the differences were significant at the 1% level.

Although the results clearly show that Hispanics had significantly lower mean scores than did non-Hispanic whites, we cannot automatically conclude that Hispanics are less ethical than non-Hispanic whites when it comes to tax evasion. To arrive at that conclusion, one must have the underlying premise that tax evasion is unethical, which may or may not be the case. One of the main purposes of the present study was to determine whether tax evasion is considered to be unethical, and under what circumstances it might be considered to be unethical. If tax evasion is determined to be ethical in certain circumstances, we cannot automatically conclude that the group that has lower scores are less ethical than the group that had higher scores. All we can conclude is that the group with the lower scores (Hispanics in this study) are less opposed to tax evasion than are the people in the group that had higher scores (non-Hispanic whites in this study).

Although Hispanics had lower scores than non-Hispanic whites, the Hispanic scores were quite high. On a scale from 1 to 7, the average Hispanic score was 5.98. How does that compare to other groups?

The survey instrument used in this study was also used in several other studies (McGee & Paláu, 2008; McGee & Goldman, 2010). Table 15.10 shows the average scores for the various other groups surveyed. As can be seen, Hispanics are near the top of the list, as the average score for this group was higher than almost every other group surveyed.

Dominant Groups

Historically, there have been three views on the ethics of tax evasion (McGee, 2006). If we arbitrarily assign numbers to the three positions, one possible assignment would be to say that those whose scores were less than 2 should be assigned to the *always or almost always* ethical group, those with scores of more than 2 but less than 6 should be in the *sometimes ethical* group, and those who gave scores of 6 or higher should be in the *never or almost never ethical* category.

Table 15.11 shows the breakdown of scores into those three categories. Each of the two groups responded to 18 statements with scores ranging from 1 to 7, for a total of 36 events. As can be seen, the Hispanics who participated in the study were in the *sometimes ethical* group 50% of the time and in the *never or almost never ethical* the other 50% of the time. Non-Hispanic whites, on the other hand, were in the *never or almost never ethical* category 88.9% of the time.

Table 15.9 Statistical data: Ethnicity

S#	Hispanic–non-Hispanic white	Probability, assuming null hypothesis	t	SD
1	Tax evasion is ethical if tax rates are too high	0.013	2.52	0.885
2	Tax evasion is ethical even if tax rates are not too high because the government is not entitled to take as much as it is taking from me	0.0013	3.29	0.706
3	Tax evasion is ethical if the tax system is unfair	0.0039	2.93	1.43
4	Tax evasion is ethical if a large portion of the money collected is wasted	0.0001	4.60	1.42
5	Tax evasion is ethical even if most of the money collected is spent wisely	0.0009	3.38	0.683
6	Tax evasion is ethical if a large portion of the money collected is spent on projects that I morally disapprove of	0.0001	4.33	1.10
7	Tax evasion is ethical even if a large portion of the money collected is spent on worthy projects	0.0001	4.51	0.774
8	Tax evasion is ethical if a large portion of the money collected is spent on projects that do not benefit me	0.0003	3.74	0.919
9	Tax evasion is ethical even if a large portion of the money collected is spent on projects that do benefit me	0.0018	3.18	0.748
10	Tax evasion is ethical if everyone is doing it	0.0016	3.21	1.22
11	Tax evasion is ethical if a significant portion of the money collected winds up in the pockets of corrupt politicians or their families and friends	0.28	1.09	1.70
12	Tax evasion is ethical if the probability of getting caught is low	0.0068	2.74	1.05
13	Tax evasion is ethical if some of the proceeds go to support a war that I consider to be unjust	0.0020	3.15	1.04
14	Tax evasion is ethical if I cannot afford to pay	0.0035	2.97	1.25
15	Tax evasion is ethical if I cannot afford to pay	0.015	2.45	0.928
16	Tax evasion would be ethical if I were a Jew living in Nazi Germany in 1940	0.92	0.105	2.41
17	Tax evasion is ethical if the government discriminates against me because of my religion, race, or ethnic background	0.47	0.719	1.83
18	Tax evasion is ethical if the government imprisons people for their political opinions	0.89	0.132	1.94

Table 15.10 Comparison of mean scores with other studies

Sample surveyed	Study	Mean score
Accounting practitioners – Florida – non-Hispanic whites	The present study	6.53
The USA – Utah accounting students	McGee & Smith, 2009	6.12
Colombia – business students	McGee, López, & Yepes, 2009	6.03
Accounting practitioners – Florida – Hispanic	The present study	5.98
The USA – Florida accounting students	McGee & Smith, 2009	5.83
The USA – Florida business students	McGee, Nickerson, & Fees, 2006	5.62
Puerto Rico – accounting and law students	McGee & López, 2007	5.62
International business academics teaching in the USA	McGee, 2006b	5.55
Estonia – business students, faculty, and practitioners	McGee, Alver, & Alver, 2008	5.54
Argentina – business, economics, and law students	McGee & Rossi, 2008	5.40
The USA – Florida business students	McGee, Ho, & Li, 2008	5.36
Hong Kong – business students	McGee, Ho, & Li, 2008	5.25
Turkey – accounting practitioners	McGee, Benk, Yildirim, & Kayikçi, 2011	5.25
Guatemala – business, economics, and law students	McGee & Lingle, 2008	5.20
Hong Kong – business students	McGee & Butt, 2008	5.06
Bosnia – business students	McGee, Basic, & Tyler, 2008	5.03
Southern China – social science, business, economics, and other students	McGee & Noronha, 2008	5.03
Germany – business students	McGee, Nickerson, & Fees, 2009	4.94
Thailand – accounting students	McGee, 2008	4.94
Macau – social science, business, economics, and other students	McGee & Noronha, 2008	4.93
Slovakia – business, economics, philosophy, and theology students	McGee & Tusan, 2008	4.91
France – MBA students	McGee & M'Zali, 2009	4.86
Turkey – business students	McGee & Benk, 2011	4.83
Australia – business, philosophy, and seminary students and faculty	McGee & Bose, 2009	4.78
Mali – executive MBA students	McGee & M'Zali, 2008	4.73
Taiwan – students	McGee & Andres, 2009	4.72
New Zealand – accounting, business, economics, and law students and accounting practitioners	Gupta & McGee, 2010	4.66
Romania – business students	McGee, Basic, & Tyler, 2008	4.59
Armenia – business, economics, and theology students	McGee & Maranjyan, 2008	4.54

(continued)

Table 15.10 (continued)

Sample surveyed	Study	Mean score
Beijing, China – business and economics students	McGee & An, 2008	4.40
Hubei, China – business, economics, law, and philosophy students	McGee & Guo, 2007	4.30
Kazakhstan – accounting and business students	McGee & Preobragenskaya, 2008	4.14

Table 15.11 Measurement of dominant groups

	Hispanics	Non-Hispanic whites	Totals
Tax evasion is always or almost always ethical (score < 2)	0	0	0
Tax evasion is sometimes ethical (2 < score < 6)	9 (50%)	2 (11.1%)	11 (30.6%)
Tax evasion is never or almost never ethical (score > 6)	9 (50%)	16 (88.9%)	25 (69.4%)
Totals	18 (100.0%)	18 (100.0%)	36 (100.0%)

References

Adams, Charles. (1982). *Fight, Flight and Fraud: The Story of Taxation*. Curacao: Euro-Dutch Publishers.

Adams, Charles. (1993). *For Good or Evil: The Impact of Taxes on the Course of Civilization*. London, New York & Lanham: Madison Books.

Ahmad, Mushtaq (1995). *Business Ethics in Islam*. Islamabad, Pakistan: The International Institute of Islamic Thought & The International Institute of Islamic Economics.

Babakus, Emin, T. Bettina Cornwell, Vince Mitchell and Bodo Schlegelmilch (2004). Reactions to Unethical Consumer Behavior across Six Countries. *The Journal of Consumer Marketing*, 21(4/5), 254–263.

Baldwin, Leland D. (1967). *Whiskey Rebels: The Story of a Frontier Uprising*. Pittsburgh: University of Pittsburgh Press.

Barnett, John H. and Marvin J. Karson. (1987). Personal Values and Business Decisions: An Exploratory Investigation. *Journal of Business Ethics*, 6(5), 371–382.

Beito, D.T. (1989). *Taxpayers in Revolt: Tax Resistance during the Great Depression*. Chapel Hill, NC: University of North Carolina Press.

Beu, Danielle S., M. Ronald Buckley & Michael G. Harvey. (2003). Ethical Decision-Making: A Multidimensional Construct. *Business Ethics: A European Review*, 12(1), 88–107.

Blum, Walter J. & Harry Kalven, Jr. (1953). *The Uneasy Case for Progressive Taxation*. Chicago & London: University of Chicago Press.

Boortz, Neal & John Linder (2005). *The Fair Tax Book: Saying Goodbye to the Income Tax and the I.R.S.* New York: HarperCollins.

Brown, Bob S. and Peggy Choong. (2005). An Investigation of Academic Dishonesty among Business Students at Public and Private United States Universities. *International Journal of Management*, 22(2), 201–214.

Buchanan, James M. (1967). *Public Finance in Democratic Process*. Chapel Hill, NC: University of North Carolina Press.

Buchanan, James M. & Marilyn R. Flowers. (1975). *The Public Finances*, 4th edition. Homewood, IL: Richard D. Irwin, Inc.

Buchanan, James M. & Richard A. Musgrave. (2001). *Public Finance and Public Choice: Two Contrasting Visions of the State*. Cambridge, MA & London. MIT Press.

Burnham, David (1989). *A Law unto Itself: Power, Politics and the IRS*. New York: Random House.

Champagne, Frank (1994). *Cancel April 15th! The Plan for Painless Taxation*. Mount Vernon, WA: Veda Vangarde.

Chodorov, Frank (1954). *The Income Tax: Root of All Evil*. New York: The Devin-Adair Company.

Cohn, Gordon. (1998). The Jewish View on Paying Taxes. *Journal of Accounting, Ethics & Public Policy*, 1(2), 109–120, reprinted in Robert W. McGee (Ed.), *The Ethics of Tax Evasion* (pp. 180–189). Dumont, NJ: The Dumont Institute for Public Policy Research, 1998, pp. 180–189.

Cowell, F.A. (1990). *Cheating the Government: The Economics of Evasion*. Cambridge, MA & London: MIT Press.

Crowe, Martin T. (1944). The Moral Obligation of Paying Just Taxes, The Catholic University of America Studies in Sacred Theology No. 84.

Cullis, J. & Philip Jones. (1998). *Public Finance and Public Choice*, 2nd edition. New York: Oxford University Press.

Curry, B. (1982). *Principles of Taxation of a Libertarian Society*. Glendale, CA: BC Publishing Company.

DeMoville, Wig. (1998). The Ethics of Tax Evasion: A Baha'i Perspective. *Journal of Accounting, Ethics & Public Policy*, 1(3), 356–368, reprinted in Robert W. McGee (Ed.), *The Ethics of Tax Evasion* (pp. 230–240). Dumont, NJ: The Dumont Institute for Public Policy Research, 1998.

DioGuardi, Joseph J. (1992). *Unaccountable Congress*. Washington, DC: Regnery Gateway.

Dubinsky, Alan J. and Michael Levy. (1985). Ethics in Retailing: Perceptions of Retail Sales People. *Journal of the Academy of Marketing Science*, 13(1), 1–16.

Frankel, Sandor & Robert S. Fink (1985). *How to Defend Yourself against the IRS*. New York: Simon & Schuster.

Grace, J. Peter (1984). *Burning Money: The Waste of Your Tax Dollars*. New York: Macmillan Publishing Company.

Graetz, M.J. & I. Shapiro. (2005). *Death by a Thousand Cuts: The Fight over Taxing Inherited Wealth*. Princeton & Oxford: Princeton University Press.

Greenwood, S. (2007). *10 Excellent Reasons not to Hate Taxes*. New York: The New Press.

Gronbacher, Gregory M.A. (1998). Taxation: Catholic Social Thought and Classical Liberalism. *Journal of Accounting, Ethics & Public Policy*, 1(1), 91–100, reprinted in Robert W. McGee (ed.), *The Ethics of Tax Evasion* (pp. 158–167). Dumont, NJ: The Dumont Institute for Public Policy Research, Dumont, NJ, 1998.

Gross, Martin L. (1995). *The Tax Racket: Government Extortion from A to Z*. New York: Ballantine Books.

Gupta, Ranjana and Robert W. McGee. (2010). A Comparative Study of New Zealanders' Opinion on the Ethics of Tax Evasion: Students v. Accountants. *New Zealand Journal of Taxation Law and Policy*, 16(1), 47–84.

Hansen, George (1984). *To Harass Our People: The IRS and Government Abuse of Power*. Washington, DC: Positive Publications.

Jalili, Ali Reza (2012). The Ethics of Tax Evasion: An Islamic Perspective. In Robert W. McGee (Ed.), *The Ethics of Tax Evasion in Theory and Practice* (forthcoming). New York: Springer.

Johnston, D.C. (2003). *Perfectly Legal: The Covert Campaign to Rig Our Tax System to Benefit the Super Rich – and Cheat Everybody Else*. New York: Penguin.

Johnston, D.C. (2007). *Free Lunch: How the Wealthiest Americans Enrich Themselves at Government Expense (and Stick You with the Bill)*. New York: Penguin.

Laffer, Arthur B. & Jan P. Seymour (Eds.) (1979). *The Economics of the Tax Revolt*. New York: Harcourt Brace Jovanovich.

Larson, M.A. (1973). *Tax Revolt: U.S.A.!* Washington, DC: Liberty Lobby.

Lewis, C. & B. Allison. (2002). *The Cheating of America: How Tax Avoidance and Evasion by the Super Rich Are Costing the Country Billions – and What You Can do About It*. New York: Perennial.

Martinez, Leo P. (1994). Taxes, Morals, and Legitimacy. *Brigham Young University Law Review*, 1994, 521–569.

McCabe, A. Catherine, Rhea Ingram and Mary Conway Dato-on. (2006). The Business of Ethics and Gender. *Journal of Business Ethics*, 64, 101–116.

McCaffery, E.J. (2002). *Fair not Flat: How To Make the Tax System Better and Simpler*. Chicago & London: University of Chicago Press.

McGee, Robert W. (1994). Is Tax Evasion Unethical? *University of Kansas Law Review*, 42(2), 411–35.

McGee, Robert W. (1997). The Ethics of Tax Evasion and Trade Protectionism from an Islamic Perspective, *Commentaries on Law & Public Policy*, 1, 250–262.

McGee, Robert W. (Ed.). (1998a). *The Ethics of Tax Evasion*. Dumont, NJ: The Dumont Institute for Public Policy Research.

McGee, Robert W. (1998b). Christian Views on the Ethics of Tax Evasion. *Journal of Accounting, Ethics & Public Policy*, 1(2), 210–225. Reprinted at http://ssrn.com/abstract=461398.

McGee, Robert W. (1998c). The Ethics of Tax Evasion in Islam, in Robert W. McGee (Ed.), *The Ethics of Tax Evasion* (pp. 214–219). Dumont, NJ: The Dumont Institute.

McGee, Robert W. (1998d). The Ethics of Tax Evasion in Islam: A Comment. *Journal of Accounting, Ethics & Public Policy*, 1(2), 162–168, reprinted in Robert W. McGee, editor, The Ethics of Tax Evasion (pp. 214–219). Dumont, NJ: The Dumont Institute for Public Policy Research, 1998.

McGee, Robert W. (1998e). Jewish Views on the Ethics of Tax Evasion, *Journal of Accounting, Ethics & Public Policy*, 1(3), 323–336.

McGee, Robert W. (1999). Is It Unethical to Evade Taxes in an Evil or Corrupt State? A Look at Jewish, Christian, Muslim, Mormon and Baha'i Perspectives. *Journal of Accounting, Ethics & Public Policy*, 2(1), 149–181. Reprinted at http://ssrn.com/abstract=251469.

McGee, Robert W. (2004). *The Philosophy of Taxation and Public Finance*. Norwell, MA and Dordrecht: Kluwer Academic Publishers.

McGee, Robert W. (2006a). Three Views on the Ethics of Tax Evasion. Journal of Business Ethics, 67(1), 15–35.

McGee, Robert W. (2006b). A Survey of International Business Academics on the Ethics of Tax Evasion. *Journal of Accounting, Ethics & Public Policy*, 6(3), 301–352.

McGee, Robert W., Inge Nickerson and Werner Fees. (2006). German and American Opinion on the Ethics of Tax Evasion. *Proceedings of the Academy of Legal, Ethical and Regulatory Issues* (Reno), 10(2), 31–34.

McGee, Robert W. and Zhiwen Guo. (2007). A Survey of Law, Business and Philosophy Students in China on the Ethics of Tax Evasion. *Society and Business Review*, 2(3), 299–315.

McGee, Robert W. and Silvia López Paláu. (2007). The Ethics of Tax Evasion: Two Empirical Studies of Puerto Rican Opinion. *Journal of Applied Business and Economics*, 7(3), 27–47 (2007). Reprinted in Robert W. McGee (editor), *Readings in Accounting Ethics* (pp. 314–342). Hyderabad, India: ICFAI University Press, 2009.

McGee, Robert W. (2008). Opinions on Tax Evasion in Thailand, in Robert W. McGee, editor, *Taxation and Public Finance in Transition and Developing Economies* (pp. 609–620). New York: Springer.

McGee, Robert W., Jaan Alver and Lehte Alver. (2008). The Ethics of Tax Evasion: A Survey of Estonian Opinion, in Robert W. McGee, editor, *Taxation and Public Finance in Transition and Developing Economies* (pp. 461–480). New York: Springer.

McGee, Robert W. and Yuhua An. (2008). A Survey of Chinese Business and Economics Students on the Ethics of Tax Evasion, in Robert W. McGee, editor, *Taxation and Public Finance in Transition and Developing Economies* (pp. 409–421). New York: Springer.

McGee, Robert W., Meliha Basic and Michael Tyler. (2008). The Ethics of Tax Evasion: A Comparative Study of Bosnian and Romanian Opinion, in Robert W. McGee, editor, *Taxation and Public Finance in Transition and Developing Economies* (pp. 167–183). New York: Springer.

McGee, Robert W. and Yiu Yu Butt. (2008). An Empirical Study of Tax Evasion Ethics in Hong Kong. Proceedings of the International Academy of Business and Public Administration Disciplines (IABPAD), Dallas, April 24–27: 72–83. Reprinted in the present volume.

McGee, Robert W., Simon S.M. Ho and Annie Y.S. Li. (2008). A Comparative Study on Perceived Ethics of Tax Evasion: Hong Kong vs. the United States. *Journal of Business Ethics*, 77(2), 147–158.

McGee, Robert W. and Christopher Lingle. (2008). The Ethics of Tax Evasion: A Survey of Guatemalan Opinion, in Robert W. McGee, editor, *Taxation and Public Finance in Transition and Developing Economies* (pp. 481–495). New York: Springer.

McGee, Robert W. and Silvia López Paláu. (2008). Tax Evasion and Ethics: A Comparative Study of the USA and Four Latin American Countries, in Robert W. McGee, editor, *Taxation and Public Finance in Transition and Developing Economies* (pp. 185–224). New York: Springer.

McGee, Robert W. and Tatyana B. Maranjyan. (2008). Opinions on Tax Evasion in Armenia, in Robert W. McGee, editor, *Taxation and Public Finance in Transition and Developing Economies* (pp. 277–307). New York: Springer.

McGee, Robert W. and Bouchra M'Zali. (2008). Attitudes toward Tax Evasion in Mali, in Robert W. McGee, editor, *Taxation and Public Finance in Transition and Developing Economies* (pp. 511–517). New York: Springer.

McGee, Robert W. and Carlos Noronha. (2008). The Ethics of Tax Evasion: A Comparative Study of Guangzhou (Southern China) and Macau Opinions. Euro Asia Journal of Management, 18(2), 133–152.

McGee, Robert W. and Galina G. Preobragenskaya. (2008). A Study of Tax Evasion Ethics in Kazakhstan, in Robert W. McGee, editor, *Taxation and Public Finance in Transition and Developing Economies* (pp. 497–510). New York: Springer.

McGee, Robert W. and Marcelo J. Rossi. (2008). A Survey of Argentina on the Ethics of Tax Evasion, in Robert W. McGee, editor, *Taxation and Public Finance in Transition and Developing Economies* (pp. 239–261). New York: Springer.

McGee, Robert W. and Radoslav Tusan. (2008). The Ethics of Tax Evasion: A Survey of Slovak Opinion, in Robert W. McGee, editor, *Taxation and Public Finance in Transition and Developing Economies* (pp. 575–601). New York: Springer.

McGee, Robert W. and Susana N. Vittadini Andres. (2009). The Ethics of Tax Evasion: Case Studies of Taiwan, in Robert W. McGee, *Readings in Business Ethics* (pp. 200–228). Hyderabad, India: ICFAI University Press. An abbreviated version was published in Marjorie G. Adams and Abbass Alkhafaji, editors, *Business Research Yearbook: Global Business Perspectives*, Volume XIV, No. 1 (pp. 34–39). Beltsville, MD: International Graphics: Beltsville, MD, 2007.

McGee, Robert W. and Sanjoy Bose. (2009). The Ethics of Tax Evasion: A Survey of Australian Opinion, in Robert W. McGee, *Readings in Business Ethics* (pp. 143–166). Hyderabad, India: ICFAI University Press.

McGee, Robert W. and Bouchra M'Zali. (2009). The Ethics of Tax Evasion: An Empirical Study of French EMBA Students, in Robert W. McGee, *Readings in Business Ethics* (pp. 185–199). Hyderabad, India: ICFAI University Press. An abbreviated version was published in Marjorie G. Adams and Abbass Alkhafaji, editors, *Business Research Yearbook: Global Business Perspectives*, Volume XIV, No. 1 (pp. 27–33). Beltsville, MD: International Graphics, 2007).

McGee, Robert W., Inge Nickerson and Werner Fees. (2009). When Is Tax Evasion Ethically Justifiable? A Survey of German Opinion, in Robert W. McGee, editor, *Readings in Accounting Ethics* (pp. 365–389). Hyderabad, India: ICFAI University Press.

McGee, Robert W., Silvia López Paláu and Gustavo A. Yepes Lopez. (2009). The Ethics of Tax Evasion: An Empirical Study of Colombian Opinion, in Robert W. McGee, *Readings in Business Ethics* (pp. 167–184). Hyderabad, India: ICFAI University Press.

McGee, Robert W. and Sheldon R. Smith. (2009). Ethics and Tax Evasion: A Comparative Study of Utah and Florida Opinion, in Robert W. McGee (Ed.), *Readings in Accounting Ethics* (pp. 343–364). Hyderabad, India: ICFAI University Press.

McGee, Robert W. & Geoff A. Goldman (2010). Ethics and Tax Evasion: A Survey of South African Opinion. *Proceedings of the Third Annual University of Johannesburg Faculty of Management Conference*, May 12–14.

McGee, Robert W. & Serkan Benk (2011). The Ethics of Tax Evasion: A Study of Turkish Opinion. *Journal of Balkan and Near Eastern Studies*, 13(2), 249–262.

McGee, Robert W., Serkan Benk, Halil Yıldırım and Murat Kayıkçı. (2011). The Ethics of Tax Evasion: A Study of Turkish Tax Practitioner Opinion, *European Journal of Social Sciences*, 18(3), 468–480.

Murtuza, Athar and S.M. Ghazanfar. (1998). Taxation as a Form of Worship: Exploring the Nature of Zakat. *Journal of Accounting, Ethics & Public Policy*, 1(2), 134–161, reprinted in Robert W. McGee (ed.), The Ethics of Tax Evasion (pp. 190–212). The Dumont Institute for Public Policy Research: Dumont, NJ, 1998.

Musgrave, Richard A. (1959). *The Theory of Public Finance: A Study in Public Economy*. New York: McGraw-Hill.

Musgrave, Richard A. (1986). *Public Finance in a Democratic Society. Volume II: Fiscal Doctrine, Growth and Institutions*. New York: New York University Press.

Musgrave, Richard A. & Peggy B. Musgrave. (1976). *Public Finance in Theory and Practice*, 2nd edition. New York: McGraw-Hill.

Musgrave, Richard A. & Alan T. Peacock (eds.) (1958). *Classics in the Theory of Public Finance*. London & New York: Macmillan.

Payne, James L. (1993). *Costly Returns: The Burdens of the U.S. Tax System*. San Francisco: ICS Press.

Pennock, Robert T. (1998). Death and Taxes: On the Justice of Conscientious War Tax Resistance. *Journal of Accounting, Ethics & Public Policy*, 1(1), 58–76, reprinted in Robert W. McGee (Ed.), *The Ethics of Tax Evasion* (pp. 124–142). Dumont, NJ: The Dumont Institute for Public Policy Research, 1998.

Rabushka, A. & P. Ryan. (1982). *The Tax Revolt*. Stanford, CA: Hoover Institution Press.

Sabrin, Murray (1995). *Tax Free 2000: The Rebirth of American Liberty*. Lafayette, LA: Prescott Press.

Schansberg, D. Eric. (1998). The Ethics of Tax Evasion within Biblical Christianity: Are There Limits to "Rendering Unto Caesar"? *Journal of Accounting, Ethics & Public Policy*, 1(1), 77–90, reprinted in Robert W. McGee (ed.), The Ethics of Tax Evasion (pp. 144–157). The Dumont Institute for Public Policy Research, Dumont, NJ, 1998.

Schlaes, Amity (1999). *The Greedy Hand: How Taxes Drive Americans Crazy and What To Do about It*. New York: Random House.

Shughart, W.F., Jr. (ed.) (1997). *Taxing Choice: The Predatory Politics of Fiscal Discrimination*. New Brunswick, NJ & London: Transaction Publishers.

Singappakdi, Anusorn, Scott J. Vitell & George R. Franke. (1999). Antecedents, Consequences and Mediating Effects of Perceived Moral Intensity and Personal Moral Philosophies. *Journal of the Academy of Marketing Science*, 27(1), 19–36.

Smith, Sheldon R. and Kevin C. Kimball. (1998). Tax Evasion and Ethics: A Perspective from Members of The Church of Jesus Christ of Latter-Day Saints. *Journal of Accounting, Ethics & Public Policy*, 1(3), 337–348, reprinted in Robert W. McGee (Ed.), *The Ethics of Tax Evasion* (pp. 220–229). Dumont, NJ: The Dumont Institute for Public Policy Research, 1998.

Tamari, Meir. (1998). Ethical Issues in Tax Evasion: A Jewish Perspective. *Journal of Accounting, Ethics & Public Policy*, 1(2), 121–132, reprinted in Robert W. McGee (Ed.), *The Ethics of Tax Evasion* (pp. 168–178). Dumont, NJ: The Dumont Institute for Public Policy Research, 1998.

Tang, S. and J. Zuo (1997). Profile of College Examination Cheaters. *College Student Journal* 31(3): 340–347, as cited in Bob S. Brown and Peggy Choong. (2005). An Investigation of Academic Dishonesty among Business Students at Public and Private United States Universities. *International Journal of Management*, 22(2), 201–214.

Webber, C. & A. Wildavsky. (1986). *A History of Taxation and Expenditure in the Western World.* New York: Simon & Schuster.

Weeks, William A., Carlos W. Moore, Joseph A. McKinney & Justin G. Longenecker. (1999). The Effects of Gender and Career Stage on Ethical Judgment. *Journal of Business Ethics*, 20(4), 301–313.

Yusuf, S.M. (1971). *Economic Justice in Islam.* Lahore: Sh. Muhammad Ashraf.

Part V
Country Studies

Chapter 16
Attitudes Toward Paying Taxes in the USA: An Empirical Analysis

Benno Torgler

Introduction

One of the key puzzles in the tax compliance literature is to understand why so many people pay their taxes, although there is a low probability of being detected. Expected utility models emphasizing the role of deterrence factors failed to convincingly solve this puzzle. Most tax compliance experiments report a higher level of income declaration than an expected utility maximization calculus would predict (see Alm, 1999; Torgler, 2002). Furthermore, in many countries the level of deterrence is too low to explain the high degree of tax compliance. It can be argued that risk aversion may help explain the high level of compliance. However, studies in Switzerland and the USA indicate that there is a big gap between the degree of risk aversion that would grant such a compliance and the degree effectively reported (see Graetz and Wilde, 1985; Alm, McClelland, and Schulze, 1992; and Frey and Feld, 2002).

Including findings of other sciences, such as psychology or sociology without losing the spirit of the economic foundation seems to be a promising step toward solving this puzzle. A few studies have tried to extend the traditional models incorporating psychological costs or social norms (Gordon, 1989; Bordignon, 1993; Erard and Feinstein, 1994, or Schnellenbach, 2002). In a broader sense these studies try to investigate attitudes toward paying taxes, which can be seen as a proxy for *tax morale*: the intrinsic motivation to comply and pay taxes and thus voluntarily contribute to the public good. However, most of the attempts failed to consider how tax morale may arise or which factors have an impact on it. Thus, tax morale is used as a residuum to capture unknown influences on tax evasion (see Frey and Feld, 2002). Another promising line is to consider empirically citizens' attitudes toward paying

B. Torgler (✉)
School of Economics and Finance, Queensland University of Technology, GPO Box 2434,
Brisbane, QLD 4001, Australia
e-mail: benno.torgler@qut.edu.au

R.W. McGee (ed.), *The Ethics of Tax Evasion: Perspectives in Theory and Practice*,
DOI 10.1007/978-1-4614-1287-8_16, © Springer Science+Business Media, LLC 2012

taxes as a proxy for tax morale and search for factors that shape it. Relatively new surveys, such as the *World Values Surveys* or *International Social Survey* allow to find a proxy for and thus to check the impact on tax morale. This attempt is in line with the growing inclination among economists to use surveys (see, e.g., Knack and Keefer, 1997, for social capital studies, or Frey and Stutzer, 2002, who intensively investigated happiness).

One reason might be that survey research now uses more sophisticated statistical techniques and designs compared to early years. Furthermore, a main advantage is that surveys include many socio-economic, demographic, and attitudinal variables. The literature on tax morale has strongly increased in the last few years (for an overview, see Torgler, 2007), but still more evidence is required. Reviewing the whole literature, Andreoni, Erard and Feinstein (1998) stress that empirical literature on tax compliance "is still in its youth, with many of the most important behavioral hypotheses and policy questions yet to be adequately investigated" (p. 835–836).

Little is known about general tendencies of tax morale in the USA, a gap this chapter intends to fill. Some information is available about the deterrence mechanism. However, this is the first study that makes an explicit empirical analysis of the tax morale for the case of the USA. It contains a number of interesting empirical results and hence makes a small contribution to our understanding of why so many people honestly pay their taxes. Furthermore, the USA is an interesting country to investigate as there is a high degree of tax morale over time (see next section). The study analyzes a cross-section of individuals throughout the USA using the World Values Survey (WVS) data of 1982, 1990, and 1995. Working with three datasets collected at three different points in time allows us to observe trends over time and it also allows us to assess the robustness of some main independent variables. Moreover, not many studies have investigated tax morale over such a long period. The findings from these data suggest that tax morale has increased over time. Furthermore, it will be shown among other results that a higher trust in the state, a stronger identification with the country and religiosity have a positive impact on tax morale.

Before considering the findings in detail, however, the next section of the paper first introduces the way tax morale is defined, thus providing information about the World Values Surveys, and presents the level of tax morale in OECD countries. Section III then introduces the models and presents our main hypotheses. In Section IV, we present the empirical findings, and Section V finishes with some concluding remarks.

Data

The data used in the present study are taken from the first three waves of the WVS. The WVS is a worldwide investigation of socio-cultural and political change, based on representative national samples. Data from these surveys are made publicly available for use by researchers interested in how views change with time.

However, economists have just started to work with the WVS. To assess the level of tax morale in the WVS, we use the following question throughout the whole paper:

> Please tell me for each of the following statements whether you think it can always be justified, never be justified, or something in between: ... Cheating on tax if you have the chance.

The question leads to a ten-scale index of tax morale with the two extreme points "never justified" and "always justified." In our case, the natural cut-off point is at the value 1, as a high amount of respondents assert that the cheating on tax is "never justifiable." Thus, our tax morale variable takes the value 1 if the respondent says that cheating on tax is "never justified," and zero otherwise.

The used datasets have the advantage that they are designed as wide-ranging surveys, which reduces the probability of participants being suspicious and of creating framing effects by other tax context questions. Certainly, it can be discussed whether it is more adequate to use an index instead of a single question to measure tax morale. However, a single question has the advantage that problems associated with the construction of an index can be avoided. Furthermore, an index might be constructed so that it best fits the theoretical argumentations.

As we analyze one specific country, problems based on differences in the interpretation of the question or a variation in the political institution which may influence the justifiability of evading taxes do not occur.[1] Working with more than one survey and thus considering different time periods allows for some determinants to reduce biases due to a "time specific mood." Certainly, there is still the problem that some individuals may excuse their noncooperative behavior in the past by declaring relatively high tax morale values.

First, we provide a comparison of the USA's tax morale levels to those of other OECD countries. This allows checking whether tax morale in the USA was substantially lower or higher in 1982 or 1990 and 1995 than in any other OECD country. We will only present a basic descriptive analysis showing the mean level of tax morale (% of people stating that tax evasion is never justifiable) in relation to the other countries. First of all, it can be seen that in 1981/1982 the average number of people among all tested OECD countries saying that tax evasion was never justified was 56%. This increased to 60% in the countries tested in 1995. While there have been some countries in the OECD that have had decreases in tax morale over time (e.g., Sweden, Germany), in general, it appears that tax morale among the OECD countries has increased slightly over time. When comparing the US figures to those of the rest of the OECD, it can be seen in Table 16.1 that the USA's level of tax morale was always quite high (above the OECD average).[2] Moreover, we observe a relatively strong increase between 1990 and 1995. In general, such high values observed for

---

[1] The justification of contributing may change if the tax revenues are collected under a dictatorship and the revenue is, e.g., used to finance war (McGee 1994).

[2] The high level of tax morale in the USA is also supported by Alm and Torgler (2006) who used the 1990 data in a multivariate analysis.

Table 16.1 Tax morale by country

Country	Year	Percentage of respondents stating tax evasion is never justified	Year	Percentage of respondents stating tax evasion is never justified	Year	Percentage of respondents stating tax evasion is never justified
Austria			1990	62.3	1995	62.1
Australia	1981	47.7				
Belgium	1981	43.3	1990	33.9		
Canada	1981	66.9	1990	59.2		
Denmark	1981	58.5	1990	57.3		
Finland	1981	58.7	1990	40.3	1996	57.4
France	1981	48.9	1990	46.5		
Germany[a]	1981	52.7	1990	53.8	1997	46.9
Great Britain	1981	58.2	1990	53.9		
Iceland	1981	56.9	1990	56		
Ireland	1981	38.5	1990	48.8		
Italy	1981	52.8	1990	69.7		
Northern Ireland	1981	74.7	1990	55.2		
Japan	1981	81.8	1990	81.9	1995	80.6
Netherlands	1981	37.9	1990	42.9		
Norway	1982	40.3	1990	43.1	1996	47.5
Portugal			1990	39.9		
Spain	1981	49.9	1990	58.4	1995	69.5
Sweden	1982	68.8	1990	56.4	1996	49.3
Switzerland			1988–1989	63.8	1996	53.5
USA	1982	67.0	1990	66.7	1995	73.6
Average		55.8		54.5		60.0

Source: authors' calculations from the WVS

[a]The 1981 value of Germany considers only West Germany

the USA make it interesting to take a closer look at tax morale and thus to search for factors that shape tax morale in the USA. Thus, we do not see a decrease of tax morale in the 1980s and the 1990s. These findings are in line with the argument of Buchanan (1999), who states that the "temperature of taxpayers" in the 1980s and the 1990s is quite low after the years of taxpayers' revolts in the late 1970s.

Models and Hypotheses

Models

If tax morale is supposed to be an explanation why tax compliance rates are so high, it might be interesting to analyze what *shapes* tax morale. The descriptive analysis only gave information about the *raw effects* and not the *partial effects*. Thus, in this section we introduce the model and develop the hypotheses to analyze in the next section in a multivariate analysis.[3] We use the following main specification to check the determinants of tax morale in USA:

$$
\begin{aligned}
\mathrm{TM}_i = {} & \beta_0 + \beta_1 \cdot \mathrm{AGE}_i + \beta_2 \cdot \mathrm{GENDER}_i + \beta_3 \cdot \mathrm{EDU}_i + \beta_4 \cdot \mathrm{MARITAL}_i + \\
& \beta_5 \cdot \mathrm{ECOSIT}_i + \beta_6 \cdot \mathrm{EMPLOY}_i + \beta_7 \cdot \mathrm{TRUST}_i + \beta_8 \cdot \mathrm{PRIDE}_i + \qquad (16.1) \\
& \beta_9 \cdot \mathrm{REL}_i + \beta_{10} \cdot \mathrm{YEAR}_t + \varepsilon_i
\end{aligned}
$$

where TM_i denotes the individual degree of tax morale. The independent variables are specified as follows:

Demographic Factors

Contrary to economics, social psychology has put more weight on analyzing theoretically and empirically the effect of demographic factors on honesty or compliance (see Tittle 1980):

- AGE_i (continuous variable, predicted sign: +): Older people may have acquired more social capital (see Tittle, 1980). They are often strongly attached to the community (see Pommerehne and Weck-Hannemann, 1996). Thus, they have a stronger dependency on others' reactions, which may act as a restriction imposing higher potential (social) costs of sanctions. Criminology findings also indicate that age is negatively correlated with rule breaking (see Gottfredson and

---

[3] For an overview of variables see *Table A1* in the Appendix.

Hirschi, 1990; Hirschi and Gottfredson, 2000; Torgler and Valev, 2006). Thus, we would predict that there is a positive correlation between age and tax morale.

- GENDER$_i$ (Dummy: WOMAN, MAN in the reference group, predicted sign: +): Although there is still a lack of empirical and experimental evidence, there is the tendency that women are more honest and also more compliant than men (e.g., Tittle, 1980). Evidence from the tax compliance literature shows the tendency that men are less compliant than women (for survey studies see, e.g., Aitken and Bonneville, 1980; Tittle, 1980; for experiments, Spicer and Becker, 1980; Spicer and Hero, 1985; Baldry, 1987). The criminology literature and some papers on corruption have shown that females are on average more compliant than males (see Tittle, 1980; Junger, 1994; Gottfredson and Hirschi, 1990; Dollar et al., 2001; Swamy et al., 2001; Mocan, 2004; Torgler and Valev, 2006b).

- EDU$_i$ (education, continuous variable, predicted sign: +/−): More educated individuals are more likely to know more about tax law and fiscal connections and thus are better aware of the benefits and services the state provides than uneducated taxpayers, but they may also be more critical about how the state acts and especially spends the tax revenues. Furthermore, they better understand opportunities for evasion and avoidance, which negatively influences tax morale. Thus, a clear prediction is difficult to make.

- MARITAL$_i$ (marital status, dummy variables: married, divorced, separate, widowed, single/living together/never married=reference group): Marital status might influence legal or illegal behavior depending on the extent to which individuals are constrained by their social networks (see Tittle, 1980). Such a constraint might have an impact on tax morale. Thus, we would predict that individuals with stronger social networks (e.g., married people) would have a higher tax morale than singles (predicted sign: +).

- ECOSIT$_i$ (economic situation, predicted sign): As a proxy for the economic situation, we have integrated a variable where people had to classify themselves in different economic classes (lower class/working class, lower middle class, upper middle class upper class). The effects of income on tax morale are difficult to assess theoretically. Depending on risk preferences and the progression of the income tax schedules, income may increase or reduce tax morale. In countries with a progressive income tax rate, taxpayers with a higher income realize a higher dollar return by evading, but with possibly less economic utility. On the other hand, lower income taxpayers might have lower social "stakes" or restrictions but are less in the position to take these risks, because of a high marginal utility loss (wealth reduction) if they are caught and penalized (Jackson and Milliron, 1986) (predicted sign: +/−, but with a stronger tendency to be negative).

- EMPLOYMENT STATUS (EMPLOY$_i$, dummy variables: part-time employed, self-employed, unemployed, at home, student, retired, other, full-time employed in the reference group): In the tax compliance literature, there is the strong argument that self-employed persons have higher compliance costs than employees (see, e.g., Lewis 1982). Taxes are more visible for self-employed people and a higher opportunity to evade or avoid taxes leads to the prediction that self-employed people have a lower tax morale than employees (full-time employees are in the reference group) (predicted sign: -).

- YEAR$_t$: Year dummy variable, $t = 1982$, 1990, and 1995. The year 1981 is in the reference group. The descriptive evaluation presented in Table 16.1 indicated that we observe an increase of tax morale between 1990 and 1995. (predicted sign: +).

SOCIETAL VARIABLES. Societal variables can be seen as (1) an indicator of the extent to which citizens can identify themselves with the state, the national institutions or the country itself. It measures the degree of individuals' trust in institutions (TRUST$_i$), such as TRUST IN THE LEGAL SYSTEM and thus is closely linked to the way taxpayers feel they are treated by the system. As a proxy for national identification we use NATIONAL PRIDE (PRIDE$_i$); (2) norms enforced by nongovernmental institutions, such as the church that promotes compliance and punishes misbehavior (REL$_i$: RELIGIOSITY, proxy: CHURCH ATTENDANCE). As one of the main contributions in this study is to investigate the correlation between societal variables and tax morale, several testable hypotheses are developed in the next subsection.

Hypotheses

Trust in the Parliament and the Legal System

We are going to use two variables that will help to investigate the impact of trust in state on tax morale. First, we are going to analyze trust in the parliament. This variable is connected to the current politico-economic level. Next, we investigate the effect of trust in the legal system. This variable allows us to analyze trust at the constitutional level (e.g., trust in the legal system), thereby focusing on how the relationship between the state and its citizens is established. If the state is seen to be acting in a trustworthy way, taxpayers' trust and also their willingness to comply with their tax obligations increase. Thus, the relationship between them and the state (relational contract) can be maintained by positive actions, well functioning institutions, implementing a positive social capital atmosphere. Such a strategy will be honored with a higher tax morale. Scholz and Lubell (1998), e.g., found that if taxpayers trusted government or other citizens, they were more likely to comply with their tax obligations than taxpayers who did not trust. Thus, trust influences citizens' incentives to commit themselves to obedience. Therefore, the following hypothesis can be developed:

Hypothesis 1: The more the citizens trust the legal system or the parliament, the higher their intrinsic motivation to pay taxes.

National Pride

Identification with the state may induce cooperation among taxpayers and thus induces similar mechanisms as the trust variables. Tyler (2000) argues that pride influences people's behavior in groups, organizations, and societies. It gives a basis for encouraging cooperative behavior. However, contrary to the trust variables, which have been thoroughly analyzed by *social capital* researchers, the variable pride has been completely neglected although it is a widespread phenomenon. The following hypothesis can be developed:

> *Hypothesis 2*: Pride might be a basis for encouraging cooperative behavior through national identification, which leads to a higher tax morale.

Religiosity

There are different measurements of religiosity. On the one hand, we have variables that can be observed, such as the frequency of church attendance. On the other hand, there are beliefs that are not observable, such as being religious. Analyzing all these different factors helps get a picture of how religiosity affects tax morale. The frequency of CHURCH ATTENDANCE indicate that people spend time devoted to religion. It has the advantage to measure the approximation of how much time individuals devote to religion, instead of asking directly the degree of religiosity. The church as an institution induces behavioral norms and moral constraints among their community. Religious organizations provide moral constitutions for a society. Religion provides a certain level of enforcement to act in the lines of accepted rules and acts as a "supernatural police" (Anderson and Tollison, 1992). Previous studies have shown that religiosity affects tax morale (see Torgler, 2006). In general, religiosity seems to affect the degree of rule breaking. Religiosity can thus be a restriction on engaging in tax evasion. Some papers in the criminology literature found a negative correlation between religious membership and crime (see, e.g., Hull, 2000; Hull and Bold, 1989; Lipford, McCormick, and Tollison, 1993). As a second variable, we include individuals' perceived RELIGIOSITY, a factor that is to a certain extent independent of any institution. Based on this assertion, the following hypothesis can be developed:

> *Hypothesis 3*: The US citizens with a higher church attendance or a higher level of religiosity are more likely to have higher levels of tax morale.

Empirical Results

As already pointed out, in our multiple regression analysis we use attitudes toward paying taxes defined as tax morale as the dependent variable. Regressions help isolate the effects of different factors from each other and thus to get the correlation of a single factor with tax morale when all other factors are constant. In the estimations, we also use a weighting variable on all observations to adjust the data to reflect the national population. In order to control for differences in the number of participants between the different time periods, the observations are also weighted to get an equal number of observations for each wave.[4]

The natural cut-off point at the value 1, showing that many respondents point out that cheating on tax is "never justifiable," allows to work with probit models. To obtain the quantitative impacts of the explanatory variables, we calculate the marginal effects of each variable.

Table 16.2 presents the results. We include the variable education sequentially in the regression due to the relatively high number of missing values. Moreover, to investigate the robustness of the impact of trust in the state on tax morale, we present estimations differentiating between TRUST IN THE PARLIAMENT and TRUST IN THE LEGAL SYSTEM. The presented pooled estimations have the big advantage that they allow not only to investigate the development of tax morale over time, but also provide us a better insight regarding the effects of the independent variables, which now show general tendencies rather than time-specific influences (Table 16.3).

In general, the results are in line with our developed predictions in the theoretical part and consistent with previously obtained results in the tax morale literature (see Torgler, 2007). In general, we find in all estimations support to the hypothesis that societal variables have a strong impact on tax morale.

The variables RELIGIOSITY and PRIDE have an especially strong effect on tax morale. An increase in the scale of the religiosity scale by one unit increases the share of individuals stating that tax evasion is never justifiable by more than 7% points, which is very high. The variable PRIDE is robust throughout all estimations with marginal effects of more than 9% points.

This means that an increase in the pride scale by one unit increases the probability of stating that tax evasion is never justifiably between 4.9 and 6% points. Also CHURCH ATTENDANCE is positive correlated with tax morale with marginal effects of around 2% points. Moreover, a higher level of trust in the state is correlated with a higher level of tax morale. This effect is especially strong for the variable TRUST IN THE PARLIAMENT. In sum, our hypotheses cannot be rejected, which indicates a strong impact of societal variables.

---

[4] This was done by taking the original weighting variable and multiplying it by a constant for each survey. If the data were not weighted, the resulting pooled estimates could be biased. The weighting variable is provided by the WVS.

Table 16.2 Determinants of tax morale

ESTIMATIONS WEIGHTED PROBIT	(17.1)			(17.2)			(17.3)		
INDEPENDENT V.	Coeff.	z-Stat.	Marg. Effect	Coeff.	z-Stat.	Marg. Effect	Coeff.	z-Stat.	Marg. Effect
Demographic factors									
AGE 30–49	0.142**	2.29	0.049	0.153**	2.34	0.053	0.155**	2.41	0.054
AGE 50–64	0.304***	4.04	0.099	0.344***	4.40	0.113	0.326***	4.21	0.107
AGE 65+	0.495***	5.07	0.155	0.520***	4.95	0.164	0.542***	5.21	0.169
WOMAN	0.101**	2.09	0.035	0.077	1.50	0.027	0.070	1.39	0.024
EDUCATION				−0.009	−1.02	−0.003	−0.012	−1.49	−0.004
Marital status									
MARRIED	0.156**	2.46	0.054	0.147**	2.19	0.052	0.151**	2.28	0.053
DIVORCED	−0.005	−0.05	−0.002	−0.058	−0.57	−0.021	−0.063	−0.63	−0.022
SEPARATED	−0.001	0.00	0.000	−0.044	−0.28	−0.016	0.025	0.16	0.009
WIDOWED	0.232**	2.17	0.076	0.198*	1.74	0.066	0.194*	1.72	0.065
Economic situation									
UPPER CLASS	−0.340***	−5.13	−0.124	−0.360***	−5.19	−0.132	−0.335***	−4.87	−0.122
UPPER MIDDLE CLASS	−0.143**	−2.16	−0.050	−0.151**	−2.04	−0.054	−0.129*	−1.77	−0.046
LOWER MIDDLE CLASS	−0.204***	−3.22	−0.072	−0.241***	−3.47	−0.086	−0.229***	−3.34	−0.082
Employment status									
PART-TIME EMPLOYED	−0.017	−0.23	−0.006	0.042	0.51	0.015	0.055	0.67	0.019
SELF-EMPLOYED	0.093	0.67	0.031	0.156	0.99	0.053	0.106	0.69	0.036
UNEMPLOYED	−0.043	−0.41	−0.015	0.011	0.10	0.004	0.043	0.40	0.015
AT HOME	0.123	1.54	0.041	0.168	1.98	0.057	0.160*	1.92	0.054
STUDENT	0.051	0.35	0.017	0.171	1.21	0.057	0.217	1.58	0.071
RETIRED	0.013	0.15	0.004	0.033	0.36	0.011	0.042	0.46	0.014
OTHER	−0.304	−1.03	−0.112	−0.594*	−1.89	−0.228	−0.575*	−1.85	−0.220

Religiosity									
RELIGIOSITY	0.216***	3.80	0.075	0.216***	3.58	0.076	0.225***	3.79	0.078
CHURCH ATTENDANCE	0.056***	4.93	0.019	0.055***	4.49	0.019	0.058***	4.81	0.020
Trust and pride									
TRUST IN THE PARLIAMENT	0.086***	2.99	0.030	0.104***	3.42	0.036			
TRUST IN THE LEG. SYSTEM							0.049*	1.71	0.017
PRIDE	0.173***	4.05	0.060	0.139***	3.12	0.049	0.159***	3.64	0.056
Time									
US 1990	0.023	0.41	0.008	0.015	0.24	0.005	-0.003	-0.04	-0.001
US 1995	0.203***	3.33	0.069	0.229***	3.00	0.077	0.214***	2.86	0.072
Number of observations	4781			4156			4288		
Pseudo R2	0.072			0.074			0.071		
Log pseudo-likelihood	-2751.189			-2411.443			-2483.903		
Prob > chi2	0.000			0.000			0.000		

Notes: Dependent variable: tax morale. In the reference group are in all three equations: AGE < 30, MAN, SINGLE/LIVING TOGETHER/NEVER MARRIED, FULL–TIME EMPLOYED, LOWEST CLASS, US 1982. Significance levels: * $0.05 < p < 0.10$, ** $0.01 < p < 0.05$, *** $p < 0.01$

Table 16.3 Derivation of variables

Variable	Derivation
TAX MORALE	Please tell me for each of the following statements whether you think it can always be justified, never be justified, or something in between: ... Cheating on tax if you have the chance
	Never justified = 1, else = 0
NATIONAL PRIDE	How proud are you to be an American? (4 = Very proud, 1 = Not at all proud)
TRUST IN THE PARLIAMENT	Could you tell me how much confidence you have in the parliament: is it a great deal of confidence, quite a lot of confidence, not very much confidence or none at all? (4 = a great deal to 1 = none at all)
TRUST IN THE LEGAL SYSTEM	Could you tell me how much confidence you have in the legal system: is it a great deal of confidence, quite a lot of confidence, not very much confidence or none at all? (4 = a great deal to 1 = none at all)
ECONOMIC SITUATION (CLASSES)	People sometimes describe themselves as belonging to the working class, the middle class, or the upper or lower class. Would you describe yourself as belonging to the:
	WVS 1990 (working class and lower class in the reference group are defined as: LOWEST CLASS)
	1. Upper class
	2. Upper middle class
	3. Lower middle class
	4. Working class
	5. Lower class
EDUCATION	At what age did you or will you complete your full-timeeducation, either at school or at an institution of higher education? Pleaseexclude apprenticeships
CHURCH ATTENDANCE	Apart from weddings, funerals, and christenings, about how often do you attend religious services these days? More than once a week, once a week, once a month, only on special holy days, once a year, less often, never, practically never
	More than once a week (coding 7)
	Once a week (6)
	Once a month (5)
	Only on special holy days (4)
	Once a year (3)
	Less often (2)
	Never, practically never (1)
RELIGIOSITY	Independently of whether you go to church or not, would you say you are:
	1. A convinced atheist
	2. Not a religious person
	3. A religious person.
MARITAL STATUS	1. Married
	2. Divorced
	3. Separated
	4. Widowed
	5. single/living together (reference group)

Source: Inglehart et al. (2000)

Looking at the control variables, we find that an increase in the level of age has a positive effect on tax morale. We find that the marginal effects increase from a lower age group to a higher one. Women report a higher morale than men, but the coefficient is only statistically significant in the first estimation. A higher education leads to a lower tax morale, but without being statistically significant. Married people seemed to have a higher tax morale than singles. Being married rather than single increases the probability of stating that tax evasion is never justifiable by more 5% points. The economic situation reports the lowest economic class has the highest tax morale. We observe to a certain extent a nonlinear negative relationship, showing the lowest tax morale values for the group UPPER CLASS, followed by the LOWER MIDDLE CLASS and the UPPER MIDDLE CLASS. Our findings also report that differences in the employment status hardly affect tax morale.

The descriptive analysis in Table 16.1 showed that tax morale has increased over time. Table 16.2 allows to check whether the increase is statistically significant, controlling in a multivariate analysis for additional factors as we pool the data using time dummy variables. We observe that inhabitants of the USA had a higher probability of reporting the highest tax morale in 1995 than in 1982. The coefficient is highly statistically significant, with high marginal effects between 6.9 and 7.8% points.

On the other hand, the small differences between 1981 and 1990 are not statistically significant. Thus, a strong improvement of tax morale between 1990 and 1995 is observable. In making this claim, it should be noted though that the present study certainly has its limitations. The data contained within the WVS is somewhat general in focus and as a result, attitudes and issues specifically related to taxation do not figure highly.

For example, it was not possible to control for expectations regarding the consequences of being detected as a cheater or the individuals' tax burden. However, it should be noted that this study has provided a newly detailed statistical analysis of tax morale as a dependent variable in the USA, analyzing how it differs from other countries in Europe, and how it has changed between 1982 and 1995. As a result, it offers the reader important insight into Americans' attitudes toward paying taxes.

Conclusions

Using data from the WVS, the aim of the present study was to investigate tax morale among the US citizens between 1982 and 1995. Thus, this paper contributes to the tax compliance literature, which still lacks empirical evidence (especially in the area of tax morale). In the last few years, economists have been showing an increasing interest in working with survey data. New survey data sources offer a good opportunity to closely investigate variables that have been neglected or strongly disregarded in the past.

The aspect of tax morale gains importance because the act of paying taxes cannot be fully explained by a standard economic expected utility approach. People pay their taxes, although there is a low probability of getting caught and being penalized. Thus, it makes sense to work with the concept of Homo Oeconomicus that is endowed with a more refined motivation structure and goes beyond a self-interested materialistic pay-off maximizer.

In this study, we found evidence that societal variables, such as trust in the state, national pride, or religiosity, have an impact on tax morale. There is a mix of internal and external norms that affects individuals' compliance attitudes. Finally, we also find an increase of tax morale over time (especially between 1990 and 1995), controlling in a multivariate analysis for additional factors. In general, the US taxpayers have a high tax morale, compared to other OECD countries. All in all, the study provides new detailed insights into the US citizens' attitudes toward paying taxes and thus contributes to understanding why so many people are willing to pay their taxes.

References

Aitken, Sherie S., and Laura Bonneville (1980) *A General Taxpayer Opinion Survey*. Washington, DC: Internal Revenue Service.

Alm, James (1999) 'Tax Compliance and Administration', in Hildreth, W. Bartley, and James A. Richardson, eds., *Handbook on Taxation*. New York: Marcel Dekker: 741–768.

Alm, James and Benno Torgler (2006) 'Culture Differences and Tax Morale in the United States and Europe', *Journal of Economic Psychology*, 27, 224–246.

Alm, James, Gary H. McClelland, and William D. Schulze (1992) 'Why Do People Pay Taxes?', *Journal of Public Economics*, 48, 21–48.

Anderson, Gary M. and Robert D. Tollison (1992) 'Morality and Monopoly: The Constitutional Political Economy of Religious Rules', *CATO Journal*, 13, 373–391.

Andreoni, James, Brian Erard, and Jonathan S. Feinstein (1998) 'Tax Compliance', *Journal of Economic Literature*, 36, 818–860.

Baldry, Jonathan C. (1987) 'Income Tax Evasion and the Tax Schedule: Some Experimental Results', *Public Finance*, 42, 357–383.

Bordignon, Massimo (1993) 'A Fairness Approach to Income Tax Evasion', *Journal of Public Economic*, 52, 345–362.

Buchanan, James M. (1999) 'Taxpayer Apathy, Institutional Inertia, and Economic Growth', *Journal of Public Finance and Public Choice*, 17, 3–10.

Dollar, David, Raymond Fisman, and Roberta Gatti (2001) 'Are Women Really the "Fairer" Sex? Corruption and Women in Government', *Journal of Economic Behavior and Organization*, 46, 423–429.

Erard, Brian, and Jonathan S. Feinstein (1994) 'The Role of Moral Sentiments and Audit Perceptions in Tax Compliance', *Public Finance*, 49, 70–89.

Frey, Bruno S., and Lars P. Feld (2002) 'Deterrence and Morale in Taxation: An Empirical Analysis', CESifo Working Paper No. 760, August 2002.

Frey, Bruno S., and Alois Stutzer (2002) *Happiness and Economics. How the Economy and Institutions Affect Well-Being*. Princeton: Princeton University Press.

Gordon, James P. F. (1989) 'Individual Morality and Reputation Costs as Deterrents to Tax Evasion', *European Economic Review*, 33, 797–805.

Gottfredson, Michael R., and Travis Hirschi (1990) *A General Theory of Crime*. Stanford: Stanford University Press.

Graetz, Michael J., and Louis L. Wilde (1985) The Economics of Tax Compliance: Facts and Fantasy, *National Tax Journal*, 38, 355–363.

Hirschi, Travis and Michael R. Gottfredson (2000) Age and the Explanation of Crime, in Crutchfield, Robert D., George S. Bridges, Joseph G. Weis, and Charis Kubrin, eds., *Crime Readings*. Thousand Oaks: Pine Forge Press: 138–142.

Hull, Brooks B. (2000) 'Religion Still Matters', *Journal of Economics*, 26, 35–48.

Hull, Brooks B., and Frederick Bold (1989) 'Towards and Economic Theory of the Church', *International Journal of Social Economics*, 16, 5–15.

Inglehart, Ronald et al. (2000) *Codebook for World Values Survey*. Ann Arbor: Institute for Social Research.

Jackson, Betty R., and Valerie C. Milliron (1986) 'Tax Compliance Research: Findings, Problems, and Prospects', *Journal of Accounting Literature*, 5, 125–166.

Knack, Stephen, and Philip Keefer (1997) 'Does Social Capital Have an Economic Payoff: A Cross-Country Investigation', *Quarterly Journal of Economics, 112,* 1251–1288.

Junger, Marianne (1994) 'Accidents', in Hirschi, Travis and Michael R. Gottfredson, eds., *The Generality of Deviance*. New Brunswick: Transaction Publishers: 81–112.

Lewis, Alan (1982) *The Psychology of Taxation*. Oxford: Martin Robertson.

Lipford, Jody, Robert E. McCormick, and Robert D. Tollison (1993) Preaching Matters, *Journal of Economic Behavior and Organization*, 21, 235–250.

McGee, Robert W. (1994). Is Tax Evasion Unethical? *University of Kansas Law Review*, 42(2), 411–35.

Mocan, Naci (2004). What Determines Corruption? International Evidence from Micro Data, NBER Working Paper Series, Nr. 10460, Cambridge, MA, April.

Pommerehne, Werner W., and Hannelore Weck-Hannemann (1996) Tax Rates, Tax Administration and Income Tax Evasion in Switzerland, *Public Choice*, 88, 161–170.

Do we Know?', CREMA Working Paper No. 2004 –03, Basel.

Schnellenbach, Jan (2002) Tax Morale, Leviathan and the Political Process: A Theoretical Approach, Paper presented at the Annual European Public Choice Society Conference in Belgirate, April 4–7.

Scholz, John T., and Mark Lubell (1998) 'Adaptive Political Attitudes: Duty, Trust and Fear as Monitors of Tax Policy', *American Journal of Political Science*, 42, 398–417.

Spicer, Michael W., and Lee A. Becker, 1980, 'Fiscal Inequity and Tax Evasion: An Experimental Approach', *National Tax Journal*, 33, 171–175.

Spicer, Michael W., and Rodney E. Hero, (1985) 'Tax Evasion and Heuristics. A Research Note', *Journal of Public Economics*, 26, 263–267.

Swamy, Anand, Stephen Knack, Young Lee and Omar Azfar (2001) 'Gender and Corruption', *Journal of Development Economics*, 64, 25–55.

Tittle, Charles (1980) *Sanctions and Social Deviance: The Question of Deterrence*. New York: Praeger.

Torgler, Benno (2002) 'Speaking to Theorists and Searching for Facts: Tax Morale and Tax Compliance in Experiments', *Journal of Economic Surveys*, 16, 657–684.

Torgler, Benno (2006) 'The Importance of Faith: Tax Morale and Religiosity', forthcoming in: *Journal of Economic Behavior and Organization*.

Torgler, B. (2007). Tax Compliance and Tax Morale: A Theoretical and Empirical Analysis, forthcoming: Edward Elgar.

Torgler, Benno and Neven T. Valev (2006) 'Corruption and Age', forthcoming in: *Journal of Bioeconomics*.

Tyler, Tom R. (2000) 'Why Do People Cooperate in Groups?', in Van Vught, Mark, Mark Snyder, Tom R. Tyler and Anders Biel, eds., *Cooperation in Modern Society*. Promoting the Welfare of Communities, States and Organizations. London, Routledge: 65–82.

Chapter 17
Tax Evasion Opinion in Estonia

Robert W. McGee, Jaan Alver, and Lehte Alver

Introduction

Most studies of tax evasion take an economic or public finance perspective. Not much has been written from a philosophical or ethical viewpoint. That is probably because most economists are utilitarians and most lawyers are legalists. However, there is a small body of literature that addresses tax evasion issues from a philosophical or theological perspective. The present study is intended to add to that small body of literature while forming a bridge to the public finance literature as well.

The authors developed a survey instrument that included 18 statements incorporating the three major views on the ethics of tax evasion that have emerged in the literature over the last 500 years. The survey was distributed to a group of accounting and business students in Estonia. This paper reports on the results of that survey.

Methodology

After reviewing the literature that exists on the ethics of tax evasion, a survey was constructed and distributed to a group of graduate and undergraduate accounting and business students and accounting professionals in order to learn their views on the ethics of tax evasion. This group was selected because they will be the future business and political leaders of Estonia. Due to space constraints, the literature is not reviewed here. However, the relevant literature is listed in the reference section.

R.W. McGee (✉)
School of Business, Florida International University, 3000 NE 151 Street,
North Miami, FL 33181, USA
e-mail: bob414@hotmail.com

J. Alver • L. Alver
Institute of Accounting, Tallinn University of Technology,
Akadeemia tee 3, Tallinn 12618, Estonia

R.W. McGee (ed.), *The Ethics of Tax Evasion: Perspectives in Theory and Practice*,
DOI 10.1007/978-1-4614-1287-8_17, © Springer Science+Business Media, LLC 2012

The survey consisted of 18 statements. Using a seven-point Likert scale, respondents were asked to place the appropriate number in the space provided to indicate the extent of their agreement or disagreement with each statement. The statements in the survey reflected the three main viewpoints on the ethics of tax evasion that have emerged over the centuries. Five hundred and thirty-nine usable responses were received.

Survey Findings

The next few sections report on the study's findings.

Demographics

Table 17.1 lists the demographics of the survey. Nearly three-quarters of the sample consisted of women. Almost half were undergraduate students, with the remainder consisting of graduate students and accounting professionals. About 60% were business and economics students. Nearly 30% were accounting students. More than half were under age 25, but a sufficient number of respondents were over 24 to conduct a statistical comparison based on age.

The 18 Statements

Table 17.2 lists the 18 statements that were used in the survey instrument and shows the mean scores. The first 15 statements reflect the main arguments that have been used in the literature over the past 500 years to justify tax evasion (Crowe, 1944). The last three statements were added so that more recent human rights issues could be included in the survey. The overall mean score was 5.25 which, on a scale from 1 to 7, indicates that there is some support for tax evasion, but also that there is more support for the position that tax evasion generally does not receive a great deal of justification.

Ranking

It was thought that some arguments justifying tax evasion might be stronger than others, so a ranking was done to determine the relative strength of each argument. Table 17.3 ranks the statements from the strongest to weakest argument justifying tax evasion.

The range of mean scores was 3.84–6.30, indicating that some arguments are indeed stronger than others. The difference between the high and low mean score was significant at the 1% level ($p < 0.001$).

Table 17.1 Demographics

	#	%		#	%
Gender			Academic major		
Male	137	25.4	Accounting	157	29.1
Female	401	74.4	Business/economics	323	59.9
Unknown	1	0.2	Law	1	0.2
Total	539	100.0	Other/unknown	58	10.8
			Total	539	100.0
Student status			Age		
Graduate	152	28.2	Under 25	307	57.0
Undergraduate	256	47.5	25–40	161	29.8
Accounting professionals	130	24.1	Over 40	70	13.0
Unknown	1	0.2	Unknown	1	0.2
Total	539	100.0	Total	539	100.0

Table 17.2 Summary of responses

S#	Statement	Mean
1	Tax evasion is ethical if tax rates are too high (S1)	5.36
2	Tax evasion is ethical even if tax rates are not too high because the government is not entitled to take as much as it is taking from me (S2)	6.17
3	Tax evasion is ethical if the tax system is unfair (S3)	4.48
4	Tax evasion is ethical if a large portion of the money collected is wasted (S4)	4.70
5	Tax evasion is ethical even if most of the money collected is spent wisely (S5)	6.30
6	Tax evasion is ethical if a large portion of the money collected is spent on projects that I morally disapprove of (S6)	5.58
7	Tax evasion is ethical even if a large portion of the money collected is spent on worthy projects (S7)	6.28
8	Tax evasion is ethical if a large portion of the money collected is spent on projects that do not benefit me (S8)	5.88
9	Tax evasion is ethical even if a large portion of the money collected is spent on projects that do benefit me (S9)	6.27
10	Tax evasion is ethical if everyone is doing it (S10)	5.85
11	Tax evasion is ethical if a significant portion of the money collected winds up in the pockets of corrupt politicians or their families and friends (S11)	3.84
12	Tax evasion is ethical if the probability of getting caught is low (S12)	5.70
13	Tax evasion is ethical if some of the proceeds go to support a war that I consider to be unjust (S13)	4.69
14	Tax evasion is ethical if I cannot afford to pay (S14)	4.81
15	Tax evasion is ethical even if it means that if I pay less, others will have to pay more (S15)	6.18
16	Tax evasion would be ethical if I were a Jew living in Nazi Germany in 1940 (S16)	4.45
17	Tax evasion is ethical if the government discriminates against me because of my religion, race, or ethnic background (S17)	4.02
18	Tax evasion is ethical if the government imprisons people for their political opinions (S18)	4.02
	Average	5.25

1 = strongly agree; 7 = strongly disagree

Table 17.3 Ranking

Rank	Statement	Mean
1	Tax evasion is ethical if a significant portion of the money collected winds up in the pockets of corrupt politicians or their families and friends (S11)	3.84
2	Tax evasion is ethical if the government discriminates against me because of my religion, race, or ethnic background (S17)	4.02
2	Tax evasion is ethical if the government imprisons people for their political opinions (S18)	4.02
4	Tax evasion would be ethical if I were a Jew living in Nazi Germany in 1940 (S16)	4.45
5	Tax evasion is ethical if the tax system is unfair (S3)	4.48
6	Tax evasion is ethical if some of the proceeds go to support a war that I consider to be unjust (S13)	4.69
7	Tax evasion is ethical if a large portion of the money collected is wasted (S4)	4.70
8	Tax evasion is ethical if I cannot afford to pay (S14)	4.81
9	Tax evasion is ethical if tax rates are too high (S1)	5.36
10	Tax evasion is ethical if a large portion of the money collected is spent on projects that I morally disapprove of (S6)	5.58
11	Tax evasion is ethical if the probability of getting caught is low (S12)	5.70
12	Tax evasion is ethical if everyone is doing it (S10)	5.85
13	Tax evasion is ethical if a large portion of the money collected is spent on projects that do not benefit me (S8)	5.88
14	Tax evasion is ethical even if tax rates are not too high because the government is not entitled to take as much as it is taking from me (S2)	6.17
15	Tax evasion is ethical even if it means that if I pay less, others will have to pay more (S15)	6.18
16	Tax evasion is ethical even if a large portion of the money collected is spent on projects that do benefit me (S9)	6.27
17	Tax evasion is ethical even if a large portion of the money collected is spent on worthy projects (S7)	6.28
18	Tax evasion is ethical even if most of the money collected is spent wisely (S5)	6.30

1 = strongly agree; 7 = strongly disagree

The strongest argument to justify tax evasion was in cases where a significant portion of the money collected winds up in the pockets of corrupt politicians or their families and friends. Tied for second place were the arguments that evasion is justified if the government discriminates on the basis of religion, race, or ethnicity or where the government imprisons people for their political opinions, both of which were human rights arguments that were added to the older arguments that have been used to justify tax evasion in the past.

In fourth place was the argument that it would be ethical to evade taxes if the taxpayer were a Jew living in Nazi Germany. This argument was included in the survey to test the limits. It was thought that, surely if tax evasion could ever be justified, it would be in the case of Jews living in Nazi Germany.

It was somewhat surprising that this reason did not rank first. However, some other surveys that have been conducted using a similar survey instrument did not rank it first, either [second in Argentina (McGee & Rossi, 2008), eighth in Bosnia

(McGee, Basic, & Tyler, 2008), fourth in Colombia (McGee, López, & Yepes, 2009), first in France (McGee & M'Zali, 2009), second in Germany (McGee, Nickerson, & Fees, 2009), third in the USA (McGee, Nickerson, & Fees, 2006), second in Guatemala (McGee, & Lingle, 2008), second among international business academics teaching in the USA (McGee, 2006b), first among Orthodox Jewish students (McGee & Cohn, 2008), eighth in Kazakhstan (McGee & Preobragenskaya, 2008), seventh in New Zealand (Gupta & McGee, 2010), fourth in Puerto Rico (McGee & López, 2007), first in Slovakia (McGee & Tusan, 2008), fifth in Thailand (McGee, 2008), and eighth in Ukraine (Nasadyuk & McGee, 2008)]. In a comparative study of accounting students in Florida and Utah, the Jewish question ranked first in Utah and sixth in Florida (McGee & Smith, 2009).

Other strong arguments to justify tax evasion were in cases, where the tax system is perceived as unfair, where the proceeds go to support an unjust war, if money is wasted, where the taxpayer cannot pay, or where tax rates are too high. Some of the weakest arguments were in cases where the funds are spent on worthy projects or where the taxpayer benefits from the government's expenditures.

Since the Jewish question had a wide disparity in the rankings from study to study, it was thought that comparing the rankings for the top six reasons in Estonia with the top six reasons found in some other studies might be interesting. Those comparisons are listed in Table 17.4.

As can be seen by comparing the relative rankings, the Estonian ranking is close to the ranking in some other studies for some arguments and not quite as close for others. The top two arguments in the present study were also ranked within the top five reasons in all of the other studies listed in Table 17.4, which indicates that there is a cross-border consistency for some arguments.

Gender

Gender is perhaps the most frequently studied demographic variable in the social science literature. In gender comparisons of ethical attitudes, some studies found that women were more ethical than men (Mason & Mudrack, 1996; Miesing & Preble, 1985; Purcell, 1977; Serwinek, 1992; Smith & Oakley, 1997; Tang & Zuo, 1997). A second group of studies found that the ethical views of men and women did not differ significantly (Kidwell et al., 1987; Posner & Schmidt, 1984; Robin & Babin, 1997; Stanga & Turpen, 1991; Swaidan, et al., 2006; Tsalikis & Ortiz-Buonafina, 1990). A third group of studies found men to be more ethical (Barnett & Karson, 1987; Weeks et al., 1999). In the studies where women were more ethical, one reason given was because women are taught to defer to authority. In some of the studies where there was no significant difference in attitudes, one reason given was because women are becoming liberated from their traditional roles, and as they become more liberated their views are having a tendency to converge with male views.

Some studies of attitudes toward tax evasion found that women were more averse to tax evasion than men. This result was found in studies of Australia (McGee & Bose, 2009), Hubei, China (McGee & Guo, 2007), Colombia (McGee, López,

Table 17.4 Comparison of relative rankings with other studies

Six strongest arguments to justify tax evasion

Statement	Rank comparisons with other studies					
	Estonia (present study)	Argentina (McGee & Rossi, 2008)	France (McGee & M'Zali, 2009)	Germany (McGee, Nickerson, & Fees, 2009)	New Zealand (Gupta & McGee, 2010)	Ukraine (Nasadyuk & McGee, 2008)
Tax evasion is ethical if a significant portion of the money collected winds up in the pockets of corrupt politicians or their families and friends	1	3	4	3	1	1
Tax evasion is ethical if the government discriminates against me because of my religion, race, or ethnic background	2	5	3	1	4	4
Tax evasion is ethical if the government imprisons people for their political opinions	2	9	2	4	5	2
Tax evasion would be ethical if I were a Jew living in Nazi Germany in 1940	4	1	1	2	7	8
Tax evasion is ethical if the tax system is unfair	5	4	7	6	2	3
Tax evasion is ethical if some of the proceeds go to support a war that I consider to be unjust	6	7	6	7	8	9

& Yepes, 2009), Germany (McGee, Nickerson, & Fees, 2006), Guatemala (McGee & Lingle, 2008), international business academics teaching in the USA (McGee, 2006b), Orthodox Jewish students (McGee & Cohn, 2008), New Zealand (Gupta McGee, 2010), Puerto Rico (McGee & López, 2007), Taiwan (McGee & Andres, 2009), and Thailand (McGee, 2008).

Another group of studies found male and female attitudes toward tax evasion to be similar. Studies in this category include Argentina (McGee & Rossi, 2008), Beijing, China (McGee & An, 2008), Southern China and Macau (McGee & Noronha, 2008), France (McGee & M'Zali, 2009), Hong Kong (McGee & Butt, 2008), Kazakhstan (McGee & Preobragenskaya, 2008), and Poland (McGee & Bernal, 2006). Men were more opposed to tax evasion in Romania (McGee, 2006c), Slovakia (McGee & Tusan, 2008), and Turkey (McGee & Benk, 2011).

The results for the present study are presented below. Table 17.5 shows the sample size, mean scores, standard deviations, and p values for each statement classified by gender.

Overall, women were more opposed to tax evasion, as indicated by the overall mean scores (men 4.78; women 5.40). A comparison of mean scores for each of the individual statements found that women were significantly more opposed to tax evasion in all 18 cases.

Age

Age is also a commonly examined demographic variable in social science studies. Ethics studies often find that older people tend to be more ethical than younger people or that older people have more respect for rules and laws than do younger people. However, that result is not found in all studies.

Ruegger and King (1992) found that people become more ethical with age. However, Sims et al. (1996) found that older students had fewer qualms about pirating software than did younger students. Babakus et al. (2004) found that age makes a difference, but the difference it makes sometimes depends on culture. Younger people from France, the UK, and the USA tended to be less-ethical consumers than older people from those countries, whereas younger Austrians tended to be more ethical consumers than their elders. Age did not matter in Hong Kong, except in the case of stealing towels from hotels and blankets from aircraft. In those cases, younger people tended to be less tolerant of these activities than older people.

Some tax evasion studies looked at age as a variable. A New Zealand study (Gupta & McGee, 2010) found that older people were more opposed to tax evasion than were younger people. Two studies of Turkey (McGee & Benk, 2011; McGee, Benk, Yildirim, & Kayikçi, 2011) had the same finding. A study of the Republic of Slovakia (McGee & Tusan, 2008) found that older people were slightly more opposed to tax evasion.

Table 17.6 shows the data based on age for the present study. The overall mean scores increased as age increased [5.03–5.51–5.59], indicating that opposition to tax

Table 17.5 Statistical data: Gender

| Stmt. | Male | | | Female | | | |
	Sample	Mean	SD	Sample	Mean	SD	p value
1	137	4.69	1.97	401	5.59	1.53	0.0001
2	137	5.78	1.67	401	6.31	1.15	0.0001
3	137	3.90	2.04	400	4.67	1.84	0.0001
4	136	4.23	2.17	399	4.86	2.01	0.0021
5	137	6.02	1.37	401	6.40	1.08	0.0010
6	137	5.29	1.78	401	5.68	1.58	0.0161
7	137	6.05	1.40	400	6.36	1.14	0.0100
8	137	5.48	1.79	400	6.03	1.34	0.0002
9	136	6.00	1.52	401	6.36	1.22	0.0055
10	135	5.60	1.86	401	5.95	1.54	0.0310
11	136	3.21	2.28	401	4.04	2.22	0.0002
12	137	5.34	1.81	401	5.83	1.56	0.0025
13	137	4.32	2.10	401	4.82	1.98	0.0123
14	137	4.34	2.07	401	4.98	1.86	0.0008
15	137	5.93	1.55	399	6.27	1.26	0.0107
16	133	3.72	2.48	386	4.71	2.29	0.0001
17	135	3.30	2.18	400	4.27	2.13	0.0001
18	135	2.90	2.08	397	4.09	2.18	0.0001
Mean Avg.		4.78			5.40		

Table 17.6 Statistical data: Age

| Stmt. | Under 25 | | | 25–40 | | | Over 40 | | |
	Sample	Mean	SD	Sample	Mean	SD	Sample	Mean	SD
1	307	5.03	1.74	161	5.83	1.51	70	5.77	1.60
2	307	5.95	1.47	161	6.45	0.99	70	6.50	1.16
3	307	4.14	1.89	161	4.86	1.92	69	5.09	1.73
4	304	4.55	2.01	161	4.96	2.15	70	4.76	2.11
5	307	6.18	1.22	161	6.55	0.89	70	6.27	1.46
6	307	5.49	1.61	161	5.74	1.68	70	5.64	1.68
7	306	6.12	1.33	161	6.48	0.98	70	6.51	1.18
8	306	5.61	1.56	161	6.23	1.26	70	6.30	1.41
9	307	6.10	1.44	161	6.51	0.98	69	6.48	1.29
10	307	5.72	1.73	160	6.08	1.44	69	5.94	1.63
11	306	3.66	2.24	161	3.96	2.28	70	4.36	2.29
12	307	5.36	1.75	161	6.06	1.40	70	6.34	1.36
13	307	4.55	1.98	161	4.86	2.09	70	4.91	2.06
14	307	4.47	1.91	161	5.19	1.91	70	5.46	1.76
15	307	6.05	1.42	161	6.30	1.27	68	6.51	1.13
16	299	4.35	2.37	154	4.62	2.39	66	4.52	2.41
17	307	3.69	2.09	160	4.38	2.27	68	4.63	2.13
18	306	3.46	2.13	159	4.05	2.30	67	4.64	2.12
Mean Avg.		5.03			5.51			5.59	

evasion intensifies with age. A comparison of the mean scores for the individual statements between the youngest and oldest group found that the mean scores for the oldest group were higher in all 18 cases, indicating consistently higher opposition to tax evasion. Calculation of the p values, shown in Table 17.7, indicates that the difference in mean scores was often significant at the 1 or 5% level.

Table 17.7 computes the p values for the age categories.

Student Status

A few studies of tax evasion opinion reported separate data for the views of graduate and undergraduate students. In some of these studies, faculty members were also polled. A study of Argentina (McGee & Rossi, 2008) found that students and faculty were equally opposed to tax evasion. An Australian study (McGee & Bose, 2009) found that, overall, undergraduate students were least opposed to tax evasion and faculty members were most opposed. A New Zealand study (Gupta & McGee, 2010) found that graduate students were more opposed to tax evasion than undergraduate students.

Table 17.8 shows the sample size, mean scores, and standard deviations for each statement classified by student status. The scores for accounting professional are also included. Overall, the mean scores for undergraduate students (5.14) and graduate students (5.17) are about the same. The overall mean score for accounting practitioners (5.61) was higher than for either student group, indicating a higher level of opposition to tax evasion. Graduate students were more opposed to tax evasion than undergraduate students in 10 of 18 cases. A comparison of individual mean scores found that accounting practitioners were more opposed to tax evasion than undergraduate students in all 18 cases and in 14 of 18 cases for graduate students.

Table 17.9 computes the p values for the various categories. Graduate students were significantly more opposed to tax evasion than undergraduate students for statements 10, 11, and 16; undergraduate students were significantly more opposed to tax evasion than graduate students for statements 4, 6, 12, and 15. The conclusion to be drawn is that, although graduate and undergraduate students generally hold the same opinion about tax evasion, for some arguments there are significant differences.

The conclusion for accounting practitioner opinion is clearer. A comparison of mean scores with undergraduate and graduate students found that accounting practitioners are often significantly more opposed to tax evasion than either of the other two groups.

Table 17.7 *P* values: Age

Statement	<25 vs. 25–40	<25 vs. >40	25–40 vs. > 40
1	0.0001	0.0012	0.7854
2	0.0001	0.0036	0.7383
3	0.0001	0.0002	0.3924
4	0.0417	0.0001	0.0001
5	0.0007	0.5922	0.0750
6	0.1166	0.4858	0.6780
7	0.0026	0.0245	0.8411
8	0.0001	0.0008	0.7087
9	0.0013	0.0444	0.8473
10	0.0245	0.3355	0.5175
11	0.1722	0.0193	0.2223
12	0.0001	0.0001	0.1602
13	0.1152	0.1739	0.8669
14	0.0001	0.0001	0.3133
15	0.0614	0.0128	0.2392
16	0.2527	0.5993	0.7769
17	0.0011	0.0009	0.4394
18	0.0061	0.0001	0.0730

Table 17.8 Statistical data: Student status

Stmt.	Undergraduate			Graduate			Professional		
	Sample	Mean	SD	Sample	Mean	SD	Sample	Mean	SD
1	256	5.15	1.76	152	5.27	1.71	130	5.89	1.45
2	256	5.99	1.47	152	6.11	1.35	130	6.59	0.83
3	256	4.34	1.90	152	4.23	1.99	129	5.05	1.75
4	254	4.82	1.93	151	4.34	2.24	130	4.86	2.09
5	256	6.20	1.20	152	6.26	1.25	130	6.54	1.01
6	256	5.65	1.47	152	5.28	1.91	130	5.78	1.57
7	255	6.13	1.30	152	6.24	1.32	130	6.62	0.86
8	255	5.63	1.57	152	5.86	1.56	130	6.41	1.06
9	256	6.13	1.41	152	5.86	1.56	129	6.57	1.01
10	256	5.86	1.60	152	6.24	1.32	128	6.16	1.40
11	255	3.76	2.24	152	5.58	1.85	130	4.11	2.30
12	256	5.51	1.68	152	3.72	2.27	130	6.32	1.21
13	256	4.78	1.92	152	5.49	1.78	130	4.85	2.05
14	256	4.58	1.90	152	4.39	2.17	130	5.38	1.78
15	256	6.10	1.39	152	4.70	2.01	128	6.50	1.11
16	252	4.45	2.31	152	6.05	1.43	125	4.54	2.41
17	255	3.82	2.10	151	3.95	2.24	129	4.50	2.22
18	254	3.64	2.13	151	3.53	2.27	127	4.38	2.22
Mean Avg.		5.14			5.17			5.61	

Table 17.9 *P* values: Student status

Stmt.	UG vs. G	UG vs. P	G vs. P
1	0.5014	0.0001	0.0013
2	0.4118	0.0001	0.0005
3	0.5789	0.0004	0.0003
4	0.0233	0.8519	0.0464
5	0.6310	0.0059	0.0417
6	0.0288	0.4228	0.0182
7	0.4121	0.0001	0.0053
8	0.1526	0.0001	0.0008
9	0.0731	0.0017	0.0001
10	0.0139	0.0721	0.6235
11	0.0001	0.1516	0.0001
12	0.0001	0.0001	0.0001
13	0.0002	0.7409	0.0054
14	0.3552	0.0001	0.0001
15	0.0001	0.0001	0.0001
16	0.0001	0.7258	0.0001
17	0.5569	0.0035	0.0407
18	0.6242	0.0018	0.0019

Academic Major

A few prior studies that used a similar survey instrument compared the views of various student majors. The results of those studies may be summarized as follows.

- Argentina (McGee & Rossi, 2008) – Business and economics students were more opposed to tax evasion than law students in 16 of 18 cases.
- Armenia (McGee & Maranjyan, 2008) – Business students were more strongly opposed to tax evasion than theology students.
- Australia (McGee & Bose, 2009) – Business and economics students were least opposed to tax evasion; seminary students were most opposed; business and economics students were significantly less opposed to tax evasion than were accounting, philosophy, health services, and seminary students. Accounting majors were significantly more opposed to tax evasion than were business, economics, and information technology students and were significantly less opposed to tax evasion than seminary and health services students.
- China (McGee & Guo, 2007) – Business and economics students were least opposed to tax evasion; law and philosophy students were equally opposed to tax evasion.
- Guatemala (McGee & Lingle, 2008) – Business students were more opposed to tax evasion than were law students.
- Kazakhstan (McGee & Preobragenskaya, 2008) – Accounting and business/ economics students were equally opposed to tax evasion.

Table 17.10 Statistical data: Academic major

	Accounting			Business/Economics			
Stmt.	Sample	Mean	SD	Sample	Mean	SD	p value
1	157	5.61	1.71	321	5.15	1.69	0.0056
2	157	6.32	1.16	321	6.07	1.38	0.0510
3	157	4.58	1.95	320	4.32	1.92	0.1674
4	156	4.67	2.14	319	4.68	2.02	0.9604
5	157	6.35	1.18	321	6.23	1.18	0.2969
6	157	5.55	1.77	321	5.58	1.57	0.8509
7	157	6.38	1.22	321	6.17	1.26	0.0844
8	157	6.08	1.37	320	5.69	1.58	0.0085
9	156	6.36	1.29	321	6.16	1.37	0.1281
10	156	5.67	1.77	320	5.88	1.61	0.1968
11	157	3.96	2.30	320	3.73	2.22	0.2939
12	157	5.79	1.60	321	5.54	1.70	0.1244
13	157	4.64	2.15	321	4.65	1.98	0.9598
14	157	5.01	1.96	321	4.63	1.91	0.0434
15	155	6.19	1.35	321	6.10	1.39	0.5044
16	147	4.49	2.44	315	4.43	2.35	0.8008
17	155	4.03	2.28	321	3.96	2.13	0.7428
18	153	3.88	2.33	321	3.68	2.16	0.3588
Mean Avg.		5.31			5.15		

- New Zealand (Gupta & McGee, 2010) – Accounting and business/economics students were equally opposed to tax evasion; law students were somewhat less opposed to tax evasion than were the other groups. Accounting practitioners were more opposed to tax evasion than were students.
- Puerto Rico (McGee & López, 2007) – Accounting students were more opposed to tax evasion in 9/18 cases; law students were more opposed in 9/18 cases.
- Slovakia (McGee & Tusan, 2008) – Philosophy/theology students were more opposed to tax evasion than were business/economics students.

Table 17.10 shows the sample size, mean scores, standard deviations, and p values for each statement classified by academic major. Only accounting majors and business/economics majors were compared, since the sample sizes for the other categories were too small to have a meaningful analysis.

The overall mean score for accounting majors (5.31) was somewhat higher than the overall mean score for business economics students (5.15), indicating somewhat more opposition by the accounting students. A comparison of individual mean scores found that accounting students were more opposed to tax evasion in 14 of 18 cases. The difference was significant at the 1% level in 2 cases, at the 5% level in 1 case, and at the 10% level in 2 cases. Thus, we can conclude that accounting majors were somewhat more opposed to tax evasion than the business/economics majors.

Concluding Comments

This study discovered several interesting things about tax evasion attitudes in Estonia. Some arguments justifying tax evasion were stronger than others. The strongest arguments to justify tax evasion were in cases of government corruption or human rights abuses, if the tax system is considered to be unfair or if the funds are used to pay for an unjust war. Women were significantly more opposed to tax evasion than were men. Older people are more averse to tax evasion than younger people. Graduate and undergraduate students were equally opposed to tax evasion, but accounting practitioners were significantly more opposed to tax evasion than either student group. Accounting majors were somewhat more opposed to tax evasion than business/economics majors.

The present study examined the attitudes toward tax evasion of accounting and business/economics majors and accounting practitioners in Estonia. The survey instrument used in this study could serve as a template for similar studies in other countries or of other groups within Estonia. A survey of a more diverse demographic group would also be interesting.

References

Babakus, Emin, T. Bettina Cornwell, Vince Mitchell and Bodo Schlegelmilch (2004). Reactions to Unethical Consumer Behavior across Six Countries. *The Journal of Consumer Marketing*, 21(4/5), 254–263.

Barnett, John H. and Marvin J. Karson. (1987). Personal Values and Business Decisions: An Exploratory Investigation. *Journal of Business Ethics*, 6(5), 371–382.

Cohn, Gordon. (1998). The Jewish View on Paying Taxes. *Journal of Accounting, Ethics & Public Policy*, 1(2), 109–120, reprinted in Robert W. McGee (Ed.), *The Ethics of Tax Evasion* (pp. 180–189). Dumont, NJ: The Dumont Institute for Public Policy Research, 1998, pp. 180–189.

Crowe, Martin T. (1944). The Moral Obligation of Paying Just Taxes, The Catholic University of America Studies in Sacred Theology No. 84.

Gupta, Ranjana and Robert W. McGee. (2010). A Comparative Study of New Zealanders' Opinion on the Ethics of Tax Evasion: Students v. Accountants. *New Zealand Journal of Taxation Law and Policy*, 16(1), 47–84.

(Ed.), *The Ethics of Tax Evasion in Theory and Practice* (forthcoming). New York: Springer.

Kidwell, Jeaneen M., Robert E. Stevens & Art L. Bethke. (1987). Differences in Ethical Perceptions Between Male and Female Managers: Myth or Reality? *Journal of Business Ethics*, 6(6), 489–493.

Mason. E. Sharon & Peter E. Mudrack. (1996). Gender and Ethical Orientation: A Test of Gender and Occupational Socialization Theories. *Journal of Business Ethics*, 15(6), 599–604.

McGee, Robert W. (2006b). A Survey of International Business Academics on the Ethics of Tax Evasion. *Journal of Accounting, Ethics & Public Policy*, 6(3), 301–352.

McGee, Robert W. (2006c). The Ethics of Tax Evasion: A Survey of Romanian Business Students and Faculty. *The ICFAI Journal of Public Finance*, 4(2), 38–68 (2006). Reprinted in Robert W. McGee and Galina G. Preobragenskaya, *Accounting and Financial System Reform in Eastern Europe and Asia* (pp. 299–334). New York: Springer, 2006.

McGee, Robert W. and Arkadiusz Bernal. (2006). The Ethics of Tax Evasion: A Survey of Business Students in Poland. In *Global Economy -- How It Works* (Mina Baliamoune-Lutz, Alojzy Z.

Nowak & Jeff Steagall, eds.) (pp. 155–174). Warsaw: University of Warsaw & Jacksonville: University of North Florida. Reprinted at http://ssrn.com/abstract=875434.

McGee, Robert W., Inge Nickerson and Werner Fees. (2006). German and American Opinion on the Ethics of Tax Evasion. *Proceedings of the Academy of Legal, Ethical and Regulatory Issues* (Reno), 10(2), 31–34.

McGee, Robert W. and Zhiwen Guo. (2007). A Survey of Law, Business and Philosophy Students in China on the Ethics of Tax Evasion. *Society and Business Review*, 2(3), 299–315.

McGee, Robert W. and Silvia López Paláu. (2007). The Ethics of Tax Evasion: Two Empirical Studies of Puerto Rican Opinion. *Journal of Applied Business and Economics*, 7(3), 27–47 (2007). Reprinted in Robert W. McGee (editor), *Readings in Accounting Ethics* (pp. 314–342). Hyderabad, India: ICFAI University Press, 2009.

McGee, Robert W. (2008). Opinions on Tax Evasion in Thailand, in Robert W. McGee, editor, *Taxation and Public Finance in Transition and Developing Economies* (pp. 609–620). New York: Springer.

McGee, Robert W. and Yuhua An. (2008). A Survey of Chinese Business and Economics Students on the Ethics of Tax Evasion, in Robert W. McGee, editor, *Taxation and Public Finance in Transition and Developing Economies* (pp. 409–421). New York: Springer.

McGee, Robert W., Meliha Basic and Michael Tyler. (2008). The Ethics of Tax Evasion: A Comparative Study of Bosnian and Romanian Opinion, in Robert W. McGee, editor, *Taxation and Public Finance in Transition and Developing Economies* (pp. 167–183). New York: Springer.

McGee, Robert W. and Yiu Yu Butt. (2008). An Empirical Study of Tax Evasion Ethics in Hong Kong. Proceedings of the International Academy of Business and Public Administration Disciplines (IABPAD), Dallas, April 24–27: 72–83.

McGee, Robert W. and Gordon M. Cohn. (2008). Jewish Perspectives on the Ethics of Tax Evasion. *Journal of Legal, Ethical and Regulatory Issues*, 11(2), 1–32.

McGee, Robert W. and Christopher Lingle. (2008). The Ethics of Tax Evasion: A Survey of Guatemalan Opinion, in Robert W. McGee, editor, *Taxation and Public Finance in Transition and Developing Economies* (pp. 481–495). New York: Springer.

McGee, Robert W. and Tatyana B. Maranjyan. (2008). Opinions on Tax Evasion in Armenia, in Robert W. McGee, editor, *Taxation and Public Finance in Transition and Developing Economies* (pp. 277–307). New York: Springer.

McGee, Robert W. and Carlos Noronha. (2008). The Ethics of Tax Evasion: A Comparative Study of Guangzhou (Southern China) and Macau Opinions. Euro Asia Journal of Management, 18(2), 133–152.

McGee, Robert W. and Galina G. Preobragenskaya. (2008). A Study of Tax Evasion Ethics in Kazakhstan, in Robert W. McGee, editor, *Taxation and Public Finance in Transition and Developing Economies* (pp. 497–510). New York: Springer.

McGee, Robert W. and Marcelo J. Rossi. (2008). A Survey of Argentina on the Ethics of Tax Evasion, in Robert W. McGee, editor, *Taxation and Public Finance in Transition and Developing Economies* (pp. 239–261). New York: Springer.

McGee, Robert W. and Radoslav Tusan. (2008). The Ethics of Tax Evasion: A Survey of Slovak Opinion, in Robert W. McGee, editor, *Taxation and Public Finance in Transition and Developing Economies* (pp. 575–601). New York: Springer.

McGee, Robert W. and Susana N. Vittadini Andres. (2009). The Ethics of Tax Evasion: Case Studies of Taiwan, in Robert W. McGee, *Readings in Business Ethics* (pp. 200–228). Hyderabad, India: ICFAI University Press. An abbreviated version was published in Marjorie G. Adams and Abbass Alkhafaji, editors, *Business Research Yearbook: Global Business Perspectives*, Volume XIV, No. 1 (pp. 34–39). Beltsville, MD: International Graphics: Beltsville, MD, 2007.

McGee, Robert W. and Sanjoy Bose. (2009). The Ethics of Tax Evasion: A Survey of Australian Opinion, in Robert W. McGee, *Readings in Business Ethics* (pp. 143–166). Hyderabad, India: ICFAI University Press.

McGee, Robert W. and Bouchra M'Zali. (2009). The Ethics of Tax Evasion: An Empirical Study of French EMBA Students, in Robert W. McGee, *Readings in Business Ethics* (pp. 185–199). Hyderabad, India: ICFAI University Press. An abbreviated version was published in Marjorie G. Adams and Abbass Alkhafaji, editors, *Business Research Yearbook: Global Business Perspectives*, Volume XIV, No. 1 (pp. 27–33). Beltsville, MD: International Graphics, 2007).

McGee, Robert W., Inge Nickerson and Werner Fees. (2009). When Is Tax Evasion Ethically Justifiable? A Survey of German Opinion, in Robert W. McGee, editor, *Readings in Accounting Ethics* (pp. 365–389). Hyderabad, India: ICFAI University Press.

McGee, Robert W., Silvia López Paláu and Gustavo A. Yepes Lopez. (2009). The Ethics of Tax Evasion: An Empirical Study of Colombian Opinion, in Robert W. McGee, *Readings in Business Ethics* (pp. 167–184). Hyderabad, India: ICFAI University Press.

McGee, Robert W. and Sheldon R. Smith. 2009. Ethics and Tax Evasion: A Comparative Study of Utah and Florida Opinion, in Robert W. McGee (Ed.), *Readings in Accounting Ethics* (pp. 343–364). Hyderabad, India: ICFAI University Press.

McGee, Robert W. & Serkan Benk (2011). The Ethics of Tax Evasion: A Study of Turkish Opinion. *Journal of Balkan and Near Eastern Studies*, 13(2), 249–262.

McGee, Robert W., Serkan Benk, Halil Yıldırım and Murat Kayıkçı. (2011). The Ethics of Tax Evasion: A Study of Turkish Tax Practitioner Opinion, *European Journal of Social Sciences*, 18(3), 468–480.

Miesing, Paul and John F. Preble. (1985). A Comparison of Five Business Philosophies. *Journal of Business Ethics*, 4(6), 465–476.

Nasadyuk, Irina and Robert W. McGee. (2008). The Ethics of Tax Evasion: An Empirical Study of Business and Economics Student Opinion in Ukraine, in Robert W. McGee (Ed.), *Taxation and Public Finance in Transition and Developing Economies* (pp. 639–661). New York: Springer.

Posner, Barry Z. & Warren H. Schmidt. (1984). Values and the American Manager: An Update. California Management Review, 26(3), 202–216.

Purcell, Theodore V. (1977). Do Courses in Business Ethics Pay Off? *California Management Review*, 19(4), 50–58.

Robin, Donald and Laurie Babin. (1997). Making Sense of the Research on Gender and Ethics in Business: A Critical Analysis and Extension. *Business Ethics Quarterly*, 7(4), 61–90.

Ruegger, Durwood and Ernest W. King. (1992). A Study of the Effect of Age and Gender upon Student Business Ethics. *Journal of Business Ethics*, 11(3), 179–186.

Serwinek, Paul J. (1992). Demographic & Related Differences in Ethical Views Among Small Businesses. *Journal of Business Ethics*, 11(7), 555–566.

Sims, Ronald R., Hsing K. Cheng & Hildy Teegen. (1996). Toward a Profile of Student Software Piraters. *Journal of Business Ethics*, 15(8), 839–849.

Smith, Patricia L. & Ellwood F. Oakley, III. (1997). Gender-Related Differences in Ethical and Social Values of Business Students: Implications for Management. *Journal of Business Ethics*, 16(1), 37–45.

Stanga, Keith G. and Richard A. Turpen. (1991). Ethical Judgments on Selected Accounting Issues: An Empirical Study. *Journal of Business Ethics*, 10(10), 739–747.

Swaidan, Ziad, Scott J. Vitell, Gregory M. Rose and Faye W. Gilbert. (2006). Consumer Ethics: The Role of Acculturation in U.S. Immigrant Populations. *Journal of Business Ethics*, 64(1), 1–16.

Tang, S. and J. Zuo (1997). Profile of College Examination Cheaters. *College Student Journal* 31(3): 340–347, as cited in Bob S. Brown and Peggy Choong. (2005). An Investigation of Academic Dishonesty among Business Students at Public and Private United States Universities. *International Journal of Management*, 22(2), 201–214.

Tsalikis, J. & M. Ortiz-Buonafina. (1990). Ethical Beliefs' Differences of Males and Females. *Journal of Business Ethics*, 9(6), 509–517.

Weeks, William A., Carlos W. Moore, Joseph A. McKinney & Justin G. Longenecker. (1999). The Effects of Gender and Career Stage on Ethical Judgment. *Journal of Business Ethics*, 20(4), 301–313.

Chapter 18
The Ethics of Tax Evasion: A Study of Haitian Opinion

Robert W. McGee and Bouchra M'Zali

Introduction

Most studies of tax evasion take an economic or public finance perspective. Not much has been written from a philosophical or ethical viewpoint. That is probably because most economists are utilitarians and most lawyers are legalists. However, there is a small body of literature that addresses tax evasion issues from a philosophical or theological perspective. The present study is intended to add to that small body of literature while forming a bridge to the public finance literature as well.

The authors developed a survey instrument that included eighteen (18) statements incorporating the three major views on the ethics of tax evasion that have emerged in the literature over the last 500 years (Crowe, 1944). The survey was distributed to a group of accounting and business students in Haiti. This chapter reports on the results of that survey.

Methodology

After reviewing the literature that exists on the ethics of tax evasion, a survey was constructed and distributed to a group of accounting and business students in order to learn their views on the ethics of tax evasion. Due to space constraints, the literature is not reviewed in depth here. However, the relevant literature is listed in the reference section.

R.W. McGee (✉)
School of Business, Florida International University, 3000 NE 151 Street,
North Miami, FL 33181, USA
e-mail: bob414@hotmail.com

B. M'Zali
School of Business, University of Quebec at Montreal,
Montreal, Quebec H2X 3X2 Canada

R.W. McGee (ed.), *The Ethics of Tax Evasion: Perspectives in Theory and Practice*,
DOI 10.1007/978-1-4614-1287-8_18, © Springer Science+Business Media, LLC 2012

The survey consisted of eighteen (18) statements. Using a seven-point Likert scale, respondents were asked to place the appropriate number in the space provided to indicate the extent of their agreement or disagreement with each statement. The statements in the survey reflected the three main viewpoints on the ethics of tax evasion that have emerged over the centuries. Thirty-two (32) usable responses were received.

Survey Findings

The next few sections report on the study's findings.

Demographics

Table 18.1 lists the demographics of the survey. More than three-quarters of the sample consisted of men. Nearly, all were first cycle accounting or business/economics majors. The average age was about 34, with a range of 25–45.

Table 18.2 shows the 18 statements and the mean scores of the responses. The overall mean score was 4.45, which indicates fairly strong support for tax evasion.

Table 18.3 ranks the responses, from strongest agreement to weakest agreement. The strongest argument to justify tax evasion was the case where tax rates were too high. The second strongest argument was in cases where the tax system is perceived to be unfair. In third place was the case of Jews living in Nazi Germany. Other arguments in the top six included where large portions of the money collected is wasted, even if the money is spent wisely, and where proceeds go to support an unjust war. What is surprising is that two of the human rights questions ranked so low – 8th and 11th. In other surveys that used a similar survey instrument, the rankings of the three human rights issues were higher.

Since a similar survey instrument was used to solicit opinions on tax evasion in other countries, it was thought that it might be interesting to compare the rankings for the various statements with some of those other surveys. Those comparisons are made in Table 18.4.

As can be seen, some of the arguments had a remarkably similar placement among countries while others had some marked differences. Tax rates that were too high ranked first in Haiti but ranked much farther down the list for the other countries. The "Tax evasion is ethical even if most of the money is spent wisely" argument ranked fifth in the Haiti sample but farther down the list for the other countries. The discrimination question ranked farther down the list for Haiti and Puerto Rico than it did for the other countries. The corrupt politician justification ranked tenth in Haiti but at or near the top of the list for the other countries. Imprisoning people for their political opinions was not as strong an argument in Haiti as it was in the other countries.

Table 18.1 Demographics

	#	%		#	%
Gender			*Academic major*		
Male	25	78.1	Accounting	5	15.6
Female	5	15.6	Business/economics	20	62.5
Unknown	2	6.3	Other	7	21.9
Total	32	100.0	Total	32	100.0
Student status			*Age*		
Premier cycle	28	87.5	Mean	34.2	
Other	4	12.5	Median	32	
Total	32	100.0	Range	25–45	

Table 18.2 Summary of responses – overall

Statement number	Statement	Mean
1	Tax evasion is ethical if tax rates are too high	3.73
2	Tax evasion is ethical even if tax rates are not too high because the government is not entitled to take as much as it is taking from me	5.03
3	Tax evasion is ethical if the tax system is unfair	3.80
4	Tax evasion is ethical if a large portion of the money collected is wasted	4.00
5	Tax evasion is ethical even if most of the money collected is spent wisely	4.07
6	Tax evasion is ethical if a large portion of the money collected is spent on projects that I morally disapprove of	4.27
7	Tax evasion is ethical even if a large portion of the money collected is spent on worthy projects	5.47
8	Tax evasion is ethical if a large portion of the money collected is spent on projects that do not benefit me	4.67
9	Tax evasion is ethical even if a large portion of the money collected is spent on projects that do benefit me	4.93
10	Tax evasion is ethical if everyone is doing it	4.93
11	Tax evasion is ethical if a significant portion of the money collected winds up in the pockets of corrupt politicians or their families and friends	4.50
12	Tax evasion is ethical if the probability of getting caught is low	4.80
13	Tax evasion is ethical if some of the proceeds go to support a war that I consider to be unjust	4.10
14	Tax evasion is ethical if I cannot afford to pay	4.40
15	Tax evasion is ethical even if it means that if I pay less, others will have to pay more	4.70
16	Tax evasion would be ethical if I were a Jew living in Nazi Germany in 1935	3.86
17	Tax evasion is ethical if the government discriminates against me because of my religion, race, or ethnic background	4.33
18	Tax evasion is ethical if the government imprisons people for their political opinions	4.53
	Average score	4.45

1 = Strongly agree; 7 = strongly disagree

Table 18.3 Ranking of arguments

Rank	Statement	Mean
1	Tax evasion is ethical if tax rates are too high	3.73
2	Tax evasion is ethical if the tax system is unfair	3.80
3	Tax evasion would be ethical if I were a Jew living in Nazi Germany in 1935	3.86
4	Tax evasion is ethical if a large portion of the money collected is wasted	4.00
5	Tax evasion is ethical even if most of the money collected is spent wisely	4.07
6	Tax evasion is ethical if some of the proceeds go to support a war that I consider to be unjust	4.10
7	Tax evasion is ethical if a large portion of the money collected is spent on projects that I morally disapprove of	4.27
8	Tax evasion is ethical if the government discriminates against me because of my religion, race, or ethnic background	4.33
9	Tax evasion is ethical if I cannot afford to pay	4.40
10	Tax evasion is ethical if a significant portion of the money collected winds up in the pockets of corrupt politicians or their families and friends	4.50
11	Tax evasion is ethical if the government imprisons people for their political opinions	4.53
12	Tax evasion is ethical if a large portion of the money collected is spent on projects that do not benefit me	4.67
13	Tax evasion is ethical even if it means that if I pay less, others will have to pay more	4.70
14	Tax evasion is ethical if the probability of getting caught is low	4.80
15	Tax evasion is ethical even if a large portion of the money collected is spent on projects that do benefit me	4.93
15	Tax evasion is ethical if everyone is doing it	4.93
17	Tax evasion is ethical even if tax rates are not too high because the government is not entitled to take as much as it is taking from me	5.03
18	Tax evasion is ethical even if a large portion of the money collected is spent on worthy projects	5.47

1 = Strongly agree; 7 = strongly disagree

Table 18.5 shows the results by gender. Although the sample size was too small to draw strong conclusions, it was felt that examining the data by gender would be an interesting exercise. Some prior studies that examined gender found that women were more opposed to tax evasion than men (McGee & Bose, 2009; McGee & Guo, 2007; McGee, López & Yepes, 2009; McGee, Alver & Alver, 2008). Another group of studies found that men and women had similar opinions about tax evasion (McGee & An, 2008; McGee & Noronha, 2008; McGee & Rossi, 2008). A third group of studies found that men were more opposed to tax evasion (McGee, 2006a, b; McGee & Benk, 2011; McGee & Tusan, 2008).

The overall mean score for females (5.03) was higher than the male mean score (4.34), which indicates that females were more opposed to tax evasion than males, on average. Table 18.5 shows the mean scores for each statement, compares them and lists the *p*-value, which determines significance. The results have to be discounted somewhat due to the small sample size. However, the results do provide some useful information about the views of men and women on the issue of tax evasion in 18 different cases.

Table 18.4 Ranking of arguments – comparison with other studies

Statement	Haiti (present study)	Puerto Rico (McGee & López, 2007)	Colombia (McGee, López & Yepes, 2009)	Argentina (McGee & Rossi, 2008)	Guatemala (McGee & Lingle, 2008)
Tax evasion is ethical if tax rates are too high	1	8	10	7	10
Tax evasion is ethical if the tax system is unfair	2	3	5	4	5
Tax evasion would be ethical if I were a Jew living in Nazi Germany in 1935	3	4	4	1	2
Tax evasion is ethical if a large portion of the money collected is wasted	4	2	3	6	4
Tax evasion is ethical even if most of the money collected is spent wisely	5	17	12	18	16
Tax evasion is ethical if some of the proceeds go to support a war that I consider to be unjust	6	6	8	7	9
Tax evasion is ethical if a large portion of the money collected is spent on projects that I morally disapprove of	7	9	8	10	8
Tax evasion is ethical if the government discriminates against me because of my religion, race, or ethnic background	8	10	2	5	3
Tax evasion is ethical if I cannot afford to pay	9	7	6	1	5
Tax evasion is ethical if a significant portion of the money collected winds up in the pockets of corrupt politicians or their families and friends	10	1	1	3	1
Tax evasion is ethical if the government imprisons people for their political opinions	11	5	7	9	7
Tax evasion is ethical if a large portion of the money collected is spent on projects that do not benefit me	12	11	13	14	12
Tax evasion is ethical even if it means that if I pay less, others will have to pay more	13	13	14	13	13
Tax evasion is ethical if the probability of getting caught is low	14	12	17	15	14
Tax evasion is ethical even if a large portion of the money collected is spent on projects that do benefit me	15	16	14	15	16
Tax evasion is ethical if everyone is doing it	15	14	18	12	14
Tax evasion is ethical even if tax rates are not too high because the government is not entitled to take as much as it is taking from me	17	17	16	15	16
Tax evasion is ethical even if a large portion of the money collected is spent on worthy projects	18	14	11	11	11

Table 18.5 Summary of responses – gender

Statement number	Statement	F	M	Larger by F	Larger by M	p
1	Tax evasion is ethical if tax rates are too high	4.60	3.56	1.04		0.3871
2	Tax evasion is ethical even if tax rates are not too high because the government is not entitled to take as much as it is taking from me	6.40	4.76	1.64		0.1896
3	Tax evasion is ethical if the tax system is unfair	4.80	3.60	1.20		0.2865
4	Tax evasion is ethical if a large portion of the money collected is wasted	4.60	3.88	0.72		0.5986
5	Tax evasion is ethical even if most of the money collected is spent wisely	3.80	4.12		0.32	0.7482
6	Tax evasion is ethical if a large portion of the money collected is spent on projects that I morally disapprove of	5.60	4.00	1.60		0.1364
7	Tax evasion is ethical even if a large portion of the money collected is spent on worthy projects	4.60	5.64		1.04	0.3385
8	Tax evasion is ethical even if a large portion of the money collected is spent on projects that do not benefit me	3.80	4.84		1.04	0.2970
9	Tax evasion is ethical even if a large portion of the money collected is spent on projects that do benefit me	5.60	4.80	0.8		0.5192
10	Tax evasion is ethical if everyone is doing it	5.60	4.80	0.80		0.5216
11	Tax evasion is ethical if a significant portion of the money collected winds up in the pockets of corrupt politicians or their families and friends	4.60	4.48	0.12		0.9333
12	Tax evasion is ethical if the probability of getting caught is low	6.00	4.56	1.44		0.1706
13	Tax evasion is ethical if some of the proceeds go to support a war that I consider to be unjust	6.20	3.68	2.52		0.0424*
14	Tax evasion is ethical if I cannot afford to pay	5.80	4.12	1.68		0.1695
15	Tax evasion is ethical even if it means that if I pay less, others will have to pay more	4.20	4.80		0.60	0.5502
16	Tax evasion would be ethical if I were a Jew living in Nazi Germany in 1935	4.75	3.71	1.04		0.4651
17	Tax evasion is ethical if the government discriminates against me because of my religion, race, or ethnic background	4.20	4.36		0.16	0.9046
18	Tax evasion is ethical if the government imprisons people for their political opinions	5.40	4.36	1.04		0.4107
	Average score	5.03	4.34			

1 = Strongly agree; 7 = strongly disagree
*Significant at 5%

Table 18.6 Statistics – gender

Statement number	Female			Male			
	Mean	SD	Sample size	Mean	SD	Sample size	*p*-Value
1	4.60	2.88	5	3.56	2.33	25	0.3871
2	6.40	0.55	5	4.76	2.68	25	0.1896
3	4.80	2.28	5	3.60	2.25	25	0.2865
4	4.60	2.88	5	3.88	2.74	25	0.5986
5	3.80	1.92	5	4.12	2.03	25	0.7482
6	5.60	2.07	5	4.00	2.14	25	0.1364
7	4.60	2.51	5	5.64	2.12	25	0.3385
8	3.80	1.79	5	4.84	2.03	25	0.2970
9	5.60	2.19	5	4.80	2.55	25	0.5192
10	5.60	2.61	5	4.80	2.50	25	0.5216
11	4.60	3.29	5	4.48	2.83	25	0.9333
12	6.00	1.00	5	4.56	2.22	25	0.1706
13	6.20	0.84	5	3.68	2.59	25	0.0424
14	5.80	1.64	5	4.12	2.54	25	0.1695
15	4.20	2.17	5	4.80	2.00	25	0.5502
16	4.75	2.87	4	3.71	2.56	24	0.4651
17	4.20	2.77	5	4.36	2.69	25	0.9046
18	5.40	2.30	5	4.36	2.58	25	0.4107

Women were more opposed to tax evasion for 13 of 18 statements. Only one difference in mean score was significant at the 5% level. A partial explanation for the dearth of significant differences might be due to the small sample size.

Table 18.6 shows the statistical information for each argument, by gender.

Concluding Comments

The Haiti study proved to be interesting for several reasons. For one, it revealed the relative importance of the various arguments that have been given over the centuries to justify tax evasion. It also found that the relative rankings for Haiti were sometimes very similar and other times quite different than the rankings for other studies that were done in the region. Part of these differences can be explained by cultural and ethnic differences. The fact that Haiti is poorer than the other countries used in the comparison might also account for some of the differences, as might the fact that Haitians have had to endure more corruption than the citizens of the other countries used for comparison purposes.

The present study has several limitations. The sample size was relatively small, which makes any conclusions reached tentative. Also, the population included in the sample was more educated than the general population. The average age might also be different. The opinions of other segments of the Haitian population might be different from the opinions of those included in the present sample. Thus, more research is needed.

References

Adams, Charles. (1993). *For Good or Evil: The Impact of Taxes on the Course of Civilization.* London, New York & Lanham: Madison Books.

Crowe, Martin T. (1944). *The Moral Obligation of Paying Just Taxes,* The Catholic University of America Studies in Sacred Theology No. 84.

McGee, Robert W. (2006a). Three Views on the Ethics of Tax Evasion. *Journal of Business Ethics,* 67(1), 15–35.

McGee, Robert W. (2006b). The Ethics of Tax Evasion: A Survey of Romanian Business Students and Faculty. *The ICFAI Journal of Public Finance,* 4(2), 38–68 (2006). Reprinted in Robert W. McGee and Galina G. Preobragenskaya, *Accounting and Financial System Reform in Eastern Europe and Asia* (pp. 299–334). New York: Springer, 2006.

McGee, Robert W. and Zhiwen Guo. (2007). A Survey of Law, Business and Philosophy Students in China on the Ethics of Tax Evasion. *Society and Business Review,* 2(3), 299–315.

McGee, Robert W. and Silvia López Paláu. (2007). The Ethics of Tax Evasion: Two Empirical Studies of Puerto Rican Opinion. *Journal of Applied Business and Economics,* 7(3), 27–47 (2007). Reprinted in Robert W. McGee (editor), *Readings in Accounting Ethics* (pp. 314–342). Hyderabad, India: ICFAI University Press, 2009.

McGee, Robert W., Jaan Alver and Lehte Alver. (2008). The Ethics of Tax Evasion: A Survey of Estonian Opinion, in Robert W. McGee, editor, *Taxation and Public Finance in Transition and Developing Economies* (pp. 461–480). New York: Springer.

McGee, Robert W. and Yuhua An. (2008). A Survey of Chinese Business and Economics Students on the Ethics of Tax Evasion, in Robert W. McGee, editor, *Taxation and Public Finance in Transition and Developing Economies* (pp. 409–421). New York: Springer.

McGee, Robert W. and Christopher Lingle. (2008). The Ethics of Tax Evasion: A Survey of Guatemalan Opinion, in Robert W. McGee, editor, *Taxation and Public Finance in Transition and Developing Economies* (pp. 481–495). New York: Springer.

McGee, Robert W. and Carlos Noronha. (2008). The Ethics of Tax Evasion: A Comparative Study of Guangzhou (Southern China) and Macau Opinions. *Euro Asia Journal of Management,* 18(2), 133–152.

McGee, Robert W. and Marcelo J. Rossi. (2008). A Survey of Argentina on the Ethics of Tax Evasion, in Robert W. McGee, editor, *Taxation and Public Finance in Transition and Developing Economies* (pp. 239–261). New York: Springer.

McGee, Robert W. and Radoslav Tusan. (2008). The Ethics of Tax Evasion: A Survey of Slovak Opinion, in Robert W. McGee, editor, *Taxation and Public Finance in Transition and Developing Economies* (pp. 575–601). New York: Springer.

McGee, Robert W. Serkan Benk, Adriana M. Ross & Harun Kılıçaslan (2009). An Empirical Study of Ethical Opinion in Germany. *Journal of Accounting, Ethics & Public Policy,* 10(2), 243–259.

McGee, Robert W., Silvia López Paláu and Gustavo A. Yepes Lopez. (2009). The Ethics of Tax Evasion: An Empirical Study of Colombian Opinion, in Robert W. McGee, *Readings in Business Ethics* (pp. 167–184). Hyderabad, India: ICFAI University Press.

McGee, Robert W. & Serkan Benk (2011). The Ethics of Tax Evasion: A Study of Turkish Opinion. *Journal of Balkan and Near Eastern Studies,* 13(2), 249–262.

Chapter 19
An Empirical Study of Tax Evasion Ethics in Hong Kong

Robert W. McGee and Yiu Yu Butt

Introduction

The vast majority of articles that have been written about tax evasion have been written from the perspective of public finance. They discuss technical aspects of tax evasion and the primary and secondary effects that tax evasion has on an economy. In many cases, there is also a discussion about how to prevent or minimize tax evasion. Very few articles discuss ethical aspects of tax evasion. Thus, there is a need for further research, which the present study is intended to partially address.

As part of this study a survey instrument was developed based on the issues that have been discussed and the arguments that have been made in the tax evasion ethics literature over the last 500 years. Similar survey instruments were used to test sample populations in Romania (McGee 2005b) and Guatemala (McGee & Lingle 2005). The survey was also distributed to professors of international business (McGee 2005a). The present study reports on the findings of a survey that was distributed to business students at a university in Hong Kong. The survey instrument consisted of 15 statements that reflect the three views on the ethics of tax evasion that have emerged over the centuries. Participants were asked to rate the extent of their agreement with each statement by placing a number from 1 to 7 in the space provided. Scores were compared to determine whether the responses were significantly different by state.

R.W. McGee (✉)
School of Business, Florida International University,
3000 NE 151 Street, North Miami, FL 33181, USA
e-mail: bob414@hotmail.com

Y.Y. Butt
Hong Kong University, Pokfulam, Hong Kong

R.W. McGee (ed.), *The Ethics of Tax Evasion: Perspectives in Theory and Practice*,
DOI 10.1007/978-1-4614-1287-8_19, © Springer Science+Business Media, LLC 2012

Review of the Literature

Although many studies have been done on tax compliance, very few have examined compliance, or rather noncompliance, primarily from the perspective of ethics. Most studies on tax evasion look at the issue from a public finance or economics perspective, although ethical issues may be mentioned briefly, in passing. The most comprehensive twentieth century work on the ethics of tax evasion was a doctoral thesis written by Martin Crowe (1944), titled *The Moral Obligation of Paying Just Taxes*. This thesis reviewed the theological and philosophical debate that had been going on, mostly within the Catholic Church, over the previous 500 years. Some of the debate took place in the Latin language. Crowe introduced this debate to an English language readership. A more recent doctoral dissertation on the topic was written by Torgler (2003), who discussed tax evasion from the perspective of public finance but also touched on some psychological and philosophical aspects of the issue.

Walter Block (1989; 1993) sought in vain to find a justification for taxation in the public finance literature. He examined a number of textbooks but found all justifications for taxation to be inadequate. Leiker (1998) speculates on how Rousseau would have viewed the ethics of tax evasion. Alfonso Morales (1998) examined the views of Mexican immigrant street vendors and found that their loyalty to their families exceeded their loyalty to the government. McGraw and Scholz (1991) examined tax compliance from the perspective of self-interest. Armstrong and Robison (1998) discuss tax evasion and tax avoidance from the perspective of an accounting practitioner and used Rawls' concept of two kinds of rules to analyze how accountants view the issue. Oliva (1998) looked at the issue from the perspective of a tax practitioner and commented on the schism that exists between a tax practitioner's ethical and legal obligations.

There have been a few studies that focus on tax evasion in a particular country. Ethics are sometimes discussed but, more often than not, the focus of the discussion is on government corruption and the reasons why the citizenry does not feel any moral duty to pay taxes to such a government. Ballas and Tsoukas (1998) discuss the situation in Greece. Smatrakalev (1998) discusses the Bulgarian case. Vaguine (1998) discusses Russia, as do Preobragenskaya and McGee (2004) to a lesser extent. A study of tax evasion in Armenia (McGee, 1999b) found the two main reasons for evasion to be the lack of a mechanism in place to collect taxes and the widespread opinion that the government does not deserve a portion of a worker's income.

A number of articles have been written from various religious perspectives. Cohn (1998) and Tamari (1998) discuss the Jewish literature on tax evasion and on ethics in general. Much of this literature is in Hebrew or a language other than English. McGee (1999a) comments on these two articles from a secular perspective.

A few articles have been written on the ethics of tax evasion from various Christian viewpoints. Gronbacher (1998) addresses the issue from the perspectives of Catholic social thought and classical liberalism. Schansberg (1998) looks at the Biblical literature for guidance. Pennock (1998) discusses just war theory in connection with the moral obligation to pay just taxes, and not to pay unjust or immoral taxes. Smith and Kimball (1998) provide a Mormon perspective. McGee (1998b; 1999a) comments on the various Christian views from a secular perspective.

The Christian Bible discusses tax evasion and the duty of the citizenry to support the government in several places. Schansberg (1998) and McGee (1994; 1998a) discuss the biblical literature on this point. When Jesus is asked whether people should pay taxes to Caesar, Jesus replied that we should give to Caesar the things that are Caesar's and give God the things that are God's [Matthew 22:17, 21]. But Jesus did not elaborate on the point. He did not say that we are only obligated to give the government 10% or 5% or any particular percent of our income.

A few other religious views are also addressed in the literature. Murtuza and Ghazanfar (1998) discuss the ethics of tax evasion from the Muslim perspective. McGee (1999a) comments on their article and also discusses the ethics of tax evasion under Islam citing Islamic business ethics literature (McGee 1997). DeMoville (1998) discusses the Baha'i perspective and cites the relevant literature to buttress his arguments. McGee (1999a) commented on the DeMoville article.

A similar survey of international business professors found that some arguments justifying tax evasion are stronger than others but none of the arguments were very strong, since most of the professors who responded to the survey were strongly against tax evasion. This survey also found that women were significantly more opposed to tax evasion than were the men (McGee, 2005a). A survey of business and law students in Guatemala reached a similar result. However, the law students felt less strongly about condemning tax evasion on ethical grounds than did the business students and female students were more opposed to tax evasion than were male students (McGee & Lingle, 2005). A survey of Romanian business students (McGee, 2005b) found that respondents often felt tax evasion was ethically justified. Males were slightly more opposed to tax evasion than were women. A survey of German business students also found that respondents were strongly against tax evasion, although some arguments were stronger than others. A comparison of male to female responses was inconclusive, in the sense that it could not be clearly determined which group of respondents was more opposed to tax evasion (McGee, Nickerson & Fees, 2005).

Three Views on the Ethics of Tax Evasion

Over the centuries, three basic views have emerged on the ethics of tax evasion. View One takes the position that tax evasion is always, or almost always, unethical. There are basically three underlying rationales for this belief. One rationale is the belief that individuals have a duty to the state to pay whatever taxes the state demands (Cohn, 1998; DeMoville, 1998; Smith & Kimball, 1998; Tamari, 1998). This view is especially prevalent in democracies where there is a strong belief that individuals should conform to majority rule.

The second rationale for an ethical duty to pay taxes is because the individual has a duty to other members of the community (Crowe, 1944; Cohn, 1998; Tamari, 1998). This view holds that individuals should not be freeloaders by taking advantage of the services the state provides while not contributing to the payment of those services. A corollary of this belief is the view that if tax dodgers do not pay their fair share, then law-abiding taxpayers must pay more than their fair share.

The third rationale is that we owe a duty to God to pay taxes, or, stated differently, God has commanded us to pay our taxes (Cohn, 1998; DeMoville, 1998; Smith & Kimball, 1998; Tamari, 1998). This view holds no water among atheists, of course, but the view is strongly held in some religious circles.

View Two might be labeled the anarchist view. This view holds that there is never any duty to pay taxes because the state is illegitimate, a mere thief that has no moral authority to take anything from anyone (Block, 1989; 1993). The state is no more than a mafia that, under democracy, has its leaders chosen by the people.

The anarchist literature does not address the ethics of tax evasion directly but rather discusses the relationship of the individual to the state. The issue of tax evasion is merely one aspect of that relationship (Spooner, 1870). There is no such thing as a social contract according to this position. Where there is no explicit agreement to pay taxes, there is also no duty. All taxation necessarily involves the taking of property by force or the threat of force, without the owner's permission. Thus, it meets the definition of theft. Stated as an equation, TAXATION = THEFT. A corollary equation is that FAIR SHARE = 0.

View Three holds that tax evasion may be ethical under some circumstances and unethical under other circumstances. This view is the prevalent view, both in the literature (Ballas & Tsoukas, 1998; Crowe, 1944; Gronbacher, 1998; McGee, 1998a, 1999b); and according to the results of some of the surveys (McGee, 2005a, b; McGee & Lingle, 2005).

The Present Study

After reviewing the literature that exists on the ethics of tax evasion, a survey instrument was constructed and distributed to a group of business students at a university in Hong Kong in order to learn the prevailing views on this issue. The survey consisted of fifteen (15) statements. Using a seven-point Likert scale, respondents were asked to place the appropriate number in the space provided to indicate the extent of their agreement or disagreement with each statement. A total of 60 usable responses were obtained.

Table 19.1 lists the 15 statements and the average scores received for each statement for both groups. A score of one (1) indicates strong agreement with the statement. Seven (7) indicates strong disagreement. An average score or 2 or less would indicate that tax evasion is always, or almost always ethical. An average score of 6 or more would indicate that tax evasion is never or almost never ethical. Scores averaging more than 2 but less than 6 would indicate that tax evasion is sometimes ethical. As can be seen from Table 19.1, the average scores are mostly in the 4 or 5 range. Only one score is above 6.00, indicating that there is widespread acceptance of tax evasion on moral grounds. The strongest obligation to pay taxes is in cases where the taxpayer receives something in exchange for tax payments.

Table 19.2 ranks the arguments from strongest to weakest. The strongest arguments to justify tax evasion are in cases where the tax system is unfair, where the funds wind up in the pockets of corrupt politicians, their family or friends or where the money is wasted. Inability to pay, unjust wars, and high tax rates were also among the top reasons to justify tax evasion.

Table 19.1 Summary of responses

Statement number	Statement	
1	Tax evasion is ethical if tax rates are too high (S1)	4.97
2	Tax evasion is ethical even if tax rates are not too high because the government is not entitled to take as much as it is taking from me (S2)	5.37
3	Tax evasion is ethical if the tax system is unfair (S3)	4.07
4	Tax evasion is ethical if a large portion of the money collected is wasted (S4)	4.47
5	Tax evasion is ethical even if most of the money collected is spent wisely (S5)	5.58
6	Tax evasion is ethical if a large portion of the money collected is spent on projects that I morally disapprove of (S6)	5.23
7	Tax evasion is ethical even if a large portion of the money collected is spent on worthy projects (S7)	5.57
8	Tax evasion is ethical if a large portion of the money collected is spent on projects that do not benefit me (S8)	5.33
9	Tax evasion is ethical even if a large portion of the money collected is spent on projects that do benefit me (S9)	6.15
10	Tax evasion is ethical if everyone is doing it (S10)	5.18
11	Tax evasion is ethical if a significant portion of the money collected winds up in the pockets of corrupt politicians or their families and friends (S11)	4.19
12	Tax evasion is ethical if the probability of getting caught is low (S12)	5.47
13	Tax evasion is ethical if some of the proceeds go to support a war that I consider to be unjust (S13)	4.53
14	Tax evasion is ethical if I cannot afford to pay (S14)	4.60
15	Tax evasion is ethical even if it means that if I pay less, others will have to pay more (S15)	5.15
	Average score	5.06

1 = Strongly agree; 7 = strongly disagree

The weakest arguments to justify tax evasion were in cases where the taxpayer benefits from the tax system and where the money is spent wisely.

Chart 19.1 shows the range of scores for the 15 statements. As can be seen, there is significant support for most of the arguments.

Since studies using a similar survey instrument were done in Macau, Taiwan, Beijing, and Hubei, China, it was thought that a comparison of relative rankings might be interesting. Since the people who live in Hong Kong have been raised in a free market, capitalist system, it is possible that the relative rankings they assign to the various arguments to justify tax evasion might be different from the rankings assigned by those who live on the Chinese mainland. It might be assumed that the rankings for Macau might be very similar to those for Hong Kong, since the two islands are very close in terms of geography, language, and culture. One might speculate about the relative rankings for Taiwan, since the people there have traditionally been vehemently anticommunist and have been raised in a form of market economy. Table 19.3 shows that comparison.

Table 19.2 Ranking of arguments (strongest to weakest)

Rank	Statement	
1	Tax evasion is ethical if the tax system is unfair (S3)	4.07
2	Tax evasion is ethical if a significant portion of the money collected winds up in the pockets of corrupt politicians or their families and friends (S11)	4.19
3	Tax evasion is ethical if a large portion of the money collected is wasted (S4)	4.47
4	Tax evasion is ethical if some of the proceeds go to support a war that I consider to be unjust (S13)	4.53
5	Tax evasion is ethical if I cannot afford to pay (S14)	4.60
6	Tax evasion is ethical if tax rates are too high (S1)	4.97
7	Tax evasion is ethical even if it means that if I pay less, others will have to pay more (S15)	5.15
8	Tax evasion is ethical if everyone is doing it (S10)	5.18
9	Tax evasion is ethical if a large portion of the money collected is spent on projects that I morally disapprove of (S6)	5.23
10	Tax evasion is ethical if a large portion of the money collected is spent on projects that do not benefit me (S8)	5.33
11	Tax evasion is ethical even if tax rates are not too high because the government is not entitled to take as much as it is taking from me (S2)	5.37
12	Tax evasion is ethical if the probability of getting caught is low (S12)	5.47
13	Tax evasion is ethical even if a large portion of the money collected is spent on worthy projects (S7)	5.57
14	Tax evasion is ethical even if most of the money collected is spent wisely (S5)	5.58
15	Tax evasion is ethical even if a large portion of the money collected is spent on projects that do benefit me (S9)	6.15

1 = Strongly agree; 7 = strongly disagree

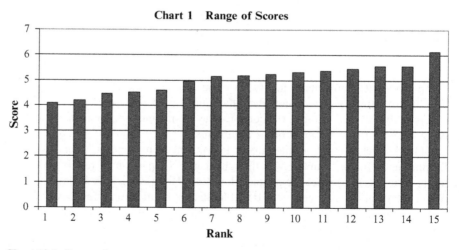

Chart 19.1 Range of scores

Table 19.3 Comparison of arguments ranking

Statement	Hong Kong (present study)	Macau (McGee, Noronha & Tyler, 2007)	Taiwan (McGee & Andres, 2009)	Beijing, China (McGee & An, 2008)	Hubei, China (McGee & Guo, 2007)
Tax evasion is ethical if the tax system is unfair (S3)	1	3	2	3	4
Tax evasion is ethical if a significant portion of the money collected winds up in the pockets of corrupt politicians or their families and friends (S11)	2	1	1	2	1
Tax evasion is ethical if a large portion of the money collected is wasted (S4)	3	4	3	1	2
Tax evasion is ethical if some of the proceeds go to support a war that I consider to be unjust (S13)	4	2	6	4	5
Tax evasion is ethical if I cannot afford to pay (S14)	5	5	5	5	6
Tax evasion is ethical if tax rates are too high (S1)	6	7	4	6	8
Tax evasion is ethical even if it means that if I pay less, others will have to pay more (S15)	7	10	13	11	11
Tax evasion is ethical if everyone is doing it (S10)	8	8	8	8	9
Tax evasion is ethical if a large portion of the money collected is spent on projects that I morally disapprove of (S6)	9	6	10	7	6

(continued)

R.W. McGee and Y.Y. Butt

Table 19.3 (continued)

Statement	Hong Kong (present study)	Macau (McGee, Noronha & Tyler, 2007)	Taiwan (McGee & Andres, 2009)	Beijing, China (McGee & An, 2008)	Hubei, China (McGee & Guo, 2007)
Tax evasion is ethical if a large portion of the money collected is spent on projects that do not benefit me (S8)	10	11	11	10	10
Tax evasion is ethical even if tax rates are not too high because the government is not entitled to take as much as it is taking from me (S2)	11	12	7	8	11
Tax evasion is ethical if the probability of getting caught is low (S12)	12	9	9	11	13
Tax evasion is ethical even if a large portion of the money collected is spent on worthy projects (S7)	13	15	15	13	14
Tax evasion is ethical even if most of the money collected is spent wisely (S5)	14	14	14	15	2
Tax evasion is ethical even if a large portion of the money collected is spent on projects that do benefit me (S9)	15	13	12	13	14

Table 19.4 Comparison by gender

Statement number	Average male score (17)	Average female score (36)	Larger by	
			Male	Female
1	5	5		
2	5.1	5.4		0.3
3	4	4.2		0.2
4	4.4	4.7		0.3
5	5.8	5.5	0.3	
6	5.2	5.3		0.1
7	5.9	5.5	0.4	
8	5.6	5.2	0.4	
9	5.7	5.7		
10	5.5	4.9	0.6	
11	4	4.2		0.2
12	5.6	5.4	0.2	
13	4.3	4.6		0.3
14	4.5	4.8		0.3
15	5.3	5.0	0.3	
Average	5.06	5.03	0.03	

1 = Strongly agree; 7 = strongly disagree

As can be seen, most of the rankings were very close together, although there were some exceptions.

Table 19.4 compares scores by gender. There were 17 males and 36 females. A few participants did not indicate their gender. The sample size was too small to do a statistical analysis. However, some information can be gained by comparing average scores for each statement.

The average male score was 5.06, compared to 5.03 for females, indicating that men were slightly more opposed to tax evasion in general than were women. However, the difference in mean score is so small and the sample size was so small that any conclusions drawn would have to be tentative.

Male scores were higher in six cases. Female scores were higher in seven cases. In two cases, the scores were identical.

Chart 19.2 shows the comparisons by gender.

Concluding Comments

The goals of this research project have been achieved. We were able to determine the extent of support for the various arguments that have been made over the last 500 years to justify tax evasion. Basically, there is a good deal of moral support for tax evasion, although some arguments are stronger than others. We were also able to determine the relative strength of the various arguments. It was also found that men and women do not place different emphasis on the various historical arguments.

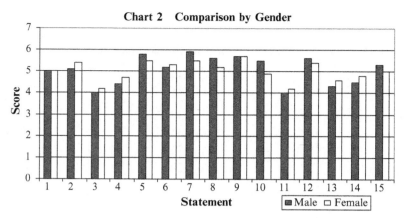

Chart 19.2 Comparison by gender

The fact that respondents are more opposed to tax evasion in some cases than others has policy implications. The survey found that opposition to tax evasion is weakest in cases where the government is corrupt or where the system is perceived as being unfair. Thus, it may be possible to reduce the extent of tax evasion by reducing government corruption and reducing the perceived unfairness of the tax system.

References

Armstrong, M.B. & Robison, J. (1998). Ethics in Taxation. *Journal of Accounting, Ethics & Public Policy*, 1(4), 535–557, reprinted in R.W. McGee (ed.), *The Ethics of Tax Evasion*, Dumont, NJ: The Dumont Institute for Public Policy Research: Dumont, NJ, 1998, pp. 330–348.

Ballas, A. A. & Tsoukas, H. (1998). Consequences of Distrust: The Vicious Circle of Tax Evasion in Greece. *Journal of Accounting, Ethics & Public Policy*, 1(4), 572–596, reprinted in R.W. McGee (ed.), *The Ethics of Tax Evasion*, Dumont, NJ: The Dumont Institute for Public Policy Research: Dumont, NJ, 1998, pp. 284–304.

Block, W. (1989). The Justification of Taxation in the Public Finance Literature: A Critique. *Journal of Public Finance and Public Choice*, 3, 141–158.

Block, W. (1993). Public Finance Texts Cannot Justify Government Taxation: A Critique. *Canadian Public Administration/Administration Publique du Canada*, 36(2), 225–262, reprinted in revised form under the title "The Justification for Taxation in the Economics Literature" in R.W. McGee (ed.), *The Ethics of Tax Evasion*, Dumont, NJ: The Dumont Institute for Public Policy Research: Dumont, NJ, 1998, pp. 36–88.

Cohn, G. (1998). The Jewish View on Paying Taxes. *Journal of Accounting, Ethics & Public Policy*, 1(2), 109–120, reprinted in R.W. McGee (ed.), *The Ethics of Tax Evasion*, Dumont, NJ: The Dumont Institute for Public Policy Research: Dumont, NJ, 1998, pp. 180–189.

Crowe, M.T. (1944). The Moral Obligation of Paying Just Taxes. *The Catholic University of America Studies in Sacred Theology No. 84.*

DeMoville, W. (1998). The Ethics of Tax Evasion: A Baha'i Perspective. *Journal of Accounting, Ethics & Public Policy*, 1(3), 356–368, reprinted in R.W. McGee (ed.), *The Ethics of Tax Evasion*, Dumont, NJ: The Dumont Institute for Public Policy Research: Dumont, NJ, 1998, pp. 230–240.

Gronbacher, G.M.A. (1998). Taxation: Catholic Social Thought and Classical Liberalism. *Journal of Accounting, Ethics & Public Policy*, 1(1), 91–100, reprinted in R.W. McGee (ed.), *The Ethics of Tax Evasion*, Dumont, NJ: The Dumont Institute for Public Policy Research: Dumont, NJ, 1998, pp. 158–167.

Leiker, B. H. (1998). Rousseau and the Legitimacy of Tax Evasion. *Journal of Accounting, Ethics & Public Policy*, 1(1), 45–57, reprinted in R.W. McGee (ed.), *The Ethics of Tax Evasion*, Dumont, NJ: The Dumont Institute for Public Policy Research: Dumont, NJ, 1998, pp. 89–101.

McGee, R.W. (1994). Is Tax Evasion Unethical? *University of Kansas Law Review*, 42(2), 411–435. Reprinted at http://ssrn.com/abstract=74420.

McGee, R.W. (1997). Ethics of Tax Evasion and Trade Protectionism from an Islamic Perspective. *Commentaries on Law & Public Policy*, 1, 250–262. Reprinted at http://ssrn.com/abstract=461397.

McGee, R.W. (Ed.). (1998a). *The Ethics of Tax Evasion*, Dumont, NJ: The Dumont Institute for Public Policy Research: Dumont, NJ.

McGee, R.W. (1998b). Christian Views on the Ethics of Tax Evasion. *Journal of Accounting, Ethics & Public Policy,* 1(2), 210–225. Reprinted at http://ssrn.com/abstract=461398.

McGee, R.W. (1999a). Is It Unethical to Evade Taxes in an Evil or Corrupt State? A Look at Jewish, Christian, Muslim, Mormon and Baha'i Perspectives. *Journal of Accounting, Ethics & Public Policy*, 2(1), 149–181. Reprinted at http://ssrn.com/abstract=251469.

McGee, R.W. (1999b). Why People Evade Taxes in Armenia: A Look at an Ethical Issue Based on a Summary of Interviews. *Journal of Accounting, Ethics & Public Policy*, 2(2), 408–416. Reprinted at http://ssrn.com/abstract=242568.

McGee, R.W. (2005a). The Ethics of Tax Evasion: A Survey of International Business Academics, Presented at the 60th International Atlantic Economic Conference, New York, October 6–9, 2005. Reprinted at http://www.ssrn.com.

McGee, R.W. (2005b). The Ethics of Tax Evasion: A Survey of Romanian Business Students and Faculty. Andreas School of Business Working Paper Series, Barry University, Miami Shores, FL 33161, USA, September. Reprinted at http://www.ssrn.com. Reprinted in R. W. McGee and G. G. Preobragenskaya, *Accounting and Financial System Reform in Eastern Europe and Asia*. Springer: New York, 2006, pp. 299–328.

McGee, Robert W. and Yuhua An. (2008). A Survey of Chinese Business and Economics Students on the Ethics of Tax Evasion, in Robert W. McGee, editor, *Taxation and Public Finance in Transition and Developing Economies* (pp. 409–421). New York: Springer.

McGee, Robert W. and Susana N. Vittadini Andres. (2009). The Ethics of Tax Evasion: Case Studies of Taiwan, in Robert W. McGee, *Readings in Business Ethics* (pp. 200–228). Hyderabad, India: ICFAI University Press. An abbreviated version was published in Marjorie G. Adams and Abbass Alkhafaji, editors, *Business Research Yearbook: Global Business Perspectives*, Volume XIV, No. 1 (pp. 34–39). Beltsville, MD: International Graphics: Beltsville, MD, 2007.

McGee, Robert W. and Zhiwen Guo. (2007). A Survey of Law, Business and Philosophy Students in China on the Ethics of Tax Evasion. *Society and Business Review*, 2(3), 299–315.

McGee, R.W. & Lingle, C. (2005). The Ethics of Tax Evasion: A Survey of Guatemalan Opinion. Presented at the 60th International Atlantic Economic Conference, New York, October 6–9, 2005. Reprinted at http://www.ssrn.com.

McGee, Robert W., Carlos Noronha and Michael Tyler. (2007). The Ethics of Tax Evasion: a Survey of Macau Opinion. *Euro Asia Journal of Management*, 17(2), 123–150. Reprinted in Robert W. McGee (editor), *Readings in Accounting Ethics* (pp. 283–313), Hyderabad, India: ICFAI University Press, 2009.

McGee, R.W., Nickerson, I. & Fees, W. (2005). When Is Tax Evasion Ethically Justifiable? A Survey of German Opinion. *Proceedings of the Academy of Legal, Ethical and Regulatory Issues*, 9(2), 35–38, Las Vegas, October 12–15. http://www.alliedacademies.org/pdf/vegas05/paleri-9-2.pdf.

McGraw, K. M. & Scholz, J.T. (1991). Appeals to Civic Virtue Versus Attention to Self-Interest: Effects on Tax Compliance. *Law and Society Review*, 25(3), 471–498.

Morales, A. (1998). Income Tax Compliance and Alternative Views of Ethics and Human Nature. *Journal of Accounting, Ethics & Public Policy*, 1(3), 380–399, reprinted in R.W. McGee (ed.), *The Ethics of Tax Evasion*, Dumont, NJ: The Dumont Institute for Public Policy Research: Dumont, NJ, 1998, pp. 242–258.

Murtuza, A. & Ghazanfar, S.M. (1998). Taxation as a Form of Worship: Exploring the Nature of Zakat. *Journal of Accounting, Ethics & Public Policy*, 1(2), 134–161, reprinted in R.W. McGee (ed.), *The Ethics of Tax Evasion*, Dumont, NJ: The Dumont Institute for Public Policy Research: Dumont, NJ, 1998, pp. 190–212.

Oliva, R. R. (1998). The Schism between Tax Practitioners' Ethical and Legal Obligations: Recommendations for the Fusion of Law and Ethics. *Journal of Accounting, Ethics & Public Policy*, 1(4), 603–628, reprinted in R.W. McGee (ed.), *The Ethics of Tax Evasion*, Dumont, NJ: The Dumont Institute for Public Policy Research: Dumont, NJ, 1998, pp. 350–371.

Pennock, R. T. (1998). Death and Taxes: On the Justice of Conscientious War Tax Resistance. *Journal of Accounting, Ethics & Public Policy*, 1(1), 58–76, reprinted in R.W. McGee (ed.), *The Ethics of Tax Evasion*, Dumont, NJ: The Dumont Institute for Public Policy Research: Dumont, NJ, 1998, pp. 124–142.

Preobragenskaya, G. G. & McGee, R.W. (2004). Taxation and Public Finance in a Transition Economy: A Case Study of Russia, in Carolyn Gardner, Jerry Biberman and Abbass Alkhafaji (Eds.), *Business Research Yearbook: Global Business Perspectives* Volume XI, Saline, MI: McNaughton & Gunn, Inc., 2004, pp. 254–258. A longer version, which was presented at the Sixteenth Annual Conference of the International Academy of Business Disciplines in San Antonio, March 25–28, 2004, is available at http://ssrn.com/abstract=480862.

Schansberg, D. E. (1998). The Ethics of Tax Evasion within Biblical Christianity: Are There Limits to 'Rendering Unto Caesar'? *Journal of Accounting, Ethics & Public Policy*, 1(1), 77–90, reprinted in R.W. McGee (ed.), *The Ethics of Tax Evasion*, Dumont, NJ: The Dumont Institute for Public Policy Research: Dumont, NJ, 1998, pp. 144–157.

Smatrakalev, G. (1998). Walking on the Edge: Bulgaria and the Transition to a Market Economy, in R.W. McGee (ed.), *The Ethics of Tax Evasion*, Dumont, NJ: The Dumont Institute for Public Policy Research: Dumont, NJ, 1998, pp. 316–329.

Smith, S. R. & Kimball, K.C. (1998). Tax Evasion and Ethics: A Perspective from Members of The Church of Jesus Christ of Latter-Day Saints. *Journal of Accounting, Ethics & Public Policy*, 1(3), 337–348, reprinted in R.W. McGee (ed.), *The Ethics of Tax Evasion*, Dumont, NJ: The Dumont Institute for Public Policy Research: Dumont, NJ, 1998, pp. 220–229.

Spooner, L. (1870). *No Treason: The Constitution of No Authority*, originally self-published by Spooner in Boston in 1870, reprinted by Rampart College in 1965, 1966 and 1971, and by Ralph Myles Publisher, Inc., Colorado Springs, Colorado in 1973.

Tamari, M. (1998). Ethical Issues in Tax Evasion: A Jewish Perspective. *Journal of Accounting, Ethics & Public Policy*, 1(2), 121–132, reprinted in R.W. McGee (ed.), *The Ethics of Tax Evasion*, Dumont, NJ: The Dumont Institute for Public Policy Research: Dumont, NJ, 1998, pp. 168–178.

Torgler, B. (2003). Tax Morale: Theory and Empirical Analysis of Tax Compliance. Dissertation der Universität Basel zur Erlangung der Würde eines Doktors der Staatswissenschaften.

Vaguine, V. V. (1998). The "Shadow Economy" and Tax Evasion in Russia, in R.W. McGee (ed.), *The Ethics of Tax Evasion*, Dumont, NJ: The Dumont Institute for Public Policy Research: Dumont, NJ, 1998, pp. 306–314.

Chapter 20
The Ethics of Tax Evasion: A Study of Indian Opinion

Robert W. McGee and Ravi Kumar Jain

Introduction

Most studies of tax evasion take an economic or public finance perspective. Not much has been written from a philosophical or ethical viewpoint. That is probably because most economists are utilitarians and most lawyers are legalists. However, there is a small body of literature that addresses tax evasion issues from a philosophical or theological perspective. The present study is intended to add to that small body of literature while forming a bridge to the public finance literature as well.

The authors developed a survey instrument that included eighteen (18) statements incorporating the three major views on the ethics of tax evasion that have emerged in the literature over the last 500 years. The survey was distributed to a group of business and engineering students and faculty in India. This paper reports on the results of that survey.

Methodology

After reviewing the literature that exists on the ethics of tax evasion, a survey was constructed and distributed to a group of graduate and undergraduate business and engineering students and faculty in order to learn their views on the ethics of tax evasion. This group was selected because they will be the future business and

R.W. McGee (✉)
School of Business, Florida International University,
3000 NE 151 Street, North Miami, FL 33181, USA
e-mail: bob414@hotmail.com

R.K. Jain
ICFAI Business School, Hyderabad Campus, IFHE University,
Survey No. 156/157 Dontanpally Village Shankerpally Mandal
Ranga Reddy District – 501 504, Andhra Pradesh, India

R.W. McGee (ed.), *The Ethics of Tax Evasion: Perspectives in Theory and Practice*,
DOI 10.1007/978-1-4614-1287-8_20, © Springer Science+Business Media, LLC 2012

political leaders of India. Due to space constraints, the literature is not reviewed here. However, the relevant literature is listed in the reference section.

The survey consisted of eighteen (18) statements. Using a seven-point Likert scale, respondents were asked to place the appropriate number in the space provided to indicate the extent of their agreement or disagreement with each statement. The statements in the survey reflected the three main viewpoints on the ethics of tax evasion that have emerged over the centuries. Four hundred and sixty-eight (468) usable responses were received.

Survey Findings

The next few sections report on the study's findings.

Demographics

Table 20.1 lists the demographics of the survey. The sample was almost evenly divided between males and females. The largest group by academic major was accounting, followed closely by other business and economics majors. There was also a fair representation of engineering majors. Slightly more than 200 participants have an unknown major because some of the surveys distributed did not ask for student major. Most of the participants were either graduate students or faculty members. The group was overwhelmingly Hindu.

The 18 Statements

Table 20.2 lists the 18 statements that were used in the survey instrument and shows the mean scores. The first 15 statements were selected based on the arguments Crowe (1944) identified to justify tax evasion in the last 500 years of literature discussion. The last three statements were added to reflect more recent human rights issues.

The average mean score was 4.88, which indicates a fair degree of support for tax evasion.

Ranking

Some arguments to justify tax evasion are stronger than others. It was thought that ranking the arguments by strength would yield some useful information.

Table 20.1 Demographics

Gender		Academic major	
Male	250	Accounting	126
Female	215	Other business/economics	95
Unknown	3	Engineering	46
Total	468	Other/unknown	201
		Total	468
Student Status		*Religion*	
Graduate	264	Hindu	423
Undergraduate	17	Muslim	11
Faculty	96	Christian	16
Other/unknown	91	Other/unknown	18
Total	468	Total	468

Table 20.2 Summary of responses

Statement number	Statement	Mean
1	Tax evasion is ethical if tax rates are too high (S1)	4.69
2	Tax evasion is ethical even if tax rates are not too high because the government is not entitled to take as much as it is taking from me (S2)	5.49
3	Tax evasion is ethical if the tax system is unfair (S3)	3.72
4	Tax evasion is ethical if a large portion of the money collected is wasted (S4)	3.57
5	Tax evasion is ethical even if most of the money collected is spent wisely (S5)	5.93
6	Tax evasion is ethical if a large portion of the money collected is spent on projects that I morally disapprove of (S6)	4.91
7	Tax evasion is ethical even if a large portion of the money collected is spent on worthy projects (S7)	5.85
8	Tax evasion is ethical if a large portion of the money collected is spent on projects that do not benefit me (S8)	5.48
9	Tax evasion is ethical even if a large portion of the money collected is spent on projects that do benefit me (S9)	5.71
10	Tax evasion is ethical if everyone is doing it (S10)	5.74
11	Tax evasion is ethical if a significant portion of the money collected winds up in the pockets of corrupt politicians or their families and friends (S11)	3.61
12	Tax evasion is ethical if the probability of getting caught is low (S12)	5.66
13	Tax evasion is ethical if some of the proceeds go to support a war that I consider to be unjust (S13)	4.85
14	Tax evasion is ethical if I can't afford to pay (S14)	4.36
15	Tax evasion is ethical even if it means that if I pay less, others will have to pay more (S15)	5.57
16	Tax evasion would be ethical if I were a victim of an oppressive regime like Nazi Germany or Stalinist Russia (S16)	4.27
17	Tax evasion is ethical if the government discriminates against me because of my religion, race, or ethnic background (S17)	4.03
18	Tax evasion is ethical if the government imprisons people for their political opinions (S18)	4.37
	Average	4.88

1 = strongly agree; 7 = strongly disagree

Table 20.3 Ranking

Rank	Statement	Mean
1	Tax evasion is ethical if a large portion of the money collected is wasted (S4)	3.57
2	Tax evasion is ethical if a significant portion of the money collected winds up in the pockets of corrupt politicians or their families and friends (S11)	3.61
3	Tax evasion is ethical if the tax system is unfair (S3)	3.72
4	Tax evasion is ethical if the government discriminates against me because of my religion, race, or ethnic background (S17)	4.03
5	Tax evasion would be ethical if I were a victim of an oppressive regime like Nazi Germany or Stalinist Russia (S16)	4.27
6	Tax evasion is ethical if I can't afford to pay (S14)	4.36
7	Tax evasion is ethical if the government imprisons people for their political opinions (S18)	4.37
8	Tax evasion is ethical if tax rates are too high (S1)	4.69
9	Tax evasion is ethical if some of the proceeds go to support a war that I consider to be unjust (S13)	4.85
10	Tax evasion is ethical if a large portion of the money collected is spent on projects that I morally disapprove of (S6)	4.91
11	Tax evasion is ethical if a large portion of the money collected is spent on projects that do not benefit me (S8)	5.48
12	Tax evasion is ethical even if tax rates are not too high because the government is not entitled to take as much as it is taking from me (S2)	5.49
13	Tax evasion is ethical even if it means that if I pay less, others will have to pay more (S15)	5.57
14	Tax evasion is ethical if the probability of getting caught is low (S12)	5.66
15	Tax evasion is ethical even if a large portion of the money collected is spent on projects that do benefit me (S9)	5.71
16	Tax evasion is ethical if everyone is doing it (S10)	5.74
17	Tax evasion is ethical even if a large portion of the money collected is spent on worthy projects (S7)	5.85
18	Tax evasion is ethical even if most of the money collected is spent wisely (S5)	5.93

1 = strongly agree; 7 = strongly disagree

Table 20.3 ranks the statements from strongest to weakest argument supporting tax evasion. The range of mean scores was 3.57–5.93, which indicates both that there is a fair degree of support for tax evasion in some cases and that some arguments are stronger or more persuasive than others. The difference in mean scores between the highest and lowest ranked arguments was significant at the 1% level ($p < 0.0001$).

The most persuasive argument to justify tax evasion was the case where a large portion of the money collected is wasted. Only slightly weaker was the case where a significant portion of the money winds up in the pockets of corrupt politicians or their families and friends. Other strong arguments to support tax evasion were in cases where the tax system is perceived as being unfair, where the government discriminates on the basis of religion, race, or ethnic background, where the taxpayer is a victim of an oppressive regime and where there is an inability to pay.

Other strong arguments to support evasion were in cases where the government imprisons people for their political opinions, where tax rates are too high, or where the proceeds go to support a war that is perceived as being unjust.

Some of the weakest arguments to justify tax evasion were in cases where the tax funds are spent wisely or for worthy projects, where everyone is doing it or where the funds are spent on projects that benefit the taxpayer.

Comparisons with Other Studies

A similar survey instrument was used to learn the opinions of students in several other countries. Table 20.4 shows the relative ranking for some other studies and compares those rankings to the rankings for the nine strongest arguments in the present study.

The comparison was interesting. In the case of Thailand, another Asian country, the same nine arguments were ranked among the top 9 statements, although the ranking was different. The same was true for Argentina and Estonia. In the cases of Germany and the USA, 8 of the 9 statements in the top 9 for India were also in the top 9 for Germany and the USA.

One conclusion that can be drawn is that the strongest arguments used to justify tax evasion are similar across a wide range of countries, ethnicities, cultures, and religions. Further research is needed to determine the reasons for the differences in rankings for particular arguments.

Gender

Gender is perhaps the most frequently studied demographic variable in the social science literature. A number of studies have examined gender in conjunction with various ethical issues or behaviors. Some studies concluded that women are more ethical than men (Akaah, 1989; Beltramini et al., 1984; Beu et al., 2003; Dawson, 1997; Ferrell and Skinner, 1988; Hoffman, 1998). Other studies found that there is no significant difference between men's and women's views on ethical issues (Babakus et al., 2004; Browning & Zabriskie, 1983; Callan, 1992; Dubinsky & Levy, 1985; Roxas & Stoneback, 2004). A few studies have found that men are more ethical than women (Barnett & Karson 1989; Weeks et al., 1999).

Several studies on attitudes toward tax evasion have also examined gender differences. Women were found to be more opposed to tax evasion in Australia (McGee & Bose, 2009), China (McGee & Guo, 2007), Colombia (McGee, López & Yepes, 2009), Estonia (McGee, Alver & Alver, 2008), Germany (McGee, Nickerson & Fees, 2006), Guatemala (McGee & Lingle, 2008), New Zealand (Gupta & McGee, 2010),

Table 20.4 Comparison of relative rankings with other studies. Nine strongest arguments to justify tax evasion

Statement	Rank comparisons with other studies					
	India (present study)	Argentina (McGee & Rossi, 2008)	Estonia (McGee, Alver & Alver, 2008)	Germany (McGee, Nickerson & Fees, 2009)	USA (McGee & Smith, 2009)	Thailand (McGee 2008)
Tax evasion is ethical if a large portion of the money collected is wasted	1	6	8	5	5	3
Tax evasion is ethical if a significant portion of the money collected winds up in the pockets of corrupt politicians or their families and friends	2	3	1	3	2	1
Tax evasion is ethical if the tax system is unfair	3	4	4	6	4	2
Tax evasion is ethical if the government discriminates against me because of my religion, race, or ethnic background	4	5	3	1	3	6
Tax evasion would be ethical if I were a victim of an oppressive regime like Nazi Germany or Stalinist Russia	5	1	5	2	6	5
Tax evasion is ethical if I can't afford to pay	6	1	7	8	7	3
Tax evasion is ethical if the government imprisons people for their political opinions	7	9	1	4	1	7
Tax evasion is ethical if tax rates are too high	8	7	9	10	9	9
Tax evasion is ethical if some of the proceeds go to support a war that I consider to be unjust	9	7	6	7	10	8

Table 20.5 Statistical data – gender

Statement	Male			Female		
	Sample	Mean	SD	Sample	Mean	SD
1	250	4.63	1.97	214	4.77	1.90
2	246	5.46	1.65	213	5.52	1.64
3	249	3.76	2.09	215	3.66	2.03
4	248	3.66	2.01	214	3.48	2.06
5	248	5.93	1.59	214	5.93	1.54
6	244	4.97	1.81	213	4.86	1.60
7	250	5.96	1.64	214	5.73	1.71
8	248	5.52	1.58	213	5.42	1.48
9	248	5.70	1.65	213	5.73	1.47
10	250	5.76	1.64	213	5.71	1.60
11	248	3.77	2.40	208	3.40	2.29
12	250	5.62	1.54	210	5.70	1.33
13	248	5.02	1.86	211	4.64	1.66
14	248	4.46	2.02	211	4.22	1.85
15	246	5.57	1.48	211	5.57	1.37
16	248	4.32	2.05	209	4.20	1.89
17	248	4.08	2.22	212	3.95	2.05
18	249	4.47	2.08	211	4.24	1.98
Mean average		4.93			4.82	

1 = strongly agree; 7 = strongly disagree

Puerto Rico (McGee & López, 2007), South Africa (McGee & Goldman, 2010), Taiwan (McGee & Andres, 2009), and Thailand (McGee, 2008). Men were found to be more opposed to tax evasion in Romania (McGee, 2006), Slovakia (McGee & Tusan, 2008), and Turkey (McGee & Benk, 2011). Other studies found that there was no significant difference between male and female opinions regarding the ethics of tax evasion. Those studies were for Argentina (McGee & Rossi, 2008), China (McGee & An, 2008), Southern China and Macau (McGee & Noronha, 2008), France (McGee & M'Zali, 2009), Hong Kong (McGee & Butt, 2008), Kazakhstan (McGee & Preobragenskaya, 2008), Macau (McGee, Noronha & Tyler, 2007), and Poland (McGee & Bernal, 2006).

One reason given for women being more ethical is because they are more likely to defer to authority. In cases where women and men had similar views on ethical issues, one reason given was because women's views are becoming closer to men's views as they become liberated.

Table 20.5 shows the sample size, mean scores, and standard deviations for each statement classified by gender.

The overall means scores indicate that men (4.93) were somewhat more opposed to tax evasion than women (4.82). Table 20.6 compares the male and female scores for each statement and shows the p value and extent of significance for each statement. Women were more opposed to tax evasion in only 4 of 18 cases. Men were more opposed in 12 cases. In 2 cases the male and female mean scores were

Table 20.6 Comparison of male and female mean scores

Statement number	Statement	Male	Female	Mean larger by Male	Mean larger by Female	p value
1	Tax evasion is ethical if tax rates are too high	4.63	4.77		0.14	0.4383
2	Tax evasion is ethical even if tax rates are not too high because the government is not entitled to take as much as it is taking from me	5.46	5.52		0.06	0.6970
3	Tax evasion is ethical if the tax system is unfair	3.76	3.66	0.10		0.6207
4	Tax evasion is ethical if a large portion of the money collected is wasted	3.66	3.48	0.18		0.3432
5	Tax evasion is ethical even if most of the money collected is spent wisely	5.93	5.93			1.0000
6	Tax evasion is ethical if a large portion of the money collected is spent on projects that I morally disapprove of	4.97	4.86	0.11		0.4944
7	Tax evasion is ethical even if a large portion of the money collected is spent on worthy projects	5.96	5.73	0.23		0.1405
8	Tax evasion is ethical if a large portion of the money collected is spent on projects that do not benefit me.	5.52	5.42	0.10		0.4858
9	Tax evasion is ethical even if a large portion of the money collected is spent on projects that do benefit me	5.70	5.73		0.03	0.8380
10	Tax evasion is ethical if everyone is doing it	5.76	5.71	0.05		0.7411
11	Tax evasion is ethical if a significant portion of the money collected winds up in the pockets of corrupt politicians or their families and friends	3.77	3.40	0.37		0.0948**
12	Tax evasion is ethical if the probability of getting caught is low	5.62	5.70		0.08	0.5553
13	Tax evasion is ethical if some of the proceeds go to support a war that I consider to be unjust	5.02	4.64	0.38		0.0224*
14	Tax evasion is ethical if I can't afford to pay	4.46	4.22	0.24		0.1880

(continued)

Table 20.6   (continued)

Statement number	Statement	Male	Female	Mean larger by		p value
				Male	Female	
15	Tax evasion is ethical even if it means that if I pay less, others will have to pay more	5.57	5.57			1.0000
16	Tax evasion would be ethical if I were a victim of an oppressive regime like Nazi Germany or Stalinist Russia	4.32	4.20	0.12		0.5186
17	Tax evasion is ethical if the government discriminates against me because of my religion, race, or ethnic background	4.08	3.95	0.13		0.5167
18	Tax evasion is ethical if the government imprisons people for their political opinions	4.47	4.24	0.23		0.2273
Average		4.93	4.82			

1 = strongly agree; 7 = strongly disagree
*Significant at the 5% level
**Significant at the 10% level

identical. Men were significantly more opposed in only one case, if significance is defined as ($p = 0.05$). Thus, we may conclude that men are slightly more opposed to tax evasion in most cases but the difference is usually not significant.

Student Status

A few other studies have examined student status in conjunction with attitudes on tax evasion. A study of Argentina (McGee & Rossi, 2008) found that students and faculty were equally opposed to tax evasion. An Australian study (McGee & Bose, 2009) found that, overall, undergraduate students were least opposed to tax evasion and faculty members were most opposed to tax evasion. An Estonian study (McGee, Alver & Alver, 2008) found that, overall, undergraduate students were least opposed to tax evasion and faculty members and practitioners were most opposed to tax evasion. A New Zealand study (Gupta & McGee, 2010) found that graduate students were more opposed to tax evasion than undergraduate students.

Table 20.7 shows the sample size, mean scores, and standard deviations for each statement classified by student status. Only the graduate student group and faculty were compared, since the sample sizes for the other categories were too small to have a meaningful analysis.

Table 20.7 Statistical data – student status

Statement	Graduate students			Faculty		
	Sample	Mean	SD	Sample	Mean	SD
1	264	4.45	1.86	95	5.36	1.97
2	261	5.41	3.47	94	5.86	1.75
3	264	3.47	1.94	95	4.59	2.17
4	263	3.30	1.85	95	4.63	2.18
5	261	5.96	1.50	96	6.27	1.36
6	262	4.85	1.64	93	5.28	1.78
7	263	6.05	1.50	96	5.64	2.00
8	262	5.42	1.49	94	5.79	1.52
9	263	5.67	1.53	93	5.95	1.55
10	263	5.66	1.60	95	6.03	1.62
11	258	3.35	2.26	93	4.53	2.50
12	261	5.57	1.46	94	6.11	1.32
13	261	4.69	1.75	94	5.35	1.71
14	260	4.11	1.82	94	4.84	2.13
15	258	5.51	1.39	94	5.86	1.49
16	261	4.08	1.97	92	4.63	1.98
17	261	3.70	2.02	94	4.79	2.22
18	260	4.14	2.00	95	4.96	2.05
Mean average		4.74			5.36	

Table 20.8 compares the graduate student and faculty scores and shows the p value and extent of significance for each statement. Overall, faculty were more opposed to tax evasion than graduate students, as indicated by the overall mean scores (graduate students = 4.74; faculty = 5.36). Faculty were more opposed to tax evasion in 17 of 18 cases. In 13 cases, the difference was significant, if one defines significance as ($p = 0.05$). In the one case where graduate students were more opposed to tax evasion, the difference was significant at the 5% level ($p = 0.0376$). Thus, we can conclude that, generally, faculty are more opposed to tax evasion than graduate students.

Academic Major

A few prior tax evasion studies have compared the views of various student majors. An Argentina study (McGee & Rossi, 2008) found that business and economics majors were more opposed to tax evasion in 16 of 18 cases, compared to law students. An Armenian study (McGee & Maranjyan, 2008) found that business students were more strongly opposed to tax evasion than theology students, although neither group showed strong opposition. An Australian study (McGee & Bose, 2009) found that business and economics students were least opposed to tax evasion among the majors included in the study and that seminary students were most opposed. Accounting majors were ranked between these two groups. A Chinese

Table 20.8 Comparison of graduate student and faculty mean scores

Statement number	Statement	Grad.	Faculty	Mean larger by Grad.	Mean larger by Faculty	p score
1	Tax evasion is ethical if tax rates are too high	4.45	5.36		0.91	0.0001*
2	Tax evasion is ethical even if tax rates are not too high because the government is not entitled to take as much as it is taking from me	5.41	5.86		0.45	0.2299
3	Tax evasion is ethical if the tax system is unfair	3.47	4.59		1.12	0.0001*
4	Tax evasion is ethical if a large portion of the money collected is wasted	3.30	4.63		1.33	0.0001*
5	Tax evasion is ethical even if most of the money collected is spent wisely	5.96	6.27		0.31	0.0769***
6	Tax evasion is ethical if a large portion of the money collected is spent on projects that I morally disapprove of	4.85	5.28		0.43	0.0344**
7	Tax evasion is ethical even if a large portion of the money collected is spent on worthy projects	6.05	5.64	0.41		0.0376**
8	Tax evasion is ethical if a large portion of the money collected is spent on projects that do not benefit me	5.42	5.79		0.37	0.0407**
9	Tax evasion is ethical even if a large portion of the money collected is spent on projects that do benefit me	5.67	5.95		0.28	0.1315
10	Tax evasion is ethical if everyone is doing it	5.66	6.03		0.37	0.0618***
11	Tax evasion is ethical if a significant portion of the money collected winds up in the pockets of corrupt politicians or their families and friends	3.35	4.53		1.18	0.0001*
12	Tax evasion is ethical if the probability of getting caught is low	5.57	6.11		0.54	0.0018*
13	Tax evasion is ethical if some of the proceeds go to support a war that I consider to be unjust	4.69	5.35		0.66	0.0017*
14	Tax evasion is ethical if I can't afford to pay	4.11	4.84		0.73	0.0016*
15	Tax evasion is ethical even if it means that if I pay less, others will have to pay more	5.51	5.86		0.35	0.0411**
16	Tax evasion would be ethical if I were a victim of an oppressive regime like Nazi Germany or Stalinist Russia	4.08	4.63		0.55	0.0221**
17	Tax evasion is ethical if the government discriminates against me because of my religion, race, or ethnic background	3.70	4.79		1.09	0.0001*
18	Tax evasion is ethical if the government imprisons people for their political opinions	4.14	4.96		0.82	0.0008*
Average		4.74	5.36			

1 = strongly agree; 7 = strongly disagree
*Significant at the 1% level
**Significant at the 5% level
***Significant at the 10% level

Table 20.9 statistical
data – academic major

Statement	Accounting			Other business/ economics		
	Sample	Mean	SD	Sample	Mean	SD
1	126	4.90	1.92	94	4.87	1.93
2	126	5.67	1.57	94	5.65	1.54
3	126	3.94	2.18	95	3.85	2.10
4	125	3.72	2.09	95	3.55	2.09
5	126	6.10	1.44	94	6.33	1.17
6	123	5.31	1.55	93	5.27	1.55
7	126	5.90	1.61	95	5.98	1.54
8	126	5.60	1.40	95	5.67	1.65
9	126	5.75	1.58	95	5.91	1.58
10	126	5.73	1.60	95	5.88	1.62
11	126	3.90	2.42	95	3.62	2.50
12	125	5.74	1.31	95	5.91	1.31
13	125	5.04	1.73	95	5.16	1.82
14	126	4.54	1.91	95	4.13	1.99
15	126	5.70	1.24	95	5.75	1.39
16	125	4.70	1.94	95	4.09	1.98
17	125	4.33	2.18	95	3.84	2.13
18	126	4.70	1.99	94	4.20	2.06
Mean average		5.07			4.98	

study (McGee & Guo, 2007) found that business and economics students were less opposed to tax evasion than law and philosophy students and that law and philosophy students were equally opposed to tax evasion. An Estonian study (McGee, Alver & Alver, 2008) found that accounting students and business and economics students were equally opposed to tax evasion.

Table 20.9 shows the sample size, mean scores, and standard deviations for each statement classified by academic major. Only accounting majors and other business/economics majors were compared, since the sample sizes for the other categories were too small to have a meaningful analysis.

Accounting majors were more opposed to tax evasion in 10 of 18 cases. However, the mean scores were significantly different in only one case, if one defines significance as ($p=0.05$). In two other cases, the difference was significant at the 10% level. Thus, all we can say is that accounting majors were slightly more opposed to tax evasion than were the other business and economics majors.

Table 20.10 compares the accounting and other business/economics scores and shows the p value and extent of significance for each statement.

Religion

Comparisons were not made by religion, since the only religion with a sufficiently large sample size was the Hindu religion.

Table 20.10 Comparison of mean scores by academic major

Statement number	Statement	Mean		larger by		p value
		Acc.	OBE	Acc.	OBE	
1	Tax evasion is ethical if tax rates are too high	4.90	4.87	0.03		0.9090
2	Tax evasion is ethical even if tax rates are not too high because the government is not entitled to take as much as it is taking from me	5.67	5.65	0.02		0.9250
3	Tax evasion is ethical if the tax system is unfair	3.94	3.85	0.09		0.7579
4	Tax evasion is ethical if a large portion of the money collected is wasted	3.72	3.55	0.17		0.5507
5	Tax evasion is ethical even if most of the money collected is spent wisely	6.10	6.33		0.23	0.2064
6	Tax evasion is ethical if a large portion of the money collected is spent on projects that I morally disapprove of	5.31	5.27	0.04		0.8512
7	Tax evasion is ethical even if a large portion of the money collected is spent on worthy projects	5.90	5.98		0.08	0.7098
8	Tax evasion is ethical if a large portion of the money collected is spent on projects that do not benefit me	5.60	5.67		0.07	0.7337
9	Tax evasion is ethical even if a large portion of the money collected is spent on projects that do benefit me	5.75	5.91		0.16	0.4568
10	Tax evasion is ethical if everyone is doing it	5.73	5.88		0.15	0.4933
11	Tax evasion is ethical if a significant portion of the money collected winds up in the pockets of corrupt politicians or their families and friends	3.90	3.62	0.28		0.4021
12	Tax evasion is ethical if the probability of getting caught is low	5.74	5.91		0.17	0.3414
13	Tax evasion is ethical if some of the proceeds go to support a war that I consider to be unjust	5.04	5.16		0.12	0.6188
14	Tax evasion is ethical if I can't afford to pay	4.54	4.13	0.41		0.1222
15	Tax evasion is ethical even if it means that if I pay less, others will have to pay more	5.70	5.75		0.05	0.7785
16	Tax evasion would be ethical if I were a victim of an oppressive regime like Nazi Germany or Stalinist Russia	4.70	4.09	0.61		0.0230*
17	Tax evasion is ethical if the government discriminates against me because of my religion, race, or ethnic background	4.33	3.84	0.49		0.0968**
18	Tax evasion is ethical if the government imprisons people for their political opinions	4.70	4.20	0.50		0.0707**
Average		5.07	4.98			

1 = strongly agree; 7 = strongly disagree
*Significant at the 5% level
**Significant at the 10% level

Concluding Comments

The present study is one of the few that have been done soliciting Indian opinion on the ethics of tax evasion. Thus, it makes a contribution to the literature. However, there is room for more research in the area. One possible study would be a comparison of other academic majors. Law and philosophy student opinion would be especially interesting.

The present study sampled Indian university students, who are both younger and more educated than the general population. Thus, the results found may not be applicable to the general population. A study that samples other demographic groups would therefore likely prove fruitful. Older people and professionals, such as accounting and law practitioners, would be logical extensions of the present study. Other possible demographic variables worth examining would be income level, marital status, religion, and region.

References

Akaah, Ishmael P. (1989). Differences in Research Ethics Judgments Between Male and Female Marketing Professionals. *Journal of Business Ethics*, 8(5), 375–381.

Babakus, Emin, T. Bettina Cornwell, Vince Mitchell and Bodo Schlegelmilch (2004). Reactions to Unethical Consumer Behavior across Six Countries. *The Journal of Consumer Marketing*, 21(4/5), 254–263.

Barnett, John H. and Marvin J. Karson. (1989). Managers, Values, and Executive Decisions: An Exploration of the Role of Gender, Career Stage, Organizational Level, Function, and the Importance of Ethics, Relationships and Results in Managerial Decision-Making. *Journal of Business Ethics*, 8(10), 747–771.

Beltramini, Richard F., Robert A. Peterson & George Kozmetsky. (1984). Concerns of College Students Regarding Business Ethics. *Journal of Business Ethics*, 3(3), 195–200.

Beu, Danielle S., M. Ronald Buckley & Michael G. Harvey. (2003). Ethical Decision-Making: A Multidimensional Construct. *Business Ethics: A European Review*, 12(1), 88–107.

Browning, John and Noel B. Zabriskie. (1983). How Ethical Are Industrial Buyers? *Industrial Marketing Management*, 12(4), 219–224.

Callan, Victor J. (1992). Predicting Ethical Values and Training Needs in Ethics. *Journal of Business Ethics*, 11(10), 761–769.

Crowe, Martin T. (1944). The Moral Obligation of Paying Just Taxes, The Catholic University of America Studies in Sacred Theology No. 84.

Dawson, Leslie M. (1997). Ethical Differences Between Men and Women in the Sales Profession. *Journal of Business Ethics*, 16(11), 1143–1152.

Dubinsky, Alan J. and Michael Levy. (1985). Ethics in Retailing: Perceptions of Retail Sales People. *Journal of the Academy of Marketing Science*, 13(1), 1–16.

Ferrell, O.C. and Steven J. Skinner. (1988). Ethical Behavior and Bureaucratic Structure in Marketing Research Organizations. *Journal of Marketing Research*, 25(1), 103–109.

Franke, George R., Deborah F. Crown & Deborah F. Spake. (1997). Gender Differences in Ethical Perceptions of Business Practices: A Social Role Theory Perspective. *Journal of Applied Psychology*, 82(6), 920–934.

Gupta, Ranjana and Robert W. McGee. (2010). A Comparative Study of New Zealanders' Opinion on the Ethics of Tax Evasion: Students v. Accountants. *New Zealand Journal of Taxation Law and Policy*, 16(1), 47–84.

Hoffman, James J. (1998). Are Women Really More Ethical Than Men? Maybe It Depends on the Situation. *Journal of Managerial Issues*, 10(1), 60–73.

McCabe, A. Catherine, Rhea Ingram and Mary Conway Dato-on. (2006). The Business of Ethics and Gender. *Journal of Business Ethics*, 64, 101–116.

McGee, Robert W. (2004). *The Philosophy of Taxation and Public Finance*. Norwell, MA and Dordrecht: Kluwer Academic Publishers.

McGee, Robert W. (2006). The Ethics of Tax Evasion: A Survey of Romanian Business Students and Faculty. *The ICFAI Journal of Public Finance*, 4(2), 38–68 (2006). Reprinted in Robert W. McGee and Galina G. Preobragenskaya, *Accounting and Financial System Reform in Eastern Europe and Asia* (pp. 299–334). New York: Springer, 2006.

McGee, Robert W. and Arkadiusz Bernal. (2006). The Ethics of Tax Evasion: A Survey of Business Students in Poland. In *Global Economy – How It Works* (Mina Baliamoune-Lutz, Alojzy Z. Nowak & Jeff Steagall, eds.) (pp. 155–174). Warsaw: University of Warsaw & Jacksonville: University of North Florida. Reprinted at http://ssrn.com/abstract=875434.

McGee, Robert W., Inge Nickerson and Werner Fees. (2006). German and American Opinion on the Ethics of Tax Evasion. *Proceedings of the Academy of Legal, Ethical and Regulatory Issues* (Reno), 10(2), 31–34.

McGee, Robert W., Carlos Noronha and Michael Tyler. (2007). The Ethics of Tax Evasion: a Survey of Macau Opinion. *Euro Asia Journal of Management*, 17(2), 123–150.

McGee, Robert W. and Silvia López Paláu. 2007. The Ethics of Tax Evasion: Two Empirical Studies of Puerto Rican Opinion. *Journal of Applied Business and Economics*, 7(3), 27–47.

McGee, Robert W. and Zhiwen Guo. (2007). A Survey of Law, Business and Philosophy Students in China on the Ethics of Tax Evasion. *Society and Business Review* 2(3): 299–315.

McGee, Robert W. (2008). Opinions on Tax Evasion in Thailand, in Robert W. McGee, editor, *Taxation and Public Finance in Transition and Developing Economies* (pp. 609–620). New York: Springer.

McGee, Robert W., Jaan Alver and Lehte Alver. (2008). The Ethics of Tax Evasion: A Survey of Estonian Opinion, in Robert W. McGee, editor, *Taxation and Public Finance in Transition and Developing Economies* (pp. 461–480). New York: Springer.

McGee, Robert W. and Yuhua An. (2008). A Survey of Chinese Business and Economics Students on the Ethics of Tax Evasion, in Robert W. McGee, editor, *Taxation and Public Finance in Transition and Developing Economies* (pp. 409–421). New York: Springer.

McGee, Robert W. and Yiu Yu Butt. (2008). An Empirical Study of Tax Evasion Ethics in Hong Kong. Proceedings of the International Academy of Business and Public Administration Disciplines (IABPAD), Dallas, April 24–27: 72–83. Reprinted in the present volume.

McGee, Robert W., Simon S.M. Ho and Annie Y.S. Li. (2008). A Comparative Study on Perceived Ethics of Tax Evasion: Hong Kong vs. the United States. *Journal of Business Ethics*, 77(2), 147–158.

McGee, Robert W. and Christopher Lingle. (2008). The Ethics of Tax Evasion: A Survey of Guatemalan Opinion, in Robert W. McGee, editor, *Taxation and Public Finance in Transition and Developing Economies* (pp. 481–495). New York: Springer.

McGee, Robert W. and Tatyana B. Maranjyan. (2008). Opinions on Tax Evasion in Armenia, in Robert W. McGee, editor, *Taxation and Public Finance in Transition and Developing Economies* (pp. 277–307). New York: Springer.

McGee, Robert W. and Carlos Noronha. (2008). The Ethics of Tax Evasion: A Comparative Study of Guangzhou (Southern China) and Macau Opinions. Euro Asia Journal of Management, 18(2), 133–152.

McGee, Robert W. and Galina G. Preobragenskaya. (2008). A Study of Tax Evasion Ethics in Kazakhstan, in Robert W. McGee, editor, *Taxation and Public Finance in Transition and Developing Economies* (pp. 497–510). New York: Springer.

McGee, Robert W. and Marcelo J. Rossi. (2008). A Survey of Argentina on the Ethics of Tax Evasion, in Robert W. McGee, editor, *Taxation and Public Finance in Transition and Developing Economies* (pp. 239–261). New York: Springer.

McGee, Robert W. and Radoslav Tusan. (2008). The Ethics of Tax Evasion: A Survey of Slovak Opinion, in Robert W. McGee, editor, *Taxation and Public Finance in Transition and Developing Economies* (pp. 575–601). New York: Springer.

McGee, Robert W. and Susana N. Vittadini Andres. (2009). The Ethics of Tax Evasion: Case Studies of Taiwan, in Robert W. McGee, *Readings in Business Ethics* (pp. 200–228). Hyderabad, India: ICFAI University Press. An abbreviated version was published in Marjorie G. Adams and Abbass Alkhafaji, editors, *Business Research Yearbook: Global Business Perspectives*, Volume XIV, No. 1 (pp. 34–39). Beltsville, MD: International Graphics: Beltsville, MD, 2007.

McGee, Robert W., Meliha Basic and Michael Tyler. (2009). The Ethics of Tax Evasion: A Survey of Bosnian Opinion, *Journal of Balkan and Near Eastern Studies*, 11(2), 197–207.

McGee, Robert W. and Sanjoy Bose. (2009). The Ethics of Tax Evasion: A Survey of Australian Opinion, in Robert W. McGee, *Readings in Business Ethics* (pp. 143–166). Hyderabad, India: ICFAI University Press.

McGee, Robert W. and Bouchra M'Zali. (2009). The Ethics of Tax Evasion: An Empirical Study of French EMBA Students, in Robert W. McGee, *Readings in Business Ethics* (pp. 185–199). Hyderabad, India: ICFAI University Press. An abbreviated version was published in Marjorie G. Adams and Abbass Alkhafaji, editors, *Business Research Yearbook: Global Business Perspectives*, Volume XIV, No. 1 (pp. 27–33). Beltsville, MD: International Graphics, 2007).

McGee, Robert W., Inge Nickerson and Werner Fees. (2009). When Is Tax Evasion Ethically Justifiable? A Survey of German Opinion, in Robert W. McGee, editor, *Readings in Accounting Ethics* (pp. 365–389). Hyderabad, India: ICFAI University Press.

McGee, Robert W., Silvia López Paláu and Gustavo A. Yepes Lopez. (2009). The Ethics of Tax Evasion: An Empirical Study of Colombian Opinion, in Robert W. McGee, *Readings in Business Ethics* (pp. 167–184). Hyderabad, India: ICFAI University Press.

McGee, Robert W. and Sheldon R. Smith. 2009. Ethics and Tax Evasion: A Comparative Study of Utah and Florida Opinion, in Robert W. McGee (Ed.), *Readings in Accounting Ethics* (pp. 343–364). Hyderabad, India: ICFAI University Press.

McGee, Robert W. & Geoffrey A. Goldman (2010). Ethics and Tax Evasion: A Survey of South African Opinion. *Proceedings of the Third Annual University of Johannesburg Faculty of Management Conference*, May 12–14. Reprinted in the present volume.

McGee, Robert W. & Serkan Benk (2011). The Ethics of Tax Evasion: A Study of Turkish Opinion. *Journal of Balkan and Near Eastern Studies*, forthcoming.

Roxas, Maria L. & Jane Y. Stoneback. (2004). The Importance of Gender Across Cultures in Ethical Decision-Making. *Journal of Business Ethics*, 50,149-165.

Torgler, Benno. (2003). To evade taxes or not to evade: that is the question. *The Journal of Socio-Economics*, 32, 283–302.

Torgler, Benno. (2006). The Importance of Faith: Tax Morale and Religiosity. *Journal of Economic Behavior & Organization*, 61, 81–109.

Weeks, William A., Carlos W. Moore, Joseph A. McKinney & Justin G. Longenecker. (1999). The Effects of Gender and Career Stage on Ethical Judgment. *Journal of Business Ethics*, 20(4), 301–313.

Chapter 21
Ethics and Tax Evasion: A Survey of South African Opinion

Robert W. McGee and Geoff A. Goldman

Introduction

The vast majority of articles that have been written about tax evasion have been written from the perspective of public finance. They discuss technical aspects of tax evasion and the primary and secondary effects that tax evasion has on an economy. In many cases, there is also a discussion about how to prevent or minimize tax evasion. Very few articles discuss ethical aspects of tax evasion. Thus, there is a need for further research which the present study is intended to partially address.

As part of this study, a survey instrument was developed based on the issues that have been discussed and the arguments that have been made in the tax evasion ethics literature over the last 500 years. Similar survey instruments were used to test sample populations in Romania (McGee 2005b) and Guatemala (McGee & Lingle 2005). The survey was also distributed to professors of international business (McGee 2005a). The present study reports on the findings of a survey that was distributed to management, economics, and finance students at a university in South Africa. The survey instrument consisted of 18 statements that reflect the three views on the ethics of tax evasion that have emerged over the centuries. Participants were asked to rate the extent of their agreement with each statement by placing a number from 1 to 7 in the space provided. Scores were compared to determine whether the responses were significantly different by gender, age, ethnicity, religion, student status, and major.

R.W. McGee (✉)
School of Business, Florida International University,
3000 NE 151 Street, North Miami, FL 33181, USA
e-mail: bob414@hotmail.com

G.A. Goldman
Department of Business Management, University of Johannesburg,
D-Ring 530 (Kingsway Campus), Auckland Park, PO Box 524,
2006 Johannesburg, Gauteng, South Africa

R.W. McGee (ed.), *The Ethics of Tax Evasion: Perspectives in Theory and Practice*,
DOI 10.1007/978-1-4614-1287-8_21, © Springer Science+Business Media, LLC 2012

Review of the Literature

Although many studies have been done on tax compliance, very few have examined compliance, or rather noncompliance, primarily from the perspective of ethics. Most studies on tax evasion look at the issue from a public finance or economics perspective, although ethical issues may be mentioned briefly, in passing. The most comprehensive twentieth century work on the ethics of tax evasion was a doctoral thesis written by Martin Crowe (1944), titled *The Moral Obligation of Paying Just Taxes*. This thesis reviewed the theological and philosophical debate that had been going on, mostly within the Catholic Church, over the previous 500 years. Some of the debate took place in the Latin language. Crowe introduced this debate to an English language readership. A more recent doctoral dissertation on the topic was written by Torgler (2003), who discussed tax evasion from the perspective of public finance but also touched on some psychological and philosophical aspects of the issue.

Walter Block (1989; 1993) sought in vain to find a justification for taxation in the public finance literature. He examined a number of textbooks but found all justifications for taxation to be inadequate. Leiker (1998) speculates on how Rousseau would have viewed the ethics of tax evasion. Alfonso Morales (1998) examined the views of Mexican immigrant street vendors and found that their loyalty to their families exceeded their loyalty to the government. McGraw and Scholz (1991) examined tax compliance from the perspective of self-interest. Armstrong and Robison (1998) discuss tax evasion and tax avoidance from the perspective of an accounting practitioner and used Rawls' concept of two kinds of rules to analyze how accountants view the issue. Oliva (1998) looked at the issue from the perspective of a tax practitioner and commented on the schism that exists between a tax practitioner's ethical and legal obligations.

There have been a few studies that focus on tax evasion in a particular country. Ethics are sometimes discussed but, more often than not, the focus of the discussion is on government corruption and the reasons why the citizenry does not feel any moral duty to pay taxes to such a government. Ballas and Tsoukas (1998) discuss the situation in Greece. Smatrakalev (1998) discusses the Bulgarian case. Vaguine (1998) discusses Russia, as do Preobragenskaya and McGee (2004) to a lesser extent. A study of tax evasion in Armenia (McGee, 1999b) found the two main reasons for evasion to be the lack of a mechanism in place to collect taxes and the widespread opinion that the government does not deserve a portion of a worker's income.

A number of articles have been written from various religious perspectives. Cohn (1998), McGee & Cohn (2006, 2008) and Tamari (1998) discuss the Jewish literature on tax evasion and on ethics in general. Much of this literature is in Hebrew or a language other than English. McGee (1999a) comments on these two articles from a secular perspective.

A few articles have been written on the ethics of tax evasion from various Christian viewpoints. Gronbacher (1998) addresses the issue from the perspectives of Catholic social thought and classical liberalism. Schansberg (1998) looks at the Biblical literature for guidance. Pennock (1998) discusses just war theory in connection with the moral obligation to pay just taxes, and not to pay unjust or immoral taxes. Smith and Kimball (1998) provide a Mormon perspective. McGee (1998b; 1999a) comments on the various Christian views from a secular perspective.

The Christian Bible discusses tax evasion and the duty of the citizenry to support the government in several places. Schansberg (1998) and McGee (1994; 1998a) discuss the biblical literature on this point. When Jesus is asked whether people should pay taxes to Caesar, Jesus replied that we should give to Caesar the things that are Caesar's and give God the things that are God's [Matthew 22:17, 21]. But Jesus did not elaborate on the point. He did not say that we are only obligated to give the government 10% or 5% or any particular percent of our income.

A few other religious views are also addressed in the literature. Murtuza and Ghazanfar (1998) discuss the ethics of tax evasion from the Muslim perspective. McGee (1999a) comments on their article and also discusses the ethics of tax evasion under Islam citing Islamic business ethics literature (McGee 1997). DeMoville (1998) discusses the Baha'i perspective and cites the relevant literature to buttress his arguments. McGee (1999a) commented on the DeMoville article.

A similar survey of international business professors found that some arguments justifying tax evasion are stronger than others but none of the arguments were very strong, since most of the professors who responded to the survey were strongly against tax evasion. This survey also found that women were significantly more opposed to tax evasion than were the men (McGee, 2005a). A survey of business and law students in Guatemala reached a similar result. However, the law students felt less strongly about condemning tax evasion on ethical grounds than did the business students, and female students were more opposed to tax evasion than were male students (McGee & Lingle, 2005). A survey of Romanian business students (McGee, 2005b) found that respondents often felt tax evasion was ethically justified. Males were slightly more opposed to tax evasion than were women. A survey of German business students also found that respondents were strongly against tax evasion, although some arguments were stronger than others. A comparison of male to female responses was inconclusive, in the sense that it could not be clearly determined which group of respondents was more opposed to tax evasion (McGee, Nickerson & Fees, 2005).

Three Views on the Ethics of Tax Evasion

Over the centuries, three basic views have emerged on the ethics of tax evasion. View One takes the position that tax evasion is always, or almost always, unethical. There are basically three underlying rationales for this belief. One rationale is the belief that individuals have a duty to the state to pay whatever taxes the state demands (Cohn, 1998; DeMoville, 1998; Smith & Kimball, 1998; Tamari, 1998). This view is especially prevalent in democracies where there is a strong belief that individuals should conform to majority rule.

The second rationale for an ethical duty to pay taxes is because the individual has a duty to other members of the community (Crowe, 1944; Cohn, 1998; Tamari, 1998). This view holds that individuals should not be freeloaders by taking advantage of the services the state provides while not contributing to the payment of those services. A corollary of this belief is the view that if tax dodgers do not pay their fair share, then law-abiding taxpayers must pay more than their fair share.

The third rationale is that we owe a duty to God to pay taxes, or, stated differently, God has commanded us to pay our taxes (Cohn, 1998; DeMoville, 1998; Smith & Kimball, 1998; Tamari, 1998). This view holds no water among atheists, of course, but the view is strongly held in some religious circles.

View Two might be labeled the anarchist view. This view holds that there is never any duty to pay taxes because the state is illegitimate, a mere thief that has no moral authority to take anything from anyone (Block, 1989; 1993). The state is no more than a mafia that, under democracy, has its leaders chosen by the people.

The anarchist literature does not address the ethics of tax evasion directly but rather discusses the relationship of the individual to the state. The issue of tax evasion is merely one aspect of that relationship (Spooner, 1870). There is no such thing as a social contract according to this position. Where there is no explicit agreement to pay taxes, there also is no duty. All taxation necessarily involves the taking of property by force or the threat of force, without the owner's permission. Thus, it meets the definition of theft. Stated as an equation, TAXATION = THEFT. A corollary equation is that FAIR SHARE = 0.

View Three holds that tax evasion may be ethical under some circumstances and unethical under other circumstances. This view is the prevalent view, both in the literature (Ballas & Tsoukas, 1998; Crowe, 1944; Gronbacher, 1998; McGee, 1998a, 1999b) and according to the results of some of the surveys (McGee and Robert 2005a&b; McGee & Lingle, 2005).

The Present Study

After reviewing the literature that exists on the ethics of tax evasion, a survey instrument was constructed and distributed to a group of management, economics, and finance students at a university in South Africa. The survey consisted of eighteen (18) statements. Using a seven-point Likert scale, respondents were asked to place the appropriate number in the space provided to indicate the extent of their agreement or disagreement with each statement. A total of 191 usable responses were obtained.

Table 21.1 lists the demographic details. The sample consisted mostly of young, African management, non-Catholic Christian students. More than half of the participants were female. Students were at the diploma, undergraduate, and graduate levels.

Table 21.2 summarizes the results for each of the 18 statements. The average for all 18 statements was 4.967, on a scale of 1–7 where 1 represents strong agreement

Table 21.1 Demographics

Gender		Age	
Male	72	Under 25	104
Female	101	25–40	53
Unknown	18	Over 40	3
Total	191	Unknown	31
		Total	191
Major		*Ethnicity*	
Management	135	White	32
Economics and finance	34	African	121
Humanities	9	Colored	13
Unknown	13	Asian	5
Total	191	Other	2
		Unknown	18
		Total	191
Religion		*Student status*	
Catholic	40	Diploma student	65
Other Christian	106	Undergraduate student	56
Jewish	2	Postgraduate student	68
Muslim	2	Unknown	2
None/atheist/agnostic	5	Total	191
Other	13		
Unknown	23		
Total	191		

Table 21.2 Summary of responses

Statement number	Statement	Mean
1	Tax evasion is ethical if tax rates are too high (S1)	4.895
2	Tax evasion is ethical even if tax rates are not too high because the government is not entitled to take as much as it is taking from me (S2)	5.217
3	Tax evasion is ethical if the tax system is unfair (S3)	4.316
4	Tax evasion is ethical if a large portion of the money collected is wasted (S4)	4.168
5	Tax evasion is ethical even if most of the money collected is spent wisely (S5)	5.314
6	Tax evasion is ethical if a large portion of the money collected is spent on projects that I morally disapprove of (S6)	5.070
7	Tax evasion is ethical even if a large portion of the money collected is spent on worthy projects (S7)	5.122
8	Tax evasion is ethical if a large portion of the money collected is spent on projects that do not benefit me (S8)	5.307
9	Tax evasion is ethical even if a large portion of the money collected is spent on projects that do benefit me (S9)	5.282
10	Tax evasion is ethical if everyone is doing it (S10)	5.516
11	Tax evasion is ethical if a significant portion of the money collected winds up in the pockets of corrupt politicians or their families and friends (S11)	4.879

(continued)

Table 21.2 (continued)

Statement number	Statement	Mean
12	Tax evasion is ethical if the probability of getting caught is low (S12)	5.720
13	Tax evasion is ethical if some of the proceeds go to support a war that I consider to be unjust (S13)	4.883
14	Tax evasion is ethical if I cannot afford to pay (S14)	4.500
15	Tax evasion is ethical even if it means that if I pay less, others will have to pay more (S15)	5.847
16	Tax evasion would be ethical if I lived under an oppressive regime like Nazi Germany or Stalinist Russia (S16)	4.317
17	Tax evasion is ethical if the government discriminates against me because of my religion, race, or ethnic background (S17)	4.457
18	Tax evasion is ethical if the government imprisons people for their political opinions (S18)	4.603
	Average score	4.967

1 = strongly agree; 7 = strongly disagree

that tax evasion is justified and 7 represents strong disagreement. Thus, it appears that there is a fair amount of opposition to tax evasion but that there is some support for it in some cases.

Table 21.3 ranks the arguments from strongest to weakest. The range of means is 4.168–5.847. All of the mean scores are below 6.0, which indicate that there is some support for tax evasion even in cases where the argument against it is strong.

Justification for tax evasion was strongest in cases where tax funds were wasted, where the system was viewed as unfair, or where the government engaged in human rights abuses. Inability to pay was also a strong reason for justifying tax evasion.

Slightly less strong reasons for justifying tax evasion were in cases where a significant portion of the funds go to corrupt politicians, their families or friends, where the funds are used to support what the taxpayer considers to be an unjust war or other purpose that the taxpayer disapproves of or where tax rates are too high.

The weakest arguments to support tax evasion involved cases where others would have to pay more if the tax evader pays less, where the probability of getting caught is low, if everybody is doing it, if the money is spent wisely, or if the participant receives benefits from the tax expenditures.

Table 21.4 shows the breakdown of scores by gender. Some prior studies found that women were more opposed to tax evasion (McGee, 2005a; McGee & Lingle, 2005) while another study found that men were more opposed (McGee, 2005b). Yet another study found men and women to be equally opposed to tax evasion (McGee, Nickerson & Fees, 2005).

The present study found that women are more opposed to tax evasion than are men for 15 of the 18 statements. However, Wilcoxon tests found that the difference was significant in only two cases.

Table 21.3 Ranking of arguments (strongest to weakest)

Rank	Statement	
1	Tax evasion is ethical if a large portion of the money collected is wasted (S4)	4.168
2	Tax evasion is ethical if the tax system is unfair (S3)	4.316
3	Tax evasion would be ethical if I lived under an oppressive regime like Nazi Germany or Stalinist Russia (S16)	4.317
4	Tax evasion is ethical if the government discriminates against me because of my religion, race, or ethnic background (S17)	4.457
5	Tax evasion is ethical if I cannot afford to pay (S14)	4.5
6	Tax evasion is ethical if the government imprisons people for their political opinions (S18)	4.603
7	Tax evasion is ethical if a significant portion of the money collected winds up in the pockets of corrupt politicians or their families and friends (S11)	4.879
8	Tax evasion is ethical if some of the proceeds go to support a war that I consider to be unjust (S13)	4.883
9	Tax evasion is ethical if tax rates are too high (S1)	4.895
10	Tax evasion is ethical if a large portion of the money collected is spent on projects that I morally disapprove of (S6)	5.07
11	Tax evasion is ethical even if a large portion of the money collected is spent on worthy projects (S7)	5.122
12	Tax evasion is ethical even if tax rates are not too high because the government is not entitled to take as much as it is taking from me (S2)	5.217
13	Tax evasion is ethical even if a large portion of the money collected is spent on projects that do benefit me (S9)	5.282
14	Tax evasion is ethical if a large portion of the money collected is spent on projects that do not benefit me (S8)	5.307
15	Tax evasion is ethical even if most of the money collected is spent wisely (S5)	5.314
16	Tax evasion is ethical if everyone is doing it (S10)	5.516
17	Tax evasion is ethical if the probability of getting caught is low (S12)	5.72
18	Tax evasion is ethical even if it means that if I pay less, others will have to pay more (S15)	5.847

1 = strongly agree; 7 = strongly disagree

Table 21.4 Responses by gender

Statement number	Statement	Male	Female	Male	Female	p-Values
1	Tax evasion is ethical if tax rates are too high (S1)	4.667	4.931		0.264	0.4961
2	Tax evasion is ethical even if tax rates are not too high because the government is not entitled to take as much as it is taking from me (S2)	5.257	5.050	0.207		0.6097
3	Tax evasion is ethical if the tax system is unfair (S3)	3.819	4.650		0.831	0.04909[a]
4	Tax evasion is ethical if a large portion of the money collected is wasted (S4)	3.833	4.257		0.424	0.3476

(continued)

Table 21.4 (continued)

Statement number	Statement	Male	Female	Male	Female	p-Values
5	Tax evasion is ethical even if most of the money collected is spent wisely (S5)	5.403	5.168	0.235		0.3677
6	Tax evasion is ethical if a large portion of the money collected is spent on projects that I morally disapprove of (S6)	4.986	4.949	0.037		0.9085
7	Tax evasion is ethical even if a large portion of the money collected is spent on worthy projects (S7)	4.843	5.198		0.355	0.5538
8	Tax evasion is ethical if a large portion of the money collected is spent on projects that do not benefit me (S8)	4.943	5.495		0.552	0.2241
9	Tax evasion is ethical even if a large portion of the money collected is spent on projects that do benefit me (S9)	5.056	5.340		0.284	0.8693
10	Tax evasion is ethical if everyone is doing it (S10)	5.333	5.643		0.310	0.7476
11	Tax evasion is ethical if a significant portion of the money collected winds up in the pockets of corrupt politicians or their families and friends (S11)	4.667	4.931		0.264	0.6552
12	Tax evasion is ethical if the probability of getting caught is low (S12)	5.472	5.770		0.298	0.4686
13	Tax evasion is ethical if some of the proceeds go to support a war that I consider to be unjust (S13)	4.583	5.030		0.447	0.2856
14	Tax evasion is ethical if I cannot afford to pay (S14)	4.000	4.590		0.590	0.1291
15	Tax evasion is ethical even if it means that if I pay less, others will have to pay more (S15)	5.681	5.851		0.170	0.7175
16	Tax evasion would be ethical if I lived under an oppressive regime like Nazi Germany or Stalinist Russia (S16)	3.929	4.470		0.541	0.1789
17	Tax evasion is ethical if the government discriminates against me because of my religion, race, or ethnic background (S17)	3.986	4.713		0.727	0.0536[b]
18	Tax evasion is ethical if the government imprisons people for their political opinions (S18)	4.194	4.752		0.558	0.153
	Average score	4.703	5.044		0.341	

1 = strongly agree; 7 = strongly disagree
[a]Significant at the 5% level
[b]Significant at the 10% level

Table 21.5 shows the scores arranged by age. Only the younger two categories are analyzed because the oldest category did not have a sufficiently large sample size to perform any kind of meaningful analysis. The 25–40 age group was more opposed to tax evasion in 8 of 18 cases; the less than 25 group was more opposed in 10 of 18 cases. In three cases, the older group was significantly more opposed to tax evasion.

Table 21.5 Responses by age

Statement number	Statement	<25	25–40	Larger by <25	Larger by 25–40	p-Values
1	Tax evasion is ethical if tax rates are too high (S1)	4.817	4.925		0.108	0.8922
2	Tax evasion is ethical even if tax rates are not too high because the government is not entitled to take as much as it is taking from me (S2)	4.981	5.538		0.557	0.1558
3	Tax evasion is ethical if the tax system is unfair (S3)	4.288	4.173	0.115		0.7084
4	Tax evasion is ethical if a large portion of the money collected is wasted (S4)	4.029	4.057		0.028	0.9926
5	Tax evasion is ethical even if most of the money collected is spent wisely (S5)	4.875	5.849		0.974	0.0281[b]
6	Tax evasion is ethical if a large portion of the money collected is spent on projects that I morally disapprove of (S6)	5.060	4.774	0.286		0.5345
7	Tax evasion is ethical even if a large portion of the money collected is spent on worthy projects (S7)	4.981	5.231		0.250	0.4938
8	Tax evasion is ethical if a large portion of the money collected is spent on projects that do not benefit me (S8)	5.223	5.212	0.011		0.7359
9	Tax evasion is ethical even if a large portion of the money collected is spent on projects that do benefit me (S9)	5.155	5.302		0.147	0.7069
10	Tax evasion is ethical if everyone is doing it (S10)	5.260	5.943		0.683	0.0884[c]
11	Tax evasion is ethical if a significant portion of the money collected winds up in the pockets of corrupt politicians or their families and friends (S11)	5.019	4.358	0.661		0.1084
12	Tax evasion is ethical if the probability of getting caught is low (S12)	5.856	5.173	0.683		0.1298
13	Tax evasion is ethical if some of the proceeds go to support a war that I consider to be unjust (S13)	4.990	4.452	0.538		0.2616

(continued)

Table 21.5 (continued)

Statement number	Statement	<25	25–40	Larger by <25	25–40	p-Values
14	Tax evasion is ethical if I cannot afford to pay (S14)	3.923	5.173		1.250	0.0016[a]
15	Tax evasion is ethical even if it means that if I pay less, others will have to pay more (S15)	5.798	5.698	0.100		0.8353
16	Tax evasion would be ethical if I lived under an oppressive regime like Nazi Germany or Stalinist Russia (S16)	4.287	4.151	0.136		0.7798
17	Tax evasion is ethical if the government discriminates against me because of my religion, race, or ethnic background (S17)	4.567	4.154	0.413		0.3349
18	Tax evasion is ethical if the government imprisons people for their political opinions (S18)	4.490	4.415	0.075		0.9956
	Average score	4.867	4.921		0.054	

1 = strongly agree; 7 = strongly disagree
[a]Significant at the 1% level
[b]Significant at the 5% level
[c]Significant at the 10% level

Table 21.6 shows the scores by ethnicity. Ethnic groups with a sample size under 30 are omitted. Whites were more opposed to tax evasion than were Africans in 17 of 18 cases. In four cases, the difference was significant.

Table 21.7 shows the scores by religion. Religions with a sample size under 30 are omitted. The only religions that were not excluded were Catholic and Other Christian. Catholics were more opposed to tax evasion in 10 of 18 cases; Other Christians were more opposed in seven cases. In one case, the groups had the same mean score. None of the differences were significant.

Table 21.8 shows the mean scores by student status. The three categories are diploma student, undergraduate student, and postgraduate student. The diploma students were less opposed to tax evasion than were the other two groups. None of the differences in mean scores were significant, with the exception of Statement 14. In that case (ability to pay), the undergraduate students were more opposed to tax evasion than were the other two groups.

Table 21.9 shows the scores by academic major. Majors with a sample size under 30 are omitted. The management students were more opposed to tax evasion than the economics and finance majors in 11 of 18 cases. However, none of the differences were significant.

Table 21.6 Responses by ethnicity

Statement number	Statement	White	African	Larger by White	Larger by African	p-Values
1	Tax evasion is ethical if tax rates are too high (S1)	4.906	4.785	0.121		0.8664
2	Tax evasion is ethical even if tax rates are not too high because the government is not entitled to take as much as it is taking from me (S2)	5.813	4.941	0.872		0.1483
3	Tax evasion is ethical if the tax system is unfair (S3)	4.407	4.250	0.157		0.8002
4	Tax evasion is ethical if a large portion of the money collected is wasted (S4)	4.125	4.066	0.059		0.9911
5	Tax evasion is ethical even if most of the money collected is spent wisely (S5)	5.969	5.050	0.919		0.2115
6	Tax evasion is ethical if a large portion of the money collected is spent on projects that I morally disapprove of (S6)	5.156	4.897	0.259		0.9539
7	Tax evasion is ethical even if a large portion of the money collected is spent on worthy projects (S7)	6.156	4.697	1.459		0.0102[b]
8	Tax evasion is ethical if a large portion of the money collected is spent on projects that do not benefit me (S8)	5.625	5.202	0.423		0.6085
9	Tax evasion is ethical even if a large portion of the money collected is spent on projects that do benefit me (S9)	5.906	5.042	0.864		0.1216
10	Tax evasion is ethical if everyone is doing it (S10)	6.219	5.339	0.880		0.1300
11	Tax evasion is ethical if a significant portion of the money collected winds up in the pockets of corrupt politicians or their families and friends (S11)	4.844	4.860		0.016	0.6635
12	Tax evasion is ethical if the probability of getting caught is low (S12)	6.188	5.625	0.563		0.1885
13	Tax evasion is ethical if some of the proceeds go to support a war that I consider to be unjust (S13)	5.188	4.750	0.438		0.6159
14	Tax evasion is ethical if I cannot afford to pay (S14)	5.531	3.942	1.589		0.0009[a]

(continued)

Table 21.6 (continued)

Statement number	Statement	White	African	Larger by White	Larger by African	p-Values
15	Tax evasion is ethical even if it means that if I pay less, others will have to pay more (S15)	6.563	5.521	1.042		0.0200[b]
16	Tax evasion would be ethical if I lived under an oppressive regime like Nazi Germany or Stalinist Russia (S16)	5.063	4.001	1.062		0.0923[c]
17	Tax evasion is ethical if the government discriminates against me because of my religion, race, or ethnic background (S17)	4.645	4.347	0.298		0.5863
18	Tax evasion is ethical if the government imprisons people for their political opinions (S18)	4.906	4.347	0.559		0.3744
	Average score	5.400	4.759	0.641		

1 = strongly agree; 7 = strongly disagree
[a]Significant at the 1% level
[b]Significant at the 5% level
[c]Significant at the 10% level

Table 21.7 Responses by religion

Statement number	Statement	Catholic	Other Christian	Larger by Catholic	Larger by Other Christian	p-Values
1	Tax evasion is ethical if tax rates are too high (S1)	4.675	4.877		0.202	0.5218
2	Tax evasion is ethical even if tax rates are not too high because the government is not entitled to take as much as it is taking from me (S2)	5.395	5.160	0.385		0.8455
3	Tax evasion is ethical if the tax system is unfair (S3)	4.333	4.425		0.092	0.8445
4	Tax evasion is ethical if a large portion of the money collected is wasted (S4)	4.275	4.123	0.152		0.5955
5	Tax evasion is ethical even if most of the money collected is spent wisely (S5)	5.125	5.264		0.139	0.7043
6	Tax evasion is ethical if a large portion of the money collected is spent on projects that I morally disapprove of (S6)	4.875	5.078		0.203	0.7269

(continued)

Table 21.7 (continued)

Statement number	Statement	Catholic	Other Christian	Larger by Catholic	Larger by Other Christian	p-Values
7	Tax evasion is ethical even if a large portion of the money collected is spent on worthy projects (S7)	5.179	4.933	0.246		0.3844
8	Tax evasion is ethical if a large portion of the money collected is spent on projects that do not benefit me (S8)	5.538	5.257	0.281		0.5499
9	Tax evasion is ethical even if a large portion of the money collected is spent on projects that do benefit me (S9)	5.350	5.114	0.236		0.7737
10	Tax evasion is ethical if everyone is doing it (S10)	5.550	5.377	0.173		0.7704
11	Tax evasion is ethical if a significant portion of the money collected winds up in the pockets of corrupt politicians or their families and friends (S11)	4.925	5.094		0.169	0.8093
12	Tax evasion is ethical if the probability of getting caught is low (S12)	5.475	5.811		0.336	0.1127
13	Tax evasion is ethical if some of the proceeds go to support a war that I consider to be unjust (S13)	5.175	4.933	0.242		0.7196
14	Tax evasion is ethical if I cannot afford to pay (S14)	4.500	4.231	0.269		0.5221
15	Tax evasion is ethical even if it means that if I pay less, others will have to pay more (S15)	5.775	5.743	0.032		0.7501
16	Tax evasion would be ethical if I lived under an oppressive regime like Nazi Germany or Stalinist Russia (S16)	4.250	4.417		0.167	0.6725
17	Tax evasion is ethical if the government discriminates against me because of my religion, race, or ethnic background (S17)	4.923	4.600	0.323		0.5927
18	Tax evasion is ethical if the government imprisons people for their political opinions (S18)	4.600	4.600			0.8874
	Average score	4.996	4.947	0.049		

1 = strongly agree; 7 = strongly disagree

Table 21.8 Responses by academic status

Statement number	Statement	Diploma	UG	PG	p-Values Diploma vs. UG	Diploma vs. PG	UG vs. PG
1	Tax evasion is ethical if tax rates are too high (S1)	4.862	4.768	5.059	0.7591	0.8553	0.5756
2	Tax evasion is ethical even if tax rates are not too high because the government is not entitled to take as much as it is taking from me (S2)	5.141	5.473	5.103	0.3806	0.8005	0.2260
3	Tax evasion is ethical if the tax system is unfair (S3)	4.308	4.255	4.426	0.9559	0.8430	0.768
4	Tax evasion is ethical if a large portion of the money collected is wasted (S4)	4.138	4.339	4.059	0.6492	0.7871	0.4574
5	Tax evasion is ethical even if most of the money collected is spent wisely (S5)	4.954	5.732	5.324	0.2028	0.8713	0.1643
6	Tax evasion is ethical if a large portion of the money collected is spent on projects that I morally disapprove of (S6)	5.206	5.091	5.015	0.9871	0.5401	0.6177
7	Tax evasion is ethical even if a large portion of the money collected is spent on worthy projects (S7)	4.831	5.564	5.045	0.2015	0.9873	0.1397
8	Tax evasion is ethical if a large portion of the money collected is spent on projects that do not benefit me (S8)	5.328	5.273	5.368	0.6992	0.9112	0.768
9	Tax evasion is ethical even if a large portion of the money collected is spent on projects that do benefit me (S9)	5.123	5.161	5.515	0.8556	0.3633	0.2704
10	Tax evasion is ethical if everyone is doing it (S10)	5.154	5.946	5.485	0.1551	0.6845	0.2650
11	Tax evasion is ethical if a significant portion of the money collected winds up in the pockets of corrupt politicians or their families and friends (S11)	5.292	4.446	4.897	0.1111	0.2338	0.4559
12	Tax evasion is ethical if the probability of getting caught is low (S12)	5.646	5.482	5.985	0.4371	0.3134	0.7932

(continued)

Table 21.8 (continued)

Statement number	Statement	Diploma	UG	PG	*p*-Values Diploma vs. UG	Diploma vs. PG	UG vs. PG
13	Tax evasion is ethical if some of the proceeds go to support a war that I consider to be unjust (S13)	5.231	4.554	4.788	0.2278	0.2114	0.8252
14	Tax evasion is ethical if I cannot afford to pay (S14)	4.047	5.125	4.373	0.0147[a]	0.4669	0.0751[b]
15	Tax evasion is ethical even if it means that if I pay less, others will have to pay more (S15)	5.538	5.929	6.060	0.3839	0.1307	0.4882
16	Tax evasion would be ethical if I lived under an oppressive regime like Nazi Germany or Stalinist Russia (S16)	4.429	4.291	4.194	0.8418	0.5463	0.7458
17	Tax evasion is ethical if the government discriminates against me because of my religion, race, or ethnic background (S17)	4.462	4.436	4.493	0.7822	0.9419	0.8915
18	Tax evasion is ethical if the government imprisons people for their political opinions (S18)	4.400	4.393	4.985	0.9565	0.1891	0.1759
	Average score	4.894	5.014	5.001			

1 = strongly agree; 7 = strongly disagree
[a]Significant at the 1% level
[b]Significant at the 10% level

Concluding Comments

The survey found that there is some support for tax evasion on ethical grounds, although the degree of support varies by reason. Support is strongest in cases where the money is wasted, where the government is corrupt or engages in human rights abuses, or where there is inability to pay. Opposition to tax evasion is weakest where the money is spent wisely and where taxpayers receive benefits in exchange for their tax payments. Women were slightly more opposed to tax evasion than were men. People between 25 and 40 years of age were somewhat more opposed to tax evasion than were people in the under age 25 group. Whites were more opposed to tax evasion than were Africans. Catholics and other Christians have the same opinion about tax evasion. The academic status of the student did not affect views toward tax evasion. Diploma students, undergraduates, and postgraduates had the same view toward tax evasion. Academic major did not make a difference. Management students had the same view toward tax evasion as economics and finance students.

Table 21.9 Responses by academic major

Statement number	Statement	Management	Economics and finance	Larger by Management	Larger by Economics and finance	p-Values
1	Tax evasion is ethical if tax rates are too high (S1)	5.148	4.324	0.824		0.2363
2	Tax evasion is ethical even if tax rates are not too high because the government is not entitled to take as much as it is taking from me (S2)	5.403	4.909	0.494		0.2805
3	Tax evasion is ethical if the tax system is unfair (S3)	4.578	3.970	0.608		0.2057
4	Tax evasion is ethical if a large portion of the money collected is wasted (S4)	4.244	4.529		0.285	0.6061
5	Tax evasion is ethical even if most of the money collected is spent wisely (S5)	5.370	5.235	0.135		0.7066
6	Tax evasion is ethical if a large portion of the money collected is spent on projects that I morally disapprove of (S6)	5.303	4.667	0.636		0.191
7	Tax evasion is ethical even if a large portion of the money collected is spent on worthy projects (S7)	5.185	5.219		0.034	0.8660
8	Tax evasion is ethical if a large portion of the money collected is spent on projects that do not benefit me (S8)	5.328	5.212	0.116		0.7161
9	Tax evasion is ethical even if a large portion of the money collected is spent on projects that do benefit me (S9)	5.254	5.758		0.504	0.4881
10	Tax evasion is ethical if everyone is doing it (S10)	5.459	5.618		0.159	0.8676

11	Tax evasion is ethical if a significant portion of the money collected winds up in the pockets of corrupt politicians or their families and friends (S11)	5.200	4.500	0.700		0.1540
12	Tax evasion is ethical if the probability of getting caught is low (S12)	5.837	5.441	0.396		0.2039
13	Tax evasion is ethical if some of the proceeds go to support a war that I consider to be unjust (S13)	5.104	4.636	0.468		0.3669
14	Tax evasion is ethical if I cannot afford to pay (S14)	4.470	4.618		0.148	0.7179
15	Tax evasion is ethical even if it means that if I pay less, others will have to pay more (S15)	5.873	5.971		0.098	0.8730
16	Tax evasion would be ethical if I lived under an oppressive regime like Nazi Germany or Stalinist Russia (S16)	4.394	4.265	0.369		0.8697
17	Tax evasion is ethical if the government discriminates against me because of my religion, race, or ethnic background (S17)	4.575	4.059	0.516		0.2466
18	Tax evasion is ethical if the government imprisons people for their political opinions (S18)	4.590	4.736		0.146	0.6713
	Average score	5.073	4.870	0.203		

1 = strongly agree; 7 = strongly disagree

These findings have policy implications. Governments that want to reduce the amount of tax evasion that occurs in their political jurisdiction need to root out corruption and human rights abuses, increase the perception of fairness, keep tax rates low, spend tax funds wisely, and give people benefits in exchange for their tax payments.

References

Armstrong, Mary Beth and Jack Robison (1998). "Ethics in Taxation." *Journal of Accounting, Ethics & Public Policy*, Volume 1, Number 4, 535–557, reprinted in Robert W. McGee (ed.), *The Ethics of Tax Evasion*, Dumont, NJ: The Dumont Institute for Public Policy Research: Dumont, NJ, 1998, pp. 330–348.

Ballas, Apostolos A. and Haridimos Tsoukas (1998). "Consequences of Distrust: The Vicious Circle of Tax Evasion in Greece." *Journal of Accounting, Ethics & Public Policy*, Volume 1, Number 4, 572–596, reprinted in Robert W. McGee (ed.), *The Ethics of Tax Evasion*, Dumont, NJ: The Dumont Institute for Public Policy Research: Dumont, NJ, 1998, pp. 284–304.

Block, Walter (1989). "The Justification of Taxation in the Public Finance Literature: A Critique." *Journal of Public Finance and Public Choice*, Volume 3, 141–158.

Block, Walter (1993). "Public Finance Texts Cannot Justify Government Taxation: A Critique." *Canadian Public Administration/Administration Publique du Canada*, Volume 36, Number 2, 225–262, reprinted in revised form under the title "The Justification for Taxation in the Economics Literature" in Robert W. McGee (ed.), *The Ethics of Tax Evasion*, Dumont, NJ: The Dumont Institute for Public Policy Research: Dumont, NJ, 1998, pp. 36–88.

Cohn, Gordon (1998). "The Jewish View on Paying Taxes." *Journal of Accounting, Ethics & Public Policy*, Volume 1, Number 2, 109–120, reprinted in Robert W. McGee (ed.), *The Ethics of Tax Evasion*, Dumont, NJ: The Dumont Institute for Public Policy Research: Dumont, NJ, 1998, pp. 180–189.

Crowe, Martin T. (1944). "The Moral Obligation of Paying Just Taxes." *The Catholic University of America Studies in Sacred Theology No. 84.*

DeMoville, Wig (1998). "The Ethics of Tax Evasion: A Baha'i Perspective." *Journal of Accounting, Ethics & Public Policy*, Volume 1, Number 3, 356–368, reprinted in Robert W. McGee (ed.), *The Ethics of Tax Evasion*, Dumont, NJ: The Dumont Institute for Public Policy Research: Dumont, NJ, 1998, pp. 230–240.

Gronbacher, Gregory M.A. (1998). "Taxation: Catholic Social Thought and Classical Liberalism." *Journal of Accounting, Ethics & Public Policy*, Volume 1, Number 1, 91–100, reprinted in Robert W. McGee (ed.), *The Ethics of Tax Evasion*, Dumont, NJ: The Dumont Institute for Public Policy Research: Dumont, NJ, 1998, pp. 158–167.

Leiker, Bret H. (1998). "Rousseau and the Legitimacy of Tax Evasion." *Journal of Accounting, Ethics & Public Policy*, Volume 1, Number 1, 45–57, reprinted in Robert W. McGee (ed.), *The Ethics of Tax Evasion*, Dumont, NJ: The Dumont Institute for Public Policy Research: Dumont, NJ, 1998, pp. 89–101.

McGee, Robert W. (1994). "Is Tax Evasion Unethical?" *University of Kansas Law Review*, Volume 42, Number 2, 411–435. Reprinted at http://ssrn.com/abstract=74420.

McGee, Robert W. (1997). "The Ethics of Tax Evasion and Trade Protectionism from an Islamic Perspective." *Commentaries on Law & Public Policy*, Volume 1, 250–262. Reprinted at http://ssrn.com/abstract=461397.

McGee, Robert W. (Ed.). (1998a). *The Ethics of Tax Evasion*, Dumont, NJ: The Dumont Institute for Public Policy Research: Dumont, NJ.

McGee, Robert W. (1998b). "Christian Views on the Ethics of Tax Evasion." *Journal of Accounting, Ethics & Public Policy*, Volume 1, Number 2, 210–225. Reprinted at http://ssrn.com/abstract=461398.

McGee, Robert W. (1999a). "Is It Unethical to Evade Taxes in an Evil or Corrupt State? A Look at Jewish, Christian, Muslim, Mormon and Baha'i Perspectives." *Journal of Accounting, Ethics & Public Policy*, Volume 2, Number 1, 149–181. Reprinted at http://ssrn.com/abstract=251469.

McGee, Robert W. (1999b). "Why People Evade Taxes in Armenia: A Look at an Ethical Issue Based on a Summary of Interviews." *Journal of Accounting, Ethics & Public Policy*, Volume 2, Number 2, 408–416. Reprinted at http://ssrn.com/abstract=242568.

McGee, Robert W. (2005a). "The Ethics of Tax Evasion: A Survey of International Business Academics," Presented at the 60th International Atlantic Economic Conference, New York, October 6–9, 2005. Reprinted at http//:www.ssrn.com.

McGee, Robert W. (2005b). "The Ethics of Tax Evasion: A Survey of Romanian Business Students and Faculty." Andreas School of Business Working Paper Series, Barry University, Miami Shores, FL 33161, USA, September. Reprinted at http://www.ssrn.com. Reprinted in R. W. McGee and G. G. Preobragenskaya, *Accounting and Financial System Reform in Eastern Europe and Asia*. Springer: New York, 2006, pp. 299–328.

McGee, Robert W. and Gordon Cohn (2006). "Jewish Perspectives on the Ethics of Tax Evasion." Andreas School of Business Working Paper, Barry University, September. Reprinted at http://www.ssrn.com.

McGee, Robert W. and Gordon Cohn (2008). 'Jewish Perspectives on the Ethics of Tax Evasion', *Academy of Accounting and Financial Studies Journal*, forthcoming.

McGee, Robert W. and Gordon M. Cohn (2008). Jewish Perspectives on the Ethics of Tax Evasion. *Journal of Legal, Ethical and Regulatory Issues*, 11(2), 1–32.

McGee, Robert W. and Christopher Lingle (2005). "The Ethics of Tax Evasion: A Survey of Guatemalan Opinion." Presented at the 60th International Atlantic Economic Conference, New York, October 6–9, 2005. Reprinted at http://www.ssrn.com.

McGee, Robert W., Inge Nickerson and Werner Fees (2005). "When Is Tax Evasion Ethically Justifiable? A Survey of German Opinion." *Proceedings of the Academy of Legal, Ethical and Regulatory Issues*, Volume 9, Number 2, 35–38, Las Vegas, October 12–15. http://www.alliedacademies.org/pdf/vegas05/paleri-9-2.pdf.

McGraw, K. M. and J.T. Scholz (1991). "Appeals to Civic Virtue Versus Attention to Self-Interest: Effects on Tax Compliance." *Law and Society Review*, 25(3), 471–498.

Morales, Alfonso (1998). "Income Tax Compliance and Alternative Views of Ethics and Human Nature." *Journal of Accounting, Ethics & Public Policy*, Volume 1, Number 3, 380–399, reprinted in Robert W. McGee (ed.), *The Ethics of Tax Evasion*, Dumont, NJ: The Dumont Institute for Public Policy Research: Dumont, NJ, 1998, pp. 242–258.

Murtuza, Athar and S.M. Ghazanfar (1998). "Taxation as a Form of Worship: Exploring the Nature of Zakat." *Journal of Accounting, Ethics & Public Policy*, Volume 1, Number 2, 134–161, reprinted in Robert W. McGee (ed.), *The Ethics of Tax Evasion*, Dumont, NJ: The Dumont Institute for Public Policy Research: Dumont, NJ, 1998, pp. 190–212.

Oliva, Robert R. (1998). "The Schism between Tax Practitioners' Ethical and Legal Obligations: Recommendations for the Fusion of Law and Ethics." *Journal of Accounting, Ethics & Public Policy*, Volume 1, Number 4, 603–628, reprinted in Robert W. McGee (ed.), *The Ethics of Tax Evasion*, Dumont, NJ: The Dumont Institute for Public Policy Research: Dumont, NJ, 1998, pp. 350–371.

Pennock, Robert. T. (1998). "Death and Taxes: On the Justice of Conscientious War Tax Resistance." *Journal of Accounting, Ethics & Public Policy*, Volume 1, Number 1, 58–76, reprinted in Robert W. McGee (ed.), *The Ethics of Tax Evasion*, Dumont, NJ: The Dumont Institute for Public Policy Research: Dumont, NJ, 1998, pp. 124–142.

Preobragenskaya, Galina G. and Robert W. McGee (2004). "Taxation and Public Finance in a Transition Economy: A Case Study of Russia," in Carolyn Gardner, Jerry Biberman and Abbass Alkhafaji (Eds.), *Business Research Yearbook: Global Business Perspectives* Volume XI, Saline, MI: McNaughton & Gunn, Inc., 2004, pp. 254–258. A longer version, which was presented at the Sixteenth Annual Conference of the International Academy of Business Disciplines in San Antonio, March 25–28, 2004, is available at http://ssrn.com/abstract=480862.

Schansberg, D. Eric (1998). "The Ethics of Tax Evasion within Biblical Christianity: Are There Limits to 'Rendering Unto Caesar'"? *Journal of Accounting, Ethics & Public Policy*, Volume

1, Number 1, 77–90, reprinted in Robert W. McGee (ed.), *The Ethics of Tax Evasion*, Dumont, NJ: The Dumont Institute for Public Policy Research: Dumont, NJ, 1998, pp. 144–157.

Smatrakalev, Gueorgui (1998). "Walking on the Edge: Bulgaria and the Transition to a Market Economy," in Robert W. McGee (ed.), *The Ethics of Tax Evasion*, Dumont, NJ: The Dumont Institute for Public Policy Research: Dumont, NJ, 1998, pp. 316–329.

Smith, Sheldon R. and Kevin C. Kimball (1998). "Tax Evasion and Ethics: A Perspective from Members of The Church of Jesus Christ of Latter-Day Saints." *Journal of Accounting, Ethics & Public Policy*, Volume 1, Number 3, 337–348, reprinted in Robert W. McGee (ed.), *The Ethics of Tax Evasion*, Dumont, NJ: The Dumont Institute for Public Policy Research: Dumont, NJ, 1998, pp. 220–229.

Spooner, Lysander (1870). *No Treason: The Constitution of No Authority*, originally self-published by Spooner in Boston in 1870, reprinted by Rampart College in 1965, 1966 and 1971, and by Ralph Myles Publisher, Inc., Colorado Springs, Colorado in 1973.

Tamari, Meir (1998). "Ethical Issues in Tax Evasion: A Jewish Perspective." *Journal of Accounting, Ethics & Public Policy*, Volume 1, Number 2, 121–132, reprinted in Robert W. McGee (ed.), *The Ethics of Tax Evasion*, Dumont, NJ: The Dumont Institute for Public Policy Research: Dumont, NJ, 1998, pp. 168–178.

Torgler, Benno (2003). "Tax Morale: Theory and Empirical Analysis of Tax Compliance." Dissertation der Universität Basel zur Erlangung der Würde eines Doktors der Staatswissenschaften.

Vaguine, Vladimir V. (1998). "The "Shadow Economy" and Tax Evasion in Russia," in Robert W. McGee (ed.), *The Ethics of Tax Evasion*, Dumont, NJ: The Dumont Institute for Public Policy Research: Dumont, NJ, 1998, pp. 306–314.

Chapter 22
Cheating on Taxes If You Have A Chance: A Comparative Study of Tax Evasion Opinion in Turkey and Germany

Robert W. McGee, Serkan Benk, Adriana M. Ross, and Harun Kılıçaslan

Introduction

Several studies on the ethics of tax evasion have been conducted in recent years. Some of them have been theoretical while others have been empirical. The present study is mostly empirical, although some theory is also discussed.

Perhaps the most comprehensive theoretical study was conducted by Martin Crowe (1944), who reviewed 500 years of Catholic literature on the ethics of tax evasion, some of which was in the Latin language. More recent comprehensive theoretical studies were conducted by Martinez (1994), McGee (1998, 2004, 2006a), and Torgler (2003, 2007), although the Torgler studies involved a good deal of empirical work as well.

Some studies on the ethics of tax evasion examined the issue from a religious perspective. The religious group most opposed to tax evasion is the Church of Jesus Christ of Latter-Day Saints (Smith & Kimball, 1998). Nothing in the Mormon literature includes an exception to the general rule that tax evasion is unethical. Next, in terms of opposition to tax evasion, is the Baha'i faith (DeMoville, 1998). They do not condone tax evasion except in cases where members of the Baha'i faith are being persecuted by some government.

R.W. McGee (✉)
School of Business, Florida International University,
3000 NE 151 Street, North Miami, FL 33181, USA
e-mail: bob414@hotmail.com

S. Benk
Zonguldak Karaelmas Universitesi I.I.B.F., Maliye Bolumu, 67100 Zonguldak, Turkey

A.M. Ross
School of Accounting, Florida International University, 11200 SW 8th Street,
Miami, FL 33199, USA

H. Kılıçaslan
Uludağ University, Ivazpasa Mah. Ivazpasa cad. No. 36, Osmangazi, Bursa, Turkey

R.W. McGee (ed.), *The Ethics of Tax Evasion: Perspectives in Theory and Practice*,
DOI 10.1007/978-1-4614-1287-8_22, © Springer Science+Business Media, LLC 2012

Cohn (1998) and Tamari (1998) discuss the Jewish view on tax evasion. Generally, tax evasion is frowned upon, although an exception may be made in cases where the rulers are corrupt and do not spend the money wisely. Catholic views are all over the map. Some Catholic theologians have said that tax evasion is a mortal sin (Saint Antoninus, 1571) while others have said it is not a sin at all (Iorio, 1939), at least in cases where the government does not provide for the common good (Angelus Carletus de Clavisio, 1494). Gronbacher (1998) and Schansberg (1998) hold that tax evasion is not always unethical. Pennock (1998) makes an exception where the government is fighting an unjust war.

At least two Muslim views have been published in the English language literature. Ahmad (1995) and Yusuf (1971) interpret the Muslim literature to permit tax evasion in cases where the tax is on income or where the effect of the tax is to raise prices, which includes value added taxes, sales taxes, use taxes, excise taxes, and tariffs. They would also see no moral need to pay inheritance taxes. Jalili (2012) disagrees with this view. According to his interpretation of the Muslim literature, one has an absolute duty to pay whatever the state demands in cases where the government follows Shariah law. In other cases, the duty to pay may be less than absolute, depending on what the government does with the tax money it collects.

A number of empirical studies have been conducted to determine views on the ethics of tax evasion. Empirical studies have been made of Asian countries (McGee, 2006d, 2007, 2008a, b; Torgler, 2004), Austria (Torgler & Schneider, 2005), Latin American and Caribbean countries (Alm & Martinez-Vazquez, 2010; McGee & López, 2008), Russia (Alm, Martinez-Vazquez & Torgler, 2005, 2006), Spain (Martinez-Vazquez and Torgler 2009), Switzerland (Torgler & Schaltegger, 2006), cultural differences in the USA (Alm & Torgler, 2006).

The Study

Methodology

The authors developed a survey instrument that asked the question: Do you think that cheating on taxes is justified if you have a chance? A similar question was asked in several *Human Beliefs and Values* surveys. The survey was distributed to a group of mostly undergraduate business students and faculty at Zonguldak Karaelmas University in Turkey and Hamburg University in Germany. They were asked to select a number from 1 (never justifiable) to 10 (always justifiable). Table 22.1 shows the demographics of the sample.

Table 22.1 Demographics

	Turkey	Germany	Combined
Student status			
Graduate student	20	22	42
Undergraduate student	364	189	553
Faculty member	13	38	51
Other/unknown	2	3	5
Total	399	252	651
Major			
Accounting	–	6	6
Other business/economics	397	189	586
Philosophy	–	2	2
Law	–	16	16
Engineering	–	1	1
Other	2	38	40
Total	399	252	651
Gender			
Male	132	141	273
Female	265	111	376
Unknown	2	–	2
Total	399	252	651
Age			
15–29	389	205	594
30–49	8	42	50
50+	–	3	3
Unknown	2	2	4
Total	399	252	651
Religion			
Christian	–	119	119
Hindu	–	2	2
Muslim	397	33	430
Agnostic or atheist	–	50	50
Other/unknown	2	48	50
Total	399	252	651
Marital status			
Married or in a committed relationship	11	38	49
Divorced or separated	–	1	1
Never married	386	210	596
Other/unknown	2	3	5
Total	399	252	651

Findings

After compiling the data, the next step was to make comparisons between relevant subsamples. Comparisons were made if the sample size for each of the subsamples to be compared was 30 or more. No analysis was made for smaller subsamples, since any findings would be statistically weak or inconclusive.

Table 22.2 Student status

	Sample	Mean	Standard deviation
Graduate students – combined	42	2.19	1.92
Undergraduate students – combined	553	2.07	2.12
Faculty – combined	47	2.06	1.66
Undergraduate students – Turkey	364	1.53	1.59
Undergraduate students – Germany	189	3.11	2.59
	p-Value	*Significant?*	
Combined graduate vs. undergraduate students	0.7221	No	
Combined graduate students vs. faculty	0.7328	No	
Combined undergraduate students vs. faculty	0.9749	No	
Undergraduate students – Turkey vs. Germany	0.0001	Yes	

1 = never justifiable; 10 = always justifiable

Prior studies that examined student status had mixed results. A study in Argentina (McGee & Rossi, 2008) found no difference between students and faculty. An Australian study (McGee & Bose, 2009) found that overall, undergraduate students were least opposed to tax evasion and faculty were most opposed. An Estonian study (McGee, Alver & Alver, 2008) found similar results. Overall, undergraduate students were least opposed to tax evasion; faculty, and accounting practitioners were most opposed. A New Zealand study (Gupta & McGee, 2010) found that undergraduate students were less opposed to tax evasion than were graduate students.

Table 22.2 shows the data and analysis based on student status. Turkish undergraduate students were most opposed to tax evasion, as evidenced by their low mean score (1.53). It was the only mean score below 2.00. Undergraduate students combined (2.06) and faculty combined (2.07) had nearly equal mean scores, followed by graduate students combined (2.19). The German undergraduate students were least opposed to tax evasion (3.11). However, the differences in mean score were significant only when comparing the German and Turkish undergraduate students ($p = 0.0001$). The Turkish undergraduate students were significantly more opposed to tax evasion than were the German undergraduate students.

Another demographic examined was academic major. Prior studies have had mixed findings. A study of Argentina (McGee & Rossi, 2008) found that business and economics students were generally more opposed to tax evasion than were law students. An Armenian study (McGee & Maranjyan, 2008) found that business students were more strongly opposed to tax evasion than were theology students. An Australian study (McGee & Bose, 2009) found that business and economics students were least opposed to tax evasion; seminary students were most opposed; business and economics students were significantly less opposed to tax evasion than were philosophy, accounting, health services, and seminary students. Accounting majors were significantly more opposed to tax evasion than were business and economics students and information technology students and were significantly less opposed to tax evasion than were seminary and health services students.

Table 22.3 Student major

	Sample	Mean	Standard deviation
Other business/economics students – Turkey	397	1.53	1.58
Other business/economics students – Germany	189	3.09	2.56
	p-Value	*Significant?*	
Turkey vs. Germany	0.0001	Yes	

1 = never justifiable; 10 = always justifiable

One Chinese study (McGee & Guo, 2007) found that business and economics students were least opposed to tax evasion and that law and philosophy students were equally opposed to tax evasion. Studies of Estonia (McGee, Alver & Alver, 2008), Kazakhstan (McGee & Preobragenskaya, 2008), and New Zealand (Gupta & McGee, 2010) found that accounting majors and business/economics majors were equally opposed to tax evasion. The New Zealand study also found that law students were somewhat less opposed to tax evasion than were the accounting and business/economics students. A Guatemalan study (McGee & Lingle, 2008) found that business students were more opposed to tax evasion than were law students.

Table 22.3 shows the data and analysis based on academic major. The only groups with sample sizes sufficiently large to compare were the German and Turkish business/economics students. The Turkish students were found to be significantly more opposed to tax evasion than were the German students ($p = 0.0001$).

Many studies have examined gender in connection with ethical decision making. The results are mixed. One group of studies that examined attitudes on ethical issues other than taxes found that women were more ethical than men (Baird, 1980; Betz, et al., 1989; Boyd, 1981; Chonko & Hunt, 1985; Franke, et al., 1997; Kohut & Corriher, 1994). Another group of studies found that the differences between male and female opinions on certain ethical issues are insignificant (Barnett & Karson, 1989; Callan, 1992; Dubinsky & Levy, 1985; Fritzsche, 1988; Harris, 1989; Kidwell, et al., 1987; Robin & Babin, 1997). A third group of studies found men to be more ethical than women (Barnett & Karson, 1987; Weeks, et al., 1999).

A few studies have examined gender ethics in conjunction with views on tax evasion. Women were found to be more strongly opposed to tax evasion in studies of Australia (McGee & Bose, 2009), Hubei, China (McGee & Guo, 2007), Colombia (McGee, López & Yepes, 2009), Estonia (McGee, Alver & Alver, 2008), the USA (McGee, Nickerson & Fees, 2006), Guatemala (McGee & Lingle, 2008), international business academics teaching in the USA (McGee, 2006b), Orthodox Jewish students (McGee & Cohn, 2008), New Zealand (Gupta & McGee, 2010), Puerto Rico (McGee & López, 2007), South Africa (McGee & Goldman, 2010), Taiwan (McGee & Andres, 2009), and Thailand (McGee, 2008a, b).

Men were found to be more strongly opposed to tax evasion in studies of Romania (McGee, 2006c), Slovakia (McGee & Tusan, 2008), and Turkey (McGee & Benk, 2011). Studies of Argentina (McGee & Rossi, 2008), Beijing, China (McGee & An, 2008), Southern China and Macau (McGee & Noronha, 2008), France (McGee & M'Zali, 2009), Hong Kong (McGee & Butt, 2008), Kazakhstan

Table 22.4 Gender

	Sample	Mean	Standard deviation
Male – Turkey	132	1.80	1.83
Male – Germany	111	2.55	2.03
Male – combined	273	2.55	2.44
Female – Turkey	265	1.40	1.41
Female – Germany	141	3.24	2.72
Female – combined	376	1.74	1.70
	p-Value	*Significant?*	
Male – Turkey vs. Germany	0.0027	Yes	
Female – Turkey vs. Germany	0.0001	Yes	
Turkey – Male vs. Female	0.0167	Yes	
Germany – Male vs. Female	0.0268	Yes	
Combined – Male vs. Female	0.0001	Yes	

1 = never justifiable; 10 = always justifiable

(McGee & Preobragenskaya, 2008), and Poland (McGee & Bernal, 2006) found no significant difference between male and female attitudes toward tax evasion.

Table 22.4 shows the data and analysis based on gender. Females in Turkey (1.40) were most opposed to tax evasion. Females in Germany (3.24) were least opposed. Turkish men (1.80) were more opposed to tax evasion than were German men (2.55). The differences were significant at the 1% or 5% level.

A number of studies have examined age in conjunction with views on various ethical issues. Some studies of ethical views on nontax issues found that people become more ethical or more respectful of authority as they get older (Barnett & Karson, 1987, 1989; Harris, 1990; Kelley et al., 1990; Longenecker et al., 1989; Ruegger & King, 1992; Serwinek, 1992). However, Sims (1996) found that older students had less reluctance when it came to pirating software than did younger students. Babakus, et al. (2004) found that age made a difference in ethical attitude, but the difference it made depended on culture and the particular topic in question.

A few studies have examined age in conjunction with views on tax evasion. An Estonian study (McGee, Alver & Alver, 2008) found that people under age 25 were significantly less opposed to tax evasion than were people in the 25–40 age group. Studies of New Zealand (Gupta & McGee, 2010) and Turkey (McGee & Benk, 2011) found older people to be more opposed to tax evasion than younger people. A study of Slovakia found older people to be slightly more opposed to tax evasion than younger people (McGee & Tusan, 2008).

Table 22.5 shows the data and analysis based on age. Only three groups had a sufficiently large sample size to make comparisons. Turkish people in the 15–29 age group were most opposed to tax evasion. German students in the same group were least opposed to tax evasion. Between those two groups in terms of opposition was the German group in the 30–49 category. The difference between the German and Turkish 15–29 age groups was significant at the 1% level ($p = 0.0001$). The difference

Table 22.5 Age

	Sample	Mean	Standard deviation
15–29 Turkey	389	1.54	1.59
15–29 Germany	205	3.08	2.55
30–49 Germany	45	2.36	1.93
	p-Value	*Significant?*	
15–29 Turkey vs. Germany	0.0001	Yes	
Germany 15–29 vs. 30–49	0.0756	Yes	

1 = never justifiable; 10 = always justifiable

Table 22.6 Religion

	Sample	Mean	Standard deviation
Combined – Christian	119	2.73	2.19
Combined – Muslim	430	1.72	1.89
Combined – agnostic/atheist	50	3.10	2.55
Muslim – Turkey	397	1.53	1.58
Muslim – Germany	33	4.00	3.36
	p-Value	*Significant?*	
Combined – Christian vs. Muslim	0.0001	Yes	
Combined – Christian vs. agnostic/atheist	0.3415	No	
Combined – Muslim vs. agnostic/atheist	0.0001	Yes	
Muslim – Turkey vs. Germany	0.0001	Yes	

1 = never justifiable; 10 = always justifiable

in mean scores between the 15–29 and 30–49 German groups was significant at the 10% level ($p = 0.0756$).

A few studies have examined religion as a demographic in connection with attitudes on tax evasion. An Australian study (McGee & Bose, 2009) found that Muslims had the least opposition to tax evasion. However, the Muslim sample size was too small to adequately measure the extent of the statistical significance. In that study, Catholics had the strongest opposition to tax evasion. A New Zealand study (Gupta & McGee, 2010) found that Catholics were most opposed to tax evasion and Buddhists were least opposed. McGee and Smith (2007) found that Mormons were significantly more opposed to tax evasion than non-Mormons. A study of Malaysia (Ross & McGee, 2011) found that Protestants were most opposed to tax evasion, followed by Roman Catholics, Muslims, Hindus, and Buddhists.

Table 22.6 shows the data and analysis based on religion. Turkish Muslims were most opposed to tax evasion. In second place was the combined Muslim sample, followed by the combined Christian sample, the combined agnostic/atheist sample, and the German Muslim sample.

Some studies on tax evasion have examined marital status as a demographic variable. Song and Yarbrough (1978) found that married people are more tax compliant than single, divorced, or widowed people. Torgler (2007) found that married people are more tax compliant than single people in Belgium, Canada, Spain, and

Table 22.7 Marital status

	Sample	Mean	Standard deviation
Combined – married	49	2.63	2.51
Combined – never married	596	2.03	2.04
Never married – Turkey	386	1.53	1.58
Never married – Germany	210	2.94	2.44
	p-Value	Significant?	
Combined – Married vs. never married	0.0526	Yes	
Never married – Turkey vs. Germany	0.0001	Yes	

1 = never justifiable; 10 = always justifiable

Switzerland but found married people were less tax compliant than single people in Costa Rica, Switzerland, and the USA. A third group of countries Torgler studied found that married and single people in Switzerland were equally compliant. In other words, the results are mixed and Switzerland represents all three positions. A Malaysian study (Ross & McGee, 2011) found that divorced individuals were most opposed to tax evasion, with a three-way tie for second place involving married, widowed, and single/never married. The living together as married group was least opposed to tax evasion.

Table 22.7 shows the data and analysis based on marital status. The category most opposed to tax evasion was the Turkish never married group, followed by the combined never married, the combined married, and the Germany never married. The sample size for the married group was too small to compare.

Concluding Comments

This study found some interesting results. The Turkish sample in general was more opposed to tax evasion than the German sample. Muslims were generally more opposed to tax evasion than were non-Muslims. Undergraduate students were most opposed to tax evasion than were graduate students. Turkish women were most opposed to tax evasion, while German women were least opposed, which was an interesting result. Younger people tended to be more opposed to tax evasion than older people, although the small sample sizes for the older groups prevented the achievement of strong results. This result, however, was unusual, since most prior studies found that people become more tax compliant and compliant with rules in general as they get older. The sample of married individuals was small, making any conclusions tentative. However, the results found that the never married Turkish group was most opposed to tax evasion while the never married German group was least opposed to tax evasion.

More research is needed to determine the causes of the similarities and differences.

References

Ahmad, Mushtaq (1995). *Business Ethics in Islam*. Islamabad, Pakistan: The International Institute of Islamic Thought & The International Institute of Islamic Economics.

Alm, James, Jorge Martinez-Vazquez and Benno Torgler. (2005). Russian Tax Morale in the 1990s. *Proceedings of the 98th Annual Conference on Taxation of the National Tax Association*, 287–292.

Alm, James and Benno Torgler. (2006). Culture differences and tax morale in the United States and in Europe. *Journal of Economic Psychology*, 27, 224–246.

Alm, James, Jorge Martinez-Vazquez and Benno Torgler. (2006). Russian attitudes toward paying taxes – before, during and after the transition. *International Journal of Social Economics*, 33(12), 832–857.

Alm, J. & J. Martinez-Vazquez. (2010). Tax Evasion, the Informal Sector, and Tax Morale in LAC Countries. In J. Alm, J. Martinez-Vazquez & B. Torgler (Eds.), *Developing Alternative Frameworks for Explaining Tax Compliance* (pp. 260–291). London & New York: Routledge.

Angelus Carletus de Clavisio (1494). *Summa Angelica*. Lyons, as cited by Martin T. Crowe, The Moral Obligation of Paying Just Taxes, The Catholic University of America Studies in Sacred Theology No. 84, 1944, pp. 28–29.

Antoninus, Saint (1571). *Summa Sacrae Theologiae, Iuris Pontificii, et Caesarei*, II, p. 63 ff, Venice, as cited by Martin T. Crowe, The Moral Obligation of Paying Just Taxes, The Catholic University of America Studies in Sacred Theology No. 84, 1944, p. 42.

Babakus, Emin, T. Bettina Cornwell, Vince Mitchell and Bodo Schlegelmilch (2004). Reactions to Unethical Consumer Behavior across Six Countries. *The Journal of Consumer Marketing*, 21(4/5), 254–263.

Baird, J.S. (1980). Current Trends in College Cheating. *Psychology in the Schools,* 17(4), 515–522, as cited in Bob S. Brown and Peggy Choong. (2005). An Investigation of Academic Dishonesty among Business Students at Public and Private United States Universities. *International Journal of Management* 22(2): 201–214.

Barnett, John H. and Marvin J. Karson. (1987). Personal Values and Business Decisions: An Exploratory Investigation. *Journal of Business Ethics*, 6(5), 371–382.

Barnett, John H. and Marvin J. Karson. (1989). Managers, Values, and Executive Decisions: An Exploration of the Role of Gender, Career Stage, Organizational Level, Function, and the Importance of Ethics, Relationships and Results in Managerial Decision-Making. *Journal of Business Ethics*, 8(10), 747–771.

Betz, Michael, Lenahan O'Connell and Jon M. Shepard. (1989). Gender Differences in Proclivity for Unethical Behavior. *Journal of Business Ethics*, 8(5), 321–324.

Boyd, David P. (1981). Improving Ethical Awareness Through the Business and Society Course. *Business and Society* 20, 21, 2, 1: 27–31.

Callan, Victor J. (1992). Predicting Ethical Values and Training Needs in Ethics. *Journal of Business Ethics*, 11(10), 761–769.

Chonko, Lawrence B. and Shelby D. Hunt. (1985). Ethics and Marketing Management: An Empirical Investigation. *Journal of Business Research*, 13(4), 339–359.

Cohn, Gordon. (1998). The Jewish View on Paying Taxes. *Journal of Accounting, Ethics & Public Policy*, 1(2), 109–120, reprinted in Robert W. McGee (Ed.), *The Ethics of Tax Evasion* (pp. 180–189). Dumont, NJ: The Dumont Institute for Public Policy Research, 1998, pp. 180–189.

Crowe, Martin T. (1944). The Moral Obligation of Paying Just Taxes, The Catholic University of America Studies in Sacred Theology No. 84.

DeMoville, Wig. (1998). The Ethics of Tax Evasion: A Baha'i Perspective. *Journal of Accounting, Ethics & Public Policy*, 1(3), 356–368, reprinted in Robert W. McGee (Ed.), *The Ethics of Tax Evasion* (pp. 230–240). Dumont, NJ: The Dumont Institute for Public Policy Research, 1998.

Dubinsky, Alan J. and Michael Levy. (1985). Ethics in Retailing: Perceptions of Retail Sales People. *Journal of the Academy of Marketing Science*, 13(1), 1–16.

Franke, George R., Deborah F. Crown & Deborah F. Spake. (1997). Gender Differences in Ethical Perceptions of Business Practices: A Social Role Theory Perspective. *Journal of Applied Psychology*, 82(6), 920–934.

Fritzsche, David J. (1988). An Examination of Marketing Ethics: Role of the Decision Maker, Consequences of the Decision, Management Position, and Sex of the Respondent. *Journal of Macromarketing*, 8(2), 29–39.

Gronbacher, Gregory M.A. (1998). Taxation: Catholic Social Thought and Classical Liberalism. *Journal of Accounting, Ethics & Public Policy*, 1(1), 91–100, reprinted in Robert W. McGee (ed.), *The Ethics of Tax Evasion* (pp. 158–167). Dumont, NJ: The Dumont Institute for Public Policy Research, Dumont, NJ, 1998.

Gupta, Ranjana and Robert W. McGee. (2010). A Comparative Study of New Zealanders' Opinion on the Ethics of Tax Evasion: Students v. Accountants. *New Zealand Journal of Taxation Law and Policy*, 16(1), 47–84.

Harris, James R. (1989). Ethical Values and Decision Processes of Male and Female Business Students. *Journal of Education for Business*, 8, 234–238, as cited in Sharon Galbraith and Harriet Buckman Stephenson. (1993). Decision Rules Used by Male and Female Business Students in Making Ethical Value Judgments: Another Look. *Journal of Business Ethics*, 12(3), 227–233.

Harris, James R. (1990). Ethical Values of Individuals at Different Levels in the Organizational Hierarchy of a Single Firm. *Journal of Business Ethics*, 9(9), 741–750.

Iorio, T. (1939). *Theologia Moralis*, 6th ed., II, n. 778, Naples: M. D'Aurea, as cited by Martin T. Crowe, The Moral Obligation of Paying Just Taxes, The Catholic University of America Studies in Sacred Theology No. 84, 1944, p. 41.

Jalili, Ali Reza (2012). The Ethics of Tax Evasion: An Islamic Perspective. In Robert W. McGee (Ed.), *The Ethics of Tax Evasion in Theory and Practice* (forthcoming). New York: Springer.

Kelley, S.W., O.C. Ferrell and S.J. Skinner. (1990). Ethical Behavior Among Marketing Researchers: An Assessment of Selected Demographic Characteristics. *Journal of Business Ethics*, 9(8), 681–688.

Kidwell, Jeaneen M., Robert E. Stevens & Art L. Bethke. (1987). Differences in Ethical Perceptions Between Male and Female Managers: Myth or Reality? *Journal of Business Ethics*, 6(6), 489–493.

Kohut, Gary F. & Susan E. Corriher. (1994). The Relationship of Age, Gender, Experience and Awareness of Written Ethics Policies to Business Decision Making. *S.A.M. Advanced Management Journal*, 59(1), 32–39.

Longenecker, Justin G., Joseph A. McKinney & Carlos W. Moore. (1989). Do Smaller Firms Have Higher Ethics? *Business and Society Review*, 71, 19–21.

Martinez, Leo P. (1994). Taxes, Morals, and Legitimacy. *Brigham Young University Law Review*, 1994, 521–569.

Martinez-Vazquez, Jorge and Benno Torgler. (2009). The Evolution of Tax Morale in Modern Spain. *Journal of Economic Issues*, 43(1), 1–28.

McGee, Robert W. (Ed.). (1998). *The Ethics of Tax Evasion*. Dumont, NJ: The Dumont Institute for Public Policy Research.

McGee, Robert W. (2004). *The Philosophy of Taxation and Public Finance*. Norwell, MA and Dordrecht: Kluwer Academic Publishers.

McGee, Robert W. (2006a). Three Views on the Ethics of Tax Evasion. Journal of Business Ethics, 67(1), 15–35.

McGee, Robert W. (2006b). A Survey of International Business Academics on the Ethics of Tax Evasion. *Journal of Accounting, Ethics & Public Policy*, 6(3), 301–352.

McGee, Robert W. (2006c). The Ethics of Tax Evasion: A Survey of Romanian Business Students and Faculty. *The ICFAI Journal of Public Finance*, 4(2), 38–68 (2006). Reprinted in Robert W. McGee and Galina G. Preobragenskaya, *Accounting and Financial System Reform in Eastern Europe and Asia* (pp. 299–334). New York: Springer, 2006.

McGee, Robert W. (2006d). A Comparative Study of Tax Evasion Ethics in Thailand and Vietnam. *Journal of Accounting, Ethics & Public Policy*, 6(1), 103–123.

McGee, Robert W. and Arkadiusz Bernal. (2006). The Ethics of Tax Evasion: A Survey of Business Students in Poland. In Global Economy -- How It Works (Mina Baliamoune-Lutz, Alojzy Z. Nowak & Jeff Steagall, eds.) (pp. 155–174). Warsaw: University of Warsaw & Jacksonville: University of North Florida. Reprinted at http://ssrn.com/abstract=875434.

McGee, Robert W., Inge Nickerson and Werner Fees. (2006). German and American Opinion on the Ethics of Tax Evasion. Proceedings of the Academy of Legal, Ethical and Regulatory Issues (Reno), 10(2), 31–34.

McGee, Robert W. (2007). Ethics and Tax Evasion in Asia. ICFAI Journal of Public Finance, 5(2), 21–33 (May). Reprinted in Business Ethics: A 360 Degree Appraisal, ICFAI University Press. Hyderabad, India.

McGee, Robert W. and Zhiwen Guo. (2007). A Survey of Law, Business and Philosophy Students in China on the Ethics of Tax Evasion. Society and Business Review, 2(3), 299–315.

McGee, Robert W. and Silvia López Paláu. (2007). The Ethics of Tax Evasion: Two Empirical Studies of Puerto Rican Opinion. Journal of Applied Business and Economics, 7(3), 27–47 (2007). Reprinted in Robert W. McGee (editor), Readings in Accounting Ethics (pp. 314–342). Hyderabad, India: ICFAI University Press, 2009.

McGee, Robert W. and Sheldon R. Smith. 2007. Ethics, Tax Evasion and Religion: A Survey of Opinion of Members of the Church of Jesus Christ of Latter-Day Saints. Western Decision Sciences Institute, Thirty-Sixth Annual Meeting, Denver, April 3–7. Published in the Proceedings. Reprinted at http://ssrn.com/abstract=934652.

McGee, Robert W. (2008a). Opinions on Tax Evasion in Asia, in Robert W. McGee, editor, Taxation and Public Finance in Transition and Developing Economies (pp. 309–320) New York: Springer.

McGee, Robert W. (2008b). Opinions on Tax Evasion in Thailand, in Robert W. McGee, editor, Taxation and Public Finance in Transition and Developing Economies (pp. 609–620). New York: Springer.

McGee, Robert W., Jaan Alver and Lehte Alver. (2008). The Ethics of Tax Evasion: A Survey of Estonian Opinion, in Robert W. McGee, editor, Taxation and Public Finance in Transition and Developing Economies (pp. 461–480). New York: Springer.

McGee, Robert W. and Yuhua An. (2008). A Survey of Chinese Business and Economics Students on the Ethics of Tax Evasion, in Robert W. McGee, editor, Taxation and Public Finance in Transition and Developing Economies (pp. 409–421). New York: Springer.

McGee, Robert W. and Yiu Yu Butt. (2008). An Empirical Study of Tax Evasion Ethics in Hong Kong. Proceedings of the International Academy of Business and Public Administration Disciplines (IABPAD), Dallas, April 24–27: 72–83.

McGee, Robert W. and Gordon M. Cohn. (2008). Jewish Perspectives on the Ethics of Tax Evasion. Journal of Legal, Ethical and Regulatory Issues, 11(2), 1–32.

McGee, Robert W. and Christopher Lingle. (2008). The Ethics of Tax Evasion: A Survey of Guatemalan Opinion, in Robert W. McGee, editor, Taxation and Public Finance in Transition and Developing Economies (pp. 481–495). New York: Springer.

McGee, Robert W. and Silvia López Paláu. (2008). Tax Evasion and Ethics: A Comparative Study of the USA and Four Latin American Countries, in Robert W. McGee, editor, Taxation and Public Finance in Transition and Developing Economies (pp. 185–224). New York: Springer.

McGee, Robert W. and Tatyana B. Maranjyan. (2008). Opinions on Tax Evasion in Armenia, in Robert W. McGee, editor, Taxation and Public Finance in Transition and Developing Economies (pp. 277–307). New York: Springer.

McGee, Robert W. and Carlos Noronha. (2008). The Ethics of Tax Evasion: A Comparative Study of Guangzhou (Southern China) and Macau Opinions. Euro Asia Journal of Management, 18(2), 133–152.

McGee, Robert W. and Galina G. Preobragenskaya. (2008). A Study of Tax Evasion Ethics in Kazakhstan, in Robert W. McGee, editor, Taxation and Public Finance in Transition and Developing Economies (pp. 497–510). New York: Springer.

McGee, Robert W. and Marcelo J. Rossi. (2008). A Survey of Argentina on the Ethics of Tax Evasion, in Robert W. McGee, editor, *Taxation and Public Finance in Transition and Developing Economies* (pp. 239–261). New York: Springer.

McGee, Robert W. and Radoslav Tusan. (2008). The Ethics of Tax Evasion: A Survey of Slovak Opinion, in Robert W. McGee, editor, *Taxation and Public Finance in Transition and Developing Economies* (pp. 575–601). New York: Springer.

McGee, Robert W. and Susana N. Vittadini Andres. (2009). The Ethics of Tax Evasion: Case Studies of Taiwan, in Robert W. McGee, Readings in Business Ethics (pp. 200–228). Hyderabad, India: ICFAI University Press. An abbreviated version was published in Marjorie G. Adams and Abbass Alkhafaji, editors, Business Research Yearbook: Global Business Perspectives, Volume XIV, No. 1 (pp. 34–39). Beltsville, MD: International Graphics: Beltsville, MD, 2007.

McGee, Robert W. and Sanjoy Bose. (2009). The Ethics of Tax Evasion: A Survey of Australian Opinion, in Robert W. McGee, *Readings in Business Ethics* (pp. 143–166). Hyderabad, India: ICFAI University Press.

McGee, Robert W. and Bouchra M'Zali. (2009). The Ethics of Tax Evasion: An Empirical Study of French EMBA Students, in Robert W. McGee, Readings in Business Ethics (pp. 185–199). Hyderabad, India: ICFAI University Press. An abbreviated version was published in Marjorie G. Adams and Abbass Alkhafaji, editors, Business Research Yearbook: Global Business Perspectives, Volume XIV, No. 1 (pp. 27–33). Beltsville, MD: International Graphics, 2007).

McGee, Robert W., Silvia López Paláu and Gustavo A. Yepes Lopez. (2009). The Ethics of Tax Evasion: An Empirical Study of Colombian Opinion, in Robert W. McGee, Readings in Business Ethics (pp. 167–184). Hyderabad, India: ICFAI University Press.

McGee, Robert W. & Geoff A. Goldman (2010). Ethics and Tax Evasion: A Survey of South African Opinion. *Proceedings of the Third Annual University of Johannesburg Faculty of Management Conference*, May 12–14. Reprinted in the present volume.

McGee, Robert W. & Serkan Benk (2011). The Ethics of Tax Evasion: A Study of Turkish Opinion. *Journal of Balkan and Near Eastern Studies*, 13(2): 249–262.

Pennock, Robert T. (1998). Death and Taxes: On the Justice of Conscientious War Tax Resistance. *Journal of Accounting, Ethics & Public Policy*, 1(1), 58–76, reprinted in Robert W. McGee (Ed.), *The Ethics of Tax Evasion* (pp. 124–142). Dumont, NJ: The Dumont Institute for Public Policy Research, 1998.

Robin, Donald and Laurie Babin. (1997). Making Sense of the Research on Gender and Ethics in Business: A Critical Analysis and Extension. *Business Ethics Quarterly*, 7(4), 61–90.

Ross, Adriana M. and Robert W. McGee (2011). A Demographic Study of Malaysian Views on the Ethics of Tax Evasion. Published in the Proceedings of the 2011 Spring International Conference of the Allied Academies, Orlando, April 6–8, 2011.

Ruegger, Durwood and Ernest W. King. (1992). A Study of the Effect of Age and Gender upon Student Business Ethics. *Journal of Business Ethics*, 11(3), 179–186.

Schansberg, D. Eric. (1998). The Ethics of Tax Evasion within Biblical Christianity: Are There Limits to "Rendering Unto Caesar"? *Journal of Accounting, Ethics & Public Policy*, 1(1), 77–90, reprinted in Robert W. McGee (ed.), The Ethics of Tax Evasion (pp. 144–157). The Dumont Institute for Public Policy Research, Dumont, NJ, 1998.

Serwinek, Paul J. (1992). Demographic & Related Differences in Ethical Views Among Small Businesses. *Journal of Business Ethics*, 11(7), 555–566.

Sims, Ronald R., Hsing K. Cheng & Hildy Teegen. (1996). Toward a Profile of Student Software Piraters. *Journal of Business Ethics*, 15(8), 839–849.

Smith, Sheldon R. and Kevin C. Kimball. (1998). Tax Evasion and Ethics: A Perspective from Members of The Church of Jesus Christ of Latter-Day Saints. *Journal of Accounting, Ethics & Public Policy*, 1(3), 337–348, reprinted in Robert W. McGee (Ed.), *The Ethics of Tax Evasion* (pp. 220–229). Dumont, NJ: The Dumont Institute for Public Policy Research, 1998.

Song, Young-dahl and Tinsley E. Yarbrough. (1978). Tax Ethics and Taxpayer Attitudes: A Survey. *Public Administration Review*, 38(5), 442–452.

Tamari, Meir. (1998). Ethical Issues in Tax Evasion: A Jewish Perspective. *Journal of Accounting, Ethics & Public Policy*, 1(2), 121–132, reprinted in Robert W. McGee (Ed.), *The Ethics of Tax Evasion* (pp. 168–178). Dumont, NJ: The Dumont Institute for Public Policy Research, 1998.

Torgler, B. (2003). Tax Morale: Theory and Empirical Analysis of Tax Compliance. Dissertation der Universität Basel zur Erlangung der Würde eines Doktors der Staatswissenschaften.

Torgler, Benno. (2004). Tax morale in Asian countries. *Journal of Asian Economics*, 15, 237–266.

Torgler, Benno and Friedrich Schneider. (2005). Attitudes Towards Paying Taxes in Austria: An Empirical Analysis. *Empirica*, 32, 231–250.

Torgler, Benno and Christoph A. Schaltegger. (2006). Tax Morale: A Survey with a Special Focus on Switzerland. *Schweizerische Zeitschrift für Volkswirtschaft und Statistik*, 142(3), 395–425.

Torgler, Benno. (2007). *Tax Compliance and Tax Morale: A Theoretical and Empirical Analysis.* Cheltenham, UK & Northampton, MA, USA: Edward Elgar.

Weeks, William A., Carlos W. Moore, Joseph A. McKinney & Justin G. Longenecker. (1999). The Effects of Gender and Career Stage on Ethical Judgment. *Journal of Business Ethics*, 20(4), 301–313.

Yusuf, S.M. (1971). *Economic Justice in Islam.* Lahore: Sh. Muhammad Ashraf.

Chapter 23
Is Tax Evasion Our National Sport?
The Bulgarian Case

Georgi Smatrakalev

Introduction

Tax evasion is illegal, fraudulent activity, and is severely prosecuted around the globe. However, many people are evading their tax obligations and they try illegally to enrich themselves either through underreporting or ordinary stealing of the previously collected taxes. Tax morale is directly connected with tax awareness and tax education of the population. Civilized societies are more or less relying on tax avoidance – formal and informal – while the newly emerged market economies are more inclined toward the evasion side.

North American and Western European governments responded rapidly to the fall of communism by creating a variety of financial and technical assistance programs for both Central and Eastern Europe. Promoting reforms and the creation of new laws in all economic areas including taxation has been a major focus within the broader rule of law. Early in the postcommunist period, it was obvious that commercial laws needed to be rewritten, replaced, or reformed to unleash market forces for growth and development. Taxes have implicit character and were mainly taken as deductions from wages and salaries or payment to the principal of the state-owned enterprises.

Consequently, donors provided numerous experts to help countries identify, adapt, and transplant best practices from a number of successful models. These experts have drafted countless laws and trained thousands of people in legal institutions in the recipient countries.

The results have varied widely. In some countries, little actual change has taken place other than the passage of new legislation. Even in the more successful transition countries, many of the new commercial laws that are now on the books are not

G. Smatrakalev (✉)
College of Business Administration, Sac, Florida Atlantic University,
3200 College Avenue 430A, Davie, FL 33314, USA
e-mail: smatraka@fau.edu

R.W. McGee (ed.), *The Ethics of Tax Evasion: Perspectives in Theory and Practice*,
DOI 10.1007/978-1-4614-1287-8_23, © Springer Science+Business Media, LLC 2012

effectively or consistently implemented, despite additional assistance to support and reform implementing institutions.

Bulgaria stepped on the road to a market economy in 1989. After an exhaustive and winding transition, the country can hardly say that the market economy has claimed victory. The economic and property ownership transition have been accomplished but the psychological transition in the mind of the population will not be finished for another generation or two. The old type of thinking is still there in many fields of the economy, in the way of doing business. The changes, although expected and wanted, are still only partially accepted.

The major goal of this chapter is to outline some of the areas of tax evasion, to look into the historical determination of this phenomenon, the literary roots and the way of limiting its influence in the national economy. For all this we shall outline the different forms of tax evasion related to the various taxes, some of the legal possibilities for inspiring tax evasion and the role of the administrative power and its instrumentation to oppose this event. The research will rely on previous authors in the field, some historical literary publications and of course investigative journalism of the newspapers in Bulgaria.

Historical and Literary Analysis

The walk between tax avoidance and tax evasion is like walking on a razor blade and one never knows when he/she will slip and cut themselves. If we have one person drafting a law for a new tax, at least ten others are already looking for loopholes or language that permits them to avoid it. Tax evasion is part of a significant and growing economic problem – the "shadow economy" that defrauds the government.[1]

Cheating the government or tax evasion is almost as old as taxation itself. With the establishment of taxation came tax avoidance and tax evasion. They are practiced by almost every layer of the population but the richest and the famous make eye-catching news copy.[2] Cowell's (1990) investigation raises questions that go to the heart of public economics and reveal the shortcomings of applying standard economic models of crime to tax evasion. He develops an analytical framework that shows how the underground economy grows and suggests simple economic mechanisms that will induce the behavior that leads to tax evasion.

Joel Slemrod defines tax evasion as cheating ourselves,[3] which unfortunately was not always understood by the taxpayer in that way and especially in Bulgaria where

---

[1] On the shadow economy, see Feige, Edgar L., The Underground Economies: Tax Evasion and Information Distortion, Cambridge University Press, 1989, 378 pages. Pashev, Konstantin, 2006. "Understanding Tax Corruption in Transition Economies: Evidence from Bulgaria," MPRA Paper 974, University Library of Munich, Germany.

[2] See Cowell, Frank A, The Economics of Evasion, MIT Press, May 1990.

[3] Slemrod, Joel, Cheating Ourselves: The Economics of Tax Evasion, Journal of Economic Perspectives – Volume 21, Number 1 – Winter 2007 – Pages 25–48.

the collective spirit is not so strong and the motto – everyone for him/herself is very widespread.

First, tax evasion is a fraud that is committed against a very special economic agent: the government. The government is special in that it has, presumably, the power to set and to enforce some of the "rules of the game" by which economic relationships are supposed to abide. It sets the structure and the level of taxes. It also has ultimate control over the mechanism used to enforce the payment of taxes and over the structure of penalties for offenders. It combines the roles of rule maker, victim, and umpire. Contrast this centralized, unitary authority with the victims of burglary and business fraud: Companies and individuals do not normally have anything like the resources, the power, or the organization available to the government with which to combat those crimes.

The second reason for singling out this subject for special treatment is the delicate interplay of information among those involved in the black economy (evaders, investigators, the government).[4]

Allingham and Sandmo (1972) analyze the individual taxpayer's decision on whether and to what extent to evade taxes by deliberate underreporting.[5] This can be viewed as economic choice of the taxpayer but it is a criminal decision that some of the tax payers are making easier than other criminal activity against the individual, like robbery or killing.

The economic choice against the government is especially easy when the cost of tax evasion is low. The marginal cost usually is established by the legal penalty multiplied by the probability of being audited. If the probability is zero or close to zero then the taxpayers are less risk averse and will utilize abusive tax shelters or simply will lean toward the "shadow economy."

Tax administration, in particular, as it relates to the penalty and detection regimes, figures prominently in determining the level and character of tax evasion.[6] Yet governance may compromise the efficacy of such tax regimes. For example, some of the transition economies of Europe and the former Soviet Union may be characterized as regimes with stiff if not draconian penalties for engaging in tax evasion. But these states are also plagued with serious governance shortcomings, with tax penalties that apply at the discretion of tax officials.[7] This raises the question of whether corruption, and in particular, bribes to tax officials, reduces tax compliance as it compromises the statutory detection and penalty regimes.

In Bulgaria, the tax and tax enforcement burden, ineffective enforcement of laws, and administrative barriers for businesses are the main factors stimulating informal economic activities.

---

[4] Ibid. p. 5.

[5] Allingham, Michael G and Agnar Sandmo, Income Tax Evasion: A Theoretical Analysis, Journal of Public Economics 1(1972) p. 323 – 338.

[6] Ibid.

[7] Himes, Susan and Martine Milliet-Einbinder (1999). "Russia's Tax Reform," OECD Observer, 215, January 2010, http://www1.oecd.org/publications/observer/215/e-himes.htm.

Bulgaria has been under foreign domination for more than half of its thirteenth century existence, the first two centuries by the Byzantine Empire and then five centuries under the Ottoman yoke. So in all these seven centuries, the government was foreign and the people were gradually alienated from it.

The Ottoman Empire, in which Bulgaria was included, used to have numerous types of taxes[8] – monetary and in kind, like food for the army, labor for building roads and fortresses. For example, in the German campaign in 1789, it was necessary to transport huge amount of cereals from the new yield into Sofia county.[9] The people at that time knew very well whose taxpayer they were, the so-called *avarisi* or additional taxes from the XVII century become in fact the major taxation issue, collected from the population. These taxes were collected on the principle of neighbor territoriality.

The whole procedure of assigning the monetary amount, in kind or labor, requires active participation from the taxable part of the population.[10] In fact, it was the Turks, the ottomans, and other independent parts of the oppressor who were collecting the tax. Since they were independent, more often the amounts collected never ended up in the treasury, which required second or multiple collections. In reality, the Ottoman Empire had very accurate accountability and detailed information about the collected amounts. It not only forced the population to finance it but also succeeded to engage it with active participation in the organization of spending the funds in some places. The scale of the Empire required some kind of autonomy in order to rule over its vast territory, since it was very centralized, granting the regions tax collecting responsibility resulted in near criminal methods of collecting taxes from the local population. The oppressed population could understand through this system not only that they pay taxes through the nose, but also for whom they pay and for what. This creates informed taxpayers and soon after that the revolts and uprisings started. Taxation without representation was not only on the American continent at that time.

The following years of the Bulgarian kingdom and socialist dictatorship did not help but further deepen this alienation. For all the years, the government is foreseen as *them*. "Let *them* do what they want." "*They* will choose but we will decide," etc. All these everyday phrases show the lack of identification of the Bulgarian taxpayer with their country. The Bulgarians love their country but always hate

---

[8] The most heavy one was the so-called "blood tax" taking away 3-, 5-, and 7-year-old boys, converting them to Islam and making them part of the ottoman army between 1395 and 1705. Hundreds of thousands of kids were trained in the army barracks even to hate and kill their own parents. This also creates inventive tax evasion as hiding their boys in the woods or dressing them as girls. See Donchev, A Vreme Razdelno (Time of Violence), 1964, Sofia, Bulgaria and the movie made after the book in 1988.

[9] Ivanova, S. The Transfigurations of Historical Time. – In: Les temps de l'Europe. V. II. Temps mythiques europeens. Delphes, Septembre, 1992. Centre European de Delphes. Conseil de '.Europe Strasbourg. Textes reunis par J. Bonnet et E. Karpodini-Diimitriadis, 1994, p. 96.

[10] Иванова, С. Данъчното облагане на населението в българските градове и формирането на неговите институции (XVII – XVIII в.) – ИДА, 1993, т. 65.

their government, even if they voted for it in the latest democratic elections. Even in the Bulgarian literature throughout the years, we have examples of either passive or active struggle against the government and the tax collectors. In the Bulgarian literature and movies, we have a couple of stories and films dealing with tax evasion and promoting it as a way for the poor to survive by outwitting the tax collector. (See "Andreshko", Elin Pelin.[11]) In the movie "Avantazh," the Cock says: "I steal from the government, from the state, never from the ordinary people. There is no poor state and whatever I steal I give back to the state. For example, I take money from one store or goods sell them and use the money in another store."[12] Numerous examples in national literature unfortunately do not relate to much research in that area. In fact only a few authors are dealing with tax evasion in the country. The Center for Studies in Democracy is one of the few institutions that carry on such research.[13] Most of the others are dealing with the shadow economy, which is related indirectly with tax evasion (Institute for Market Economy and Institute of Economic Studies).

Types of Tax Evasion in Bulgaria

No government can announce a tax system and then rely on the taxpayers' sense of duty to remit what is owed. Some dutiful people will undoubtedly pay what they owe, but many others will not.[14] In fact, people get innovative in the ways they find to avoid or evade taxation. During the third century, many wealthy Romans buried their jewelry or stocks of gold coin to evade the luxury tax, and homeowners in eighteenth-century England temporarily bricked up their fireplaces to escape notice of the hearth tax collector.[15] In the Netherlands, all the old houses have small windows, because the property tax was based on the number of the windows and their size. Taxpayers in old Quebec avoided taxes by bricking up their windows.

Evasion of taxes in Bulgaria is very wide ranging and examples can be found in every single area of taxation. All taxes can be avoided, shifted, or evaded and samples of that can be found in every sector of the economy – beginning with not reporting of income and ending with pure stealing of the collected excises and value

---

[11] Elin Pelin. (2010). In *Encyclopædia Britannica*. Retrieved November 9, 2010, from Encyclopædia Britannica Online: http://www.britannica.com/EBchecked/topic/449221/Elin-Pelin and http://balgarin.bravehost.com/elinpelin/andreshko.htm.

[12] In the socialism, all the stores were government operated. http://www.imdb.com/title/tt0077190/plotsummary retrieved November 9, 2010.

[13] See Скритата Икономика в България, София 2004, Център за Изследване на Демокрацията 200 стр. and also http://ideas.repec.org/f/ppa244.html#details retrieved November 17, 2010.

[14] Slemrod, Joel, Cheating Ourselves: The Economics of Tax Evasion, Journal of Economic Perspectives – Volume 21, Number 1 – Winter 2007 – Pages 25–48.

[15] Webber, Carolyn, and Aaron B. Wildavsky. 1986. *History of Taxation and Expenditure in the Western World*. New York: Simon & Schuster. p. 141.

added taxes. It is always claimed that income taxes are voluntary taxes and the self-assessment mechanism opens the door wide for tax avoidance and sometime to tax evasion.

Income Tax Evasion

In a recent study of the Association of Italian Taxpayers, Bulgaria is in third place in the European Union in terms of income tax evasion, after Italy and Romania. Italy has 51% nonreported income subject to taxation, while Romania has 42.7% and Bulgaria 39.2%.[16] This is due to several reasons:

1. Income tax evasion sometimes is based on the complexity of the compliance regulations. If people are to spend time in compliance and also in the tax office soon they simply divert to tax evasion.
2. Evasion is also stimulated by the examples around us. If he/she is doing it and there are no consequences, why then should I pay is a common religion among taxpayers. I remember a story by a friend of mine who was visited by two tax agents in the early nineties "to see the dummy" who paid such a huge amount of income tax, as they did not have such a case before, and the other one that in the early 2000s the widely publicized best taxpayer, a big businessmen who turned out not to have paid a penny in taxes. All this is demoralizing to ordinary taxpayers.
3. There are also political will for tax evasion. It is a widely held belief that those who are paying to different parties are not paying the government and, respectively, the government is lax toward its duties. Unfortunately, these are most difficult to prove since there are no official data for corruption, except some sensational interviews in the electronic media.[17]

In personal income tax evasion, the examples are similar to those of all developed countries; most of the scandals are with rich people or celebrities. There is one peculiarity in Bulgarian tax evasion, the lower the education level of the taxpayer the higher the evasion simply because these taxpayers do not know the opportunity cost and they are part of criminal organizations, so the origin of their income is unclear. That is why they do not declare their income. Some of them have accrued their wealth in the transition period with unclear laws and great uncertainty, low enforcement, and corrupt governments. All this contributes to the development of a high level of tax evasion expressed by simply not filing tax returns and not complying with the tax regulations, combined with low tax morale.

---

[16] Трети сме по укриване на данъци в ЕС, 20 август 2009 / News.dir.bg http://dnes.dir.bg/news.php?id=4950800 retrieved November 23, 2010.

[17] Танов: Костов и Станишев с куфарчета от митниците Не знам да има разработка срещу мен в МВР, категоричен беше бившият шеф на антимафиотите, http://www.standartnews.com retrieved November 27, 2010.

The newspapers are filled with articles and commentaries about the tax audits of celebrities in Bulgaria. Wealthy Bulgarians made up new ways of evading taxes. Instead of proving the purchases of luxurious things with loans from friends, they claim that they live an affluent life out of presents from friends. If a Bentley car and diamonds are grants, there is no need to declare them in the tax return. This is what the instructions from the National Revenue Agency sent to the tax inspections read.

Loans should be registered in the tax declarations even if received from close relatives such as brothers or sisters. Thus, luxurious cars, yachts, and expensive presents will be hidden from the state until tax officers conduct an audit. At the time of the tax inspections, the owners of expensive things give explanations of where their posh belongings came from. Only then will the tax officers approach the rich man who gives luxurious presents.[18]

The tax administration also audits some of the folk and pop divas, who also are underreporting income, claiming they live on loans or underestimating their assets for tax purposes. All these are just for the public, as there is not one lawsuit for tax evasion or some effective measures for proclaiming how much was collected from these audits.

Business tax compliance is extremely important for the fiscal health of the government. It is not only the corporate income tax, which is a small amount but the businesses themselves, which are charged with the duty of collecting VAT and sales taxes, income tax withholding, and employment taxes. This opens another possibility for tax evasion – stealing the already collected revenue. Although it is important, little is known about business tax compliance and the behavioral consequences of the various tax regimes. Indeed, the empirical literature on business tax evasion is scant, in sharp contrast to the voluminous work on individual income tax compliance.

The existing inertia from socialist times when the nationalized enterprises were paying directly to the government and the communist party continues, simply because the CEOs of these "privatized" companies are the same old "comrades" with the same old feelings for the renamed socialist party or its derivatives. They keep transferring money toward the party and ignoring the treasury payments for taxes and other collections. During the last government of the Bulgarian Socialist party, the CEO of a huge chemical enterprise was promoted as the Bulgarian Biggest Taxpayer and just a few weeks later the press investigation showed that he did not pay any taxes at all.

It is clear that not all businesses are involved in tax evasion. The common belief is that if someone is not paying taxes, then he is paying bribes or kickbacks[19] either to the tax authorities or directly to the government and is under the protection of the so-called political umbrella.

---

[18] Стоянова, Стела, Данъчен ме гони мамо, в. Стандарт, 27 февруару 2010 http://paper.standartnews.com/bg/category.php?d=2010-02-27&cat=9 retrieved February 27, 2010.

[19] See more in Joulfaian, David, Bribes and Business Tax Evasion, The European Journal of Comparative Economics, 2009, Vol. 6, n. 2, pp. 227–244.

Presumptive Taxation and Tax Evasion

Presumptive taxation was introduced in Bulgaria[20] in 1995 in order to mitigate the losses from tax collection from small business owners. It is somewhere in between the personal and corporate income tax. The creation of the so-called patent tax supposedly eased the small- and medium-sized companies (SME) with tax compliance by collecting a lump sum tax from them, established out of nowhere.

This tax is unconstitutional and lacks a reason for existence. Over the years, the changes made to it have been chaotic and unsystematic. The range is from 0 to 200% and even higher for various activities. I am impressed also by the special tendency for increasing it in Sofia and by the large gap between the capital and the provinces. For example, the increase in the hotel business is from 50 to 150%, in catering from 50 to 122%, in the wholesale trade from 300 to 500%, etc., which forces the medium and small producers into the shadow economy.

According to the Corlett–Hague Rule, every thing that is close to free time activities has to be taxed higher because the free time cannot be taxed. But when talking about kids' free time activities, this is not only about following the rules of the public finances. Anyway, all entertainment activities related to the free time of the kids are taxed at over 50% higher.

The drastic increase of the patent tax on the one hand put a significant part of the economy's agents in the shadow economy and decreases the well-being of the population as a whole because the possibility of transferring these taxes to consumers could be easily realized by raising the prices of goods and services.

Those who pay the patent tax are not exempt from all the taxes in the corporate income tax law, such as those related to expenditures in the social sphere, promotional expenditures and automobile maintenance, etc. These SMEs that pay the patent tax have the same obligations and compliance rules with the tax legislation as all the other economic agents – keeping accounting records, making social and health insurance payments, purchasing control equipment "in case the state defines its application with a decree" etc., but they do not have the opportunity to deduct all these expenditures like all the others big enterprises.

The most frequent method of evading the patent tax is registering in a similar but lower tax classification, for example, instead of plumber – handyman, because of the ten times tax savings as a handyman. The most ridiculous example was the absence of any escort agency but numerous massage shops, since the tax is half as much for the latter. On the other hand, underreporting the number of seats for the catering and hotel businesses is a common practice, which forced the authorities to charge based on square meters, which brings to life the movable walls in the premises.

---

[20] The detailed analysis of presumptive taxation can be found in Konstantin V. Pashev, 2006. "Presumptive Taxation: Lessons from Bulgaria," Post-Communist Economies, Taylor and Francis Journals, vol. 18(4), pages 399–418, December.

Since 2008, the patent tax has been moved into the bailiwick of the local tax authorities, which makes it easy to control and more difficult to evade, since the local authorities closely monitor the local businesses and their activities.

Evasion of Indirect Taxation

Indirect taxes are always the ones that have been evaded, stolen, and underreported. Again we are facing the difference in reporting, collection but common for all of them is shifting them to consumers in the form of higher prices. Imports or exports foster opportunities to evade three taxes at the same time – customs duties, excise, and value added tax (VAT). This fraudulent evasion cannot happen without active participation of the customs officers. They are the ones who legitimize the false exports or do not charge the proper rate for certain imported goods. Usually it relates to heavily taxed goods like cigarettes and alcoholic beverages. For example, a container filled with kids toys (or even empty) is exported out of the country and the firm exporter claims a refund for the amounts paid for excise and taxes on "documented" cigarettes or brandy, that can easily be a couple of millions.[21]

Or importing a container filled with cigarettes or whiskey, documented as VAT exempt items, so the profit is collected after selling them on the internal market.

The so-called customs officer's villages next to Svilengrad and Plovdiv are like urban legends, where everyone can see houses of two or three stories that belong to people with an ordinary level of income, who by no means can afford them if they rely only on their regular work pay. Again, we face the lack of enforcement or a law without teeth. Distributing the control among a few agencies makes most of the transition bills uncontrollable and unenforceable and helps the growth of the scale of tax evasion and the shadow economy.

Evasion of excise taxes and the value added tax (VAT) are often linked with fraud, since we have issues of crowding out the budget or simply not paying the collected amount to the government in any of those cases the evasion is criminalized and linked with severe penalties and jail time.

VAT fraud is a serious problem that undermines the entire tax system. Ever since the establishment of the VAT, fraudulent activity was one of its characteristics in the EU.[22] With the expansion of the Union, the organized crime of the postsocialist

---

[21] The Treasury lost 2.5 billion levs (about $2 billion) over 5 years (1999–2004) due to crowding out of VAT which was caught by the service. According to the Chief Tax Commissioner Nikola Popov, there are over 4 billion levs that were not revealed by the tax agents. See News.bg http://news.ibox.bg/news/id_110452666 retrieved November 29, 2010. Konstantin Pashev, 2006."VAT Frauds and the Challenges to Bulgarian Tax Policy and Administration in Enlarged Europe," Economic Thought Journal, Bulgarian Academy of Sciences – Institute of Economics, issue 1, pages 57–80.

[22] Report from the Commission to the Council and The European Parliament on the use of administrative cooperation arrangements in the fight against VAT fraud, Brussels, 16.4.2004, COM(2004) 260 final.

countries united with their western partners and now has a greater area of operation. As a UK tax official stated recently, "VAT fraud is an attack on the system, often carried out by organized criminals. We are committed to defeating this crime." Estimates for losses attributable to *VAT fraud* vary between EUR 40 million and 60 million. The system works well enough when all the entities in a transaction account properly for VAT, but the zero-rating of cross-border transactions is the weak point in the system, which is exploited by fraudsters. This is approximately the entire amount of VAT collected by France. A recent report estimated that Belgium alone is losing approximately 10% of VAT to fraud. Traders may not pay the correct amount of VAT for a number of reasons, including error, misunderstanding of the system, deliberately understating their VAT liabilities, or through an organized, systematic attack on the system – fraud.

Since the introduction of the value added tax in April 1, 1994 (yes, almost like a joke this important tax was introduced on April Fool's Day), all governments try to fight VAT fraud.

Types of VAT Fraud

The types of VAT fraud are numerous and it is not the subject of this research, so only a few points will be mentioned here. The fraudulent agents are really innovative and always increase their arsenal with new methods, answering to the changes that have occurred in the trade around us and the rapid increase in Internet commerce. This also requires more sources for control and involvement of agencies in a couple of countries sometimes due to globalization.[23]

Missing Trader intracommunity (MTIC) frauds – involves companies that register for VAT in their home country, buy inventory for export VAT free from another EU member country, import and sell that inventory at VAT inclusive prices, then disappear without remitting the VAT collected to their home country's taxing authorities.

The VAT arrangements are designed so that intracommunity supplies of goods between taxable persons are exempt in the goods' Member State of origin, with taxation taking place in the Member State of destination. These "normal" arrangements have been supplemented by many special, often complex arrangements in areas in which the Member States wanted to maintain more extensive control over taxation.

This exemption mechanism exposes the VAT system to fraud, and in particular intracommunity "carousel" fraud. Since goods can move without being taxed, it is important that the Community administrative cooperation arrangements be used as effectively as possible and that national control systems be adapted to these challenges.

Carousel fraud – an extension of the MTIC fraud. The goods pass through several companies or "buffers" in the trader's home country, before being sold VAT

---

[23] Крантов, Красимир, ДДС измами по интернет, в. „24 часа" 29 April 2005 p. 19.

free by an exporter or "broker" to a company in another EU member country. The same goods are then resold VAT free to the original trader who re-imports them to begin the circle again, completing the carousel.

Carousel fraud involves a circular trade of cross-border purchases, typically computer chips or mobile phones, between connected companies, sometimes controlled by criminal syndicates.

In 2006, according to the Center Studies in Democracy, about 10% of the registered firms for VAT collection in Bulgaria have fraudulent activity and are crowding out the budget.[24]

Shadow economy fraud – involves legitimate businesses with turnovers above the VAT registration threshold of their home country, who do not register for VAT, either deliberately, or due to not understanding the requirements of the tax system.

The annual *hidden economy index* in Bulgaria for 2008 has registered a moderate decline. In comparison, the index was 40% higher in 2002 when it was first constructed. The decline is due to the shrinking of the hidden economy in all its dimensions – tax evasion, hidden turnover, and employment. However, business perceptions regarding the extent of the hidden economy in Bulgaria have kept on rising since 2006. There is a major risk of a rise in the levels of hidden economic activity in Bulgaria with the increased risks of an economic slowdown or recession in most developed countries in the world, including the Euro zone.[25]

Repayment frauds – involved in VAT repayment frauds register for VAT, make false claims for repayments, then disappear. In some of these cases, the chain ends high up in the government. [26]

Suppression fraud – This VAT fraud is perpetrated by legitimate businesses that deliberately understate a portion of their sales and/or inflate claims for VAT refunds on their purchases. This is extremely valid for e-commerce. A picture of Kamchia River was claimed to be sold for 15 million levs?![27] (about $10 million) This borders on a high level of ignorance and stupidity.

Recent Examples

There are many examples of VAT fraud in the European Union. Several selected cases are noted below. A recent UK case highlights carousel fraud, which is on the rise. In the UK case, two traders bought and sold mobile phones across Europe, and evaded VAT through businesses they set up in Spain, Ireland, and the UK. They were sentenced to 16 years in prison for the resulting 38 million pound sterling fraud.

---

[24] 8000 фирми източват ДДС, в. Стандарт 28 януари 2006.

[25] The informal economy in Bulgaria: Policy responses in an economic crisis, CSD, http://www.csd.bg/artShow.php?id=9553 retrieved November 20, 2010.

[26] Гамбит с ДДС носи тройна печалба, в Стандарт, 13 декевмври 2005.

[27] Крантов, Красимир, ДДС измами по интернет, в. „24 часа" 29 April 2005 p. 19.

Also in the UK, tax enforcement officials reported that a recent carousel shipment of computer chips through Ireland involved quantities so large that it would have supplied the entire annual market for that chip in Europe, Asia, and Africa combined.

In a Slovakian case, authorities charged 19 people with repayment fraud. The group operated through at least 15 Slovakian companies, all registered VAT payers. However, the companies issued fraudulent invoices for fictitious purchases between them. The group received over 16 million euro in fraudulent refunds before being detected.

In another case, Bulgarian tax enforcement officials report that one of their tax officers, Mario Kamishev, Chief of Sofia's Vitosha Territorial Tax Directorate in 2005, along with another tax officer, was the mastermind of an organized crime group that paid others to register VAT companies controlled by the perpetrators, into their own names. These companies then issued fraudulent invoices for fictitious imports of various goods, including consumer electronics and appliances, and applied for VAT refunds. Upon investigation, addresses, warehouse, inventory, and staff were all found to be fictitious. Usually, Roma firms are the end-users, the so-called "fuses" of any VAT fraud. If they are caught, the investigation is often hampered, since they are mostly illiterate and some of them do not speak the Bulgarian language properly.[28]

Further examples of VAT fraud surface almost daily, with criminal prosecution and jail time on the rise. For example, a Scottish trader was recently sentenced to 4 years in prison in a Missing Trader intracommunity fraud involving computer chips. He used the proceeds to maintain a lavish lifestyle, including a palatial mansion and a fleet of luxury automobiles.

Suppression fraud often involves larger companies and is usually vigorously denied. In an example from outside the EU, officials of the US Company Procter and Gamble were shocked when Russian tax inspectors arrived to audit its detergent factory south of Moscow. The result was that P&G was billed over $1 million for disputed back VAT taxes.[29]

The Administration Role in Tax Evasion

Tax evasion and corruption are related insofar as that substituting corruption expenses for expenditure caused by legal actions can alter the costs of evading taxes. Every tax law can be enforced in a good and bad manner. In a good manner means more money for the treasury and in a bad manner means more money for the administrator enforcing the law.

---

[28] Томова, Поля, Банкери и данъчни служители помагат на "белите якички", сп Конфликти, 16/2005 http://www.bgsever.info/konflikti/br-16-2005.htm retrieved 5/13/2005.

[29] The company was able to use its clout with senior government officials to resolve the situation, but other companies have been less fortunate or do not have the financial ability to pay "overheads" to the officials.

The fiscal corruption causes a direct impact on tax collection and can also have an indirect effect. Individual behavior is influenced by social norms and usually these norms apply equally to tax evasion and corruption. On the other hand, tax evasion is only feasible for income generated unofficially and, in addition, activities in the shadow economy require bribing government employees, so corruption and tax evasion are closely correlated. The corruption among tax officials is one of the feasible connections between the two illegal activities.

Ascertaining the existence of such a link and also its details can be important for a number of reasons: first, since evasion reduces tax revenues and, thereby, the supply of public goods, a positive association between corruption and tax evasion will further question the "efficient grease hypothesis"[30] according to which corruption can enhance the efficiency of an economy strangled by excessive government regulation. Second, a positive relationship between evasion and corruption can provide an additional explanation for the observation that countries with higher levels of corruption collect fewer taxes per unit of GDP than those with less corruption.[31]

Tax enforcement officials have issued the following list of suspicious activities that individual citizens should be aware of to help combat VAT fraud:

- Establishments where cash is placed into open registers without being rung up or receipts issued.
- Contractors who request payment in cash and are reluctant to provide invoices.
- Businesses that offer discounts for cash and are reluctant to accept cash or credit cards.
- Traders who sell from unusual locations, such as car trunks or parking lots.
- Heavily discounted consumer electronics and appliances being sold for cash from nontraditional providers, such as bars and restaurants.
- Businesses that do not number their sales invoices and request that payment be made to different names than the business's.
- Tobacco products and alcoholic beverages without proper duty paid stamps and/ or markings not in the home country language.
- Fuel being sold directly from tankers, instead of through pumps, often away from established refueling centers.

Tax enforcement officials advise that individuals should refuse to do business in the manners described and to report such suspicious activity to tax enforcement officials immediately.

The advisory continues with a warning that businesses, as well as individuals, must be alert for VAT fraud. Businesses that do not report suspected fraudulent activities risk becoming responsible for the VAT liabilities of their trading partners,

---

[30] Kaufmann D, Wei S (1999) Does "grease money" speed up the wheels of commerce? NBER Working Paper No. 7093.

[31] See also Goerke Laszlo, Bureaucratic corruption and profit tax evasion, Published online: July 26, 2006. © Springer-Verlag 2006 Economics of Governance (2008) 9:177–196.

both up and down the supply chain, if it is found that they should have known that they were involved in potentially fraudulent transactions.

While taxpayer education, civil investigations, and fines are the most used methods to reduce VAT fraud, tax officials list the following specific activities that are likely to result in criminal prosecution:

- Setting up fraudulent companies specifically to cheat the VAT system.
- Deliberately deceiving tax investigators during the course of civil investigations.
- Combining VAT fraud with other crimes, such as smuggling and/or dealing in stolen goods.

Criminal penalties can include seizure of assets, jail terms, heavy fines, and disqualification from being company directors.

Tax enforcement officials have also stepped up checks on applications for VAT registrations to detect fictitious companies. For example, in 2003, the UK verified the authenticity of approximately 2.8% of the 250,000 applications it received. As a result, 1.5% of applications were either refused, or the trader was required to post-bond. Stated differently, over 50% of applications audited were found to be potentially fraudulent. Undercover investigators are being increasingly used in suspect businesses to identify fraudulent trading practices, especially within the shadow economy. However, this work is labor intensive and costly due to the high turnover of businesses in the shadow economy, and has been allocated limited resources.

Cooperation between EU member countries is also increasing compliance. Additional detection will result from increased use of data matching and data sharing.

The VAT Information Exchange System (VIES) is one such mechanism for exchanging information about VAT registered traders and the values of their supplies of goods. However, the value of VIES is limited as data integrity is not assured, due to inaccurate entries by traders, and the fact that the information will always be at least 3 months old.

A possible solution to Missing Trader intercommunity fraud would be to impose the tax in the country of origin, instead of the consuming country. However, while supported by tax authorities, EU member states have rejected this solution outright. It is unlikely that a political agreement can be reached on this measure.

EU members have concluded that the disadvantages far outweigh any potential benefits and have suggested that increased cooperation and information exchange between members is sufficient to control the situation. As with all efforts, cost of enforcement and political considerations are major hurdles.

Conclusion

Tax evasion has a century long history in Bulgaria. The Bulgarian taxpayers involved in tax evasion can be found in every aspect o f this phenomenon – on the inventive side, hiding their yield, changing the clothes of their kids to prevent their

Islamization; from underreporting techniques in personal and corporate income taxation to expanding the deductions and creating inappropriate expenses; from crowding out the budget and draining no existing VAT to the pure hiding and stealing of already collected from the consumer excises and VAT.

In personal income taxation, the variety of evaders ranges from those who are doing it because "of poverty and stupidity,"[32] which only shows that the mentality has not been changed since the last century, to the new types of employers who are evading and even stealing the social security, Medicare and income taxes due by them or collected from their employees.

The introduction of the flat tax and becoming a member of the European Union somehow lowers these types of evasion, since no western partner would like to do business with a tinted "fraudulent" firm or firm under investigation. In 2009, there is an increase of charged and sentenced individuals for tax and financial charges but their relative share is extremely low. Only 112 people were sentenced in 2009 and just in one fraudulent scheme in VAT there are about 40 firms and some tax officials.[33]

VAT fraud is a significant problem within the EU. Efforts are being made to reduce it, including cooperation between member states, taxpayer education, fines, and both civil and criminal prosecution.

However, long established business practices are in place, and political agreements are hard to come by. While major offenders are being targeted, and increased resources are being allocated, cost and political considerations remain big concerns.

Overall, it appears that while increased compliance would be preferable and that organized crime is unacceptable, some level of VAT fraud is viewed as unavoidable within the EU. It further appears that the general consensus among members is that aggressive enforcement is not really worth the price, either in financial or political terms.

More likely, long-term improvements in compliance rates will come through increased taxpayer education and an evolution in attitudes regarding taxation, rather than through aggressive law enforcement and criminal prosecution.

The alienation and the cynicism of the citizens in tax evasion are far from being a reason for pride or to show off but the coin always has a second side. So on one side is the reason for paying taxes and on the other one is the extraordinary way of spending the taxpayer's money. The renewal of the car park at the Bulgarian parliament with newer and newer limos every time after election is one of the reasons for this alienation and tax evasion in recent times. The second one is the personal example of the elected officials, as recently the newspapers are full with steno grams, recorded phone calls of different corruption and fraud deals which additionally undermine the fragile tax moral of the ordinary taxpayer. If we as taxpayers cannot see good ways of spending our money by the government why should we pay that money? Everyone can say to himself – I can waste my money way better.

---

[32] Пелин,   Елин,   Андрешко,   http://books2.my.contact.bg/pelin/andreshko.html   retrieved November 20, 2010

[33] *112 осъдени за финансови и данъчни престъпления, http://www.economynews.bg retrieved 10/28/2010 Разбиха ДДС афера за 60 млн. Лева, в Стандарт, 18 януари 2006 г.*

Chapter 24
Ethics and Tax Evasion: A Survey of Mexican Opinion

Robert W. McGee, Yanira Petrides, and Adriana M. Ross

Introduction

Several studies on the ethics of tax evasion have been conducted in recent years. Some of them have been theoretical while others have been empirical. The present study is mostly empirical, although some theory is also discussed.

Perhaps the most comprehensive theoretical study was conducted by Martin Crowe (1944), who reviewed 500 years of Catholic literature on the ethics of tax evasion, some of which was in the Latin language. More recent comprehensive theoretical studies were conducted by Martinez (1994), McGee (1998, 2004, 2006a), and Torgler (2003, 2007), although the Torgler studies involved a good deal of empirical work as well.

Some studies on the ethics of tax evasion examined the issue from a religious perspective. The religious group most opposed to tax evasion is the Church of Jesus Christ of Latter-Day Saints (Smith & Kimball, 1998). Nothing in the Mormon literature includes an exception to the general rule that tax evasion is unethical. Next, in terms of opposition to tax evasion, is the Baha'i faith (DeMoville, 1998). They do not condone tax evasion except in cases where members of the Baha'i faith are being persecuted by some government.

R.W. McGee (✉)
School of Business, Florida International University,
3000 NE 151 Street, North Miami, FL 33181, USA
e-mail: bob414@hotmail.com

Y. Petrides
Instituto Tecnológico Autónomo de México, Río Hondo No. 1,
Tizapán San Ángel C.P. 01080, Distrito Federal, Mexico

A.M. Ross
School of Accounting, Florida International University, 11200 SW 8th Street,
Miami, FL 33199, USA

R.W. McGee (ed.), *The Ethics of Tax Evasion: Perspectives in Theory and Practice*,
DOI 10.1007/978-1-4614-1287-8_24, © Springer Science+Business Media, LLC 2012

Cohn (1998) and Tamari (1998) discuss the Jewish view on tax evasion. Generally, tax evasion is frowned upon, although an exception may be made in cases where the rulers are corrupt and do not spend the money wisely. Catholic views are all over the map. Some Catholic theologians have said that tax evasion is a mortal sin (Saint Antoninus, 1571) while others have said it is not a sin at all (Iorio, 1939), at least in cases where the government does not provide for the common good (Angelus Carletus de Clavisio, 1494). Gronbacher (1998) and Schansberg (1998) hold that tax evasion is not always unethical. Pennock (1998) makes an exception where the government is fighting an unjust war.

At least two Muslim views have been published in the English language literature. Ahmad (1995) and Yusuf (1971) interpret the Muslim literature to permit tax evasion in cases where the tax is on income or where the effect of the tax is to raise prices, which includes value added taxes, sales taxes, use taxes, excise taxes, and tariffs. They would also see no moral need to pay inheritance taxes. Jalili (2012) disagrees with this view. According to his interpretation of the Muslim literature, one has an absolute duty to pay whatever the state demands in cases where the government follows Shariah law. In other cases, the duty to pay may be less than absolute, depending on what the government does with the tax money it collects.

A number of empirical studies have been conducted to determine views on the ethics of tax evasion. Empirical studies have been made of Asian countries (McGee, 2006d, 2007, 2008a, b; Torgler, 2004), Austria (Torgler & Schneider, 2005), Latin American and Caribbean countries (Alm & Martinez-Vazquez, 2010; McGee & López, 2008), Russia (Alm, Martinez-Vazquez & Torgler, 2005, 2006), Spain (Martinez-Vazquez and Torgler 2009), Switzerland (Torgler & Schaltegger, 2006), cultural differences in the United States (Alm & Torgler, 2006).

Methodology

After reviewing the literature that exists on the ethics of tax evasion, a survey was constructed and distributed to a group of graduate and undergraduate accounting, business, engineering, philosophy, and law students, as well as faculty and non-students in order to learn their views on the ethics of tax evasion. Due to space constraints, the literature is not fully reviewed here. However, the relevant literature is listed in the reference section.

The survey consisted of eighteen (18) statements. Using a seven-point Likert scale, respondents were asked to place the appropriate number in the space provided to indicate the extent of their agreement or disagreement with each statement. The statements in the survey reflected the three main viewpoints on the ethics of tax evasion that have emerged over the centuries. Four hundred and one (401) usable responses were received.

Survey Findings

The next few sections report on the study's findings.

Demographics

Table 24.1 lists the demographics of the survey. Both graduate and undergraduate students were included in the survey, as well as faculty and a sampling of nonstudents. Most students were accounting, business, or engineering students, although some other majors were also represented. Data were also analyzed by gender and age.

Table 24.2 lists the 18 statements and their mean scores. The overall mean score was 5.61, which indicates some opposition to tax evasion but also a fair degree of acceptability.

One reason for the present study was to determine which arguments that have been used in the past to justify tax evasion were the strongest and which were the weakest. Table 24.3 ranks the arguments from strongest to weakest.

The strongest arguments to justify tax evasion were in the cases of corruption, waste, unfairness, and inability to pay. High tax rates was another reason given to justify tax evasion. Three of the top eight reasons to justify tax evasion were in cases where the government engages in human rights abuses.

Table 24.1 Demographic information

	#	%		#	%
Status			*Major*		
Graduate student	98	24	Accounting	51	12.7
Undergraduate student	147	37	Other business/economics	112	27.9
Faculty	42	10	Theology/Religious Studies	9	2.2
Other	95	24	Philosophy	24	6
Unknown	19	5	Law	19	4.7
Total	401	100.0	Engineering	81	20.2
			Other	0	0
			Unknown	105	26.2
			Total	401	100.0
Gender			*Age*		
Male	204	51	<25	162	40.4
Female	185	46.3	25–40	131	32.7
Unknown	12	2.7	>40	98	24.4
Total	401	100.0	Unknown	10	2.5
			Total	401	100.0

Table 24.2 Summary of responses

Statement number	Statement	Mean
1	Tax evasion is ethical if tax rates are too high (S1)	5.40
2	Tax evasion is ethical even if tax rates are not too high because the government is not entitled to take as much as it is taking from me (S2)	6.10
3	Tax evasion is ethical if the tax system is unfair (S3)	5.10
4	Tax evasion is ethical if a large portion of the money collected is wasted (S4)	5.09
5	Tax evasion is ethical even if most of the money collected is spent wisely (S5)	6.02
6	Tax evasion is ethical if a large portion of the money collected is spent on projects that I morally disapprove of (S6)	5.61
7	Tax evasion is ethical even if a large portion of the money collected is spent on worthy projects (S7)	5.79
8	Tax evasion is ethical if a large portion of the money collected is spent on projects that do not benefit me (S8)	5.88
9	Tax evasion is ethical even if a large portion of the money collected is spent on projects that do benefit me (S9)	5.85
10	Tax evasion is ethical if everyone is doing it (S10)	6.03
11	Tax evasion is ethical if a significant portion of the money collected winds up in the pockets of corrupt politicians or their families and friends (S11)	5.02
12	Tax evasion is ethical if the probability of getting caught is low (S12)	6.13
13	Tax evasion is ethical if some of the proceeds go to support a war that I consider to be unjust (S13)	5.51
14	Tax evasion is ethical if I can't afford to pay (S14)	5.19
15	Tax evasion is ethical even if it means that if I pay less, others will have to pay more (S15)	6.04
16	Tax evasion would be ethical if I lived under an oppressive regime like Nazi Germany or Stalinist Russia (S16)	5.46
17	Tax evasion is ethical if the government discriminates against me because of my religion, race, or ethnic background (S17)	5.25
18	Tax evasion is ethical if the government imprisons people for their political opinions (S18)	5.48
	Average	5.61

1 = strongly agree; 7 = strongly disagree

Table 24.3 Ranking of arguments – strongest to weakest

Rank	Statement	Mean
1	Tax evasion is ethical if a significant portion of the money collected winds up in the pockets of corrupt politicians or their families and friends (S11)	5.02
2	Tax evasion is ethical if a large portion of the money collected is wasted (S4)	5.09
3	Tax evasion is ethical if the tax system is unfair (S3)	5.10
4	Tax evasion is ethical if I can't afford to pay (S14)	5.19
5	Tax evasion is ethical if the government discriminates against me because of my religion, race, or ethnic background (S17)	5.25

(continued)

Table 24.3 (continued)

Rank	Statement	Mean
6	Tax evasion is ethical if tax rates are too high (S1)	5.40
7	Tax evasion would be ethical if I lived under an oppressive regime like Nazi Germany or Stalinist Russia (S16)	5.46
8	Tax evasion is ethical if the government imprisons people for their political opinions (S18)	5.48
9	Tax evasion is ethical if some of the proceeds go to support a war that I consider to be unjust (S13)	5.51
10	Tax evasion is ethical if a large portion of the money collected is spent on projects that I morally disapprove of (S6)	5.61
11	Tax evasion is ethical even if a large portion of the money collected is spent on worthy projects (S7)	5.79
12	Tax evasion is ethical even if a large portion of the money collected is spent on projects that do benefit me (S9)	5.85
13	Tax evasion is ethical if a large portion of the money collected is spent on projects that do not benefit me (S8)	5.88
14	Tax evasion is ethical even if most of the money collected is spent wisely (S5)	6.02
15	Tax evasion is ethical if everyone is doing it (S10)	6.03
16	Tax evasion is ethical even if it means that if I pay less, others will have to pay more (S15)	6.04
17	Tax evasion is ethical even if tax rates are not too high because the government is not entitled to take as much as it is taking from me (S2)	6.10
18	Tax evasion is ethical if the probability of getting caught is low (S12)	6.13

1 = strongly agree; 7 = strongly disagree

Gender

Many studies have examined gender in connection with ethical decision making. The results are mixed. One group of studies that examined attitudes on ethical issues other than taxes found that women were more ethical than men (Baird, 1980; Betz, et al., 1989; Boyd, 1981; Chonko & Hunt, 1985; Franke, et al., 1997; Kohut & Corriher, 1994). Another group of studies found that the differences between male and female opinions on certain ethical issues are insignificant (Barnett & Karson, 1989; Callan, 1992; Dubinsky & Levy. 1985; Fritzsche, 1988; Harris, 1989; Kidwell, et al., 1987; Robin & Babin, 1997). A third group of studies found men to be more ethical than women (Barnett & Karson, 1987; Weeks, et al., 1999).

A few studies have examined gender ethics in conjunction with views on tax evasion. Women were found to be more strongly opposed to tax evasion in studies of Australia (McGee & Bose, 2009), Hubei, China (McGee & Guo, 2007), Colombia (McGee, López & Yepes, 2009), Estonia (McGee, Alver & Alver, 2008), the USA (McGee, Nickerson & Fees, 2006), Guatemala (McGee & Lingle, 2008), international business academics teaching in the United States (McGee, 2006b), Orthodox Jewish students (McGee & Cohn, 2008), New Zealand (Gupta & McGee, 2010),

Table 24.4 Statistical data – gender

Statement	Male			Female			p value
	Sample	Mean	SD	Sample	Mean	SD	
1	204	5.52	1.73	186	5.32	2.02	0.2931
2	204	6.12	1.38	186	6.15	1.33	0.8274
3	204	5.09	2.06	186	5.15	2.04	0.7730
4	204	5.04	2.10	186	5.22	2.03	0.3909
5	204	6.01	1.53	185	6.09	1.58	0.6124
6	204	5.66	1.63	186	5.66	1.68	1.0000
7	204	5.84	1.69	184	5.77	1.69	0.6839
8	204	5.88	1.52	185	5.95	1.57	0.6554
9	204	5.96	1.65	185	5.88	1.79	0.6467
10	204	6.08	1.58	185	6.07	1.75	0.9528
11	204	4.89	2.25	186	5.25	2.30	0.1192
12	204	6.26	1.28	185	6.03	1.52	0.1063
13	204	5.48	1.84	184	5.62	1.99	0.4720
14	204	5.18	1.99	184	5.27	1.99	0.6567
15	204	6.00	1.50	183	6.13	1.46	0.3892
16	200	5.30	2.26	181	5.69	1.98	0.0753
17	204	5.05	2.25	184	5.47	2.04	0.0558
18	203	5.25	2.06	183	5.75	1.72	0.0105
Mean average		5.59			5.69		

1 = strongly agree; 7 = strongly disagree

Puerto Rico (McGee & López, 2007), South Africa (McGee & Goldman, 2010), Taiwan (McGee & Andres, 2009), and Thailand (McGee 2008a, b).

Men were found to be more strongly opposed to tax evasion in studies of Romania (McGee, 2006a, b, c, d), Slovakia (McGee & Tusan, 2008), and Turkey (McGee & Benk, 2011). Studies of Argentina (McGee & Rossi, 2008); Beijing, China (McGee & An, 2008); Southern China and Macau (McGee & Noronha, 2008); France (McGee & M'Zali, 2009); Hong Kong (McGee & Butt, 2008); Kazakhstan (McGee & Preobragenskaya, 2008); and Poland (McGee & Bernal, 2006) found no significant difference between male and female attitudes toward tax evasion.

Table 24.4 shows the data summarized by gender. The women's overall mean score (5.69) was slightly higher than the men's overall mean score (5.59), indicating that women were more strongly opposed to tax evasion. Women had higher mean scores in 12 of 18 cases, indicating stronger opposition to tax evasion. Men were more opposed to tax evasion in five cases. In one case, the mean scores were identical. However, the difference in mean score was significant at the 5% level in only one case (Statement 18 – where the government imprisons people for their political opinions). The difference in mean score was significant at the 10% level for the other two human rights questions (S16 – living under an oppressive regime; S17 – discrimination). Thus, it can be said that, although women were slightly more opposed to tax evasion, the differences based on gender were generally insignificant.

Table 24.5 Statistical data – age

Statement	Under 25			25–40			Over 40		
	Sample	Mean	SD	Sample	Mean	SD	Sample	Mean	SD
1	162	5.24	1.94	131	5.66	1.80	98	5.36	1.89
2	162	5.99	1.52	131	6.11	1.28	98	6.39	1.13
3	162	4.88	2.11	131	5.37	1.98	98	5.18	2.03
4	162	4.78	2.12	131	5.44	1.95	98	5.27	2.05
5	161	5.92	1.74	131	6.27	1.13	98	5.99	1.70
6	162	5.49	1.67	131	5.95	1.39	98	5.58	1.82
7	161	5.47	1.89	129	6.09	1.42	98	6.02	1.57
8	161	5.68	1.74	131	6.11	1.33	98	6.04	1.41
9	161	5.67	1.87	131	6.25	1.36	98	5.88	1.87
10	161	5.85	1.86	131	6.35	1.35	98	6.09	1.64
11	162	4.72	2.33	131	5.31	2.22	98	5.28	2.23
12	161	6.02	1.48	131	6.20	1.37	98	6.32	1.33
13	162	5.20	2.13	130	6.01	1.52	98	5.44	1.92
14	162	4.62	2.06	130	5.86	1.60	98	5.32	2.08
15	162	5.85	1.63	129	6.36	1.07	98	6.01	1.61
16	160	5.42	2.04	127	5.83	1.95	96	5.09	2.48
17	162	4.87	2.15	130	5.61	1.97	98	5.36	2.35
18	161	5.23	2.07	129	5.78	1.66	98	5.43	2.02
Mean average		5.38			5.92			5.67	

1 = strongly agree; 7 = strongly disagree

Age

A number of studies have examined age in conjunction with views on various ethical issues. Some studies of ethical views on nontax issues found that people become more ethical or more respectful of authority as they get older (Barnett & Karson, 1987, 1989; Harris, 1990; Kelley et al., 1990; Longenecker et al., 1989; Ruegger & King, 1992; Serwinek, 1992). However, Sims (1996) found that older students had less reluctance when it came to pirating software than did younger students. Babakus, et al. (2004) found that age made a difference in ethical attitude, but the difference it made depended on culture and the particular topic in question.

A few studies have examined age in conjunction with views on tax evasion. An Estonian study (McGee, Alver & Alver, 2008) found that people under age 25 were significantly less opposed to tax evasion than were people in the 25–40 age group. Studies of New Zealand (Gupta & McGee, 2010) and Turkey (McGee & Benk, 2011) found older people to be more opposed to tax evasion than younger people. A study of Slovakia found older people to be slightly more opposed to tax evasion than younger people (McGee & Tusan, 2008).

Table 24.5 shows the statistical data for three age groups. The sample sizes for each age category were sufficiently large to do some comparisons.

A comparison of mean scores from Table 24.5 yields some interesting results, which are summarized in Table 24.6. The youngest group was least opposed to tax evasion in 17 of 18 cases. The middle group was most opposed to tax evasion in 16

Table 24.6 Age – comparison of mean scores

	Under 25	25–40	Over 40
Most opposed to tax evasion	0	16	2
Least opposed to tax evasion	17	0	1

Table 24.7 Statistical data – age (p values)

Statement	Under 25 vs. 25–40	Under 25 vs. Over 40	25–40 vs. over 40
1	0.0581	0.6259	0.2232
2	0.4719	0.0250	0.0866
3	0.0431	0.2608	0.4780
4	0.0064	0.0686	0.5238
5	0.0478	0.7514	0.1363
6	0.0121	0.6843	0.0824
7	0.0022	0.0163	0.7256
8	0.0206	0.0847	0.7013
9	0.0032	0.3816	0.0843
10	0.0106	0.2937	0.1900
11	0.0285	0.0574	0.9197
12	0.2862	0.1016	0.5073
13	0.0003	0.3620	0.0131
14	0.0001	0.0087	0.0277
15	0.0024	0.4417	0.0508
16	0.0857	0.2495	0.0133
17	0.0026	0.0868	0.3838
18	0.0148	0.4474	0.1535

of 18 cases. The only time the oldest group was least opposed to taxation was the case where the taxpayer lived under a repressive regime.

These results were somewhat surprising. Most other ethical studies that examined the age variable found that people have more respect for authority and law as they become older. Thus, one might predict a priori that the oldest group would be the group that has the strongest opposition to tax evasion while the youngest group would have the least opposition. Although it was true that the youngest group had the least opposition to tax evasion, it was the middle group (25–40) that usually had the most opposition, making the pattern curvilinear rather than linear.

Table 24.7 summarizes the extent of the significance of the differences in mean scores. The differences in mean scores were significant at the 1% level in 8 cases; at the 5% level in 12 cases; at the 10% level in 10 cases; and not significant in 24 cases. Thus, we can conclude that the middle group (25–40) was most opposed to tax evasion, while the youngest group (under 25) was least opposed.

Academic Major

Another demographic examined was academic major. Prior studies have had mixed findings. A study of Argentina (McGee & Rossi, 2008) found that business and

Table 24.8 Statistical data – major

Statement	Accounting			Other business/economics			Engineering		
	Sample	Mean	SD	Sample	Mean	SD	Sample	Mean	SD
1	51	5.22	2.06	112	5.02	2.01	81	5.58	1.66
2	51	5.90	1.64	112	6.11	1.38	81	5.95	1.56
3	51	4.98	1.96	112	4.62	2.15	81	4.99	2.17
4	51	4.92	2.09	112	4.43	2.07	81	5.12	2.05
5	51	5.86	1.77	111	6.05	1.63	81	5.90	1.60
6	51	5.65	1.53	112	5.48	1.67	81	5.57	1.75
7	51	5.82	1.71	110	5.64	1.83	81	5.89	1.57
8	51	6.04	1.40	111	5.86	1.61	81	5.79	1.51
9	51	5.88	1.76	111	5.72	1.86	81	6.07	1.56
10	51	6.35	1.34	111	5.79	1.96	81	6.09	1.54
11	51	5.14	2.24	112	4.54	2.28	81	4.91	2.42
12	51	5.94	1.75	111	6.21	1.45	81	6.30	1.05
13	50	5.18	2.06	112	5.34	1.88	80	5.48	2.06
14	50	5.00	2.07	112	4.79	2.05	80	5.44	1.87
15	50	6.14	1.54	112	5.91	1.54	79	6.25	1.08
16	50	5.74	1.89	110	5.21	2.20	79	5.65	2.11
17	50	4.70	2.27	112	4.88	2.20	80	5.39	2.11
18	50	5.12	2.10	112	5.07	2.09	79	5.48	1.80
Mean average		5.53			5.37			5.66	

1 = strongly agree; 7 = strongly disagree

economics students were generally more opposed to tax evasion than were law students. An Armenian study (McGee & Maranjyan, 2008) found that business students were more strongly opposed to tax evasion than were theology students. An Australian study (McGee & Bose, 2009) found that business and economics students were least opposed to tax evasion; seminary students were most opposed; business and economics students were significantly less opposed to tax evasion than were philosophy, accounting, health services, and seminary students. Accounting majors were significantly more opposed to tax evasion than were business and economics students and information technology students and were significantly less opposed to tax evasion than were seminary and health services students.

One Chinese study (McGee & Guo, 2007) found that business and economics students were least opposed to tax evasion and that law and philosophy students were equally opposed to tax evasion. Studies of Estonia (McGee, Alver & Alver, 2008), Kazakhstan (McGee & Preobragenskaya, 2008), and New Zealand (Gupta & McGee, 2010) found that accounting majors and business/economics majors were equally opposed to tax evasion. The New Zealand study also found that law students were somewhat less opposed to tax evasion than were the accounting and business/economics students. A Guatemalan study (McGee & Lingle, 2008) found that business students were more opposed to tax evasion than were law students.

Table 24.8 shows the data for the three majors having the largest sample sizes. Based on overall mean scores, the engineering majors (5.66) were most opposed to

Table 24.9 Academic major – comparison of mean scores

	Accounting	Other business	Engineering
Most opposed to tax evasion	5	2	11
Least opposed to tax evasion	5	12	1

Table 24.10 Statistical data – major

Statement	Accounting vs. other business/economics	Accounting vs. engineering	Other business/economics vs. engineering
1	0.5597	0.2716	0.0416
2	0.3976	0.8607	0.4528
3	0.3101	0.9787	0.2413
4	0.1643	0.5890	0.0228
5	0.5035	0.8935	0.5264
6	0.5373	0.7890	0.7177
7	0.5543	0.8100	0.3234
8	0.4927	0.3427	0.7604
9	0.6058	0.5180	0.1703
10	0.0662	0.3231	0.2542
11	0.1192	0.5853	0.2796
12	0.3047	0.3047	0.6354
13	0.6279	0.4207	0.6256
14	0.5490	0.2128	0.0259
15	0.3812	0.6345	0.0926
16	0.1426	0.8064	0.1694
17	0.6345	0.0805	0.1089
18	0.8885	0.3018	0.1594

tax evasion, the business/economics majors (5.37) were least opposed, and the accounting majors (5.53) were in the middle.

Table 24.9 shows the results for comparing mean scores from Table 24.8. The engineering majors were most opposed to tax evasion in 11 of 18 cases. The other business/economics majors were least opposed to tax evasion in 12 of 18 cases. Comparing the overall mean scores and the data in Table 24.9 might lead one to reasonably conclude that engineering majors were more opposed to tax evasion than were the other two groups and the other business/economics majors were least opposed to tax evasion, with accounting majors falling in between these two groups.

Table 24.10 shows the extent of the significance in mean score differences. Only three of the differences were significant at the 5% level.

Student Status

Prior studies that examined student status had mixed results. A study in Argentina (McGee & Rossi, 2008) found no difference between students and faculty. An Australian study (McGee & Bose, 2009) found that overall, undergraduate students were least opposed to tax evasion and faculty were most opposed. An Estonian study (McGee, Alver & Alver, 2008) found similar results. Overall, undergraduate students were least opposed to tax evasion; faculty and accounting practitioners were most opposed. A New Zealand study (Gupta & McGee, 2010) found that undergraduate students were less opposed to tax evasion than were graduate students.

Table 24.11 shows the data for the present study. A comparison of overall mean scores shows that the nonstudents (6.11) were most opposed to tax evasion while undergraduate students were least opposed (5.26), with graduate students (5.65) and faculty (5.84) falling in between.

Table 24.12 shows the significance of the differences in mean score for graduate students, undergraduate students, and faculty. Differences were significant at the 1% level in 9 cases, significant at the 5% level in 10 cases, significant at the 10% level in 1 case, and not significant in 34 cases.

Concluding Comments

The study found some interesting results. Women were slightly more opposed to tax evasion but the differences in mean scores were not significant. Regarding age, the 25–40-year-old group was most opposed to tax evasion, while the under 25 group was least opposed. Surprisingly, the oldest group was not the group that was most opposed to tax evasion. Engineering majors were most opposed to tax evasion, while business and economics majors were least opposed, with accounting majors falling in the middle. In the student status category, the nonstudents polled were more opposed to tax evasion than any of the other groups, which might lead one to conclude that using student surveys may result in biased samples. Faculty members were not the group that was most opposed to tax evasion, although they were more opposed than were either of the two student groups, which is consistent with other studies. Undergraduate students were least opposed to tax evasion, which is also consistent with other studies.

Table 24.11 Statistical data – status

Statement	Graduate students			Undergraduate students			Faculty			Nonstudents		
	Sample	Mean	SD	Sample	Mean	SD	Sample	Mean	SD	Sample	Mean	SD
1	98	5.35	1.94	147	5.10	1.93	42	5.60	1.61	95	6.03	1.58
2	98	6.16	1.34	147	5.84	1.61	42	6.50	0.94	95	6.38	0.99
3	98	5.02	2.08	147	4.63	2.12	42	5.19	1.80	95	5.94	1.76
4	98	5.09	2.16	147	4.62	2.09	42	5.10	1.81	95	5.91	1.82
5	98	6.03	1.58	147	5.80	1.79	41	6.63	0.86	95	6.22	1.32
6	98	5.54	1.65	147	5.35	1.70	42	5.90	1.57	95	6.22	1.34
7	96	5.67	1.71	147	5.29	1.92	41	6.63	0.94	95	6.35	1.20
8	98	5.77	1.55	147	5.65	1.71	41	6.51	0.81	95	6.22	1.37
9	98	5.94	1.72	147	5.54	2.03	41	6.66	0.62	95	6.15	1.41
10	98	6.16	1.62	147	5.78	1.92	41	6.51	1.10	95	6.26	1.43
11	98	4.96	2.33	147	4.73	2.35	42	4.45	2.42	95	6.00	1.76
12	98	6.02	1.53	147	6.04	1.53	41	6.61	1.05	95	6.27	1.22
13	98	5.73	1.67	147	5.01	2.15	42	5.50	1.92	95	6.09	1.64
14	98	5.49	1.91	147	4.37	2.09	42	5.64	1.78	95	5.95	1.62
15	97	6.20	1.22	147	5.78	1.75	42	6.48	0.83	95	6.24	1.31
16	95	5.44	2.30	146	5.34	2.14	42	4.98	2.36	93	5.94	1.82
17	98	5.49	2.23	147	4.75	2.16	42	4.90	2.25	95	5.82	1.89
18	98	5.63	1.78	146	5.05	2.14	42	5.26	2.01	95	5.97	1.65
Mean average		5.65			5.26			5.84			6.11	

1 = strongly agree; 7 = strongly disagree

Table 24.12 Statistical data – status

Statement	Graduate students vs. undergraduate students	Graduate students vs. faculty	Undergraduate students vs. faculty
1	0.3226	0.4645	0.1270
2	0.1050	0.1377	0.0121
3	0.1565	0.6458	0.1209
4	0.0901	0.9791	0.1786
5	0.3032	0.0235	0.0045
6	0.3867	0.2322	0.0275
7	0.1169	0.0010	0.0001
8	0.5771	0.0045	0.0021
9	0.1100	0.0102	0.0006
10	0.1080	0.2079	0.0210
11	0.4521	0.2427	0.4995
12	0.9202	0.0257	0.0262
13	0.0055	0.4768	0.1843
14	0.0001	0.6647	0.0004
15	0.0408	0.6647	0.1772
16	0.7310	0.2862	0.3491
17	0.0101	0.1548	0.6946
18	0.0276	0.2804	0.5708

References

Ahmad, Mushtaq (1995). *Business Ethics in Islam*. Islamabad, Pakistan: The International Institute of Islamic Thought & The International Institute of Islamic Economics.

Alm, James, Jorge Martinez-Vazquez and Benno Torgler. (2005). Russian Tax Morale in the 1990s. *Proceedings of the 98th Annual Conference on Taxation of the National Tax Association*, 287–292.

Alm, James and Benno Torgler. (2006). Culture differences and tax morale in the United States and in Europe. *Journal of Economic Psychology*, 27, 224–246.

Alm, James, Jorge Martinez-Vazquez and Benno Torgler. (2006). Russian attitudes toward paying taxes – before, during and after the transition. *International Journal of Social Economics*, 33(12), 832–857.

Alm, J. & J. Martinez-Vazquez. (2010). Tax Evasion, the Informal Sector, and Tax Morale in LAC Countries. In J. Alm, J. Martinez-Vazquez & B. Torgler (Eds.), *Developing Alternative Frameworks for Explaining Tax Compliance* (pp. 260–291). London & New York: Routledge.

Angelus Carletus de Clavisio (1494). *Summa Angelica*. Lyons, as cited by Martin T. Crowe, The Moral Obligation of Paying Just Taxes, The Catholic University of America Studies in Sacred Theology No. 84, 1944, pp. 28–29.

Antoninus, Saint (1571). *Summa Sacrae Theologiae, Iuris Pontificii, et Caesarei*, II, p. 63 ff, Venice, as cited by Martin T. Crowe, The Moral Obligation of Paying Just Taxes, The Catholic University of America Studies in Sacred Theology No. 84, 1944, p. 42.

Babakus, Emin, T. Bettina Cornwell, Vince Mitchell and Bodo Schlegelmilch (2004). Reactions to Unethical Consumer Behavior across Six Countries. *The Journal of Consumer Marketing*, 21(4/5), 254–263.

Baird, J.S. (1980). Current Trends in College Cheating. *Psychology in the Schools,* 17(4), 515–522, as cited in Bob S. Brown and Peggy Choong. (2005). An Investigation of Academic Dishonesty among Business Students at Public and Private United States Universities. *International Journal of Management* 22(2): 201–214.

Barnett, John H. and Marvin J. Karson. (1987). Personal Values and Business Decisions: An Exploratory Investigation. *Journal of Business Ethics*, 6(5), 371–382.

Barnett, John H. and Marvin J. Karson. (1989). Managers, Values, and Executive Decisions: An Exploration of the Role of Gender, Career Stage, Organizational Level, Function, and the Importance of Ethics, Relationships and Results in Managerial Decision-Making. *Journal of Business Ethics*, 8(10), 747–771.

Betz, Michael, Lenahan O'Connell and Jon M. Shepard. (1989). Gender Differences in Proclivity for Unethical Behavior. *Journal of Business Ethics*, 8(5), 321–324.

Boyd, David P. (1981). Improving Ethical Awareness Through the Business and Society Course. *Business and Society* 20, 21, 2, 1: 27–31.

Callan, Victor J. (1992). Predicting Ethical Values and Training Needs in Ethics. *Journal of Business Ethics*, 11(10), 761–769.

Chonko, Lawrence B. and Shelby D. Hunt. (1985). Ethics and Marketing Management: An Empirical Investigation. *Journal of Business Research*, 13(4), 339–359.

Cohn, Gordon. (1998). The Jewish View on Paying Taxes. *Journal of Accounting, Ethics & Public Policy*, 1(2), 109–120, reprinted in Robert W. McGee (Ed.), *The Ethics of Tax Evasion* (pp. 180–189). Dumont, NJ: The Dumont Institute for Public Policy Research, 1998, pp. 180–189.

Crowe, Martin T. (1944). The Moral Obligation of Paying Just Taxes, The Catholic University of America Studies in Sacred Theology No. 84.

DeMoville, Wig. (1998). The Ethics of Tax Evasion: A Baha'i Perspective. *Journal of Accounting, Ethics & Public Policy*, 1(3), 356–368, reprinted in Robert W. McGee (Ed.), *The Ethics of Tax Evasion* (pp. 230–240). Dumont, NJ: The Dumont Institute for Public Policy Research, 1998.

Dubinsky, Alan J. and Michael Levy. (1985). Ethics in Retailing: Perceptions of Retail Sales People. *Journal of the Academy of Marketing Science*, 13(1), 1–16.

Franke, George R., Deborah F. Crown & Deborah F. Spake. (1997). Gender Differences in Ethical Perceptions of Business Practices: A Social Role Theory Perspective. *Journal of Applied Psychology*, 82(6), 920–934.

Fritzsche, David J. (1988). An Examination of Marketing Ethics: Role of the Decision Maker, Consequences of the Decision, Management Position, and Sex of the Respondent. *Journal of Macromarketing*, 8(2), 29–39.

Gronbacher, Gregory M.A. (1998). Taxation: Catholic Social Thought and Classical Liberalism. *Journal of Accounting, Ethics & Public Policy*, 1(1), 91–100, reprinted in Robert W. McGee (ed.), *The Ethics of Tax Evasion* (pp. 158–167). Dumont, NJ: The Dumont Institute for Public Policy Research, Dumont, NJ, 1998.

Gupta, Ranjana and Robert W. McGee. (2010). A Comparative Study of New Zealanders' Opinion on the Ethics of Tax Evasion: Students v. Accountants. *New Zealand Journal of Taxation Law and Policy*, 16(1), 47–84.

Harris, James R. (1989). Ethical Values and Decision Processes of Male and Female Business Students. *Journal of Education for Business*, 8, 234–238, as cited in Sharon Galbraith and Harriet Buckman Stephenson. (1993). Decision Rules Used by Male and Female Business Students in Making Ethical Value Judgments: Another Look. *Journal of Business Ethics*, 12(3), 227–233.

Harris, James R. (1990). Ethical Values of Individuals at Different Levels in the Organizational Hierarchy of a Single Firm. *Journal of Business Ethics*, 9(9), 741–750.

Iorio, T. (1939). *Theologia Moralis,* 6th ed., II, n. 778, Naples: M. D'Aurea, as cited by Martin T. Crowe, The Moral Obligation of Paying Just Taxes, The Catholic University of America Studies in Sacred Theology No. 84, 1944, p. 41.

Jalili, Ali Reza (2012). The Ethics of Tax Evasion: An Islamic Perspective. In Robert W. McGee (Ed.), *The Ethics of Tax Evasion in Theory and Practice* (forthcoming). New York: Springer.

Kelley, S.W., O.C. Ferrell and S.J. Skinner. (1990). Ethical Behavior Among Marketing Researchers: An Assessment of Selected Demographic Characteristics. *Journal of Business Ethics*, 9(8), 681–688.

Kidwell, Jeaneen M., Robert E. Stevens & Art L. Bethke. (1987). Differences in Ethical Perceptions Between Male and Female Managers: Myth or Reality? *Journal of Business Ethics*, 6(6), 489–493.

Kohut, Gary F. & Susan E. Corriher. (1994). The Relationship of Age, Gender, Experience and Awareness of Written Ethics Policies to Business Decision Making. *S.A.M. Advanced Management Journal*, 59(1), 32–39.

Longenecker, Justin G., Joseph A. McKinney & Carlos W. Moore. (1989). Do Smaller Firms Have Higher Ethics? *Business and Society Review*, 71, 19–21.

Martinez, Leo P. (1994). Taxes, Morals, and Legitimacy. *Brigham Young University Law Review*, 1994, 521–569.

Martinez-Vazquez, Jorge and Benno Torgler. (2009). The Evolution of Tax Morale in Modern Spain. *Journal of Economic Issues*, 43(1), 1–28.

McGee, Robert W. (Ed.). (1998). *The Ethics of Tax Evasion*. Dumont, NJ: The Dumont Institute for Public Policy Research.

McGee, Robert W. (2004). *The Philosophy of Taxation and Public Finance*. Norwell, MA and Dordrecht: Kluwer Academic Publishers.

McGee, Robert W. (2006a). Three Views on the Ethics of Tax Evasion. Journal of Business Ethics, 67(1), 15–35.

McGee, Robert W. (2006b). A Survey of International Business Academics on the Ethics of Tax Evasion. *Journal of Accounting, Ethics & Public Policy*, 6(3), 301–352.

McGee, Robert W. (2006c). The Ethics of Tax Evasion: A Survey of Romanian Business Students and Faculty. *The ICFAI Journal of Public Finance*, 4(2), 38–68 (2006). Reprinted in Robert W. McGee and Galina G. Preobragenskaya, *Accounting and Financial System Reform in Eastern Europe and Asia* (pp. 299–334). New York: Springer, 2006.

McGee, Robert W. (2006d). A Comparative Study of Tax Evasion Ethics in Thailand and Vietnam. *Journal of Accounting, Ethics & Public Policy*, 6(1), 103–123.

McGee, Robert W. and Arkadiusz Bernal. (2006). The Ethics of Tax Evasion: A Survey of Business Students in Poland. In Global Economy -- How It Works (Mina Baliamoune-Lutz, Alojzy Z. Nowak & Jeff Steagall, eds.) (pp. 155–174). Warsaw: University of Warsaw & Jacksonville: University of North Florida. Reprinted at http://ssrn.com/abstract=875434.

McGee, Robert W., Inge Nickerson and Werner Fees. (2006). German and American Opinion on the Ethics of Tax Evasion. *Proceedings of the Academy of Legal, Ethical and Regulatory Issues* (Reno), 10(2), 31–34.

McGee, Robert W. (2007). Ethics and Tax Evasion in Asia. *ICFAI Journal of Public Finance*, 5(2), 21–33 (May). Reprinted in Business Ethics: A 360 Degree Appraisal, ICFAI University Press. Hyderabad, India.

McGee, Robert W. and Zhiwen Guo. (2007). A Survey of Law, Business and Philosophy Students in China on the Ethics of Tax Evasion. *Society and Business Review*, 2(3), 299–315.

McGee, Robert W. and Silvia López Paláu. (2007). The Ethics of Tax Evasion: Two Empirical Studies of Puerto Rican Opinion. *Journal of Applied Business and Economics*, 7(3), 27–47 (2007). Reprinted in Robert W. McGee (editor), *Readings in Accounting Ethics* (pp. 314–342). Hyderabad, India: ICFAI University Press, 2009.

McGee, Robert W. (2008a). Opinions on Tax Evasion in Asia, in Robert W. McGee, editor, *Taxation and Public Finance in Transition and Developing Economies* (pp. 309–320) New York: Springer.

McGee, Robert W. (2008b). Opinions on Tax Evasion in Thailand, in Robert W. McGee, editor, *Taxation and Public Finance in Transition and Developing Economies* (pp. 609–620). New York: Springer.

McGee, Robert W., Jaan Alver and Lehte Alver. (2008). The Ethics of Tax Evasion: A Survey of Estonian Opinion, in Robert W. McGee, editor, *Taxation and Public Finance in Transition and Developing Economies* (pp. 461–480). New York: Springer.

McGee, Robert W. and Yuhua An. (2008). A Survey of Chinese Business and Economics Students on the Ethics of Tax Evasion, in Robert W. McGee, editor, *Taxation and Public Finance in Transition and Developing Economies* (pp. 409–421). New York: Springer.

McGee, Robert W. and Yiu Yu Butt. (2008). An Empirical Study of Tax Evasion Ethics in Hong Kong. Proceedings of the International Academy of Business and Public Administration Disciplines (IABPAD), Dallas, April 24–27: 72–83. Reprinted in the present volume.

McGee, Robert W. and Gordon M. Cohn. (2008). Jewish Perspectives on the Ethics of Tax Evasion. *Journal of Legal, Ethical and Regulatory Issues*, 11(2), 1–32.

McGee, Robert W. and Christopher Lingle. (2008). The Ethics of Tax Evasion: A Survey of Guatemalan Opinion, in Robert W. McGee, editor, *Taxation and Public Finance in Transition and Developing Economies* (pp. 481–495). New York: Springer.

McGee, Robert W. and Silvia López Paláu. (2008). Tax Evasion and Ethics: A Comparative Study of the USA and Four Latin American Countries, in Robert W. McGee, editor, *Taxation and Public Finance in Transition and Developing Economies* (pp. 185–224). New York: Springer.

McGee, Robert W. and Tatyana B. Maranjyan. (2008). Opinions on Tax Evasion in Armenia, in Robert W. McGee, editor, *Taxation and Public Finance in Transition and Developing Economies* (pp. 277–307). New York: Springer.

McGee, Robert W. and Carlos Noronha. (2008). The Ethics of Tax Evasion: A Comparative Study of Guangzhou (Southern China) and Macau Opinions. *Euro Asia Journal of Management*, 18(2), 133–152.

McGee, Robert W. and Galina G. Preobragenskaya. (2008). A Study of Tax Evasion Ethics in Kazakhstan, in Robert W. McGee, editor, *Taxation and Public Finance in Transition and Developing Economies* (pp. 497–510). New York: Springer.

McGee, Robert W. and Marcelo J. Rossi. (2008). A Survey of Argentina on the Ethics of Tax Evasion, in Robert W. McGee, editor, *Taxation and Public Finance in Transition and Developing Economies* (pp. 239–261). New York: Springer.

McGee, Robert W. and Radoslav Tusan. (2008). The Ethics of Tax Evasion: A Survey of Slovak Opinion, in Robert W. McGee, editor, *Taxation and Public Finance in Transition and Developing Economies* (pp. 575–601). New York: Springer.

McGee, Robert W. and Susana N. Vittadini Andres. (2009). The Ethics of Tax Evasion: Case Studies of Taiwan, in Robert W. McGee, *Readings in Business Ethics* (pp. 200–228). Hyderabad, India: ICFAI University Press. An abbreviated version was published in Marjorie G. Adams and Abbass Alkhafaji, editors, *Business Research Yearbook: Global Business Perspectives*, Volume XIV, No. 1 (pp. 34–39). Beltsville, MD: International Graphics: Beltsville, MD, 2007.

McGee, Robert W. and Sanjoy Bose. (2009). The Ethics of Tax Evasion: A Survey of Australian Opinion, in Robert W. McGee, *Readings in Business Ethics* (pp. 143–166). Hyderabad, India: ICFAI University Press.

McGee, Robert W. and Bouchra M'Zali. (2009). The Ethics of Tax Evasion: An Empirical Study of French EMBA Students, in Robert W. McGee, *Readings in Business Ethics* (pp. 185–199). Hyderabad, India: ICFAI University Press. An abbreviated version was published in Marjorie G. Adams and Abbass Alkhafaji, editors, *Business Research Yearbook: Global Business Perspectives*, Volume XIV, No. 1 (pp. 27–33). Beltsville, MD: International Graphics, 2007).

McGee, Robert W., Silvia López Paláu and Gustavo A. Yepes Lopez. (2009). The Ethics of Tax Evasion: An Empirical Study of Colombian Opinion, in Robert W. McGee, *Readings in Business Ethics* (pp. 167–184). Hyderabad, India: ICFAI University Press.

McGee, Robert W. & Geoff A. Goldman (2010). Ethics and Tax Evasion: A Survey of South African Opinion. *Proceedings of the Third Annual University of Johannesburg Faculty of Management Conference*, May 12–14. Reprinted in the present volume.

McGee, Robert W. & Serkan Benk. (2011). The Ethics of Tax Evasion: A Study of Turkish Opinion. *Journal of Balkan and Near Eastern Studies*, 13(2), 249–262.

Pennock, Robert T. (1998). Death and Taxes: On the Justice of Conscientious War Tax Resistance. *Journal of Accounting, Ethics & Public Policy*, 1(1), 58–76, reprinted in Robert W. McGee (Ed.), *The Ethics of Tax Evasion* (pp. 124–142). Dumont, NJ: The Dumont Institute for Public Policy Research, 1998.

Robin, Donald and Laurie Babin. (1997). Making Sense of the Research on Gender and Ethics in Business: A Critical Analysis and Extension. *Business Ethics Quarterly*, 7(4), 61–90.

Ruegger, Durwood and Ernest W. King. (1992). A Study of the Effect of Age and Gender upon Student Business Ethics. *Journal of Business Ethics*, 11(3), 179–186.

Schansberg, D. Eric. (1998). The Ethics of Tax Evasion within Biblical Christianity: Are There Limits to "Rendering Unto Caesar"? *Journal of Accounting, Ethics & Public Policy*, 1(1),

77–90, reprinted in Robert W. McGee (ed.), The Ethics of Tax Evasion (pp. 144–157). The Dumont Institute for Public Policy Research, Dumont, NJ, 1998.

Serwinek, Paul J. (1992). Demographic & Related Differences in Ethical Views Among Small Businesses. *Journal of Business Ethics*, 11(7), 555–566.

Sims, Ronald R., Hsing K. Cheng & Hildy Teegen. (1996). Toward a Profile of Student Software Piraters. *Journal of Business Ethics*, 15(8), 839–849.

Smith, Sheldon R. and Kevin C. Kimball. (1998). Tax Evasion and Ethics: A Perspective from Members of The Church of Jesus Christ of Latter-Day Saints. *Journal of Accounting, Ethics & Public Policy*, 1(3), 337–348, reprinted in Robert W. McGee (Ed.), *The Ethics of Tax Evasion* (pp. 220–229). Dumont, NJ: The Dumont Institute for Public Policy Research, 1998.

Tamari, Meir. (1998). Ethical Issues in Tax Evasion: A Jewish Perspective. *Journal of Accounting, Ethics & Public Policy*, 1(2), 121–132, reprinted in Robert W. McGee (Ed.), *The Ethics of Tax Evasion* (pp. 168–178). Dumont, NJ: The Dumont Institute for Public Policy Research, 1998.

Torgler, B. (2003). Tax Morale: Theory and Empirical Analysis of Tax Compliance. Dissertation der Universität Basel zur Erlangung der Würde eines Doktors der Staatswissenschaften.

Torgler, Benno. (2004). Tax morale in Asian countries. *Journal of Asian Economics*, 15, 237–266.

Torgler, Benno and Friedrich Schneider. (2005). Attitudes Towards Paying Taxes in Austria: An Empirical Analysis. *Empirica*, 32, 231–250.

Torgler, Benno and Christoph A. Schaltegger. (2006). Tax Morale: A Survey with a Special Focus on Switzerland. *Schweizerische Zeitschrift für Volkswirtschaft und Statistik*, 142(3), 395–425.

Torgler, Benno. (2007). *Tax Compliance and Tax Morale: A Theoretical and Empirical Analysis*. Cheltenham, UK & Northampton, MA, USA: Edward Elgar.

Weeks, William A., Carlos W. Moore, Joseph A. McKinney & Justin G. Longenecker. (1999). The Effects of Gender and Career Stage on Ethical Judgment. *Journal of Business Ethics*, 20(4), 301–313.

Yusuf, S.M. (1971). *Economic Justice in Islam*. Lahore: Sh. Muhammad Ashraf.

Chapter 25
How Serious Is Tax Evasion? A Survey of Mexican Opinion

Robert W. McGee, Yanira Petrides, and Adriana M. Ross

Introduction

The goal of this study is to determine the relative seriousness of tax evasion compared to other crimes or acts that are considered to be unethical. A few other studies have examined this issue and have used methodologies similar to the one used in the present study. Karlinsky, Burton and Blanthorne (2004) measured the perceptions of students in North Carolina and California as to the seriousness of tax evasion and found that it ranked 11th out of 21 offenses. Burton, Karlinsky and Blanthorne (2005) surveyed MBA and graduate tax students from California and North Carolina as well as a few tax professors from across the USA using the same methodology and list of crimes and found the same result with regard to tax evasion; it ranked 11th out of 21 crimes. Gupta (2007) replicated the 2004 study using a New Zealand student population and found that tax evasion ranked 12th out of 21 crimes.

A comparison of the results of those three studies is presented in Table 25.1. The rankings are quite similar. Violent crimes are seen as more serious than nonviolent crimes. The three surveys were not identical. Insurance fraud was included in the New Zealand list but not in the two US studies. Prostitution is legal in New Zealand, and thus is not a crime there. In all the studies, tax evasion ranked in the middle, more serious than some crimes but less serious than others.

R.W. McGee (✉)
School of Business, Florida International University,
3000 NE 151 Street, North Miami, FL 33181, USA
e-mail: bob414@hotmail.com

Y. Petrides
Instituto Tecnológico Autónomo de México, Río Hondo No. 1, Tizapán San Ángel C.P. 01080, Distrito Federal, Mexico

A.M. Ross
School of Accounting, Florida International University,
11200 SW 8th Street, Miami, FL 33199, USA

R.W. McGee (ed.), *The Ethics of Tax Evasion: Perspectives in Theory and Practice*,   405
DOI 10.1007/978-1-4614-1287-8_25, © Springer Science+Business Media, LLC 2012

Table 25.1 Ranking of crimes in terms of seriousness

Crime	Karlinsky, Burton and Blanthorne (2004)	Burton, Karlinsky and Blanthorne (2005)	Gupta (2007)
Murder	1	1	1
Rape	2	2	3
Child molestation	3	2	2
Robbery	4	4	5
DWI	5	5	4
Carjacking	6	5	7
Child labor	7	7	6
Accounting fraud	8	7	9
Insider trading	9	9	14
Welfare fraud	10	10	8
Tax evasion	11	11	12
Minimum wage	12	11	10
Insurance fraud	NA	NA	11
Shoplifting	13	13	15
Prostitution	14	14	NA – legal in NZ
Running a red light	15	15	13
Bike theft	16	16	18
Smoking marijuana	17	17	21
Speeding	18	18	16
Ticket scalping	19	19	17
Illegal parking	20	20	19
Jaywalking	21	21	20

The Present Study

Wave 5 of the World Values Surveys (2008) asked hundreds of questions to participants in 57 countries. One of those questions asked whether it was justifiable to evade taxes if one had the opportunity to do so. Another question asked whether it was justifiable to pay cash to avoid paying taxes. It also asked questions on other ethical issues such as bribery, avoiding a fare on public transport, claiming government benefits, and buying stolen goods. The present study included those questions in a survey that was distributed to 369 students, faculty, and nonstudents at a university in Mexico City to determine the relative seriousness of each act. They were asked to select a number from 1 (never justifiable) to 10 (always justifiable) to show the extent of their agreement or disagreement with the commission of the six acts. The goal was to determine how serious tax evasion was compared to other acts that might be considered unethical.

Table 25.2 shows the demographic information. The sample included graduate and undergraduate students as well as faculty and others who were not students. The students were mostly accounting and business/economics majors, along with some engineering students and a smattering of other majors. Most participants were under age 25, although there was a sufficient number of older participants to compare opinions by age.

Table 25.2 Demographic information

	#	%		#	%
Status			*Major*		
Graduate student	114	30.9	Accounting	46	12.5
Undergraduate student	127	34.4	Other business/economics	85	23
Faculty	42	11.4	Theology/religious studies	9	2.4
Other (nonstudents)	84	22.8	Philosophy	17	4.6
Unknown	2	0.5	Law	15	4.1
			Engineering	36	9.8
			Other	157	42.5
			Unknown	4	1.1
Total	369	100.0	Total	369	100.0
Gender			*Age*		
Male	201	54.5	<25	188	50.9
Female	167	45.3	25–40	140	37.9
Unknown	1	0.2	>40	38	10.4
			Unknown	3	0.8
Total	369	100.0	Total	369	100.0

Table 25.3 Summary of responses (1=never justifiable; 10=always justifiable)

Act number	Act	Mean
1	Claiming government benefits to which you are not entitled	5.43
2	Avoiding a fare on public transport	2.80
3	Cheating on taxes if you have a chance	2.60
4	Someone accepting a bribe in the course of their duties	2.57
5	Prostitution	2.48
6	Buy stolen goods	2.35

Table 25.4 Ranking of acts: strongest opposition to weakest (1=never justifiable; 10=always justifiable)

Rank	Act	Mean
1	Buy stolen goods	2.35
2	Prostitution	2.48
3	Someone accepting a bribe in the course of their duties	2.57
4	Cheating on taxes if you have a chance	2.60
5	Avoiding a fare on public transport	2.80
6	Claiming government benefits to which you are not entitled	5.43

Table 25.3 lists the six acts and their mean scores.

Table 25.4 ranks the acts, from most serious to least serious. Buying stolen goods was the most serious of the acts listed, followed by prostitution. Accepting a bribe was ranked third, followed by cheating on taxes if you have a chance. Avoiding a fare on public transport was in fifth place. Least serious was claiming government benefits to which you are not entitled.

Table 25.5 Comparison of studies

	Mexico	Germany	Turkey
Buy stolen goods	1	2	3
Prostitution	2	NA	NA
Someone accepting a bribe in the course of their duties	3	1	1
Cheating on taxes if you have a chance	4	4	2
Avoiding a fare on public transport	5	6	5
Claiming government benefits to which you are not entitled	6	3	4
Paying cash for services to avoid taxes	NA	5	6

Table 25.6 Statistical data: gender (1 = never justifiable; 10 = always justifiable)

	Male			Female			
Act	Sample	Mean	SD	Sample	Mean	SD	p-Value
1	201	5.46	3.77	166	5.36	3.91	0.8037
2	201	2.85	2.80	167	2.76	2.81	0.7594
3	201	2.63	2.53	167	2.57	2.66	0.8250
4	201	2.61	2.55	167	2.54	2.63	0.7962
5	201	2.79	2.64	167	2.11	2.25	0.0089
6	201	2.32	2.63	167	2.40	2.69	0.7739
Mean average		3.11			2.96		

Studies of Germany (McGee, Benk, Ross and Kılıçaslan 2009) and Turkey (Benk, McGee and Ross 2009) used a similar survey instrument to determine the opinions of the populations in those countries on most of the same issues. Table 25.5 compares the results of those studies to the results of the present study. Tax evasion was ranked second in Turkey, but fourth in both Mexico and Germany. The most serious offense in Mexico was buying stolen goods. Accepting a bribe was ranked first in both Germany and Turkey.

Table 25.6 shows the data for the gender variable. In general, women were more opposed to the six acts than were men, as evidenced by their overall mean scores – 3.11 for men and 2.96 for women. Women were also more strongly opposed to each of the first five acts listed, although the extent of their opposition was not significant except for Act 5 (prostitution), where the difference was significant at the 1% level ($p = 0.0089$). The differences in mean scores were not significant for any of the acts other than prostitution.

Table 25.7 shows the data for the age demographic. A comparison of mean scores reveals some interesting results. In many other studies, the results found people tend to become more respectful of authority and the law as they get older. That is not quite the case here. The group most opposed to the six acts overall was the 30–49 age group. The group least opposed was the youngest group (15–29). The oldest group (50+) had mean scores that fell between the other two groups. However, a comparison of mean scores for the individual acts found that the oldest group was most opposed for Act 1 (Claiming government benefits to which you are not entitled).

Table 25.7 Statistical data: age (1 = never justifiable; 10 = always justifiable)

	15–29			30–49			50+		
Act	Sample	Mean	SD	Sample	Mean	SD	Sample	Mean	SD
1	187	5.61	3.75	140	5.40	3.95	38	4.29	3.68
2	188	3.33	3.04	140	2.05	2.20	38	3.11	3.04
3	188	2.86	2.84	140	2.09	1.98	38	3.26	3.05
4	188	2.73	2.74	140	2.19	2.20	38	3.11	2.91
5	188	2.76	2.73	140	2.06	1.97	38	2.76	2.79
6	188	2.83	2.96	140	1.54	1.70	38	3.05	3.24
Mean average		3.35			2.55			3.26	

Table 25.8 Statistical data: age (p-values)

Statement number	15–29 vs. 30–49	15–29 vs. 50+	30–49 vs. 50+
1	0.6247	0.0485	0.1210
2	0.0001	0.6845	0.0168
3	0.0063	0.4350	0.0050
4	0.0562	0.0562	0.4411
5	0.0105	1.0000	0.0793
6	0.0001	0.6813	0.0001

Table 25.9 Statistical data: major (1 = never justifiable; 10 = always justifiable)

	Accounting			Other business/economics			Engineering		
Act	Sample	Mean	SD	Sample	Mean	SD	Sample	Mean	SD
1	46	4.43	3.77	85	5.02	3.66	36	6.00	3.85
2	46	3.11	3.16	85	2.78	2.70	36	2.36	2.22
3	46	2.59	2.41	85	2.47	2.38	36	1.61	1.27
4	46	2.61	2.63	85	2.60	2.63	36	2.17	2.27
5	46	2.59	2.76	85	3.06	2.80	36	2.61	2.98
6	46	2.70	2.94	85	2.58	2.73	36	2.33	2.78
Mean average		3.00			3.08			2.85	

The cheating on tax item was Act 3. For that act, the 30–49 age group was most opposed and the 50+ age group was least opposed.

Table 25.8 compares the mean scores of the three age groups and shows the significance of the differences in mean scores for each of the six acts. The most significant differences were between the 15–29 and 30–49 age groups.

Table 25.9 shows the data by academic major. Three majors had a sufficiently large sample size to do some statistical comparisons. Overall, the engineering majors (2.85) were the most opposed to the six acts. The other business and economics majors were least opposed, with the accounting majors falling between the other two groups.

Table 25.10 Statistical data: major

Statement number	Accounting vs. other business/economics	Accounting vs. engineering	Other business/ economics vs. engineering
1	0.3851	0.0674	0.1874
2	0.5308	0.2303	0.4125
3	0.7843	0.0300	0.0145
4	0.9835	0.4274	0.3943
5	0.3584	0.9750	0.4294
6	0.8156	0.5641	0.6478

Table 25.11 Statistical data: status (1 = never justifiable; 10 = always justifiable)

	Graduate students			Undergraduate students			Faculty		
Act	Sample	Mean	SD	Sample	Mean	SD	Sample	Mean	SD
1	113	5.78	3.73	127	4.93	3.67	42	3.33	3.30
2	114	1.82	1.92	127	3.50	3.07	42	2.12	1.88
3	114	2.43	2.32	127	2.98	2.90	42	1.90	1.88
4	114	2.40	2.34	127	2.97	2.85	42	1.50	1.52
5	114	2.00	1.90	127	3.30	2.99	42	2.55	2.75
6	114	1.65	1.90	127	2.96	3.09	42	1.55	1.50
Mean average		2.68			3.44			2.16	

Table 25.12 Statistical data: status (p-value)

Statement number	Graduate students vs. undergraduate students	Graduate students vs. faculty	Undergraduate students vs. faculty
3	0.1079	0.1862	0.0252

For the tax question (Act 3), the engineering students were most opposed (1.61) and the accounting majors were least opposed (2.59). Table 25.10 shows the difference in mean scores between the engineering students, and the students in the other two majors were significant at the 5% level.

Table 25.10 shows that some of the other differences in mean scores were significant at the 5 or 10% level.

Table 25.11 shows the results by student status. Overall, the faculty (2.16) was more opposed to the six acts than were the other two groups. Undergraduate students (3.44) were least opposed to the six acts, overall. Faculty was also more opposed to the cheating on taxes question (Act 3) than were the other two groups; undergraduate students were least opposed for that act.

Table 25.12 shows the significance of the differences in mean scores between groups. Faculty was significantly more opposed to the tax question than were the undergraduate students. The differences in mean scores for the other comparisons were not significant for the tax item.

References

Benk, Serkan, Robert W. McGee and Adriana M. Ross (2009). An Empirical Study of Ethical Opinion in Turkey. *Journal of Accounting, Ethics & Public Policy*, 10(1), 83–99.

Burton, Hughlene A., Stewart S. Karlinsky and Cynthia Blanthorne (2005). Perception of a White-Collar Crime: Tax Evasion. *The ATA Journal of Legal Tax Research* 3, 35–48.

Gupta, Ranjana (2007). Perception of Tax Evasion as a Crime: Evidence from New Zealand. New Zealand Journal of Taxation Law and Policy 12(3), 199–223.

Karlinsky, Stewart, Hughlene Burton and Cindy Blanthorne (2004). Perceptions of Tax Evasion as a Crime. *eJournal of Tax Research* 2(2), 226–240.

McGee, Robert W. Serkan Benk, Adriana M. Ross & Harun Kılıçaslan (2009). An Empirical Study of Ethical Opinion in Germany. *Journal of Accounting, Ethics & Public Policy*, 10(2), 243–259.

World Values Survey (2008). www.wvsevsdb.com/wvs/WVSAnalizeStudy.jsp.

Part VI
Demographic Studies

Chapter 26
Gender and the Ethics of Tax Evasion: An Empirical Study of 82 Countries

Robert W. McGee

Introduction

Gender is perhaps the most widely studied demographic variable. It is an interesting variable from the perspectives of economics, law, philosophy, political science, psychology, sociology, anthropology, religion, history, and culture, to name a few. What makes women different from men? How are they different from men? Is female thinking becoming closer to male thinking as women gain equal rights and liberation?

These are a few of the questions that might be asked. However, the present study will not attempt to provide answers to these and the many other questions that could be asked about gender differences and similarities. The goal of the present study is more modest, to categorize some of the existing literature and summarize it to provide a background, then to examine some data collected by the many social scientists who worked on the World Values and Beliefs surveys to see what men's and women's views are on the ethics of tax evasion.

The World Values and Beliefs surveys consist of hundreds of questions asked to as many as 200,000 people in over 80 countries. The first surveys were conducted in the early 1980s and various groups of social scientists have coordinated their efforts to conduct additional surveys every few years since then. The present study utilized this data for 82 countries and examines the responses to the question whether it is justifiable to cheat on taxes if you have a chance, which is one of the questions asked in the surveys. But first some background information.

Many studies have been conducted in recent decades that compare male and female views on a wide range of issues. One of those issues was ethical beliefs.

R.W. McGee (✉)
School of Business, Florida International University,
3000 NE 151 Street, North Miami, FL 33181, USA
e-mail: bob414@hotmail.com

R.W. McGee (ed.), *The Ethics of Tax Evasion: Perspectives in Theory and Practice*,
DOI 10.1007/978-1-4614-1287-8_26, © Springer Science+Business Media, LLC 2012

Are men's and women's ethical beliefs different, and if so, how are they different and what makes them different? Space does not permit a full discussion of these questions. Entire books have been written to address these questions. However, a few things can be said.

For example, when one asks the question, "Who is more ethical, men or women?" the results of studies have been mixed. Numerous scholars have examined this question and they have not been able to agree on the answer. Much of this research has been conducted by Americans or professors who teach in American universities, although some studies have involved non-US participants. A variety of methodologies have been used, including surveys, role playing, and various forms of experiments.

Some studies have found that women are more ethical than men. Other studies have found that there is no significant difference between male and female views on ethical issues. A third group of studies found that men are more ethical than women. Sometimes the result depends on which ethical issue is being examined. Other times, it might depend on how one defines ethical or how one phrases the questions that survey participants are asked to reply to.

For example, if one tested ethical views by asking "Is it unethical to cheat on taxes?" the responses might depend on the age, income level, and country of residence of the individual being asked the question as well as the amount of taxes they pay and what the government does with the money it collects. Marital status and religion might also influence the response.

If one asks the question slightly differently, such as "Is it unethical for a Jew living in Nazi Germany to evade taxes?" or "Is it ethical to evade taxes in an evil or corrupt state?," the percentages of those answering in the affirmative might be different than if one asked, "Is it unethical to evade taxes if others have to pay more because I pay less?"

Numerous studies have asked these and similar questions and the results show that opinions on the ethics of tax evasion differ, depending on which question is asked. Some of these surveys are discussed in this book.

Several studies have found that women are more compliant in general (Dollar et al., 2001; Swamy et al. 2001). Tittle (1980) found that women are more compliant and less self-reliant than men. Other studies have found that women are more compliant when it comes to tax matters (Aitken & Bonneville, 1980; Mason & Calvin, 1978). Mears et al. (2000) found that women are significantly less likely to engage in crime and delinquency regardless of age, ethnic, or racial group. Kastlunger et al. (2010) found that women and less male "typical" individuals were more tax compliant than males and male "typical" individuals and that prenatal testosterone levels did not make a difference. One reason given for women being more tax compliant in the Orthodox Jewish community is because they are taught from an early age to defer to authority (McGee & Cohn, 2008).

A number of reasons have been offered to explain the different behavioral patterns of men and women. Byrnes et al. (1999) found that men and women have different risk propensities. Eagly (1987) said that differences may be due to gender-role orientation. Several scholars have predicted that as more women enter the work force and assume male positions, the differences between men and women will diminish when it comes to ethical decision making (Grasmick et al., 1984; Jackson & Milliron, 1986).

Another point needs to be made. If some survey finds that women are more opposed to tax evasion than men, which many surveys have found, it cannot automatically be said that women are more ethical than men, since that would depend on whether tax evasion constitutes an unethical act. All that one can say is that women are more opposed to tax evasion than men.

One goal of the present study is to determine whether women are more opposed, less opposed, or equally opposed to tax evasion than men. I will let the readers to decide for themselves whether that also means one gender is more or less ethical than the other gender. If one begins with the premise that there is an affirmative duty to evade taxes, which has been argued in the case of living under an evil or corrupt regime, those who prefer not to evade taxes may actually be acting unethically or, stated differently, those who choose to evade taxes for moral reasons, such as cutting off funding to a corrupt or evil regime, may be acting more ethically than those who pay their taxes. As Dietrich Bonhoeffer has said:

> Silence in the face of evil is itself evil, God will not hold us guiltless. Not to speak is to speak. Not to act is to act (Dietrich Bonhoeffer)

Table 26.1 lists 66 studies that have compared ethical views on a wide range of topics by gender (McGee, 2006c). As can be seen, the results are mixed, although

Table 26.1 Comparisons of ethical attitudes: males and females

Study	Males are more ethical	Females are more ethical	No difference
Akaah (1989)		x	
Akaah & Riordan (1989)		x	
Ameen, Guffey & McMillan (1996)		x	
Babakus, Cornwell, Mitchell & Schlegelmilch (2004)			x
Baird (1980)		x	
Barnett & Karson (1989)			x
Barnett & Karson (1987)	x		
Beltramini, Peterson & Kozmetsky (1984)		x	
Betz, O'Connell & Shepard (1989)		x	
Beu, Buckley & Harvey (2003)		x	
Brown & Choong (2005)		x	
Browning & Zabriskie (1983)			x
Boyd (1981)		x	
Callan (1992)			x
Chonko & Hunt (1985)		x	
Dawson (1997)		x	
Derry (1989)			x
Dubinsky & Levy (1985)			x
Ferrell & Skinner (1988)		x	
Franke, Crown & Spake (1997)		x	

(continued)

Table 26.1 (continued)

Study	Males are more ethical	Females are more ethical	No difference
Friedman, Robinson & Friedman (1987)			x
Fritzsche (1988)			x
Glover (1991)		x	
Glover, Bumpus & Logan (1993)		x	
Glover, Bumpus, Logan & Ciesla (1997)		x	
Glover, Bumpus, Sharp & Munchus (2002)		x	
Harris (1990)		x	x
Harris (1989)			x
Hegarty & Sims (1978)			x
Hoffman (1998)		x	x
Kelley, Ferrell & Skinner (1990)		x	
Kidwell, Stevens & Bethke (1987)			x
Kohut & Corriher (1994)		x	
Lampe, Finn, Gaa & O'Malley (1992)		x	
Loo (2003)			x
Luthar, DiBattista & Gautschi (1997)		x	
Mason & Mudrack (1996)		x	
McCabe, Ingram & Dato-on (2006)			x
McCuddy & Peery (1996)			x
McDonald & Kan (1997)			x
McNichols & Zimmerer (1985)			x
Miesing & Preble (1985)		x	
Nyaw & Ng (1994)			x
Ondrack (1973)		x	
Posner & Schmidt (1984)			x
Purcell (1977)		x	
Robin & Babin (1997)			x
Roxas & Stoneback (2004)			x
Ruegger & King (1992)		x	
Schaub (1994)		x	
Schmidt & Posner (1992)		x	
Serwinek (1992)		x	x
Sierles, Hendrickx & Circle (1980)		x	
Sikula & Costa (1994)			x
Sims, Cheng & Teegen (1996)		x	
Singappakdi, Vitell & Franke (1999)		x	
Smith & Oakely (1997)		x	
Stanga & Turpen (1991)			x
Stern & Havlicek (1986)			x
Su (2006)		x	
Swaidan, Vitell, Rose & Gilbert (2006)			x
Tang & Zuo (1997)		x	
Tsalikis & Ortiz-Buonafina (1990)			x
Weeks, Moore, McKinney & Longenecker (1999)	x	x	x
Whitley (1998)		x	

the studies that have found men to be more ethical than women have been fewer in number than the studies that found women to be either more ethical or equally (un)ethical.

Some studies have examined ethical attitudes toward tax evasion through the prism of gender. Table 26.2 summarizes and classifies some of these studies. The studies listed below used a survey instrument that was distributed mostly to students in various countries. One contribution to the literature these studies make is that many of them sample non-USA populations, which is an area that has been

Table 26.2 Summary of tax evasion opinion surveys

Study	Sample	Findings
Women were more opposed to tax evasion than men		
McGee & Maranjyan, 2012	Accounting practitioners in South Florida	Women were slightly more opposed to tax evasion
McGee & Bose, 2009	Australia – business, philosophy and seminary students, and faculty	Women were more opposed to tax evasion in 12 of 18 cases; opposition was significant in 2/18 cases. Men were significantly more opposed in 2/18 cases
McGee & Guo, 2007	Hubei, China – graduate and advanced undergraduate business and economics, law and philosophy students	Women were significantly more opposed to tax evasion
McGee, López & Yepes, 2009	Colombia – business students	Women were more opposed to tax evasion in all 18 cases. Opposition was significant in 6 of 18 cases
McGee, López & Jaramillo, 2007	Ecuador – business students	Women were slightly more opposed to tax evasion than were men but none of the mean scores were significantly different
McGee, Alver & Alver, 2008	Estonia – graduate and under-graduate business students, faculty, and practitioners	Women were significantly more opposed to tax evasion
McGee, Alver & Alver, 2012	Estonia – accounting and business students	Women were significantly more opposed to tax evasion in all 18 cases
McGee, Benk, Ross & Kılıçaslan, 2009	Germany – business students	Women were more opposed to tax evasion and five other acts
McGee, Nickerson & Fees, 2006	Germany and the USA – graduate and undergraduate business students	American women were more opposed to tax evasion than American men. Gender differences were not tested in the German sample
McGee & Lingle, 2008	Guatemala – business and economics and law students	Women were more opposed to tax evasion
McGee & M'Zali, 2012	Haiti – accounting and business/ economics students	Women were somewhat more opposed to tax evasion

(continued)

Table 26.2 (continued)

Study	Sample	Findings
McGee, 2006a	USA – international business academics who taught in US universities.	Women were more opposed to tax evasion in all 18 cases
McGee & Cohn, 2008	Orthodox Jewish students in New York City	Women were significantly more opposed to tax evasion
McGee & Smith, 2007	Mormon accounting, business and economics, legal studies, and technology students	Women were significantly more opposed to tax evasion
Gupta & McGee, 2010	New Zealand – graduate and undergraduate accounting, business and economics and law students, and accounting practitioners	Women were more opposed to tax evasion
McGee, 2012	Philosophy professors	Women were significantly more opposed to tax evasion
McGee & López, 2007	Puerto Rico – accounting and law students	Women were more opposed to tax evasion in 16 of 18 cases. Opposition was significant in 3 of 18 cases
McGee & Goldman, 2010	South Africa – management, economics and finance graduate and undergraduate students, mostly Christian, mostly under age 41, mostly African	Women were somewhat more opposed to tax evasion
McGee & Andres, 2009	Taiwan – students	Women were more opposed to tax evasion
McGee, 2008	Thailand – advanced undergraduate accounting students	Women were more opposed to tax evasion
Benk, McGee & Ross, 2009	Turkey – business students	Women were significantly more opposed to tax evasion
McGee & López, 2008	USA, Colombia, Ecuador, Puerto Rico, and the Dominican Republic – accounting, business and economics students	Women were more opposed to tax evasion in general. The difference in mean scores was often significant. Gender differences were the most significant for the three human rights issues

Men were more opposed to tax evasion than women

Study	Sample	Findings
McGee & Jain, 2012	India – accounting, business, and engineering (mostly graduate) students and faculty	Men were slightly more opposed to tax evasion but the difference was significant in only 1 of 18 cases
McGee, 2006b	Romania – graduate and upper division undergraduate business students	Men were more opposed to tax evasion in 12 of 18 cases
McGee & Tusan, 2008	Slovakia – business and economics, philosophy and theology students	Men were significantly more opposed to tax evasion
McGee & Benk, 2011	Turkey – undergraduate business and economics students at three Turkish universities	Men were significantly more opposed to tax evasion

(continued)

Table 26.2 (continued)

Study	Sample	Findings
McGee, Benk, Yıldırım and Kayıkçı. 2011	Turkey – tax practitioners	Men were significantly more opposed to tax evasion
Gender differences were not significant or results were mixed		
McGee & Rossi, 2008	Argentina – business, economics and law students, and faculty	Men and women were equally opposed to tax evasion
McGee & An, 2008	Beijing, China – graduate and advanced undergraduate business and economics students	Men and women were equally opposed to tax evasion
McGee & Noronha, 2008	Southern China and Macau – social science, business and economics graduate and undergraduate students	Men and women were equally opposed to tax evasion
McGee & M'Zali, 2009	France – executive MBA students	Men and women were equally opposed to tax evasion
McGee, Djatej & Sarikas, forthcoming	Hispanic students in South Texas	Men and women were equally opposed to tax evasion
McGee & Butt, 2008	Hong Kong – business students	Men and women were equally opposed to tax evasion
McGee & George, 2008	India – graduate business students in Kerala	Men and women were equally opposed to tax evasion
McGee & Ardakani, 2009	Iran – master's degree accounting students	Men and women were equally opposed to tax evasion
McGee & Preobragenskaya, 2008	Kazakhstan – accounting and business students	Men and women were equally opposed to tax evasion
McGee, Noronha & Tyler, 2007	Macau – graduate and under-graduate business and economics students	Men and women were equally opposed to tax evasion, overall. Although the overall mean scores were not significantly different, male mean scores were significantly higher [men were more opposed to tax evasion] in 3 of 15 cases
McGee, Petrides & Ross, 2012	Mexico – accounting, business and engineering students; faculty; nonstudents	Men and women were equally opposed to tax evasion
McGee & Bernal, 2006	Poland – economics students at Poznan University of economics	Men and women were equally opposed to tax evasion
Nasadyuk & McGee, 2007	Ukraine – law students in Odessa	Men and women were equally opposed to tax evasion

previously underreported. One limitation of these studies is that most of the surveys gathered student opinions. University students are generally younger and more educated than the general population, so the results may not necessarily be extrapolated to the general population, although it would be fair to say that the opinions expressed in those surveys express the views of the country's future opinion leaders, especially when the sample consists of law students, although the same could be said, perhaps to a lesser extent, for students with other majors. A few of the studies solicited the opinions of faculty or accounting practitioners.

Now that the prior research has been summarized, the next step is to examine the World Values data for the 82 countries where data is available to determine what the gender views are for each country. The next section does that.

Methodology and Findings

Methodology

The World Values survey data for 82 countries was examined to determine the views of men and women on the ethics of tax evasion. The question posed to them was whether it was ever justifiable to cheat on taxes if they had an opportunity to do so.

Findings

The overall mean was 2.44 for males and 2.18 for females, which was significant ($p < 0.0001$), meaning that females for the total sample were significantly more opposed to evading taxes than were males.

Table 26.3 shows the sample sizes, means, standard deviations, and p-values for each country, listed alphabetically and by gender.

Table 26.3 Cheating on taxes if you could gender

	Male			Female			
	Sample size	Mean	SD	Sample size	Mean	SD	p-Value
Total	53,031	2.44	2.403	55,235	2.18	2.171	<0.0001
Albania	491	1.94	1.482	494	1.83	1.374	0.2273
Algeria	640	2.19	2.377	607	1.83	2.005	0.004
Argentina	594	2.1	2.288	676	1.67	1.777	0.0002
Armenia	918	3.85	3.107	1,028	3.52	2.99	0.0171
Australia	1,003	2.43	2.254	1,036	1.89	1.651	<0.0001
Austria	722	2.38	2.1	775	2.02	1.848	0.0004
Azerbaijan	923	3.84	3.329	937	3.4	3.146	0.0034

(continued)

Table 26.3 (continued)

	Male			Female			
	Sample size	Mean	SD	Sample size	Mean	SD	p-Value
Bangladesh	829	1.09	0.671	666	1.02	0.361	0.0154
Belarus	421	4.42	2.858	492	4.05	2.848	0.051
Belgium	918	3.98	2.909	972	3.36	2.743	<0.0001
Bosnia	573	1.89	1.959	624	1.63	1.617	0.0121
Brazil	568	3.74	3.261	570	3.43	3.07	0.099
Bulgaria	465	2.13	2.002	483	1.89	1.838	0.0547
Canada	947	2.36	2.333	975	1.82	1.823	<0.0001
Chile	558	2.16	2.314	618	2.15	2.273	0.9405
China	492	1.53	1.338	493	1.61	1.568	0.3893
Colombia	1,570	2.35	2.28	1,425	2.22	2.188	0.1123
Croatia	471	2.77	2.722	526	2.31	2.262	0.0037
Czech Republic	911	2.23	1.915	973	1.92	1.618	0.0001
Denmark	500	2.25	1.944	517	1.77	1.62	<0.0001
Dominican Republic	165	2.06	2.211	239	1.85	1.88	0.3054
Egypt	1,534	1.7	1.625	1,449	1.44	1.267	<0.0001
El Salvador	584	1.94	2.334	636	1.89	2.296	0.7063
Estonia	438	3.36	2.571	536	2.98	2.406	0.0176
Finland	487	3.01	2.688	537	1.97	1.636	<0.0001
France	757	3.25	2.741	819	2.88	2.553	0.0056
Georgia	893	2.79	2.455	1,094	2.69	2.319	0.3518
Germany, East	443	2.64	2.389	525	2.2	2.18	0.0028
Germany, West	441	2.54	2.184	588	2.2	1.836	0.0069
Great Britain	483	2.63	2.199	507	2.22	2.056	0.0025
Greece	459	3.31	2.634	631	3.04	2.323	0.0737
Hungary	455	2.26	2.249	520	1.99	1.822	0.0388
Iceland	476	2.48	2.178	485	1.98	1.669	<0.0001
India	1,097	2.1	2.53	786	2.2	2.789	0.4179
Indonesia	499	1.63	1.466	500	1.45	1.271	0.0384
Iran	1,324	1.49	1.666	1,131	1.44	1.556	0.4449
Ireland	483	2.52	2.152	506	2.16	2.014	0.0067
Italy	949	2.5	2.253	1,018	2.29	2.106	0.0327
Japan	615	1.59	1.596	697	1.35	1.189	0.0019
Jordan	590	1.57	1.65	614	1.54	1.486	0.7401
Kyrgyzstan	464	2.73	2.654	572	2.72	2.575	0.9511
Latvia	454	2.62	2.501	535	2.14	2.028	0.0009
Lithuania	449	3.93	3.084	519	3.64	3.03	0.1411
Luxembourg	573	3.59	2.852	594	3.18	2.671	0.0114
Macedonia	526	2.37	2.56	499	2.19	2.32	0.2393
Malta	484	1.73	1.698	518	1.37	1.137	<0.0001
Mexico	703	2.4	2.529	744	2.22	2.372	0.1626
Moldova	447	4.27	3.028	484	4.13	2.858	0.4682
Montenegro	505	2.59	2.137	494	2.49	2.101	0.4561
Morocco	613	1.27	1.28	622	1.11	0.876	0.0104
Netherlands	489	3	2.324	511	2.5	2.087	0.0004

(continued)

Table 26.3 (continued)

	Male			Female			
	Sample size	Mean	SD	Sample size	Mean	SD	p-Value
New Zealand	516	2.64	2.458	635	2.03	1.96	<0.0001
Nigeria	1,032	2.11	1.913	990	1.95	1.722	0.0485
Northern Ireland	455	2.7	2.377	495	2.14	1.968	<0.0001
Norway	545	3.13	2.486	575	2.32	2.102	<0.0001
Pakistan	1,001	1.2	0.783	939	1.18	0.667	0.5461
Peru	724	2.23	2.027	749	2	1.917	0.0254
Philippines	594	3.34	2.589	589	2.93	2.401	0.0048
Poland	502	2.31	2.265	564	2.15	2.025	0.2236
Portugal	457	2.48	2.167	505	2.42	2.147	0.6666
Puerto Rico	250	2.14	2.543	452	1.94	2.239	0.281
Romania	533	2.91	2.836	547	2.67	2.674	0.1527
Russia	1,093	3.4	2.797	1,288	2.83	2.426	<0.0001
Serbia	562	2.19	2.028	601	2.01	1.885	0.117
Singapore	745	1.97	1.916	760	1.8	1.675	0.0669
Slovakia	628	2.37	2.129	679	1.96	1.769	0.0002
Slovenia	457	2.58	2.403	542	2.13	2.046	0.0014
South Africa	1,584	2.99	2.844	1,340	2.35	2.253	<0.0001
South Korea	604	1.63	1.358	595	1.55	1.403	0.3159
Spain	579	2.31	2.086	611	2.03	1.801	0.0132
Sweden	502	2.61	2.12	507	2.21	1.866	0.0015
Switzerland	599	2.98	2.692	588	2.22	2.094	<0.0001
Taiwan	379	1.85	1.66	388	2.07	1.873	0.0858
Tanzania	641	1.7	2.151	502	1.77	2.207	0.5894
Turkey	602	1.22	1.005	600	1.14	0.778	0.1231
Uganda	474	3.27	3.334	525	3.56	3.475	0.1797
Ukraine	519	3.69	2.86	589	3.23	2.696	0.006
Uruguay	417	1.78	1.849	559	1.69	1.735	0.4359
USA	599	2.54	2.336	599	2.01	2.023	<0.0001
Venezuela	602	1.86	1.878	592	1.77	1.643	0.3786
Vietnam	489	1.28	1.056	500	1.36	1.16	0.2573
Zimbabwe	457	1.69	1.713	523	1.37	1.295	0.0009

1 = never justifiable; 10 = always justifiable

Table 26.4 categorizes the results by country.

It is clear that in most countries women are more opposed to tax evasion, often significantly, although the reasons in each case are not clear. More research is needed, since the reasons could be different in every country. Another interesting finding is that Taiwan is the only country where men were significantly more opposed to tax evasion, and even there it was only at the 10% level. More research is needed to determine why Taiwanese men are different from the men in the other 81 countries included in the present study.

Table 26.5 shows the categorical breakdown. Women were significantly more opposed to tax evasion in more than 63% of the countries included in the survey and

Table 26.4 Gender opinion differences: categorization by country

Women more opposed – statistically significant (10%)

Algeria	Croatia	Indonesia	Peru
Argentina	Czech Republic	Ireland	Philippines
Armenia	Denmark	Italy	Russia
Australia	Egypt	Japan	Singapore
Austria	Estonia	Latvia	Slovakia
Azerbaijan	Finland	Luxembourg	Slovenia
Bangladesh	France	Malta	South Africa
Belarus	Great Britain	Morocco	Spain
Belgium	Germany, East	New Zealand	Sweden
Bosnia	Germany, West	Northern Ireland	Switzerland
Brazil	Greece	Netherlands	Ukraine
Bulgaria	Hungary	Nigeria	USA
Canada	Iceland	Norway	Zimbabwe

Women more opposed – not statistically significant

Albania	Iran	Mexico	Puerto Rico
Chile	Jordan	Moldova	Romania
Colombia	Korea	Montenegro	Serbia
Dominican Republic	Kyrgyzstan	Pakistan	Turkey
El Salvador	Lithuania	Poland	Uruguay
Georgia	Macedonia	Portugal	Venezuela

Men more opposed – not statistically significant

China	Tanzania	Uganda	Vietnam
India			

Men more opposed – statistically significant

Taiwan

Table 26.5 Relative opposition in percentage terms

	Number of countries	%Age
Woman significantly more opposed	52	63.4
Women somewhat more opposed	24	29.3
Men somewhat more opposed	5	6.1
Men significantly more opposed	1	1.2
	82	100.0

1 = never justified; 10 = always justified

were somewhat more opposed in another 29%. Men were more opposed in only 7.3% of the countries.

Chart 26.1 shows the relative scores graphically. It is broken down into four categories:

Women significantly more opposed (W SMO)
Woman more opposed, but not statistically significant (W MO)
Men more opposed, but not statistically significant (M MO)
Men significantly more opposed (M SMO)

Table 26.6 ranks each group based on the extent of opposition to tax evasion, from most opposed to least opposed. It is not surprising that women dominate the first half of the ranking and men dominate the second half. One interesting point that could be made is that each of the top 8 in the rankings, whether male or female, is from predominantly Muslim countries. Thirteen of the top 20 are from predominantly Muslim countries as well.

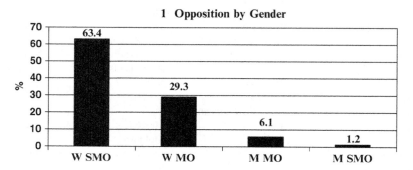

Chart 26.1 Opposition by gender

Table 26.6 Ranking based on opposition to tax evasion

Rank	Gender	Mean	Country	Rank	Gender	Mean	Country
1	F	1.02	Bangladesh	81	F	2.20	India
2	M	1.09	Bangladesh	84	F	2.21	Sweden
3	F	1.11	Morocco	85	F	2.22	Colombia
4	F	1.14	Turkey	85	F	2.22	Great Britain
5	F	1.18	Pakistan	85	F	2.22	Mexico
6	M	1.2	Pakistan	85	F	2.22	Switzerland
7	M	1.22	Turkey	89	M	2.23	Czech
8	M	1.27	Morocco	89	M	2.23	Peru
9	M	1.28	Vietnam	91	M	2.25	Denmark
10	F	1.35	Japan	92	M	2.26	Hungary
11	F	1.36	Vietnam	93	F	2.29	Italy
12	F	1.37	Malta	94	F	2.31	Croatia
12	F	1.37	Zimbabwe	94	M	2.31	Poland
14	F	1.44	Egypt	94	M	2.31	Spain
14	F	1.44	Iran	97	F	2.32	Norway
16	F	1.45	Indonesia	98	F	2.35	South Africa
17	M	1.49	Iran	98	M	2.35	Colombia
18	M	1.53	China	100	M	2.36	Canada
19	F	1.54	Jordan	101	M	2.37	Macedonia
20	F	1.55	South Korea	101	M	2.37	Slovakia
21	M	1.57	Jordan	103	M	2.38	Austria
22	M	1.59	Japan	104	M	2.4	Mexico
23	F	1.61	China	105	F	2.42	Portugal

(continued)

Table 26.6 (continued)

Rank	Gender	Mean	Country	Rank	Gender	Mean	Country
24	F	1.63	Bosnia	106	M	2.43	Australia
24	M	1.63	Indonesia	107	M	2.48	Iceland
24	M	1.63	South Korea	107	M	2.48	Portugal
27	F	1.67	Argentina	109	F	2.49	Montenegro
28	F	1.69	Uruguay	110	F	2.50	Netherlands
28	M	1.69	Zimbabwe	110	M	2.50	Italy
30	M	1.7	Egypt	112	M	2.52	Ireland
30	M	1.7	Tanzania	113	M	2.54	Germany, West
32	M	1.73	Malta	113	M	2.54	USA
33	F	1.77	Denmark	115	M	2.58	Slovenia
33	F	1.77	Tanzania	116	M	2.59	Montenegro
33	F	1.77	Venezuela	117	M	2.61	Sweden
36	M	1.78	Uruguay	118	M	2.62	Latvia
37	F	1.8	Singapore	119	M	2.63	Great Britain
38	F	1.82	Canada	120	M	2.64	Germany, East
39	F	1.83	Albania	120	M	2.64	New Zealand
39	F	1.83	Algeria	122	F	2.67	Romania
41	F	1.85	Dominican Republic	123	F	2.69	Georgia
41	M	1.85	Taiwan	124	M	2.70	Northern Ireland
43	M	1.86	Venezuela	125	F	2.72	Kyrgyzstan
44	F	1.89	Australia	126	M	2.73	Kyrgyzstan
44	F	1.89	Bulgaria	127	M	2.77	Croatia
44	F	1.89	El Salvador	128	M	2.79	Georgia
44	M	1.89	Bosnia	129	F	2.83	Russia
48	F	1.92	Czech	130	F	2.88	France
49	M	1.94	Albania	131	M	2.91	Romania
49	F	1.94	Puerto Rico	132	F	2.93	Philippines
49	M	1.94	El Salvador	133	F	2.98	Estonia
52	F	1.95	Nigeria	133	M	2.98	Switzerland
53	F	1.96	Slovakia	135	M	2.99	South Africa
54	F	1.97	Finland	136	M	3.00	Netherlands
54	M	1.97	Singapore	137	M	3.01	Finland
56	F	1.98	Iceland	138	F	3.04	Greece
57	F	1.99	Hungary	139	M	3.13	Norway
58	F	2	Peru	140	F	3.18	Luxembourg
59	F	2.01	Serbia	141	F	3.23	Ukraine
59	F	2.01	USA	142	M	3.25	France
61	F	2.02	Austria	143	M	3.27	Uganda
62	F	2.03	New Zealand	144	M	3.31	Greece
62	F	2.03	Spain	145	M	3.34	Philippines
64	M	2.06	Dominican Republic	146	F	3.36	Belgium
65	F	2.07	Taiwan	146	M	3.36	Estonia
66	M	2.1	Argentina	148	F	3.40	Azerbaijan
66	M	2.1	India	148	M	3.40	Russia
68	M	2.11	Nigeria	150	F	3.43	Brazil

(continued)

Table 26.6 (continued)

Rank	Gender	Mean	Country	Rank	Gender	Mean	Country
69	F	2.13	Slovenia	151	F	3.52	Armenia
69	M	2.13	Bulgaria	152	F	3.56	Uganda
71	F	2.14	Latvia	153	M	3.59	Luxembourg
71	F	2.14	Northern Ireland	154	F	3.64	Lithuania
71	M	2.14	Puerto Rico	155	M	3.69	Ukraine
74	F	2.15	Chile	156	M	3.74	Brazil
74	F	2.15	Poland	157	M	3.84	Azerbaijan
76	F	2.16	Ireland	158	M	3.85	Armenia
76	M	2.16	Chile	159	M	3.93	Lithuania
78	F	2.19	Macedonia	160	M	3.98	Belgium
78	M	2.19	Algeria	161	F	4.05	Belarus
78	M	2.19	Serbia	162	F	4.13	Moldova
81	F	2.2	Germany, East	163	M	4.27	Moldova
81	F	2.2	Germany, West	164	M	4.42	Belarus

1 = never justified; 10 = always justified

Table 26.7 Gender, age, and attitude toward tax evasion

	Male	Female	p-Value
15–29			
Sample size	16,197	16,352	0.0001
Mean	2.7	2.4	
SD	2.59	2.3	
30–49			
Sample size	21,887	22,888	0.0001
Mean	2.5	2.2	
SD	2.43	2.2	
50+			
Sample size	15,405	16,475	0.0001
Mean	2.1	2	
SD	2.09	1.97	

1 = never justified; 10 = always justified

At the other end of the scale, 8 of the 10 least opposed are from former Soviet republics; 13 of the 20 least opposed are also from former Soviet republics. This result is not surprising. It is reasonable to expect that people who lived under repressive, corrupt regimes for three-quarters of a century would have little respect, and a large amount of distrust for their governments, and that these attitudes would flow over into their attitude toward tax evasion.

Although it can reasonably be said that women are generally more opposed to tax evasion than men, is that true for every age group, or do the results differ by age? Table 26.7 attempts to answer that question, in the aggregate, at least. It shows the sample size, mean, and standard deviation for three age groups. The p-value calculations show that women are significantly more opposed to tax evasion in all age groups.

Table 26.8 Gender, education, and attitude toward tax evasion

	Male	Female	p-Value
Education – lower			
Sample size	18,358	21,449	0.0001
Mean	2.3	2	
SD	2.29	2.01	
Education – middle			
Sample size	23,130	23,367	0.0001
Mean	2.60	2.3	
SD	2.51	2.27	
Education – upper			
Sample size	11,828	10,668	0.0010
Mean	2.4	2.3	
SD	2.33	2.22	

1 = never justified; 10 = always justified

Table 26.9 Gender, marital status, and attitude toward tax evasion

	Male	Female	p-Value
Married			
Sample size	31,287	30,896	0.0001
Mean	2.3	2.1	
SD	2.27	2.1	
Living together			
Sample size	2,388	2,458	0.0001
Mean	2.6	2.3	
SD	2.55	2.28	
Divorced			
Sample size	1,535	2,746	0.0001
Mean	3	2.5	
SD	2.75	2.36	
Separated			
Sample size	678	1,128	0.0102
Mean	2.6	2.3	
SD	2.51	2.33	
Widowed			
Sample size	1,418	5,578	0.0008
Mean	2.2	2	
SD	2.26	1.94	
Single/never married			
Sample size	16,069	12,813	0.0001
Mean	2.7	2.4	
SD	2.55	2.31	

1 = never justified; 10 = always justified

Table 26.8 compares the statistics at three different education levels. Again, women are significantly more opposed to tax evasion at each level of education.

Table 26.9 shows that women are significantly more opposed to tax evasion regardless of marital status.

Table 26.10 Gender, religion, and attitude toward tax evasion

	Male	Female	p-Value	Result
Al-Hadis				
Sample size	74	71	0.0996	Women were more opposed to tax evasion but opposition was significant only at the 10% level
Mean	1.3	1.1		
SD	0.88	0.52		
Ancestral worshipping				
Sample size	141	161	0.1001	Men were more opposed to tax evasion but opposition was significant only slightly above the 10% level
Mean	1.1	1.3		
SD	0.85	1.2		
Armenian Apostolic church				
Sample size	724	897	0.0077	Women were significantly more opposed to tax evasion
Mean	3.8	3.4		
SD	3.07	2.94		
Buddhist				
Sample size	816	949	1.0000	No difference. Mean scores were identical
Mean	1.7	1.7		
SD	1.56	1.65		
Catholic (don't follow rules)				
Sample size	165	163	0.4467	No significant difference
Mean	2	1.8		
SD	2.54	2.2		
Christian				
Sample size	98	85	0.7258	No significant difference
Mean	1.9	1.8		
SD	1.93	1.91		
Evangelical				
Sample size	580	758	0.0857	Women were more opposed to tax evasion. The difference is significant only at the 10% level
Mean	2.1	1.9		
SD	2.32	1.93		
Free church (nondenominational)				
Sample size	288	383	0.1509	Women were more opposed but the difference is significant only at slightly above the 15% level
Mean	2.1	1.9		
SD	1.9	1.69		
Gregorian				
Sample size	22	20	0.9051	No significant difference
Mean	3.2	3.3		
SD	2.68	2.72		
Hindu				
Sample size	947	696	0.4170	No significant difference
Mean	2	2.1		
SD	2.34	2.63		

(continued)

Table 26.10 (continued)

	Male	Female	*p*-Value	Result
Iglesia ni Cristo				
Sample size	26	20	0.4268	No significant difference
Mean	4.1	3.5		
SD	2.68	2.28		
Independent African church				
Sample size	278	353	0.0286	Women were significantly more
Mean	2.5	2.1		opposed to tax evasion
SD	2.55	2.03		
Independent church				
Sample size	15	27	0.6656	No significant difference
Mean	1.5	1.7		
SD	1.3	1.49		
Jehovah witnesses				
Sample size	61	64	0.7445	No significant difference
Mean	1.8	1.7		
SD	1.94	1.46		
Jewish				
Sample size	176	148	0.4586	No significant difference
Mean	2.4	2.6		
SD	2.38	2.46		
Muslim				
Sample size	8,756	8,241	0.0012	Women were significantly more
Mean	1.9	1.8		opposed to tax evasion
SD	2.1	1.92		
Orthodox				
Sample size	3,759	4,844	0.0644	Women were more opposed to tax
Mean	2.8	2.7		evasion but opposition was
SD	2.56	2.43		significantly more only at the 10% level
Protestant				
Sample size	6,480	7,273	0.0001	Women were significantly more
Mean	2.5	2		opposed to tax evasion
SD	2.36	1.89		
Roman Catholic				
Sample size	15,129	17,819	0.0001	Women were significantly more
Mean	2.5	2.3		opposed to tax evasion
SD	2.4	2.2		
Seventh day Adventist				
Sample size	23	19	0.8893	No significant difference
Mean	1.9	2		
SD	2.37	2.22		

(continued)

Table 26.10 (continued)

	Male	Female	*p*-Value	Result
Shenism (Chinese religion)				
Sample size	28	37	0.6430	No significant difference
Mean	2.3	2.5		
SD	1.72	1.71		
Shia Muslim				
Sample size	74	115	0.1315	Women were more opposed to tax
Mean	1.4	1.2		evasion but the difference was
SD	1.03	0.78		significant only about the 13%
				level
Sikh				
Sample size	36	32	0.4313	No significant difference
Mean	2.3	1.8		
SD	2.74	2.43		
Sunni Muslim				
Sample size	534	502	0.0239	Men were significantly more
Mean	1.1	1.2		opposed to tax evasion
SD	0.73	0.69		
Taoist				
Sample size	65	50	0.4275	No significant difference
Mean	1.7	1.9		
SD	1.39	1.26		

1 = never justified; 10 = always justified

The World Values surveys also gathered data on the basis of religion. Table 26.10 shows the results for all religions that had a sample size of 30 or more. The results are mixed. In some cases, women were significantly more opposed to tax evasion than men but in many other cases they were not. In a few cases, men were more opposed to tax evasion.

Table 26.11 shows the frequency with which people attend religious services and provides a gender comparison. It was thought that frequency might make a difference but what difference it makes regarding gender was unclear. The results show that women were generally significantly more opposed to tax evasion, but that there was no significant difference where attendance was more than once a week or where attendance was only on certain days.

Concluding Comments

The study found that women are almost always more opposed to tax evasion than men and that the difference is often significant, but not always so. More research is needed to find the reasons why women are more opposed in some cases but not in others.

Table 26.11 Gender, religious practice, and attitude toward tax evasion

	Male	Female	p-Value	Result
More than once a week				
Sample size	6,609	6,739	1.0000	No significant difference.
Mean	1.7	1.7		Identical means
SD	1.82	1.75		
Once a week				
Sample size	8,838	10,666	0.0001	Women were significantly
Mean	2.2	2		more opposed to tax
SD	2.21	2.07		evasion
Once a month				
Sample size	5,855	6,858	0.0001	Women were significantly
Mean	2.5	2.2		more opposed to tax
SD	2.47	2.17		evasion
Only on special holy days (Christmas, Easter)				
Sample size	8,400	9,389	0.0001	Women were significantly
Mean	2.5	2.3		more opposed to tax
SD	2.37	2.22		evasion
Other specific holy days				
Sample size	1,144	1,468	0.2875	No significant difference
Mean	2.8	2.7		
SD	2.45	2.33		
Once a year				
Sample size	3,945	3,745	0.0001	Women were significantly
Mean	2.8	2.5		more opposed to tax
SD	2.6	2.44		evasion
Less than once a year				
Sample size	4,982	4,904	0.0001	Women were significantly
Mean	2.6	2.3		more opposed to tax
SD	2.41	2.25		evasion
Never, practically never				
Sample size	13,454	11,702	0.0001	Women were significantly
Mean	2.8	2.2		more opposed to tax
SD	2.58	2.23		evasion

References

Aitken, Sherie S. and Laura Bonneville, (1980). A General Taxpayer Opinion Survey. IRS, Office of Planning and Research, (CSR Incorporated) (March). Cited in Betty R. Jackson and Valerie C. Milliron. 1986. Tax Compliance Research: Findings, Problems, and Prospects. Journal of Accounting Literature 5, 125–165, at p. 127.

Akaah, Ishmael P. (1989). Differences in Research Ethics Judgments Between Male and Female Marketing Professionals. *Journal of Business Ethics*, 8(5), 375–381.

Akaah, Ishmael P. and Edward A. Riordan. (1989). Judgments of Marketing Professionals About Ethical Issues in Marketing Research: A Replication and Extension. *Journal of Marketing Research*, 26(1), 112–120.

Ameen, Elsice C., Daryl M. Guffey & Jeffrey J. McMillan (1996). Gender Differences in Determining the Ethical Sensitivity of Future Accounting Professionals. *Journal of Business Ethics*, 15(5), 591–597.

Babakus, Emin, T. Bettina Cornwell, Vince Mitchell and Bodo Schlegelmilch (2004). Reactions to Unethical Consumer Behavior across Six Countries. *The Journal of Consumer Marketing*, 21(4/5), 254–263.

Baird, J.S. (1980). Current Trends in College Cheating. *Psychology in the Schools*, 17(4), 515–522, as cited in Bob S. Brown and Peggy Choong. (2005). An Investigation of Academic Dishonesty among Business Students at Public and Private United States Universities. *International Journal of Management* 22(2): 201–214.

Barnett, John H. and Marvin J. Karson. (1987). Personal Values and Business Decisions: An Exploratory Investigation. *Journal of Business Ethics*, 6(5), 371–382.

Barnett, John H. and Marvin J. Karson. (1989). Managers, Values, and Executive Decisions: An Exploration of the Role of Gender, Career Stage, Organizational Level, Function, and the Importance of Ethics, Relationships and Results in Managerial Decision-Making. *Journal of Business Ethics*, 8(10), 747–771.

Beltramini, Richard F., Robert A. Peterson & George Kozmetsky. (1984). Concerns of College Students Regarding Business Ethics. *Journal of Business Ethics*, 3(3), 195–200.

Benk, Serkan, Robert W. McGee and Adriana M. Ross (2009). An Empirical Study of Ethical Opinion in Turkey. *Journal of Accounting, Ethics & Public Policy*, 10(1), 83–99.

Betz, Michael, Lenahan O'Connell and Jon M. Shepard. (1989). Gender Differences in Proclivity for Unethical Behavior. *Journal of Business Ethics*, 8(5), 321–324.

Beu, Danielle S., M. Ronald Buckley & Michael G. Harvey. (2003). Ethical Decision-Making: A Multidimensional Construct. *Business Ethics: A European Review*, 12(1), 88–107.

Boyd, David P. (1981). Improving Ethical Awareness Through the Business and Society Course. *Business and Society* 20, 21, 2, 1: 27–31.

Brown, Bob S. and Peggy Choong. (2005). An Investigation of Academic Dishonesty among Business Students at Public and Private United States Universities. *International Journal of Management*, 22(2), 201–214.

Browning, John and Noel B. Zabriskie. (1983). How Ethical Are Industrial Buyers? *Industrial Marketing Management*, 12(4), 219–224.

Byrnes, J. P., D.C. Miller and W.D. Schafer. (1999). Gender Differences in Risk Taking: A Meta-analysis. *Psychological Bulletin*, 125, 367–383.

Callan, Victor J. (1992). Predicting Ethical Values and Training Needs in Ethics. *Journal of Business Ethics*, 11(10), 761–769.

Chonko, Lawrence B. and Shelby D. Hunt. (1985). Ethics and Marketing Management: An Empirical Investigation. *Journal of Business Research*, 13(4), 339–359.

Dawson, Leslie M. (1997). Ethical Differences Between Men and Women in the Sales Profession. *Journal of Business Ethics*, 16(11), 1143–1152.

Derry, Robin. (1989). An Empirical Study of Moral Reasoning Among Managers. *Journal of Business Ethics*, 8(11), 855–862.

Dollar, David, Raymond Fisman, and Roberta Gatti. (2001). Are Women Really the "Fairer" Sex? Corruption and Women in Government, *Journal of Economic Behavior and Organization*, 46, 423–429.

Dubinsky, Alan J. and Michael Levy. (1985). Ethics in Retailing: Perceptions of Retail Sales People. *Journal of the Academy of Marketing Science*, 13(1), 1–16.

Eagly, A. H. 1987. *Sex Differences in Social Behavior: A Social-role Interpretation*. Hillsdale, NJ: Lawrence Erlbaum.

Ferrell, O.C. and Steven J. Skinner. (1988). Ethical Behavior and Bureaucratic Structure in Marketing Research Organizations. *Journal of Marketing Research*, 25(1), 103–109.

Franke, George R., Deborah F. Crown & Deborah F. Spake. (1997). Gender Differences in Ethical Perceptions of Business Practices: A Social Role Theory Perspective. *Journal of Applied Psychology*, 82(6), 920–934.

Friedman, William J., Amy B. Robinson & Britt L. Friedman. (1987). Sex Differences in Moral Judgments? A Test of Gilligan's Theory. *Psychology of Women Quarterly*, 11, 37–46.

Fritzsche, David J. (1988). An Examination of Marketing Ethics: Role of the Decision Maker, Consequences of the Decision, Management Position, and Sex of the Respondent. *Journal of Macromarketing*, 8(2), 29–39.

Glover, Saundra H. (1991). The Influences of Individual Values on Ethical Decision Making. Unpublished doctoral dissertation, University of South Carolina, Columbia, as cited in Saundra H. Glover, Minnette A. Bumpus, Glynda F. Sharp & George A. Munchus. (2002). Gender Differences in Ethical Decision Making. *Women in Management Review*, 17(5), 217–227.

Glover, Saundra H., Minnette Bumpus and J. Logan. (1993). Putting Values into Decision Making: the Influence of the Value Honesty/Integrity on the Decision Choice. *Proceedings of the Southern Management Association* 428–431, as cited in Saundra H. Glover, Minnette A. Bumpus, Glynda F. Sharp & George A. Munchus. (2002). Gender Differences in Ethical Decision Making. *Women in Management Review*, 17(5), 217–227.

Glover, Saundra H., Minnette Bumpus, John E. Logan & James R. Ciesla. (1997). Re-examining the Influence of Individual Values on Ethical Decision Making. *Journal of Business Ethics*, 16(12/13), 1319–1329.

Glover, Saundra H., Minnette A. Bumpus, Glynda F. Sharp & George A. Munchus. (2002). Gender Differences in Ethical Decision Making. *Women in Management Review*, 17(5), 217–227.

Grasmick, H., N. Finley and D. Glaser. (1984). Labor Force Participation, Sex-Role Attitudes, and Female Crime: Evidence from a Survey of Adults. *Social Science Quarterly* 65, 703–718.

Gupta, Ranjana and Robert W. McGee. (2010). A Comparative Study of New Zealanders' Opinion on the Ethics of Tax Evasion: Students v. Accountants. *New Zealand Journal of Taxation Law and Policy*, 16(1), 47–84.

Harris, James R. (1989). Ethical Values and Decision Processes of Male and Female Business Students. *Journal of Education for Business*, 8, 234–238, as cited in Sharon Galbraith and Harriet Buckman Stephenson. (1993). Decision Rules Used by Male and Female Business Students in Making Ethical Value Judgments: Another Look. *Journal of Business Ethics*, 12(3), 227–233.

Harris, James R. (1990). Ethical Values of Individuals at Different Levels in the Organizational Hierarchy of a Single Firm. *Journal of Business Ethics*, 9(9), 741–750.

Hegarty, W.H. and H.P. Sims, Jr. (1978). Some Determinants of Unethical Decision Behavior: An Experiment. *Journal of Applied Psychology*, 63(4), 451–457.

Hoffman, James J. (1998). Are Women Really More Ethical Than Men? Maybe It Depends on the Situation. *Journal of Managerial Issues*, 10(1), 60–73.

Jackson, Betty R. and Valerie C. Milliron. (1986). Tax Compliance Research: Findings, Problems, and Prospects. *Journal of Accounting Literature*, 5, 125–165.

Kastlunger, Barbara, Stefan G. Dressler, Erich Kirchler, Luigi Mittone and Martin Voracek. (2010). Sex Differences in Tax Compliance: Differentiating between Demographic Sex, Gender-Role Orientation, and Prenatal Masculinization (2D:4D). *Journal of Economic Psychology* 31, 542–552.

Kelley, S.W., O.C. Ferrell and S.J. Skinner. (1990). Ethical Behavior Among Marketing Researchers: An Assessment of Selected Demographic Characteristics. *Journal of Business Ethics*, 9(8), 681–688.

Kidwell, Jeaneen M., Robert E. Stevens & Art L. Bethke. (1987). Differences in Ethical Perceptions Between Male and Female Managers: Myth or Reality? *Journal of Business Ethics*, 6(6), 489–493.

Kohut, Gary F. & Susan E. Corriher. (1994). The Relationship of Age, Gender, Experience and Awareness of Written Ethics Policies to Business Decision Making. *S.A.M. Advanced Management Journal*, 59(1), 32–39.

Lampe, James C., Don W. Finn, James Gaa & Patricia L. O'Malley. (1992). A Model of Auditors' Ethical Decision Processes; Discussions; Reply. *Auditing: A Journal of Practice and Theory*, 11 (Supplement), 33–78.

Loo, Robert. (2003). Are Women More Ethical Than Men? Findings from Three Independent Studies. *Women in Management Review*, 18(3/4), 169–181.

Luthar, Harsh K., Ron A. DiBattista & Theodore Gautschi (1997). Perception of What the Ethical Climate Is and What It Should Be: The Role of Gender, Academic Status, and Ethical Education. *Journal of Business Ethics*, 16(2), 205–217.

Mason, R. and L. Calvin, (1978). A Study of Admitted Income Tax Evasion. *Law and Society Review*, 13(1), 73–89.

Mason. E. Sharon & Peter E. Mudrack. (1996). Gender and Ethical Orientation: A Test of Gender and Occupational Socialization Theories. *Journal of Business Ethics*, 15(6), 599–604.

McCabe, A. Catherine, Rhea Ingram and Mary Conway Dato-on. (2006). The Business of Ethics and Gender. *Journal of Business Ethics*, 64, 101–116.

McCuddy, Michael K. and Barbara L. Peery (1996). Selected Individual Differences and Collegian's Ethical Beliefs. *Journal of Business Ethics*, 15(3), 261–272.

McDonald, Gael M. and Pak Cho Kan (1997). Ethical Perceptions of Expatriate and Local Managers in Hong Kong. Journal of Business Ethics, 16(15), 1605–1623.

McGee, Robert W. (2006a). A Survey of International Business Academics on the Ethics of Tax Evasion. *Journal of Accounting, Ethics & Public Policy*, 6(3), 301–352.

McGee, Robert W. (2006b). The Ethics of Tax Evasion: A Survey of Romanian Business Students and Faculty. *The ICFAI Journal of Public Finance*, 4(2), 38–68 (2006). Reprinted in Robert W. McGee and Galina G. Preobragenskaya, *Accounting and Financial System Reform in Eastern Europe and Asia* (pp. 299–334). New York: Springer, 2006.

McGee, Robert W. (2006c). Gender, Age and the Ethics of Tax Evasion. Andreas School of Business Working Paper Series, Barry University, September.

McGee, Robert W. and Arkadiusz Bernal. (2006). The Ethics of Tax Evasion: A Survey of Business Students in Poland. In *Global Economy -- How It Works* (Mina Baliamoune-Lutz, Alojzy Z. Nowak & Jeff Steagall, eds.) (pp. 155–174). Warsaw: University of Warsaw & Jacksonville: University of North Florida. Reprinted at http://ssrn.com/abstract=875434.

McGee, Robert W., Inge Nickerson and Werner Fees. (2006). German and American Opinion on the Ethics of Tax Evasion. *Proceedings of the Academy of Legal, Ethical and Regulatory Issues* (Reno), 10(2), 31–34.

McGee, Robert W. and Zhiwen Guo. (2007). A Survey of Law, Business and Philosophy Students in China on the Ethics of Tax Evasion. *Society and Business Review*, 2(3), 299–315.

McGee, Robert W., Carlos Noronha and Michael Tyler. (2007). The Ethics of Tax Evasion: a Survey of Macau Opinion. *Euro Asia Journal of Management*, 17(2), 123–150. Reprinted in Robert W. McGee (editor), *Readings in Accounting Ethics* (pp. 283–313), Hyderabad, India: ICFAI University Press, 2009.

McGee, Robert W. and Silvia López Paláu. (2007). The Ethics of Tax Evasion: Two Empirical Studies of Puerto Rican Opinion. *Journal of Applied Business and Economics*, 7(3), 27–47 (2007). Reprinted in Robert W. McGee (editor), *Readings in Accounting Ethics* (pp. 314–342). Hyderabad, India: ICFAI University Press, 2009.

McGee, Robert W., Silvia López-Paláu and Fabiola Jarrín Jaramillo. (2007). The Ethics of Tax Evasion: An Empirical Study of Ecuador. American Society of Business and Behavioral Sciences 14th Annual Meeting, Las Vegas, February 22–25, 2007. Published in the Proceedings of the American Society of Business and Behavioral Sciences 14(1): 1186–1198.

McGee, Robert W. and Sheldon R. Smith. (2007). Ethics, Tax Evasion and Religion: A Survey of Opinion of Members of the Church of Jesus Christ of Latter-Day Saints. Western Decision Sciences Institute, Thirty-Sixth Annual Meeting, Denver, April 3–7. Published in the Proceedings. Reprinted at http://ssrn.com/abstract=934652.

McGee, Robert W. (2008). Opinions on Tax Evasion in Thailand, in Robert W. McGee, editor, *Taxation and Public Finance in Transition and Developing Economies* (pp. 609–620). New York: Springer.

McGee, Robert W., Jaan Alver and Lehte Alver. (2008). The Ethics of Tax Evasion: A Survey of Estonian Opinion, in Robert W. McGee, editor, *Taxation and Public Finance in Transition and Developing Economies* (pp. 461–480). New York: Springer.

McGee, Robert W. and Yuhua An. (2008). A Survey of Chinese Business and Economics Students on the Ethics of Tax Evasion, in Robert W. McGee, editor, *Taxation and Public Finance in Transition and Developing Economies* (pp. 409–421). New York: Springer.

McGee, Robert W. and Yiu Yu Butt. (2008). An Empirical Study of Tax Evasion Ethics in Hong Kong. Proceedings of the International Academy of Business and Public Administration Disciplines (IABPAD), Dallas, April 24–27: 72–83.

McGee, Robert W. and Gordon M. Cohn. (2008). Jewish Perspectives on the Ethics of Tax Evasion. *Journal of Legal, Ethical and Regulatory Issues*, 11(2), 1–32.

McGee, Robert W. and Beena George (2008). Tax Evasion and Ethics: A Survey of Indian Opinion. *Journal of Accounting, Ethics & Public Policy*, 9(3), 301–332.

McGee, Robert W. and Christopher Lingle. (2008). The Ethics of Tax Evasion: A Survey of Guatemalan Opinion, in Robert W. McGee, editor, *Taxation and Public Finance in Transition and Developing Economies* (pp. 481–495). New York: Springer.

McGee, Robert W. and Paláu Silvia López. (2008). Tax Evasion and Ethics: A Comparative Study of the USA and Four Latin American Countries, in Robert W. McGee, editor, *Taxation and Public Finance in Transition and Developing Economies* (pp. 185–224). New York: Springer.

McGee, Robert W. and Carlos Noronha. (2008). The Ethics of Tax Evasion: A Comparative Study of Guangzhou (Southern China) and Macau Opinions. Euro Asia Journal of Management, 18(2), 133–152.

McGee, Robert W. and Galina G. Preobragenskaya. (2008). A Study of Tax Evasion Ethics in Kazakhstan, in Robert W. McGee, editor, *Taxation and Public Finance in Transition and Developing Economies* (pp. 497–510). New York: Springer.

McGee, Robert W. and Marcelo J. Rossi. (2008). A Survey of Argentina on the Ethics of Tax Evasion, in Robert W. McGee, editor, *Taxation and Public Finance in Transition and Developing Economies* (pp. 239–261). New York: Springer.

McGee, Robert W. and Radoslav Tusan. (2008). The Ethics of Tax Evasion: A Survey of Slovak Opinion, in Robert W. McGee, editor, *Taxation and Public Finance in Transition and Developing Economies* (pp. 575–601). New York: Springer.

McGee, Robert W. and Susana N. Vittadini Andres. (2009). The Ethics of Tax Evasion: Case Studies of Taiwan, in Robert W. McGee, *Readings in Business Ethics* (pp. 200–228). Hyderabad, India: ICFAI University Press. An abbreviated version was published in Marjorie G. Adams and Abbass Alkhafaji, editors, *Business Research Yearbook: Global Business Perspectives*, Volume XIV, No. 1 (pp. 34–39). Beltsville, MD: International Graphics: Beltsville, MD, 2007.

McGee, Robert W. and Mahdi Nazemi Ardakani (2009). The Ethics of Tax Evasion: A Case Study of Opinion in Iran. Florida International University Working Paper.

McGee, Robert W. Serkan Benk, Adriana M. Ross & Harun Kılıçaslan (2009). An Empirical Study of Ethical Opinion in Germany. *Journal of Accounting, Ethics & Public Policy*, 10(2), 243–259.

McGee, Robert W. and Sanjoy Bose. (2009). The Ethics of Tax Evasion: A Survey of Australian Opinion, in Robert W. McGee, *Readings in Business Ethics* (pp. 143–166). Hyderabad, India: ICFAI University Press.

McGee, Robert W. and Bouchra M'Zali. (2009). The Ethics of Tax Evasion: An Empirical Study of French EMBA Students, in Robert W. McGee, *Readings in Business Ethics* (pp. 185–199). Hyderabad, India: ICFAI University Press. An abbreviated version was published in Marjorie G. Adams and Abbass Alkhafaji, editors, *Business Research Yearbook: Global Business Perspectives*, Volume XIV, No. 1 (pp. 27–33). Beltsville, MD: International Graphics, 2007.

McGee, Robert W., Silvia López Paláu and Gustavo A. Yepes Lopez. (2009). The Ethics of Tax Evasion: An Empirical Study of Colombian Opinion, in Robert W. McGee, *Readings in Business Ethics* (pp. 167–184). Hyderabad, India: ICFAI University Press.

McGee, Robert W. & Geoff A. Goldman (2010). Ethics and Tax Evasion: A Survey of South African Opinion. *Proceedings of the Third Annual University of Johannesburg Faculty of Management Conference*, May 12–14. Reprinted in the present volume.

McGee, Robert W. & Serkan Benk (2011). The Ethics of Tax Evasion: A Study of Turkish Opinion. *Journal of Balkan and Near Eastern Studies*, 13(2): 249–262.

McGee, Robert W., Serkan Benk, Halil Yıldırım and Murat Kayıkçı. (2011). The Ethics of Tax Evasion: A Study of Turkish Tax Practitioner Opinion, *European Journal of Social Sciences*, 18(3), 468–480.

McGee, Robert W., Arsen M. Djatej and Robert H.S. Sarikas. (2012). The Ethics of Tax Evasion: A Survey of Hispanic Opinion. *Accounting & Taxation*, 4(1), 53–74.

McGee, Robert W. (2012). Attitudes on the Ethics of Tax Evasion: A Survey of Philosophy Professors. In Robert W. McGee (Ed.), *The Ethics of Tax Evasion: Perspectives in Theory and Practice*. New York: Springer.

McGee, Robert W., Jaan Alver and Lehte Alver (2012). Tax Evasion Opinion in Estonia. In Robert W. McGee (Ed.), *The Ethics of Tax Evasion: Perspectives in Theory and Practice*. New York: Springer.

McGee, Robert W. and Bouchra M'Zali (2012). Opinions on Tax Evasion in Haiti. In Robert W. McGee (Ed.), *The Ethics of Tax Evasion: Perspectives in Theory and Practice*. New York: Springer.

McGee, Robert W. and Ravi Kumar Jain (2012). The Ethics of Tax Evasion: A Study of Indian Opinion. In Robert W. McGee (Ed.), *The Ethics of Tax Evasion: Perspectives in Theory and Practice*. New York: Springer.

McGee, Robert W. and Tatyana B. Maranjyan (2012). Attitudes toward Tax Evasion: An Empirical Study of Florida Accounting Practitioners. In Robert W. McGee (Ed.), *The Ethics of Tax Evasion: Perspectives in Theory and Practice*. New York: Springer.

McGee, Robert W., Yanira Petrides and Adriana M. Ross (2012). Ethics and Tax Evasion: A Survey of Mexican Opinion. In Robert W. McGee (Ed.), *The Ethics of Tax Evasion: Perspectives in Theory and Practice*. New York: Springer.

McNichols, Charles W. and Thomas W. Zimmerer (1985). Situational Ethics: An Empirical Study of Differentiators of Student Attitudes. *Journal of Business Ethics* 4, 175–180.

Mears, D.P., M. Ploeger and M. Warr. (2000). Explaining the Gender Gap in Delinquency: Peer Influence and Moral Evaluations of Behavior. In Robert D. Crutchfield, George S. Bridges, Joseph G. Weis and Charis Kubrin (eds.), *Crime Readings* (pp. 143–148), Thousand Oaks, CA: Pine Forge Press.

Miesing, Paul and John F. Preble. (1985). A Comparison of Five Business Philosophies. *Journal of Business Ethics*, 4(6), 465–476.

Nasadyuk, Irina and Robert W. McGee. (2007). The Ethics of Tax Evasion: Lessons for Transitional Economies. . In Greg N. Gregoriou and C. Read (eds.), *International Taxation* (pp. 291–310). Elsevier.

Nyaw, Mee-Kau and Ignace Ng. (1994). A Comparative Analysis of Ethical Beliefs: A Four Country Study. *Journal of Business Ethics*, 13(7), 543–555.

Ondrack, D.A. (1973). Emerging Occupational Values: A Review and Some Findings. *Academy of Management Journal*, 16, 423–432.

Posner, Barry Z. & Warren H. Schmidt. (1984). Values and the American Manager: An Update. *California Management Review*, 26(3), 202–216.

Purcell, Theodore V. (1977). Do Courses in Business Ethics Pay Off? *California Management Review*, 19(4), 50–58.

Robin, Donald and Laurie Babin. (1997). Making Sense of the Research on Gender and Ethics in Business: A Critical Analysis and Extension. *Business Ethics Quarterly*, 7(4), 61–90.

Roxas, Maria L. & Jane Y. Stoneback. (2004). The Importance of Gender Across Cultures in Ethical Decision-Making. *Journal of Business Ethics*, 50, 149–165.

Ruegger, Durwood and Ernest W. King. (1992). A Study of the Effect of Age and Gender upon Student Business Ethics. *Journal of Business Ethics*, 11(3), 179–186.

Schaub, Michael K. (1994). An Analysis of the Association of Traditional Demographic Variables with the Moral Reasoning of Auditing Students and Auditors. *Journal of Accounting Education*, 12(1), 1–26.

Schmidt, Warren W. & Barry Z. Posner. (1992). The Values of American Managers Then and Now. *Management Review*, 81(2), 37–40.

Serwinek, Paul J. (1992). Demographic & Related Differences in Ethical Views Among Small Businesses. *Journal of Business Ethics*, 11(7), 555–566.

Sierles, F., I. Hendrickx and S. Circle (1980). Cheating in Medical School. *Medical Education*, 55(2), 124–125, as cited in Bob S. Brown and Peggy Choong. (2005). An Investigation of Academic Dishonesty among Business Students at Public and Private United States Universities. *International Journal of Management*, 22(2), 201–214.

Sikula, Andrew, Sr. and Adelmiro D. Costa. (1994). Are Women More Ethical than Men? *Journal of Business Ethics,* 13(11), 859–871.

Sims, Ronald R., Hsing K. Cheng & Hildy Teegen. (1996). Toward a Profile of Student Software Piraters. *Journal of Business Ethics*, 15(8), 839–849.

Singappakdi, Anusorn, Scott J. Vitell & George R. Franke. (1999). Antecedents, Consequences and Mediating Effects of Perceived Moral Intensity and Personal Moral Philosophies. *Journal of the Academy of Marketing Science*, 27(1), 19–36.

Smith, Patricia L. & Ellwood F. Oakley, III. (1997). Gender-Related Differences in Ethical and Social Values of Business Students: Implications for Management. *Journal of Business Ethics*, 16(1), 37–45.

Stanga, Keith G. and Richard A. Turpen. (1991). Ethical Judgments on Selected Accounting Issues: An Empirical Study. *Journal of Business Ethics*, 10(10), 739–747.

Stern, E.B. and L. Havlicek (1986). Academic Misconduct: results of Faculty and Undergraduate Student Surveys. *Journal of Allied Health*, 15(2), 129–142, as cited in Bob S. Brown and Peggy Choong. (2005). An Investigation of Academic Dishonesty among Business Students at Public and Private United States Universities. *International Journal of Management*, 22(2), 201–214.

Su, Shu-Hui. (2006). Cultural Differences in Determining the Ethical Perception and Decision-making of Future Accounting Professionals: A Comparison between Accounting Students from Taiwan and the United States. *Journal of American Academy of Business*, 9(1), 147–158.

Swaidan, Ziad, Scott J. Vitell, Gregory M. Rose and Faye W. Gilbert. (2006). Consumer Ethics: The Role of Acculturation in U.S. Immigrant Populations. *Journal of Business Ethics*, 64(1), 1–16.

Swamy, Anand, Stephen Knack, Young Lee and Omar Azfar. (2001). Gender and Corruption. *Journal of Development Economics*, 64, 25–55.

Tang, S. and J. Zuo (1997). Profile of College Examination Cheaters. *College Student Journal* 31(3): 340–347, as cited in Bob S. Brown and Peggy Choong. (2005). An Investigation of Academic Dishonesty among Business Students at Public and Private United States Universities. *International Journal of Management*, 22(2), 201–214.

Tittle, C. (1980). *Sanctions and Social Deviance: The Question of Deterrence*. New York: Praeger.

Tsalikis, J. & M. Ortiz-Buonafina. (1990). Ethical Beliefs' Differences of Males and Females. *Journal of Business Ethics*, 9(6), 509–517.

Weeks, William A., Carlos W. Moore, Joseph A. McKinney & Justin G. Longenecker. (1999). The Effects of Gender and Career Stage on Ethical Judgment. *Journal of Business Ethics*, 20(4), 301–313.

Whitley, Bernard E. (1998). Factors Associated with Cheating among College Students: A Review. *Research in Higher Education*, 39(3), 235–274.

World Values Survey Data. http://www.wvsevsdb.com/

Chapter 27
Age and the Ethics of Tax Evasion

Robert W. McGee

Introduction

Some studies have found that people become more respectful of authority and the rule of law as they get older. However, other studies have had contrary findings. The next few pages analyze the relationship between age and attitudes toward the ethics of tax evasion, using the World Values survey data.

Findings

Table 27.1 shows the data for each country for each of the three age groups. Overall, the oldest group (50+) was most opposed to tax evasion and the youngest group (15–29) was least opposed to tax evasion. The oldest group was the group most opposed to tax evasion in 72 countries. The 30–49 age group was most opposed to tax evasion in eight cases (Algeria, Armenia, Bangladesh, Moldova, Philippines, Uganda, Venezuela, and Vietnam). The 15–29 age group was most opposed in two countries (India and Vietnam). The mean scores for the 30–49 and 50+ groups were identical for Vietnam.

Table 27.2 shows the p-values for various comparisons. Many of the differences in mean scores were significant at the 1 or 5% level.

Table 27.3 shows the ANOVA calculations between groups and within groups. Almost all of the differences are significant.

R.W. McGee (✉)
School of Business, Florida International University,
3000 NE 151 Street, North Miami, FL 33181, USA
e-mail: bob414@hotmail.com

R.W. McGee (ed.), *The Ethics of Tax Evasion: Perspectives in Theory and Practice*,
DOI 10.1007/978-1-4614-1287-8_27, © Springer Science+Business Media, LLC 2012

Table 27.1 Cheating on taxes if you could – age

	15–29			30–49			50+		
	Sample size	Mean	SD	Sample size	Mean	SD	Sample size	Mean	SD
Total	32,257	2.53	2.456	44,405	2.35	2.322	31,407	2.03	2.029
Albania	253	2.08	1.635	440	1.94	1.473	292	1.64	1.105
Algeria	535	2.24	2.397	466	1.79	1.891	246	1.95	2.309
Argentina	393	2.15	2.359	458	1.84	1.891	420	1.65	1.850
Armenia	745	3.82	2.958	734	3.57	3.045	467	3.61	3.192
Australia	610	2.56	2.163	771	2.22	2.030	657	1.71	1.656
Austria	313	2.76	2.397	586	2.23	2.011	597	1.87	1.611
Azerbaijan	695	3.83	3.464	877	3.51	3.117	287	3.40	3.035
Bangladesh	605	1.11	0.793	744	1.02	0.295	141	1.04	0.313
Belarus	239	5.00	2.937	364	4.27	2.826	310	3.56	2.678
Belgium	362	4.23	2.854	737	3.84	2.876	787	3.22	2.740
Bosnia	354	1.91	1.915	485	1.80	1.859	358	1.54	1.542
Brazil	451	3.81	3.131	468	3.61	3.178	219	3.07	3.186
Bulgaria	191	2.63	2.296	354	2.27	2.134	403	1.48	1.306
Canada	409	2.45	2.376	811	2.17	2.161	697	1.78	1.821
Chile	323	2.23	2.306	507	2.15	2.341	347	2.08	2.208
China	193	1.73	1.542	566	1.55	1.443	226	1.50	1.415
Colombia	969	2.52	2.355	1,558	2.21	2.212	467	2.08	2.027
Croatia	235	3.80	3.380	409	2.20	2.095	353	2.05	1.883
Czech Republic	419	2.43	1.957	680	2.31	1.982	784	1.67	1.357
Denmark	209	2.11	1.918	413	2.15	1.880	395	1.80	1.632
Dominican Republic	256	2.00	2.076	137	1.84	1.956	10	1.70	1.636
Egypt	1,015	1.62	1.494	1,313	1.58	1.509	652	1.50	1.338
El Salvador	468	2.07	2.481	462	1.90	2.340	290	1.68	1.947
Estonia	220	3.90	2.647	356	3.47	2.589	398	2.45	2.101
Finland	208	3.07	2.525	367	2.70	2.491	425	1.98	1.780
France	311	3.78	2.707	622	3.18	2.784	643	2.59	2.388

Georgia	638	3.10	2.594	757	2.65	2.274	592	2.46	2.226
Germany, East	180	2.74	2.570	414	2.53	2.418	374	2.10	1.938
Germany, West	180	2.82	2.288	428	2.49	2.140	419	2.00	1.630
Great Britain	216	3.41	2.461	357	2.56	2.241	390	1.78	1.549
Greece	461	3.30	2.433	426	3.14	2.542	180	2.70	2.217
Hungary	233	2.58	2.226	355	2.50	2.286	384	1.47	1.408
Iceland	257	2.63	2.213	404	2.27	1.920	300	1.82	1.668
India	523	2.00	2.395	900	2.15	2.670	454	2.28	2.832
Indonesia	181	1.76	1.855	423	1.56	1.375	395	1.42	1.071
Iran	1,234	1.57	1.792	770	1.38	1.440	451	1.34	1.360
Ireland	246	2.60	2.118	383	2.47	2.188	336	1.98	1.856
Italy	441	2.93	2.411	723	2.39	2.175	803	2.10	1.990
Japan	242	1.64	1.326	505	1.45	1.337	565	1.40	1.477
Jordan	470	1.72	1.735	511	1.52	1.509	223	1.28	1.263
Kyrgyzstan	388	2.84	2.612	442	2.69	2.615	207	2.58	2.594
Latvia	184	3.32	2.644	362	2.43	2.316	443	1.92	1.910
Lithuania	254	4.67	3.105	347	4.06	3.064	366	2.87	2.774
Luxembourg	278	3.85	2.772	470	3.24	2.769	419	3.23	2.737
Macedonia	262	2.62	2.447	445	2.45	2.696	318	1.77	1.957
Malta	258	1.82	1.698	360	1.60	1.613	384	1.30	0.990
Mexico	487	2.51	2.475	615	2.39	2.614	340	1.88	2.037
Moldova	264	4.44	2.870	362	3.90	2.818	306	4.33	3.114
Montenegro	232	3.18	2.587	399	2.70	2.132	371	2.00	1.636
Morocco	487	1.23	1.190	500	1.22	1.196	246	1.05	0.562
Netherlands	210	3.26	2.290	402	2.91	2.277	389	2.29	2.031
New Zealand	173	3.30	2.711	478	2.37	2.221	489	1.89	1.895
Nigeria	1,096	2.06	1.901	782	2.04	1.771	144	1.74	1.444
Northern Ireland	200	2.66	2.372	324	2.77	2.472	391	1.96	1.727
Norway	266	2.73	2.207	479	2.98	2.427	375	2.36	2.253
Pakistan	653	1.2	0.775	942	1.22	0.759	345	1.08	0.519

(continued)

Table 27.1 (continued)

	15–29			30–49			50+		
	Sample size	Mean	SD	Sample size	Mean	SD	Sample size	Mean	SD
Peru	595	2.12	1.891	622	2.19	2.109	256	1.92	1.816
Philippines	382	3.21	2.463	529	3.09	2.554	272	3.13	2.471
Poland	237	2.92	2.566	445	2.12	2.045	384	1.92	1.858
Portugal	239	2.45	2.174	338	2.73	2.299	386	2.21	1.983
Puerto Rico	144	2.58	2.820	244	2.18	2.553	316	1.63	1.841
Romania	239	3.35	2.996	414	3.01	2.881	427	2.27	2.386
Russia	537	4.25	2.943	1,001	3.23	2.643	844	2.20	1.973
Serbia	222	2.62	2.267	452	2.21	2.030	493	1.75	1.647
Singapore	721	2.07	1.891	582	1.74	1.757	202	1.64	1.505
Slovakia	344	2.36	2.051	523	2.24	2.085	440	1.89	1.691
Slovenia	254	3.04	2.665	388	2.26	2.157	355	1.93	1.812
South Africa	1,136	2.52	2.520	1,343	3.04	2.792	445	2.11	2.061
South Korea	313	1.73	1.532	619	1.58	1.362	267	1.45	1.217
Spain	311	2.37	2.084	403	2.31	2.050	475	1.90	1.732
Sweden	235	2.51	2.029	378	2.64	2.153	396	2.12	1.805
Switzerland	249	3.19	2.624	515	2.95	2.731	414	1.83	1.641
Taiwan	120	2.02	1.732	467	2.04	1.923	180	1.70	1.320
Tanzania	391	1.84	2.446	526	1.76	2.133	215	1.43	1.624
Turkey	489	1.20	0.929	523	1.19	0.989	190	1.11	0.452
Uganda	502	3.67	3.474	394	3.11	3.307	102	3.41	3.415
Ukraine	252	4.45	2.999	430	3.66	2.789	426	2.64	2.389
Uruguay	193	2.01	2.229	338	1.83	1.825	445	1.52	1.493
USA	314	2.73	2.443	515	2.26	2.197	369	1.90	1.898
Venezuela	494	1.86	1.855	468	1.76	1.641	232	1.85	1.813
Vietnam	223	1.31	1.178	467	1.31	0.955	299	1.33	1.275
Zimbabwe	459	1.61	1.655	343	1.48	1.487	178	1.37	1.111

1 = Never justifiable; 10 = always justifiable

Table 27.2 Cheating on taxes if you could – age

	15–29 vs. 30–49	15–29 vs. 50+	30–49 vs. 50+
Albania	0.2478	0.0002	0.0031
Algeria	0.0011	0.1125	0.3211
Argentina	0.0337	0.0008	0.1333
Armenia	0.1095	0.2437	0.8276
Australia	0.0027	0.0001	0.8490
Austria	0.0005	0.0001	0.0007
Azerbaijan	0.0545	0.0672	0.6016
Bangladesh	0.0043	0.3037	0.4650
Belarus	0.0024	0.0001	0.0012
Belgium	0.0344	0.0001	0.0001
Bosnia	0.4035	0.0046	0.0314
Brazil	0.9643	0.8827	0.9162
Bulgaria	0.9147	0.6415	0.7460
Canada	0.9359	0.8230	0.8922
Chile	0.9816	0.9625	0.9834
China	0.9455	0.9125	0.9837
Colombia	0.9266	0.9047	0.9735
Croatia	0.6713	0.6266	0.9581
Czech Republic	0.3275	0.0001	0.0001
Denmark	0.8035	0.0373	0.0049
Dominican Republic	0.4581	0.6522	0.8257
Egypt	0.5242	0.0959	0.2511
El Salvador	0.2828	0.0230	0.1817
Estonia	0.0553	0.0001	0.0001
Finland	0.0891	0.0001	0.0001
France	0.0018	0.0001	0.0001
Georgia	0.0006	0.0001	01245
Germany, East	0.3404	0.0012	0.0064
Germany, West	0.0896	0.0001	0.0002
Great Britain	0.0001	0.0001	0.0001
Greece	0.3385	0.0042	0.0438
Hungary	0.6751	0.0001	0.0001
Iceland	0.0272	0.0001	0.0012
India	0.2891	0.0944	0.4075
Indonesia	0.1427	0.0057	0.1063
Iran	0.0131	0.0133	0.6327
Ireland	0.4618	0.0002	0.0011
Italy	0.0001	0.0001	0.0066
Japan	0.0688	0.0296	0.5634
Jordan	0.0539	0.0008	0.0380
Kyrgyzstan	0.4096	0.2468	0.6167
Latvia	0.0001	0.0001	0.0006
Lithuania	0.0168	0.0001	0.0001
Luxembourg	0.0037	0.0037	0.9569
Macedonia	0.4026	0.0001	0.0001

(continued)

Table 27.2 (continued)

	15–29 vs. 30–49	15–29 vs. 50+	30–49 vs. 50+
Malta	0.1024	0.0001	0.0022
Mexico	0.4387	0.0001	0.0019
Moldova	0.0191	0.6630	0.0616
Montenegro	0.0121	0.0001	0.0001
Morocco	0.8953	0.0248	0.0346
Netherlands	0.0721	0.0001	0.0001
New Zealand	0.0001	0.0001	0.0003
Nigeria	0.8172	0.0571	0.0554
Northern Ireland	0.6155	0.0001	0.0001
Norway	0.1647	0.0392	0.0001
Pakistan	0.6080	0.0099	0.0016
Peru	0.5428	0.1526	0.0733
Philippines	0.4777	0.6828	0.8320
Poland	0.0001	0.0001	0.1434
Portugal	0.1411	0.1570	0.0011
Puerto Rico	0.1525	0.0001	0.0032
Romania	0.1528	0.0001	0.0001
Russia	0.0001	0.0001	0.0001
Serbia	0.0180	0.0001	0.0001
Singapore	0.0013	0.0030	04704
Slovakia	0.4043	0.0005	0.0048
Slovenia	0.0001	0.0001	0.0249
South Africa	0.0001	0.0023	0.0001
South Korea	0.1284	0.0164	0.1790
Spain	0.7004	0.0006	0.0014
Sweden	0.4578	0.0125	0.0003
Switzerland	0.2493	0.0001	0.0001
Taiwan	0.9175	0.0790	0.0295
Tanzania	0.5980	0.0279	0.0418
Turkey	0.8686	0.2019	0.2829
Uganda	0.0146	0.4898	0.4177
Ukraine	0.0005	0.0001	0.0001
Uruguay	0.3144	0.0012	0.0092
USA	0.0043	0.0001	0.0112
Venezuela	0.3771	0.9456	0.5099
Vietnam	1.0000	0.8548	0.8046
Zimbabwe	0.2509	0.0748	0.3853

Age – p-values (t-test)

Table 27.3 Cheating on taxes if you could – ANOVA data

Country	Between groups Σ Squares	df	Mean squares	Within groups Σ Squares	df	Mean squares	Fisher F-value	p-Value
Albania	28.475	2	14.237	1981.482	982	2.018	7.056	0.001
Algeria	51.715	2	25.857	6037.153	1,244	4.853	5.328	0.005
Argentina	51.539	2	25.770	5249.638	1,268	4.140	6.224	0.002
Armenia	25.729	2	12.864	18054.229	1,943	9.292	1.384	0.251
Australia	233.404	2	116.702	7821.314	2,035	3.843	30.364	<0.0001
Austria	163.686	2	81.843	7512.980	1,493	5.032	16.264	<0.0001
Azerbaijan	55.052	2	27.526	19472.865	1,856	10.492	2.624	0.073
Bangladesh	2.756	2	1.378	458.200	1,487	0.308	4.471	0.012
Belarus	281.354	2	140.677	7168.049	910	7.877	17.859	<0.0001
Belgium	293.828	2	146.914	14929.165	1,883	7.928	18.530	<0.0001
Bosnia	26.035	2	13.018	3816.039	1,194	3.196	4.073	0.017
Brazil	81.209	2	40.604	11340.805	1,135	9.992	4.064	0.017
Bulgaria	210.543	2	105.272	3294.819	945	3.487	30.193	<0.0001
Canada	125.170	2	62.585	8393.914	1,914	4.386	14.271	<0.0001
Chile	3.765	2	1.883	6172.142	1,174	5.257	0.358	0.699
China	6.260	2	3.130	2083.502	982	2.122	1.475	0.229
Colombia	81.826	2	40.913	14901.534	2,991	4.982	8.212	<0.0001
Croatia	504.867	2	252.434	5712.114	994	5.747	43.928	<0.0001
Czech Republic	218.910	2	109.455	5710.063	1,880	3.037	36.037	<0.0001
Denmark	27.587	2	13.793	3446.125	1,014	3.399	4.059	0.018
Dominican Republic	2.866	2	1.433	1643.409	400	4.109	0.349	0.706
Egypt	5.752	2	2.876	6416.264	2,977	2.155	1.334	0.263
El Salvador	27.358	2	13.679	6494.349	1,217	5.336	2.563	0.077
Estonia	355.224	2	177.612	5666.422	971	5.836	30.436	<0.0001
Finland	196.336	2	98.168	4934.216	997	4.949	19.836	<0.0001
France	312.209	2	156.105	10745.824	1,573	6.831	22.851	<0.0001

(continued)

Table 27.3 (continued)

Country	Between groups Σ Squares	df	Mean squares	Within groups Σ Squares	df	Mean squares	Fisher F-value	p-Value
Georgia	135.220	2	67.610	11124.052	1,984	5.607	12.058	<0.0001
Germany, East	61.456	2	30.728	4997.904	965	5.179	5.933	0.003
Germany, West	99.474	2	49.737	4003.128	1,024	3.909	12.723	<0.0001
Great Britain	378.233	2	189.116	4023.380	960	4.191	45.124	<0.0001
Greece	46.622	2	23.311	6349.016	1,064	5.967	3.907	0.020
Hungary	262.747	2	131.373	3758.793	969	3.879	33.867	<0.0001
Iceland	92.179	2	46.090	3571.231	958	3.728	12.364	<0.0001
India	19.239	2	9.619	13036.248	1,874	6.956	1.383	0.251
Indonesia	14.617	2	7.308	1869.162	996	1.877	3.894	0.021
Iran	26.191	2	13.095	6112.899	2,452	2.493	5.253	0.005
Ireland	66.594	2	33.297	4081.803	962	4.243	7.847	<0.0001
Italy	196.114	2	98.057	9149.197	1,964	4.658	21.049	<0.0001
Japan	9.909	2	4.955	2555.062	1,309	1.952	2.538	0.079
Jordan	30.284	2	15.142	2927.234	1,201	2.437	6.212	0.002
Kyrgyzstan	10.024	2	5.012	7042.122	1,034	6.811	0.736	0.479
Latvia	257.063	2	128.531	4828.117	986	4.897	26.249	<0.0001
Lithuania	531.383	2	265.691	8496.163	964	8.813	30.146	<0.0001
Luxembourg	80.046	2	40.023	8855.765	1,164	7.608	5.261	0.005
Macedonia	125.853	2	62.927	6004.057	1,022	5.875	10.711	<0.0001
Malta	43.639	2	21.819	2050.397	999	2.052	10.631	<0.0001
Mexico	86.282	2	43.141	8579.149	1,439	5.962	7.236	0.001
Moldova	52.926	2	26.463	7990.634	929	8.601	3.077	0.047
Montenegro	213.282	2	106.641	4345.366	999	4.350	24.517	<0.0001
Morocco	6.051	2	3.025	1479.384	1,230	1.203	2.515	0.081
Netherlands	147.168	2	73.584	4775.578	998	4.785	15.378	<0.0001
New Zealand	257.512	2	128.756	5369.015	1,137	4.723	27.264	<0.0001
Nigeria	13.174	2	6.587	6704.847	2,019	3.321	1.984	0.138

Northern Ireland	133.573	2	66.787	4256.620	912		4.667	14.309	<0.0001
Norway	80.953	2	40.476	6004.780	1,117		5.376	7.529	0.001
Pakistan	5.082	2	2.541	1026.360	1,937		0.530	4.796	0.008
Peru	13.248	2	6.624	5727.161	1,470		3.896	1.700	0.183
Philippines	3.217	2	1.608	7410.069	1,180		6.280	0.256	0.774
Poland	155.104	2	77.552	4732.906	1,063		4.452	17.418	<0.0001
Portugal	48.729	2	24.364	4419.965	960		4.604	5.292	0.005
Puerto Rico	99.450	2	49.725	3788.644	701		5.405	9.200	<0.0001
Romania	210.441	2	105.221	7989.475	1,077		7.418	14.184	<0.0001
Russia	1,410.680	2	705.340	14909.449	2,379		6.267	112.546	<0.0001
Serbia	125.844	2	62.922	4328.912	1,164		3.719	16.919	<0.0001
Singapore	49.038	2	24.519	4823.480	1,502		3.211	7.635	0.001
Slovakia	49.132	2	24.566	4967.428	1,304		3.809	6.449	0.002
Slovenia	186.617	2	93.309	4759.742	994		4.788	19.486	<0.0001
South Africa	346.925	2	173.462	19554.936	2,921		6.695	25.911	<0.0001
South Korea	11.430	2	5.715	2272.658	1,196		1.900	3.008	0.050
Spain	54.888	2	24.444	4457.669		1.186	3.759	7.302	0.001
Sweden	55.631	2	27.815	3997.810	1,006		3.974	6.999	0.001
Switzerland	395.165	2	197.583	6653.331	1,175		5.662	34.894	<0.0001
Taiwan	15.582	2	7.791	2392.104	764		3.131	2.488	0.084
Tanzania	24.526	2	12.263	5286.322	1,129		4.682	2.619	0.073
Turkey	1.176	2	0.588	970.357	1,199		0.809	0.727	0.484
Uganda	69.243	2	34.622	11522.237	995		11.580	2.990	0.051
Ukraine	550.455	2	275.227	8020.091	1,105		7.258	37.921	<0.0001
Uruguay	38.103	2	19.052	3066.059	973		3.151	6.046	0.002
USA	117.004	2	58.502	5674.726	1,195		4.749	12.319	<0.0001
Venezuela	2.682	2	1.341	3713.291	1,191		3.118	0.430	0650
Vietnam	0.083	2	0.042	1217.506	986		1.235	0.034	0.967
Zimbabwe	8.271	2	4.135	2229.168	977		2.282	1.812	0.164

Chapter 28
Education Level and the Ethics of Tax Evasion

Robert W. McGee

Introduction

Some studies have found that the more education a person has, the more averse they are to tax evasion, while other studies have found just the opposite. Part of the reason for the differing results is because several behavioral factors are at work that pull taxpayers' opinions in opposite directions. Richer taxpayers tend to be more educated than the general population, and they may have a tendency to have more respect for the rule of law. On the other hand, rich people are taxed more than poor people and they may resent paying so much in taxes, causing them to view tax evasion more favorably.

The next few pages analyze the relationship between level of education and attitudes toward the ethics of tax evasion, using the World Values survey data.

Findings

Table 28.1 shows the data for each country for each of the three education groups. Overall, the group with the lowest level of education was most opposed to tax evasion The middle education group had the least aversion to tax evasion. The overall mean score for the group with the most education fell between the other two mean scores. Thus, it appears that the relationship is curvilinear rather than linear.

Table 28.2 shows the degree of significance for various comparisons between groups. Many of the differences in mean score are significant.

R.W. McGee (✉)
School of Business, Florida International University,
3000 NE 151 Street, North Miami, FL 33181, USA
e-mail: bob414@hotmail.com

R.W. McGee (ed.), *The Ethics of Tax Evasion: Perspectives in Theory and Practice*,   451
DOI 10.1007/978-1-4614-1287-8_28, © Springer Science+Business Media, LLC 2012

Table 28.1 Cheating on taxes if you could – education level

	Low			Middle			Upper		
	Sample size	Mean	SD	Sample size	Mean	SD	Sample size	Mean	SD
Average mean		2.21			2.38			2.31	
Albania	415	1.97	1.498	408	1.84	1.341	162	1.77	1.459
Algeria	292	2.13	2.378	544	1.91	2.072	407	2.06	2.246
Argentina	749	1.87	2.091	401	1.90	1.986	120	1.78	1.935
Armenia	165	3.79	3.121	1,373	3.74	3.048	408	3.43	3.018
Australia	527	2.07	1.981	818	2.16	2.040	661	2.21	1.939
Austria	738	1.93	1.760	566	2.30	2.002	192	2.89	2.470
Azerbaijan	98	3.77	3.116	1,148	3.51	3.230	614	3.79	3.290
Bangladesh	789	1.03	0.397	404	1.09	0.695	289	1.10	.697
Belarus	220	3.71	2.728	553	4.38	2.841	140	4.37	3.042
Belgium	435	3.38	2.868	858	3.83	2.58	578	3.62	2.607
Bosnia	204	1.45	1.422	751	1.82	1.826	242	1.83	1.942
Brazil	499	3.72	3.317	498	3.55	3.102	141	3.23	2.845
Bulgaria	320	1.68	1.559	440	2.16	2.047	188	2.21	2.114
Canada	462	1.97	2.235	908	2.19	2.220	542	1.98	1.731
Chile	428	2.27	2.417	538	2.04	2.206	210	2.19	2.247
China	405	1.36	1.057	537	1.71	1.676	43	1.81	1.547
Colombia	717	2.09	2.005	1,250	2.52	2.418	1,028	2.16	2.138
Croatia	380	2.30	2.336	490	2.63	2.601	127	2.79	2.537
Czech Republic	962	2.08	1.857	725	2.02	1.667	195	2.21	1.747
Denmark	538	1.99	1.841	145	2.26	2.071	270	1.89	1.545
Dominican Republic	29	1.52	1.805	98	2.42	2.616	272	1.80	1.767
Egypt	1,504	1.58	1.457	923	1.54	1.417	555	1.62	1.578
El Salvador	634	1.86	2.237	343	2.01	2.433	241	1.88	2.291

Estonia	296	3.12	2.386	501	3.19	2.570	177	3.11	2.426
Finland	574	2.52	2.407	304	2.45	2.071	127	2.21	2.020
France	912	2.82	2.586	309	3.54	2.639	356	3.25	2.756
Georgia	290	2.65	2.390	1,287	2.77	2.394	410	2.71	2.336
Germany, East	341	2.42	2.306	500	2.49	2.357	118	1.98	1.913
Germany, West	482	2.33	2.041	452	2.45	1.987	82	2.02	1.877
Great Britain	423	2.35	2.129	367	2.58	2.169	134	2.42	2.114
Greece	100	2.64	2.299	455	3.19	2.622	536	3.23	2.342
Hungary	632	1.96	1.945	236	2.34	2.177	104	2.57	2.168
Iceland	392	2.11	2.066	371	2.32	1.902	188	2.19	1.666
India	938	2.56	3.056	477	1.81	2.238	461	1.63	1.880
Indonesia	247	1.33	.943	411	1.59	1.443	334	1.65	1.544
Iran	746	1.41	1.546	970	1.46	1.600	638	1.56	1.756
Ireland	517	2.43	2.233	271	2.35	1.939	196	2.09	1.894
Italy	855	2.45	2.271	817	2.43	2.214	295	2.14	1.766
Japan	124	1.44	1.478	828	1.42	1.331	318	1.56	1.501
Jordan	573	1.36	1.287	329	1.68	1.794	299	1.79	1.748
Kyrgyzstan	153	2.76	2.557	516	2.35	2.418	365	3.24	2.802
Latvia	229	1.98	1.940	583	2.53	2.418	169	2.34	2.127
Lithuania	243	3.15	2.822	593	4.02	3.109	131	3.82	3.097
Luxembourg	389	2.94	2.651	533	3.61	2.791	216	3.61	2.841
Macedonia	328	2.51	2.893	502	2.16	2.166	195	2.22	2.290
Malta	278	1.31	1.054	612	1.62	1.534	112	1.71	1.714
Mexico	775	2.19	2.395	515	2.53	2.594	154	2.14	2.129
Moldova	222	4.34	2.997	451	4.37	2.983	257	3.77	2.775
Montenegro	395	2.29	1.858	420	2.89	2.427	184	2.34	1.828

(continued)

Table 28.1 (continued)

	Low			Middle			Upper		
	Sample size	Mean	SD	Sample size	Mean	SD	Sample size	Mean	SD
Morocco-1	998	1.17	1.067	166	1.22	1.037	71	1.46	1.547
Morocco-2	782	1.29	1.419	159	1.22	1.210	64	1.27	1.130
Netherlands	313	2.65	2.304	362	2.68	2.115	327	2.91	2.246
New Zealand	447	2.22	2.247	261	2.20	2.133	406	2.47	2.218
Nigeria	769	2.16	1.969	775	1.95	1.685	470	1.97	1.797
Northern Ireland	422	2.37	2.214	353	2.51	2.227	170	2.28	2.058
Norway	337	2.69	2.478	427	2.88	2.382	353	2.53	2.113
Pakistan	1,053	1.21	0.787	605	1.13	0.557	280	1.25	.822
Peru	304	2.10	1.893	699	2.14	2.024	466	2.08	1.961
Philippines	384	3.27	2.525	472	3.17	2.511	327	2.95	2.468
Poland	586	2.21	2.171	339	2.33	2.205	138	2.09	1.867
Portugal	640	2.35	2.094	249	2.87	2.382	73	1.92	1.609
Puerto Rico	71	1.45	1.240	214	1.91	2.188	415	2.16	2.541
Romania	361	2.62	2.693	513	2.94	2.752	200	2.72	2.878
Russia	279	2.22	2.036	1,583	3.09	2.594	519	3.58	2.841
Serbia	391	2.18	2.023	499	2.10	1.971	270	1.93	1.769
Singapore	518	1.73	1.675	796	2.01	1.939	191	1.81	1.463
Slovakia	397	2.18	2.010	791	2.14	1.929	119	2.16	2.016
Slovenia	274	2.18	2.099	571	2.37	2.293	151	2.52	2.206

South Africa	1,611	2.79	2.439	1,204	2.59	2.760	109	2.65	3.246
South Korea	56	1.50	1.514	680	1.52	1.306	463	1.71	1.464
Spain	696	2.04	1.867	300	2.33	2.019	192	2.38	2.105
Sweden	236	2.19	2.013	477	2.60	2.051	296	2.27	1.899
Switzerland	234	2.20	2.152	838	2.71	2.523	113	2.65	2.350
Taiwan	279	1.83	1.497	176	1.95	1.791	310	2.08	1.981
Tanzania	615	1.73	2.224	352	1.73	2.100	171	1.75	2.186
Turkey	693	1.15	0.689	398	1.24	1.129	109	1.19	1.118
Uganda	281	3.37	3.523	643	3.62	3.439	67	1.77	2.081
Ukraine	135	2.69	2.405	681	3.54	2.803	292	3.59	2.848
Uruguay	572	1.63	1.648	318	1.81	1.876	86	2.08	2.226
USA	235	2.43	2.410	354	2.34	2.302	605	2.17	2.027
Venezuela	304	1.93	1.894	633	1.84	1.812	257	1.63	1.455
Vietnam	529	1.32	1.130	382	1.26	0.831	67	1.69	2.009
Zimbabwe	564	1.45	1.437	408	1.61	1.598	8	1.84	2.039

1 = Never justifiable; 10 = always justifiable

Table 28.2 Cheating on taxes if you could – education level p-values

	Low vs. middle	Low vs. upper	Middle vs. upper
Albania	0.1902	0.1471	0.5839
Algeria	0.1653	0.6919	0.2869
Argentina	0.8135	0.6585	0.5594
Armenia	0.8426	0.2010	0.0708
Australia	0.4245	0.2210	0.6319
Austria	0.0004	0.0001	0.0010
Azerbaijan	0.4433	0.9551	0.0851
Bangladesh	0.05830	0.0401	0.8521
Belarus	0.0029	0.0331	0.9708
Belgium	0.0044	0.1651	0.1322
Bosnia	0.0075	0.0208	0.9419
Brazil	0.4035	0.1110	0.2714
Bulgaria	0.0005	0.0013	0.7814
Canada	0.0838	0.9364	0.0595
Chile	0.0863	0.6879	0.4061
China	0.0002	0.0120	0.7052
Colombia	0.0001	0.4902	0.0002
Croatia	0.0527	0.0458	0.5349
Czech Republic	0.4927	0.3682	0.1623
Denmark	0.1277	0.4432	0.0402
Dominican Republic	0.0857	0.4188	0.0098
Egypt	0.5071	0.5890	0.0001
El Salvador	0.3324	0.9066	0.5152
Estonia	0.7030	0.9651	0.7181
Finland	0.6675	0.1775	0.2699
France	0.0001	0.0091	0.1680
Georgia	0.4406	0.7403	0.6567
Germany, East	0.6698	0.0632	0.0292
Germany, West	0.3633	0.1990	0.0696
Great Britain	0.1337	0.7398	0.4622
Greece	0.0529	0.0207	0.7999
Hungary	0.0134	0.0037	0.3694
Iceland	0.1451	0.6432	0.4269
India	0.0001	0.0001	0.1833
Indonesia	0.0118	0.0041	0.5832
Iran	0.5150	0.0913	0.2385
Ireland	0.6177	0.0593	0.1494
Italy	0.8554	0.0332	0.0427
Japan	0.8778	0.4486	0.1244
Jordan	0.0020	0.0001	0.4376
Kyrgyzstan	0.0696	0.0687	0.0001
Latvia	0.0022	0.0798	0.3562
Lithuania	0.0002	0.0350	0.5051
Luxembourg	0.0003	0.0038	1.0000
Macedonia	0.0471	0.2327	0.7468

(continued)

Table 28.2 (continued)

	Low vs. middle	Low vs. upper	Middle vs. upper
Malta	0.0023	0.0054	0.5755
Mexico	0.0159	0.8097	0.0892
Moldova	0.9026	0.0313	0.0085
Montenegro	0.0001	0.7620	0.0061
Morocco-1	0.5747	0.0328	0.1638
Morocco-2	0.5617	0.9125	0.7764
Netherlands	0.8601	0.1488	0.1668
New Zealand	0.9074	0.1029	0.1199
Nigeria	0.0245	0.0888	0.8431
Northern Ireland	0.3822	0.6482	0.2575
Norway	0.2825	0.3610	0.0320
Pakistan	0.0293	0.4585	0.0111
Peru	0.7694	0.8885	0.6158
Philippines	0.5634	0.0892	0.2205
Poland	0.4208	0.5493	0.2612
Portugal	0.0014	0.0900	0.0015
Puerto Rico	0.0935	0.0215	0.2214
Romania	0.0881	0.6812	0.3441
Russia	0.0001	0.0001	0.0003
Serbia	0.5526	0.1009	0.2373
Singapore	0.0071	0.5600	0.1816
Slovakia	0.7396	0.9242	0.9165
Slovenia	0.2489	0.1181	0.4715
South Africa	0.0421	0.5712	0.8306
South Korea	0.9134	0.3129	0.0217
Spain	0.0285	0.0302	0.7923
Sweden	0.0117	0.6385	0.0256
Switzerland	0.0049	0.0775	0.8110
Taiwan	0.4411	0.0872	0.4722
Tanzania	1.0000	0.9169	0.9197
Turkey	0.1024	0.6102	0.6816
Uganda	0.3132	0.0004	0.0001
Ukraine	0.0010	0.0016	0.7997
Uruguay	0.1379	0.0252	0.2566
USA	0.6486	0.1145	0.2338
Venezuela	0.4833	0.0385	0.0985
Vietnam	0.3791	0.0237	0.0030
Zimbabwe	0.1026	0.4490	0.6886

Chapter 29
Religious Practice and the Ethics of Tax Evasion

Robert W. McGee

Introduction

One might assume that the more religious a person is, the more likely he/she is to pay taxes, but such an assumption must be tested. The purpose of this chapter is to do that. Religiosity may be estimated by the frequency with which someone attends religious services. The World Values surveys collected data on this variable. The results are reported below.

Findings

Tables 29.1–29.3 show the data for each country for each of the frequency groups.

Table 29.4 shows the mean scores for each of the seven categories as well as the overall mean scores. The columns use letters to identify each category in the interests of conserving space. The letters represent the following categories:

A. More than once a week
B. Once a week
C. Once a month
D. Only on special holy days
E. Once a year
F. Less than once a year
G. Never/practically never

R.W. McGee (✉)
School of Business, Florida International University,
3000 NE 151 Street, North Miami, FL 33181, USA
e-mail: bob414@hotmail.com

R.W. McGee (ed.), *The Ethics of Tax Evasion: Perspectives in Theory and Practice*,
DOI 10.1007/978-1-4614-1287-8_29, © Springer Science+Business Media, LLC 2012

Table 29.1 Cheating on taxes if you could – Religious practice

	More than once a week			Once a week			Once a month		
	Sample size	Mean	SD	Sample size	Mean	SD	Sample size	Mean	SD
Albania	38	1.66	1.169	165	1.78	1.288	89	1.73	1.105
Algeria	319	1.76	1.952	255	1.98	2.215	35	2.74	2.964
Argentina	103	1.58	1.788	210	1.66	1.623	232	1.64	1.487
Armenia	37	1.38	0.924	106	3.08	2.907	421	3.55	2.772
Australia	125	1.21	0.682	217	1.66	1.486	166	1.85	1.612
Austria	38	2.11	2.128	302	1.85	1.573	294	1.77	1.551
Azerbaijan	47	3.53	3.175	60	4.40	3.585	137	3.36	3.022
Bangladesh	555	1.04	0.568	286	1.07	0.498	167	1.13	0.660
Belarus	16	3.12	2.754	34	3.15	2.653	72	4.04	2.860
Belgium	67	2.45	2.223	261	3.04	2.463	183	3.39	2.684
Bosnia	141	1.31	1.090	189	1.78	1.772	210	1.98	2.087
Brazil	143	2.94	2.917	264	3.30	3.052	441	3.76	3.191
Bulgaria	24	1.28	0.708	61	1.78	1.561	110	2.00	1.898
Canada	124	1.54	1.634	355	1.70	1.741	207	2.05	1.973
Chile	129	2.20	2.273	229	2.15	2.368	165	2.20	2.270
China	7	1.57	1.512	14	1.29	1.069	9	1.67	1.414
Colombia	320	1.99	1.968	1,032	2.23	2.204	638	2.25	2.120
Croatia	58	1.95	1.992	256	2.39	2.086	209	2.40	2.440
The Czech Republic	34	1.43	1.455	96	1.76	1.393	89	1.79	1.387
Denmark	7	1.14	0.378	20	1.30	0.657	91	1.45	1.310
Dom Republic	90	1.54	1.573	86	1.99	2.038	44	2.02	2.017
Egypt	669	1.58	1.481	592	1.55	1.436	75	1.71	1.683
El Salvador	349	1.62	1.980	360	1.98	2.360	132	2.11	2.507
Estonia	13	2.27	2.103	23	2.16	1.971	72	2.92	2.265
Finland	22	1.36	1.009	33	1.35	1.045	90	1.67	1.413
France	27	2.08	2.215	90	2.22	2.305	69	2.50	2.153
Georgia	55	2.82	2.554	129	2.42	2.171	353	2.67	2.286

Germany E	3	4.14	3.594	51	1.82	1.620	62	2.08	1.705
Germany W	27	1.92	1.556	132	1.86	1.508	192	2.26	1.917
G Britain	57	1.63	1.465	85	1.79	1.593	44	2.49	2.335
Greece	35	3.14	2.647	116	2.65	2.188	209	3.01	2.432
Hungary	12	1.42	1.010	91	1.35	0.851	69	1.71	1.571
Iceland	9	1.22	0.667	22	1.68	1.427	85	1.68	1.274
India	301	1.86	2.187	317	2.28	2.826	371	2.19	2.703
Indonesia	309	1.54	1.567	337	1.42	1.154	108	1.57	1.402
Iran	287	1.19	0.964	366	1.33	1.372	453	1.34	1.287
Ireland	134	1.77	1.547	455	2.15	1.923	105	2.92	2.255
Italy	198	2.13	2.168	590	2.19	1.967	258	2.47	2.275
Japan	22	1.86	1.885	31	1.42	0.958	107	1.31	1.085
Jordan	345	1.50	1.595	191	1.37	1.249	32	2.20	2.432
Kyrgyzstan	120	2.56	2.428	80	3.04	2.772	53	3.30	3.067
Latvia	17	2.12	2.233	48	1.90	1.905	79	2.08	1.927
Lithuania	30	2.32	1.951	134	2.80	2.660	129	3.63	3.066
Luxembourg	37	2.88	2.721	206	2.96	2.512	118	2.96	2.359
Macedonia	106	3.09	3.214	117	3.12	3.240	117	1.91	1.911
Malta	320	1.29	1.067	504	1.57	1.424	44	1.77	1.277
Mexico	193	2.17	2.358	615	2.22	2.303	266	2.25	2.348
Moldova	40	3.86	2.664	90	4.70	3.098	131	4.11	3.002
Montenegro	12	2.58	1.881	50	2.66	2.273	114	2.52	1.947
Morocco	452	1.20	1.127	132	1.29	1.317	34	1.13	0.724
The Netherlands	43	1.30	0.828	96	1.61	1.299	113	2.69	2.121
New Zealand	59	1.20	0.637	132	1.45	1.121	58	1.78	1.351
Nigeria	1,289	2.00	1.881	576	2.10	1.676	61	2.20	2.023
N. Ireland	121	1.56	1.193	341	2.12	1.952	142	2.42	2.017
Norway	22	1.50	1.406	34	1.44	0.960	84	1.56	1.101

(continued)

Table 29.1 (continued)

	More than once a week			Once a week			Once a month		
	Sample size	Mean	SD	Sample size	Mean	SD	Sample size	Mean	SD
Pakistan	981	1.16	0.609	464	1.27	0.943	331	1.18	0.730
Peru	241	1.85	1.712	451	2.02	1.910	356	2.12	1.913
The Philippines	156	3.11	2.473	535	3.07	2.500	247	3.35	2.721
Poland	92	1.89	1.856	534	2.07	1.921	206	2.34	2.174
Portugal	74	1.64	1.248	273	2.66	2.321	139	2.38	2.034
Puerto Rico	200	1.58	1.769	201	1.96	2.252	93	1.95	2.375
Romania	39	1.85	2.059	221	2.76	2.689	225	2.88	2.742
Russia	29	2.03	1.716	44	3.19	2.775	137	2.62	2.288
Serbia	36	1.97	1.934	73	1.86	1.910	118	1.87	1.418
Singapore	173	1.55	1.522	289	1.93	1.859	200	2.27	2.117
Slovakia	192	1.73	1.482	337	2.02	1.874	123	2.12	1.972
Slovenia	22	2.00	1.718	144	2.37	2.209	134	2.31	2.108
South Africa	562	2.23	2.319	953	2.63	2.618	475	3.35	3.280
S. Korea	157	1.64	1.498	205	1.46	1.096	96	1.34	0.856
Spain	85	1.80	1.689	210	1.82	1.713	132	2.08	1.877
Sweden	5	1.88	1.343	33	1.88	2.007	56	1.85	1.284
Switzerland	29	1.78	2.417	109	1.71	1.322	142	2.04	1.769
Taiwan	23	2.00	2.486	28	2.54	1.710	55	1.76	1.515
Tanzania	559	1.59	1.988	416	1.87	2.340	20	1.70	2.155
Uganda	270	2.19	2.544	527	3.70	3.470	87	4.19	3.951
Ukraine	28	2.45	1.672	67	3.32	2.637	79	3.68	2.930
Uruguay	43	1.21	0.915	85	1.22	0.870	98	1.48	1.549
The USA	196	1.76	1.617	345	1.94	1.954	180	2.49	2.186
Venezuela	101	1.82	2.109	261	1.77	1.613	206	1.75	1.576
Vietnam	13	1.23	0.832	25	1.44	1.044	90	1.36	1.042
Zimbabwe	347	1.30	1.088	374	1.55	1.683	74	1.79	1.613

1=never justifiable; 10=always justifiable

Table 29.2 Cheating on taxes if you could – Religious practice

	Only on special holy days			Once a year		
	Sample size	Mean	SD	Sample size	Mean	SD
Albania	317	1.85	1.253	49	2.22	1.447
Algeria	107	1.60	1.553	18	1.28	1.179
Argentina	108	1.76	1.719	111	1.88	2.289
Armenia	454	4.07	3.047	409	3.37	3.027
Australia	225	2.40	2.070	215	2.23	1.981
Austria	226	2.53	2.256	72	2.05	1.725
Azerbaijan	725	3.58	3.209	276	3.81	3.309
Bangladesh	74	1.01	0.116	87	1.10	0.965
Belarus	259	4.40	2.871	118	4.21	2.917
Belgium	125	3.84	2.820	104	3.55	2.857
Bosnia	352	1.89	1.918	55	1.67	1.678
Brazil	105	3.68	3.021	95	3.85	3.534
Bulgaria	226	2.07	1.965	62	2.20	2.376
Canada	309	2.17	2.233	203	2.09	1.992
Chile	80	1.88	2.069	126	2.42	2.637
China	54	1.44	1.127	8	2.00	1.927
Colombia	149	2.06	1.932	225	2.58	2.419
Croatia	240	2.68	2.533	52	3.57	3.509
The Czech Republic	201	2.21	1.934	172	2.07	1.768
Denmark	163	1.83	1.534	173	2.05	1.750
Dom Republic	55	2.60	2.622	18	2.39	2.477
Egypt	743	1.57	1.416	155	1.60	1.582
El Salvador	74	1.66	1.946	77	2.29	2.892
Estonia	238	2.85	2.316	103	3.33	2.332
Finland	213	2.05	1.642	136	2.21	1.977
France	89	3.02	2.349	103	2.71	2.694
Georgia	735	2.77	2.372	205	2.97	2.496
Germany E	86	2.44	2.361	36	2.36	2.157
Germany W	176	2.39	1.945	84	2.36	2.026
G Britain	75	2.82	2.139	53	2.57	2.128
Greece	497	3.22	2.467	85	3.71	2.685
Hungary	177	1.98	1.673	70	2.01	1.750
Iceland	208	1.99	1.765	169	2.41	2.153
India	484	1.82	2.183	152	2.88	3.395
Indonesia	144	1.56	1.133	5	1.00	0.000
Iran	992	1.52	1.666	70	1.63	1.819
Ireland	107	2.40	2.319	49	3.33	2.759
Italy	307	2.55	2.223	78	2.67	2.350
Japan	563	1.42	1.258	283	1.50	1.505
Jordan	84	1.42	1.373	37	2.39	2.004
Kyrgyzstan	327	2.29	2.356	74	3.31	2.794
Latvia	186	2.40	2.333	125	2.66	2.332
Lithuania	151	4.05	3.189	76	4.55	3.344
Luxembourg	148	3.40	2.718	75	3.64	2.901

(continued)

Table 29.2 (continued)

	Only on special holy days			Once a year		
	Sample size	Mean	SD	Sample size	Mean	SD
Macedonia	442	1.92	1.961	49	2.04	2.007
Malta	23	2.21	2.213	12	2.72	2.450
Mexico	141	2.61	2.648	70	2.22	2.592
Moldova	370	4.05	2.840	141	3.93	2.895
Montenegro	350	2.51	2.139	118	2.35	1.923
Morocco	72	1.51	1.978	15	1.29	1.017
The Netherlands	75	3.02	2.313	63	3.35	2.459
New Zealand	103	2.10	2.234	103	2.61	2.352
Nigeria	15	1.40	0.737	9	1.89	0,928
N. Ireland	28	2.57	2.539	30	3.24	2.762
Norway	207	2.70	2.071	156	2.42	2.146
Pakistan	98	1.22	0.740	66	1.15	0.588
Peru	160	2.28	2.134	98	2.50	2.321
The Philippines	61	3.01	2.193	52	3.20	2.071
Poland	101	2.82	2.809	18	3.24	3.061
Portugal	75	2.83	2.521	39	3.06	2.458
Puerto Rico	59	2.53	2.687	37	2.76	2.910
Romania	338	2.92	2.878	79	3.01	2.840
Russia	359	2.96	2.496	236	3.65	2.862
Serbia	518	2.15	1.981	137	2.37	2.216
Singapore	324	1.55	1.101	46	2.90	2.856
Slovakia	149	2.24	1.931	39	2.20	2.029
Slovenia	166	2.01	2.002	71	2.94	2.688
South Africa	177	2.79	2.239	56	2.63	2.492
S. Korea	134	1.72	1.661	83	1.36	1.164
Spain	169	2.12	1.749	54	1.87	1.858
Sweden	106	2.35	1.854	215	2.38	2.069
Switzerland	227	2.30	2.005	117	2.74	2.630
Taiwan	163	1.65	1.284	17	1.71	1.359
Tanzania	39	2.21	2.755	6	1.00	0.000
Uganda	62	3.65	3.346	8	3.70	2.895
Ukraine	245	3.08	2.535	82	4.42	3.190
Uruguay	42	2.91	2.796	62	1.88	1.911
The USA	126	2.54	2.331	83	2.97	2.775
Venezuela	166	1.82	1.645	108	1.84	1.890
Vietnam	198	1.37	1.231	35	1.37	1.457
Zimbabwe	27	1.88	2.049	6	1.09	0.313

1 = never justifiable; 10 = always justifiable

Table 29.3 Cheating on taxes if you could – Religious practice

	Less than once a year			Never/practically never		
	Sample size	Mean	SD	Sample size	Mean	SD
Albania	97	2.14	1.871	230	1.91	1.656
Algeria	145	2.08	2.222	326	2.22	2.390
Argentina	151	1.87	2.074	356	2.26	2.539
Armenia	218	3.94	3.159	257	4.03	3.371
Australia	191	2.42	2.004	899	2.33	2.186
Austria	216	2.07	1.820	254	2.91	2.530
Azerbaijan	217	4.01	3.342	313	3.73	3.361
Bangladesh	271	1.01	0.136	55	1.18	0.964
Belarus	96	3.77	2.654	255	4.51	2.962
Belgium	80	4.21	2.843	875	3.93	3.019
Bosnia	85	1.59	1.522	165	1.65	1.727
Brazil	95	3.85	3.534	86	4.19	3.383
Bulgaria	77	1.96	1.764	250	2.04	2.002
Canada	162	2.19	1.978	558	2.40	2.399
Chile	169	1.95	1.907	261	2.07	2.241
China	10	2.30	1.636	875	1.57	1.453
Colombia	422	2.59	2.515	209	2.46	2.449
Croatia	45	2.26	2.721	104	2.56	2.720
The Czech Republic	149	1.97	1.591	1,071	2.13	1.840
Denmark	75	1.77	1.485	433	2.29	2.084
Dom Republic	51	1.88	2.151	54	1.78	1.939
Egypt	4	1.50	1.000	745	1.59	1.490
El Salvador	84	2.04	2.387	143	2.12	2.505
Estonia	88	3.78	2.859	362	3.31	2.652
Finland	189	2.69	2.482	265	3.47	2.818
France	107	3.19	2.740	953	3.29	2.754
Georgia	222	2.86	2.595	270	2.61	2.311
Germany E	116	2.93	2.737	546	2.37	2.345
Germany W	141	2.69	2.156	229	2.42	2.250
G Britain	90	2.47	2.054	547	2.45	2.140
Greece	6	4.50	4.183	51	2.88	2.286
Hungary	127	2.17	1.837	413	2.43	2.464
Iceland	104	2.29	1.815	309	2.56	2.180
India	214	2.60	3.159	44	1.36	1.163
Indonesia	88	1.91	1.672	8	2.12	1.727
Iran	110	1.85	2.322	93	2.57	2.958
Ireland	34	3.04	2.356	86	2.62	2.367
Italy	58	2.90	2.447	274	2.65	2.477
Japan	179	1.45	1.387	111	1.68	1.850
Jordan	15	1.67	1.364	500	1.58	1.570
Kyrgyzstan	61	2.97	2.720	320	2.88	2.679
Latvia	78	2.45	2.448	335	2.51	2.430
Lithuania	70	4.49	3.115	154	4.14	3.102
Luxembourg	83	3.06	2.400	372	3.79	3.039

(continued)

Table 29.3 (continued)

	Less than once a year			Never/practically never		
	Sample size	Mean	SD	Sample size	Mean	SD
Macedonia	131	2.54	2.557	63	2.29	2.626
Malta	25	2.16	2.605	42	1.85	2.190
Mexico	70	2.68	2.858	88	2.75	3.082
Moldova	91	4.75	3.148	68	4.47	3.028
Montenegro	193	2.53	2.069	167	2.78	2.423
Morocco	92	1.18	0.820	437	1.09	0.748
The Netherlands	62	2.56	1.596	483	3.02	2.386
New Zealand	179	2.59	2.367	513	2.60	2.448
Nigeria	60	2.08	2.069	12	1.42	1.165
N. Ireland	70	2.65	2.202	183	3.18	2.682
Norway	149	2.81	2.229	467	3.14	2.651
Pakistan	98	1.22	0.740	66	1.15	0.588
Peru	91	2.38	2.230	72	2.29	2.204
The Philippines	121	3.16	2.447	11	2.58	2.490
Poland	32	2.55	2.144	54	2.60	2.697
Portugal	171	2.36	1.972	144	2.57	2.315
Puerto Rico	10	2.40	2.797	98	2.50	2.926
Romania	26	2.77	2.776	78	2.47	2.809
Russia	194	3.28	2.790	1,189	3.04	2.607
Serbia	123	2.39	2.220	161	1.75	1.721
Singapore	284	1.89	1.918	190	2.04	1.849
Slovakia	126	2.40	2.199	299	2.43	2.197
Slovenia	74	2.43	2.107	296	2.40	2.344
South Africa	398	2.62	2.071	302	2.83	2.571
S. Korea	331	1.73	1.403	192	1.59	1.566
Spain	137	2.09	1.679	393	2.52	2.241
Sweden	131	2.28	1.899	460	2.58	2.103
Switzerland	158	2.40	2.269	391	3.36	2.916
Taiwan	175	1.88	1.634	296	2.18	2.065
Tanzania	80	1.79	2.133	26	1.85	2.525
Uganda	35	5.48	4.076	10	6.71	3.691
Ukraine	83	4.57	2.993	343	3.23	2.720
Uruguay	114	1.65	1.481	531	1.80	1.880
The USA	87	2.34	2.280	178	2.74	2.565
Venezuela	176	1.76	1.678	168	2.02	2.082
Vietnam	141	1.14	0.650	487	1.34	1.157
Zimbabwe	43	1.73	1.705	110	1.77	1.702

1 = never justifiable; 10 = always justifiable

Table 29.4 Cheating on taxes if you could – Summary of mean scores (religious practice)

	A	B	C	D	E	F	G
Albania	1.66	1.78	1.73	1.85	2.22	2.14	1.91
Algeria	1.76	1.98	2.74	1.60	1.28	2.08	2.22
Argentina	1.58	1.66	1.64	1.76	1.88	1.87	2.26
Armenia	1.38	3.08	3.55	4.07	3.37	3.94	4.03
Australia	1.21	1.66	1.85	2.40	2.23	2.42	2.33
Austria	2.11	1.85	1.77	2.53	2.05	2.07	2.91
Azerbaijan	3.53	4.40	3.36	3.58	3.81	4.01	3.73
Bangladesh	1.04	1.07	1.13	1.01	1.10	1.01	1.18
Belarus	3.12	3.15	4.04	4.40	4.21	3.77	4.51
Belgium	2.45	3.04	3.39	3.84	3.55	4.21	3.93
Bosnia	1.31	1.78	1.98	1.89	1.67	1.59	1.65
Brazil	2.94	3.30	3.76	3.68	3.85	3.85	4.19
Bulgaria	1.28	1.78	2.00	2.07	2.20	1.96	2.04
Canada	1.54	1.70	2.05	2.17	2.09	2.19	2.40
Chile	2.20	2.15	2.20	1.88	2.42	1.95	2.07
China	1.57	1.29	1.67	1.44	2.00	2.30	1.57
Colombia	1.99	2.23	2.25	2.06	2.58	2.59	2.46
Croatia	1.95	2.39	2.40	2.68	3.57	2.26	2.56
The Czech Republic	1.43	1.76	1.79	2.21	2.07	1.97	2.13
Denmark	1.14	1.30	1.45	1.83	2.05	1.77	2.29
Dom Republic	1.54	1.99	2.02	2.60	2.39	1.88	1.78
Egypt	1.58	1.55	1.71	1.57	1.60	1.50	1.59
El Salvador	1.62	1.98	2.11	1.66	2.29	2.04	2.12
Estonia	2.27	2.16	2.92	2.85	3.33	3.78	3.31
Finland	1.36	1.35	1.67	2.05	2.21	2.69	3.47
France	2.08	2.22	2.50	3.02	2.71	3.19	3.29
Georgia	2.82	2.42	2.67	2.77	2.97	2.86	2.61
Germany E	4.14	1.82	2.08	2.44	2.36	2.93	2.37
Germany W	1.92	1.86	2.26	2.39	2.36	2.69	2.42
G Britain	1.63	1.79	2.49	2.82	2.57	2.47	2.45
Greece	3.14	2.65	3.01	3.22	3.71	4.50	2.88
Hungary	1.42	1.35	1.71	1.98	2.01	2.17	2.43
Iceland	1.22	1.68	1.68	1.99	2.41	2.29	2.56
India	1.86	2.28	2.19	1.82	2.88	2.60	1.36
Indonesia	1.54	1.42	1.57	1.56	1.00	1.91	2.12
Iran	1.19	1.33	1.34	1.52	1.63	1.85	2.57
Ireland	1.77	2.15	2.92	2.40	3.33	3.04	2.62
Italy	2.13	2.19	2.47	2.55	2.67	2.90	2.65
Japan	1.86	1.42	1.31	1.42	1.50	1.45	1.68
Jordan	1.50	1.37	2.20	1.42	2.39	1.67	1.58
Kyrgyzstan	2.56	3.04	3.30	2.29	3.31	2.97	2.88
Latvia	2.12	1.90	2.08	2.40	2.66	2.45	2.51
Lithuania	2.32	2.80	3.63	4.05	4.55	4.49	4.14
Luxembourg	2.88	2.96	2.96	3.40	3.64	3.06	3.79
Macedonia	3.09	3.12	1.91	1.92	2.04	2.54	2.29

(continued)

Table 29.4 (continued)

	A	B	C	D	E	F	G
Malta	1.29	1.57	1.77	2.21	2.72	2.16	1.85
Mexico	2.17	2.22	2.25	2.61	2.22	2.68	2.75
Moldova	3.86	4.70	4.11	4.05	3.93	4.75	4.47
Montenegro	2.58	2.66	2.52	2.51	2.35	2.53	2.78
Morocco	1.20	1.29	1.13	1.51	1.29	1.18	1.09
The Netherlands	1.30	1.61	2.69	3.02	3.35	2.56	3.02
New Zealand	1.20	1.45	1.78	2.10	2.61	2.59	2.60
Nigeria	2.00	2.10	2.20	1.40	1.89	2.08	1.42
N. Ireland	1.56	2.12	2.42	2.57	3.24	2.65	3.18
Norway	1.50	1.44	1.56	2.70	2.42	2.81	3.14
Pakistan	1.16	1.27	1.18	1.22	1.15	1.22	1.15
Peru	1.85	2.02	2.12	2.28	2.50	2.38	2.29
The Philippines	3.11	3.07	3.35	3.01	3.20	3.16	2.58
Poland	1.89	2.07	2.34	2.82	3.24	2.55	2.60
Portugal	1.64	2.66	2.38	2.83	3.06	2.36	2.57
Puerto Rico	1.58	1.96	1.95	2.53	2.76	2.40	2.50
Romania	1.85	2.76	2.88	2.92	3.01	2.77	2.47
Russia	2.03	3.19	2.62	2.96	3.65	3.28	3.04
Serbia	1.97	1.86	1.87	2.15	2.37	2.39	1.75
Singapore	1.55	1.93	2.27	1.55	2.90	1.89	2.04
Slovakia	1.73	2.02	2.12	2.24	2.20	2.40	2.43
Slovenia	2.00	2.37	2.31	2.01	2.94	2.43	2.40
South Africa	2.23	2.63	3.35	2.79	2.63	2.62	2.83
S. Korea	1.64	1.46	1.34	1.72	1.36	1.73	1.59
Spain	1.80	1.82	2.08	2.12	1.87	2.09	2.52
Sweden	1.88	1.88	1.85	2.35	2.38	2.28	2.58
Switzerland	1.78	1.71	2.04	2.30	2.74	2.40	3.36
Taiwan	2.00	2.54	1.76	1.65	1.71	1.88	2.18
Tanzania	1.59	1.87	1.70	2.21	1.00	1.79	1.85
Uganda	2.19	3.70	4.19	3.65	3.70	5.48	6.71
Ukraine	2.45	3.32	3.68	3.08	4.42	4.57	3.23
Uruguay	1.21	1.22	1.48	2.91	1.88	1.65	1.80
The USA	1.76	1.94	2.49	2.54	2.97	2.34	2.74
Venezuela	1.82	1.77	1.75	1.82	1.84	1.76	2.02
Vietnam	1.23	1.44	1.36	1.37	1.37	1.14	1.34
Zimbabwe	1.30	1.55	1.79	1.88	1.09	1.73	1.77
Avg. mean	1.91	2.12	2.27	2.38	2.53	2.53	2.55

1 = never justifiable; 10 = always justifiable

Table 29.5 shows the ranking of the overall mean scores. As might be expected, the relationship between religious service attendance and aversion to tax evasion is a linear relationship. The more frequently one attends religious services, the more aversion there is to tax evasion.

Table 29.5 Ranking of mean scores

Rank	Frequency	Mean
1	More than once a week	1.91
2	Once a week	2.12
3	Once a month	2.27
4	Only on special holy days	2.38
5	Once a year	2.53
5	Less than once a year	2.53
7	Never/practically never	2.55

Chapter 30
Religion and the Ethics of Tax Evasion

Robert W. McGee

Introduction

Religion is another variable that has an influence on ethical beliefs and attitude toward paying taxes. The World Values surveys collected data on this variable. The results are reported below.

Findings

Table 30.1 lists the data for all the religions in the World Values surveys that had a sample size of 30 or more.

Table 30.2 ranks the various religions in terms of attitude toward tax evasion, from most opposed to least opposed. There is a three-way tie for first place involving Al-Hadis, ancestral worshipping, and Sunni Muslims, followed closely by Shia Muslims. The various Christian groups are farther down the list.

R.W. McGee (✉)
School of Business, Florida International University,
3000 NE 151 Street, North Miami, FL 33181, USA
e-mail: bob414@hotmail.com

R.W. McGee (ed.), *The Ethics of Tax Evasion: Perspectives in Theory and Practice*,
DOI 10.1007/978-1-4614-1287-8_30, © Springer Science+Business Media, LLC 2012

Table 30.1 Religion

	Sample	Mean	SD
Al-Hadis	145	1.2	0.73
Ancestral worshipping	302	1.2	1.05
Armenian Apostolic church	1,621	3.6	3.00
Buddhist	1,765	1.7	1.61
Catholic (do not follow rules)	328	1.9	2.38
Christian	183	1.9	1.91
Evangelical	1,338	2.0	2.11
Free Church (nondenominational)	671	2.0	1.79
Gregorian	42	3.2	2.67
Hindu	1,644	2.0	2.47
Iglesia ni Cristo (INC)	47	3.8	2.50
Independent African church	631	2.3	2.28
Independent church	42	1.6	1.42
Jehovah witnesses	125	1.7	1.70
Jewish	324	2.5	2.41
Muslim	17,004	1.8	2.01
Orthodox	8,611	2.8	2.49
Protestant	13,757	2.2	2.14
Roman Catholic	32,959	2.4	2.30
Seventh day adventist	42	1.9	2.28
Shenism (Chinese religion)	65	2.4	1.70
Shia	189	1.3	0.89
Sikh	68	2.0	2.59
Sunni	1,036	1.2	0.71
Taoist	115	1.8	1.33

1 = Never justifiable; 10 = always justifiable

Table 30.2 Ranking of religions

Rank	Religion	Mean
1	Al-Hadis	1.2
1	Ancestral worshipping	1.2
1	Sunni Muslim	1.2
4	Shia Muslim	1.3
5	Independent church	1.6
6	Buddhist	1.7
6	Jehovah witnesses	1.7
7	Muslim	1.8
7	Taoist	1.8
10	Catholic (do not follow rules)	1.9
10	Christian	1.9
10	Seventh day adventist	1.9
13	Evangelical	2.0
13	Free church (nondenominational)	2.0
13	Hindu	2.0
13	Sikh	2.0
17	Protestant	2.2
18	Independent African church	2.3
19	Roman Catholic	2.4
19	Shenism (Chinese religion)	2.4
21	Jewish	2.5
22	Orthodox	2.8
23	Gregorian	3.2
24	Armenian Apostolic church	3.6
25	Iglesia ni Cristo (INC)	3.8

1 = Never justifiable; 10 = always justifiable

Chapter 31
Marital Status and the Ethics of Tax Evasion

Robert W. McGee

Introduction

Marital status is another variable that has an influence on ethical beliefs and attitude toward paying taxes. The World Values surveys collected data on this variable. It was thought that marital status might have some effect on attitudes toward tax evasion but the effect it has is unclear. One might assume a priori that married people are more responsible than single people and thus would be more averse to tax evasion. On the other hand, married people might have more expenses than younger people and might have less ability to pay taxes, which could have just the opposite effect on their opinion on the issue of tax evasion. Thus, it is necessary to test the a priori assumptions. The results are reported below.

Findings

Tables 31.1 and 31.2 list the data for various categories in the World Values surveys.

Table 31.3 ranks the various categories by mean score. Widows are the group most opposed to tax evasion, followed by married, separated, living together as married, single or never married, and divorced.

Table 31.4 shows the data for gender and marital status. Women are significantly more opposed to tax evasion for each category.

R.W. McGee (✉)
School of Business, Florida International University,
3000 NE 151 Street, North Miami, FL 33181, USA
e-mail: bob414@hotmail.com

R.W. McGee (ed.), *The Ethics of Tax Evasion: Perspectives in Theory and Practice*,
DOI 10.1007/978-1-4614-1287-8_31, © Springer Science+Business Media, LLC 2012

Table 31.1 Cheating on taxes if you could – marital status

	Married			LT			Divorced		
	Sample Size	Mean	SD	Sample Size	Mean	SD	Sample Size	Mean	SD
Total	61,519	2.19	2.191	4,848	2.43	2.427	4,269	2.66	2.521
Albania	705	1.80	1.341	11	2.18	1.940	4	1.50	0.577
Algeria	541	1.72	1.870	85	2.40	2.656	30	2.23	2.254
Argentina	603	1.66	1.727	141	1.99	2.082	25	1.91	2.078
Armenia	1,157	3.62	3.059	25	4.08	3.341	65	3.88	3.300
Australia	1,032	1.92	1.805	137	3.00	2.539	118	2.23	2.129
Austria	920	1.98	1.696	81	2.77	2.573	7	2.37	2.837
Azerbaijan	1,163	3.62	3.165	13	4.08	3.662	40	3.48	3.351
Bangladesh	1,169	1.02	0.256	7	1.43	1.134	10	1.00	0.000
Belarus	558	4.10	2.816	–	–	–	73	4.78	2.973
Belgium	1,131	3.47	2.704	140	4.04	3.232	27	4.79	3.054
Bosnia	737	1.71	1.735	7	1.86	0.900	30	2.00	2.197
Brazil	540	3.36	3.109	107	3.85	3.235	40	4.32	3.547
Bulgaria	588	1.87	1.757	–	–	–	44	2.73	2.477
Canada	1,053	1.95	2.007	207	2.37	2.172	86	2.06	2.242
Chile	666	2.11	2.283	103	2.04	2.279	11	1.98	1.830
China	858	1.54	1.398	3	4.00	2.646	9	1.00	0.000
Colombia	1,257	2.12	2.107	549	2.39	2.290	25	2.24	2.471
Croatia	627	2.21	2.087	–	–	–	40	1.62	1.351
Czech Republic	1,201	2.04	1.771	–	–	–	7	185	348
Denmark	537	1.91	1.650	–	–	–	86	2.20	2.141
Dominican Republic	124	1.98	2.249	37	1.51	1.170	19	2.05	2.527
Egypt	2,017	1.55	1.441	–	–	–	34	1.62	1.074

El Salvador	468	1.81	2.184	272	2.18	2.622	18	2.00	2.473
Estonia	512	2.94	2.373	84	3.27	2.511	20	3.65	2.591
Finland	459	2.15	1.923	144	2.92	2.528	133	2.79	2.621
France	695	2.61	2.458	–	–	–	126	3.24	2.578
Georgia	1,196	2.63	2.305	28	2.18	1.827	56	2.61	2.278
Germany, East	573	2.36	2.276	–	–	–	86	2.53	2.259
Germany, West	679	2.27	1.911	–	–	–	50	2.36	2.039
Great Britain	496	2.12	1.873	–	–	–	102	2.77	2.340
Greece	451	3.06	2.483	–	–	–	23	2.57	2.332
Hungary	564	2.05	1.991	–	–	–	85	2.49	2.294
Iceland	457	1.95	1.697	14	2.64	2.560	75	2.48	2.023
India	1,476	2.20	2.706	121	1.61	1.976	6	2.33	1.633
Indonesia	144	1.60	1.601	603	1.49	1.209	4	1.50	1.000
Iran	1,395	1.35	1.383	10	1.00	0.000	19	2.16	2.544
Ireland	535	2.12	1.906	36	3.21	2.373	9	2.72	2.113
Italy	1,143	2.24	2.057	–	–	–	29	3.21	2.993
Japan	948	1.42	1.379	14	1.14	0.535	38	1.42	1.605
Jordan	813	1.53	1.546	–	–	–	5	2.49	1.863
Kyrgyzstan	617	2.61	2.528	20	3.50	3.035	60	2.63	2.668
Latvia	514	2.30	2.188	–	–	–	145	2.20	2.146
Lithuania	587	3.79	3.096	–	–	–	72	4.21	3.344
Luxembourg	665	3.23	2.741	–	–	–	56	3.45	3.199
Macedonia	713	2.29	2.519	25	1.49	1.339	15	2.40	2.530
Malta	632	1.55	1.473	–	–	–	2	1.00	0.000
Mexico	876	2.25	2.410	90	2.73	2.747	24	2.39	3.018
Moldova	625	4.03	2.859	29	3.99	2.709	26	4.73	3.297
Montenegro	652	2.36	1.914	21	3.57	2.657	20	3.10	2.918

(continued)

Table 31.1 (continued)

	Married			LT			Divorced		
	Sample Size	Mean	SD	Sample Size	Mean	SD	Sample Size	Mean	SD
Morocco	684	1.19	1.096	3	1.00	0.000	44	1.32	1.578
Netherlands	498	2.53	2.104	–	–	–	75	3.23	2.356
New Zealand	665	2.06	2.045	108	2.94	2.572	60	2.58	2.465
Nigeria	938	1.93	1.663	67	2.79	2.556	20	2.45	2.282
Northern Ireland	554	2.20	2.010	38	2.54	2.480	34	2.75	2.297
Norway	603	2.64	2.289	183	2.97	2.401	59	2.53	2.452
Pakistan	1,280	1.17	0.665	–	–	–	–	–	–
Peru	606	2.08	1.982	247	2.19	2.080	16	1.25	0.775
Philippines	877	3.08	2.519	26	2.89	1.978	3	3.00	2.384
Poland	708	2.05	1.959	32	1.84	2.111	2	5.59	4.586
Portugal	613	2.46	2.122	–	–	–	33	2.98	2.739
Puerto Rico	367	1.77	2.037	41	2.54	3.195	74	1.96	2.338
Romania	722	2.75	2.804	–	–	–	40	2.75	2.509
Russia	1,265	3.04	2.604	307	3.44	2.696	56	3.34	2.488
Serbia	742	1.96	1.836	27	2.63	2.498	59	2.36	1.945
Singapore	678	1.68	1.711	2	2.00	0.000	22	2.13	1.752
Slovakia	367	1.77	2.037	–	–	–	41	2.54	3.195
Slovenia	584	2.17	2.056	–	–	–	38	1.68	1.491

South Africa	1,113	2.78	2.602	322	3.33	3.206	64	1.62	1.637
South Korea	823	1.56	1.336	7	3.00	2.236	14	1.07	0.267
Spain	659	2.03	1.836	51	2.52	2.059	18	2.37	2.394
Sweden	480	2.20	1.807	119	2.86	2.240	136	2.50	2.300
Switzerland	676	2.36	2.303	92	3.51	3.011	83	2.59	2.552
Taiwan	589	1.95	1.809	3	3.00	1.732	12	1.83	1.267
Tanzania	582	1.66	2.033	100	1.90	2.254	39	1.08	0.354
Turkey	824	1.17	0.879	3	1.00	0.000	17	1.00	0.000
Uganda	367	2.91	3.197	140	3.12	3.270	4	5.40	3.331
Ukraine	713	3.36	2.770	—	—	—	90	3.79	3.017
Uruguay	520	1.72	1.769	58	1.92	1.910	74	1.62	1.484
USA	578	2.01	1.987	87	2.80	2.522	128	2.11	2.215
Venezuela	482	1.72	1.630	191	1.90	1.809	38	1.87	1.563
Vietnam	758	1.31	1.073	34	1.35	1.252	6	1.67	1.633
Zimbabwe	578	1.43	1.356	40	1.77	1.515	29	1.81	2.089

1 = Never justifiable; 10 = always justifiable

Table 31.2 Cheating on taxes if you could – marital status

	Separated			Widow			Single/NM		
	Sample size	Mean	SD	Sample size	Mean	SD	Sample size	Mean	SD
Total	1,787	2.41	2.387	6,909	2.01	2.018	28,536	2.56	2.455
Albania	3	2.00	1.732	56	1.71	0.948	206	2.20	1.738
Algeria	8	1.00	0.000	37	1.86	1.917	527	2.24	2.406
Argentina	68	2.00	2.382	101	1.75	2.081	333	2.22	2.399
Armenia	20	3.45	3.300	144	3.79	3.245	535	3.73	2.927
Australia	75	1.98	1.938	135	1.53	1.450	537	2.58	2.124
Austria	7	2.37	2.837	118	1.70	1.663	366	2.76	2.400
Azerbaijan	10	3.80	3.645	88	3.30	3.056	546	3.66	3.423
Bangladesh	10	1.00	0.000	6	1.00	0.000	15	1.00	0.000
Belarus	9	5.56	4.157	96	3.22	2.290	176	4.82	2.976
Belgium	27	4.79	3.054	164	3.01	2.843	415	4.17	2.940
Bosnia	7	1.71	1.496	99	1.60	1.641	317	1.89	1.943
Brazil	40	2.30	2.514	36	3.11	3.050	375	3.94	3.214
Bulgaria	8	3.29	1.993	148	1.60	1.509	155	2.68	2.438
Canada	67	2.29	2.324	125	1.59	1.650	383	2.42	2.335
Chile	63	2.06	1.972	64	2.20	2.268	269	2.33	2.420
China	1	2.00	0.000	20	1.95	2.460	92	1.80	1.672
Colombia	162	2.19	2.196	66	2.74	2.819	936	2.44	2.317
Croatia	5	2.94	3.630	94	1.88	1.755	178	3.80	3.338
Czech Republic	7	5.52	4.446	185	1.46	0.953	348	2.45	1.946
Denmark	14	2.71	3.361	72	1.68	1.276	308	2.17	1.941
Dominican Republic	19	2.05	2.527	11	2.91	3.562	5	1.00	0.000
Egypt	12	2.83	2.918	201	1.30	1.030	719	1.70	1.604

El Salvador	49	1.55	1.803	65	1.54	1.937	347	1.95	2.328
Estonia	20	3.65	2.591	106	2.41	2.080	243	3.80	2.714
Finland	6	2.23	2.404	92	1.72	1.465	179	3.00	2.607
France	67	2.95	2.614	121	2.43	2.435	504	3.70	2.819
Georgia	15	3.40	2.798	172	2.59	2.354	520	3.06	2.556
Germany, East	9	1.90	1.547	71	1.94	1.774	225	2.65	2.481
Germany, West	8	2.08	1.510	80	1.74	1.486	209	2.84	2.345
Great Britain	17	2.69	2.234	83	1.43	0.966	265	3.23	2.500
Greece	17	2.88	2.595	40	2.18	1.551	543	3.39	2.499
Hungary	8	2.66	2.421	119	1.37	1.062	198	2.58	2.323
Iceland	11	2.00	1.265	51	1.78	1.514	350	2.57	2.224
India	10	1.90	2.846	93	1.78	2.176	177	2.22	2.697
Indonesia	3	1.00	0.000	80	1.35	0.858	165	1.78	1.848
Iran	6	1.00	0.000	36	1.44	1.647	974	1.63	1.889
Ireland	23	2.15	1.887	77	1.90	1.932	309	2.71	2.324
Italy	36	2.64	2.554	136	2.00	1.947	612	2.68	2.320
Japan	10	1.90	1.663	51	1.51	1.912	233	1.60	1.204
Jordan	4	1.00	0.000	40	1.16	0.884	342	1.66	1.675
Kyrgyzstan	20	2.15	2.390	61	2.26	2.529	259	3.10	2.748
Latvia	21	2.10	1.895	134	1.82	1.875	172	3.15	2.723
Lithuania	16	2.88	2.336	117	2.67	2.428	176	4.36	3.048
Luxembourg	8	1.73	1.389	88	3.06	2.519	317	3.75	2.784
Macedonia	10	1.88	1.652	74	1.41	1.261	189	2.72	2.561
Malta	21	2.18	2.263	57	1.16	0.632	290	1.55	1.421
Mexico	40	2.35	2.667	71	2.03	2.285	338	2.34	2.376

(continued)

Table 31.2 (continued)

	Separated			Widow			Single/NM		
	Sample size	Mean	SD	Sample size	Mean	SD	Sample size	Mean	SD
Moldova	12	2.35	2.070	87	4.43	3.214	154	4.82	3.035
Montenegro	6	2.00	0.894	79	2.14	1.886	220	3.14	2.558
Morocco	–	–	–	39	1.00	0.000	432	1.49	1.828
Netherlands	20	2.81	2.136	82	1.80	1.607	322	3.20	2.376
New Zealand	40	2.85	2.694	78	1.36	1.128	181	3.04	2.476
Nigeria	7	1.71	1.254	55	1.93	1.631	935	2.07	1.905
Northern Ireland	25	2.80	2.109	56	1.83	1.718	239	2.89	2.534
Norway	18	2.94	2.155	53	2.19	2.076	203	2.86	2.426
Pakistan	–	–	–	30	1.37	0.928	630	1.22	0.835
Peru	61	1.92	2.108	26	1.73	1.343	512	2.18	1.922
Philippines	12	2.02	1.189	50	3.22	2.459	215	3.45	2.551
Poland	2	5.59	4.586	112	1.97	1.942	212	3.00	2.594
Portugal	10	2.36	2.683	100	2.11	1.946	205	2.50	2.216
Puerto Rico	31	2.45	2.528	74	2.15	2.546	119	2.41	2.666
Romania	6	2.50	1.761	115	1.90	1.906	195	3.45	2.904
Russia	56	3.34	2.488	349	2.08	1.836	396	3.84	2.898
Serbia	10	2.40	2.413	108	1.66	1.566	221	2.62	2.291
Singapore	8	3.08	2.413	23	1.65	1.305	773	2.05	1.866
Slovakia	11	2.85	3.160	116	1.75	1.539	297	2.37	2.009
Slovenia	2	5.50	6.364	82	2.06	1.848	279	2.83	2.587

South Africa	32	1.92	1.858	126	2.14	1.878	1,267	2.59	2.525
South Korea	6	1.67	1.633	27	1.15	0.770	322	1.69	1.509
Spain	27	2.34	2.340	93	1.96	1.839	341	2.38	2.084
Sweden	51	2.62	2.123	32	2.45	2.301	189	2.48	1.959
Switzerland	16	2.01	1.374	85	1.84	1.504	230	3.26	2.661
Taiwan	3	3.00	3.464	23	1.70	1.063	137	2.00	1.719
Tanzania	39	1.79	2.080	44	1.84	2.614	345	1.85	2.417
Turkey	4	1.00	0.000	46	1.17	0.529	308	1.23	1.022
Uganda	30	3.79	3.956	53	3.59	3.545	405	3.92	3.522
Ukraine	10	2.93	2.914	120	2.47	2.006	168	4.27	2.903
Uruguay	44	1.72	1.702	113	1.33	1.069	167	2.00	2.228
USA	31	2.45	2.303	49	2.01	2.103	325	2.70	2.385
Venezuela	47	1.83	1.672	47	1.87	1.996	386	1.90	1.907
Vietnam	6	1.17	0.408	37	1.59	1.554	148	1.30	1.134
Zimbabwe	18	1.36	0.974	67	1.14	0.839	249	1.75	1.876

1 = Never justifiable; 10 = always justifiable

Table 31.3 Ranking of mean scores

Rank	Category	Mean
1	Widow	2.01
2	Married	2.19
3	Separated	2.41
4	Living together as married	2.43
5	Single/never married	2.56
6	Divorced	2.66

1 = Never justifiable; 10 = always justifiable

Table 31.4 Gender and marital status

	Male	Female	p-Value
Married			
Sample size	31,287	30,896	0.0001
Mean	2.3	2.1	
SD	2.27	2.1	
Living together			
Sample size	2,388	2,458	0.0001
Mean	2.6	2.3	
SD	2.55	2.28	
Divorced			
Sample size	1,535	2,746	0.0001
Mean	3.0	2.5	
SD	2.75	2.36	
Separated			
Sample size	678	1,128	0.0102
Mean	2.6	2.3	
SD	2.51	2.33	
Widowed			
Sample size	1,418	5,578	0.0008
Mean	2.2	2	
SD	2.26	1.94	
Single/never married			
Sample size	16,069	12,813	0.0001
Mean	2.7	2.4	
SD	2.55	2.31	

1 = Never justifiable; 10 = always justifiable

Chapter 32
Income Level and the Ethics of Tax Evasion

Robert W. McGee

Introduction

Income was another variable tracked in the World Values surveys. One might assume a priori that the more income one has, the less aversion there will be to tax evasion because of the feeling by the relatively rich that they are being overtaxed and exploited. On the other hand, those in the poorer income groups might have less aversion to tax evasion because of their inability to pay. Thus, there is a need to conduct a test to learn what the relationship is between income level and attitude toward tax evasion.

Table 32.1 shows the data for each country as well as the significance of the differences in mean scores.

Table 32.2 shows the comparisons of low- and medium-income people by country.

Table 32.3 shows the comparisons between high- and low-income groups.

Table 32.4 compares the data for the medium- and high-income levels.

Table 32.5 shows the trend analysis.

Although there was no discernible trend between income level and aversion to tax evasion for 35 countries, a few countries had trends that reversed direction. For example, Hungary, Iran, and Turkey had mean scores that dropped significantly from low- to middle-income categories, then rose significantly from medium- to high-income levels, meaning that medium-income people were significantly more averse to tax evasion than were either low-income or high-income people. The trend for Portugal was just the opposite. Middle-income people were significantly less averse to tax evasion than either low-income or high-income people.

R.W. McGee (✉)
School of Business, Florida International University,
3000 NE 151 Street, North Miami, FL 33181, USA
e-mail: bob414@hotmail.com

R.W. McGee (ed.), *The Ethics of Tax Evasion: Perspectives in Theory and Practice*,
DOI 10.1007/978-1-4614-1287-8_32, © Springer Science+Business Media, LLC 2012

Table 32.1 Income level and attitude toward tax evasion

Country	Income level			p-Values		
	Low	Medium	High	Low vs. medium	Low vs. high	Medium vs. high
Albania						
Sample size	348	300	328	0.0037	0.0487	0.4105
Mean	1.7	2.0	1.9			
SD	1.09	1.52	1.52			
Algeria						
Sample size	430	297	285	1.0000	0.2317	0.2629
Mean	1.9	1.9	2.1			
SD	2.11	2.00	2.30			
Argentina						
Sample size	378	509	382	0.4759	0.4855	1.0000
Mean	1.8	1.9	1.9			
SD	1.96	2.14	1.99			
Austria						
Sample size	322	438	446	0.4871	0.5013	0.1290
Mean	2.2	2.1	2.3			
SD	2.05	1.89	2.02			
Bangladesh						
Sample size	422	618	435	0.0030	0.0017	1.0000
Mean	1.0	1.1	1.1			
SD	0.28	0.65	0.59			
Belgium						
Sample size	399	546	604	0.1141	0.0011	0.0687
Mean	3.3	3.6	3.9			
SD	2.96	2.82	2.76			
Bosnia and Herzegovina						
Sample size	252	612	275	1.0000	0.0034	0.0001
Mean	1.6	1.6	2.1			
SD	1.86	1.59	2.03			
Bulgaria						
Sample size	317	262	311	0.1558	0.0001	0.0034
Mean	1.7	1.9	2.4			
SD	1.63	1.75	2.23			
Belarus						
Sample size	307	416	185	0.0593	0.0094	0.2368
Mean	3.9	4.3	4.6			
SD	2.82	2.81	2.99			
Canada						
Sample size	529	537	635	0.4415	0.0197	0.1138
Mean	2.0	2.1	2.3			
SD	2.15	2.09	2.21			
Chile						
Sample size	456	400	271	0.2162	0.0289	0.2265
Mean	2.3	2.1	1.9			
SD	2.55	2.12	2.07			

(continued)

Table 32.1 (continued)

Country	Income level			p-Values		
	Low	Medium	High	Low vs. medium	Low vs. high	Medium vs. high
China						
Sample size	371	340	233	0.3326	0.0160	0.1333
Mean	1.5	1.6	1.8			
SD	1.31	1.44	1.73			
Croatia						
Sample size	209	429	329	0.0001	0.0001	0.3018
Mean	1.7	2.8	2.6			
SD	1.53	2.65	2.63			
Czech Republic						
Sample size	489	688	535	0.0509	0.0001	0.0035
Mean	1.8	2.0	2.3			
SD	1.73	1.73	1.84			
Denmark						
Sample size	298	405	202	1.0000	1.0000	1.0000
Mean	2.0	2.0	2.0			
SD	1.87	1.71	1.71			
Egypt						
Sample size	927	698	1,040	0.2054	0.0029	0.1394
Mean	1.7	1.6	1.5			
SD	1.65	1.47	1.32			
Estonia						
Sample size	209	305	350	0.1522	0.0017	0.0453
Mean	2.7	3.0	3.4			
SD	2.27	2.37	2.69			
Finland						
Sample size	310	296	307	0.3044	0.2532	0.0286
Mean	2.5	2.7	2.3			
SD	2.33	2.46	2.00			
France						
Sample size	400	509	353	0.0950	0.1157	1.0000
Mean	2.8	3.1	3.1			
SD	2.59	2.76	2.63			
Germany						
Sample size	568	582	315	0.1290	0.2073	1.0000
Mean	2.4	2.6	2.6			
SD	2.16	2.30	2.42			
Great Britain						
Sample size	258	213	218	0.6226	1.0000	0.6197
Mean	2.4	2.5	2.4			
SD	2.26	2.11	2.07			
Greece						
Sample size	298	326	302	0.6173	0.1422	0.3197
Mean	3.1	3.2	3.4			
SD	2.48	2.51	2.52			

(continued)

Table 32.1 (continued)

Country	Income level			p-Values		
	Low	Medium	High	Low vs. medium	Low vs. high	Medium vs. high
Hungary						
Sample size	207	383	357	0.0723	0.3009	0.0006
Mean	2.2	1.9	2.4			
SD	2.23	1.75	2.20			
Iceland						
Sample size	268	341	290	0.5183	0.2517	0.0538
Mean	2.2	2.1	2.4			
SD	2.01	1.80	2.10			
India						
Sample size	381	700	784	0.0016	0.0001	0.0001
Mean	2.9	2.3	1.7			
SD	3.31	2.77	2.02			
Indonesia						
Sample size	357	392	138	0.3325	1.0000	0.4881
Mean	1.5	1.6	1.5			
SD	1.29	1.51	1.29			
Iran						
Sample size	828	982	376	0.0065	1.0000	0.0331
Mean	1.6	1.4	1.6			
SD	1.76	1.36	1.95			
Ireland						
Sample size	257	278	308	0.1063	0.2556	0.5720
Mean	2.2	2.5	2.4			
SD	2.08	2.20	2.08			
Italy						
Sample size	524	471	510	0.1464	0.4746	0.0236
Mean	2.4	2.2	2.5			
SD	2.33	1.97	2.16			
Japan						
Sample size	444	383	389	0.3299	0.2772	1.0000
Mean	1.4	1.5	1.5			
SD	1.37	1.58	1.27			
Jordan						
Sample size	406	395	313	1.0000	0.3871	0.4039
Mean	1.6	1.6	1.5			
SD	1.62	1.70	1.42			
Republic of Korea						
Sample size	456	320	423	0.3170	0.2885	1.0000
Mean	1.5	1.6	1.6			
SD	1.39	1.34	1.40			
Kyrgyzstan						
Sample size	280	534	184	0.0001	0.0001	0.3926
Mean	2.1	2.9	3.1			
SD	2.17	2.78	2.60			

(continued)

Table 32.1 (continued)

Country	Income level			p-Values		
	Low	Medium	High	Low vs. medium	Low vs. high	Medium vs. high
Latvia						
Sample size	442	207	281	0.5840	0.0856	0.0601
Mean	2.3	2.2	2.6			
SD	2.18	2.14	2.44			
Lithuania						
Sample size	213	245	347	0.7216	0.4309	0.2248
Mean	3.5	3.4	3.7			
SD	2.94	3.04	2.90			
Luxembourg						
Sample size	220	224	184	0.2414	0.1446	0.7268
Mean	3.0	3.3	3.4			
SD	2.56	2.82	2.94			
Macedonia						
Sample size	369	370	257	0.2772	1.0000	0.3004
Mean	2.2	2.4	2.2			
SD	2.49	2.51	2.17			
Malta						
Sample size	235	229	249	0.0122	0.0024	0.5169
Mean	1.3	1.6	1.7			
SD	0.94	1.56	1.79			
Mexico						
Sample size	379	395	364	1.0000	0.5641	0.5542
Mean	2.3	2.3	2.2			
SD	2.41	2.34	2.31			
Republic of Moldova						
Sample size	227	315	321	0.0072	0.0003	0.3979
Mean	3.6	4.3	4.5			
SD	2.84	3.08	2.88			
Morocco						
Sample size	568	481	300	0.1994	0.2893	1.0000
Mean	1.2	1.3	1.3			
SD	1.21	1.31	1.51			
Netherlands						
Sample size	308	348	266	1.0000	0.2849	0.2660
Mean	2.7	2.7	2.9			
SD	2.26	2.21	2.20			
Nigeria						
Sample size	733	663	542	0.3223	0.3362	1.0000
Mean	2.1	2.0	2.0			
SD	1.96	1.74	1.65			
Northern Ireland						
Sample size	232	213	225	0.1715	1.0000	0.1657
Mean	2.4	2.7	2.4			
SD	2.23	2.39	2.13			

(continued)

Table 32.1 (continued)

Country	Income level			p-Values		
	Low	Medium	High	Low vs. medium	Low vs. high	Medium vs. high
Pakistan						
Sample size	586	767	462	1.0000	1.0000	1.0000
Mean	1.2	1.2	1.2			
SD	0.77	0.72	0.66			
Peru						
Sample size	618	511	344	0.4023	0.0276	0.1312
Mean	2.2	2.1	1.9			
SD	2.08	1.89	1.91			
Philippines						
Sample size	331	491	353	0.2591	0.0085	0.0861
Mean	2.9	3.1	3.4			
SD	2.46	2.51	2.49			
Poland						
Sample size	409	463	167	0.4985	0.6217	0.2865
Mean	2.3	2.2	2.4			
SD	2.27	2.09	2.04			
Portugal						
Sample size	127	319	227	0.0003	0.3539	0.0006
Mean	2.1	3.0	2.3			
SD	1.78	2.54	2.03			
Puerto Rico						
Sample size	193	262	222	0.1528	0.0105	0.1876
Mean	1.7	2.0	2.3			
SD	2.00	2.35	2.65			
Romania						
Sample size	297	285	421	0.0258	0.3206	0.1649
Mean	2.5	3.0	2.7			
SD	2.50	2.89	2.76			
Russian Federation						
Sample size	759	694	778	0.1232	0.0001	0.0001
Mean	2.7	2.9	3.6			
SD	2.44	2.50	2.79			
Singapore						
Sample size	369	493	516	0.4516	0.4294	1.0000
Mean	2.0	1.9	1.9			
SD	2.03	1.85	1.72			
Slovakia						
Sample size	358	401	452	0.4733	1.0000	0.4343
Mean	2.1	2.0	2.1			
SD	2.03	1.81	1.91			
Slovenia						
Sample size	258	212	175	1.0000	0.1733	0.1895
Mean	2.2	2.2	2.5			
SD	2.12	2.07	2.42			

(continued)

Table 32.1   (continued)

Country	Income level			p-Values		
	Low	Medium	High	Low vs. medium	Low vs. high	Medium vs. high
South Africa						
Sample size	1,079	1,058	482	0.3447	0.0001	0.0001
Mean	2.7	2.6	3.3			
SD	2.38	2.51	2.28			
Spain						
Sample size	417	792	427	0.0003	0.0001	0.0921
Mean	1.8	2.2	2.4			
SD	1.61	1.90	2.11			
Sweden						
Sample size	367	326	279	0.5201	1.0000	0.5307
Mean	2.4	2.5	2.4			
SD	2.12	1.95	1.96			
Tanzania						
Sample size	459	374	221	0.5187	1.0000	0.5712
Mean	1.8	1.7	1.8			
SD	2.39	2.00	2.21			
Turkey						
Sample size	450	481	252	0.0369	0.2010	0.0066
Mean	1.2	1.1	1.3			
SD	0.77	0.69	1.30			
Uganda						
Sample size	218	125	178	0.7832	0.5341	0.4100
Mean	3.0	3.1	2.8			
SD	3.27	3.18	3.07			
Ukraine						
Sample size	417	362	303	0.0105	0.0002	0.1780
Mean	3.1	3.6	3.9			
SD	2.67	2.76	2.97			
USA						
Sample size	425	401	305	0.5074	0.5477	0.2294
Mean	2.3	2.2	2.4			
SD	2.19	2.14	2.25			
Venezuela						
Sample size	319	301	383	0.0071	0.0001	0.1010
Mean	2.2	1.8	1.6			
SD	2.03	1.62	1.55			
Vietnam						
Sample size	199	415	358	1.0000	0.3475	0.1984
Mean	1.3	1.3	1.4			
SD	1.26	0.99	1.17			
Zimbabwe						
Sample size	329	316	178	1.0000	0.4649	0.4849
Mean	1.5	1.5	1.6			
SD	1.40	1.49	1.59			

Mean score: 1 = never acceptable; 10 = always acceptable

Table 32.2 Comparison of low- to medium-income levels

Low-income people were significantly *more* averse to tax evasion than were medium-income people (at 10% level)	Low-income people were *more* averse to tax evasion than were medium-income people, but not significantly more averse (at 10% level)	No difference
Albania	Argentina	Algeria
Bangladesh	Belgium	Bosnia and Herzegovina
Belarus	Bulgaria	Denmark
Croatia	Canada	Jordan
Czech Republic	China	Mexico
France	Estonia	Netherlands
Kyrgyzstan	Finland	Pakistan
Malta	Germany	Slovenia
Moldova	Great Britain	Vietnam
Portugal	Greece	Zimbabwe
Romania	Indonesia	[10 Countries]
Spain	Ireland	
Ukraine	Japan	
[13 Countries]	Korea	
	Luxembourg	
	Macedonia	
	Morocco	
	Northern Ireland	
	Philippines	
	Puerto Rico	
	Russia	
	Sweden	
	Uganda	
	[23 Countries]	
Low-income people were significantly *less* averse to tax evasion than were medium-income people (at 10% level)	Low-income people were *less* averse to tax evasion than were medium-income people, but not significantly less averse (at 10% level)	
Hungary	Austria	
India	Chile	
Iran	Egypt	
Turkey	Iceland	
Venezuela	Italy	
[5 Countries]	Latvia	
	Lithuania	
	Nigeria	
	Peru	
	Poland	
	Singapore	
	Slovakia	
	South Africa	
	Tanzania	
	USA	
	[15 Countries]	

Table 32.3 Comparison of low- to high-income levels

Low-income people were significantly *more* averse to tax evasion than were high-income people (at 10% level)	Low-income people were *more* averse to tax evasion than were high-income people, but not significantly more averse (at 10% level)	No difference
Albania	Algeria	Denmark
Bangladesh	Argentina	Great Britain
Belarus	Austria	Indonesia
Belgium	France	Iran
Bosnia & Herzegovina	Germany	Macedonia
Bulgaria	Greece	Northern Ireland
Canada	Hungary	Pakistan
China	Iceland	Slovakia
Croatia	Ireland	Sweden
Czech Republic	Italy	Tanzania
Estonia	Japan	[10 Countries]
Kyrgyzstan	Korea	
Latvia	Lithuania	
Malta	Luxembourg	
Moldova	Morocco	
Philippines	Netherlands	
Puerto Rico	Poland	
Russia	Portugal	
South Africa	Romania	
Spain	Slovenia	
Ukraine	Turkey	
[21 Countries]	USA	
	Vietnam	
	Zimbabwe	
	[24 Countries]	
Low-income people were significantly *less* averse to tax evasion than were higher-income people (at 10% level)	Low-income people were *less* averse to tax evasion than were high-income people, but not significantly less averse (at 10% level)	
Chile	Finland	
Egypt	Jordan	
India	Mexico	
Peru	Nigeria	
Venezuela	Singapore	
[5 Countries]	Uganda	
	[6 Countries]	

Table 32.4 Comparison of medium- to high-income levels

Medium-income people were significantly *more* averse to tax evasion than were high-income people (at 10% level)	Medium-income people were *more* averse to tax evasion than were high-income people, but not significantly more averse (at 10% level)	No difference
Belgium	Algeria	Argentina
Bosnia and Herzegovina	Austria	Bangladesh
Bulgaria	Belarus	Denmark
Czech Republic	Canada	France
Estonia	China	Germany
Hungary	Greece	Japan
Iceland	Kyrgyzstan	Korea
Iran	Lithuania	Morocco
Italy	Luxembourg	Nigeria
Latvia	Malta	Pakistan
Philippines	Moldova	Singapore
Russia	Netherlands	[11 Countries]
South Africa	Poland	
Spain	Puerto Rico	
Turkey	Slovakia	
[15 Countries]	Slovenia	
	Tanzania	
	Ukraine	
	USA	
	Vietnam	
	Zimbabwe	
	[21 Countries]	
Medium-income people were significantly *less* averse to tax evasion than were higher-income people (at 10% level)	Medium-income people were *less* averse to tax evasion than were high-income people, but not significantly less averse (at 10% level)	
Finland	Albania	
India	Chile	
Portugal	Croatia	
[3 Countries]	Egypt	
	Great Britain	
	Indonesia	
	Ireland	
	Jordan	
	Macedonia	
	Mexico	
	Northern Ireland	
	Peru	
	Romania	
	Sweden	
	Uganda	
	Venezuela	
	[16 Countries]	

Table 32.5 Trend analysis

Upward trend – People become less averse to tax evasion as income increases	Downward trend – People become more averse to tax evasion as income increases	No discernible trend
Albania	Chile	Algeria
Bangladesh	Egypt	Argentina
Belarus	Finland	Austria
Belgium	India	Denmark
Bosnia & Herzegovina	Peru	Germany
Bulgaria	Venezuela	Great Britain
Canada	[6 Countries]	Greece
China		Hungary
Croatia		Indonesia
Czech Republic		Iran
Estonia		Ireland
France		Japan
Iceland		Jordan
Italy		Korea
Kyrgyzstan		Lithuania
Latvia		Luxembourg
Malta		Macedonia
Moldova		Mexico
Philippines		Morocco
Puerto Rico		Netherlands
Romania		Nigeria
Russia		Northern Ireland
South Africa		Pakistan
Spain		Poland
Ukraine		Portugal
[25 Countries]		Singapore
		Slovakia
		Slovenia
		Sweden
		Tanzania
		Turkey
		Uganda
		USA
		Vietnam
		Zimbabwe
		[35 Countries]

Part VII
Annotated Bibliographies

Chapter 33
Annotated Bibliography: 18 Statement Surveys*

Robert W. McGee

Introductory Remarks

The studies summarized below were based on survey research conducted by Robert W. McGee, sometimes with coauthors. The studies usually consisted of 18 statements beginning with the phrase, "Tax evasion is ethical if ...." The first 15 statements are based on arguments used in prior studies over the last 500 years to justify tax evasion. The last three statements were added to survey views on three human rights issues that had not been addressed in prior research.

One of those human rights statements (#16) differed slightly depending on the study. The usual statement was "Tax evasion would be ethical if I were a Jew living in Nazi Germany." For some studies this statement was changed to "Tax evasion would be ethical if I lived under an oppressive regime like Nazi Germany or Stalinist Russia" because some bureaucrats at the institution where the surveys were distributed considered the original version of the statement to be offensive (poor babies). Some of the Chinese studies omitted the three human rights questions to avoid getting a coauthor in potential trouble (Human rights is a touchy issue in China).

A seven-point Likert Scale was used to determine the extent of agreement or disagreement with each statement. Usually, the scale was from 1 to 7, where 1 indicated strong agreement and 7 indicated strong disagreement. For some of the studies conducted in former Soviet republics the scale was changed from 0 to 6, where 0 indicated strong disagreement with the statement and 6 indicated strong agreement. The reason for changing the scale was because people in those republics are accustomed to perceiving zero (0) as the number that should be used to indicate strong disagreement.

---

*Note: Some of the studies listed below are available online at http://ssrn.com/author=2139.

R.W. McGee (✉)
School of Business, Florida International University, 3000 NE 151 Street,
North Miami, FL 33181, USA
e-mail: bob414@hotmail.com

R.W. McGee (ed.), *The Ethics of Tax Evasion: Perspectives in Theory and Practice*,
DOI 10.1007/978-1-4614-1287-8_33, © Springer Science+Business Media, LLC 2012

Earlier versions of some of these studies are published on the Social Science Research Network Web site at http://ssrn.com/author=2139. This link will take you to the abstract. It is possible to download the full paper by selecting the "One-click Download" link.

The statements used in the surveys are listed below:

1. ——Tax evasion is ethical if tax rates are too high.
2. ——Tax evasion is ethical even if tax rates are not too high because the government is not entitled to take as much as it is taking from me.
3. ——Tax evasion is ethical if the tax system is unfair.
4. ——Tax evasion is ethical if a large portion of the money collected is wasted.
5. ——Tax evasion is ethical even if most of the money collected is spent wisely.
6. ——Tax evasion is ethical if a large portion of the money collected is spent on projects that I morally disapprove of.
7. ——Tax evasion is ethical even if a large portion of the money collected is spent on worthy projects.
8. ——Tax evasion is ethical if a large portion of the money collected is spent on projects that do not benefit me.
9. ——Tax evasion is ethical even if a large portion of the money collected is spent on projects that do benefit me.
10. ——Tax evasion is ethical if everyone is doing it.
11. ——Tax evasion is ethical if a significant portion of the money collected winds up in the pockets of corrupt politicians or their families and friends.
12. ——Tax evasion is ethical if the probability of getting caught is low.
13. ——Tax evasion is ethical if some of the proceeds go to support a war that I consider to be unjust.
14. ——Tax evasion is ethical if I can't afford to pay.
15. ——Tax evasion is ethical even if it means that if I pay less, others will have to pay more.
16. ——Tax evasion would be ethical if I were a Jew living in Nazi Germany.
17. ——Tax evasion is ethical if the government discriminates against me because of my religion, race, or ethnic background.
18. ——Tax evasion is ethical if the government imprisons people for their political opinions.

The studies are summarized below.

Accounting Practitioners: Florida

McGee, Robert W., and Tatyana B. Maranjyan (2012). Attitudes toward Tax Evasion: An Empirical Study of Florida Accounting Practitioners. In Robert W. McGee (Ed.), *The Ethics of Tax Evasion: Perspectives in Theory and Practice* (pp. 247–265). New York: Springer.

Methodology

18 Statement Survey: Tax evasion is ethical if ...
Sample: 171 accounting practitioners in South Florida.
Range of scores (1 = strongly agree; 7 = strongly disagree): 5.37–6.81
Mean score: 6.45

Overall Findings

- Some arguments justifying tax evasion were significantly stronger than others.
- Comparisons were made with more than 20 other studies.
- Gender: Women were slightly more opposed to tax evasion.
- Ethnicity: Non-Hispanic whites were significantly more opposed to tax evasion than were Hispanics.

Ranking

Strongest Arguments to Justify Tax Evasion

1	Tax evasion would be ethical if I were a Jew living in Nazi Germany in 1940	(5.37)
2	Tax evasion is ethical if the government discriminates against me because of my religion, race, or ethnic background	(5.93)
3	Tax evasion is ethical if the government imprisons people for their political opinions	(5.98)
4	Tax evasion is ethical if a significant portion of the money collected winds up in the pockets of corrupt politicians or their families and friends	(6.06)
5	Tax evasion is ethical if the tax system is unfair	(6.34)
6	Tax evasion is ethical if a large portion of the money collected is wasted	(6.37)

Weakest Arguments to Justify Tax Evasion

18	Tax evasion is ethical even if most of the money collected is spent wisely	(6.81)
17	Tax evasion is ethical even if a large portion of the money collected is spent on worthy projects	(6.80)
16	Tax evasion is ethical even if a large portion of the money collected is spent on projects that do benefit me	(6.76)

14 Tax evasion is ethical if a large portion of the money collected
    is spent on projects that do not benefit me   (6.71)
14 Tax evasion is ethical even if tax rates are not too high because
    the government is not entitled to take as much as it is taking
    from me   (6.71)
13 Tax evasion is ethical if the probability of getting caught is low   (6.68)

Gender

Overall Mean Scores

Female: 6.55
Male: 6.39

Findings

Women were more opposed to tax evasion in 13 of 18 cases. However, the difference in mean score was significant in just one case.

Conclusion: Women are slightly more opposed to tax evasion than are men.

Ethnicity

Overall Mean Scores

Hispanics: 5.98
Non-Hispanic Whites: 6.53

Findings

Non-Hispanic whites were more opposed to tax evasion in 17 of 18 cases. In many cases the differences were significant at the 1% level.

Argentina

McGee, Robert W. and Marcelo J. Rossi. 2008. A Survey of Argentina on the Ethics of Tax Evasion, in Robert W. McGee, editor, *Taxation and Public Finance in Transition and Developing Economies* (pp. 239–261). New York: Springer.

Methodology

18 Statement Survey: Tax evasion is ethical if …
Sample: 218 business and economics and law students and faculty.
Range of scores (1 = strongly agree; 7 = strongly disagree): 4.1–6.6
Mean score: 5.4

Overall Findings

- Some arguments justifying tax evasion were significantly stronger than others.
- Status: Students and faculty were equally opposed to tax evasion.
- Gender: Males were more opposed to tax evasion in 9/18 cases; females were more opposed to tax evasion in 7/18 cases; opposition was equal in 2/18 cases.
- Major: Business and economics students were more opposed to tax evasion in 16/18 cases; law students were more opposed to tax evasion in 1/18 cases; opposition was equal in 1/18 cases.

Ranking

Strongest Arguments to Justify Tax Evasion

1	Tax evasion is ethical if I can't afford to pay	(4.1)
2	Tax evasion would be ethical if I were a Jew living in Nazi Germany	(4.1)
3	Tax evasion is ethical if a significant portion of the money collected winds up in the pockets of corrupt politicians or their families and friends	(4.2)
4	Tax evasion is ethical if the tax system is unfair	(4.4)
5	Tax evasion is ethical if the government discriminates against me because of my religion, race, or ethnic background	(4.6)
6	Tax evasion is ethical if a large portion of the money collected is wasted	(4.7)

Weakest Arguments to Justify Tax Evasion

18	Tax evasion is ethical even if most of the money collected is spent wisely	(6.6)
15	Tax evasion is ethical if the probability of getting caught is low	(6.5)
15	Tax evasion is ethical even if a large portion of the money collected is spent on projects that do benefit me	(6.5)

15 Tax evasion is ethical even if tax rates are not too high because the government is not entitled to take as much as it is taking from me   (6.5)

14 Tax evasion is ethical if a large portion of the money collected is spent on projects that do not benefit me   (6.4)

13 Tax evasion is ethical even if it means that if I pay less, others will have to pay more   (6.3)

Gender

Overall Mean Scores

Female: 5.41
Male: 5.38

Major

Overall Mean Scores

Business and Economics: 5.6
Law: 5.2

Armenia

McGee, Robert W. and Tatyana B. Maranjyan. 2008. Opinions on Tax Evasion in Armenia, in Robert W. McGee, editor, *Taxation and Public Finance in Transition and Developing Economies* (pp. 277–307). New York: Springer.

Methodology

14 Statement Survey: Tax evasion is ethical if …

Sample: 52 business and economics students and 33 theology students. It was at times difficult to get approval to distribute the survey instrument. One administrator accused the person collecting the data of being a CIA agent who wanted to show the people of Armenia in a bad light. Permission to distribute was sometimes denied.

Range of scores (1 = strongly agree; 7 = strongly disagree): 2.75–6.06

Mean score: 4.54

Overall Findings

- Some arguments justifying tax evasion were significantly stronger than others.
- Major: Business students were more strongly opposed to tax evasion than were theology students, although neither group was strongly opposed to tax evasion.
- There was a widespread perception that tax evasion is ethical in at least some cases.
- Some arguments for tax evasion were significantly stronger than others.
- At first it was difficult to find an acceptable explanation to explain why the theology students were less opposed to tax evasion than were the business students. However, when an earlier version of this paper was presented at a conference in Armenia, several participants explained that theology was a business in Armenia. The tenor of the conversations seemed to indicate that there was a certain amount of cynicism regarding the perception of religious fervor of some members of the Armenian Orthodox Church.
- A comparison of mean scores with 40 other studies that used a similar survey instrument found that Armenian theology students ranked sixth (sixth lowest mean score) and Armenian business students ranked tenth (tenth lowest mean score) in terms of weak opposition to tax evasion. Of the 40 study comparisons, Chinese business and economics students and Moldovan students tied for first place in terms of lowest means core (4.10). Episcopal seminarians and accounting practitioners tied for the fortieth place with the highest mean scores (6.45).

Ranking

Strongest Arguments to Justify Tax Evasion

1	Tax evasion is ethical if the system is unfair	(2.75)
2	Tax evasion is ethical if a significant portion of the money collected winds up in the pockets of corrupt politicians or their families and friends	(3.01)
3	Tax evasion is ethical if a large portion of the money collected is wasted	(3.51)
4	Tax evasion is ethical if tax rates are too high	(3.71)
5	Tax evasion is ethical if a large portion of the money collected is spent on projects that I morally disapprove of	(3.80)
6	Tax evasion is ethical if I can't afford to pay	(4.33)
7	Tax evasion is ethical if the probability of getting caught is low	(4.65)

Weakest Arguments to Justify Tax Evasion

14 Tax evasion is ethical even if it means that if I pay less, others
    will have to pay more   (6.06)
13 Tax evasion is ethical even if most of the money collected is
    spent wisely   (5.65)
12 Tax evasion is ethical even if tax rates are not too high   (5.64)
11 Tax evasion is ethical if a large portion of the money collected
    is spent on projects that do not benefit me   (5.41)
10 Tax evasion is ethical even if a large portion of the money
    collected is spent on worthy projects   (5.29)
9   Tax evasion is ethical if everyone is doing it   (4.99)
8   Tax evasion is ethical even if a large portion of the money
    collected is spent on projects that do benefit me   (4.80)

Major

Overall Mean Scores

Theology: 4.40
Business: 4.64

Business students more opposed to tax evasion in 10/14 cases.
Theology students more opposed to tax evasion in 3/14 cases.
Equally opposed in 1/14 cases.

Conclusion: Business students are more opposed to tax evasion, although nei-
    ther group is strongly opposed.

Australia

McGee, Robert W. and Sanjoy Bose. 2009. The Ethics of Tax Evasion: A Survey of
Australian Opinion, in Robert W. McGee, *Readings in Business Ethics* (pp. 143–
166). Hyderabad, India: ICFAI University Press.

Methodology

18 Statement Survey: Tax evasion is ethical if …
Sample: 315 business, philosophy, and seminary students and faculty.
Range of scores (1 = strongly agree; 7 = strongly disagree): 4.30–5.14
Mean score: 4.78

Overall Findings

- Some arguments justifying tax evasion were significantly stronger than others.
- Gender: Females were more opposed to tax evasion in 12/18 cases; females were significantly more opposed to tax evasion in 2/18 cases.
- Males were significantly more opposed to tax evasion in 2/18 cases.
- Student status: Overall, undergraduate students were least opposed to tax evasion and faculty members were most opposed to tax evasion. Differences between undergraduate students and faculty members were significant at the 5% level.
- Major: Business and economics students were least opposed to tax evasion; seminary students were most opposed; Business and economics students were significantly less opposed to tax evasion than were philosophy, accounting, health services, and seminary students. Accounting majors were significantly more opposed to tax evasion than were business and economics, and information technology students and were significantly less opposed to tax evasion than were seminary and health services students. Some other comparisons were not made because of small sample size.
- Religion: Muslims had the least opposition to tax evasion, but the Muslim sample size was 12, which was too small to measure the extent of statistical significance. Catholics had the strongest opposition to tax evasion. Many of the differences between religious groups were significant.
- Ethnicity: Asians were least opposed to tax evasion; Anglos were most opposed to tax evasion.

Ranking

Strongest Arguments to Justify Tax Evasion

1	Tax evasion is ethical if tax rates are too high	(4.30)
2	Tax evasion is ethical if the tax system is unfair	(4.53)
3	Tax evasion is ethical if a large portion of the money collected is wasted	(4.53)
4	Tax evasion is ethical if the government discriminates against me because of my religion, race, or ethnic background	(4.58)
5	Tax evasion is ethical if a significant portion of the money collected winds up in the pockets of corrupt politicians or their families and friends	(4.61)
6	Tax evasion is ethical if the government imprisons people for their political opinions	(4.71)

Weakest Arguments to Justify Tax Evasion

18 Tax evasion is ethical even if tax rates are not too high because
    the government is not entitled to take as much as it is taking
    from me   (5.14)
17 Tax evasion is ethical if the probability of getting caught is low   (4.98)
16 Tax evasion is ethical even if it means that if I pay less, others
    will have to pay more   (4.96)
15 Tax evasion would be ethical if I were a Jew living in Nazi
    Germany   (4.93)
14 Tax evasion is ethical even if most of the money collected is
    spent wisely   (4.91)
13 Tax evasion is ethical even if a large portion of the money
    collected is spent on projects that do benefit me   (4.90)

Gender

Overall Mean Scores

Female: 4.82
Male: 4.74

Student Status

Overall Mean Scores

Undergraduate students: 4.50
Graduate students: 4.68
Faculty: 4.84

Major

Overall Mean Scores

Accounting: 5.05
Business and Economics: 4.37
Health Services: 5.26
Seminary: 6.46
Theology: 4.64
Philosophy: 4.92
Information Technology: 4.57

Religion

Overall Mean Scores

Catholic: 5.23
Anglican: 4.92
Christian: 5.16
Jewish: 4.56
Hindu: 4.69
Buddhist: 4.83
Muslim: 4.24
Atheist/Agnostic/None: 4.40

Ethnicity

Overall Mean Scores

Asian: 4.50
African and Middle Eastern: 4.87
Anglo: 5.00

Bosnia and Herzegovina

McGee, Robert W., Meliha Basic, and Michael Tyler. 2009. The Ethics of Tax Evasion: A Survey of Bosnian Opinion, *Journal of Balkan and Near Eastern Studies* 11(2): 197–207.

Methodology

18 Statement Survey: Tax evasion is ethical if …
Sample: 132 third and fourth year undergraduate business students at the University of Sarajevo.
Range of scores (1 = strongly agree; 7 = strongly disagree): 3.44–6.11
Mean score: 5.03

Overall Findings

- Some arguments justifying tax evasion were significantly stronger than others.

Ranking

Strongest Arguments to Justify Tax Evasion

1   Tax evasion is ethical if a significant portion of the money
    collected winds up in the pockets of corrupt politicians or their
    families and friends   (3.44)
1   Tax evasion is ethical if the government discriminated against
    me because of my religion, race, or ethnic background   (3.44)
3   Tax evasion is ethical if the government imprisons people for
    their political opinions   (3.92)
4   Tax evasion is ethical if tax system is unfair   (3.93)
5   Tax evasion is ethical if a large portion of the money collected
    is wasted   (4.14)
6   Tax evasion is ethical if I can't afford to pay   (4.30)

Weakest Arguments to Justify Tax Evasion

18 Tax evasion is ethical even if a large portion of the money
    collected is spent on worthy projects   (6.11)
16 Tax evasion is ethical even if a large portion of the money
    collected is spent on projects that do benefit me   (6.09)
16 Tax evasion is ethical even if most of the money collected is
    spent wisely   (6.09)
15 Tax evasion is ethical even if it means that if I pay less, others will
    have to pay more   (5.81)
14 Tax evasion is ethical if a large portion of the money collected
    is spent on projects that do not benefit me   (5.80)
13 Tax evasion is ethical even if tax rates are not too high because
    the government is not entitles to take as much as it is taking
    from me   (5.76)

Bosnia and Romania

McGee, Robert W., Meliha Basic, and Michael Tyler. 2008. The Ethics of Tax Evasion: A Comparative Study of Bosnian and Romanian Opinion, in Robert W. McGee, editor, *Taxation and Public Finance in Transition and Developing Economies* (pp. 167–183). New York: Springer.

Methodology

18 Statement Survey: Tax evasion is ethical if …
Sample: 132 Bosnian business students; 134 Romanian business students.
Range of scores (1 = strongly agree; 7 = strongly disagree): Bosnia 3.44–6.11;
   Romania 3.87–5.24
Mean score: Bosnia 5.03; Romania 4.59

Overall Findings

- Some arguments justifying tax evasion were significantly stronger than others.
- Nationality: Bosnians were more opposed to tax evasion in 14/18 cases.
- Bosnians were significantly more opposed to tax evasion in 10/18 cases.
- Romanians were significantly more opposed to tax evasion in 2/18 cases.
- The Corruption Perceptions Index ranked Romania #69 and Bosnia #84 out of 180 countries, where #1 is least corrupt.

Ranking: Bosnia

Strongest Arguments to Justify Tax Evasion

1	Tax evasion is ethical if a significant portion of the money collected winds up in the pockets of corrupt politicians or their families and friends	(3.44)
2	Tax evasion is ethical if the government discriminates against me because of my religion, race, or ethnic background	(3.44)
3	Tax evasion is ethical if the government imprisons people for their political opinions	(3.92)
4	Tax evasion is ethical if the tax system is unfair	(3.93)
5	Tax evasion is ethical if a large portion of the money collected is wasted	(4.14)
6	Tax evasion is ethical if I can't afford to pay	(4.30)

Weakest Arguments to Justify Tax Evasion

18	Tax evasion is ethical even if a large portion of the money collected is spent on worthy projects	(6.11)
17	Tax evasion is ethical even if a large portion of the money collected is spent on projects that do benefit me	(6.09)

16 Tax evasion is ethical even if most of the money collected is
   spent wisely   (6.09)
15 Tax evasion is ethical even if it means that if I pay less, others will
   have to pay more   (5.81)
14 Tax evasion is ethical if a large portion of the money collected
   is spent on projects that do not benefit me   (5.80)
13 Tax evasion is ethical even if tax rates are not too high because
   the government is not entitled to take as much as it is taking
   from me   (5.76)

Ranking: Romania

Strongest Arguments to Justify Tax Evasion

1 Tax evasion is ethical if the tax system is unfair   (3.87)
2 Tax evasion is ethical if the government discriminates against
  me because of my religion, race, or ethnic background   (4.07)
3 Tax evasion is ethical if I can't afford to pay   (4.16)
4 Tax evasion is ethical if tax rates are too high   (4.17)
5 Tax evasion is ethical if a significant portion of the money
  collected winds up in the pockets of corrupt politicians or their
  families and friends   (4.18)
6 Tax evasion is ethical if the government imprisons people for their
  political opinions   (4.32)

Weakest Arguments to Justify Tax Evasion

18 Tax evasion is ethical if everyone is doing it   (5.24)
17 Tax evasion is ethical if the probability of getting caught is low (5.16)
16 Tax evasion is ethical even if it means that if I pay less, others will
   have to pay more   (5.03)
15 Tax evasion is ethical even if tax rates are not too high   (5.00)
14 Tax evasion is ethical if a large portion of the money collected
   is spent on projects that do not benefit me   (4.95)
13 Tax evasion is ethical even if a large portion of the money
   collected is spent on projects that do benefit me   (4.86)

China

McGee, Robert W. and Zhiwen Guo. 2007. A Survey of Law, Business and
Philosophy Students in China on the Ethics of Tax Evasion. *Society and Business
Review* 2(3): 299–315.

Methodology

15 Statement Survey (omitted the three human rights issues): Tax evasion is
   ethical if …
Sample: 256 graduate and advanced undergraduate business and economics,
   law, and philosophy students in the city of Hubei in Central China.
Range of scores (1 = strongly agree; 7 = strongly disagree): 2.9–6.0
Mean score: 4.3

Overall Findings

- Some arguments justifying tax evasion were significantly stronger than
  others.
- Gender: Women were significantly more opposed to tax evasion than were
  men.
- Major: Business and Economics students are least opposed to tax evasion;
  law and philosophy students are equally opposed to tax evasion.

Ranking

Strongest Arguments to Justify Tax Evasion

1	Tax evasion is ethical if a significant portion of the money collected winds up in the pockets of corrupt politicians or their families and friends	(2.9)
2	Tax evasion is ethical if a large portion of the money collected is wasted	(3.1)
3	Tax evasion is ethical even if most of the money collected is spent wisely	(3.1)
4	Tax evasion is ethical if the tax system is unfair	(3.2)
5	Tax evasion is ethical if some of the proceeds go to support a war that I consider to be unjust	(3.3)

Weakest Arguments to Justify Tax Evasion

15	Tax evasion is ethical even if a large portion of the money collected is spent on projects that benefit me	(6.0)
14	Tax evasion is ethical even if a large portion of the money collected is spent on worthy projects	(6.0)
13	Tax evasion is ethical if the probability of getting caught is low	(5.8)

12 Tax evasion is ethical even if it means that if I pay less, others
   will have to pay more   (5.7)
11 Tax evasion is ethical even if tax rates are not too high because
   the government is not entitled to take as much as it is taking
   from me   (5.7)

Gender

Overall Mean Scores

Female: 4.42
Male: 4.27

Findings

Women more opposed to tax evasion: 9/15
Men more opposed to tax evasion: 3/15
Equally opposed to tax evasion: 3/15
Conclusion: Women are more opposed to tax evasion ($p = 0.0238$).

Academic Major

Overall Mean Scores

Law: 4.8
Business and Economics: 4.1
Philosophy: 4.7

Findings

Law students are most opposed to tax evasion: 9/15
Business and Economics students are most opposed to tax evasion: 0/15
Philosophy students are most opposed to tax evasion: 6/15
Law students are least opposed to tax evasion: 1/15
Business and Economics students are least opposed to tax evasion: 15/15
Philosophy students are least opposed to tax evasion: 1/15
Note: The total of the fractions is 17/15 because there were two ties.
Conclusions: Business and Economics students are least opposed to tax eva-
   sion; law and philosophy students are equally opposed to tax evasion
   ($p = 0.7872$).

China

McGee, Robert W. and Yuhua An. 2008. A Survey of Chinese Business and Economics Students on the Ethics of Tax Evasion, in Robert W. McGee, editor, *Taxation and Public Finance in Transition and Developing Economies* (pp. 409–421). New York: Springer.

Methodology

15 Statement Survey (omitted the 3 human rights issues): Tax evasion is ethical if …

Sample: 173 graduate and advanced undergraduate business and economics students at the University of International Business and Economics in Beijing.

Range of scores (1 = strongly agree; 7 = strongly disagree): 3.1–5.3

Mean: 4.4

Overall Findings

- Some arguments justifying tax evasion were significantly stronger than others.
- Gender: Men and women are equally opposed to tax evasion.

Ranking

Strongest Arguments to Justify Tax Evasion

1	Tax evasion is ethical if a larger portion of the money collected is wasted	(3.1)
2	Tax evasion is ethical if a significant portion of the money collected winds up in the pockets of corrupt politicians or their family and friends	(3.2)
3	Tax evasion is ethical if the tax system is unfair	(3.4)
4	Tax evasion is ethical if some of the proceeds go to support a war I consider to be unjust	(3.6)
5	Tax evasion is ethical if I cannot afford to pay	(3.9)

Weakest Arguments to Justify Tax Evasion

15	Tax evasion is ethical even if most of the money collected is spent wisely	(5.3)

14 Tax evasion is ethical even if a large portion of the money
    collected is spent on projects that benefit me   (5.2)
14 Tax evasion is ethical even if a large portion of the money
    collected is spent on worthy projects   (5.2)
12 Tax evasion is ethical even if it means that if I pay less, others
    will have to pay more   (5.1)
12 Tax evasion is ethical if the probability of getting caught is low   (5.1)

Gender

Overall Mean Scores

Female: 4.37
Male: 4.41

Findings

Women more opposed to tax evasion: 6/15
Men more opposed to tax evasion: 7/15
Equally opposed to tax evasion: 2/15
Conclusion: Men and women are equally opposed to tax evasion
    ($p = 0.5157$).

China and Macau

McGee, Robert W. and Carlos Noronha. 2008. The Ethics of Tax Evasion:
A Comparative Study of Guangzhou (Southern China) and Macau Opinions. *Euro
Asia Journal of Management* 18(2): 133–152.

Methodology

15 Statement Survey (omitted the three human rights issues): Tax evasion is
    ethical if …
Sample: 186 social science, business, and economics and other undergraduate
    students from Zhongshan University in China and 187 undergraduate and
    graduate business students from the University of Macau.

Overall Mean Scores

China: 5.0318
Macau: 4.9374
Conclusion: Mainland Chinese and Macau students are equally opposed to tax evasion (p = 0.2891). Note: Although the overall differences were not significant, responses of the two groups to individual statements were significantly different for 5 of the 15 statements.
Range of scores: (1 = strongly agree; 7 = strongly disagree)
China: 3.7849–5.8564
Macau: 3.5806–5.7957

Overall Findings

- Some arguments justifying tax evasion were significantly stronger than others.
- Mainland Chinese and Macau students were equally opposed to tax evasion.
- Gender: Men and women were equally opposed to tax evasion.

Ranking: China

Strongest Arguments to Justify Tax Evasion

1	Tax evasion is ethical if the tax system is unfair	(3.7849)
2	Tax evasion is ethical if a large portion of the money collected is wasted	(4.1129)
3	Tax evasion is ethical if a significant portion of the money collected winds up in the pockets of corrupt politicians or their families and friends	(4.1135)
4	Tax evasion is ethical if some of the proceeds go to support a war that I consider to be unjust	(4.2688)
5	Tax evasion is ethical if tax rates are too high	(4.5484)

Weakest Arguments to Justify Tax Evasion

15	Tax evasion is ethical even if most of the money collected is spent wisely	(5.8564)
14	Tax evasion is ethical even if it means that if I pay less, others will have to pay more	(5.8495)
13	Tax evasion is ethical even if a large portion of the money collected is spent on projects that benefit me	(5.7946)

12 Tax evasion is ethical if the probability of getting caught is
    low   (5.7419)
11 Tax evasion is ethical even if tax rates are not too high
    because the government is not entitled to take as much as it
    is taking from me   (5.6022)

Ranking: Macau

Strongest Arguments to Justify Tax Evasion

1   Tax evasion is ethical if a significant portion of the money
    collected winds up in the pockets of corrupt politicians or
    their families and friends   (3.5806)
2   Tax evasion is ethical if some of the proceeds go to support a
    war that I consider to be unjust   (3.6310)
3   Tax evasion is ethical if the tax system is unfair   (3.9519)
4   Tax evasion is ethical if a large portion of the money
    collected is wasted   (4.0376)
5   Tax evasion is ethical if I can't afford to pay   (4.3209)

Weakest Arguments to Justify Tax Evasion

15 Tax evasion is ethical even if a large portion of the money
    collected is spent on worthy projects   (5.7957)
14 Tax evasion is ethical even if most of the money collected is
    spent wisely   (5.7568)
13 Tax evasion is ethical even if a large portion of the money
    collected is spent on projects that benefit me   (5.7433)
13 Tax evasion is ethical even if tax rates are not too high
    because the government is not entitled to take as much as it
    is taking from me   (5.7433)
11 Tax evasion is ethical if a large portion of the money
    collected is spent on projects that do not benefit me   (5.5775)

Gender

Overall Mean Scores

Female: 4.9913
Male: 5.1284

Findings

Women more opposed to tax evasion: 4/15
Men more opposed to tax evasion: 11/15
Conclusion: Males and females were equally opposed to tax evasion. None of
    the mean scores for any of the 15 statements were significantly different.

Colombia

McGee, Robert W., Silvia López Paláu, and Gustavo A. Yepes Lopez. 2009. The
Ethics of Tax Evasion: An Empirical Study of Colombian Opinion, in Robert W.
McGee, *Readings in Business Ethics* (pp. 167–184). Hyderabad, India: ICFAI
University Press.

Methodology

18 Statement Survey: Tax evasion is ethical if …
Sample: 205 business students.
Range of scores (1 = strongly agree; 7 = strongly disagree): 5.33–6.61
Mean score: 6.03

Overall Findings

- Some arguments justifying tax evasion were significantly stronger than
  others.
- Gender: Females were more opposed to tax evasion in all 18 cases. They
  were significantly more opposed in 6 of 18 cases.

Ranking

Strongest Arguments to Justify Tax Evasion

1 Tax evasion is ethical if a significant portion of the money
   collected winds up in the pocket of corrupt politicians or their
   families and friends   (5.33)
2 Tax evasion is ethical if the government discriminated against
   me because of my religion, race, or ethnic background   (5.38)

3 Tax evasion is ethical if a large portion of the money collected
   is wasted   (5.48)
4 Tax evasion would be ethical if I were a Jew living in Nazi
   Germany   (5.51)
5 Tax evasion is ethical if the tax system is unfair   (5.72)
6 Tax evasion is ethical if I can't afford to pay   (5.74)

Weakest Arguments to Justify Tax Evasion

18 Tax evasion is ethical if everyone is doing it   (6.61)
17 Tax evasion is ethical if the probability of getting caught is
    low   (6.60)
16 Tax evasion is ethical even if tax rates are not too high
    because the government is not entitled to take as much as it is
    taking from me   (6.50)
14 Tax evasion is ethical even if it means that if I pay less,
    others will have to pay more   (6.43)
14 Tax evasion is ethical even if a large portion of the money
    collected is spent on projects that do benefit me   (6.43)
13 Tax evasion is ethical if a large portion of the money col-
    lected is spent on projects that do not benefit me   (6.40)

Gender

Overall Mean Scores

Female: 6.21
Male: 5.83

Ecuador

McGee, Robert W., Silvia López-Paláu, and Fabiola Jarrín Jaramillo. 2007. The Ethics of Tax Evasion: An Empirical Study of Ecuador. American Society of Business and Behavioral Sciences 14th Annual Meeting, Las Vegas, February 22–25, 2007. Published in the Proceedings of the American Society of Business and Behavioral Sciences 14(1): 1186–1198.

Methodology

18 Statement Survey: Tax evasion is ethical if ...
Sample: 140 business students.
Range of scores (1 = strongly agree; 7 = strongly disagree): 4.41–6.38
Mean score: 5.67

Overall Findings

- Some arguments justifying tax evasion were significantly stronger than others.
- Gender: Women were slightly more opposed to tax evasion than were men but none of the mean scores were significantly different.

Ranking

Strongest Arguments to Justify Tax Evasion

1	Tax evasion is ethical if a significant portion of the money collected winds up in the pockets of corrupt politicians or their families and friends	(4.41)
2	Tax evasion is ethical if a large portion of the money collected is wasted	(4.57)
3	Tax evasion is ethical if the tax system is unfair	(4.95)
4	Tax evasion is ethical if some of the proceeds go to support a war that I consider to be unjust	(5.11)
5	Tax evasion would be ethical if I were a Jew living in Nazi Germany in 1940	(5.24)
6	Tax evasion is ethical if I can't afford to pay	(5.34)

Weakest Arguments to Justify Tax Evasion

18	Tax evasion is ethical even if tax rates are not too high because the government is not entitled to take as much as it is taking from me	(6.38)
17	Tax evasion is ethical if the probability of getting caught is low	(6.36)
15	Tax evasion is ethical if everyone is doing it	(6.30)
15	Tax evasion is ethical even if most of the money collected is spent wisely	(6.30)
14	Tax evasion is ethical even if a large portion of the money collected is spent on projects that do benefit me	(6.13)
13	Tax evasion is ethical even if it means that if I pay less, others will have to pay more	(6.11)

Gender

Overall Mean Scores

Female: 5.78
Male: 5.55

Findings

Although females were more opposed to tax evasion in 16 of 18 cases, none of the mean scores were significantly different.

Conclusion: Women were slightly more opposed to tax evasion than were men.

ESTONIA

McGee, Robert W., Jaan Alver, and Lehte Alver. 2008. The Ethics of Tax Evasion: A Survey of Estonian Opinion, in Robert W. McGee, editor, *Taxation and Public Finance in Transition and Developing Economies* (pp. 461–480). New York: Springer.

Methodology

18 Statement Survey: Tax evasion is ethical if …
Sample: 300 graduate and undergraduate business students, faculty, and practitioners.
Range of scores (1 = strongly agree; 7 = strongly disagree):
Mean score: 5.54

Overall Findings

- Some arguments justifying tax evasion were significantly stronger than others.
- Gender: Women were significantly more opposed to tax evasion.
- Status: Overall, undergraduate students were least opposed to tax evasion; faculty members and practitioners were most opposed to tax evasion.

- Age: People under age 25 were significantly less opposed to tax evasion than were people in the 25–40 age-group. Differences in mean scores were not significant for other comparisons.
- Major: Accounting students and business and economics students were equally opposed to tax evasion.

Ranking

Strongest Arguments to Justify Tax Evasion

1. Tax evasion is ethical if a significant portion of the money collected winds up in the pockets of corrupt politicians or their families and friends (4.44)
2. Tax evasion is ethical if the government imprisons people for their political opinions (4.44)
3. Tax evasion is ethical if the government discriminates against me because of my religion, race, or ethnic background (4.66)
4. Tax evasion is ethical if the tax system is unfair (4.79)
5. Tax evasion is ethical if I were a Jew living in Nazi Germany (4.87)
6. Tax evasion is ethical if some of the proceeds go to support a war that I consider to be unjust (5.06)

Weakest Arguments to Justify Tax Evasion

18. Tax evasion is ethical even if it means that if I pay less, others will have to pay more (6.38)
17. Tax evasion is ethical even if most of the money collected is spent wisely (6.31)
16. Tax evasion is ethical even if tax rates are not too high because the government is not entitled to take as much as it is taking from me (6.29)
14. Tax evasion is ethical even if a large portion of the money collected is spent on worthy projects (6.25)
14. Tax evasion is ethical even if a large portion of the money collected is spent on projects that do benefit me (6.25)
13. Tax evasion is ethical if a large portion of the money collected is spent on projects that do not benefit me (6.22)

Gender

Overall Mean Scores

Female: 5.70
Male: 5.07
Females were more opposed to tax evasion in all 18 cases.

Status

Overall Mean Scores

Undergraduate students: 5.35
Graduate students: 5.60
Faculty: 5.78
Practitioners: 5.78

Overall, undergraduate students were least opposed to tax evasion; faculty members and practitioners were most opposed to tax evasion.

Age

Overall Mean Scores

<25: 5.40
25–40: 5.78
>40: 5.70

People under age 25 were significantly less opposed to tax evasion than were people in the 25–40 age-group. Differences in mean scores were not significant for other comparisons.

Major

Overall Mean Scores

Accounting students: 5.66
Business and economics students: 5.47

Overall, the differences in mean scores were not significant.

Estonia

McGee, Robert W., Jaan Alver, and Lehte Alver (2012). Tax Evasion Opinion in Estonia. In Robert W. McGee (Ed.), *The Ethics of Tax Evasion: Perspectives in Theory and Practice* (pp. 285–299). New York: Springer.

Methodology

18 Statement Survey: Tax evasion is ethical if ...
Sample: 539 accounting and other business students.
Range of scores (1 = strongly agree; 7 = strongly disagree): 3.84–6.30
Mean score: 5.25

Overall Findings

- Some arguments justifying tax evasion were significantly stronger than others.
- Gender: Women were significantly more opposed to tax evasion in all 18 cases.
- Age: People in the oldest age-group (over 40) were significantly more opposed to tax evasion than were people in the youngest age-group (under 25). People in the middle group (25–40) were significantly more opposed to tax evasion than were people in the younger group (under 25) in 13 of 18 cases.
- Student status: Accounting practitioners were often significantly more opposed to tax evasion than either graduate or undergraduate students.
- Major: Accounting majors were somewhat more opposed to tax evasion than the business/economics majors.

Ranking

Strongest Arguments to Justify Tax Evasion

1	Tax evasion is ethical if a significant portion of the money collected winds up in the pockets of corrupt politicians or their families and friends	(3.84)
2	Tax evasion is ethical if the government discriminates against me because of my religion, race, or ethnic background	(4.02)
2	Tax evasion is ethical if the government imprisons people for their political opinions	(4.02)
4	Tax evasion would be ethical if I were a Jew living in Nazi Germany in 1940	(4.45)
5	Tax evasion is ethical if the tax system is unfair	(4.48)
6	Tax evasion is ethical if some of the proceeds go to support a war that I consider to be unjust	(4.69)

Weakest Arguments to Justify Tax Evasion

18 Tax evasion is ethical even if most of the money collected is
     spent wisely   (6.30)
17 Tax evasion is ethical even if a large portion of the money
     collected is spent on worthy projects   (6.28)
16 Tax evasion is ethical even if a large portion of the money
     collected is spent on projects that do benefit me   (6.27)
15 Tax evasion is ethical even if it means that if I pay less, others
     will have to pay more   (6.18)
14 Tax evasion is ethical even if tax rates are not too high because
     the government is not entitled to take as much as it is taking
     from me   (6.17)
13 Tax evasion is ethical if a large portion of the money collected
     is spent on projects that do not benefit me   (5.88)

Gender

Overall Mean Scores

Female: 5.40
Male: 4.78

Findings

Women were significantly more opposed to tax evasion in all 18 cases.

Age

Overall Mean Scores

Under 25: 5.03
25–40: 5.51
Over 40:5.59

Findings

A comparison of the mean scores for the individual statements between the youngest and oldest group found that the mean scores for the oldest group were higher in all 18 cases, indicating consistently higher opposition to tax evasion. Calculation of the p values indicates that the difference in mean scores was often significant at the 1 or 5% level.

Conclusion: People in the oldest age-group (over 40) were significantly more opposed to tax evasion than were people in the youngest age-group (under 25). People in the middle group (25–40) were significantly more opposed to tax evasion than were people in the younger group (under 25) in 13 of 18 cases.

Student Status

Overall Mean Scores

Undergraduate Students: 5.14
Graduate Students: 5.17
Accounting Practitioners: 5.61

Findings

Although graduate students and undergraduate students generally hold the same opinion about tax evasion, for some arguments there are significant differences. Accounting practitioners were often significantly more opposed to tax evasion than either of the other two groups.

Academic Major

Overall Mean Scores

Accounting: 5.31
Other Business and Economics: 5.15

Findings

Accounting students were more opposed to tax evasion in 14 of 18 cases. The difference was significant at the 1% level in two cases, at the 5% level in one case and at the 10% level in two cases.

Conclusion: Accounting majors were somewhat more opposed to tax evasion than the business/economics majors.

France

McGee, Robert W. and Bouchra M'Zali. 2009. The Ethics of Tax Evasion: An Empirical Study of French EMBA Students, in Robert W. McGee, *Readings in Business Ethics* (pp. 185–199). Hyderabad, India: ICFAI University Press. An abbreviated version was published in Marjorie G. Adams and Abbass Alkhafaji, editors, *Business Research Yearbook: Global Business Perspectives*, Volume XIV, No. 1 (International Graphics: Beltsville, MD., 2007), 27–33.

Methodology

18 Statement Survey: Tax evasion is ethical if ...
Sample: 31 French MBA students.
Range of scores (1 = strongly agree; 7 = strongly disagree): 2.24–6.26
Mean score: 4.86

Overall Findings

- Some arguments justifying tax evasion were significantly stronger than others.
- Gender: Males were more opposed to tax evasion in 9/18 cases; women were more opposed in 9/18 cases. Statistical tests of significance were not done because of the small sample size.
- The three strongest arguments to justify tax evasion all had to do with human rights issues.

Ranking

Strongest Arguments to Justify Tax Evasion

1	Tax evasion would be ethical if I were a Jew living in Nazi Germany	(2.24)
2	Tax evasion is ethical if the government imprisons people for their political opinions	(3.00)
3	Tax evasion is ethical if the government discriminates against me because of my religion, race, or ethnic background	(3.45)
4	Tax evasion is ethical if a significant portion of the money collected winds up in the pockets of corrupt politicians or their families and friends	(3.81)
5	Tax evasion is ethical if a large portion of the money collected is wasted	(4.06)
6	Tax evasion is ethical if some of the proceeds go to support a war that I consider to be unjust	(4.26)

Weakest Arguments to Justify Tax Evasion

18	Tax evasion is ethical even if a large portion of the money collected is spent on projects that do benefit me	(6.26)
16	Tax evasion is ethical even if it means that if I pay less, others will have to pay more	(6.06)
16	Tax evasion is ethical even if most of the money collected is spent wisely	(6.06)
15	Tax evasion is ethical if the probability of getting caught is low	(6.03)
14	Tax evasion is ethical if a large portion of the money collected is spent on projects that do not benefit me	(6.00)
13	Tax evasion is ethical even if tax rates are not too high	(5.94)

Gender

Overall Mean Scores

Female: 4.74
Male: 4.89

Germany

McGee, Robert W., Inge Nickerson, and Werner Fees. 2009. When Is Tax Evasion Ethically Justifiable? A Survey of German Opinion, in Robert W. McGee, editor, *Readings in Accounting Ethics* (pp. 365–389). Hyderabad, India: ICFAI University Press.

Methodology

18 Statement Survey: Tax evasion is ethical if …
Sample: 71 German graduate and upper division undergraduate business school students.
Range of scores (1 = strongly agree; 7 = strongly disagree): 3.41–6.38
Mean score: 4.94

Overall Findings

- Some arguments justifying tax evasion were significantly stronger than others.

Ranking

Strongest Arguments to Justify Tax Evasion

1   Tax evasion is ethical if the government discriminates against
    me because of my religion, race, or ethnic background   (3.41)
2   Tax evasion would be ethical if I were a Jew living in Nazi
    Germany   (3.59)
3   Tax evasion is ethical if a significant portion of the money
    collected winds up in the pockets of corrupt politicians or their
    family and friends   (3.65)
4   Tax evasion is ethical if the government imprisons people for
    their political opinions   (3.69)
5   Tax evasion is ethical if a large portion of the money collected
    is wasted   (4.03)
6   Tax evasion is ethical if the tax system is unfair   (4.24)

Weakest Arguments to Justify Tax Evasion

18 Tax evasion is ethical even if most of the money collected is
    spent wisely   (6.38)
17 Tax evasion is ethical even if a large portion of the money
    collected is spent on projects that do benefit me   (6.31)
16 Tax evasion is ethical even if a large portion of the money
    collected is spent on worthy projects   (6.21)
15 Tax evasion is ethical if a large portion of the money collected
    is spent on projects that do not benefit me   (6.04)
14 Tax evasion is ethical if the probability of getting caught is low (6.00)
13 Tax evasion is ethical even if tax rates are not too high because
    government is not entitled to take as much as it is taking
    from me   (5.97)

Germany and USA

McGee, Robert W., Inge Nickerson, and Werner Fees. 2006. German and American Opinion on the Ethics of Tax Evasion. *Proceedings of the Academy of Legal, Ethical and Regulatory Issues* (Reno) 10(2): 31–34.

Methodology

18 Statement Survey: Tax evasion is ethical if …

Sample: 71 German graduate and upper division undergraduate business school students and 119 business students from St. Thomas University in Miami, USA.

Range of scores (1 = strongly agree; 7 = strongly disagree)

American Students: 4.91–6.17

German Students: 3.41–6.38

Mean scores

American Students: 5.62

German Students: 4.94

Overall Findings

- Some arguments justifying tax evasion were significantly stronger than others.
- Americans more opposed to tax evasion in 13/18 cases.
- Americans significantly more opposed to tax evasion in 11/18 cases.
- Germans significantly more opposed to tax evasion in 1/18 cases.
- Gender: American women were more opposed to tax evasion than were American men.

Ranking (American Only. The German Rankings Are Given Above for the 2009 German Study)

Strongest Arguments to Justify Tax Evasion

1	Tax evasion is ethical if the government discriminates against me because of my religion, race, or ethnic background	(4.91)
2	Tax evasion is ethical if the government imprisons people for their political opinions	(4.95)
3	Tax evasion would be ethical if I were a Jew living in Nazi Germany	(4.99)
4	Tax evasion is ethical if a large portion of the money collected is wasted	(5.15)
5	Tax evasion is ethical if the tax system is unfair	(5.19)
6	Tax evasion is ethical if I can't afford to pay	(5.43)

Weakest Arguments to Justify Tax Evasion

18 Tax evasion is ethical if everyone is doing it   (6.17)
17 Tax evasion is ethical if the probability of getting caught is low   (6.08)
16 Tax evasion is ethical even if most of the money collected is
    spent wisely   (6.00)
15 Tax evasion is ethical if a large portion of the money collected
    is spent on projects that do not benefit me   (5.98)
14 Tax evasion is ethical even if a large portion of the money
    collected is spent on worthy projects   (5.97)
13 Tax evasion is ethical even if a large portion of the money
    collected is spent on projects that do benefit me   (5.97)

Gender Findings

Gender data was not compiled for the German sample.
  For the American sample:

- Women were more opposed to tax evasion in all 18 cases.
- Women were significantly more opposed to tax evasion in 9 cases.

Guatemala

McGee, Robert W. and Christopher Lingle. 2008. The Ethics of Tax Evasion: A Survey of Guatemalan Opinion, in Robert W. McGee, editor, *Taxation and Public Finance in Transition and Developing Economies* (pp. 481–495). New York: Springer.

Methodology

18 Statement Survey: Tax evasion is ethical if …
Sample: 114 business/economics and law students.
Range of scores (1 = strongly agree; 7 = strongly disagree): 3.7–6.3
Mean score: 5.2

Overall Findings

- Some arguments justifying tax evasion were significantly stronger than others.

- Gender: Women were more opposed to tax evasion than were men.
- Major: Business students were more opposed to tax evasion than were law students.

Ranking

Strongest Arguments to Justify Tax Evasion

1 Tax evasion is ethical if a significant portion of the money collected winds up in the pockets of corrupt politicians or their families and friends   (3.7)
2 Tax evasion would be ethical if I were a Jew living in Nazi Germany   (4.0)
3 Tax evasion is ethical if the government discriminates against me because of my religion, race, or ethnic background   (4.3)
4 Tax evasion is ethical if a large portion of the money collected is wasted   (4.4)
5 Tax evasion is ethical if the tax system is unfair   (4.5)
6 Tax evasion is ethical if I can't afford to pay   (4.5)

Weakest Arguments to Justify Tax Evasion

18 Tax evasion is ethical even if a large portion of the money collected is spent on projects that do benefit me   (6.3)
17 Tax evasion is ethical even if most of the money collected is spent wisely   (6.3)
16 Tax evasion is ethical even if tax rates are not too high   (6.3)
15 Tax evasion is ethical if the probability of getting caught is low   (6.2)
14 Tax evasion is ethical if everyone is doing it   (6.2)
13 Tax evasion is ethical even if it means that if I pay less, others will have to pay more   (6.1)

Gender

Overall Mean Scores

Female: 5.49
Male: 5.14

Findings

Women were more opposed to tax evasion in 12/18 cases; Men were more opposed in 4/18 cases; opposition was equal in 2/18 cases.

Major

Overall Mean Scores

Business students: 5.3
Law students: 4.9

Findings

Business students were more opposed to tax evasion in 16/18 cases; law students were more opposed in 1/18 cases; both groups were equally opposed to tax evasion in 1/18 cases.

Haiti

McGee, Robert W. and Bouchra M'Zali (2012) The Ethics of Tax Evasion: A Study of Haitian Opinion. In Robert W. McGee (Ed.). *The Ethics of Tax Evasion: Perspectives in Theory and Practice* (pp. 301–308). New York: Springer.

Methodology

18 Statement Survey: Tax evasion is ethical if …
Sample: 32 accounting and business/economics students.
Range of scores (1 = strongly agree; 7 = strongly disagree): 3.73–5.47
Mean score: 4.45

Overall Findings

- Some arguments justifying tax evasion were significantly stronger than others.
- Gender: Women were somewhat more opposed to tax evasion than were men.

Ranking

Strongest Arguments to Justify Tax Evasion

1	Tax evasion is ethical if tax rates are too high	(3.73)
2	Tax evasion is ethical if the tax system is unfair	(3.80)
3	Tax evasion would be ethical if I were a Jew living in Nazi Germany in 1935	(3.86)
4	Tax evasion is ethical if a large portion of the money collected is wasted	(4.00)
5	Tax evasion is ethical even if most of the money collected is spent wisely	(4.07)
6	Tax evasion is ethical if some of the proceeds go to support a war that I consider to be unjust	(4.10)

Weakest Arguments to Justify Tax Evasion

18	Tax evasion is ethical even if a large portion of the money collected is spent on worthy projects	(5.47)
17	Tax evasion is ethical even if tax rates are not too high because the government is not entitled to take as much as it is taking from me	(5.03)
15	Tax evasion is ethical if everyone is doing it	(4.93)
15	Tax evasion is ethical even if a large portion of the money collected is spent on projects that do benefit me	(4.93)
14	Tax evasion is ethical if the probability of getting caught is low	(4.80)
13	Tax evasion is ethical even if it means that if I pay less, others will have to pay more	(4.70)

Gender

Overall Mean Scores

Female: 5.03
Male: 4.34

Findings

Women were more opposed to tax evasion for 13 of 18 statements. Only one difference in mean score was significant at the 5% level. A partial explanation for the dearth of significant differences might be due to the small sample size

Hispanics (Texas)

McGee, Robert W., Arsen M. Djatej and Robert H.S. Sarikas. (2012). The Ethics of Tax Evasion: A Survey of Hispanic Opinion. *Accounting & Taxation* 4(1): 53–74.

Methodology

18 Statement Survey: Tax evasion is ethical if ...
Sample: 316 business students at a university in South Texas.
Range of scores (1 = strongly agree; 7 = strongly disagree): 4.76–5.94
Mean score: 5.39

Overall Findings

- Some arguments justifying tax evasion were significantly stronger than others.
- Gender: No significant difference between male and female views.
- Age: No significant difference between the under 25 and 25+ groups.
- Major: Accounting students were significantly more opposed to tax evasion than were business and economics students.

Ranking

Strongest Arguments to Justify Tax Evasion

1	Tax evasion would be ethical if I were a victim of an oppressive regime or dictatorship similar to that in Stalinist Russia or Nazi Germany	(4.76)
2	Tax evasion is ethical if the tax system is unfair	(4.86)
3	Tax evasion is ethical if the government imprisons people for their political opinions	(4.91)
4	Tax evasion is ethical if the government discriminates against me because of my religion, race, or ethnic background	
5	Tax evasion is ethical if a significant portion of the money collected winds up in the pockets of corrupt politicians or their families and friends	(5.00)
6	Tax evasion is ethical if a large portion of the money collected is wasted	(5.06)

Weakest Arguments to Justify Tax Evasion

18 Tax evasion is ethical if the probability of getting caught is low   (5.94)
17 Tax evasion is ethical even if tax rates are not too high because
    the government is not entitled to take as much as it is taking
    from me   (5.81)
16 Tax evasion is ethical if everyone is doing it   (5.80)
15 Tax evasion is ethical even if it means that if I pay less, others will
    have to pay more   (5.79)
14 Tax evasion is ethical even if a large portion of the money
    collected is spent on projects that do benefit me   (5.76)
13 Tax evasion is ethical even if most of the money collected is
    spent wisely   (5.71)

Hong Kong and USA

McGee, Robert W., Simon S.M. Ho, and Annie Y.S. Li. 2008. A Comparative Study on Perceived Ethics of Tax Evasion: Hong Kong vs. the United States. *Journal of Business Ethics* 77(2): 147–158.

Methodology

15 Statement Survey (the 3 human rights issues were omitted): Tax evasion is ethical if …

Sample: 90 advanced undergraduate Hong Kong business students and 173 advanced undergraduate business students from Barry University in Miami.

Range of scores (1 = strongly agree; 7 = strongly disagree):

Hong Kong: 3.66–6.49

USA: 4.69–5.77

Mean score:

Hong Kong students: 5.25

US students: 5.36

Overall Findings

- Some arguments justifying tax evasion were significantly stronger than others.
- There were often significant differences when comparing the mean scores for individual statements but the overall difference in mean scores was not very significant.

Ranking: Hong Kong Sample

Strongest Arguments to Justify Tax Evasion

1 Tax evasion is ethical if a significant portion of the money
   collected winds up in the pockets of corrupt politicians or their
   families and friends   (3.66)
2 Tax evasion is ethical if some of the proceeds go to support a
   war that I consider to be unjust   (4.00)
3 Tax evasion is ethical if a large portion of the money collected
   is wasted   (4.18)
4 Tax evasion is ethical even if a large portion of the money
   collected is spent wisely   (4.39)
5 Tax evasion is ethical if the tax system is unfair   (4.54)

Weakest Arguments to Justify Tax Evasion

15 Tax evasion is ethical even if a large portion of the money
   collected is spent on projects that benefit me   (6.49)
14 Tax evasion is ethical even if a large portion of the money
   collected is spent on worthy projects   (6.42)
13 Tax evasion is ethical if a large portion of the funds collected
   are spent on projects that do not benefit me   (6.17)
12 Tax evasion is ethical even if tax rates are not too high because
   the government is not entitled to take as much as it is taking
   from me   (6.03)
11 Tax evasion is ethical even if it means that if I pay less, others
   will have to pay more   (6.02)

Ranking: US Sample

Strongest Arguments to Justify Tax Evasion

1 Tax evasion is ethical if a significant portion of the money
   collected winds up in the pockets of corrupt politicians or their
   families and friends   (4.69)
2 Tax evasion is ethical if the tax system is unfair   (4.80)
3 Tax evasion is ethical if I cannot afford to pay   (4.82)
4 Tax evasion is ethical if a large portion of the money collected
   is wasted   (4.92)
5 Tax evasion is ethical if some of the proceeds go to support a war
   that I consider unjust   (5.24)

Weakest Arguments to Justify Tax Evasion

15 Tax evasion is ethical if everyone is doing it (5.77)
14 Tax evasion is ethical even if most of the money collected is
   spent wisely (5.77)
13 Tax evasion is ethical even if it means that if I pay less, others
   will have to pay more (5.64)
12 Tax evasion is ethical even if a large portion of the money
   collected is spent on projects that benefit me (5.62)
11 Tax evasion is ethical even if a large portion of the money
   collected is spent on worthy projects (5.61)

Conclusion: There were often significant differences when comparing the mean scores for individual statements but the overall difference in mean scores was not very significant.

Hong Kong

McGee, Robert W. and Yiu Yu Butt. 2008. An Empirical Study of Tax Evasion Ethics in Hong Kong. Proceedings of the International Academy of Business and Public Administration Disciplines (IABPAD), Dallas, April 24–27: 72–83. Reprinted in Robert W. McGee (Ed.), *The Ethics of Tax Evasion: Perspectives in Theory and Practice*. New York, Springer, 2012, 309–320.

Methodology

15 Statement Survey (3 human rights arguments were omitted): Tax evasion is ethical if …
Sample: 60 Hong Kong business students.
Range of scores (1 = strongly agree; 7 = strongly disagree): 4.07–6.15
Mean: 5.06

Overall Findings

• Some arguments justifying tax evasion were significantly stronger than others.
• Gender: Males and females are equally opposed to tax evasion.

Ranking

Strongest Arguments to Justify Tax Evasion

1   Tax evasion is ethical if the tax system is unfair   (4.07)
2   Tax evasion is ethical if a significant portion of the money
    collected winds up in the pockets of corrupt politicians or their
    families and friends   (4.19)
3   Tax evasion is ethical if a large portion of the money collected
    is wasted   (4.47)
4   Tax evasion is ethical if some of the proceeds go to support a
    war that I consider to be unjust   (4.53)
5   Tax evasion is ethical if I can't afford to pay   (4.60)

Weakest Arguments to Justify Tax Evasion

15 Tax evasion is ethical even if a large portion of the money
    collected is spent on projects that benefit me   (6.15)
14 Tax evasion is ethical even if most of the money collected is
    spent wisely   (5.58)
13 Tax evasion is ethical even if a large portion of the money
    collected is spent on worthy projects   (5.57)
12 Tax evasion is ethical if the probability of getting caught is low   (5.47)
11 Tax evasion is ethical even if tax rates are not too high because
    the government is not entitled to take as much as it is taking
    from me   (5.37)

Gender

Overall Mean Scores

Female: 5.03
Male: 5.06

Findings

Women more opposed to tax evasion: 7/15
Men more opposed to tax evasion: 6/15
Equally opposed to tax evasion: 2/15
Conclusion: Males and females are equally opposed to tax evasion. The sample size was too small to do a valid statistical comparison.

India

McGee, Robert W. and Beena George (2008). Tax Evasion and Ethics: A Survey of Indian Opinion. *Journal of Accounting, Ethics & Public Policy*, 9(3), 301–332.

Methodology

18 Statement Survey: Tax evasion is ethical if ...
Sample: 149 graduate business students in Kerala.
Range of scores (1 = strongly agree; 7 = strongly disagree): 3.114–5.878
Mean score: 4.634

Overall Findings

- Some arguments justifying tax evasion were significantly stronger than others.
- Gender: The difference in male and female opinion is not significant.
- Religion: Hindus were slightly more opposed to tax evasion than were Christians.

Ranking

Strongest Arguments to Justify Tax Evasion

1	Tax evasion is ethical if the tax system is unfair	(3.114)
2	Tax evasion is ethical if a large portion of the money collected is wasted	(3.128)
3	Tax evasion is ethical if a significant portion of the money collected winds up in the pockets of corrupt politicians or their families and friends	(3.345)
4	Tax evasion is ethical if the government discriminates against me because of my religion, race, or ethnic background	(3.466)
5	Tax evasion is ethical if I can't afford to pay	(3.624)
6	Tax evasion is ethical if the government imprisons people for their political opinions	(3.811)

Weakest Arguments to Justify Tax Evasion

18	Tax evasion is ethical even if a large portion of the money collected is spent on worthy projects	(5.878)

17 Tax evasion is ethical even if a large portion of the money
    collected is spent on projects that do benefit me   (5.836)
16 Tax evasion is ethical even of most of the money collected is
    spent wisely   (5.819)
15 Tax evasion is ethical if everyone is doing it   (5.797)
14 Tax evasion is ethical if a large portion of the money collected
    is spent on projects that do not benefit me   (5.631)
13 Tax evasion is ethical if the probability of getting caught is
    low   (5.615)

Gender

Overall Mean Scores

Female: 4.591
Male: 4.689

Findings

Men were more opposed to tax evasion in 12 of 18 cases. Only one of the differences in mean scores was significant and only at the 10% level.

Conclusion: The difference in male and female opinion is not significant.

Religion

Overall Mean Scores

Christians: 4.541
Hindus: 4.673

Findings

Hindus were more opposed to tax evasion overall and also in 15 of 18 cases, but they were significantly more opposed (at the 5% level) in only one case.

Conclusion: Hindus were slightly more opposed to tax evasion than were Christians.

India

McGee, Robert W. and Ravi Kumar Jain. 2012. The Ethics of Tax Evasion: A Study of Indian Opinion, in Robert W. McGee (Ed.), *The Ethics of Tax Evasion: Perspectives in Theory and Practice* (pp. 321–336). New York: Springer.

Methodology

18 Statement Survey: Tax evasion is ethical if …
Sample: 468 accounting, business, and engineering (mostly graduate) students and faculty.
Range of scores (1 = strongly agree; 7 = strongly disagree): 3.57–5.93
Mean score: 4.88

Overall Findings

- Some arguments justifying tax evasion were significantly stronger than others.
- Gender: Men were slightly more opposed to tax evasion but the difference was significant in only 1 of 18 cases.
- Student status: Faculty were significantly more opposed to tax evasion than were graduate students. The undergraduate sample was too small to make comparisons.
- Major: Accounting students were slightly more opposed to tax evasion than were business/economics majors.

Ranking

Strongest Arguments to Justify Tax Evasion

1	Tax evasion is ethical if a large portion of the money collected is wasted	(3.57)
2	Tax evasion is ethical if a significant portion of the money collected winds up in the pockets of corrupt politicians or their families and friends	(3.61)
3	Tax evasion is ethical if the tax system is unfair	(3.72)
4	Tax evasion is ethical if the government discriminates against me because of my religion, race, or ethnic background	(4.03)
5	Tax evasion would be ethical if I were a victim of an oppressive regime like Nazi Germany or Stalinist Russia	(4.27)
6	Tax evasion is ethical if I can't afford to pay	(4.36)

Weakest Arguments to Justify Tax Evasion

18 Tax evasion is ethical even if most of the money collected is
    spent wisely   (5.93)
17 Tax evasion is ethical even if a large portion of the money
    collected is spent on worthy projects   (5.85)
16 Tax evasion is ethical if everyone is doing it   (5.74)
15 Tax evasion is ethical even if a large portion of the money
    collected is spent on projects that do benefit me   (5.71)
14 Tax evasion is ethical if the probability of getting caught is low   (5.66)
13 Tax evasion is ethical even if it means that if I pay less, others
    will have to pay more   (5.57)

Gender

Overall Mean Scores

Female: 4.82
Male: 4.93

Findings

Women were more opposed in 4 of 18 cases. Men were more opposed in 12 of 18 cases. Mean scores were identical in 2 cases. Men were significantly more opposed in only one case.

Conclusion: Men were slightly more opposed to tax evasion but the difference was only significant in one case.

Student Status

Overall Mean Scores (Only Two Groups Were Large
Enough for Comparison)

Graduate Students: 4.74
Faculty: 5.36

Findings

Overall, faculty were more opposed to tax evasion. Faculty were more opposed in 17 of 18 cases. In 13 cases, the difference was significant.

Conclusion: Faculty are significantly more opposed to tax evasion than are graduate students.

Academic Major

Overall Mean Scores

Accounting: 5.07
Other Business/Economics: 4.98

Findings

Accounting majors were more opposed to tax evasion in 10 of 18 cases. The mean scores were significantly different in only 1 case. (3 cases if one defines significance as 10%).

Conclusion: Accounting majors were slightly more averse to tax evasion than were business/economics majors.

International Business Academics

McGee, Robert W. 2006. A Survey of International Business Academics on the Ethics of Tax Evasion. *Journal of Accounting, Ethics & Public Policy* 6(3): 301–352.

Methodology

18 Statement Survey: Tax evasion is ethical if …
Sample: 79 international business professors and students.
Range of scores (1 = strongly agree; 7 = strongly disagree): 4.06–6.52
Mean score: 5.55

Overall Findings

- Some arguments justifying tax evasion were significantly stronger than others.
- Gender: Females were more opposed to tax evasion in all 18 cases.

Ranking

Strongest Arguments to Justify Tax Evasion

1 Tax evasion is not unethical if the government imprisons people
   for their political opinions   (4.06)
2 Tax evasion would not be unethical if I were a Jew living in
   Nazi Germany in 1935   (4.23)
3 Tax evasion is not unethical if a significant portion of the
   money collected winds up in the pockets of corrupt politicians
   or their families and friends   (4.35)
4 Tax evasion is not unethical if the government discriminates
   against me because of my religion, race, or ethnic background   (4.45)
5 Tax evasion is not unethical if the tax system is unfair   (5.03)
6 Tax evasion is not unethical if some of the proceeds go to
   support a war that I consider to be unjust   (5.03)

Weakest Arguments to Justify Tax Evasion

18 Tax evasion is not unethical even if a large portion of the
    money collected is spent on projects that do benefit me   (6.52)
17 Tax evasion is not unethical even if most of the money col-
    lected is spent wisely   (6.49)
16 Tax evasion is not unethical if the probability of getting caught
    is low   (6.48)
15 Tax evasion is not unethical even if a large portion of the
    money collected is spent on worthy projects   (6.43)
14 Tax evasion is not unethical if a large portion of the money
    collected is spent on projects that do not benefit me   (6.34)
13 Tax evasion is not unethical even if it means that if I pay less,
    others will have to pay more   (6.28)

Gender

Overall Mean Scores

Female: 5.60
Male: 4.95

Females were more opposed to tax evasion in all 18 cases.

Iran

McGee, Robert W. and Mahdi Nazemi Ardakani (2009). The Ethics of Tax Evasion: A Case Study of Opinion in Iran. Florida International University Working Paper.

Methodology

18 Statement Survey: Tax evasion is ethical if ...
Sample: 131 master's degree accounting students.
Range of scores (1 = strongly agree; 7 = strongly disagree): 3.58–6.45
Mean score: 5.06

Overall Findings

- Some arguments justifying tax evasion were significantly stronger than others.
- Gender: Men and women were equally opposed to tax evasion.

Ranking

Strongest Arguments to Justify Tax Evasion

1	Tax evasion is ethical if the tax system is unfair	(3.58)
2	Tax evasion is ethical if a significant portion of the money collected winds up in the pockets of corrupt politicians or their families and friends	(3.64)
3	Tax evasion is ethical if some of the proceeds go to support a war that I consider to be unjust	(3.67)
4	Tax evasion is ethical if a large portion of the money collected is wasted	(4.15)
5	Tax evasion is ethical if I can't afford to pay	(4.28)
6	Tax evasion is ethical if a large portion of the money collected is spent on projects that I morally disapprove of	(4.50)

Weakest Arguments to Justify Tax Evasion

18	Tax evasion is ethical even if a large portion of the money collected is spent on projects that do benefit me	(6.45)
17	Tax evasion is ethical even if a large portion of the money collected is spent on worthy projects	(6.41)

16 Tax evasion is ethical even if most of the money collected is
    spent wisely   (6.09)
15 Tax evasion is ethical if a large portion of the money collected
    is spent on projects that do not benefit me   (5.93)
13 Tax evasion is ethical if the probability of getting caught is low   (5.90)
13 Tax evasion is ethical if everyone is doing it   (5.90)

Gender

Overall Mean Scores

Female: 5.04
Male: 5.09

Findings

Women were more opposed to tax evasion in 9 cases. Men were more opposed
in 9 cases. None of the differences in mean scores were significant.

Jewish

McGee, Robert W. and Gordon M. Cohn. 2008. Jewish Perspectives on the Ethics
of Tax Evasion. *Journal of Legal, Ethical and Regulatory Issues*, 11(2): 1–32.

Methodology

18 Statement Survey: Tax evasion is ethical if …
Sample: 107 undergraduate Orthodox Jewish students at Touro College in
    New York. Many of the male students had rabbinical training. Most of the
    female students had a strong high school background in Jewish studies as
    well as post high school education.
Range of scores (1 = strongly agree; 7 = strongly disagree): 3.12–6.57
Mean score: 5.57

Overall Findings

• Some arguments justifying tax evasion were significantly stronger than
  others.
• Gender: Women were significantly more opposed to tax evasion than men.

Ranking

Strongest Arguments to Justify Tax Evasion

1	Tax evasion would be ethical if I were a Jew living in Nazi Germany in 1940	(3.12)
2	Tax evasion is ethical if the government discriminates against me because of my religion, race, or ethnic background	(3.30)
3	Tax evasion is ethical if a significant portion of the money collected winds up in the pockets of corrupt politicians or their families and friends	(4.61)
4	Tax evasion is ethical if the government imprisons people for their political opinions	(4.81)
5	Tax evasion is ethical if the tax system is unfair	(4.84)
6	Tax evasion is ethical if a large portion of the money collected is wasted	(5.24)

Weakest Arguments to Justify Tax Evasion

18	Tax evasion is ethical even if a large portion of the money collected is spent on projects that do benefit me	(6.57)
17	Tax evasion is ethical if the probability of getting caught is low	(6.54)
16	Tax evasion is ethical even if a large portion of the money collected is spent on worthy projects	(6.49)
15	Tax evasion is ethical even if most of the money collected is spent wisely	(6.44)
14	Tax evasion is ethical even if it means that if I pay less, others will have to pay more	(6.39)
13	Tax evasion is ethical if some of the proceeds go to support a war that I consider to be unjust	(6.38)

Gender

Overall Mean Scores

Female: 6.02
Male: 5.29

Findings

Females were more opposed to tax evasion in all 18 cases. Differences were significant in 8 cases (10 cases if significance is defined at 10%).

Conclusion: Females are significantly more averse to tax evasion than are men.

Kazakhstan

McGee, Robert W. and Galina G. Preobragenskaya. 2008. A Study of Tax Evasion Ethics in Kazakhstan, in Robert W. McGee, editor, *Taxation and Public Finance in Transition and Developing Economies* (pp. 497–510). New York: Springer.

Methodology

18 Statement Survey: Tax evasion is ethical if ...
Sample: 79 accounting and business students.
Range of scores (1 = strongly agree; 7 = strongly disagree): 3.190–5.241
Mean score: 4.143

Overall Findings

- Some arguments justifying tax evasion were significantly stronger than others.
- Gender: Men and women were equally opposed to tax evasion.
- Major: Accounting students and business/economics students were equally opposed to tax evasion.

Ranking

Strongest Arguments to Justify Tax Evasion

1	Tax evasion is ethical if the government discriminates against me because of my religion, race, or ethnic background	(3.190)
2	Tax evasion is ethical if a significant portion of the money collected winds up in the pockets of corrupt politicians or their families and friends	(3.253)
3	Tax evasion is ethical if the tax system is unfair	(3.316)
4	Tax evasion is ethical if I can't afford to pay	(3.582)
5	Tax evasion is ethical if a large portion of the money collected is wasted	(3.595)
6	Tax evasion is ethical if the government imprisons people for their political opinions	(3.7)

Weakest Arguments to Justify Tax Evasion

18	Tax evasion is ethical even if it means that if I pay less, others will have to pay more	(5.241)
17	Tax evasion is ethical if everyone is doing it	(4.987)
16	Tax evasion is ethical even if a large portion of the money collected is spent on projects that do benefit me	(4.949)
15	Tax evasion is ethical even if tax rates are not too high because the government is not entitled to take as much as it is taking from me	(4.835)
14	Tax evasion is ethical even if most of the money collected is spent wisely	(4.734)
13	Tax evasion is ethical if a large portion of the money collected is spent on projects that do not benefit me	(4.481)

Gender

Overall Mean Scores

Female: 4.172
Male: 4.112

Findings

Males were more opposed to tax evasion in 8/18 cases; females were more opposed to tax evasion in 10/18 cases. The overall differences and the differences for individual cases were not statistically significant.

Major

Overall Mean Scores

Accounting students: 4.103
Business/economics students: 4.192

Findings

Accounting students were more opposed to tax evasion in 8/18 cases; business/economics students were more opposed in 10/18 cases. The overall differences and the differences for individual cases were not statistically significant.

Macau

McGee, Robert W., Carlos Noronha, and Michael Tyler. 2007. The Ethics of Tax Evasion: A Survey of Macau Opinion. *Euro Asia Journal of Management* 17(2): 123–150. Reprinted in Robert W. McGee (editor), *Readings in Accounting Ethics* (pp. 283–313), Hyderabad, India: ICFAI University Press, 2009.

Methodology

15 Statement Survey (three human rights arguments were omitted): Tax evasion is ethical if …
Sample: 187 graduate and undergraduate business and economics students.
Range of scores (1 = strongly agree; 7 = strongly disagree): 3.5806–5.7957
Mean score: 4.94

Overall Findings

- Some arguments justifying tax evasion were significantly stronger than others.
- Gender: Men and women were equally opposed to tax evasion. Although the overall means were not significantly different, male mean scores were significantly higher than female mean scores for 3 of 15 statements.

Ranking

Strongest Arguments to Justify Tax Evasion

1	Tax evasion is ethical if a significant portion of the money collected winds up in the pockets of corrupt politicians or their families and friends	(3.5806)
2	Tax evasion is ethical if some of the proceeds go to support a war that I consider to be unjust	(3.6310)
3	Tax evasion is ethical if the tax system is unfair	(3.9519)
4	Tax evasion is ethical if a large portion of the money collected is wasted	(4.0376)
5	Tax evasion is ethical if I can't afford to pay	(4.3209)

Weakest Arguments to Justify Tax Evasion

15	Tax evasion is ethical even if a large portion of the money collected is spent on worthy projects	(5.7957)

14 Tax evasion is ethical even if most of the money collected is
    spent wisely   (5.7568)
13 Tax evasion is ethical even if a large portion of the money
    collected is spent on projects that benefit me   (5.7433)
13 Tax evasion is ethical even if tax rates are not too high
    because the government is not entitled to take as much as it
    is taking from me   (5.7433)
11 Tax evasion is ethical if a large portion of the money
    collected is spent on projects that do not benefit me   (5.5775)

Gender

Overall Mean Scores

Female: 4.9007
Male: 4.9973

Findings

Women more opposed to tax evasion: 7/15
Men more opposed to tax evasion: 7/15
Equally opposed to tax evasion: 1/15
Conclusion: Men and women were equally opposed to tax evasion. Although
    the overall means were not significantly different, male mean scores were
    significantly higher than female mean scores for 3 of 15 statements (1 at
    1%; 2 at 10%).

Mali

McGee, Robert W. and Bouchra M'Zali. 2008. Attitudes toward Tax Evasion in
Mali, in Robert W. McGee, editor, *Taxation and Public Finance in Transition and
Developing Economies* (pp. 511–517). New York: Springer.

Methodology

18 Statement Survey: Tax evasion is ethical if …
Sample: 25 executive MBA students.
Range of scores (1 = strongly agree; 7 = strongly disagree): 3.601–5.792
Mean score: 4.728526

Overall Findings

- Some arguments justifying tax evasion were significantly stronger than others.
- None of the scores were greater than 5.8, indicating that there is widespread support for tax evasion.

Ranking

Strongest Arguments to Justify Tax Evasion

1	Tax evasion is ethical if a large portion of the money collected is wasted	(3.601)
2	Tax evasion is ethical if I were a Jew living in Nazi Germany	(3.727)
3	Tax evasion is ethical if the tax system is unfair	(3.833)
4	Tax evasion is ethical if the government discriminates against me because of my religion, race, or ethnic background	(4.091)
5	Tax evasion is ethical if the government imprisons people for their political opinions	(4.091)
6	Tax evasion is ethical if a large portion of the money collected is spent on projects that I morally disapprove of	(4.348)

Weakest Arguments to Justify Tax Evasion

18	Tax evasion is ethical if a large portion of the money collected is spent on projects that do not benefit me	(5.792)
17	Tax evasion is ethical even if a large portion of the money collected is spent on projects that do benefit me	(5.522)
16	Tax evasion is ethical even if tax rates are not too high because the government is not entitled to take as much as it is taking from me	(5.478)
15	Tax evasion is ethical even if it means that if I pay less, others will have to pay more	(5.455)
14	Tax evasion is ethical if the probability of getting caught is low	(5.261)
13	Tax evasion is ethical if everyone is doing it	(5.174)

Mexico

McGee, Robert W., Yanira Petrides, and Adriana M. Ross (2012). Ethics and Tax Evasion: A Survey of Mexican Opinion. In Robert W. McGee (Ed.), *The Ethics of Tax Evasion: Perspectives in Theory and Practice* (pp. 387–403). New York: Springer.

Methodology

18 Statement Survey: Tax evasion is ethical if ...
Sample: 401 business and engineering students, faculty, and nonstudents.
Range of scores (1 = strongly agree; 7 = strongly disagree): 5.02–6.13
Mean score: 5.61

Overall Findings

- Some arguments justifying tax evasion were significantly stronger than others.
- Gender: although women were slightly more opposed to tax evasion, the differences based on gender were generally insignificant.
- Age: The under 25 group was significantly less opposed to tax evasion than the other two groups. The 25–40 group was most opposed to tax evasion. The over 40 group was between the other two groups.
- Major: Engineering students were most opposed to tax evasion. Other business/economics students were least opposed to tax evasion. Accounting students were in between the other two groups.
- Student status: Nonstudents were more opposed to tax evasion than were any other group. Undergraduate students were least opposed to tax evasion. Faculty were more opposed to tax evasion than either graduate or undergraduate students.

Ranking

Strongest Arguments to Justify Tax Evasion

1 Tax evasion is ethical if a significant portion of the money collected winds up in the pockets of corrupt politicians or their families and friends   (5.02)
2 Tax evasion is ethical if a large portion of the money collected is wasted   (5.09)
3 Tax evasion is ethical if the tax system is unfair   (5.10)
4 Tax evasion is ethical if I can't afford to pay   (5.19)
5 Tax evasion is ethical if the government discriminates against me because of my religion, race, or ethnic background   (5.25)
6 Tax evasion is ethical if tax rates are too high   (5.40)

Weakest Arguments to Justify Tax Evasion

18 Tax evasion is ethical if the probability of getting caught is low   (6.13)
17 Tax evasion is ethical even if tax rates are not too high because
    the government is not entitled to take as much as it is taking
    from me   (6.10)
16 Tax evasion is ethical even if it means that if I pay less, others
    will have to pay more   (6.04)
15 Tax evasion is ethical if everyone is doing it   (6.03)
14 Tax evasion is ethical even if most of the money collected is
    spent wisely   (6.02)
13 Tax evasion is ethical if a large portion of the money collected
    is spent on projects that do not benefit me   (5.88)

Gender

Overall Mean Scores

Female: 5.69
Male: 5.59

Findings

Although women were slightly more opposed to tax evasion, the differences based on gender were generally insignificant.

Age

Overall Mean Scores

Under 25: 5.38
25–40: 5.92
Over 40: 5.67

Findings

The under 25 group was significantly less opposed to tax evasion than the other two groups. The 25–40 group was most opposed to tax evasion. The Over 40 group was between the other two groups.

Academic Major

Overall Mean Scores

Accounting students: 5.53
Other business/economics students: 5.37
Engineering students: 5.66

Findings

Engineering students were most opposed to tax evasion. Other business/ economics students were least opposed to tax evasion. Accounting students were in between the other two groups.

Student Status

Overall Mean Scores

Graduate students: 5.65
Undergraduate students: 5.26
Faculty: 5.84
Nonstudents: 6.11

Findings

Nonstudents were more opposed to tax evasion than were any other group. Undergraduate students were least opposed to tax evasion. Faculty were more opposed to tax evasion than either graduate or undergraduate students.

Mormon [Church of Jesus Christ of Latter-Day Saints]

McGee, Robert W. and Sheldon R. Smith. 2007. Ethics, Tax Evasion and Religion: A Survey of Opinion of Members of the Church of Jesus Christ of Latter-Day Saints. Western Decision Sciences Institute, Thirty-Sixth Annual Meeting, Denver, April 3–7. Published in the Proceedings. Reprinted at http://ssrn.com/abstract=934652. Reprinted in Robert W. McGee (Ed.), *The Ethics of Tax Evasion: Perspectives in Theory and Practice*. New York, Springer, 2012, 211–226.

Methodology

18 Statement Survey: Tax evasion is ethical if ...
Sample: 638 accounting, business and economics, legal studies, and technol-
    ogy students at a large college in the Western United States (562 were
    Mormons).
Range of scores (1=strongly agree; 7=strongly disagree): 5.144–6.566
Mean score: 6.191 (LDS); 5.279 (non-LDS)

Overall Findings

- Some arguments justifying tax evasion were significantly stronger than
  others.
- Gender: Mormon women were significantly more opposed to tax evasion
  than Mormon men.
- LDS V. non-LDS: LDS mean scores were significantly (at 1%) higher than
  non-LDS scores in all 18 cases.

Ranking

Strongest Arguments to Justify Tax Evasion [LDS Only]

1 Tax evasion would be ethical if I were a Jew living in Nazi
   Germany in 1940   (5.144)
2 Tax evasion is ethical if the government imprisons people for
   their political opinions   (5.641)
3 Tax evasion is ethical if the government discriminates against
   me because of my religion, race, or ethnic background   (5.742).
4 Tax evasion is ethical if a significant portion of the money
   collected winds up in the pockets of corrupt politicians or
   their families and friends   (5.815)
5 Tax evasion is ethical if the tax system is unfair.   (5.973)
6 Tax evasioOn is ethical if a large portion of the money
   collected is wasted   (6.044)

Weakest Arguments to Justify Tax Evasion [LDS Only]

18 Tax evasion is ethical even if it means that if I pay less, others
   will have to pay more   (6.566)
17 Tax evasion is ethical if the probability of getting caught is low (6.553)
16 Tax evasion is ethical if everyone is doing it   (6.523)

15 Tax evasion is ethical even if most of the money collected is spent wisely (6.507)

14 Tax evasion is ethical even if a large portion of the money collected is spent on projects that do benefit me (6.48)

13 Tax evasion is ethical if a large portion of the money collected is spent on projects that do not benefit me (6.468)

Gender

Overall Mean Scores

Female: 6.349
Male: 6.123

Findings

Women were more opposed in 16/18 cases. They were significantly more opposed in 4 cases (at 1 or 5% level, or in five cases if significance is defined as 10%).

Conclusion: Women were significantly more opposed to tax evasion.

New Zealand

Gupta, Ranjana and Robert W. McGee. 2010. A Comparative Study of New Zealanders' Opinion on the Ethics of Tax Evasion: Students v. Accountants. *New Zealand Journal of Taxation Law and Policy* 16(1): 47–84.

Methodology

18 Statement Survey: Tax evasion is ethical if …
Sample: 620 graduate and undergraduate accounting, business/economics, and law students from the greater Auckland metropolitan area and 51 accounting practitioners.
Student survey results:
Range of scores (1 = strongly agree; 7 = strongly disagree): 3.717–5.477
Mean score: 4.659

Overall Findings

- Some arguments justifying tax evasion were significantly stronger than others.
- Gender: Women were more opposed to tax evasion.
- Age: Older people are more opposed to tax evasion than are younger people.
- Student status: Graduate students are more opposed to tax evasion than are undergraduate students.
- Major: Accounting and business and economics students are equally opposed to tax evasion; law students are somewhat less opposed to tax evasion than are the other groups.
- Ethnicity: The European group was significantly more opposed to tax evasion than were the other two groups. The Asian and Pasifika groups were equally opposed to tax evasion.
- Religion: Catholics were most opposed to tax evasion; Buddhists were least opposed.

Ranking

Strongest Arguments to Justify Tax Evasion

1	Tax evasion is ethical if a significant portion of the money collected winds up in the pockets of corrupt politicians or their families and friends	(3.717)
2	Tax evasion is ethical if the tax system is unfair	(3.771)
3	Tax evasion is ethical if a large portion of the money collected is wasted	(3.790)
4	Tax evasion is ethical if the government discriminates against me because of my religion, race, or ethnic background	(3.981)
5	Tax evasion is ethical if the government imprisons people for their political opinions	(4.053)
6	Tax evasion is ethical if I can't afford to pay	(4.344)

Weakest Arguments to Justify Tax Evasion

18	Tax evasion is ethical even if most of the money collected is spent wisely	(5.477)
17	Tax evasion is ethical even if it means that if I pay less, others will have to pay more	(5.402)
16	Tax evasion is ethical even if a large portion of the money collected is spent on worthy projects	(5.385)

15 Tax evasion is ethical even if a large portion of the money
    collected is spent on projects that do benefit me   (5.318)
14 Tax evasion is ethical if the probability of getting caught is
    low   (5.271)
13 Tax evasion is ethical if a large portion of the money collected
    is spent on projects that do not benefit me   (5.139)

Gender

Overall Mean Scores

Female: 4.743
Male: 4.583

Findings

Women more opposed to tax evasion: 14/18
Women significantly more opposed to tax evasion: 6/18
Men more opposed to tax evasion: 4/18
Conclusion: Women are more opposed to tax evasion.

Age

Overall Mean Scores

<25: 4.502
25–40: 4.940
40+: 5.239

Findings

The differences were significant for 30 of 54 comparisons.

Conclusion: People tend to become more opposed to tax evasion as they get
older.

Student Status

Overall Mean Scores

Graduate Students: 4.812
Undergraduate Students: 3.948

Findings

Graduate students more opposed to tax evasion: 15/18
Graduate students significantly more opposed to tax evasion: 6/18
Undergraduate students more opposed to tax evasion: 2/18
Equal opposition: 1/18
Conclusion: Graduate students are more opposed to tax evasion.

Academic Major

Overall Mean Scores

Accounting: 4.784
Business and Economics: 4.756
Law: 4.599

Findings

Accounting students most opposed to tax evasion: 9/18
Business and economics students most opposed to tax evasion: 9/18
Accounting students least opposed to tax evasion: 1/18
Business and economics students least opposed to tax evasion: 5/18
Law students least opposed to tax evasion: 12/18

Law students were significantly less opposed to tax evasion in only 3 of 36 comparisons to the other two groups.

Conclusions: Accounting and business and economics students are equally opposed to tax evasion; law students are somewhat less opposed to tax evasion than are the other groups.

Ethnicity

Overall Mean Scores

European: 5.012
Asian: 4.558
Pasifika: 4.575

Findings

Europeans most opposed to tax evasion: 16/18
Asians most opposed to tax evasion: 1/18
Pasifika most opposed to tax evasion: 1/18

Europeans least opposed to tax evasion: 1/18
Asians least opposed to tax evasion: 10/18
Pasifika least opposed to tax evasion: 7/18

None of the differences between the Asian and Pasifika groups were statistically significant. Differences between the European and Asian groups were significant in 15/18 cases; differences between the European and Pasifika groups were significant in 6/18 cases.

Conclusions: The European group was significantly more opposed to tax evasion than were the other two groups. The Asian and Pasifika groups were equally opposed to tax evasion.

Religion

Overall Mean Scores

Catholic: 4.949
Other Christian: 4.877
Muslim: 4.640
Buddhist: 4.293
Hindu: 4.439
None: 4.678
Conclusion: Catholics were most opposed to tax evasion; Buddhists were
    least opposed.

Accounting Practitioner Survey Results

Range of scores (1 = strongly agree; 7 = strongly disagree): 4.588–6.706
Mean score: 6.143

Overall Findings

• Some arguments justifying tax evasion were significantly stronger than others.

    Ranking (1 = strongly agree; 7 = strongly disagree)

Strongest Arguments to Justify Tax Evasion
1   Tax evasion would be ethical if I were a Jew living in Nazi
    Germany in 1940   (4.588)

2   Tax evasion would be ethical if a significant portion of the
    money collected winds up in the pockets of corrupt politi-
    cians or their families and friends   (5.078)
3   Tax evasion is ethical if the government discriminates
    against me because of my religion, race, or ethnic
    background   (5.392)
4   Tax evasion is ethical if the government imprisons people
    for their political opinions   (5.569)
5   Tax evasion is ethical if a large portion of the money
    collected is wasted   (5.902)
6   Tax evasion is ethical if the tax system is unfair   (5.961)

Weakest Arguments to Justify Tax Evasion

18 Tax evasion is ethical if the probability of getting caught is
    low   (6.706)
17 Tax evasion is ethical if everyone is doing it   (6.667)
16 Tax evasion is ethical even if the money collected is spent
    wisely   (6.647)
15 Tax evasion is ethical even if a large portion of the money
    collected is spent on worthy projects   (6.627)
14 Tax evasion is ethical even if tax rates are not too high
    because the government is not entitled to take as much as it is
    taking from me   (6.549)
13 Tax evasion is ethical even if it means that if I pay less, others
    will have to pay more   (6.490)

Comparison of students vs. Accounting practitioners:

Overall Mean Scores

Accounting Practitioners: 6.143
Students: 4.659

Overall Findings

*   Some arguments justifying tax evasion were significantly stronger than
    others.
*   Accounting practitioners were more opposed to tax evasion in 17/18 cases.
    The differences were significant at the 1% level in all 17 cases.
*   Accounting practitioners are significantly more opposed to tax evasion
    than are students.

Philosophy Professors

McGee, Robert W. (2012). Attitudes on the Ethics of Tax Evasion: A Survey of Philosophy Professors. In Robert W. McGee (Ed.), *The Ethics of Tax Evasion: Perspectives in Theory and Practice* (pp. 125–132). New York: Springer.

Methodology

18 Statement Survey: Tax evasion is ethical if …
Sample: 39 philosophy professors.
Range of scores (1 = strongly agree; 7 = strongly disagree): 3.82–6.46
Mean score: 5.36

Overall Findings

- Some arguments justifying tax evasion were significantly stronger than others.
- Gender: Women were significantly more opposed to tax evasion.

Ranking

Strongest Arguments to Justify Tax Evasion

1	Tax evasion would be ethical if I were a Jew living in Nazi Germany in 1940	(3.82)
2	Tax evasion is ethical if the government discriminates against me because of my religion, race, or ethnic background	(4.06)
3	Tax evasion is ethical if the government imprisons people for their political opinions	(4.14)
4	Tax evasion is ethical if a significant portion of the money collected winds up in the pockets of corrupt politicians or their families and friends	(4.53)
5	Tax evasion is ethical if the tax system is unfair	(4.59)
6	Tax evasion is ethical if some of the proceeds go to support a war that I consider to be unjust	(5.04)

Weakest Arguments to Justify Tax Evasion

18	Tax evasion is ethical if the probability of getting caught is low	(6.46)
17	Tax evasion is ethical even if it means that if I pay less, others will have to pay more	(6.37)

16 Tax evasion is ethical even if most of the money collected is
    spent wisely   (6.23)
15 Tax evasion is ethical even if a large portion of the money
    collected is spent on projects that do benefit me   (6.22)
14 Tax evasion is ethical if a large portion of the money collected
    is spent on projects that do not benefit me   (6.19)
13 Tax evasion is ethical even if a large portion of the money
    collected is spent on worthy projects   (6.16)

Gender

Overall Mean Scores

Female: 6.21
Male: 5.07

Findings

Women were more opposed to tax evasion in all 18 cases. The difference was
significant.

Poland

McGee, Robert W. and Arkadiusz Bernal. 2006. The Ethics of Tax Evasion:
A Survey of Business Students in Poland. In *Global Economy – How It Works* (Mina
Baliamoune-Lutz, Alojzy Z. Nowak & Jeff Steagall, eds.) (pp. 155–174). Warsaw:
University of Warsaw & Jacksonville: University of North Florida.

Methodology

18 Statement Survey: Tax evasion is ethical if …
Sample: 279 economics students at Poznan University of Economics.
Range of scores (1 = strongly agree; 7 = strongly disagree): 3.4–5.8
Mean score: 4.7

Overall Findings

- Some arguments justifying tax evasion were significantly stronger than others.
- Gender: No significant difference between male and female attitudes toward tax evasion.

Ranking

Strongest Arguments to Justify Tax Evasion

1	Tax evasion is ethical if a significant portion of the money collected winds up in the pockets of corrupt politicians or their families and friends	(3.4)
1	Tax evasion is ethical if the government discriminates against me because of my religion, race, or ethnic background	(3.4)
3	Tax evasion is ethical if a large portion of the money collected is wasted	(3.7)
3	Tax evasion is ethical if a large portion of the money collected is spent on projects that I morally disapprove of	(3.7)
5	Tax evasion would be ethical if I were a Jew living in Nazi Germany in 1940	(3.9)
6	Tax evasion is ethical if I can't afford to pay	(4.1)

Weakest Arguments to Justify Tax Evasion

18	Tax evasion is ethical even if most of the money collected is spent wisely	(5.8)
16	Tax evasion is ethical even if a large portion of the money collected is spent on projects that do benefit me	(5.7)
16	Tax evasion is ethical even if a large portion of the money collected is spent on worthy projects	(5.7)
14	Tax evasion is ethical even if it means that if I pay less, others will have to pay more	(5.6)
14	Tax evasion is ethical if the probability of getting caught is low	(5.6)
13	Tax evasion is ethical even if tax rates are not too high because the government is not entitled to take as much as it is taking from me	(5.5)

Gender

Overall Mean Scores

Female: 4.73
Male: 4.67

Findings

Males had higher scores for 5 of the 18 questions. Women had higher scores for 8 statements. In 5 cases, the male and female scores were the same.

Conclusion: There is no significant difference between male and female attitudes toward tax evasion.

Puerto Rico

McGee, Robert W. and Silvia López Paláu. 2007. The Ethics of Tax Evasion: Two Empirical Studies of Puerto Rican Opinion. *Journal of Applied Business and Economics* 7(3): 27–47 (2007). Reprinted in Robert W. McGee (editor), *Readings in Accounting Ethics* (pp. 314–342). Hyderabad, India: ICFAI University Press, 2009.

Methodology

18 Statement Survey: Tax evasion is ethical if …
Sample: 233 accounting and law students from the University of Puerto Rico.
Range of scores (1 = strongly agree; 7 = strongly disagree): 4.29–6.46
Mean score: 5.62

Overall Findings

- Some arguments justifying tax evasion were significantly stronger than others.
- Gender: Women more opposed to tax evasion in 16/18 cases.
- Women significantly more opposed in 3/18 cases.
- Major: Accounting students more opposed to tax evasion in 9/18 cases.
- Law students more opposed to tax evasion in 9/18 cases.
- Accounting students were significantly more opposed to tax evasion in only one case, where the money is spent on projects that do not benefit the taxpayer.

Ranking

Strongest Arguments to Justify Tax Evasion

1. Tax evasion is ethical if a significant portion of the money collected winds up in the pockets of corrupt politicians or their families and friends
2. Tax evasion is ethical if a large portion of the money collected is wasted

3 Tax evasion is ethical if the tax system is unfair
4 Tax evasion would be ethical if I were a Jew living in Nazi Germany
5 Tax evasion is ethical if the government imprisons people for their
   political opinions
6 Tax evasion is ethical if some of the proceeds go to support a war that I
   consider to be unjust

Weakest Arguments to Justify Tax Evasion

18 Tax evasion is ethical even if most of the money collected is spent
    wisely
17 Tax evasion is ethical even if tax rates are not too high because the
    government is not entitled to take as much as it is taking from me
16 Tax evasion is ethical even if a large portion of the money collected is
    spent on projects that do benefit me
15 Tax evasion is ethical if everyone is doing it
14 Tax evasion is ethical even if a large portion of the money collected is
    spent on worthy projects
13 Tax evasion is ethical even if it means that if I pay less, others will have
    to pay more

Gender

Overall Mean Scores

Female: 5.68
Male: 5.50

Major

Overall Mean Scores

Accounting: 5.63
Law: 5.45

Romania

McGee, Robert W. 2006. The Ethics of Tax Evasion: A Survey of Romanian
Business Students and Faculty. *The ICFAI Journal of Public Finance* 4(2): 38–68
(2006). Reprinted in Robert W. McGee and Galina G. Preobragenskaya, *Accounting
and Financial System Reform in Eastern Europe and Asia* (pp. 299–334). New
York: Springer, 2006.

Methodology

18 Statement Survey: Tax evasion is ethical if …
Sample: 134 graduate and upper division undergraduate business students.
Range of scores (1 = strongly agree; 7 = strongly disagree): 3.87–5.24
Mean score: 4.59

Overall Findings

- Some arguments justifying tax evasion were significantly stronger than others.
- Gender: Males were more opposed to tax evasion in 12/18 cases.

Ranking

Strongest Arguments to Justify Tax Evasion

1	Tax evasion is ethical if the tax system is unfair	(3.87)
2	Tax evasion is ethical if the government discriminates against me because of my religion, race, or ethnic background	(4.07)
3	Tax evasion is ethical if I can't afford to pay	(4.16)
4	Tax evasion is ethical if tax rates are too high	(4.17)
5	Tax evasion is ethical if a significant portion of the money collected winds up in the pockets of corrupt politicians or their families and friends	(4.18)
6	Tax evasion is ethical if the government imprisons people for their political opinions	(4.32)

Weakest Arguments to Justify Tax Evasion

18	Tax evasion is ethical if everyone is doing it	(5.24)
17	Tax evasion is ethical if the probability of getting caught is low	(5.16)
16	Tax evasion is ethical even if it means that if I pay less, others will have to pay more	(5.03)
15	Tax evasion is ethical even if tax rates are not too high	(5.00)
14	Tax evasion is ethical if a large portion of the money collected is spent on projects that do not benefit me	(4.95)
13	Tax evasion is ethical even if a large portion of the money collected is spent on projects that do benefit me	(4.86)

Gender

Overall Mean Scores

Female: 4.54
Male: 4.67

Six Countries (USA, Argentina, Guatemala, Poland, Romania, UK)

Nickerson, Inge, Larry P. Pleshko and Robert W. McGee. Presenting the Dimensionality of an Ethics Scale Pertaining to Tax Evasion. Journal of Legal, Ethical and Regulatory Issues, 12(1): 1–14 (2009).

Methodology

18 Statement Survey: Tax evasion is ethical if ...
Sample: 1,100 students in six countries.
Mean score:
USA: 5.62
Argentina: 5.4
Guatemala: 5.2
Poland: 4.7
Romania: 4.59
UK: 4.15

Overall Findings

- Some arguments justifying tax evasion were significantly stronger than others.
- Findings suggest that tax evasion has three overall perceptual dimensions across the items tested: (1) fairness, as related to the positive use of the money, (2) tax system, as related to the tax rates and negative use of the money, and (3) discrimination, as related to avoidance under certain conditions.

Ranking (Six Countries Combined)

Strongest Arguments to Justify Tax Evasion

1   Tax evasion is ethical if a significant portion of the money collected winds up in the pockets of corrupt politicians or their friends and family   (4.06)

2   Tax evasion is ethical if the government discriminates against
    me because of my religion, race, or ethnic background   (4.15)
3   Tax evasion is ethical if the tax system is unfair   (4.24)
4   Tax evasion would be ethical if I were a Jew living in Nazi
    Germany in 1940   (4.27)
5   Tax evasion is ethical if I cannot afford to pay   (4.29)
6   Tax evasion is ethical if a large proportion of the money
    collected is wasted   (4.33)

Weakest Arguments to Justify Tax Evasion

18 Tax evasion is ethical if the probability of getting caught is low   (5.73)
17 Tax evasion is ethical even if most of the money collected is
    spent wisely   (5.71)
16 Tax evasion is ethical if a large proportion of the money
    collected is spent on projects which do benefit me   (5.67)
15 Tax evasion is ethical if everyone is doing it   (5.66)
13 Tax evasion is ethical even if it means that if I pay less, others
    will have to pay more   (5.64)
13 Tax evasion is ethical even if tax rates are not too high   (5.64)

Slovakia

McGee, Robert W. and Radoslav Tusan. 2008. The Ethics of Tax Evasion: A Survey
of Slovak Opinion, in Robert W. McGee, editor, *Taxation and Public Finance in
Transition and Developing Economies* (pp. 575–601). New York: Springer.

Methodology

18 Statement Survey: Tax evasion is ethical if …
Sample: 184 business/economics, philosophy, and theology students.
Range of scores (1 = strongly agree; 7 = strongly disagree): 2.80–6.11
Mean score: 4.91

Overall Findings

• Some arguments justifying tax evasion were significantly stronger than
  others.

- Gender: Men were significantly more opposed to tax evasion than were women.
- Age: The older group was slightly more opposed to tax evasion than was the younger group.
- Major: Philosophy/Theology students were more opposed to tax evasion than were business/economics students.
- The study also analyzed the results of 66 other gender studies.

Ranking

Strongest Arguments to Justify Tax Evasion

1	Tax evasion would be ethical if I were a Jew living in Nazi German	(2.80)
2	Tax evasion is ethical if the government discriminates against me because of my religion, race, or ethnic background	(3.35)
3	Tax evasion is ethical if the government imprisons people for their political opinions	(3.95)
4	Tax evasion is ethical if a significant portion of the money collected winds up in the pockets of corrupt politicians or their families and friends	(4.04)
5	Tax evasion is ethical even if a large portion of the money collected is spent on projects that do benefit me	(4.61)
6	Tax evasion is ethical if a large portion of the money collected is wasted	(4.74)

Weakest Arguments to Justify Tax Evasion

18	Tax evasion is ethical even if tax rates are not too high because the government is not entitled to take as much as it is taking from me	(6.11)
17	Tax evasion is ethical even if most of the money collected is spent wisely	(5.91)
16	Tax evasion is ethical even if a large portion of the money collected is spent on worthy projects	(5.89)
15	Tax evasion is ethical if a large portion of the money collected is spent on projects that do not benefit me	(5.66)
14	Tax evasion is ethical if everyone is doing it	(5.41)
13	Tax evasion is ethical even if it means that if I pay less, others will have to pay more	(5.38)

Gender

Overall Mean Scores

Female: 4.84
Male: 5.13

Findings

Males were more opposed to tax evasion in 14/18 cases. Many of the mean scores were significantly different.

Major

Overall Mean Scores

Business: 5.01
Philosophy/Theology: 5.44

Philosophy/Theology students were more opposed to tax evasion in 17/18 cases.

Age

Overall Mean Scores

<25: 4.932
25 and older: 5.167

Findings

The older group was more opposed to tax evasion in 14/18 cases. The difference was significant at the 10% level in only two cases.

South Africa

McGee, Robert W. and Geoff A. Goldman (2010). Ethics and Tax Evasion: A Survey of South African Opinion. *Proceedings of the Third Annual University of Johannesburg Faculty of Management Conference*, May 12–14. Reprinted in Robert W. McGee (Ed.), *The Ethics of Tax Evasion: Perspectives in Theory and Practice*. New York, Springer, 2012, 337–356.

Methodology

18 Statement Survey: Tax evasion is ethical if …
Sample: 191 management, economics, and finance graduate and undergraduate students, mostly Christian, mostly under age 41, mostly African.
Range of scores (1 = strongly agree; 7 = strongly disagree): 4.168–5.847
Mean score: 4.967

Overall Findings

- Some arguments justifying tax evasion were significantly stronger than others.
- Gender: Women were somewhat more strongly opposed to tax evasion than men.
- Age: The 25–40-year-old group was somewhat more opposed to tax evasion than the under-25 group.
- Ethnicity: Whites were significantly more opposed to tax evasion than were Africans.
- Religion: Catholics and Other Christians were equally opposed to tax evasion (the difference in mean scores was not significant).
- Student status: Diploma students, undergraduate students, and postgraduate students were more or less equally opposed to tax evasion.
- Major: Management students and economics and finance students were equally opposed to tax evasion.

Ranking

Strongest Arguments to Justify Tax Evasion

1	Tax evasion is ethical if a large portion of the money collected is wasted	(4.168)
2	Tax evasion is ethical if the tax system is unfair	(4.316)
3	Tax evasion would be ethical if I lived under an oppressive regime like Nazi Germany or Stalinist Russia	(4.317)
4	Tax evasion is ethical if the government discriminates against me because of my religion, race, or ethnic background	(4.457)
5	Tax evasion is ethical if I can't afford to pay	(4.500)
6	Tax evasion is ethical if the government imprisons people for their political opinions	(4.603)

Weakest Arguments to Justify Tax Evasion

18 Tax evasion is ethical even if it means that if I pay less, others
      will have to pay more   (5.847)
17 Tax evasion is ethical if the probability of getting caught is low (5.720)
16 Tax evasion is ethical if everyone is doing it   (5.516)
15 Tax evasion is ethical even if most of the money collected is
      spent wisely   (5.314)
14 Tax evasion is ethical if a large portion of the money collected
      is spent on projects that do not benefit me   (5.307)
13 Tax evasion is ethical even if a large portion of the money
      collected is spent on projects that do benefit me   (5.282)

Gender

Overall Mean Scores

Female: 5.044
Male: 4.703

Findings

Women were more opposed to tax evasion in 15 of 18 cases. The difference
was significant in only two cases.

Conclusion: Women were somewhat more opposed to tax evasion than men.

Age

Overall Mean Scores

< 25: 4.867
25–40: 4.921

Findings

The older group was more opposed to tax evasion in 8 of 18 cases. The
difference was significant in 2 cases (or 3 cases if significance is defined
as 10%).

Ethnicity

Overall Mean Scores

White: 5.400
African: 4.759

Findings

Whites were more opposed to tax evasion in 17 of 18 cases. The difference was significant in 3 cases (4 if significance is defined as 10%).

Conclusion: Whites were significantly more opposed to tax evasion than were Africans.

Religion

Overall Mean Scores

Catholic: 4.996
Other Christian: 4.947

Findings

Catholics were more opposed to tax evasion in 10 of 18 cases. Other Christians were more opposed in 7 of 18 cases. In one case the mean scores were the same. None of the differences were significant.

Conclusion: Religion is not a significant variable.

Student Status

Overall Mean Scores

Diploma Students: 4.894
Undergraduate Students: 5.014
Postgraduate Students: 5.001

Findings

The diploma students were less opposed to tax evasion than were the other two groups. None of the differences in mean scores were significant, with the exception of Statement 14 (ability to pay). In that case, the undergraduate students were more opposed to tax evasion than were the other two groups.

Conclusion: Student status is not a significant variable.

Major

Overall Mean Scores

Management Majors: 5.073
Economics and Finance Majors: 4.870

Findings

Management students were more opposed to tax evasion in 11 of 18 cases. However, none of the differences were significant.

Conclusion: Major is not a significant variable.

Taiwan

McGee, Robert W. and Susana N. Vittadini Andres. 2009. The Ethics of Tax Evasion: Case Studies of Taiwan, in Robert W. McGee, *Readings in Business Ethics* (pp. 200–228). Hyderabad, India: ICFAI University Press. An abbreviated version was published in Marjorie G. Adams and Abbass Alkhafaji, editors, *Business Research Yearbook: Global Business Perspectives*, Volume XIV, No. 1 (pp. 34–39). Beltsville, MD: International Graphics: Beltsville, MD, 2007.

Methodology

15 Statement Survey (3 human rights arguments were omitted): Tax evasion is ethical if …
Sample: 196 students.
Range of scores (1 = strongly agree; 7 = strongly disagree): 3.27–5.78
Mean score: 4.72

Overall Findings

- Some arguments justifying tax evasion were significantly stronger than others.
- Gender: Women were more opposed to tax evasion.

Ranking

Strongest Arguments to Justify Tax Evasion

1	Tax evasion is ethical if a significant portion of the money collected winds up in the pockets of corrupt politicians or their families and friends	(3.27)
2	Tax evasion is ethical if the tax system is unfair	(3.28)
3	Tax evasion is ethical if a large portion of the money collected is wasted	(3.49)
4	Tax evasion is ethical if tax rates are too high	(4.12)
5	Tax evasion is ethical if I can't afford to pay	(4.24)

Weakest Arguments to Justify Tax Evasion

15	Tax evasion is ethical even if a large portion of the money collected is spent on worthy projects	(5.78)
14	Tax evasion is ethical even if most of the money collected is spent wisely	(5.70)
13	Tax evasion is ethical even if it means that if I pay less, others will have to pay more	(5.46)
12	Tax evasion is ethical even if a large portion of the money collected is spent on projects that benefit me	(5.45)
11	Tax evasion is ethical if a large portion of the money collected is spent on projects that do not benefit me	(5.17)

Gender

Overall Mean Scores

Female: 4.91
Male: 4.45

Findings

Women more opposed to tax evasion: 13/15
Men more opposed to tax evasion: 2/15

Conclusion: Overall, women were significantly more opposed to tax evasion ($p = 0.0027$). Females were significantly more opposed to tax evasion in 6 of 15 cases.

Taiwan and USA

Andres, Susana N. Vittadini and Robert W. McGee. 2007. The Ethics of Tax Evasion: A Comparative Study of Taiwan and the USA. Kaoshiung Hsien, Republic of China. Chinese Association of Political Science, September 29–30.

Methodology

15 Statement Survey: Tax evasion is ethical if … (The three human rights arguments were omitted from this survey.)
Sample: 196 (Taiwan); 232 (USA) students. 428 total.
Range of scores (1 = strongly agree; 7 = strongly disagree):
Taiwan: 3.27–5.78
USA: 5.40–6.22
Mean score:
Taiwan: 4.72
USA: 6.00
Conclusion: The US students were significantly more opposed to tax evasion than were the Taiwan students.

Overall Findings

- Some arguments justifying tax evasion were significantly stronger than others.
- The US students were significantly more opposed to tax evasion than were the Taiwan students.
- Gender: Taiwan women were significantly more opposed to tax evasion than were Taiwan men. The differences in mean scores for the USA sample were not significant.

Ranking (Taiwan)

Strongest Arguments to Justify Tax Evasion

1   Tax evasion is ethical if a significant portion of the money
    collected winds up in the pockets of corrupt politicians or their
    families and friends   (3.27)
2   Tax evasion is ethical if the system is unfair   (3.28)
3   Tax evasion is ethical if a large portion of the money collected
    is wasted   (3.49)
4   Tax evasion is ethical if tax rates are too high   (4.12)
5   Tax evasion is ethical if I can't afford to pay   (4.24)
6   Tax evasion is ethical if some of the proceeds go to support a
    war that I consider to be unjust   (4.33)

Weakest Arguments to Justify Tax Evasion

15 Tax evasion is ethical even if a large portion of the money
    collected is spent on worthy projects   (5.78)
14 Tax evasion is ethical even if most of the money collected is
    spent wisely   (5.70)
13 Tax evasion is ethical even if it means that if I pay less, others
    will have to pay more   (5.46)

Ranking (USA)

Strongest Arguments to Justify Tax Evasion

1   Tax evasion is ethical if a significant portion of the money
    collected winds up in the pockets of corrupt politicians or their
    families and friends   (5.40)
2   Tax evasion is ethical if the tax system is unfair   (5.45)
3   Tax evasion is ethical if a large portion of the money collected
    is wasted   (5.51)
4   Tax evasion is ethical if tax rates are too high   (6.05)
5   Tax evasion is ethical if a large portion of the money collected
    is spent on projects that I morally disapprove of   (5.94)
6   Tax evasion is ethical if tax rates are too high   (6.05)

Weakest Arguments to Justify Tax Evasion

15 Tax evasion is ethical even if most of the money is spent wisely   (6.39)
14 Tax evasion is ethical even if it means that if I pay less, others
    will have to pay more   (6.26)

13 Tax evasion is ethical if a large portion of the money collected
  is spent on projects that do not benefit me   (6.25)

Gender

Overall Mean Scores (Taiwan)

Female: 4.91
Male: 4.45

Findings

Taiwan: Females were more opposed to tax evasion in 13 of 15 cases. The
  differences were significant in 6 of 15 cases.
Conclusion: Women were significantly more opposed to tax evasion than men
  in Taiwan. Male and female differences were not significant for the USA
  sample.

Thailand

McGee, Robert W. 2008. Opinions on Tax Evasion in Thailand, in Robert
W. McGee, editor, *Taxation and Public Finance in Transition and Developing
Economies* (pp. 609–620). New York: Springer.

Methodology

18 Statement Survey: Tax evasion is ethical if ...
Sample: 41 undergraduate accounting students.
Range of scores (1 = strongly agree; 7 = strongly disagree): 3.13–6.28
Mean score: 4.94

Overall Findings

- Some arguments justifying tax evasion were significantly stronger than
  others.
- Gender: Females were more opposed to tax evasion than were men.

Ranking

Strongest Arguments to Justify Tax Evasion

1	Tax evasion is ethical if a significant portion of the money collected winds up in the pockets of corrupt politicians or their families and friends	(3.13)
2	Tax evasion is ethical if the tax system is unfair	(3.75)
3	Tax evasion is ethical if a large portion of the money collected is wasted	(3.81)
4	Tax evasion is ethical if I can't afford to pay	(3.81)
5	Tax evasion would be ethical if I were a Jew living in Nazi Germany	(3.93)
6	Tax evasion is ethical if the government discriminates against me because of my religion, race, or ethnic background	(3.96)

Weakest Arguments to Justify Tax Evasion

18	Tax evasion is ethical even if a large portion of the money collected is spent on worthy projects	(6.28)
17	Tax evasion is ethical even if most of the money collected is spent wisely	(6.06)
16	Tax evasion is ethical if a large portion of the money collected is spent on projects that do not benefit me	(5.97)
15	Tax evasion is ethical if the probability of getting caught is low	(5.91)
14	Tax evasion is ethical even if a large portion of the money collected is spent on projects that do benefit me	(5.91)
13	Tax evasion is ethical even if it means that if I pay less, others will have to pay more	(5.90)

Gender

Overall Mean Scores

Female: 5.00
Male: 3.98

Findings

Females were more opposed to tax evasion in 15/18 cases. In 5 cases, the difference in mean score was significant. However, the sample size was small and there were only 8 males in the class, so the statistical finding is weak.

Turkey

McGee, Robert W. and Serkan Benk. The Ethics of Tax Evasion: A Study of Turkish Opinion, *Journal of Balkan & Near Eastern Studies* 13(2): 249–262 (2011).

Methodology

18 Statement Survey: Tax evasion is ethical if ...
Sample: 291 undergraduate business and economics students at 3 Turkish universities.
Range of scores (1 = strongly agree; 7 = strongly disagree): 3.609–6.038
Mean score: 4.826

Overall Findings

* Some arguments justifying tax evasion were significantly stronger than others.
* Gender: Men were significantly more opposed to tax evasion.
* Age: Older people are more opposed to tax evasion than are younger people.

Ranking

Strongest Arguments to Justify Tax Evasion

1	Tax evasion is ethical if a significant portion of the money collected winds up in the pockets of corrupt politicians or their families and friends	(3.609)
2	Tax evasion is ethical if a large portion of the money collected is wasted	(3.766)
3	Tax evasion would be ethical if I lived under an oppressive regime like Nazi Germany or Stalinist Russia	(3.855)
4	Tax evasion is ethical if the tax system is unfair	(3.955)
5	Tax evasion is ethical if the government discriminates against me because of my religion, race, or ethnic background	(3.951)
6	Tax evasion is ethical if some of the proceeds go to support a war that I consider to be unjust	(4.031)

Weakest Arguments to Justify Tax Evasion

18	Tax evasion is ethical even if a large portion of the money collected is spent on worthy projects	(6.038)
17	Tax evasion is ethical even if a large portion of the money collected is spent on projects that do benefit me	(5.931)
16	Tax evasion is ethical even if most of the money collected is spent wisely	(5.890)
15	Tax evasion is ethical even if it means that if I pay less, others will have to pay more	(5.760)
14	Tax evasion is ethical even if tax rates are not too high because the government is not entitled to take as much as it is taking from me	(5.735)
13	Tax evasion is ethical if the probability of getting caught is low	(5.699)

Gender

Overall Mean Scores

Female: 4.649
Male: 5.048

Findings

Men more opposed to tax evasion: 18/18
Men significantly more opposed to tax evasion 8/18

Conclusion: Men were significantly more opposed to tax evasion.

Age

Overall Mean Scores

<25: 4.804
25–40: 5.121

Findings

The younger group was *less opposed* to tax evasion in 17 of 18 cases.
    The younger group was *significantly less opposed* to tax evasion in 4 of 18 cases.

Conclusion: People tend to become more opposed to tax evasion as they get older.

Turkey

McGee, Robert W., Serkan Benk, Halil Yıldırım, and Murat Kayıkçı. 2011. The Ethics of Tax Evasion: A Study of Turkish Tax Practitioner Opinion, *European Journal of Social Sciences* 18(3): 468–480.

Methodology

18 Statement Survey: Tax evasion is ethical if …
Sample: 176 Turkish accounting practitioners.
Range of scores (1 = strongly agree; 7 = strongly disagree): 3.8807–6.2670
Mean score: 5.2544

Overall Findings

- Some arguments justifying tax evasion were significantly stronger than others.
- Gender: Men were significantly more opposed to tax evasion.
- Age: Older people are more opposed to tax evasion than are younger people.

Ranking

Strongest Arguments to Justify Tax Evasion

1	Tax evasion is ethical if a significant portion of the money collected winds up in the pockets of corrupt politicians or their families and friends	(3.8807)
2	Tax evasion is ethical if the tax system is unfair	(4.3409)
3	Tax evasion is ethical if a large portion of the money collected is wasted	(4.4716)
4	Tax evasion would be ethical if I lived under an oppressive regime like Nazi Germany or Stalinist Russia	(4.6193)
5	Tax evasion is ethical if some of the proceeds go to support a war that I consider to be unjust	(4.6591)
6	Tax evasion is ethical if tax rates are too high	(4.7159)

Weakest Arguments to Justify Tax Evasion

18	Tax evasion is ethical even if most of the money collected is spent wisely	(6.2670)
17	Tax evasion is ethical even if a large portion of the money collected is spent on worthy projects	(6.1705)
16	Tax evasion is ethical even if a large portion of the money collected is spent on projects that do benefit me	(6.1591)
15	Tax evasion is ethical even if it means that if I pay less, others will have to pay more	(6.0966)
14	Tax evasion is ethical if the probability of getting caught is low	(5.9886)
13	Tax evasion is ethical even if tax rates are not too high because the government is not entitled to take as much as it is taking from me	(5.9545)

Gender

Overall Mean Scores

Female: 4.9693
Male: 5.4297

Findings

Men more opposed to tax evasion: 18/18
Men significantly more opposed to tax evasion: 11/18

Conclusion: Men were significantly more opposed to tax evasion.

Age

Overall Mean Scores

<26: 4.8889
26–40: 5.3012
>40: 5.3092

Findings

The younger group was *least opposed* to tax evasion in 16 of 18 cases.
    The 26–40 group and the 41+ group were equally opposed to tax evasion.

Conclusion: Older people are more opposed to tax evasion than are younger people.

Ukraine

Nasadyuk, Irina and Robert W. McGee. 2007. The Ethics of Tax Evasion: Lessons for Transitional Economies. In Greg N. Gregoriou and C. Read (eds.), *International Taxation* (pp. 291–310). Elsevier.

Methodology

18 Statement Survey: Tax evasion is ethical if …
Note: The scale used in this study is different from the scale used in most other studies.
Sample: 99 law students from the Odessa National Law Academy.
Range of scores (0 = strongly disagree; 6 = strongly agree): 1.18–4.24.
Mean score: 2.575

Overall Findings

- Some arguments justifying tax evasion were significantly stronger than others.
- Gender: Men and women were equally opposed to tax evasion.

Ranking

Strongest Arguments to Justify Tax Evasion

1	Tax evasion is ethical if tax rates are too high	(4.24)
2	Tax evasion is ethical if the government imprisons people for their political opinions	(4.08)
3	Tax evasion is ethical if the tax system is unfair	(4.00)
4	Tax evasion is ethical if a significant portion of the money collected winds up in the pockets of corrupt politicians or their families and friends	(3.94)
5	Tax evasion is ethical if the government discriminates against me because of my religion, race, or ethnic background	(3.75)
6	Tax evasion is ethical if I can't afford to pay	(3.61)

Weakest Arguments to Justify Tax Evasion

18	Tax evasion is ethical even if a large portion of the money collected is spent on worthy projects	(1.18)

17 Tax evasion is ethical even if a large portion of the money
     collected is spent on projects that do benefit me   (1.23)
15 Tax evasion is ethical even if tax rates are not too high   (1.36)
15 Tax evasion is ethical even if most of the money collected is
     spent wisely   (1.36)
14 Tax evasion is ethical if everyone is doing it   (1.47)
13 Tax evasion is ethical even if it means that if I pay less, others
     will have to pay more   (1.48)

Gender

Overall Mean Scores

Female: 2.51
Male: 2.74

Findings

Women were more opposed to tax evasion in 13 of 18 cases. However, none
of the differences in mean score were significant.

Ukraine

Nasadyuk, Irina and Robert W. McGee. 2008. The Ethics of Tax Evasion: An
Empirical Study of Business and Economics Student Opinion in Ukraine, in Robert
W. McGee (Ed.), *Taxation and Public Finance in Transition and Developing
Economies* (pp. 639–661). New York: Springer. A different version of this study
that included comparative data was published under the title Ethics and Tax Evasion
in Ukraine: An Empirical and Comparative Study, in *Accounting and Finance in
Transition* 5: 169–198 (2008).

Methodology

18 Statement Survey: Tax evasion is ethical if …
NOTE: The scale is different for this study than for most other studies.
Sample: 161 graduate and advanced undergraduate accounting and econom-
     ics students.
Range of scores (0 = strongly disagree; 6 = strongly agree): 1.01–4.24
Mean score: 2.69

Overall Findings

- Some arguments justifying tax evasion were significantly stronger than others.

Ranking

Strongest Arguments to Justify Tax Evasion

1   Tax evasion is ethical if a significant portion of the money collected winds up in the pockets of corrupt politicians or their families and friends   (4.24)
2   Tax evasion is ethical if the government imprisons people for their political opinions   (4.23)
3   Tax evasion is ethical if the tax system is unfair   (4.13)
4   Tax evasion is ethical if the government discriminates against me because of my religion, race, or ethnic background   (4.10)
5   Tax evasion is ethical if tax rates are too high   (3.71)
6   Tax evasion is ethical if a large portion of the money collected is wasted   (3.66)

Weakest Arguments to Justify Tax Evasion

18 Tax evasion is ethical even if most of the money collected is   (1.01)
    spent wisely
17 Tax evasion is ethical even if a large portion of the money   (1.32)
    collected is spent on projects that do benefit me
16 Tax evasion is ethical even if tax rates are not too high   (1.34)
15 Tax evasion is ethical even if a large portion of the money   (1.48)
    collected is spent on worthy projects
14 Tax evasion is ethical even if it means that if I pay less, others   (1.57)
    will have to pay more
13 Tax evasion is ethical if everyone is doing it   (1.66)

USA and Four Latin American Countries

McGee, Robert W. and Silvia López Paláu. 2008. Tax Evasion and Ethics: A Comparative Study of the USA and Four Latin American Countries, in Robert W. McGee, editor, *Taxation and Public Finance in Transition and Developing Economies* (pp. 185–224). New York: Springer.

Methodology

18 Statement Survey: Tax evasion is ethical if …

Sample: 1,195 accounting, business and economics students in the USA, Colombia, Ecuador, Puerto Rico, and the Dominican Republic.

Range of scores (1 = strongly agree; 7 = strongly disagree): 4.73–6.05 for five countries

Mean score: 5.53 average for five countries

Overall Findings

- Some arguments justifying tax evasion were significantly stronger than others.
- Countries: The USA was more opposed to tax evasion than was the Latin American sample in total, but Colombia was more opposed to tax evasion than were any of the other countries.
- Ethnicity: US Hispanics were more opposed to tax evasion than was the total US sample.
- Countries: Scores for the Dominican Republic were substantially and consistently lower than for the other countries, indicating that tax evasion was less of a moral problem for the average Dominican than for the other four groups sampled.
- Gender: Women were more opposed to tax evasion in 17/18 cases; women were significantly more opposed to tax evasion in 5/18 cases.
- Gender differences were most significant for the three human rights arguments.
- Major: Business students were more opposed to tax evasion than were accounting students in 17/18 cases; the difference was significant in 14/18 cases.

Ranking: Average for Five Countries

Strongest Arguments to Justify Tax Evasion

1 Tax evasion is ethical if a large portion of the money collected is wasted   (4.73)
2 Tax evasion is ethical if a significant portion of the money collected winds up in the pockets of corrupt politicians or their families and friends   (4.75)
3 Tax evasion is ethical if the tax system is unfair   (4.92)
4 Tax evasion is ethical if I can't afford to pay   (5.11)

5   Tax evasion is ethical would be ethical if I were a Jew living in
    Nazi Germany   (5.15)
6   Tax evasion is ethical if some of the proceeds go to support a
    war that I consider to be unjust   (5.39)

Weakest Arguments to Justify Tax Evasion

18 Tax evasion is ethical if the probability of getting caught is low   (6.05)
17 Tax evasion is ethical even if tax rates are not too high because
    the government is not entitled to take as much as it is taking
    from me   (6.03)
16 Tax evasion is ethical even if it means that if I pay less, others
    will have to pay more   (6.01)
15 Tax evasion is ethical even if most of the money collected is
    spent wisely   (5.98)
14 Tax evasion is ethical if everyone is doing it   (5.96)
13 Tax evasion is ethical even if a large portion of the money
    collected is spent on projects that do benefit me   (5.93)

Country

Overall Mean Scores

USA: 5.78
US Hispanics: 5.84
Four Latin American Countries Combined: 5.49
Colombia: 6.03
Ecuador: 5.67
Puerto Rico: 5.62
Dominican Republic: 4.57

Gender

Overall Mean Scores

Female: 5.65
Male: 5.53

Major

Overall Mean Scores

Accounting: 5.42
Business: 5.75

USA: Utah

McGee, Robert W. and Sheldon R. Smith (2007). Ethics and Tax Evasion: A Comparative Study of Accounting and Business Student Opinion in Utah. American Society of Business and Behavioral Sciences 14th Annual Meeting, Las Vegas, February 22–25, 2007. Published in the Proceedings of the American Society of Business and Behavioral Sciences 14(1): 1175–1185.

Methodology

18 Statement Survey: Tax evasion is ethical if …
Sample: 202 accounting majors and 300 other business majors [502 total].
Range of scores (1 = strongly agree; 7 = strongly disagree): 5.075–6.138
Mean score:
Accounting Students: 6.119
Business Students: 6.151

Overall Findings

- Some arguments justifying tax evasion were significantly stronger than others.
- Major: Business students were slightly more opposed to tax evasion than were accounting students but the difference was not significant.

Ranking

Strongest Arguments to Justify Tax Evasion

1	Tax evasion would be ethical if I were a Jew living in Nazi Germany in 1940	(5.075)
2	Tax evasion is ethical if the government imprisons people for their political opinions	(5.569)
3	Tax evasion is ethical if a significant portion of the money collected winds up in the pockets of corrupt politicians or their families and friends	(5.683)
4	Tax evasion is ethical if the government discriminates against me because of my religion, race, or ethnic background	(5.688)
5	Tax evasion is ethical if the tax system is unfair	(5.861)
6	Tax evasion is ethical if a large portion of the money collected is wasted	(6.010)

Weakest Arguments to Justify Tax Evasion

18 Tax evasion is ethical even if it means that if I pay less, others
    will have to pay more   (6.518)
17 Tax evasion is ethical if the probability of getting caught is low   (6.516)
16 Tax evasion is ethical if everyone is doing it   (6.490)
15 Tax evasion is ethical even if most of the money collected is
    spent wisely   (6.486)
14 Tax evasion is ethical even if a large portion of the money
    collected is spent on projects that do benefit me   (6.454)
13 Tax evasion is ethical even if a large portion of the money
    collected is spent on worthy projects   (6.452)

Major

Overall Mean Scores

Accounting: 6.119
Business: 6.151

Findings

Business majors were more opposed to tax evasion than were accounting
majors in 15 of 18 cases. However, none of the differences were significant.

USA: Utah and Florida

McGee, Robert W. and Sheldon R. Smith. 2009. Ethics and Tax Evasion:
A Comparative Study of Utah and Florida Opinion, in Robert W. McGee (Ed.),
Readings in Accounting Ethics (pp. 343–364). Hyderabad, India: ICFAI University
Press.

Methodology

18 Statement Survey: Tax evasion is ethical if …
Sample: 319 accounting majors in Utah (202) and Florida (117).
Range of scores (1 = strongly agree; 7 = strongly disagree): Florida 5.24–6.36;
    Utah 5.26–6.51
Mean score: Utah 6.12; Florida 5.83

Overall Findings

- Some arguments justifying tax evasion were significantly stronger than others.
- Utah students were more opposed to tax evasion in 17/18 cases.
- The differences in mean scores were significant in only 4/18 cases.

Ranking

Strongest Arguments to Justify Tax Evasion

	Rank	
Statement	FL	UT
Tax evasion is ethical if the government imprisons people for their political opinions	1	2
Tax evasion is ethical if a significant portion of the money collected winds up in the pockets of corrupt politicians or their families and friends	2	4
Tax evasion is ethical if the government discriminates against me because of my religion, race, or ethnic background	3	3
Tax evasion is ethical if the tax system is unfair	4	5
Tax evasion is ethical if a large portion of the money collected is wasted	5	6
Tax evasion would be ethical if I were a Jew living in Nazi Germany	6	1

Weakest Arguments to Justify Tax Evasion

	Rank	
Statement	FL	UT
Tax evasion is ethical even if most of the money collected is spent wisely	18	14
Tax evasion is ethical if the probability of getting caught is low	17	18
Tax evasion is ethical if a large portion of the money collected is spent on projects that do not benefit me	16	11
Tax evasion is ethical even if it means that if I pay less, others will have to pay more	15	17
Tax evasion is ethical even if a large portion of the money collected is spent on worthy projects	14	14
Tax evasion is ethical if everyone is doing it	13	16

USA: Utah and New Jersey

McGee, Robert W. and Sheldon R. Smith. 2008. Opinions on the Ethics of Tax Evasion: A Comparative Study of Utah and New Jersey. Presented at the 39th Annual Meeting of the Decision Sciences Institute, Baltimore, November 22–26, 2008. Published in the Proceedings at pp. 3981–3986.

Methodology

18 Statement Survey: Tax evasion is ethical if ...
Sample: 379 business students at a large college in Utah and three universities in New Jersey.
Range of scores (1 = strongly agree; 7 = strongly disagree): 4.71–5.75 (New Jersey); 5.26–6.51 (Utah)
Mean score:
Utah: 6.12
New Jersey: 5.27

Overall Findings

- Some arguments justifying tax evasion were significantly stronger than others.
- Utah students were significantly more opposed to tax evasion in all 18 cases (17 at 1% level and 1 at 5% level).

Ranking (New Jersey)

Strongest Arguments to Justify Tax Evasion

1	Tax evasion is ethical if a significant portion of the money collected winds up in the pockets of corrupt politicians or their families and friends	(4.71)
2	Tax evasion is ethical if the tax system is unfair	(4.79)
3	Tax evasion would be ethical if I were a Jew living in Nazi Germany in 1940	(4.80)
3	Tax evasion is ethical if the government discriminates against me because of my religion, race, or ethnic background	(4.80)
5	Tax evasion is ethical if I can't afford to pay	(4.81)
6	Tax evasion is ethical if the government imprisons people for their political opinions	(4.87)

Weakest Arguments to Justify Tax Evasion

17	Tax evasion is ethical if everyone is doing it	(5.75)
17	Tax evasion is ethical even if most of the money collected is spent wisely	(5.75)
16	Tax evasion is ethical even if it means that if I pay less, others will have to pay more	(5.65)
15	Tax evasion is ethical even if a large portion of the money collected is spent on projects that do benefit me	(5.64)
14	Tax evasion is ethical even if a large portion of the money collected is spent on worthy projects	(5.62)
11	Tax evasion is ethical if the probability of getting caught is low	(5.59)
11	Tax evasion is ethical if a large portion of the money collected is spent on projects that do not benefit me	(5.59)
11	Tax evasion is ethical even if tax rates are not too high because the government is not entitled to take as much as it is taking from me	(5.59)

Ranking (Utah)

Strongest Arguments to Justify Tax Evasion

1	Tax evasion would be ethical if I were a Jew living in Nazi Germany in 1940	(5.26)
2	Tax evasion is ethical if the government imprisons people for their political opinions	(5.54)
3	Tax evasion is ethical if the government discriminates against me because of my religion, race, or ethnic background	(5.58)
4	Tax evasion is ethical if a significant portion of the money collected winds up in the pockets of corrupt politicians or their families and friends	(5.66)
5	Tax evasion is ethical if the tax system is unfair	(5.88)
6	Tax evasion is ethical if a large portion of the money collected is wasted	(5.97)

Weakest Arguments to Justify Tax Evasion

18	Tax evasion is ethical if the probability of getting caught is low	(6.51)
17	Tax evasion is ethical even if it means that if I pay less, others will have to pay more	(6.50)
16	Tax evasion is ethical if everyone is doing it	(6.44)
14	Tax evasion is ethical even if a large portion of the money collected is spent on worthy projects	(6.42)

14 Tax evasion is ethical even if most of the money collected is
    spent wisely   (6.42)
12 Tax evasion is ethical if some of the proceeds go to support a
    war that I consider to be unjust   (6.41)
12 Tax evasion is ethical even if a large portion of the money
    collected is spent on projects that do benefit me   (6.41)

Chapter 34
Annotated Bibliography: World Values Surveys*

Robert W. McGee

Introduction

The Human Beliefs and Values Surveys have been collecting opinion and demographic data on countries all over the world since the early 1980s. Some surveys collected responses to hundreds of questions from 200,000 people in more than 80 countries representing 85% of the world's population. The samples for each country were generally large, in some cases exceeding 2,000 participants. The surveys generally used a 10-point Likert Scale where 1 = never justified and 10 = always justified. The studies listed below used the data from these surveys.

Some surveys asked one or more questions about tax evasion. The surveys summarized below usually examined responses to the following question:

> Please tell me for each of the following statements whether you think it can always be justified, never be justified, or something in between: Cheating on taxes if you have a chance.

In studies where a different question was chosen, that is clearly indicated in the summary.

Earlier versions of some of these studies are published on the Social Science Research Network Web site at http://ssrn.com/author=2139. This link will take you to the abstract. It is possible to download the full paper by selecting the "One-click Download" link.

---

*Note: Some of the studies listed below are available online at http://ssrn.com/author=2139.

R.W. McGee (✉)
School of Business, Florida International University,
3000 NE 151 Street, North Miami, FL 33181, USA
e-mail: bob414@hotmail.com

R.W. McGee (ed.), *The Ethics of Tax Evasion: Perspectives in Theory and Practice*,
DOI 10.1007/978-1-4614-1287-8_34, © Springer Science+Business Media, LLC 2012

Asia

McGee, Robert W. 2008. Opinions on Tax Evasion in Asia, in Robert W. McGee, editor, *Taxation and Public Finance in Transition and Developing Economies* (pp. 309–320). New York: Springer.

METHODOLOGY; Human Beliefs and Values Survey, "Is tax evasion ever justified if you have a chance?" (1 = never justifiable; 10 = always justifiable).

SAMPLE SIZE: 16,809 from 13 Asian countries.

Overall Findings

- Attitude toward tax evasion varied by country.
- GENDER: Women were more opposed to tax evasion in 9 of 13 countries.
- AGE: Older people are generally more opposed to tax evasion than are younger people.

RANGE OF MEAN SCORES: 1.06–3.14

Overall Mean Score

Bangladesh 1.06
Turkey 1.18
Pakistan 1.19
Vietnam 1.32
Japan 1.46
Indonesia 1.54
China 1.57
Korea (South) 1.59
Singapore 1.89
Taiwan 1.96
India 2.14
Kyrgyzstan 2.73
Philippines 3.14

Gender

- Women were more opposed to tax evasion in Bangladesh, Indonesia, Japan, South Korea, Kyrgyzstan, Pakistan, Philippines, Singapore, and Turkey.
- Men were more opposed to tax evasion in China, India, Taiwan, and Vietnam.

Age

- Older people were more opposed to tax evasion than were younger people in 11 of 13 countries.
- Younger people were more opposed to tax evasion in India.

  Age mean scores were about the same for all age groups in Vietnam.

Australia and New Zealand

Gupta, Ranjana and Robert W. McGee. 2010. Study on Tax Evasion Perceptions in Australasia. *Australian Tax Forum* 25(4): 507–534.

METHODOLOGY; Human Beliefs and Values Survey, "Is tax evasion ever justified if you have a chance?" (1 = never justifiable; 10 = always justifiable).

Overview

The authors conducted a survey of 967 undergraduate and graduate accounting, business and economics, law and medical students, and faculty in New Zealand drawn from the Auckland area to determine their views on cheating on taxes (Study 1). The survey instrument asked whether it was justifiable to cheat on taxes if you had a chance. The survey instrument used a 10-point Likert scale that ranged from never justifiable to always justifiable. Results were tabulated and comparisons were made based on student status (graduate or undergraduate), academic major, gender, religion, and age to determine whether any of these demographic variables made a difference. All the interaction effects between the variables were studied and were found to be insignificant. The results were then compared to data from similar surveys of 2,270 nonstudents conducted in Australia (Study 2) and New Zealand (Study 3) that used different methodologies, had different sample populations and different demographics to determine if the findings of Study 1 confirmed the data collected from those two other surveys that used a different methodology and had different demographics. The results suggest that there is some support for tax evasion and that demographic variables do play a role.

STUDY 1

SAMPLE: 967 undergraduate and graduate accounting, business and economics, law and medical students, and faculty in New Zealand.

Gender

Mean Scores

Female: 2.57
Male: 3.02

Findings

- Females were significantly more opposed to tax evasion.

Age

Mean Scores

15–29: 2.79
30–49: 2.74
50+: 1.55

Findings

- People over 49 were significantly more opposed to tax evasion than were people in the younger age groups.

Major

Mean Scores

Accounting: 2.70
Business and Economics: 2.97
Law: 1.97
Medical Sciences: 3.22

Findings

- Law majors were significantly more opposed to tax evasion than were any other majors.
- Accounting majors were more opposed to tax evasion than were business and economics majors ($p = 0.070$).
- Medical sciences majors were least opposed to tax evasion.

Student Status

Mean Scores

Undergraduate students: 2.92
Graduate students: 2.64
Faculty: 1.45

Findings

- Faculty were significantly more opposed to tax evasion than either student group.
- Graduate students were significantly more opposed to tax evasion than were undergraduate students.

Religion

Mean Scores

Agnostic: 3.20
Atheist: 3.01
Buddhist: 2.92
Christian: 2.79
Hindu: 2.18
Jewish: 3.25
Muslim: 2.66
Sikh: 1.90
Taoist: 3.08

Findings

- Hindus were significantly more opposed to tax evasion than any other religion.
- No significant differences were found for any other religious comparisons. Some comparisons were not significant because some of the religions had small sample sizes.

Other Findings

The study also compared tax evasion to other acts to determine the relative seriousness of tax evasion. The survey found that tax evasion was not considered as serious as most other acts. Tax evasion was found to be more justifiable than:

- Accepting a bribe
- Buying stolen goods
- Claiming government benefits to which you are not entitled
- Cheating on taxes and avoiding a fare on public transport were found to be equally reprehensible compared to cheating on taxes.
- Cheating on taxes was found to be less justifiable than prostitution (which is legal in New Zealand).

STUDY 2 (Australia) and 3 (New Zealand)

SAMPLE: World Values Surveys

Gender

- Women were significantly more opposed to tax evasion in both studies.
- Australian men and New Zealand men were equally opposed to tax evasion.
- Australian women and New Zealand women were equally opposed to tax evasion.
- In Study 1, males and females were significantly less opposed to tax evasion than they were in either of the two other studies.

Age

- Older people are more averse to tax evasion than are younger people in both Australia and New Zealand.

Religion

- For the Australian study (Study 2), Buddhists were significantly less opposed to tax evasion than were Roman Catholics, Protestants, or Orthodox Christians.
- Roman Catholics were significantly less opposed to tax evasion than were Protestants (Study 2).
- Differences in mean scores for other religion comparisons were not statistically significant.

- The four religions most opposed to tax evasion were all from Australia in Study 2 (Jehovah Witnesses, Hindu, Protestant, and Orthodox).
- Most of the religions least opposed to tax evasion were from New Zealand in Study 1 (Taoist, Jewish, Buddhist).

Comparisons with Other Acts

- Tax evasion was not considered to be as serious an offense as most other acts included in the comparison.
- The least justifiable act was accepting a bribe and the most justifiable act was prostitution.

Australia, New Zealand, and the USA

McGee, Robert W. and Sanjoy Bose. 2009. The Ethics of Tax Evasion: A Comparative Study of Australian, New Zealand and USA Opinion, in Robert W. McGee, *Readings in Business Ethics* (pp. 125–142). Hyderabad, India: ICFAI University Press.

METHODOLOGY; Human Beliefs and Values Survey, "Is tax evasion ever justified if you have a chance?" (1 = never justifiable; 10 = always justifiable).

SAMPLE SIZE: 2,039 (Australia), 1155 (New Zealand), 1198 (USA).

Overall Mean Score

Australia: 2.16
New Zealand: 2.30
USA: 2.28
Finding: Country differences in mean scores are not statistically significant.

Gender

Mean Scores

	Australia	New Zealand	USA
Male	2.43	2.64	2.54
Female	1.89	2.03	2.01
Overall	2.16	3.30	2.28

Findings

- Men's views on tax evasion did not differ significantly between countries.
- Women's views on tax evasion did not differ significantly between countries.
- Women were significantly more opposed to tax evasion in all three countries.

Age

Mean Scores

Age	Australia	New Zealand	USA
15–29	2.56	3.30	2.73
30–49	2.22	2.37	2.26
50+	1.71	1.89	1.90

Findings

- Older people are more averse to tax evasion than are younger people. Differences in mean scores were significant in all cases.
- New Zealanders in the 15–29 age group were significantly less opposed to tax evasion than were the Australians or Americans in the same age group. Other differences were not significant.

Education

Mean Scores

Level of education	Australia	New Zealand	USA
Lower	2.07	2.22	2.43
Middle	2.16	2.20	2.34
Upper	2.21	2.47	2.17

Findings

- Australia and New Zealand: More educated people tend to be less opposed to tax evasion than less educated people. The differences in mean scores were often significant.
- USA: The differences in mean scores were not significant, although there was slightly more opposition to tax evasion as the level of education increased.

- At the upper education level, New Zealanders were significantly less opposed to tax evasion than were their US counterparts, but for all other country comparisons by level of education the differences were not significant.

Egypt, Iran and Jordan

McGee, Robert W. and Sanjoy Bose. 2006. Attitudes toward Tax Evasion in the Middle East: A Comparative Study of Egypt, Iran and Jordan. *Accounting and Finance in Transition* 3: 23–34.

METHODOLOGY; Human Beliefs and Values Survey, "Is tax evasion ever justified if you have a chance?" (1 = never justifiable; 10 = always justifiable).

SAMPLE SIZE: 6,642

Gender

Mean Scores

	Egypt	Iran	Jordan
Male	1.70	1.49	1.57
Female	1.44	1.44	1.54

Conclusion: Egyptian women were significantly more opposed to tax evasion than Egyptian men. Gender differences were not significant for Iran and Jordan.

Age

Mean Scores

Age	Egypt	Iran	Jordan
15–29	1.62	1.57	1.72
30–49	1.58	1.38	1.52
50+	1.50	1.34	1.28

Conclusion: Although older people in all three countries were more opposed to tax evasion than younger people, the difference was significant only for Jordan.

Education

Mean Scores

Level of education	Egypt	Iran	Jordan
Lower	1.58	1.41	1.36
Middle	1.54	1.46	1.68
Upper	1.62	1.58	1.79

Conclusion: Although people in all three countries tended to become less opposed to tax evasion as the level of education increased, the difference in mean scores was significant only for Jordan.

Fifteen Transition Economies and Two Developed Economies

McGee, Robert W. 2006. Cheating on Taxes: A Comparative Study of Tax Evasion Ethics of Fifteen Transition Economies and Two Developed Economies. *Accounting and Finance in Transition* 3: 273–289.

METHODOLOGY; Human Beliefs and Values Survey, "Is tax evasion ever justified if you have a chance?" (1 = never justifiable; 10 = always justifiable).

Overall Mean Score

Country	Mean	Country	Mean
Belarus	4.22	Latvia	2.36
Bulgaria	2.01	Lithuania	3.77
Croatia	2.53	Poland	2.23
Czech Republic	2.07	Romania	2.79
Denmark	2.00	Russia	3.09
East Germany	2.40	Slovakia	2.15
Estonia	3.15	Slovenia	2.34
Finland	2.46	Ukraine	3.45
Hungary	2.12	Average	2.66

Gender

Conclusion: Women were more opposed to tax evasion in all 17 countries.

Age

Conclusion: In all 17 countries the oldest group (50+) was more opposed to tax evasion than the youngest group (15–29).

Education

Mean Scores

Lower: 2.41
Middle: 2.76
Upper: 2.72

- Generally, individuals in the lower education group have a stronger aversion to tax evasion than do individuals in the other two groups.
- Individuals in the middle and upper education groups have about the same views on tax evasion.
- About half of the time the upper education group is slightly more opposed to tax evasion than the middle group; about half the time the middle education group is slightly more opposed to tax evasion than the upper group.

Marital Status

Conclusion: Married people were more opposed to tax evasion than were single people in all 17 countries.

Germany (East and West) and USA

McGee, Robert W., Inge Nickerson and Werner Fees. 2006. The Ethics of Tax Evasion: A Comparative Study of Germany and the United States. Working Paper, Barry University, October.

QUESTION: Is tax evasion ever justified if you have a chance? (1 = never justified; 10 = always justified).

	Mean scores		
	West Germany	East Germany	USA
Gender			
Male	2.54	2.64	2.54
Female	2.20	2.20	2.01
Age			
15–29	2.82	2.74	2.73
30–49	2.49	2.53	2.26
50 and older	2.00	2.10	1.90

Findings

Gender

Females were more opposed to tax evasion than were males in all three samples.

East German males were less averse to tax evasion than were males in West Germany and the USA.

USA females were more opposed to tax evasion than were the females in the other two samples.

Age

People became more averse to tax evasion as they got older in all 3 samples.

Jewish

McGee, Robert W. and Gordon M. Cohn. 2008. Jewish Perspectives on the Ethics of Tax Evasion. *Journal of Legal, Ethical and Regulatory Issues*, 11(2): 1–32.

METHODOLOGY; Human Beliefs and Values Survey, "Is tax evasion ever justified if you have a chance?" (1 = never justifiable; 10 = always justifiable).

SAMPLE SIZE: 324 Jews from more than 40 countries. Only 4 countries had at least 20 Jews in the sample. The only samples used were from those four countries: France, Georgia, Tanzania, and the USA.

Overall Mean Score

Overall: 2.412
France: 2.665
Georgia: 2.056
Tanzania: 2.447
USA: 2.912

Religion

Mean Scores (Ranked: Most Opposed to Least Opposed;
Sample Size 82,589)

Buddhist: 1.68
Muslim: 1.83
Hindu: 2.00
Protestant: 2.22
Roman Catholic: 2.40
Jewish: 2.49
Orthodox: 2.76

Korea, Japan, and China

McGee, Robert W. 2008. Tax Evasion, Tax Misery and Ethics: Comparative Studies of Korea, Japan and China, in Robert W. McGee (Ed.), *Taxation and Public Finance in Transition and Developing Economies* (pp. 137–165). New York: Springer.

METHODOLOGY; Human Beliefs and Values Survey, "Is tax evasion ever justifiable if you have a chance?" (1 = never justifiable; 10 = always justifiable).
SAMPLE SIZE: 985 (China), 1,312 (Japan), 1,199 (Korea).
OVERALL MEAN SCORE: 1.57 (China), 1.46 (Japan), 1.59 (Korea).

Finding

Japan was significantly more opposed to tax evasion than China or Korea. The difference in mean scores between China and Korea was not significant.

Gender

Mean Scores

	China	Japan	Korea
Female	1.61	1.35	1.55
Male	1.53	1.59	1.63

Findings

Japanese women were significantly more opposed to tax evasion than were Japanese men. Gender differences for China and Korea were not significant.

Age

Mean Scores

	China	Japan	Korea
15–29	1.73	1.64	1.73
30–49	1.55	1.45	1.58
50+	1.50	1.40	1.45

Findings

Older people were more averse to tax evasion in all three countries. However, the differences in mean scores for China were not significant.

Education

Mean Scores

	China	Japan	Korea
Lower	1.36	1.44	1.50
Middle	1.71	1.42	1.52
Upper	1.81	1.56	1.71

Findings

Opposition to tax evasion deteriorates somewhat as the level of education increases for all three countries. The difference between lower and middle was significant for China. The differences in mean scores were not significant for Japan. The difference between middle and upper was significant at the 10% level for Korea.

Religion

Mean Scores

Roman Catholic: 1.60
Buddhist: 1.52
Protestant: 1.64
Not applicable: 1.52

Findings

Buddhists were significantly more opposed to tax evasion than were Roman Catholics at the 5% level. None of the other comparisons were significant at the 5% level. However, Buddhists were significantly more opposed to tax evasion than were Protestants at the 10% level.

Marital Status

Mean Scores

Married: 1.50
Divorced: 1.28
Widowed: 1.50
Single/never married: 1.67

Findings

Married were significantly more opposed to tax evasion than single/never married at the 1% significance level. Widowed were significantly more opposed to tax evasion than single/never married at the 1% level. Divorced were significantly more opposed to tax evasion than single/never married at the 5% level. None of the other comparisons were significant.

Malaysia

Ross, Adriana M. and Robert W. McGee (2011). A Demographic Study of Malaysian Views on the Ethics of Tax Evasion. Published in the Proceedings of the 2011 Spring International Conference of the Allied Academies, Orlando, April 6–8, 2011. Reprinted as Attitudes toward Tax Evasion: A Demographic Study of Malaysia, *Asian Journal of Law & Economics*, Vol. 2, Issue 3, article 5 (2011): 1–49. Available at: http://www.bepress.com/ajle/vol2/iss3/5.

METHODOLOGY; Human Beliefs and Values Survey, "Is tax evasion ever justified if you have a chance?" (1 = never justifiable; 10 = always justifiable).

SAMPLE SIZE: 1,200

Gender

Mean Scores

Female: 3.4
Male: 3.6
Findings: The difference in mean scores was not significant.

Age

Mean Scores

15–24: 3.6
25–34: 3.5
35–44: 3.4
45–54: 3.5
55–64: 3.7
65+: 3.5
Findings: The differences in mean scores were not significant.

Education

Findings: In general, the more education one has, the less opposition there is to tax evasion. However, a comparison of mean scores found that the differences were insignificant.

Religion

Findings: Of religions that had a sample size of 30 or more, Protestants were most opposed to tax evasion, followed by Roman Catholics, Muslims, Hindus, and Buddhists.

Importance of God in Your Life

Findings: The group most opposed to tax evasion was the group where God was least important in their life. However, the group that ranked third (out of 10) was the group where God was most important in their life. In general, those who were in the middle of the God is important spectrum were least opposed to tax evasion.

Employment Status

Mean Scores

Full-time: 3.5
Part-time: 4.4
Self-employed: 3.5
Housewife: 3.2
Retired: 4.0
Students: 3.6
Unemployed: 3.4
Findings: Housewives were most opposed to tax evasion, followed by the unemployed, full-time and self-employed, students, and retired. Part-time employees were least opposed to tax evasion.

Income Level

Findings: The group most opposed to tax evasion was the highest income group. The group second most opposed to tax evasion was the lowest income group. There appears to be a tendency for those at higher income levels to be more opposed to tax evasion than people in the lower income groups.

Institution of Occupation

Findings: Those in private business tended to be more opposed to tax evasion than either public institution employees or those who work in private non-profit organizations. However, the differences in mean scores were not significant.

Occupation

Findings: Of groups that had a sample size of 30 or more, semi-skilled manual workers were most opposed to tax evasion, followed by unskilled manual workers, farmers, and members of the armed forces. The groups least opposed to tax evasion tended to be managers, skilled workers, and professionals.

Marital Status

Findings: Divorced people were the group most opposed to tax evasion. People living together as married were least opposed. However, the differences in mean scores among the various groups were not significant.

Number of Children

Findings: The four groups that were least opposed to tax evasion were the four groups with the most children. However, the group most opposed to tax evasion was the group with 4 children.

Size of Town

Findings: People who lived in cities with populations between 20,000 and 50,000 were significantly more opposed to tax evasion than were people who live in cities of other sizes. However, the relationship between size of the community and attitude toward tax evasion is not linear. All that can be said is that some comparisons had significant differences.

Region

Findings: The data was divided into 11 regions. The differences in mean scores were often significant. Those from North Sembilan were most opposed to tax evasion. Those from Pahang were least opposed.

Social Class

Findings: The upper class and the lower middle class had identical mean scores and were the two groups most opposed to tax evasion. The lower class was least opposed. However, the differences in mean scores generally were not significant.

Ethnicity

Findings: A comparison of mean scores found no significant differences based on ethnicity.

Feeling of Happiness

Findings: Happy people were more averse to tax evasion than unhappy people but the differences in mean scores were not significant.

Satisfaction with Life

Findings: Those who were most dissatisfied with life were also the most opposed to tax evasion. However, those who were most satisfied with life ranked second in terms of opposition to tax evasion. The two groups least opposed to tax evasion were also highly dissatisfied with life.

State of Health

Findings: Those who were in fair health were most opposed to tax evasion. Those in poor health were least opposed. Those in good or very good health were between the two extremes.

Income Equality

Findings: There seemed to be little relationship between views on income equality and attitude toward tax evasion. The two groups most opposed to tax evasion were at the two extremes – incomes should be more equal and we need larger income differences as incentives.

Competition: Good or Harmful

Findings: Those who felt most strongly that competition was good and those who thought most strongly that competition was harmful were the two groups that were most opposed to tax evasion and had equal mean scores. However, the overall trend tended to be linear. Those who think competition is good tended to be more firmly opposed to tax evasion than people who believed competition to be harmful.

Private vs. State Ownership of Business

Findings: It was difficult to determine the relationship between attitude toward tax evasion and opinion on tax evasion. The group most opposed to tax evasion (out of 10 groups) was the group that most firmly believed that government ownership of business should be increased. The group ranked third in terms of opposition to tax evasion was the group that most firmly believed private ownership of business should be increased. The group having the least opposition to tax evasion strongly believed that private ownership of business should be increased.

Government vs. Individual Responsibility

Findings: Those who most strongly believed that individuals should take more responsibility and those who most strongly believed that the government should take more responsibility were the two groups most strongly opposed to tax evasion. Those in the middle of the spectrum had less opposition to tax evasion. The two groups least opposed to tax evasion believed the government should take more responsibility.

Success: Hard Work vs. Luck and Connections

Findings: Those most opposed to tax evasion were the group who most firmly believed that success is more a matter of luck or connections than hard work. Those ranked second (out of 10 groups) were in the group that most strongly believed that success comes about as a result of hard work. There was no clear relationship between opinion on the cause of success and attitude toward tax evasion.

Wealth Accumulation

Findings: The group most opposed to tax evasion was the group that most firmly believed that wealth can grow, so there is enough for everyone. In general, those who held this belief were more opposed to tax evasion than were those who believed that people can get rich only at the expense of others.

Confidence in Government

Findings: The groups most opposed to tax evasion were the groups that had the most confidence in government. The groups that had the least confidence in government were the least averse to tax evasion.

Confidence in the Justice System

Findings: People who had more confidence in the justice system had the most aversion to tax evasion and those who had the least confidence in the justice system had the least opposition to tax evasion.

Confidence in the Police

Findings: People who had more confidence in the police had the most aversion to tax evasion and those who had the least confidence in the police had the least opposition to tax evasion.

Relative Seriousness of Tax Evasion

Findings: Tax evasion was considered to be more serious than divorce, avoiding a fare on public transport, and claiming government benefits to which you are not entitled. Tax evasion was less serious than homosexuality, prostitution, abortion, suicide, wife beating, accepting a bribe, and euthanasia.

Trend Analysis

Moldova and Romania

McGee, Robert W. 2009. Views toward Tax Evasion: A Comparative Study of Moldova and Romania. *ICFAI Journal of Public Finance* 7(3&4): 7–24.

The question was whether it is justified to cheat on taxes if you have a chance.	
Moldova	Gender: not significant
	Age: People in the 30–49 group were significantly more opposed to tax evasion than people in the 15–29 and 50+ groups; people in the 15–29 and 50+ age groups were equally opposed to tax evasion
	Education Level: People in the upper education level were significantly more opposed to tax evasion than were people in the lower or middle education groups
	Marital Status: Married people were significantly more opposed to tax evasion than were single people; married vs. divorced were equally opposed; divorced vs. single were equally opposed

(continued)

(continued)	
Romania	Gender: no significant difference
	Age: the 50+ group was significantly more opposed to tax evasion than either the 15–29 or 30–49 age groups; the 15–29 and 30–49 groups were equally opposed
	Education Level: People with lower level education were somewhat more opposed to tax evasion than were people in the middle education group ($p=0.0881$); No difference between lower vs. upper or middle vs. upper
	Marital Status: Married were significantly more opposed to tax evasion than were single individuals; no difference between married vs. divorced or divorced vs. single
Moldova vs. Romania	Overall: Romanians were significantly more opposed to tax evasion
	Gender: Romanian males were significantly more opposed to tax evasion than were Moldovan males; Romanian females were significantly more opposed to tax evasion than were Moldovan females
	Age: Romanians in all age groups were significantly more opposed to tax evasion than were Moldovans in the same age group
	Marital status: Romanians were significantly more opposed to tax evasion for all marital status categories

The Netherlands

Ross, Adriana M. and Robert W. McGee (2011). A Demographic Study of the Netherlands Attitudes toward Tax Evasion. Published in the Proceedings of the 2011 Spring International Conference of the Allied Academies, Orlando, April 6–8, 2011, forthcoming in the *Journal of International Business Research*, 2012 under the title Attitudes toward Tax Evasion: A Demographic Study of the Netherlands.

METHODOLOGY; Human Beliefs and Values Survey, "Is tax evasion ever justified if you have a chance?" (1 = never justifiable; 10 = always justifiable).

SAMPLE SIZE: 1,035

Gender

Mean Scores

Female: 2.1
Male: 2.5
Findings: Women are significantly more averse to tax evasion.

Age

Mean Scores

15–24: 2.2
25–34: 1.9
35–44: 2.6
45–54: 2.3
55–64: 2.8
65+: 1.8

Conclusion: Although the oldest group (65+) was also the group that was most firmly opposed to tax evasion, the groups that ranked second and third in terms of opposition were the two youngest groups. The second group was least opposed to tax evasion. Thus, it could fairly be said that the pattern in the Netherlands does not conform neatly to the pattern found in some other countries. An ANOVA found that the difference between groups was significant at the 1% level.

Education

Findings: People with no formal education were most opposed to tax evasion. Those with inadequately completed elementary education ranked second in terms of opposition. However, those with some university education ranked third, which breaks the linear pattern. Those who completed secondary education and those with college degrees were among the groups least opposed to tax evasion. In general, aversion to tax evasion tended to decrease as the level of education increased.

Religion

Findings: Differences between groups was not significant.

Religious Practice

Findings: Those who attend religious services more than once a week were most opposed to tax evasion. Those who attend once a week ranked second in terms of opposition. In general, those who attend less frequently were less opposed to tax evasion.

Importance of God in Their Life

Findings: Generally, the more important God is in their life, the more opposed people are to tax evasion. The ANOVA found the difference in mean scores to be significant at the 5% level.

Employment Status

Mean Scores

Full-time: 2.7
Part-time: 2.1
Self-employed: 2.7
Housewife: 1.7
Retired: 2.0
Students: 2.3
Unemployed: 2.1

Findings: Housewives and retired people were the two groups most opposed to tax evasion. Full-time employees and self-employed individuals were least opposed.

Income Level

Findings: The group most opposed to tax evasion was the lowest income group. However, the highest income group ranked third out of 10 groups. There seemed to be no pattern between income group and ranking. Some p values were significant.

Institution of Occupation

Findings: Those who worked for nonprofit organizations were most opposed to tax evasion. Those who worked in private business were least opposed. Public institution workers ranked between the other two groups. However, the differences in mean score were not significant at the 5% level (ANOVA $p=0.131$).

Occupation

Findings: Semi-skilled manual workers were most opposed to tax evasion, followed by skilled manual workers. Employers/managers of establishments with fewer than 10 employees were least opposed. In general, managers, supervisors, and professionals were less opposed to tax evasion than were manual workers.

Marital Status

Findings: Divorced and widowed people had equal mean scores and were the most opposed to tax evasion. Married people ranked third. There was a tie for fourth place between people living together as married and single/never married. Separated people were least opposed to tax evasion.

Number of Children

Findings: In general, people with more children were more opposed to tax evasion than people with fewer children, although the sample sizes for people having more than 4 children were too small to draw solid conclusions. People having 1 child were least opposed to tax evasion, followed by people with 0, 2, or 3 children.

Region

Findings: Data were subdivided into 12 regions. Opposition to tax evasion did differ by region and some differences were significant.

Feeling of Happiness

Findings: The groups that are very happy and quite happy are significantly more firmly opposed to tax evasion than are people who are not very happy.

Satisfaction with Life

Findings: The two groups that were most dissatisfied with life were also the groups that were most opposed to tax evasion (out of 10 groups). However, the sample sizes were so small for those groups that their mean scores should be disregarded. There seemed to be no clear pattern, although it was clear that some of the differences between groups were significant.

State of Health

Findings: Those in poor health were more opposed to tax evasion than any of the other three groups. However, the differences in mean scores were not significant.

Self Positioning on Political Scale

Findings: Those in the center of the left-right political spectrum were most opposed to tax evasion, while those at the extreme right and left were least opposed. Comparisons between mean scores found some differences to be significant.

Income Equality

Findings: No clear pattern could be found between those who believe incomes should be more equal and those who believe that larger income differences are needed to provide incentives. However, comparisons of mean scores found some differences between groups to be significant.

Government vs. Individual Responsibility

Findings: The groups least opposed to tax evasion tended to be the groups who supported individual responsibility over government responsibility.

Success: Hard Work vs. Luck and Connections

Findings: Those who believed that hard work was the key to success and those who believed that good luck and connections were responsible for success were more or less equally opposed to tax evasion. Differences in mean scores were not significant.

Confidence in Government

Findings: The groups who have the most confidence in government were also most opposed to tax evasion.

Confidence in the Justice System

Findings: The groups who have the most confidence in the justice system were also most opposed to tax evasion.

Confidence in the Police

Findings: The two groups (out of 4) who had the most confidence in the police were also the two groups most opposed to tax evasion.

Relative Seriousness of Tax Evasion

Findings: Cheating on taxes ranked fifth out of 11 ethical issues. It was less serious than wife beating, claiming government benefits to which you are not entitled, accepting a bribe, and avoiding a fare on public transit and more serious than suicide, abortion, prostitution, euthanasia, divorce, and homosexuality.

Trend Analysis

Findings: There is a clear trend toward increased opposition to tax evasion since 1981.

Poland

Ross, Adriana M. and Robert W. McGee (2011). A Demographic Study of Polish Attitudes toward Tax Evasion. Published in the Proceedings of the 2011 Spring International Conference of the Allied Academies, Orlando, April 6–8, 2011, forthcoming in the *Academy of Accounting and Financial Studies Journal*.

METHODOLOGY; Human Beliefs and Values Survey, "Is tax evasion ever justified if you have a chance?" (1 = never justifiable; 10 = always justifiable).

SAMPLE SIZE: 949

Gender

Mean Scores

Female: 2.4
Male: 2.5
Findings: The difference in mean scores was not significant.

Age

Mean Scores

15–24: 3.2
25–34: 2.8
35–44: 2.2
45–54: 2.5
55–64: 2.4
65+: 1.6

Conclusion: Older people are more averse to tax evasion than are younger people. The 65+ group was the most opposed to tax evasion; the two youngest groups were least opposed.

Education

Findings: The differences between groups were significant at the 5% level. People at the lower ends of education tended to be more averse to tax evasion than people with more education.

Religious Practice

Findings: Some of the differences were highly significant but no clear pattern could be found. Those who attended religious services once a week and once a year were the two groups that were most opposed to tax evasion and their mean scores were identical. Those who never or practically never attended religious services were least opposed.

Employment Status

Mean Scores

Full-time: 2.4
Part-time: 2.7
Self-employed: 3.3
Housewife: 3.1
Retired: 1.9
Students: 3.0
Unemployed: 2.9
Findings: Full-time employees were more opposed to tax evasion than were the other groups except for the retired category. Self-employed individuals were least opposed, followed by housewives, students, and unemployed.

Income Level

Findings: There was no clear pattern for the divergence of opinion. All that can be said is that income level is sometimes correlated to view of tax evasion.

Institution of Occupation

Findings: People who work at public institutions were significantly more opposed to tax evasion than people who work in private business.

Occupation

Findings: Members of the armed forces were most opposed to tax evasion, followed by semi-skilled manual workers, unskilled manual workers, and farmers who have their own farm. Agricultural workers were the least opposed group but the sample size for this group was small. The general pattern seems to show that managers and supervisory workers are less opposed to tax evasion than unskilled and blue-collar workers.

Marital Status

Findings: Widows was the group most opposed to tax evasion, followed by married, divorced, single/never married, and living together as married. Some of the differences were highly significant.

Number of Children

Findings: People with no children were least opposed to tax evasion. People with three, two, or four children were the three groups that were most opposed to tax evasion.

Size of Town

Findings: People who live in small towns generally were more opposed to tax evasion than other groups. However, some small town categories were less opposed to tax evasion than some big city groups.

Social Class

Findings: The differences in mean scores were not significant.

Feeling of Happiness

Findings: People who were very happy and quite happy were more opposed to tax evasion than were people who were not very happy and not at all happy, but the differences in mean scores were not significant.

State of Health

Findings: People in poor health were significantly more opposed to tax evasion than were people in the other categories. As health improved, people became significantly less opposed to tax evasion.

Self Positioning on Political Scale

Findings: Centrists were the most opposed to tax evasion; leftists and rightists were least opposed. However, the differences in mean scores were not significant.

Income Equality

Findings: Those who strongly believed that income should be more equal and those who strongly believed that we need larger income differences as incentives were the two groups most opposed to tax evasion. Centrists tended to have less opposition to tax evasion. The differences in mean scores were significant.

Private vs. State Ownership of Business

Findings: The views of those who believed that government ownership of business should be increased were not significantly different from the view of those who believed that private ownership of business should be increased.

Government vs. Individual Responsibility

Findings: The views of those who believed that government should take more responsibility were not significantly different from the views of those who thought individuals should take more responsibility.

Competition: Good or Harmful

Findings: This question compared the views of those who believed competition is good with those who believed competition is harmful. Those at both extremes were more opposed to tax evasion than were people who were more centrist. Comparisons of differences in mean scores between groups was significant.

Success: Hard Work vs. Luck and Connections

Findings: The views toward tax evasion of those who believed that hard work usually brings a better life were compared to those who believed that success is more a matter of luck or connections. Differences between groups were not significant.

Wealth Accumulation

Findings: Those who believed that people can get rich only at the expense of others and those who believed that wealth can grow and that there is enough for everyone were equally opposed to tax evasion. Differences in mean scores were not significant.

Confidence in Government

Findings: People who have the most confidence in government also have the strongest aversion to tax evasion and people who have the least confidence in government have the least aversion to tax evasion. The difference in mean scores between groups was highly significant.

Confidence in the Justice System

Findings: People who have the most confidence in the justice system also have the strongest aversion to tax evasion and people who have the least confidence in the justice system have the least aversion to tax evasion. The difference in mean scores between groups was highly significant.

Relative Seriousness of Tax Evasion

Findings: Wife beating, accepting a bribe, claiming government benefits to which you are not entitled, and suicide are considered more serious ethical breaches than tax evasion, whereas avoiding a fare on public transport, prostitution, abortion, homosexuality, euthanasia, and divorce were considered less serious ethical breaches.

Trend Analysis

Findings: Differences in mean scores were significant over the years but the trend was not linear. Aversion to tax evasion was strongest in 1999. It was somewhat weaker in 2005 and weaker yet in 1997.The least aversion to tax evasion was in 1989–1990, which was about the same time the Berlin Wall was dismantled.

Puerto Rico

McGee, Robert W. and Silvia López Paláu. 2007. The Ethics of Tax Evasion: Two Empirical Studies of Puerto Rican Opinion. *Journal of Applied Business and Economics* 7(3): 27–47. Reprinted in Robert W. McGee (Ed.), *Readings in Accounting Ethics* (pp. 314–342). Hyderabad, India: ICFAI University Press, 2009.

METHODOLOGY; Human Beliefs and Values Survey, Wave 4
(1 = never justifiable; 10 = always justifiable).
More than three out of four respondents (77.8%) said that tax evasion is never justified, which ranked it as the fourth most opposed to tax evasion from among 11 Latin American countries that were included in the survey.

SAMPLE SIZE: 706
OVERALL MEAN SCORE: 2.06

Gender

Mean Scores

Female: 1.94
Male: 2.43

Conclusion: Women are more opposed to tax evasion.

Age

Mean Scores

15–29: 2.58
30–49: 2.18
50+: 1.63
Conclusion: Older people are more averse to tax evasion than are younger people.

Education

Mean Scores

Lower: 1.45
Middle: 1.91
Upper: 2.16
Conclusion: People tend to become less averse to tax evasion as the level of
education increases.

Religion

Mean Scores

Roman Catholic: 2.00
Buddhist: 1.16
Protestant: 1.73
Conclusion: Attitude toward tax evasion does not differ by religion.
Although the mean scores showed that Buddhists and Protestants are more
averse to tax evasion than are Roman Catholics, the sample sizes for the
non-Catholic groups were small. Differences were not significant at
the 5% level.

Six Countries (Brazil, Russia, India, China, USA, Germany)

Ross, Adriana M. and Robert W. McGee (2011). Education Level and Ethical
Attitude toward Tax Evasion: A Six-Country Study. Published in the Proceedings of
the 2011 Spring International Conference of the Allied Academies, Orlando, April
6–8, 2011. Forthcoming in the *Journal of Legal, Ethical and Regulatory Issues.*

METHODOLOGY; Human Beliefs and Values Survey, "Is tax evasion ever
justified if you have a chance?" (1 = never justifiable; 10 = always justifiable).

SAMPLE SIZE: 10,034
NOTE: This study summarizes more than 30 surveys conducted in various
countries that solicited opinions on the ethics of tax evasion.

Mean Scores

China: 2.0
USA: 2.1
Germany: 2.2
Russia: 3.0
India: 3.0
Brazil: 3.6

Gender: Brazil

Mean Scores

Female: 3.5
Male: 3.4
Findings: Overall, men were somewhat more opposed to tax evasion than women, but the difference in mean score was not significant. However, men were significantly more opposed to tax evasion for the categories of incomplete secondary school: technical and university degree.

Gender: Russia

Mean Scores

Female: 2.9
Male: 3.1
Findings: Women were more opposed to tax evasion, but the difference in mean scores was significant only at the 11% level ($p = 0.1084$).

Gender: India

Mean Scores

Female: 2.9
Male: 3.1
Findings: Women were more opposed to tax evasion but the difference in mean scores was not significant.

Gender: China

Mean Scores

Female: 1.9
Male: 2.0
Findings: Women were more opposed to tax evasion but the difference in
mean scores was not significant.

Gender: USA

Mean Scores

Female: 1.9
Male: 2.3
Findings: Overall, women were significantly more opposed to tax evasion
than men. However, men were more opposed to tax evasion in the categories of completed elementary education and some university.

Gender: Germany

Mean Scores

Female: 2.2
Male: 2.2
Findings: Overall, the mean scores were identical, meaning there was no sig-
nificant difference between male and female attitudes toward tax evasion.
However, men with university degrees were significantly more opposed to
tax evasion than women with university degrees.

Age

Findings: Older people tend to be more opposed to tax evasion than young
people in Brazil, Russia, China, the USA, and Germany.
   In India, the youngest age group (15–24) (out of 6 groups) was most
opposed to tax evasion and the second youngest age group (25–34) was least
opposed. However, none of the differences in mean scores were
significant.

Education Level

Findings: The relationship between the level of education and attitude toward tax evasion differed by country. Three distinct patterns were identified.

- No clear pattern: Brazil, USA, and Germany
- The more education, the less opposition to tax evasion: Russia and China
- The more education, the more opposition to tax evasion: India

South Africa

Ross, Adriana M. and Robert W. McGee (2011). A Demographic Study of South African Attitudes on Tax Evasion. Published in the Proceedings of the 2011 Spring International Conference of the Allied Academies, Orlando, April 6–8, 2011, forthcoming in the *Journal of Economics and Economic Education Journal*.

METHODOLOGY; Human Beliefs and Values Survey, "Is tax evasion ever justified if you have a chance?" (1 = never justifiable; 10 = always justifiable).

SAMPLE SIZE: 2,911

Gender

Mean Scores

Female: 2.4
Male: 2.6
Findings: Women were significantly more opposed to tax evasion.

Age

Mean Scores

15–24: 2.5
25–34: 2.6
35–44: 2.6
45–54: 2.4
55–64: 2.3
65+: 2.4

Findings: Older people tended to be more opposed to tax evasion than younger people, but the differences in mean scores between some younger groups and some older groups were only significant at the 10% level.

Education

Findings: Those with university degrees were most opposed to tax evasion. Those who had some university education were least opposed. Aside from this anomaly, there seemed to be a pattern that the most educated groups were most opposed to tax evasion while those with the least education were least opposed to tax evasion.

Religion

Findings: Of the groups having a sample size of 30 or more, Muslims were most opposed to tax evasion, followed by Pentecostals, Evangelicals, Independent African Church members, Protestants, Roman Catholics, and Jehovah Witnesses.

Religious Practice

Findings: The results did not follow a clear pattern. The two groups most opposed to tax evasion were the groups that attended religious services once a year and more than once a week, which were at opposite ends of the spectrum. Those who attended religious services once a week and once a month had similar mean scores. Those who never or practically never attended, those who attended less than once a year and those who attended only on special hold days were the three groups least opposed to tax evasion.

Importance of God in Your Life

Findings: The ANOVA found that the difference between groups was highly significant, although it was difficult to see a clear-cut pattern. The two groups most opposed to tax evasion were at opposite ends of the spectrum (God was important/not important).

Employment Status

Mean Scores

Full-time: 2.5
Part-time: 2.8

Self-employed: 2.4
Housewife: 2.0
Retired: 2.4
Students: 2.4
Unemployed: 2.7

Findings: Housewives were most opposed to tax evasion. Part-time workers, unemployed, and full-time workers were least opposed. Differences between groups were highly significant.

Income Level

Findings: The middle income groups tended to be more opposed to tax evasion than either the low-income or high-income groups. Those in the higher income groups were least opposed to tax evasion.

Institution of Occupation

Findings: Employees of public (government) institutions were most opposed to tax evasion, followed by employees in private businesses. Those who worked for private nonprofit organizations were least opposed to tax evasion.

Occupation

Findings: The two groups most opposed to tax evasion were supervisory non-manual workers and non-manual office workers. Office workers and professionals tended to be more averse to tax evasion than other groups, in general. Groups least opposed to tax evasion were farmers and agricultural workers and various categories of manual workers. If one could generalize, one might say that people who work with their hands are less averse to tax evasion than people who work with their brains.

Marital Status

Findings: The group most opposed to tax evasion was divorced people. The second most opposed group was married people, followed by widowed people. The group least opposed to tax evasion was people who were living together as married. The differences in mean scores were highly significant.

Number of Children

Findings: The group most opposed to tax evasion was the group that had 6 children. Those who had 8 or more children ranked second. Those who had 0, 1, or 3 children were least opposed to tax evasion. Those who had 2 or 7 children were equally opposed, in the sense that their mean scores were identical. The relationship was not linear, although one could say that those who have 0, 1, or 3 children were less opposed to tax evasion than those who had more than 3 children.

Ethnicity

Findings: Whites were most opposed to tax evasion, followed by colored (dark). South Asians and blacks were least opposed to tax evasion and had identical mean scores.

Region

Findings: Data were grouped into 9 regions and there were significant differences in attitudes toward tax evasion between regions. Those in Western Cape were most opposed to tax evasion, while those in Northern Cape were least opposed.

Social Class

Findings: Working class people tended to be the most averse to tax evasion, while people from the lower class tended to be least averse to tax evasion. The upper and middle class groups ranked in the middle.

Feeling of Happiness

Findings: People who are very happy and people who are not very happy were most opposed to tax evasion and had identical mean scores. Those who were not happy at all were least opposed to tax evasion.

Satisfaction with Life

Findings: The ranking by mean scores did not show a discernible pattern. Those most dissatisfied with life were most opposed to tax evasion, while those who were almost as dissatisfied with life were least opposed to tax evasion.

State of Health

Findings: Those who were in fair health were most opposed to tax evasion, while those in poor health were least opposed. However, the differences in mean scores for all categories were not significant.

Self Positioning on Political Scale

Findings: The three groups (out of 10) most opposed to tax evasion were all left of center and the two groups most opposed to tax evasion were right of center. Some of the centrist groups were in the middle of the ranking. However, the farthest right group was also in the middle of the ranking.

Income Equality

Findings: Those who strongly believed that incomes should be more equal were more strongly opposed to tax evasion than were other groups. Those who believed that larger income differences are needed to provide incentives were least opposed to tax evasion.

Private vs. State Ownership of Business

Findings: Those who favored more private ownership of business tended to be more opposed to tax evasion than those who favored more government ownership.

Government vs. Individual Responsibility

Findings: Those who believed that government should take more responsibility were more strongly opposed to tax evasion than were those who believed individuals should take more responsibility.

Success: Hard Work vs. Luck and Connections

Findings: In general, those who believe that hard work brings success were more opposed to tax evasion than those who believe that success comes from luck and connections.

Confidence in Government

Findings: Those who had quite a lot of confidence in government and those who did not have confidence in government at all had equal mean scores and both groups were most strongly opposed to tax evasion. The group that was least opposed to tax evasion was the group that had a great deal of confidence in government.

Confidence in the Justice System

Findings: Those who did not have any confidence in the justice system were most opposed to tax evasion, whereas those who had a great deal of confidence in the justice system were least opposed to tax evasion.

Confidence in the Police

Findings: Those most opposed to tax evasion had quite a lot of confidence in the police, while those who had a great deal of confidence in the police had the least opposition to tax evasion.

Relative Seriousness of Tax Evasion

Findings: Evading taxes was found to be less serious than accepting a bribe, suicide, or wife beating and more serious than prostitution, claiming government benefits to which you are not entitled, abortion, avoiding a fare on public transport, homosexuality, euthanasia, or divorce.

Trend Analysis

Findings: Attitude toward tax evasion has changed over time but not in a linear pattern. South Africans were most opposed to tax evasion in 1996. Opposition was less in 2007 and even less in 1990 and 2001.

Switzerland

Ross, Adriana M. and Robert W. McGee (2011). Attitudes toward Tax Evasion in Switzerland: A Demographic Study. Published in the Proceedings of the 2011 Spring International Conference of the Allied Academies, Orlando, April 6–8, 2011. Reprinted as Attitudes toward Tax Evasion: A Demographic Study of Switzerland, *Business Studies Journal* 3(2): 1–47 (2011).

METHODOLOGY; Human Beliefs and Values Survey, "Is tax evasion ever justified if you have a chance?" (1 = never justifiable; 10 = always justifiable).

SAMPLE SIZE: 1,238

Gender

Mean Scores

Female: 1.7
Male: 2.3
Findings: Women were significantly more opposed to tax evasion.

Age

Mean Scores

15–24: 2.5
25–34: 2.5
35–44: 2.1
45–54: 2.1
55–64: 1.7
65+: 1.9
Findings: In general, older people are more averse to tax evasion than are younger people.

Language Group

Findings: German speakers were most opposed to tax evasion, followed by Italian and French speakers. The difference in mean scores between the German and Italian speakers was not significant. The difference between the German and French speakers was significant at the 1% level.

Language and Gender

Findings: In all three cases women were more opposed to tax evasion than men, but the difference in mean score was significant only for the French and German groups.

Education

Findings: Those with less education tended to be more averse to tax evasion than those who had more education, although the differences in mean scores were not significant.

Religion

Findings: Those in the "Other" category, which presumably included atheists and agnostics, were most opposed to tax evasion, followed by Protestants, Roman Catholics, and Muslims. However, none of the differences in mean scores were significant at the 5% level.

Religious Practice

Findings: Those who attend religious services more frequently are more opposed to tax evasion than those who attend less frequently.

Importance of God in Life

Findings: The more important God is in one's life, the more opposition there is to tax evasion.

Employment Status

Mean Scores

Full-time: 2.3
Part-time: 1.8
Self-employed: 2.2
Housewife: 1.3
Retired: 1.8
Students: 2.1
Unemployed: 2.3
Findings: Housewives were most opposed to tax evasion, followed by part-time and retired workers, students, the self-employed, full-time workers, and unemployed individuals. An ANOVA found that the difference between groups was significant at the 1% level.

Income Level

Findings: Differences in mean scores were not significant.

Institution of Occupation

Findings: People employed in public institutions (government) were somewhat more opposed to tax evasion than people who worked for private non-profit organizations and private sector business employees. The difference in mean scores between public institution and private business employees was significant at the 5% level.

Marital Status

Findings: Widowed was the group most opposed to tax evasion, followed closely by married and divorced. The group least opposed to tax evasion was the single/never married category. An ANOVA found the difference between groups to be significant at the 1% level.

Number of Children

Findings: In general, people with fewer children are less averse to tax evasion than people with more children.

Region

Findings: The German speaking region was most opposed to tax evasion; the French-speaking region was least opposed. The difference was significant.

Social Class

Findings: The differences in mean scores were not significant.

Feeling of Happiness

Findings: Those most opposed to tax evasion are the happiest people and those least opposed are the least happy groups. An ANOVA found the difference between groups to be significant at the 10% level.

Satisfaction with Life

Findings: An ANOVA of differences among the 10 categories found the difference to be significant at the 1% level, although no pattern could be identified. Those most satisfied with life were most opposed to tax evasion but some groups that were highly dissatisfied with life were also strongly opposed to tax evasion.

State of Health

Findings: those in the best health were most opposed to tax evasion while those in the poorest health were least opposed. However, the differences in mean scores were not significant.

Self Positioning on Political Scale

Findings: The position on the left-right political spectrum made a significant difference at times but it was unclear what that difference is. The far left group was most opposed to tax evasion but some centrists and far rights groups were almost equally opposed to tax evasion. Some centrist groups were least opposed to tax evasion.

Income Equality

Findings: There was no significant difference in mean scores between those who believed that incomes should be made more equal and those who believed that larger income differences are needed to provide incentives.

Private vs. State Ownership of Business

Findings: The group most strongly in favor of increasing government ownership of business and the group most strongly in favor of increasing private ownership of business were the two groups least opposed to tax evasion. However, none of the differences in mean scores among the 10 groups were significant at the 5% level.

Government vs. Individual Responsibility

Findings: Those who most strongly believed that individuals should take more responsibility and those who most strongly believed that government should take more responsibility were the groups most opposed to tax evasion, while the groups between these two extremes were least opposed to tax evasion.

Success: Hard Work vs. Luck and Connections

Findings: Those who most firmly believe that hard work brings success are most opposed to tax evasion, compared to those who believe that success is the result of luck and connections. The difference was significant.

Confidence in Government

Findings: Those who had a great deal or quite a lot of confidence in government were more strongly opposed to tax evasion than were those who had little or no trust in government. The difference was significant at the 1% level.

Confidence in the Justice System

Findings: Those who had a great deal of confidence in the justice system were more firmly opposed to tax evasion than were those who had little or no confidence in the justice system.

Confidence in the Police

Findings: Those who had the most confidence in the police were also most opposed to tax evasion.

Relative Seriousness of Tax Evasion

Findings: In terms of seriousness, tax evasion was ranked fifth out of 11 ethical issues. Tax evasion was more serious than suicide, prostitution, abortion, euthanasia, divorce, and homosexuality and less serious than claiming government benefits to which you are not entitled, accepting a bribe, wife beating, and avoiding a fare on public transport.

Trend Analysis

Findings: Views toward tax evasion have shifted over time, but not in a linear pattern. The Swiss were most opposed to tax evasion in 2007 and least opposed in 1996. In 1989 they were between these two extremes.

Taiwan

McGee, Robert W. and Susana N. Vittadini Andres. 2009. The Ethics of Tax Evasion: Case Studies of Taiwan, in Robert W. McGee, *Readings in Business Ethics* (pp. 200–228). Hyderabad, India: ICFAI University Press. An abbreviated version was published in Marjorie G. Adams and Abbass Alkhafaji (Eds.), *Business Research Yearbook: Global Business Perspectives*, Volume XIV, No. 1 (pp. 34–39). Beltsville, MD: International Graphics, 2007.

METHODOLOGY; Human Beliefs and Values Survey, Wave 4 (1 = never justifiable; 10 = always justifiable).

SAMPLE SIZE: 780
OVERALL MEAN SCORE: 1.96

Gender

Mean Scores

Female: 2.07
Male: 1.85
Conclusion: Men are more opposed to tax evasion.

Age

Mean Scores

15–29: 2.02
30–49: 2.04
50+: 1.70

Conclusion: People become more averse to tax evasion as they get older.

Education

Mean Scores

Lower: 1.83
Middle: 1.95
Upper: 2.08
Conclusion: People tend to become less averse to tax evasion as the level of education increases.

Marital Status

Mean Scores

Widowed: 1.70
Divorced: 1.83
Married: 1.95
Single/Never Married: 2.00
Living together as married: 3.00
Separated: 3.00
Conclusion: Attitude toward tax evasion differs by marital status.

Religion

Mean Scores

Roman Catholic: 1.69
Other: 1.88
Buddhist: 2.00
Protestant: 2.21
Conclusion: Attitude toward tax evasion differs by religion.

Ten Transition Economies

McGee, Robert W. and Wendy Gelman. 2008. Opinions on the Ethics of Tax Evasion: A Comparative Study of 10 Transition Economies, in Robert W. McGee (Ed.), *Accounting Reform in Transition and Developing Economies* (pp. 495–508). New York: Springer.

METHODOLOGY; Human Beliefs and Values Survey, "Is tax evasion ever justified if you have a chance?" (1 = never justifiable; 10 = always justifiable).

SAMPLE SIZE: 12,320

Overall Mean Score

China 1.57
Czech Republic 2.07

Estonia 3.15
Hungary 2.12
Latvia 2.36
Lithuania 3.77
Poland 2.23
Russia 3.09
Ukraine 3.45
Vietnam 1.32
Overall 2.55

Gender

Women were significantly more opposed to tax evasion in 5 cases (Czech Republic, Estonia, Latvia, Russia, Ukraine).

Women were more opposed to tax evasion in 3 cases but the difference was not significant (Hungary, Lithuania, Poland).

Men were more opposed to tax evasion in 2 cases (China, Vietnam) but the differences in mean scores were not significant.

Age

In 9 cases older people were significantly more averse to tax evasion than were younger people. In the case of Vietnam, opposition to tax evasion was the same for all age groups.

Ten Transition Economies

McGee, Robert W. 2008. Changing Attitudes toward the Ethics of Tax Evasion: An Empirical Study of 10 Transition Economies. *Accounting and Finance in Transition* 5: 145–154. Also Fifth International Conference on Accounting and Finance in Transition. London, July 12–14, 2007. Reprinted in Robert W. McGee (Ed.), *Taxation and Public Finance in Transition and Developing Economies* (pp. 119–136). New York: Springer, 2008, under the title Trends in the Ethics of Tax Evasion: An Empirical Study of Ten Transition Economies.

METHODOLOGY; Human Beliefs and Values Survey. (1 = never justifiable; 10 = always justifiable).

This study examined trends of tax evasion opinion in ten countries. The goal was to determine whether people became more or less opposed to tax evasion over time.

Became Significantly Less Opposed Over Time

Belarus (1990; 1999)
Estonia (1990; 1999)
Lithuania (1990; 1999)
Russia (1990; 1999)
Slovenia (1992; 1999)
East Germany (1990; 1999)

Became Significantly More Opposed Over Time

Bulgaria (1990; 1999)
Poland (1989; 1999)

Became More Opposed But Not Significantly

China (1990; 2001)
Latvia (1990; 1999)

Thailand and Vietnam

McGee, Robert W. 2006. A Comparative Study of Tax Evasion Ethics in Thailand and Vietnam. *Journal of Accounting, Ethics & Public Policy* 6(1): 103–123.
QUESTION: Is tax evasion ever justified if you have a chance? (1 = never justified; 10 = always justified).

Overall

Mean

Thailand 2.8
Vietnam 1.7

Gender	Mean scores	
	Thailand	Vietnam
Male	2.9	1.7
Female	2.6	1.6

Findings

Overall

Vietnamese are significantly more opposed to tax evasion, at the 1% level.

Gender

Females were more strongly opposed to tax evasion in both countries. The difference was significant in Thailand but not in Vietnam.

Age

Older people are more averse to tax evasion than are younger people.

Confidence in Government

Although there was no significant difference for the Thai sample, an analysis of the Vietnamese sample found that individuals became significantly less averse to tax evasion as their confidence in government declined.

Happiness

Although the differences in the Thai sample were not significant, an analysis of the Vietnamese sample found that people who were very happy were significantly less opposed to tax evasion than were people who were quite happy.

Thirty-Three Countries

McGee, Robert W. and Michael Tyler. 2007. Tax Evasion and Ethics: A Demographic Study of Thirty-Three Countries. *International Journal of Business, Accounting, and Finance* 1(1): 95–114.

METHODOLOGY; Human Beliefs and Values Survey, "Is tax evasion ever justified if you have a chance?" (1 = never justifiable; 10 = always justifiable).

Gender

Combined Mean Scores

Female: 2.38
Male: 2.77

Findings

Women were more opposed to tax evasion in 32 countries. Opposition was equal in one country (Portugal).

Age

In almost all cases, the percentage of people who think tax evasion is always unethical rises as they get older. Mann-Whitney U tests were used to determine whether the differences were significant. The test result comparing the 16–29 and 30–49-year-old groups was significant at the 1% level ($p \leq 0.003$). A comparison of the 30–49 and 50+ age groups was also found to be significantly different at the 1% level ($p \leq 3.21014\text{e-}05$). These findings confirm the belief that people have more respect for government and authority as they get older.

Education

People are less likely to view tax evasion as always unethical if they are more educated, or at least as they move out of the lowest category of education. The difference between the lower and middle education categories was statistically significant at the 1% level. But there was no statistical difference between the middle and upper level educated groups. Results indicate that the lower educated group tends to be more opposed to tax evasion than the higher educated groups.

Income

The percentage of people who view tax evasion as always unethical declines as income increases. A comparison of the scores for the lower and middle income groups found the difference to be significant at the 10% level.

Comparing the scores for the middle and upper income groups found the difference not to be significant, but a comparison of the lower and upper income scores found the difference to be significant at the 1% level. Results indicate that the lower income group tends to be more opposed to tax evasion than the upper income group.

USA and 6 Latin American Countries

McGee, Robert W. and Wendy Gelman. 2009. Opinions on the Ethics of Tax Evasion: A Comparative Study of the USA and Six Latin American Countries. *Akron Tax Journal* 24: 69–91.

METHODOLOGY; Human Beliefs and Values Survey. (1 = never justifiable; 10 = always justifiable).

Overall Mean Scores

Venezuela 1.82
Argentina 1.87
Puerto Rico 2.01
Peru 2.11
Chile 2.15
USA 2.28
Mexico 2.31

Gender

Argentina – females significantly more opposed to tax evasion
Chile – females more opposed but not significantly
Mexico – females more opposed but not significantly
Peru – females significantly more opposed
Puerto Rico – females more opposed but not significantly
USA – females significantly more opposed
Venezuela – females more opposed but not significantly

Age

Argentina – become significantly more opposed with age
Chile – become more opposed with age but not significantly
Mexico – become significantly more opposed with age
Peru – become more opposed with age but not significantly
Puerto Rico – become significantly more opposed with age
USA – become significantly more opposed with age
Venezuela – age makes no difference

Education

Argentina – no difference
Chile – no difference
Mexico – people with a secondary education are significantly less opposed to tax evasion than are people with either more or less education
Peru – no difference
Puerto Rico – no difference
USA – no difference
Venezuela – no difference

Religious Observance

Argentina – no difference
Chile – no difference
Mexico – no difference
Peru – those who attend services more than once a week are significantly more opposed to tax evasion than are people who attend services once a month.
Puerto Rico – no difference
USA – those who attend services more than once a week are significantly more opposed to tax evasion than are people who attend services once a month or never/practically never.
Venezuela – no difference

Vietnam

McGee, Robert W. 2008. A Survey of Vietnamese Opinion on the Ethics of Tax Evasion, in Robert W. McGee (Ed.), *Taxation and Public Finance in Transition and Developing Economies* (pp. 663–674). New York: Springer.

METHODOLOGY; Human Beliefs and Values Survey, "Is tax evasion ever justified if you have a chance?" (1 = never justifiable; 10 = always justifiable).

SAMPLE SIZE: 989
OVERALL MEAN SCORE: 1.32

Gender

Mean Scores

Female: 1.36
Male: 1.28
Conclusion: Men are more opposed to tax evasion.

Age

Mean Scores

15–29: 1.31
30–49: 1.31
50+: 1.33
Conclusion: People of all ages are equally opposed to tax evasion.

Education

Mean Scores

Lower: 1.32
Middle: 1.26
Upper: 1.69
Conclusion: People with a middle-level education are more opposed to tax evasion than are people with either a higher or lower education. People with an upper education are least opposed to tax evasion.

Religion

Mean Scores

Roman Catholic: 1.47
Buddhist: 1.42
Ancestral Worshipping: 1.23
Conclusion: Ancestral worshippers were most opposed to tax evasion. Roman Catholics were least opposed to tax evasion.

Religions Service Attendance

Mean Scores

More than once a week: 1.23
Once a week: 1.44
Once a month: 1.36
Only on special days: 1.37
Once a year: 1.37
Less often: 1.14
Never/practically never: 1.34

Conclusion: People who attend religious services infrequently were most opposed to tax evasion, followed by people who attend more than once a week. Those who attend once a week were least opposed to tax evasion. However, all mean scores were less than 1.5, indicating that all groups were strongly opposed to tax evasion.

Marital Status

Mean Scores

Married: 1.31
Living together as married: 1.35
Divorced: 1.67
Separated: 1.17
Widowed: 1.59
Single/never married: 1.30

Conclusion. Separated people were the most strongly opposed to tax evasion. Divorced people were least opposed to tax evasion. However, all mean scores were less than 1.5, indicating that all groups were strongly opposed to tax evasion.

Chapter 35
Annotated Bibliography: Other Studies*

Robert W. McGee

Germany

McGee, Robert W. Serkan Benk, Adriana M. Ross & Harun Kılıçaslan (2009). An Empirical Study of Ethical Opinion in Germany. *Journal of Accounting, Ethics & Public Policy*, 10(2), 243–259.

Methodology

Examined six ethical issues that were included in the World Values Surveys. Students were asked to determine the justifiability of six acts using a ten-point Likert scale (1 = never justifiable; 10 = always justifiable).

Sample: A total of 252 business students and faculty at Hamburg University. The sample consisted mostly of undergraduate unmarried Christian business students under age 30.

Ranking (strongest to weakest opposition)

Rank	Act	Mean
1	Someone accepting a bribe in the course of their duties	1.77
2	Buy stolen goods	2.31
3	Claiming government benefits to which you are not entitled	2.82
4	Cheating on taxes if you have a chance	2.94
5	Paying cash for services to avoid taxes	4.11
6	Avoiding a fare on public transport	4.17

*Note: Some of the studies listed below are available online at http://ssrn.com/author=2139.

R.W. McGee (✉)
School of Business, Florida International University, 3000 NE 151 Street,
North Miami, FL 33181, USA
e-mail: bob414@hotmail.com

R.W. McGee (ed.), *The Ethics of Tax Evasion: Perspectives in Theory and Practice*,
DOI 10.1007/978-1-4614-1287-8_35, © Springer Science+Business Media, LLC 2012

Overall Findings

- Ranking: Three acts were found to be more serious an offense than tax evasion. The two tax evasion issues were ranked 4 and 5 out of six acts.
- Gender: Women found all six acts less justifiable than men. The differences were significant (at 5%) in three cases.

Mexico

McGee, Robert W., Yanira Petrides and Adriana M. Ross (2012). How Serious Is Tax Evasion: A Survey of Mexican Opinion. In Robert W. McGee (Ed.), *The Ethics of Tax Evasion: Perspectives in Theory and Practice* (pp. 405–411). New York: Springer.

Methodology

Examined six ethical issues that were included in the World Values Surveys. Students were asked to determine the justifiability of six acts using a ten-point Likert scale (1 = never justifiable; 10 = always justifiable).

Sample: A total of 369 accounting, business and engineering students, and faculty at a university in Mexico city.
Ranking (strongest to weakest opposition)

Rank	Act	Mean
1	Buy stolen goods	2.35
2	Prostitution	2.48
3	Someone accepting a bribe in the course of their duties	2.57
4	Cheating on taxes if you have a chance	2.60
5	Avoiding a fare on public transport	2.80
6	Claiming government benefits to which you are not entitled	5.43

Overall Findings

- Ranking: Three acts were found to be more serious an offense than tax evasion.
- Gender: Mean scores were not significantly different except for the prostitution question, where women were significantly more opposed.

- Age: The group most opposed to the six acts overall was the 30–49 age group. The group least opposed was the youngest group (15–29). The oldest group (50+) had mean scores that fell between the other two groups.
- Major: Overall, the engineering majors were the most opposed to the six acts. The other business and economics majors were least opposed, with the accounting majors falling between the other two groups.
- Status: Overall, the faculty was more opposed to the six acts than were the other two groups. Undergraduate students were least opposed to the six acts, overall. Faculty were also more opposed to the cheating on taxes question (Act 3) than were the other two groups; undergraduate students were least opposed for that act.

Turkey

Benk, Serkan, Robert W. McGee and Adriana M. Ross (2009). An Empirical Study of Ethical Opinion in Turkey. *Journal of Accounting, Ethics & Public Policy*, 10(1), 83–99.

Methodology

Examined six ethical issues that were included in the World Values Surveys. Students were asked to determine the justifiability of six acts using a ten-point Likert scale (1 = never justifiable; 10 = always justifiable).

Sample: A total of 399 business students and faculty at Zonguldak University in Turkey. The sample consisted mostly of undergraduate unmarried Muslim business students under age 30.

Ranking (strongest to weakest opposition)

Rank	Act	Mean
1	Someone accepting a bribe in the course of their duties	1.42
2	Cheating on taxes if you have a chance	1.53
3	Buy stolen goods	1.68
4	Claiming government benefits to which you are not entitled	1.69
5	Avoiding a fare on public transport	1.83
6	Paying cash for services to avoid taxes	3.35

Overall Findings

- Ranking: One act was found to be more serious an offense than tax evasion. The two tax evasion issues were ranked 2 and 6 out of six acts.
- Gender: Women found to be significantly more opposed to acts 2, 5, and 6. The differences in mean scores for the other three acts were not significant.

References

Adams, Charles. (1982). *Fight, Flight and Fraud: The Story of Taxation*. Curacao: Euro-Dutch Publishers.

Adams, Charles. (1993). *For Good or Evil: The Impact of Taxes on the Course of Civilization*. London, New York & Lanham: Madison Books.

Ahmad, Mushtaq (1995). *Business Ethics in Islam*. Islamabad, Pakistan: The International Institute of Islamic Thought & The International Institute of Islamic Economics.

Aitken, Sherie S. and Laura Bonneville, (1980). A General Taxpayer Opinion Survey. IRS, Office of Planning and Research, (CSR Incorporated) (March). Cited in Betty R. Jackson and Valerie C. Milliron. 1986. Tax Compliance Research: Findings, Problems, and Prospects. Journal of Accounting Literature 5, 125–165, at p. 127.

Akaah, Ishmael P. (1989). Differences in Research Ethics Judgments Between Male and Female Marketing Professionals. *Journal of Business Ethics*, 8(5), 375–381.

Akaah, Ishmael P. (1996). The Influence of Organizational Rank and Role on Marketing Professionals' Ethical Judgments. *Journal of Business Ethics*, 15(6), 605–613.

Akaah, Ishmael P. and Edward A. Riordan. (1989). Judgments of Marketing Professionals About Ethical Issues in Marketing Research: A Replication and Extension. *Journal of Marketing Research*, 26(1), 112–120.

Alm, James and Benno Torgler. (2004). Estimating the Determinants of Tax Morale. *Proceedings of the 97th Annual Conference on Taxation of the National Tax Association – Tax Institute of America*, 269–274.

Alm, James, Jorge Martinez-Vazquez and Benno Torgler. (2005). Russian Tax Morale in the 1990s. *Proceedings of the 98th Annual Conference on Taxation of the National Tax Association*, 287–292.

Alm, James and Benno Torgler. (2006). Culture differences and tax morale in the United States and in Europe. *Journal of Economic Psychology*, 27, 224–246.

Alm, James, Jorge Martinez-Vazquez and Benno Torgler. (2006). Russian attitudes toward paying taxes – before, during, and after the transition. *International Journal of Social Economics*, 33(12), 832–857.

Alm, James, Jorge Martinez-Vazquez & Mark Rider (eds.) (2006). *The Challenges of Tax Reform in a Global Economy*. New York: Springer.

Alm, J., J. Martinez-Vazquez & B. Torgler (2010). Developing Alternative Frameworks for Explaining Tax Compliance. In J. Alm, J. Martinez-Vazquez & B. Torgler (Eds.), *Developing Alternative Frameworks for Explaining Tax Compliance* (pp. 3–12). London & New York: Routledge.

Alm, J. & J. Martinez-Vazquez. (2010). Tax Evasion, the Informal Sector, and Tax Morale in LAC Countries. In J. Alm, J. Martinez-Vazquez & B. Torgler (Eds.), *Developing Alternative Frameworks for Explaining Tax Compliance* (pp. 260–291). London & New York: Routledge.

References

Ameen, Elsice C., Daryl M. Guffey & Jeffrey J. McMillan (1996). Gender Differences in Determining the Ethical Sensitivity of Future Accounting Professionals. *Journal of Business Ethics*, 15(5), 591–597.

Angelus Carletus de Clavisio (1494). *Summa Angelica.* Lyons, as cited by Martin T. Crowe, The Moral Obligation of Paying Just Taxes, The Catholic University of America Studies in Sacred Theology No. 84, 1944, pp. 28–29.

Antoninus, Saint (1571). *Summa Sacrae Theologiae, Iuris Pontificii, et Caesarei*, II, p. 63 ff, Venice, as cited by Martin T. Crowe, The Moral Obligation of Paying Just Taxes, The Catholic University of America Studies in Sacred Theology No. 84, 1944, p. 42.

Aristotle. *Nicomachean Ethics.*

Aristotle. *The Politics.*

Armstrong, Mary Beth and Jack Robison. (1998). Ethics in Taxation. *Journal of Accounting, Ethics & Public Policy*, 1(4), 535–557, reprinted in Robert W. McGee (Ed.), *The Ethics of Tax Evasion* (pp. 330–348). Dumont, NJ: The Dumont Institute for Public Policy Research, 1998.

Babakus, Emin, T. Bettina Cornwell, Vince Mitchell and Bodo Schlegelmilch (2004). Reactions to Unethical Consumer Behavior across Six Countries. *The Journal of Consumer Marketing*, 21(4/5), 254–263.

Baird, J.S. (1980). Current Trends in College Cheating. *Psychology in the Schools*, 17(4), 515–522, as cited in Bob S. Brown and Peggy Choong. (2005). An Investigation of Academic Dishonesty among Business Students at Public and Private United States Universities. *International Journal of Management* 22(2): 201–214.

Baldwin, Leland D. (1967). *Whiskey Rebels: The Story of a Frontier Uprising.* Pittsburgh: University of Pittsburgh Press.

Ballas, Apostolos A. and Haridimos Tsoukas. (1998). Consequences of Distrust: The Vicious Circle of Tax Evasion in Greece. *Journal of Accounting, Ethics & Public Policy*, 1(4), 572–596, reprinted in Robert W. McGee (Ed.), *The Ethics of Tax Evasion.* Dumont, NJ: The Dumont Institute for Public Policy Research, 1998, pp. 284–304.

Barker, Dan. (1992). *Losing Faith in Faith.* Madison, WI: Freedom from Religion Foundation.

Barnett, John H. and Marvin J. Karson. (1987). Personal Values and Business Decisions: An Exploratory Investigation. *Journal of Business Ethics*, 6(5), 371–382.

Barnett, John H. and Marvin J. Karson. (1989). Managers, Values, and Executive Decisions: An Exploration of the Role of Gender, Career Stage, Organizational Level, Function, and the Importance of Ethics, Relationships and Results in Managerial Decision-Making. *Journal of Business Ethics*, 8(10), 747–771.

Bastiat, Frédéric. (1968). *The Law.* Irvington-on-Hudson, NY: Foundation for Economic Education. Originally published in 1850 as a pamphlet, *La Loi*, reprinted in *Sophismes Économiques*, Vol. I. *Oeuvres Complètes de Frédéric Bastiat*, 4th edition, Paris: Guillaumin et Cⁱᵉ, 1878, pp. 343–394.

Beia, F. Lodovicus de (1591). *Responsiones Casuum Conscientiae.* Venice, at cas. 13, p. 53 ff., as cited by Martin T. Crowe, The Moral Obligation of Paying Just Taxes, The Catholic University of America Studies in Sacred Theology No. 84, 1944, p. 32.

Beito, D.T. (1989). *Taxpayers in Revolt: Tax Resistance during the Great Depression.* Chapel Hill, NC: University of North Carolina Press.

Beltramini, Richard F., Robert A. Peterson & George Kozmetsky. (1984). Concerns of College Students Regarding Business Ethics. *Journal of Business Ethics*, 3(3), 195–200.

Benk, Serkan, Robert W. McGee and Adriana M. Ross (2009). An Empirical Study of Ethical Opinion in Turkey. *Journal of Accounting, Ethics & Public Policy*, 10(1), 83–99.

Berardi, Aemilio (1898). *Praxis Confessariorum II*, as cited in Martin T. Crowe, *The Moral Obligation of Paying Just Taxes*, The Catholic University of America Studies in Sacred Theology No. 84, 1944 at p. 35.

Betz, Michael, Lenahan O'Connell and Jon M. Shepard. (1989). Gender Differences in Proclivity for Unethical Behavior. *Journal of Business Ethics*, 8(5), 321–324.

Beu, Danielle S., M. Ronald Buckley & Michael G. Harvey. (2003). Ethical Decision-Making: A Multidimensional Construct. *Business Ethics: A European Review*, 12(1), 88–107.

Bird, Richard M., Jorge Martinez-Vazquez and Benno Torgler. (2004). Tax Performance in Developing Countries: the Role of Demand Factors. *Proceedings of the 97th Annual Conference on Taxation of the National Tax Association – Tax Institute of America*, 284–289.

Bird, Richard M., Jorge Martinez-Vazquez and Benno Torgler. (2007). Tax Effort: The Impact of Corruption, Voice and Accountability. Working Paper No. 2007–13, Center for Research in Economics, Management and the Arts, Basel, Switzerland.

Blackwell, C. (2010). A Meta-analysis of Incentive Effects in Tax Compliance Experiments. In J. Alm, J. Martinez-Vazquez & B. Torgler (Eds.), *Developing Alternative Frameworks for Explaining Tax Compliance* (pp. 97–112). London & New York: Routledge.

Block, Walter. (1989). The Justification of Taxation in the Public Finance Literature: A Critique. *Journal of Public Finance and Public Choice*, 3, 141–158.

Block, Walter. (1993). Public Finance Texts Cannot Justify Government Taxation: A Critique. *Canadian Public Administration/Administration Publique du Canada*, 36(2), 225–262, reprinted in revised form under the title "The Justification for Taxation in the Economics Literature" in Robert W. McGee (ed.), *The Ethics of Tax Evasion* (pp. 36–88) The Dumont Institute for Public Policy Research, Dumont, NJ, 1998.

Block, Walter, William Kordsmeier and Joseph Horton (2012). The Failure of Public Finance. In Robert W. McGee (Ed.), *The Ethics of Tax Evasion: Perspectives in Theory and Practice* (pp. 229–244). New York, Springer.

Bloomquist, Kim M. (2003a). Tax Evasion, Income Inequality and Opportunity Costs of Compliance. Presented at the 96th Annual Conference of the National Tax Association, Drake Hotel, Chicago (November). www.irs.gov/pub/irs-soi/bloomq.pdf

Bloomquist, Kim M. (2003b). Trends as Changes in Variance: The Case of Tax Noncompliance. 2003 IRS Research Conference (June).

Blum, Walter J. & Harry Kalven, Jr. (1953). *The Uneasy Case for Progressive Taxation*. Chicago & London: University of Chicago Press.

Boétie, Étienne de la (1577). *Discours de la Servitude Volontaire*.

Boétie, Étienne de la (1974). *The Will to Bondage*. Colorado Springs: Ralph Myles Publisher.

Boétie, Étienne de la (1975). *The Politics of Obedience: The Discourse of Voluntary Servitude*. New York: Free Life Editions.

Bonacina, Martinus (1687). *Operum de Morali Theologia*, "Tractatus de Restitutione," disp. II, q. IX, n. 5 (Venice), II, p. 449, as cited by Martin T. Crowe, The Moral Obligation of Paying Just Taxes, The Catholic University of America Studies in Sacred Theology No. 84, 1944, p. 46.

Boortz, Neal & John Linder (2005). *The Fair Tax Book: Saying Goodbye to the Income Tax and the I.R.S.* New York: HarperCollins.

Bose, Sanjoy (2012). Hindu Ethical Considerations in Relation to Tax Evasion. In Robert W. McGee (Ed.), *The Ethics of Tax Evasion: Perspectives in Theory and Practice* (pp. 135–147). New York, Springer.

Boyd, David P. (1981). Improving Ethical Awareness Through the Business and Society Course. *Business and Society* 20, 21, 2, 1: 27–31.

Braithwaite, V., M. Reinhart & M. Smart. (2010). Tax Non-compliance among the Under-30s: Knowledge, Obligation or Skepticism? In J. Alm, J. Martinez-Vazquez & B. Torgler (Eds.), *Developing Alternative Frameworks for Explaining Tax Compliance* (pp. 217–237). London & New York: Routledge.

Brown, Bob S. and Peggy Choong. (2005). An Investigation of Academic Dishonesty among Business Students at Public and Private United States Universities. *International Journal of Management*, 22(2), 201–214.

Browning, John and Noel B. Zabriskie. (1983). How Ethical Are Industrial Buyers? *Industrial Marketing Management*, 12(4), 219–224.

Buchanan, James M. (1967). *Public Finance in Democratic Process*. Chapel Hill, NC: University of North Carolina Press.

Buchanan, James M. & Marilyn R. Flowers. (1975). *The Public Finances*, 4th edition. Homewood, IL: Richard D. Irwin, Inc.

Buchanan, James M. & Richard A. Musgrave. (2001). *Public Finance and Public Choice: Two Contrasting Visions of the State*. Cambridge, MA & London. MIT Press.

Bulluart, F.C.R. (1874). *Summa Sancti Thomae hodiernis academiarum moribus accommodate*, VI, dissert. IX, art. VII, para. II (Lyons), VI, as cited in Martin T. Crowe, *The Moral Obligation of Paying Just Taxes*. The Catholic University of America Studies in Sacred Theology No. 84, p. 56.

Burnham, David (1989). *A Law unto Itself: Power, Politics and the IRS*. New York: Random House.

Burr, William Henry. (1987). *Self-Contradictions in the Bible*. Buffalo: Prometheus Books. Originally published in 1860 in New York by A.J. Davis & Company.

Burton, Hughlene A., Stewart S. Karlinsky and Cynthia Blanthorne (2005). Perception of a White-Collar Crime: Tax Evasion. *The ATA Journal of Legal Tax Research* 3, 35–48.

Byrnes, J. P., D.C. Miller and W.D. Schafer. (1999). Gender Differences in Risk Taking: A Meta-analysis. *Psychological Bulletin*, 125, 367–383.

Callan, Victor J. (1992). Predicting Ethical Values and Training Needs in Ethics. *Journal of Business Ethics*, 11(10), 761–769.

Chamberlain, Andrew and Gerald Prante (2007). Who Pays Taxes and Who Receives Government Spending? An Analysis of Federal, State and Local Tax and Spending Distributions, 1991–2004. Tax Foundation Working Paper No. 1 (March). Washington, DC: Tax Foundation.

Champagne, Frank (1994). *Cancel April 15th! The Plan for Painless Taxation*. Mount Vernon, WA: Veda Vangarde.

Chesher, James E. and Tibor R. Machan. (1999). *The Business of Commerce: Examining an Honorable Profession*. Stanford: Hoover Institution Press.

Chodorov, Frank (1954). *The Income Tax: Root of All Evil*. New York: The Devin-Adair Company.

Chonko, Lawrence B. and Shelby D. Hunt. (1985). Ethics and Marketing Management: An Empirical Investigation. *Journal of Business Research*, 13(4), 339–359.

CIA World Factbook (2011). https://www.cia.gov/library/publications/the-world-factbook/

Cohn, Gordon. (1998). The Jewish View on Paying Taxes. *Journal of Accounting, Ethics & Public Policy*, 1(2), 109–120, reprinted in Robert W. McGee (Ed.), *The Ethics of Tax Evasion* (pp. 180–189). Dumont, NJ: The Dumont Institute for Public Policy Research, 1998, pp. 180–189.

Cohn, Gordon (2012). The Traditional Jewish View of Paying Taxes. In Robert W. McGee (Ed.), *The Ethics of Tax Evasion: Perspectives in Theory and Practice* (pp. 149–158). New York, Springer.

Concina, F. Daniel (1774). *Theologia Christiana Dogmatico-Moralis* (Naples), as cited in Martin T. Crowe, *The Moral Obligation of Paying Just Taxes*. The Catholic University of America Studies in Sacred Theology No. 84, p. 55.

Cowell, F.A. (1990). *Cheating the Government: The Economics of Evasion*. Cambridge, MA & London: MIT Press.

Crolly, George (1877). *Disputationes Theologicae de Justitia et Jure*. Dublin: Gill and Son, as cited by Martin T. Crowe, The Moral Obligation of Paying Just Taxes, The Catholic University of America Studies in Sacred Theology No. 84, 1944, p. 38.

Crowe, Martin T. (1944). The Moral Obligation of Paying Just Taxes, The Catholic University of America Studies in Sacred Theology No. 84.

Cullis, J. & Philip Jones. (1998). *Public Finance and Public Choice*, 2nd edition. New York: Oxford University Press.

Cullis, John, Jones, Philip and Lewis, Alan, (2006). Tax Framing, Instrumentality and Individual Differences: Are There Two Different Cultures? *Journal of Economic Psychology*, 27, 304–320.

Cullis, J., P. Jones & A. Lewis. (2010). Tax Compliance: Social Norms, Culture, and Endogeneity. In J. Alm, J. Martinez-Vazquez & B. Torgler (Eds.), *Developing Alternative Frameworks for Explaining Tax Compliance* (pp. 35–55). London & New York: Routledge.

Cummings, Ronald G., Jorge Martinez-Vazquez, Michael McKee and Benno Torgler. (2004). Effects of Culture on Tax Compliance: A Cross Check of experimental and Survey Evidence. Presented at the Meeting of the Public Choice Society, Baltimore, March 11–14.

Cummings, Ronald G., Jorge Martinez-Vazquez, Michael McKee and Benno Torgler. (2009). Tax morale affects tax compliance: Evidence from surveys and an artefactual field experiment. *Journal of Economic Behavior & Organization*, 70, 447–457.

Curry, B. (1982). *Principles of Taxation of a Libertarian Society*. Glendale, CA: BC Publishing Company.

Davis, Henry (1938). Moral and Pastoral Theology, 3rd ed. New York: Sheed and Ward, as cited in Martin T. Crowe, *The Moral Obligation of Paying Just Taxes*. The Catholic University of America Studies in Sacred Theology No. 84, p. 40.

Dawson, Leslie M. (1997). Ethical Differences Between Men and Women in the Sales Profession. *Journal of Business Ethics*, 16(11), 1143–1152.

DeMoville, Wig. (1998). The Ethics of Tax Evasion: A Baha'i Perspective. *Journal of Accounting, Ethics & Public Policy*, 1(3), 356–368, reprinted in Robert W. McGee (Ed.), *The Ethics of Tax Evasion* (pp. 230–240). Dumont, NJ: The Dumont Institute for Public Policy Research, 1998.

Derry, Robin. (1989). An Empirical Study of Moral Reasoning Among Managers. *Journal of Business Ethics*, 8(11), 855–862.

DioGuardi, Joseph J. (1992). *Unaccountable Congress*. Washington, DC: Regnery Gateway.

Dollar, David, Raymond Fisman, and Roberta Gatti. (2001). Are Women Really the "Fairer" Sex? Corruption and Women in Government, *Journal of Economic Behavior and Organization*, 46, 423–429.

Dubinsky, Alan J. and Michael Levy. (1985). Ethics in Retailing: Perceptions of Retail Sales People. *Journal of the Academy of Marketing Science*, 13(1), 1–16.

Eabrasu, Marian (2012). Towards a Convergence of the Ethics of Tax Evasion and Secession. In Robert W. McGee (Ed.), *The Ethics of Tax Evasion: Perspectives in Theory and Practice* (pp. 107–123). New York, Springer.

Edwards, C. & D.J. Mitchell. (2008). *Global Tax Revolution: The Rise of Tax Competition and the Battle to Defend It*. Washington, DC: Cato Institute.

Ekin, M.G. Serap (Atakan) and S. Hande Tezolmez. (1999). Business Ethics in Turkey: An Empirical Investigation with Special Emphasis on Gender. *Journal of Business Ethics*, 18(1), 17–34.

Erard, B. & J.S. Feinstein. (2010). Econometric Models for Multi-Stage Audit Processes: An Application to the IRS National Research Program. In J. Alm, J. Martinez-Vazquez & B. Torgler (Eds.), *Developing Alternative Frameworks for Explaining Tax Compliance* (pp. 113–137). London & New York: Routledge.

Feld, L.P. & B.S. Frey. (2010). Tax Evasion and the Psychological Tax Contract. In J. Alm, J. Martinez-Vazquez & B. Torgler (Eds.), *Developing Alternative Frameworks for Explaining Tax Compliance* (pp. 74–94). London & New York: Routledge.

Ferrell, O.C. and Steven J. Skinner. (1988). Ethical Behavior and Bureaucratic Structure in Marketing Research Organizations. *Journal of Marketing Research*, 25(1), 103–109.

Fischer, Justina A.V. and Benno Torgler. (2006). Does Envy Destroy Social Fundamentals? The Impact of Relative Income Position on Social Capital. Working Paper No. 2006–04, Center for Research in Economics, Management and the Arts, Basel, Switzerland.

Fitzgerald, Randall (1988). *When Government Goes Private: Successful Alternatives to Public Services*. New York: Universe Books.

Fitzgerald, Randall & Gerald Lipson (1984). *Pork Barrel: The Unexpurgated Grace Commission Story of Congressional Profligacy*. Washington, DC: Cato Institute.

Franke, George R., Deborah F. Crown & Deborah F. Spake. (1997). Gender Differences in Ethical Perceptions of Business Practices: A Social Role Theory Perspective. *Journal of Applied Psychology*, 82(6), 920–934.

Frankel, Sandor & Robert S. Fink (1985). *How to Defend Yourself against the IRS*. New York: Simon & Schuster.

Frey, Bruno S. and Benno Torgler. (2007). Tax morale and conditional cooperation. *Journal of Comparative Economics*, 35, 136–159.

Friedman, William J., Amy B. Robinson & Britt L. Friedman. (1987). Sex Differences in Moral Judgments? A Test of Gilligan's Theory. *Psychology of Women Quarterly*, 11, 37–46.

Fritzsche, David J. (1988). An Examination of Marketing Ethics: Role of the Decision Maker, Consequences of the Decision, Management Position, and Sex of the Respondent. *Journal of Macromarketing*, 8(2), 29–39.

Galbraith, Sharon and Harriet Buckman Stephenson. (1993). Decision Rules Used by Male and Female Business Students in Making Ethical Value Judgments: Another Look. *Journal of Business Ethics*, 12(3), 227–233.

García-Valiñas, María A., Roberto Fernández Llera and Benno Torgler. (2005). More Income Equality or Not? An Empirical Analysis of Individuals' Preferences. Working Paper No. 2005-23, Center for Research in Economics, Management and the Arts, Basel, Switzerland.

Glover, Saundra H. (1991). The Influences of Individual Values on Ethical Decision Making. Unpublished doctoral dissertation, University of South Carolina, Columbia, as cited in Saundra H. Glover, Minnette A. Bumpus, Glynda F. Sharp & George A. Munchus. (2002). Gender Differences in Ethical Decision Making. *Women in Management Review*, 17(5), 217–227.

Glover, Saundra H., Minnette Bumpus and J. Logan. (1993). Putting Values into Decision Making: the Influence of the Value Honesty/Integrity on the Decision Choice. *Proceedings of the Southern Management Association* 428–431, as cited in Saundra H. Glover, Minnette A. Bumpus, Glynda F. Sharp & George A. Munchus. (2002). Gender Differences in Ethical Decision Making. *Women in Management Review*, 17(5), 217–227.

Glover, Saundra H., Minnette Bumpus, John E. Logan & James R. Ciesla. (1997). Re-examining the Influence of Individual Values on Ethical Decision Making. *Journal of Business Ethics*, 16(12/13), 1319–1329.

Glover, Saundra H., Minnette A. Bumpus, Glynda F. Sharp & George A. Munchus. (2002). Gender Differences in Ethical Decision Making. *Women in Management Review*, 17(5), 217–227.

Grace, J. Peter (1984). *Burning Money: The Waste of Your Tax Dollars*. New York: Macmillan Publishing Company.

Graetz, M.J. & I. Shapiro. (2005). *Death by a Thousand Cuts: The Fight over Taxing Inherited Wealth*. Princeton & Oxford: Princeton University Press.

Grasmick, H., N. Finley and D. Glaser. (1984). Labor Force Participation, Sex-Role Attitudes, and Female Crime: Evidence from a Survey of Adults. *Social Science Quarterly* 65, 703–718.

Greene, Jeffrey D. (2001). *Cities and Privatization: Prospects for the New Century*. Upper Saddle River, NJ: Prentice Hall.

Greenwood, S. (2007). *10 Excellent Reasons not to Hate Taxes*. New York: The New Press.

Gronbacher, Gregory M.A. (1998). Taxation: Catholic Social Thought and Classical Liberalism. *Journal of Accounting, Ethics & Public Policy*, 1(1), 91–100, reprinted in Robert W. McGee (ed.), *The Ethics of Tax Evasion* (pp. 158–167). Dumont, NJ: The Dumont Institute for Public Policy Research, Dumont, NJ, 1998.

Gross, Martin L. (1995). *The Tax Racket: Government Extortion from A to Z*. New York: Ballantine Books.

Gupta, Ranjana (2006). Perceptions of Tax Evasion as a Crime: Evidence from New Zealand. *New Zealand Journal of Taxation Law and Policy* 12, 1–25.

Gupta, Ranjana and Robert W. McGee. (2010). A Comparative Study of New Zealanders' Opinion on the Ethics of Tax Evasion: Students v. Accountants. *New Zealand Journal of Taxation Law and Policy*, 16(1), 47–84.

Gupta, Ranjana and Robert W. McGee. (2010). Study on Tax Evasion Perceptions in Australasia. *Australian Tax Forum*, 25(4), 507–534.

Hall, R.E. & A. Rabushka. (1985). *The Flat Tax*. Stanford: Hoover Institution Press.

Hansen, George (1984). *To Harass Our People: The IRS and Government Abuse of Power.* Washington, DC: Positive Publications.

Harris, James R. (1989). Ethical Values and Decision Processes of Male and Female Business Students. *Journal of Education for Business*, 8, 234–238, as cited in Sharon Galbraith and Harriet Buckman Stephenson. (1993). Decision Rules Used by Male and Female Business Students in Making Ethical Value Judgments: Another Look. *Journal of Business Ethics*, 12(3), 227–233.

Harris, James R. (1990). Ethical Values of Individuals at Different Levels in the Organizational Hierarchy of a Single Firm. *Journal of Business Ethics*, 9(9), 741–750.

Hasseldine, D. John, Steven E. Kaplan and Lori R. Fuller. (1994). Characteristics of New Zealand Tax Evaders: A Note. *Accounting and Finance*, 34(2), 79–93.

Hegarty, W.H. and H.P. Sims, Jr. (1978). Some Determinants of Unethical Decision Behavior: An Experiment. *Journal of Applied Psychology*, 63(4), 451–457.

Hite, Peggy A. (1988). An Examination of the Impact of Subject Selection of Hypothetical and Self-reported Taxpayer Noncompliance. *Journal of Economic Psychology*, 9, 445–466.

Hite, Peggy A. (1997). Identifying and Mitigating Taxpayer Non-compliance. *Australian Tax Forum*, 13, 155–180.

Hobbes, Thomas. (1651). *Leviathan*.

Hoffman, James J. (1998). Are Women Really More Ethical Than Men? Maybe It Depends on the Situation. *Journal of Managerial Issues*, 10(1), 60–73.

Holmes, S. & C.R. Sunstein. (1999). *The Cost of Rights: Why Liberty Depends on Taxes*. New York & London: W.W. Norton & Co.

Hultberg, N. (1996). *Why We Must Abolish the Income Tax and the IRS: A Special Report on the National Sales Tax*. Dallas: AFR Publications.

Internal Revenue Service. (1978). A Dictionary of Compliance Factors, Office of the Assistant Commissioner Research Division.

Internal Revenue Service. (1983). Income Tax Compliance Research: Estimates for 1973–1981. Office of the Assistant Commissioner Research Division.

Iorio, T. (1939). *Theologia Moralis*, 6th ed., II, n. 778, Naples: M. D'Aurea, as cited by Martin T. Crowe, The Moral Obligation of Paying Just Taxes, The Catholic University of America Studies in Sacred Theology No. 84, 1944, p. 41.

Izraeli, Dove. (1988). Ethical Beliefs and Behavior among Managers: A Cross-Cultural Perspective. *Journal of Business Ethics*, 7(4), 263–271.

Jackson, Betty R. and Valerie C. Milliron. (1986). Tax Compliance Research: Findings, Problems, and Prospects. *Journal of Accounting Literature*, 5, 125–165.

Jalili, Ali Reza (2012). The Ethics of Tax Evasion: An Islamic Perspective. In Robert W. McGee (Ed.), *The Ethics of Tax Evasion in Theory and Practice* (pp. 167–199). New York: Springer.

Jefferson, Thomas. (1789). "Letter of Thomas Jefferson to James Madison," Paris, September 6, 1789, reprinted in *Thomas Jefferson: Writings*. New York: The Library of America, 1984, pp. 959–964.

Jefferson, Thomas. (1813). "Letter of Thomas Jefferson to John Wayles Eppes," June 24, 1813, reprinted in *Thomas Jefferson: Writings*. New York: The Library of America, 1984, pp. 1280–1281.

Johnston, D.C. (2003). *Perfectly Legal: The Covert Campaign to Rig Our Tax System to Benefit the Super Rich – and Cheat Everybody Else*. New York: Penguin.

Johnston, D.C. (2007). *Free Lunch: How the Wealthiest Americans Enrich Themselves at Government Expense (and Stick You with the Bill)*. New York: Penguin.

Jouvenel, Bertrand de (1952). *The Ethics of Redistribution*. Cambridge: Cambridge University Press. Reprinted by The Liberty Fund, Indianapolis, 1990.

Kant, Immanuel. (1952a). *Fundamental Principles of the Metaphysics of Morals*. Great Books of the Western World, Volume 42, Chicago: Encyclopedia Britannica, pp. 251–287.

Kant, Immanuel. (1952b). *General Introduction to the Metaphysics of Morals*. Great Books of the Western World, Volume 42, Chicago: Encyclopedia Britannica, pp. 381–394.

Kant, Immanuel. (1952c). Preface and Introduction to the *Metaphysical Elements of Ethics*. Great Books of the Western World, Volume 42, Chicago: Encyclopedia Britannica, pp. 363–379.

Kant, Immanuel. (1952d). *Introduction to the Science of Right. Great Books of the Western World*, Volume 42, Chicago: Encyclopedia Britannica, pp. 397–458.

Kant, Immanuel. (1983). *Ethical Philosophy*, James W. Ellington, translator. Indianapolis and Cambridge: Hackett Publishing Company.

Kaplan, Martin (1999). *What the IRS Doesn't Want You to Know*. New York: Villard.

Kaplow, Louis. (2008). *The Theory of Taxation and Public Economics*. Princeton & Oxford: Princeton University Press.

Karlinsky, Stewart, Hughlene Burton and Cindy Blanthorne (2004). Perceptions of Tax Evasion as a Crime. *eJournal of Tax Research* 2(2), 226–240.

Kastlunger, Barbara, Stefan G. Dressler, Erich Kirchler, Luigi Mittone and Martin Voracek. (2010). Sex Differences in Tax Compliance: Differentiating between Demographic Sex, Gender-Role Orientation, and Prenatal Masculinization (2D:4D). *Journal of Economic Psychology* 31, 542–552.

Kelley, S.W., O.C. Ferrell and S.J. Skinner. (1990). Ethical Behavior Among Marketing Researchers: An Assessment of Selected Demographic Characteristics. *Journal of Business Ethics*, 9(8), 681–688.

Kemp, Roger L. (2007). *Privatization: The Provision of Public Services by the Private Sector.* Jefferson, NC: McFarland & Co.

Keohane, Nannerl O. (1977). The Radical Humanism of Étienne de la Boétie. *Journal of the History of Ideas* 38(1): 119–130.

Kidwell, Jeaneen M., Robert E. Stevens & Art L. Bethke. (1987). Differences in Ethical Perceptions Between Male and Female Managers: Myth or Reality? *Journal of Business Ethics*, 6(6), 489–493.

Kirchler, Erich. (2007). *The Economic Psychology of Tax Behaviour.* New York & Cambridge: Cambridge University Press.

Kirchler, E., S. Muehlbacher, B. Kastlunger & I. Wahl. (2010). Why Pay Taxes? A Review of Tax Compliance Decisions. In J. Alm, J. Martinez-Vazquez & B. Torgler (Eds.), *Developing Alternative Frameworks for Explaining Tax Compliance* (pp. 15–31). London & New York: Routledge.

Kohut, Gary F. & Susan E. Corriher. (1994). The Relationship of Age, Gender, Experience and Awareness of Written Ethics Policies to Business Decision Making. *S.A.M. Advanced Management Journal*, 59(1), 32–39.

La Croix, C. (1739). *Theologia Moralis*, III, pars. II (Coloniae), as cited in Martin T. Crowe, *The Moral Obligation of Paying Just Taxes.* The Catholic University of America Studies in Sacred Theology No. 84, p. 55.

Laffer, Arthur B. & Jan P. Seymour (Eds.) (1979). *The Economics of the Tax Revolt.* New York: Harcourt Brace Jovanovich.

Lampe, James C., Don W. Finn, James Gaa & Patricia L. O'Malley. (1992). A Model of Auditors' Ethical Decision Processes; Discussions; Reply. *Auditing: A Journal of Practice and Theory*, 11 (Supplement), 33–78.

Larson, M.A. (1973). *Tax Revolt: U.S.A.!* Washington, DC: Liberty Lobby.

Lehmkuhl, A. (1902). *Theologia Moralis I*, as cited in Martin T. Crowe, *The Moral Obligation of Paying Just Taxes*, The Catholic University of America Studies in Sacred Theology No. 84, 1944 at p. 76.

Leiker, Bret H. (1998). Rousseau and the Legitimacy of Tax Evasion. *Journal of Accounting, Ethics & Public Policy*, 1(1), 45–57, reprinted in Robert W. McGee (Ed.), *The Ethics of Tax Evasion* (pp. 89–101). Dumont, NJ: The Dumont Institute for Public Policy Research, 1998.

Lewis, Alan, Sonia Carrera, John Cullis, and Philip Jones. (2009). Individual, Cognitive and Cultural Differences in Tax Compliance: UK and Italy Compared. *Journal of Economic Psychology*, 30(3), 431–445.

Lewis, C. & B. Allison. (2002). *The Cheating of America: How Tax Avoidance and Evasion by the Super Rich Are Costing the Country Billions – and What You Can do About It.* New York: Perennial.

Lewis, Joseph. (1926). *The Bible Unmasked.* New York: The Freethought Press Association.

Liguori, St. Alphonsus (1907). *Theologia Moralis* (ed. Gaudé, Rome), III, as cited in Martin T. Crowe, *The Moral Obligation of Paying Just Taxes.* The Catholic University of America Studies in Sacred Theology No. 84, p. 58. Crowe does not cite the exact page number.

Locke, John. (1689). *Two Treatises on Government.*

Longenecker, Justin G., Joseph A. McKinney & Carlos W. Moore. (1989). Do Smaller Firms Have Higher Ethics? *Business and Society Review*, 71, 19–21.

Loo, Robert. (2003). Are Women More Ethical Than Men? Findings from Three Independent Studies. *Women in Management Review*, 18(3/4), 169–181.

Luthar, Harsh K., Ron A. DiBattista & Theodore Gautschi (1997). Perception of What the Ethical Climate Is and What It Should Be: The Role of Gender, Academic Status, and Ethical Education. *Journal of Business Ethics*, 16(2), 205–217.

Machan, Tibor (2012). Taxation: The Ethics of Its Avoiding or Dodging. In Robert W. McGee (Ed.), *The Ethics of Tax Evasion: Perspectives in Theory and Practice* (pp. 73–82). New York, Springer.

Marta, Janet K. Mullin, Anusorn Singhapakdi, Ashraf Attia & Scott J. Vitell. (2004). Some Important Factors Underlying Ethical Decisions of Middle-Eastern Marketers. *International Marketing Review*, 21(1), 53–67.

Martinez, Leo P. (1994). Taxes, Morals, and Legitimacy. *Brigham Young University Law Review*, 1994, 521–569.

Martinez-Vazquez, Jorge and Benno Torgler. (2009). The Evolution of Tax Morale in Modern Spain. *Journal of Economic Issues*, 43(1), 1–28.

Mason. E. Sharon & Peter E. Mudrack. (1996). Gender and Ethical Orientation: A Test of Gender and Occupational Socialization Theories. *Journal of Business Ethics*, 15(6), 599–604.

McCabe, A. Catherine, Rhea Ingram and Mary Conway Dato-on. (2006). The Business of Ethics and Gender. *Journal of Business Ethics*, 64, 101–116.

McCaffery, E.J. (2002). *Fair not Flat: How To Make the Tax System Better and Simpler.* Chicago & London: University of Chicago Press.

McCuddy, Michael K. and Barbara L. Peery (1996). Selected Individual Differences and Collegian's Ethical Beliefs. *Journal of Business Ethics*, 15(3), 261–272.

McDonald, Gael M. and Pak Cho Kan (1997). Ethical Perceptions of Expatriate and Local Managers in Hong Kong. *Journal of Business Ethics*, 16(15), 1605–1623.

McGee, Robert W. (1994). Is Tax Evasion Unethical? *University of Kansas Law Review*, 42(2), 411–35.

McGee, Robert W. (1997). The Ethics of Tax Evasion and Trade Protectionism from an Islamic Perspective, *Commentaries on Law & Public Policy*, 1, 250–262.

McGee, Robert W. (Ed.). (1998). *The Ethics of Tax Evasion*. Dumont, NJ: The Dumont Institute for Public Policy Research.

McGee, Robert W. (1998). Christian Views on the Ethics of Tax Evasion. *Journal of Accounting, Ethics & Public Policy*, 1(2), 210–225. Reprinted at http://ssrn.com/abstract=461398.

McGee, Robert W. (1998). When Is Tax Evasion Unethical? In Robert W. McGee (Ed.), *The Ethics of Tax Evasion* (pp. 5–35). Dumont, NJ: The Dumont Institute.

McGee, Robert W. (1998). The Ethics of Tax Evasion in Islam, in Robert W. McGee (Ed.), *The Ethics of Tax Evasion* (pp. 214–219). Dumont, NJ: The Dumont Institute.

McGee, Robert W. (1998). The Ethics of Tax Evasion in Islam: A Comment. *Journal of Accounting, Ethics & Public Policy,* 1(2), 162–168, reprinted in Robert W. McGee, editor, The Ethics of Tax Evasion (pp. 214–219). Dumont, NJ: The Dumont Institute for Public Policy Research, 1998.

McGee, Robert W. (1998). Should Accountants be Punished for Aiding and Abetting Tax Evasion? *Journal of Accounting, Ethics & Public Policy*, 1(1), 16–44.

McGee, Robert W. (1998). Jewish Views on the Ethics of Tax Evasion, *Journal of Accounting, Ethics & Public Policy*, 1(3), 323–336.

McGee, Robert W. (1998). Ethical Views on Tax Evasion among Swedish CEOs: A Comment, *Journal of Accounting, Ethics & Public Policy*, 1(3), 460–467.

McGee, Robert W. 1998d. "Is the Ability to Pay Principle Ethically Bankrupt?" *Journal of Accounting*, Ethics & Public Policy, 1 (3): 503–511.

McGee, Robert W. (1998). Are Discriminatory Tax Rates Ethically Justifiable? *Journal of Accounting, Ethics & Public Policy,* 1(4), 527–534.

McGee, Robert W. (1998). The Political Economy of Excise Taxation: Some Ethical and Legal Issues, *Journal of Accounting, Ethics & Public Policy*, 1(4), 558–571.

McGee, Robert W. (1999). Is It Unethical to Evade Taxes in an Evil or Corrupt State? A Look at Jewish, Christian, Muslim, Mormon and Baha'i Perspectives. *Journal of Accounting, Ethics & Public Policy*, 2(1), 149–181. Reprinted at http://ssrn.com/abstract=251469.

McGee, Robert W. (1999). Is It Unethical to Evade the Estate Tax? *Journal of Accounting, Ethics & Public Policy*, 2(2), 266–285. Reprinted at http://ssrn.com/abstract=242536.

McGee, Robert W. (1999). An Ethical Look at Paying Your "Fair Share" of Taxes. *Journal of Accounting, Ethics & Public Policy*, 2(2), 318–328. Reprinted at http://ssrn.com/abstract=242549.

McGee, Robert W. (1999). Tariffs as a Form of Taxation: Is Evasion Unethical? *Journal of Accounting, Ethics & Public Policy*, 2(2), 376–385. Reprinted at http://ssrn.com/abstract=242565.

McGee, Robert W. (1999). Why People Evade Taxes in Armenia: A Look at an Ethical Issue Based on a Summary of Interviews. *Journal of Accounting, Ethics & Public Policy*, 2(2), 408–416. Reprinted at http://ssrn.com/abstract=242568.

McGee, Robert W. (1999). Is It Unethical to Evade the Capital Gains Tax? *Journal of Accounting, Ethics & Public Policy*, 2(3), 567–581. Reprinted at http://ssrn.com/abstract=251491.

McGee, Robert W. (1999). Is It Unethical to Evade the Social Security Tax? *Journal of Accounting, Ethics & Public Policy*, 2(3), 585–596. Reprinted at http://ssrn.com/abstract=242507.

McGee, Robert W. (2000). Taxation in the Republic of Armenia: An Overview and Discussion from the Perspectives of Law, Economics and Ethics, *ILSA Journal of International & Comparative Law*, 7(1), 97–109.

McGee, Robert W. (2001). Some Ethical Problems with Using Public Finance as a Tool of Social Engineering. *Public Finance & Management*, 1(3), 363–369. Reprinted at http://spaef.com/PFM_PUB/pubv1n3.html.

McGee, Robert W. (2004). *The Philosophy of Taxation and Public Finance*. Norwell, MA and Dordrecht: Kluwer Academic Publishers.

McGee, Robert W. (2006). Three Views on the Ethics of Tax Evasion. *Journal of Business Ethics*, 67(1), 15–35.

McGee, Robert W. (2006). A Survey of International Business Academics on the Ethics of Tax Evasion. *Journal of Accounting, Ethics & Public Policy*, 6(3), 301–352.

McGee, Robert W. (2006). The Ethics of Tax Evasion: A Survey of Romanian Business Students and Faculty. *The ICFAI Journal of Public Finance*, 4(2), 38–68 (2006). Reprinted in Robert W. McGee and Galina G. Preobragenskaya, *Accounting and Financial System Reform in Eastern Europe and Asia* (pp. 299–334). New York: Springer, 2006.

McGee, Robert W. (2006). Gender, Age and the Ethics of Tax Evasion. Andreas School of Business Working Paper Series, Barry University, September.

McGee, Robert W. (2006). A Comparative Study of Tax Evasion Ethics in Thailand and Vietnam. *Journal of Accounting, Ethics & Public Policy*, 6(1), 103–123.

McGee, Robert W. and Arkadiusz Bernal. (2006). The Ethics of Tax Evasion: A Survey of Business Students in Poland. In *Global Economy – How It Works* (Mina Baliamoune-Lutz, Alojzy Z. Nowak & Jeff Steagall, eds.) (pp. 155–174). Warsaw: University of Warsaw & Jacksonville: University of North Florida. Reprinted at http://ssrn.com/abstract=875434.

McGee, Robert W. and Tatyana Maranjyan. (2006). Tax Evasion in Armenia: An Empirical Study. Working Paper No. 06/10, Armenian International Policy Research Group, Washington, DC.

McGee, Robert W., Inge Nickerson and Werner Fees. (2006). German and American Opinion on the Ethics of Tax Evasion. *Proceedings of the Academy of Legal, Ethical and Regulatory Issues* (Reno), 10(2), 31–34.

McGee, Robert W. (2007). Ethics and Tax Evasion in Asia. *ICFAI Journal of Public Finance*, 5(2), 21–33 (May). Reprinted in Business Ethics: A 360 Degree Appraisal, ICFAI University Press. Hyderabad, India.

McGee, Robert W. and Zhiwen Guo. (2007). A Survey of Law, Business and Philosophy Students in China on the Ethics of Tax Evasion. *Society and Business Review*, 2(3), 299–315.

McGee, Robert W., Carlos Noronha and Michael Tyler. (2007). The Ethics of Tax Evasion: a Survey of Macau Opinion. *Euro Asia Journal of Management*, 17(2), 123–150. Reprinted in Robert W. McGee (editor), *Readings in Accounting Ethics* (pp. 283–313), Hyderabad, India: ICFAI University Press, 2009.

McGee, Robert W. and Silvia López Paláu. (2007). The Ethics of Tax Evasion: Two Empirical Studies of Puerto Rican Opinion. *Journal of Applied Business and Economics*, 7(3), 27–47 (2007). Reprinted in Robert W. McGee (editor), *Readings in Accounting Ethics* (pp. 314–342). Hyderabad, India: ICFAI University Press, 2009.

McGee, Robert W., Silvia López-Paláu and Fabiola Jarrín Jaramillo. (2007). The Ethics of Tax Evasion: An Empirical Study of Ecuador. American Society of Business and Behavioral

Sciences 14th Annual Meeting, Las Vegas, February 22–25, 2007. Published in the Proceedings of the American Society of Business and Behavioral Sciences 14(1): 1186–1198.

McGee, Robert W. and Sheldon R. Smith. 2007. Ethics, Tax Evasion and Religion: A Survey of Opinion of Members of the Church of Jesus Christ of Latter-Day Saints. Western Decision Sciences Institute, Thirty-Sixth Annual Meeting, Denver, April 3–7. Published in the Proceedings. Reprinted at http://ssrn.com/abstract=934652.

McGee, Robert W. and Michael Tyler. (2007). Tax Evasion and Ethics: A Demographic Study of Thirty-three Countries. *International Journal of Business, Accounting, and Finance*, 1(1), 95–114.

McGee, Robert W. (2008). Is It Unethical to Evade Taxes in an Evil or Corrupt State? In David M. Gross (Ed.), *We Won't Pay: A Tax Resistance Reader* (pp. 516–539) Creativecommons.org.

McGee, Robert W. (2008). Opinions on Tax Evasion in Asia, in Robert W. McGee, editor, *Taxation and Public Finance in Transition and Developing Economies* (pp. 309–320) New York: Springer.

McGee, Robert W. (2008). Changing Attitudes toward the Ethics of Tax Evasion: An Empirical Study of 10 Transition Economies. *Accounting and Finance in Transition*, 5, 145–154. Also Fifth International Conference on Accounting and Finance in Transition. London, July 12–14, 2007. Reprinted in Robert W. McGee (Ed.), *Taxation and Public Finance in Transition and Developing Economies* (pp. 119–136). New York: Springer, 2008, under the title Trends in the Ethics of Tax Evasion: An Empirical Study of Ten Transition Economies.

McGee, Robert W. (2008). Tax Evasion, Tax Misery and Ethics: Comparative Studies of Korea, Japan and China, in Robert W. McGee (Ed.), *Taxation and Public Finance in Transition and Developing Economies* (pp. 137–165). New York: Springer.

McGee, Robert W. (2008). Opinions on Tax Evasion in Thailand, in Robert W. McGee, editor, *Taxation and Public Finance in Transition and Developing Economies* (pp. 609–620). New York: Springer.

McGee, Robert W. (2008). A Survey of Vietnamese Opinion on the Ethics of Tax Evasion, in Robert W. McGee (Ed.), *Taxation and Public Finance in Transition and Developing Economies* (pp. 663–674). New York: Springer.

McGee, Robert W., Jaan Alver and Lehte Alver. (2008). The Ethics of Tax Evasion: A Survey of Estonian Opinion, in Robert W. McGee, editor, *Taxation and Public Finance in Transition and Developing Economies* (pp. 461–480). New York: Springer.

McGee, Robert W. and Yuhua An. (2008). A Survey of Chinese Business and Economics Students on the Ethics of Tax Evasion, in Robert W. McGee, editor, *Taxation and Public Finance in Transition and Developing Economies* (pp. 409–421). New York: Springer.

McGee, Robert W., Meliha Basic and Michael Tyler. (2008). The Ethics of Tax Evasion: A Comparative Study of Bosnian and Romanian Opinion, in Robert W. McGee, editor, *Taxation and Public Finance in Transition and Developing Economies* (pp. 167–183). New York: Springer.

McGee, Robert W. and Yiu Yu Butt. (2008). An Empirical Study of Tax Evasion Ethics in Hong Kong. Proceedings of the International Academy of Business and Public Administration Disciplines (IABPAD), Dallas, April 24–27: 72–83.

McGee, Robert W. and Gordon M. Cohn. (2008). Jewish Perspectives on the Ethics of Tax Evasion. *Journal of Legal, Ethical and Regulatory Issues*, 11(2), 1–32.

McGee, Robert W. and Wendy Gelman. (2008). Opinions on the Ethics of Tax Evasion: A Comparative Study of 10 Transition Economies, in Robert W. McGee (Ed.), *Accounting Reform in Transition and Developing Economies* (pp. 495–508). New York: Springer.

McGee, Robert W. and Beena George (2008). Tax Evasion and Ethics: A Survey of Indian Opinion. *Journal of Accounting, Ethics & Public Policy*, 9(3), 301–332.

McGee, Robert W., Simon S.M. Ho and Annie Y.S. Li. (2008). A Comparative Study on Perceived Ethics of Tax Evasion: Hong Kong vs. the United States. *Journal of Business Ethics*, 77(2), 147–158.

McGee, Robert W. and Christopher Lingle. (2008). The Ethics of Tax Evasion: A Survey of Guatemalan Opinion, in Robert W. McGee, editor, *Taxation and Public Finance in Transition and Developing Economies* (pp. 481–495). New York: Springer.

McGee, Robert W. and Silvia López Paláu. (2008). Tax Evasion and Ethics: A Comparative Study of the USA and Four Latin American Countries, in Robert W. McGee, editor, *Taxation and Public Finance in Transition and Developing Economies* (pp. 185–224). New York: Springer.

McGee, Robert W. and Tatyana B. Maranjyan. (2008). Opinions on Tax Evasion in Armenia, in Robert W. McGee, editor, *Taxation and Public Finance in Transition and Developing Economies* (pp. 277–307). New York: Springer.

McGee, Robert W. and Bouchra M'Zali. (2008). Attitudes toward Tax Evasion in Mali, in Robert W. McGee, editor, *Taxation and Public Finance in Transition and Developing Economies* (pp. 511–517). New York: Springer.

McGee, Robert W. and Carlos Noronha. (2008). The Ethics of Tax Evasion: A Comparative Study of Guangzhou (Southern China) and Macau Opinions. *Euro Asia Journal of Management*, 18(2), 133–152.

McGee, Robert W. and Galina G. Preobragenskaya. (2008). A Study of Tax Evasion Ethics in Kazakhstan, in Robert W. McGee, editor, *Taxation and Public Finance in Transition and Developing Economies* (pp. 497–510). New York: Springer.

McGee, Robert W. and Marcelo J. Rossi. (2008). A Survey of Argentina on the Ethics of Tax Evasion, in Robert W. McGee, editor, *Taxation and Public Finance in Transition and Developing Economies* (pp. 239–261). New York: Springer.

McGee, Robert W. and Sheldon R. Smith. (2008). Opinions on the Ethics of Tax Evasion: A Comparative Study of Utah and New Jersey. Presented at the 39th Annual Meeting of the Decision Sciences Institute, Baltimore, November 22–26, 2008. Published in the Proceedings at pp. 3981–3986.

McGee, Robert W. and Radoslav Tusan. (2008). The Ethics of Tax Evasion: A Survey of Slovak Opinion, in Robert W. McGee, editor, *Taxation and Public Finance in Transition and Developing Economies* (pp. 575–601). New York: Springer.

McGee, Robert W. (2009). Views toward Tax Evasion: A Comparative Study of Moldova and Romania. *ICFAI University Journal of Public Finance*, 7(3&4), 7–24.

McGee, Robert W. and Susana N. Vittadini Andres. (2009). The Ethics of Tax Evasion: Case Studies of Taiwan, in Robert W. McGee, *Readings in Business Ethics* (pp. 200–228). Hyderabad, India: ICFAI University Press. An abbreviated version was published in Marjorie G. Adams and Abbass Alkhafaji, editors, *Business Research Yearbook: Global Business Perspectives*, Volume XIV, No. 1 (pp. 34–39). Beltsville, MD: International Graphics: Beltsville, MD, 2007.

McGee, Robert W. and Mahdi Nazemi Ardakani (2009). The Ethics of Tax Evasion: A Case Study of Opinion in Iran. Florida International University Working Paper.

McGee, Robert W., Meliha Basic and Michael Tyler. (2009). The Ethics of Tax Evasion: A Survey of Bosnian Opinion, *Journal of Balkan and Near Eastern Studies*, 11(2), 197–207.

McGee, Robert W. Serkan Benk, Adriana M. Ross & Harun Kılıçaslan (2009). An Empirical Study of Ethical Opinion in Germany. *Journal of Accounting, Ethics & Public Policy*, 10(2), 243–259.

McGee, Robert W. and Sanjoy Bose. (2009). The Ethics of Tax Evasion: A Comparative Study of Australian, New Zealand and USA Opinion, in Robert W. McGee, *Readings in Business Ethics* (pp. 125–142). Hyderabad, India: ICFAI University Press.

McGee, Robert W. and Sanjoy Bose. (2009). The Ethics of Tax Evasion: A Survey of Australian Opinion, in Robert W. McGee, *Readings in Business Ethics* (pp. 143–166). Hyderabad, India: ICFAI University Press.

McGee, Robert W. and Wendy Gelman. (2009). Opinions on the Ethics of Tax Evasion: A Comparative Study of the USA and Six Latin American Countries. *Akron Tax Journal*, 24, 69–91.

McGee, Robert W. and Bouchra M'Zali. (2009). The Ethics of Tax Evasion: An Empirical Study of French EMBA Students, in Robert W. McGee, *Readings in Business Ethics* (pp. 185–199). Hyderabad, India: ICFAI University Press. An abbreviated version was published in Marjorie G. Adams and Abbass Alkhafaji, editors, *Business Research Yearbook: Global Business Perspectives*, Volume XIV, No. 1 (pp. 27–33). Beltsville, MD: International Graphics, 2007.

McGee, Robert W., Inge Nickerson and Werner Fees. (2009). When Is Tax Evasion Ethically Justifiable? A Survey of German Opinion, in Robert W. McGee, editor, *Readings in Accounting Ethics* (pp. 365–389). Hyderabad, India: ICFAI University Press.

McGee, Robert W., Silvia López Paláu and Gustavo A. Yepes Lopez. (2009). The Ethics of Tax Evasion: An Empirical Study of Colombian Opinion, in Robert W. McGee, *Readings in Business Ethics* (pp. 167–184). Hyderabad, India: ICFAI University Press.

McGee, Robert W. and Sheldon R. Smith. (2009). Ethics and Tax Evasion: A Comparative Study of Utah and Florida Opinion, in Robert W. McGee (Ed.), *Readings in Accounting Ethics* (pp. 343–364). Hyderabad, India: ICFAI University Press.

McGee, Robert W. & Geoff A. Goldman (2010). Ethics and Tax Evasion: A Survey of South African Opinion. *Proceedings of the Third Annual University of Johannesburg Faculty of Management Conference*, May 12–14. Reprinted in Robert W. McGee (Ed.), *The Ethics of Tax Evasion: Perspectives in Theory and Practice*. New York, Springer, 2012, 337–356.

McGee, Robert W. & Serkan Benk (2011). The Ethics of Tax Evasion: A Study of Turkish Opinion. *Journal of Balkan and Near Eastern Studies*, 13(2), 249–262.

McGee, Robert W., Serkan Benk, Halil Yıldırım and Murat Kayıkçı. (2011). The Ethics of Tax Evasion: A Study of Turkish Tax Practitioner Opinion, *European Journal of Social Sciences*, 18(3), 468–480.

McGee, Robert W., Arsen M. Djatej and Robert H.S. Sarikas. (2012). The Ethics of Tax Evasion: A Survey of Hispanic Opinion. *Accounting & Taxation*, 4(1), 53–74.

McGee, Robert W. (Ed.) (2012). *The Ethics of Tax Evasion: Perspectives in Theory and Practice*. New York: Springer.

McGee, Robert W. (2012). Four Views on the Ethics of Tax Evasion. In Robert W. McGee (Ed.), *The Ethics of Tax Evasion: Perspectives in Theory and Practice* (pp. 3–33). New York, Springer.

McGee, Robert W. (2012). Duty to Whom? In Robert W. McGee (Ed.), *The Ethics of Tax Evasion: Perspectives in Theory and Practice* (pp. 35–45). New York, Springer.

McGee, Robert W. (2012). An Analysis of Some Arguments. In Robert W. McGee (Ed.), *The Ethics of Tax Evasion: Perspectives in Theory and Practice* (pp. 47–71). New York, Springer.

McGee, Robert W. (2012). Attitudes on the Ethics of Tax Evasion: A Survey of Philosophy Professors. In Robert W. McGee (Ed.), *The Ethics of Tax Evasion: Perspectives in Theory and Practice* (pp. 125–132). New York, Springer.

McGee, Robert W. (2012). The Ethics of Tax Evasion in Islam: A Comment. In Robert W. McGee (Ed.), *The Ethics of Tax Evasion: Perspectives in Theory and Practice* (pp. 159–165). New York, Springer.

McGee, Robert W. (2012). Christian Views on the Ethics of Tax Evasion. In Robert W. McGee (Ed.), *The Ethics of Tax Evasion: Perspectives in Theory and Practice* (pp. 201–210). New York, Springer.

McGee, Robert W. (2012). Gender and the Ethics of Tax Evasion: An Empirical Study of 82 Countries. In Robert W. McGee (Ed.), *The Ethics of Tax Evasion: Perspectives in Theory and Practice* (pp. 415–439). New York, Springer.

McGee, Robert W. (2012). Age and the Ethics of Tax Evasion. In Robert W. McGee (Ed.), *The Ethics of Tax Evasion: Perspectives in Theory and Practice* (pp. 441–449). New York, Springer.

McGee, Robert W. (2012). Education Level and the Ethics of Tax Evasion. In Robert W. McGee (Ed.), *The Ethics of Tax Evasion: Perspectives in Theory and Practice* (pp. 451–457). New York, Springer.

McGee, Robert W. (2012). Religious Practice and the Ethics of Tax Evasion. In Robert W. McGee (Ed.), *The Ethics of Tax Evasion: Perspectives in Theory and Practice* (pp. 459–469). New York, Springer.

McGee, Robert W. (2012). Religion and the Ethics of Tax Evasion. In Robert W. McGee (Ed.), *The Ethics of Tax Evasion: Perspectives in Theory and Practice* (pp. 471–473). New York, Springer.

McGee, Robert W. (2012). Marital Status and the Ethics of Tax Evasion. In Robert W. McGee (Ed.), *The Ethics of Tax Evasion: Perspectives in Theory and Practice* (pp. 475–484). New York, Springer.

McGee, Robert W. (2012). Income Level and the Ethics of Tax Evasion. In Robert W. McGee (Ed.), *The Ethics of Tax Evasion: Perspectives in Theory and Practice* (pp. 485–495). New York, Springer.

McGee, Robert W., Jaan Alver and Lehte Alver (2012). Tax Evasion Opinion in Estonia. In Robert W. McGee (Ed.), *The Ethics of Tax Evasion: Perspectives in Theory and Practice* (pp. 285–299). New York: Springer.

McGee, Robert W. Serkan Benk, Adriana M. Ross & Harun Kılıçaslan (2012). Cheating on Taxes if You Have a Chance: A Comparative Study of Tax Evasion Opinion in Turkey and Germany. In Robert W. McGee (Ed.), *The Ethics of Tax Evasion: Perspectives in Theory and Practice* (pp. 357–369). New York: Springer.

McGee, Robert W. and Yiu Yu Butt (2012). An Empirical Study of Tax Evasion Ethics in Hong Kong. In Robert W. McGee (Ed.), *The Ethics of Tax Evasion: Perspectives in Theory and Practice* (pp. 309–320). New York, Springer.

McGee, Robert W. and Geoff A. Goldman (2012). Ethics and Tax Evasion: A Survey of South African Opinion. In Robert W. McGee (Ed.), *The Ethics of Tax Evasion: Perspectives in Theory and Practice* (pp. 337–356). New York, Springer.

McGee, Robert W. and Ravi Kumar Jain (2012). The Ethics of Tax Evasion: A Study of Indian Opinion. In Robert W. McGee (Ed.), *The Ethics of Tax Evasion: Perspectives in Theory and Practice* (pp. 321–336). New York, Springer.

McGee, Robert W. and Bouchra M'Zali (2012) Opinions on Tax Evasion in Haiti. In Robert W. McGee (Ed.), *The Ethics of Tax Evasion: Perspectives in Theory and Practice* (pp. 301–308). New York: Springer.

McGee, Robert W. and Tatyana B. Maranjyan (2012). Attitudes toward Tax Evasion: An Empirical Study of Florida Accounting Practitioners. In Robert W. McGee (Ed.), *The Ethics of Tax Evasion: Perspectives in Theory and Practice* (pp. 247–265). New York: Springer.

McGee, Robert W., Yanira Petrides and Adriana M. Ross (2012). Ethics and Tax Evasion: A Survey of Mexican Opinion. In Robert W. McGee (Ed.), *The Ethics of Tax Evasion: Perspectives in Theory and Practice* (pp. 387–403). New York: Springer.

McGee, Robert W., Yanira Petrides and Adriana M. Ross (2012). How Serious Is Tax Evasion: A Survey of Mexican Opinion. In Robert W. McGee (Ed.), *The Ethics of Tax Evasion: Perspectives in Theory and Practice* (pp. 405–411). New York: Springer.

McGee, Robert W. and Sheldon R. Smith (2012). Ethics, Tax Evasion and Religion: A Survey of Opinion of Members of the Church of Jesus Christ of Latter-Day Saints. In Robert W. McGee (Ed.), *The Ethics of Tax Evasion: Perspectives in Theory and Practice* (pp. 211–226). New York: Springer.

McKinsey, C. Dennis. (1995). *The Encyclopedia of Biblical Errancy*. Amherst, NY: Prometheus Books.

McKinsey, C. Dennis. (2000). *Biblical Errancy: A Reference Guide*. Amherst, NY: Prometheus Books.

McNichols, Charles W. and Thomas W. Zimmerer. (1985). Situational Ethics: An Empirical Study of Differentiators of Student Attitudes. *Journal of Business Ethics*, 4, 175–180 (June).

Mears, D.P., M. Ploeger and M. Warr. (2000). Explaining the Gender Gap in Delinquency: Peer Influence and Moral Evaluations of Behavior. In Robert D. Crutchfield, George S. Bridges, Joseph G. Weis and Charis Kubrin (eds.), *Crime Readings* (pp. 143–148), Thousand Oaks, CA: Pine Forge Press.

Merkelbach, H.B. (1938). *Theologiae Moralis*, 3rd ed., I. Paris: Dersclee De Brouwer & Soc., as cited by Martin T. Crowe, The Moral Obligation of Paying Just Taxes, The Catholic University of America Studies in Sacred Theology No. 84, 1944, p. 28.

Miesing, Paul and John F. Preble. (1985). A Comparison of Five Business Philosophies. *Journal of Business Ethics*, 4(6), 465–476.

Molina, Louis (1611). *De Justitia et Jure*, tr. II., Disp. 674, n.3, III, col. 555 ff., Venice, as cited by Martin T. Crowe, The Moral Obligation of Paying Just Taxes, The Catholic University of America Studies in Sacred Theology No. 84, 1944, p. 43.

Morales, Alfonso. (1998). Income Tax Compliance and Alternative Views of Ethics and Human Nature. *Journal of Accounting, Ethics & Public Policy*, 1(3), 380–399, reprinted in Robert W. McGee (ed.), *The Ethics of Tax Evasion* (pp. 242–258). The Dumont Institute for Public Policy Research: Dumont, NJ, 1998.

Morales, Alfonso (2012). Understanding and Interpreting Tax Compliance Strategies Among Street Vendors. In Robert W. McGee (Ed.), *The Ethics of Tax Evasion: Perspectives in Theory and Practice* (pp. 83–106). New York, Springer.

Murphy, K. (2010). Procedural Justice and the Regulation of Tax Compliance Behavior: The Moderating Role of Personal Norms. In J. Alm, J. Martinez-Vazquez & B. Torgler (Eds.), *Developing Alternative Frameworks for Explaining Tax Compliance* (pp. 191–213). London & New York: Routledge.

Murtuza, Athar and S.M. Ghazanfar. (1998). Taxation as a Form of Worship: Exploring the Nature of Zakat. *Journal of Accounting, Ethics & Public Policy*, 1(2), 134–161, reprinted in Robert W. McGee (ed.), The Ethics of Tax Evasion (pp. 190–212). The Dumont Institute for Public Policy Research: Dumont, NJ, 1998.

Musgrave, Richard A. (1959). *The Theory of Public Finance: A Study in Public Economy*. New York: McGraw-Hill.

Musgrave, Richard A. (1986). *Public Finance in a Democratic Society. Volume II: Fiscal Doctrine, Growth and Institutions*. New York: New York University Press.

Musgrave, Richard A. & Peggy B. Musgrave. (1976). *Public Finance in Theory and Practice*, 2nd edition. New York: McGraw-Hill.

Musgrave, Richard A. & Alan T. Peacock (eds.) (1958). *Classics in the Theory of Public Finance*. London & New York: Macmillan.

Mutti, J.H. (2003). *Foreign Direct Investment and Tax Competition*. Washington, DC: Institute for International Economics.

Myddelton, D.R. (1994). *The Power to Destroy: A study of the British tax system*. London: Society for Individual Freedom.

Nasadyuk, Irina and Robert W. McGee. (2007). The Ethics of Tax Evasion: Lessons for Transitional Economies. . In Greg N. Gregoriou and C. Read (eds.), *International Taxation* (pp. 291–310). Elsevier.

Nasadyuk, Irina and Robert W. McGee. (2008). The Ethics of Tax Evasion: An Empirical Study of Business and Economics Student Opinion in Ukraine, in Robert W. McGee (Ed.), *Taxation and Public Finance in Transition and Developing Economies* (pp. 639–661). New York: Springer.

Navarrus, Martinus (1618). *Opera Omnia*. Venice, as cited by Martin T. Crowe, The Moral Obligation of Paying Just Taxes, The Catholic University of America Studies in Sacred Theology No. 84, 1944, p. 31.

Nozick, Robert (1974). *Anarchy, State & Utopia*. New York: Basic Books.

Nyaw, Mee-Kau and Ignace Ng. (1994). A Comparative Analysis of Ethical Beliefs: A Four Country Study. *Journal of Business Ethics*, 13(7), 543–555.

Nylén, Ulrica (1998). Ethical Views on Tax Evasion Among Swedish CEOs, in Robert W. McGee (Ed.), *The Ethics of Tax Evasion* (pp. 260–282). Dumont, NJ: The Dumont Institute.

Oliva, Robert R. (1998). The Schism between Tax Practitioners' Ethical and Legal Obligations: Recommendations for the Fusion of Law and Ethics. *Journal of Accounting, Ethics & Public Policy*, 1(4), 603–628, reprinted in Robert W. McGee (Ed.), *The Ethics of Tax Evasion* (pp. 350–371). Dumont, NJ: The Dumont Institute for Public Policy Research, 1998.

Ondrack, D.A. (1973). Emerging Occupational Values: A Review and Some Findings. *Academy of Management Journal*, 16, 423–432.

Pashev, Konstantin V. (2008). Monitoring of Tax Corruption in Transition Economies: Evidence from Bulgaria, in Robert W. McGee, editor, *Taxation and Public Finance in Transition and Developing Economies* (pp. 321–362). New York: Springer.

Pashev, Konstantin V. (2008). Tax Compliance of Small Business in Transition Economies: Lessons from Bulgaria, in Robert W. McGee, editor, *Taxation and Public Finance in Transition and Developing Economies* (pp. 363–388). New York: Springer.

Patuzzi, J. (1770). Ethica Christiana sive Theologia Moralis (Venice), I, as cited in Martin T. Crowe, *The Moral Obligation of Paying Just Taxes*. The Catholic University of America Studies in Sacred Theology No. 84, p. 57.

Payne, James L. (1993). *Costly Returns: The Burdens of the U.S. Tax System*. San Francisco: ICS Press.

Pennock, Robert T. (1998). Death and Taxes: On the Justice of Conscientious War Tax Resistance. *Journal of Accounting, Ethics & Public Policy*, 1(1), 58–76, reprinted in Robert W. McGee (Ed.), *The Ethics of Tax Evasion* (pp. 124–142). Dumont, NJ: The Dumont Institute for Public Policy Research, 1998.

Plato. *The Laws*.

Plato. *The Republic*.

Poole, Robert W. (1980). *Cutting Back City Hall*. New York: Universe Books.

Posner, Barry Z. & Warren H. Schmidt. (1984). Values and the American Manager: An Update. California Management Review, 26(3), 202–216.

Prante, Gerald and Mark Robyn: 2010. Summary of Latest Federal Individual Income Tax Data. Fiscal Fact No. 249 (October 6). Washington, DC: Tax Foundation.

Preobragenskaya, Galina G. and Robert W. McGee. (2004). Taxation and Public Finance in a Transition Economy: A Case Study of Russia. In Carolyn Gardner, Jerry Biberman and Abbass Alkhafaji (Eds.), *Business Research Yearbook: Global Business Perspectives* Volume XI, Saline, MI: McNaughton & Gunn, Inc., 2004, pp. 254–258. A longer version, which was presented at the Sixteenth Annual Conference of the International Academy of Business Disciplines in San Antonio, March 25–28, 2004, is available at http://ssrn.com/abstract=480862.

Purcell, Theodore V. (1977). Do Courses in Business Ethics Pay Off? *California Management Review*, 19(4), 50–58.

Rabushka, A. & P. Ryan. (1982). *The Tax Revolt*. Stanford, CA: Hoover Institution Press.

Rand, Ayn (1961). *For the New Intellectual*. New York: Penguin.

Ricardo, D. (1817; 1996). *Principles of Political Economy and Taxation*. Amherst, NY: Prometheus Books.

Ritsema, Christina M., Deborah W. Thomas & Gary D. Ferrier (2003). Economic and Behavioral Determinants of Tax Compliance: Evidence from the 1997 Arkansas Tax Penalty Amnesty Program. Presented at the 2003 IRS Research Conference (June). www.irs.gov/pub/irs-soi/ritsema.pdf

Robin, Donald and Laurie Babin. (1997). Making Sense of the Research on Gender and Ethics in Business: A Critical Analysis and Extension. *Business Ethics Quarterly*, 7(4), 61–90.

Ross, Adriana M. and Robert W. McGee (2011). A Demographic Study of Polish Attitudes toward Tax Evasion. Published in the Proceedings of the 2011 Spring International Conference of the Allied Academies, Orlando, April 6–8, 2011, forthcoming in *the Academy of Accounting and Financial Studies Journal*.

Ross, Adriana M. and Robert W. McGee (2011). Attitudes toward Tax Evasion in Switzerland: A Demographic Study. Published in the Proceedings of the 2011 Spring International Conference of the Allied Academies, Orlando, April 6–8, 2011. Reprinted as Attitudes toward Tax Evasion: A Demographic Study of Switzerland, *Business Studies Journal* 3(2): 1–47 (2011).

Ross, Adriana M. and Robert W. McGee (2011). A Demographic Study of South African Attitudes on Tax Evasion. Published in the Proceedings of the 2011 Spring International Conference of the Allied Academies, Orlando, April 6–8, 2011, forthcoming in the *Journal of Economics and Economic Education Journal*.

Ross, Adriana M. and Robert W. McGee (2011). A Demographic Study of the Netherlands Attitudes toward Tax Evasion. Published in the Proceedings of the 2011 Spring International Conference of the Allied Academies, Orlando, April 6–8, 2011. To be reprinted as Attitudes toward Tax Evasion: A Demographic Study of the Netherlands in the *Journal of International Business Research*, forthcoming.

Ross, Adriana M. and Robert W. McGee (2011). A Demographic Study of Malaysian Views on the Ethics of Tax Evasion. Published in the Proceedings of the 2011 Spring International Conference of the Allied Academies, Orlando, April 6–8, 2011. Reprinted as Attitudes toward Tax Evasion: A Demographic Study of Malaysia, *Asian Journal of Law & Economics*, Vol. 2, Issue 3, article 5 (2011): 1–49.

Ross, Adriana M. and Robert W. McGee (2011). Education Level and Ethical Attitude toward Tax Evasion: A Six-Country Study. Published in the Proceedings of the 2011 Spring International Conference of the Allied Academies, Orlando, April 6–8, 2011. Forthcoming in the *Journal of Legal, Ethical and Regulatory Issues.*

Rousseau, Jean Jacques. (1762). *The Social Contract.*

Roxas, Maria L. & Jane Y. Stoneback. (2004). The Importance of Gender Across Cultures in Ethical Decision-Making. *Journal of Business Ethics*, 50,149–165.

Ruegger, Durwood and Ernest W. King. (1992). A Study of the Effect of Age and Gender upon Student Business Ethics. *Journal of Business Ethics*, 11(3), 179–186.

Sabrin, M. (1995). *Tax Free 2000: The Rebirth of American Liberty.* Lafayette, LA: Prescott Press.

Savas, E.S. (1982). *Privatizing the Public Sector: How To Shrink Government.* Chatham, NJ: Chatham House Publishers.

Savas, E.S. (2005). *Privatization in the City: Successes, Failures, Lessons.* Washington, DC: CQ Press.

Schaltegger, Christoph A. and Benno Torgler. (2005). Trust in Government and Public Debt: An Empirical Analysis. *Proceedings of the 98th Annual Conference on Taxation of the National Tax Association*, 217–222.

Schansberg, D. Eric. (1998). The Ethics of Tax Evasion within Biblical Christianity: Are There Limits to "Rendering Unto Caesar"? *Journal of Accounting, Ethics & Public Policy*, 1(1), 77–90, reprinted in Robert W. McGee (ed.), The Ethics of Tax Evasion (pp. 144–157). The Dumont Institute for Public Policy Research, Dumont, NJ, 1998.

Schaub, Michael K. (1994). An Analysis of the Association of Traditional Demographic Variables with the Moral Reasoning of Auditing Students and Auditors. *Journal of Accounting Education*, 12(1), 1–26.

Schlaes, Amity (1999). *The Greedy Hand: How Taxes Drive Americans Crazy and What To Do about It.* New York: Random House.

Schmidt, Warren W. & Barry Z. Posner. (1992). The Values of American Managers Then and Now. *Management Review*, 81(2), 37–40.

Schnellenbach, J. (2010). Vertical and Horizontal Reciprocity in a Theory of Taxpayer Compliance. In J. Alm, J. Martinez-Vazquez & B. Torgler (Eds.), *Developing Alternative Frameworks for Explaining Tax Compliance* (pp. 56–73). London & New York: Routledge.

Seligman, E.R. (1931). *Essays in Taxation.* New York: Macmillan.

Serwinek, Paul J. (1992). Demographic & Related Differences in Ethical Views Among Small Businesses. *Journal of Business Ethics*, 11(7), 555–566.

Shughart, W.F., Jr. (ed.) (1997). *Taxing Choice: The Predatory Politics of Fiscal Discrimination.* New Brunswick, NJ & London: Transaction Publishers.

Sierles, F., I. Hendrickx and S. Circle (1980). Cheating in Medical School. *Medical Education*, 55(2), 124–125, as cited in Bob S. Brown and Peggy Choong. (2005). An Investigation of Academic Dishonesty among Business Students at Public and Private United States Universities. *International Journal of Management*, 22(2), 201–214.

Sikula, Andrew, Sr. and Adelmiro D. Costa. (1994). Are Women More Ethical than Men? *Journal of Business Ethics,* 13(11), 859–871.

Sims, Ronald R., Hsing K. Cheng & Hildy Teegen. (1996). Toward a Profile of Student Software Piraters. *Journal of Business Ethics*, 15(8), 839–849.

Singappakdi, Anusorn, Scott J. Vitell & George R. Franke. (1999). Antecedents, Consequences and Mediating Effects of Perceived Moral Intensity and Personal Moral Philosophies. *Journal of the Academy of Marketing Science*, 27(1), 19–36.

Smatrakalev, Gueorgui. (1998). Walking on the Edge: Bulgaria and the Transition to a Market Economy. In Robert W. McGee (Ed.), *The Ethics of Tax Evasion* (pp. 316–329). Dumont, NJ: The Dumont Institute for Public Policy Research.

Smatrakalev, Georgi (2012). Is Tax Evasion Our National Sport? The Bulgarian Case. In Robert W. McGee (Ed.), *The Ethics of Tax Evasion: Perspectives in Theory and Practice* (pp. 371–385). New York, Springer.

Smith, Patricia L. & Ellwood F. Oakley, III. (1997). Gender-Related Differences in Ethical and Social Values of Business Students: Implications for Management. *Journal of Business Ethics*, 16(1), 37–45.

Smith, Sheldon R. and Kevin C. Kimball. (1998). Tax Evasion and Ethics: A Perspective from Members of The Church of Jesus Christ of Latter-Day Saints. *Journal of Accounting, Ethics & Public Policy*, 1(3), 337–348, reprinted in Robert W. McGee (Ed.), *The Ethics of Tax Evasion* (pp. 220–229). Dumont, NJ: The Dumont Institute for Public Policy Research, 1998.

Song, Young-dahl and Tinsley E. Yarbrough. (1978). Tax Ethics and Taxpayer Attitudes: A Survey. *Public Administration Review*, 38(5), 442–452.

Spooner, Lysander. (1870). *No Treason: The Constitution of No Authority*, originally self-published by Spooner in Boston in 1870, reprinted by Rampart College in 1965, 1966 and 1971, and by Ralph Myles Publisher, Inc., Colorado Springs, Colorado in 1973.

Stanga, Keith G. and Richard A. Turpen. (1991). Ethical Judgments on Selected Accounting Issues: An Empirical Study. *Journal of Business Ethics*, 10(10), 739–747.

Stern, E.B. and L. Havlicek (1986). Academic Misconduct: results of Faculty and Undergraduate Student Surveys. *Journal of Allied Health*, 15(2), 129–142, as cited in Bob S. Brown and Peggy Choong. (2005). An Investigation of Academic Dishonesty among Business Students at Public and Private United States Universities. *International Journal of Management*, 22(2), 201–214.

Su, Shu-Hui. (2006). Cultural Differences in Determining the Ethical Perception and Decision-making of Future Accounting Professionals: A Comparison between Accounting Students from Taiwan and the United States. *Journal of American Academy of Business*, 9(1), 147–158.

Swaidan, Ziad, Scott J. Vitell, Gregory M. Rose and Faye W. Gilbert. (2006). Consumer Ethics: The Role of Acculturation in U.S. Immigrant Populations. *Journal of Business Ethics*, 64(1), 1–16.

Swamy, Anand, Stephen Knack, Young Lee and Omar Azfar. (2001). Gender and Corruption. *Journal of Development Economics*, 64, 25–55.

Tamari, Meir. (1998). Ethical Issues in Tax Evasion: A Jewish Perspective. *Journal of Accounting, Ethics & Public Policy*, 1(2), 121–132, reprinted in Robert W. McGee (Ed.), *The Ethics of Tax Evasion* (pp. 168–178). Dumont, NJ: The Dumont Institute for Public Policy Research, 1998.

Tang, S. and J. Zuo (1997). Profile of College Examination Cheaters. *College Student Journal* 31(3): 340–347, as cited in Bob S. Brown and Peggy Choong. (2005). An Investigation of Academic Dishonesty among Business Students at Public and Private United States Universities. *International Journal of Management*, 22(2), 201–214.

Templeton, Charles. (1996). *Farewell to God*. Toronto: McClelland & Stewart.

Thorndike, Joseph J. & Dennis J. Ventry, Jr. (2002). *The Ongoing Debate on Tax Justice*. Washington, DC: The Urban Institute Press.

Tittle, C. (1980). *Sanctions and Social Deviance: The Question of Deterrence*. New York: Praeger.

Torgler, Benno. (2002). Speaking to Theorists and Searching for Facts: Tax Morale and Tax Compliance in Experiments. *Journal of Economic Surveys*, 16(5), 657–683.

Torgler, B. (2003). Tax Morale: Theory and Empirical Analysis of Tax Compliance. Dissertation der Universität Basel zur Erlangung der Würde eines Doktors der Staatswissenschaften.

Torgler, Benno. (2003). Tax Morale in Transition Countries. *Post-Communist Economies*, 15(3), 357–381.

Torgler, Benno. (2003). Tax Morale and Tax Compliance: A Cross Culture Comparison. *Proceedings of the 96th Annual Conference on Taxation of the National Tax Association-Tax Institute of America*, 63–74.

Torgler, Benno. (2003). Tax Morale, Rule-Governed Behaviour and Trust. *Constitutional Political Economy*, 14(2), 119–140.

Torgler, Benno. (2003). To evade taxes or not to evade: that is the question. *The Journal of Socio-Economics*, 32, 283–302.

Torgler, Benno. (2003). Beyond Punishment: A Tax Compliance Experiment with Taxpayers in Costa Rico. *Revista de Análisis Económico*, 18(1), 27–56.

Torgler, Benno, Christoph A. Schaltegger and Markus Schaffner. (2003). Is Forgiveness Divine? A Cross-Culture Comparison of Tax Amnesties. *Schweizerische Zeitschrift für Volkswirtschaft und Statistik*, 139(3), 375–396.

Torgler, Benno. (2004). Moral suasion: An alternative tax policy strategy? Evidence from a controlled field experiment in Switzerland. *Economics of Governance*, 5(3), 235–253.

Torgler, Benno. (2004). Tax morale in Asian countries. *Journal of Asian Economics*, 15, 237–266.

Torgler, Benno and Neven T. Valev. (2004). Corruption and Age. Working Paper No. 2004–24, Center for Research in Economics, Management and the Arts, Basel, Switzerland.

Torgler, Benno. (2005). A Knight without a Sword? The Effects of Audit Courts on Tax Morale. *Journal of Institutional and Theoretical Economics*, 161, 735–760.

Torgler, Benno and Friedrich Schneider. (2005). Attitudes Towards Paying Taxes in Austria: An Empirical Analysis. *Empirica*, 32, 231–250.

Torgler, Benno. (2005). Tax morale in Latin America. *Public Choice*, 122, 133–157.

Torgler, Benno. (2006). The Importance of Faith: Tax Morale and Religiosity. *Journal of Economic Behavior & Organization*, 61, 81–109.

Torgler, Benno. (2006). Compliance in India: An Empirical Analysis. *The Icfai University Journal of Public Finance*, 4(2), 7–18.

Torgler, Benno and Christoph A. Schaltegger. (2006). Tax Morale: A Survey with a Special Focus on Switzerland. *Schweizerische Zeitschrift für Volkswirtschaft und Statistik*, 142(3), 395–425.

Torgler, Benno and Neven T. Valev. (2006). Women and Illegal Activities: Gender Differences and Women's Willingness to Comply over Time. Working Paper No. 2006–15, Center for Research in Economics, Management and the Arts, Basel, Switzerland.

Torgler, Benno. (2007). *Tax Compliance and Tax Morale: A Theoretical and Empirical Analysis*. Cheltenham, UK & Northampton, MA, USA: Edward Elgar.

Torgler, Benno. (2007). The Impact of Direct Democracy and Local Autonomy on Tax Morale in Switzerland. Institute of Local Public Finance, Working Paper 06–2007, December, Switzerland.

Torgler, Benno, Friedrich Schneider & Christoph A. Schaltegger. (2007). With or Against the People? The Impact of a Bottom-Up Approach on Tax Morale and the Shadow Economy. Working Paper No. 2007–4, Center for Research in Economics, Management and the Arts, Basel, Switzerland.

Torgler, Benno and Friedrich Schneider. (2007). What Shapes Attitudes Toward Paying Taxes? Evidence from Multicultural European Countries. *Social Science Quarterly*, 88(2), 443–470.

Torgler, Benno and Neven T. Valev. (2007). Public Attitudes Toward Corruption and Tax Evasion: Investigating the Role of Gender Over Time. Working/Discussion Paper #214, Queensland University of Technology, QUT School of Economics and Finance, Australia.

Torgler, Benno. (2008). What Do We Know about Tax Fraud? An Overview of Recent Developments. *Social Research*, 75(4), 1239–1270.

Torgler, Benno, María A. García-Valiñas and Alison Macintyre. (2008). Differences in Preferences Towards the Environment: The Impact of a Gender, Age and Parental effect. Working Paper No. 2008–1, Center for Research in Economics, Management and the Arts, Basel, Switzerland.

Torgler, Benno, Ihsan C. Demir, Alison Macintyre and Markus Schaffner. (2008). Causes and Consequences of Tax Morale: An Empirical Investigation. *Economic Analysis & Policy*, 38(2), 313–339.

Torgler, Benno and Friedrich Schneider. (2009). The impact of tax morale and institutional quality on the shadow economy. *Journal of Economic Psychology*, 30, 228–245.

Torgler, Benno. (2010). Serious Tax noncompliance: Motivation and Guardianship. *Criminology & Public Policy*, 9(3), 535–542.

Torgler, Benno & Neven T. Valev. (2010). Gender and Public Attitudes toward Corruption and Tax Evasion. *Contemporary Economic Policy*, 28(4), 554–568.

Torgler, Benno, M. Schaffner & A. Macintyre. (2010). Tax Compliance, Tax Morale, and Governance Quality. In J. Alm, J. Martinez-Vazquez & B. Torgler (Eds.), *Developing Alternative Frameworks for Explaining Tax Compliance* (pp. 141–173). London & New York: Routledge.

Torgler, Benno (2012). Attitudes Toward Paying Taxes in the USA: An Empirical Analysis. In Robert W. McGee (Ed.), *The Ethics of Tax Evasion: Perspectives in Theory and Practice* (pp. 269–283). New York, Springer.

Tsalikis, J. & M. Ortiz-Buonafina. (1990). Ethical Beliefs' Differences of Males and Females. *Journal of Business Ethics*, 9(6), 509–517.

Tullock, Gordon (1970). *Private Wants, Public Means: An Economic Analysis of the Desirable Scope of Government*. New York: Basic Books.

Tullock, Gordon (1989). *The Economics of Special Privilege and Rent Seeking*. Boston, Dordrecht & London: Kluwer Academic Publishers.

Tullock, Gordon (1993). *Rent Seeking*. Hants, UK & Brookfield, VT: Edward Elgar Publishing.

Uslaner, E.M. (2010). Tax Evasion, Corruption, and the Social Contract in Transition. In J. Alm, J. Martinez-Vazquez & B. Torgler (Eds.), *Developing Alternative Frameworks for Explaining Tax Compliance* (pp. 174–190). London & New York: Routledge.

Vaguine, Vladimir V. (1998). The "Shadow Economy" and Tax Evasion in Russia. In Robert W. McGee (Ed.), *The Ethics of Tax Evasion* (pp. 306–314). Dumont, NJ: The Dumont Institute for Public Policy Research.

Valentine, P. (2005). *Tax Revolt*. Nashville: Nelson Current.

Walter, Nicolas (1966). Etienne de la Boetie's Discourse of Voluntary Servitude: Introduction. *Anarchy* 6(5): 129–152.

Webber, C. & A. Wildavsky. (1986). *A History of Taxation and Expenditure in the Western World*. New York: Simon & Schuster.

Webley, P. & J. Ashby. (2010). The Economic Psychology of Value Added Tax Compliance. In J. Alm, J. Martinez-Vazquez & B. Torgler (Eds.), *Developing Alternative Frameworks for Explaining Tax Compliance* (pp. 238–259). London & New York: Routledge.

Weeks, William A., Carlos W. Moore, Joseph A. McKinney & Justin G. Longenecker. (1999). The Effects of Gender and Career Stage on Ethical Judgment. *Journal of Business Ethics*, 20(4), 301–313.

Whitley, Bernard E. (1998). Factors Associated with Cheating among College Students: A Review. *Research in Higher Education*, 39(3), 235–274.

Williams, Walter (1987). *All It Takes Is Guts: A Minority View*. Washington, DC: Regnery Books.

Wilson, J. Eugene (1980). *How to Fight the I.R.S. – And Win!* College Park, GA: J.C. Printing Co.

Wood, John A., Justin G. Longenecker, Joseph A. McKinney & Carlos W. Moore. (1988). Ethical Attitudes of Students and Business Professionals: A Study of Moral Reasoning. *Journal of Business Ethics*, 7(4), 249–257.

World Values Survey Data. http://www.wvsevsdb.com/

Yusuf, S.M. (1971). *Economic Justice in Islam*. Lahore: Sh. Muhammad Ashraf.

Index